GLOBAL HOOPS:

MIND, BODY & SOUL

GREGG SCOTT

<u>FOREWORD BY: DONALD SPARKS</u>

G' FLIGHT

YouTube.com/MentalAthlete

Order this book online at www.trafford.com
or email orders@trafford.com

Most Trafford titles are also available at major online book retailers.

Print information available on the last page.

ISBN: 978-1-4120-1125-9 (sc)
ISBN: 978-1-4669-6328-3 (e)

Trafford rev. 12/22/2015

www.trafford.com

North America & international
toll-free: 1 888 232 4444 (USA & Canada)
fax: 812 355 4082

DEDICATION

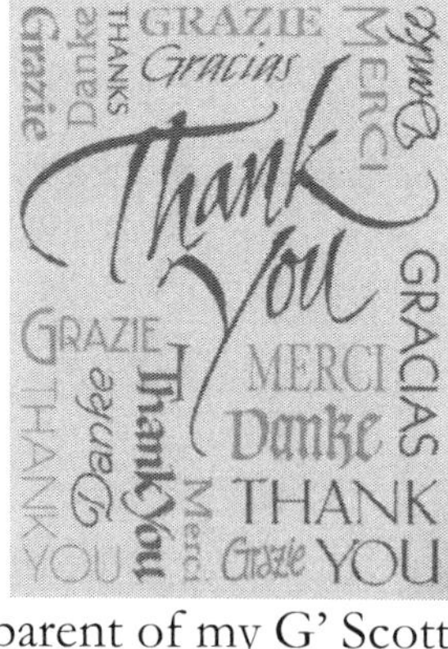

TO MY MOM

For all your Love! I never knew your true sacrifices, and pride until I became a parent of my G' Scott!

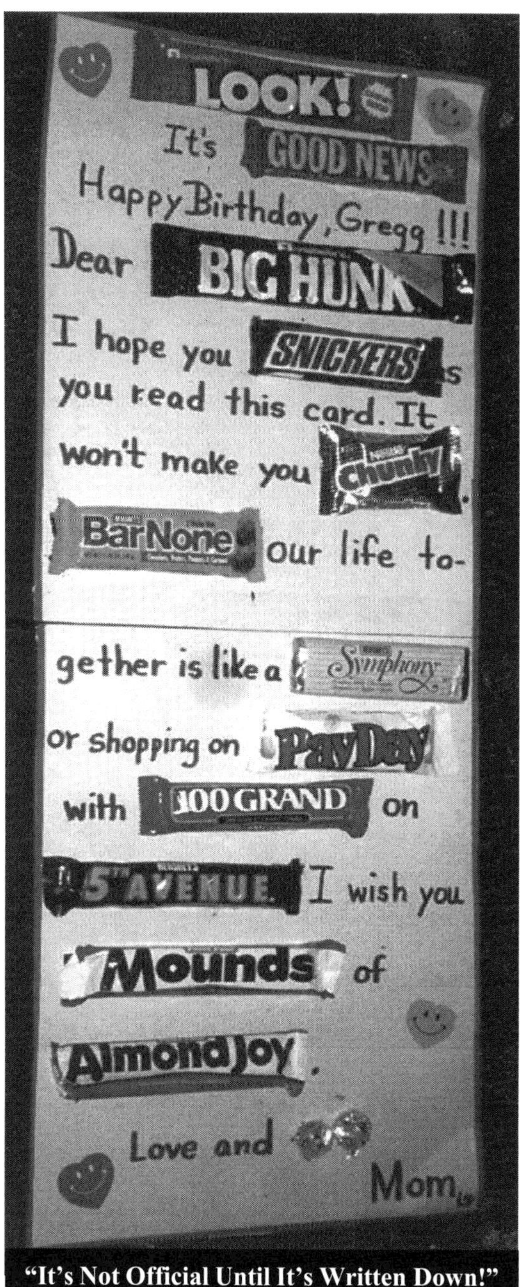

"It's Not Official Until It's Written Down!"

TO AGE 15 GABRIELA SABATINI

September 13, 1987 Buenos Aires, ARG G' MVP & Promise the crowd I'd write this book. G'$ Fan: I promised you I'd name my daughter after YOU!

TO GABRIELLA SCOTT

Sometimes when I need a miracle, I look into my daughters eyes, and realize I've already created one

The Greatest Bond EVER! **My Blessing & My Bestie!** A True G' & A Champion!

FOREWARD: DONALD SPARKS

Competition! Whether we realize it, acknowledge it or accept it, competition is a reality of our daily lives. Competition for grades, competition for jobs or even competition for a good parking space at the local mall; competition is always a fact of life. So how does one learn to compete and become comfortable competing? That's why GHMBS is very special.

From an early age, the majority of us learn how to compete in youth sports leagues where all too often the emphasis is placed on winning. Coaches, parents, friends and teammates are all so overly preoccupied with the end result that the mental aspect of competition is often overlooked. Focusing solely on physical performance fails to address whether or not the young athlete is actually comfortable being in a true competition. Many young athletes never reach their potential simply because a parent or coach or mentor has not addressed or prepared their young athlete to be comfortable in a competitive environment. The emphasis on winning or losing is the only way a young athlete is taught to measure success. The main focus of our efforts are then "backed into" depending on the net result of our competition. If you win, "Great job!". If you lose, "Don't worry. You'll get 'em next time."

Over the years, I've had the great pleasure of standing on the sidelines and watching young athletes compete. One such athlete, your author Gregg Scott, was someone whom I have truly enjoyed mentoring and witnessing his acute evolution as an athlete and a competitor.

Being gifted with great physical talents, Gregg, like he was taught, often put the end result as the ultimate goal - winning. His focus was on simply winning, and in many cases, doing whatever it takes to win. However, as Gregg continued his competitive journey, he like many athletes before him, started to encounter other athletes who were just as physically gifted, if not more, than he was. Competing and winning were no longer as easy as before. As a true competitor, Gregg started to look for other methods to increase his competitive advantage. It was at that point when Gregg Scott began his journey as a 'Mental Athlete'.

I was fortunate to come along at the right time. I knew Gregg had all the physical tools to achieve his competitive objectives. However, I also saw a young athlete who became easily frustrated when skills were limited by circumstances beyond his control: Bad Referee Calls!

Not wanting him to squander his opportunity, I took Gregg under my wing and shared all I could to aid and impact his Mental Athlete journey. He was a diligent and dutiful protégé.

GHMBS is a testament to Gregg's true life tales, tools, and teachings of his unique journey in competitive sports. Through purgatory of his injuries, his set-backs, his pain and defeats, the Mental Athlete found ways to be resilliant and persevere. His journey is one that we all can embrace and learn from because in Sports and in Life we all Compete on a Daily Basis!

PREFACE

Persevere! Athlete to Athlete: I empathize with each of you, so I share my personal heartbreaks and painful experiences that trump the highlights and triumphs. True life tales of trials and tribulations, injuries, setbacks and comebacks. PAID DUES!! Young athletes put a tremendous amount of time, effort and, someone's money towards their athletic pursuits and dreams. For better or worse, self-image is dictated and skewed by athletic skills, attributes and ultimately, performance. I strive to shorten the learning curve and soften the inevitable hurts and hardships in the **Pursuit of Peak Performance & Athletic Excellence!** Inherently, **blood, sweat and tears** must be shed, and eventually coveted, as you travel the path of a **Competitive Athlete**. It is my quest to mentor athletes, especially those in their formative years, with life skills in a sports context that will provide a compass that is life-changing and lifelong. Creating Achievers from the Inside, Out! And, Teaching not only What to Think, but, How to Think! 'VW Ventures & Porsche Pursuits'!

***HAIL: Homage to my Helpers** | ***TOUT: Tributes to my Teammates**
***PROMOTE: Props to my Protégées** | ***GIVE: Gratuities to my Generation Next**

Memoir

Scrapbook

Self-Help Workbook

Basketball IQ Blueprint for Excellence

The Modern Day Mental Athlete Manifesto

> *"The Thrill of Victory or the Agony of Defeat"*

AMATEUR BASKETBALL ASSOCIATION OF THE UNITED STATES OF AMERICA
INTERNATIONAL PLAYER TRAVEL PERMIT
This will certify that . . .
Gregory T. Scott
is a registered amateur player eligible for FIBA basketball competition during 1986-87.
William L. Wall, Executive Director
Nº 6 499

Mom archived all of my articles and pictures. Interviewed so many individuals with prophetic purpose. Flowcharted and forecasted my manuscript mission. And, instructed me to: **"Put your noble humility aside and share the G'$ tales."** So, I present to you the tangible evidence of an obedient son. The fruit of her labor and proof of my 'work' on full display! In that vien, Global Hoops is a dirty game and not all of my tales are Rated G. Some are duly noted: **'Do Not Emulate!'**

Pay Forward! The Next Generation of Mental Athletes!

HIGH SCHOOL SWEETHEARTS: GENETIC POTENTIAL

My father, Henry T. Scott and my mother (formally) Janet K. Dicks were high school sweethearts in Cincinnati, Ohio. Being two years older my dad graduated and attended Ohio University on both academic and football scholarships. He was a starting half-back and a kicker. An odd mix. He graduated with two B.A. degrees. Psychology and Sociology.

My mom earned academic and volleyball scholarships to Eastern Kentucky University. She was 5'8", extremely athletic and had great jumping ability like her 6'3" brother, Uncle Mike! Alas, her athletic and college pursuits were sidetracked when she got pregnant in her Frosh year and Frosh (first) 'experience.' "I didn't even get to enjoy it.", she often lamented later. She dropped out, returned to Cincy and they got married. March 18, 1961: Mark was born.

Henry Scott: Half-back Ohio U. ~ Army Psychologist Vietnam

My dad enlisted in the Army and was a psychologist for the troops dealing with what we now call PTSD. So many tales!

Landstuhl, Germany: September 3, 1964

Dad waa stationed at Ramstein Air Force Base. **Army Brat:** Born in the famous Landstuhl Medical Hospital on 9/3/64.

Old Skool Motown Jam:

"It was the 3rd of September! A day I'll always remember. 'Cause that was the day..."

~Papa was a Rolling Stone~

My Birthday Present: A Cast on my Leg!

When I was 5, I recall going through family trinkets and pictures when I noticed two pair of baby booty's, a pair of soft baby shoes and a pair of hard baby shoes. I asked my mom about them. She told me the soft pair were my brothers and the hard pair were mine. Why? At birth my leg was slightly bent and they had to put a tiny cast on it so I couldn't wear the normal soft baby shoes. Then, I asked about the booty's. Shocker! My mom had given birth to twins who both passed away within a week. It was somewhat of a taboo familial subject. Sadly.

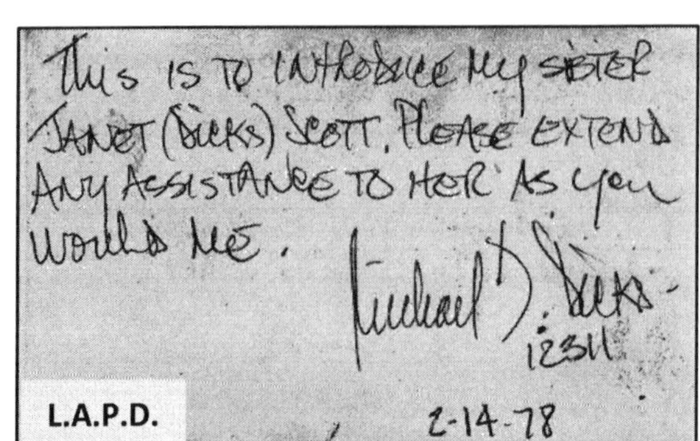
THIS IS TO INTRODUCE MY SISTER JANET (DICKS) SCOTT. PLEASE EXTEND ANY ASSISTANCE TO HER AS YOU WOULD ME.

Michael D. Dicks
12311

L.A.P.D.

2-14-78

Manifest Destiny: To West L.A.

After 8 years of service we moved to West L.A. into apt. 9 in a complex on Pointview St.

Uncle Mike & Kin Moved Too!

FORMATIVE YEARS: 'IRON SHARPENS IRON'

The environment, in which my parents became high school sweethearts, Walnut Hills High School in Cincinnati, would become the core of their childrearing. Walnut Hills was, and is, a highly acclaimed private college prep institution with a stellar academic tradition. Latin was a required course each year. In that vein, we were molded to be highly educated and articulate while exhibiting proper social graces, appropriate table manners, etiquette, humility and a respect for our elders, at all times. Beyond being 'color blind', they also stressed that we accept, embrace and experience various other cultures and their traditions.

My Mom: A Literal Den Mother ~ Young G': 'I'm No Cub Scout'

When I was 6, my brother joined the Cub Scouts. My mom was the Den Mother for him and his buds, Marvin Mensies, Glenn Webb and Steven Van Arden. All cool dudes. Still, when mom asked me if I wanted to join I said, 'Oh, no! I'd never wear such a get-up. Nah, I want to wear a uniform with **my name** on the back, not a nameplate on the front. Sorry.'

When I was age ten, we had a family dinner at the renowned Benihana restaurant in nearby Beverly Hills. The chef's classic culinary preparation show concluded. A waitress asked if we needed anything. 'May I have ketchup, please?' My Mom Meddled: "This isn't Sizzler!"

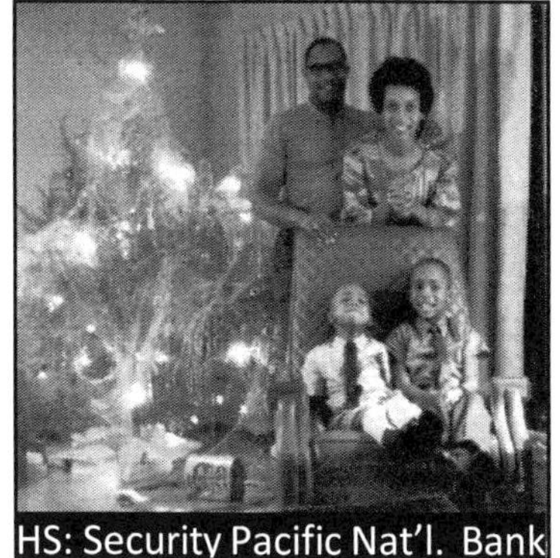
HS: Security Pacific Nat'l. Bank

We were expected to know when to be seen and not heard, with the ability to comfortably engage in adult conversations on cue, and represent them properly, without any exceptions! Although both my parents were college athletes, excellence as a student-athlete was to be achieved in that order; student first. Sports were an 'extra-curricular'. For us, maximizing the inherent Scott 'genetic potential' was embedded and enforced from my earliest memories. When I was twelve, I brought home my 7th grade mid-semester progress report with my first-ever 'C' grade, in ONE class. Pops had a full-on sh... (correction) hissy fit. His Epic and Unforgettable Conniption: "In this Scott house we do not applaud, nor do we accept average in anything that we do."

Swank Sweet & Smart Scott Shelter

"You Are Genetically Inclined To Be Better! Bred To Be Better! And, Young Man, BETTER, You Shall Most Certainly Be!" 'Yes Dad'! Final Report Card: 'B'!

***Mark inherited Dads genius IQ.**

***I got my Moms genius memory!**

Wise Mom
The Shortest Pencil Is Greater Than The Longest Memory

Family Values, Lifestyles & Pursuits ~ Eats, Beats, Camp & Bowl

We tend to gravitate towards the chosen pursuits, mindsets and motivations of our parents. In our case, an affinity for good cuisine, love of music, passion for camping or fishing trips and the captivation of competitive bowling were all perpetual parts of our family lifestyle. But, camping trips, from A-frame chalets in Mammoth to our pop-up camper at Campland on Mission Bay to deep sea fishing, lake or river angling ventures. Dad obsessed over his love for camping and fishing get-aways, near and far. It brought him much peace and joy. **Perfect Example:** Age 8! Pops was V.P. & Manager at the SPNB Malibu Branch on PCH. We were alone inside the bank on a Friday with the camper and Dads VW Squareback in the lot. We were going on a camping trip to nearby Leo Carillo. I got permission to look around but, "Don't Touch"! At the shiny vault I held my hand up close to the mirroring metal. POP! OUCH! ELECTRIC SHOCK! I back up, scurry out and go back to the lobby. No harm done. Minutes later I notice a glare in the parking lot. LIGHTS! Get This: LAPD, Santa Monica PD, Culver City PD, Sheriffs, and CHP! All geeked up! Shock! Silent Alarm! Dad calmly spoke to the Head Honcho and they left swiftly. He never mentioned it at all. Years, no, decades later I asked him why he never got mad. "Going Camping Trumps All!"

My Preferred Periodicals: The Pacific Bowler and Bowling News. Two must-reads for competitive bowlers. Mark and I competed far beyond the Saturday morning Jr. Leagues at Midtown Bowl and later West Pico Bowl. We competed in junior bowling tournaments! Singles, doubles, adult-junior, no-tap, you name it, we went. My first sports road trips were to the Western Regional Tournaments at the revered Showboat Lanes in Las Vegas. Mom and I enjoyed yearly Circus Circus trips. An annual tradition that I continue with my G'13. As Mom taught me at Circus Circus, I also taught G'13: Basic Strategy for Blackjack. **'21'!**

My brother had legitimate pro potential and opportunities. We differ in 'Risk vs. Reward'! My brother and I also kept score for our parents' adult bowling leagues at Tropicana Bowl. Manually! A tiny pencil that wrote in yellow on a long three-game plastic sheet laid across a hot overhead projector system. No auto-score back in the day. Twice a week we kept score and homework had to be done before or afterwards. Gigs Unanticipated Dividends: Mark and I both became **very acute with NUMBERS** as a result.

1st Jersey: A Bowling Shirt?
The Cisco Kid was a Friend of Mine!
WAR

While, to this day, I have never worn another man's jersey, not even MJ, I did purchase the exact same bowling ball used by the initial 'athlete' (debatable term for that sport) I wanted to emulate. A tall, slender and smooth lefty who always exhibited a calm demeanor, razor sharp focus, and a constantly calculating mind. Sustained class, concentration and quiet confidence, without any overt displays of emotion. Champions Mettle and Oh So Clutch! **I Tribute: The (late) great Earl Anthony, PBA HOF ~ R.I.P.**

Age 9: Movin' On Up to Alfred St. ~ 'Big Crib'

Backyard hoop where Mark abused & taught me to shoot!

Haughty Carthay Center Elementary School

The first coach to be included on my personal Board of Directors, Mr. Bernie Bucholtz, was a great teacher and Sports Director at my elementary school, Carthay Center. Mr. 'B' took a vested interest in my development as a student and multi-sport athlete. He uniquely recognized that my mental aptitude, arm and athleticism could be molded into a top-flight football quarterback. I was a porous sponge absorbing his input and dutiful in applying it, which I knew delighted him. His nurturing manner, motivation and guidance were all true blessings and key assets to my maturation and evolution as a student-athlete, a young man, and as a future QB. At my sixth grade culmination he hugged me with such pride and joy!

Chavez Ravine: Bleeding Dodger Blue! ~ Legendary Vin Scully!

Our family spent more time at Dodger Stadium than the Forum. Pops proudly wore his Big Red Machine Cincinnati gear. **Pops Perk:** Bank VIP Field Level seats over the dugout! Blessed: Listening to Vin Scully at the ballpark while enjoying their famous Dodger Dogs!

Tommy Lasorda ~ Steve Yeager ~ Steve Garvey ~ Davey Lopes ~ Bill Russell ~ Ron Cey ~ Dusty Baker ~ Jimmy Wynnn ~ Reggie Smith Tommy John ~ Claude Osteen ~ Joe Ferguson

#44 Trivia: Lefty Al Downing gave up the famed 715th home run by Hank Aaron. Both wore #44

The Dodger Pepsi Fan Club Promos!

"Fernandomania"

G'$: 20/15 Vision & Ambidextrous!

Swing Sports entail acute hand-eye coordination. As a switch-hitter blessed with keen 20/15 vision, 4.4 speed, a laser arm, and a solid infield glove: Baseball was a true natural calling. Yet, **so boring!** Hindsight: MLB wages trump bordom & NBA $.

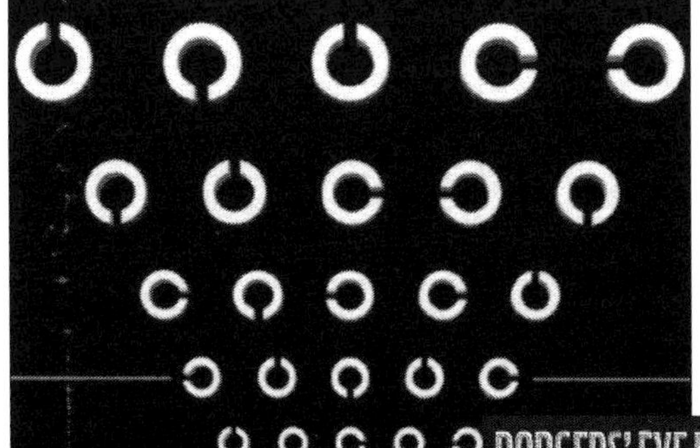

DODGERS' EYE EXAM This illustration simulates a test involving Landolt rings—each of which has a space in one side—in decreasing sizes. Two decades ago members of the L.A. organization were asked which side of each ring contained the gap, down to the smallest they could see. Eighty-one percent proved to have at least 20/15 vision, meaning they could see things 20 feet away that most people could see only at 15 feet.

MY HOMETOWN: L.A. THE CITY OF CHAMPIONS

JOHN HALL Los Angeles Times, 1971

Some Cagey Cops

Their names are Ellis, Day, Bridges, Ervin, Nelson, Dillard, Dicks, Harper, Gordon and Harvey. They're cops.

"We're pretty proud of them," said Danny Roberts of Youth Services in the Los Angeles Police Dept. Roberts also happens to be a sometimes player as well as coach of the above men who form the LAPD basketball team.

You may remember Officer Roberts. Danny once was an All City center at Belmont High, lettered two years at the University of Washington and later performed for Kirby's Shoes when AAU basketball was major league in Southern California.

There is evidence, if you will excuse the cop talk, to support the growing view that this may be the banner basketball season of them all hereabouts.

The Lakers have been going a little crazy—winning a club record 17 in-a-row and aiming, without apology, for the NBA mark of 20. College action began with three local schools—UCLA, Cal State Long Beach and USC—ranked by most among the nation's top ten. The Bruins opened their bid for an eighth national championship by scoring a modest 211 points in their first two games and turning loose again the flashiest blur in the blue yonder in senior guard Henry Bibby.

Pepperdine displays one of the finest sophomores in flight over land or sea—William (The Bird) Averitt. A total of 49,503 paid to see four games last weekend at Pauley Pavilion, the Forum and Sports Arena. The oven is hot.

Not as well known a member of the fraternity, perhaps, the LAPD basketball squad is nonetheless a part of the mushroom. Our cops recently won the police national championship and they will be at their specialty again this weekend—defending their California title in the second annual Santa Maria Police tournament hosted by Santa Maria's finest.

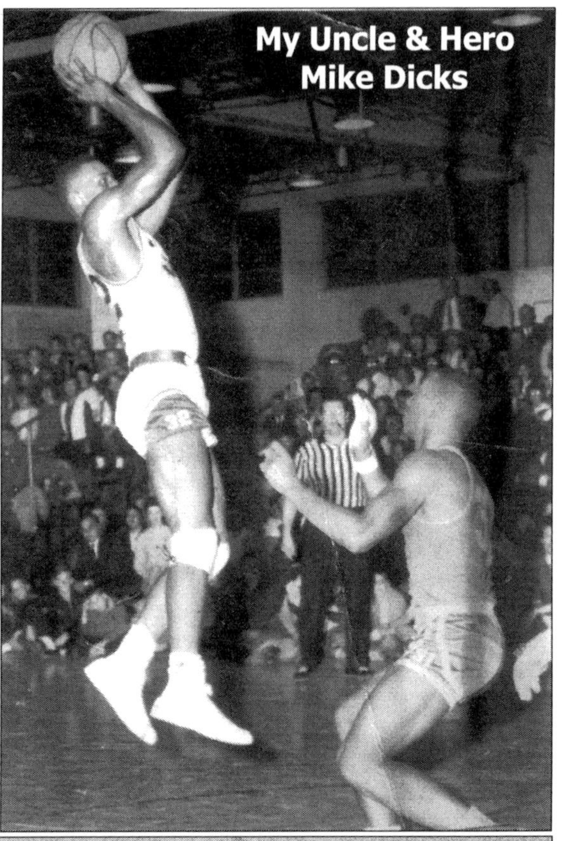

Those representing the championship LAPD:

Bill Ellis: investigator, narcotics division. Remember Bill, the human? He was co-captain of John Wooden's 1961 UCLA team.

Joe Day: patrol car, Newton division. He was a starting guard on Utah's 1966 NCAA Western Regional champs, a teammate of ex-Laker Jerry Chambers.

Ted Bridges: patrol car, 77th Street Division. All City at Washington High in 1959, starred three seasons for Pepperdine, was high scorer in the 1962 third place win over Utah State in the NCAA regionals.

Dick Ervin: patrol car, Wilshire Division. Arizona State 1962-1965, team's second-highest scorer in his senior season.

Russ Nelson: patrol car, Venice Division. Harbor College, 1955-1966.

Cecil Dillard: Southwest Division. Portland State, center on the San Diego Marine team that won the All-Marine title in 1962.

Mike Dicks: Advance Planning Division. Knoxville College, former All-Army and tryout finalist for the 1964 Olympic team.

Dick Harper: motorcycle officer, Traffic Division. Did not play in college. Athletics after joining the force.

Sterling Gordon: patrol car, 77th Division. No college. But was named MVP of the first Santa Maria tournament and the LAPD's outstanding player of 1971.

These are the people. Their badges glow on you.

Setting the Bar: Victory! Core Conditioning!

We are products of our environment. I was enamored, I studied, and later emulated the Champions Pedigree of my City & my Uncle!

~He was promoted to Detective in 1977~

He was also a personal bodyguard for boxer (& friend) Ken Norton. On TV at his Las Vegas fight vs. Muhammad Ali!

The stories along with personally witnessing my Uncle Mike and the LAPD team play was a unique perk. These guys could ball and put a new 'hoop spin' on their motto, 'To Protect and Serve'. 'Protect your space at all times'; 'Serve your man on offense'; and 'Secure your man on defense'! They were a talented, tough and, at times, straight up nasty squad. No Joke!! Their games and tourneys were simply a form of hubris in a hoop context, badges be damned. Yet, playing fundamental basketball with team work, chemistry and synergy, constant verbilization, and a stellar man-to-man defense were their trademarks. Games, practices, even a few camping trips exposed me to LAPD Hoopla, and I embody the tips and tools my 'Uncles' shared. Beyond hoops, I'm indebted for their personal time schooling me on street-smart self-defense. Still, the most formidable clique in L.A. is the Police.

Mastering 'Self-Defense' from the "PoPo" (LAPD) Perspective!

Uncle Mike taught me the '3 Elements' of defending myself in any hostile situation:

- **<u>DISSUADE:</u> Diffuse the Situation! Don't Provoke! Give Suitable Warnings!**
- **<u>DISARM:</u>** Hands vs. Weapons ~ gun; knife; short stick (baton); long stick (bat/ax)
    - Cognizance ~ Stance ~ Footwork ~Balance ~ Technique ~ Leverage
      Defense ~ Up-block ~ Down-block ~ Cross-block ~ Holds & Grabs
- **<u>DISABLE:</u> 'Close-quarters combat'** tactics with <u>swift resolution</u>. Basic anatomy!
    - Proper Striking ~ Pressure Points ~ Vital Organs ~ Joint Manipulation
    - **Vertical Vulnerables: Gut ~ Sternum ~ 'Adams Apple' ~ Jaw ~ Nose**

I was equally masterful with a Jump Rope & Nunchuks! Mimic: Ali & Bruce Lee!

Having the ability to defend yourself will <u>increase</u> your ability to avoid conflicts. As for on the court, it gives the confidence to compete and protect with No Fear! No bravado! Yet, L.A., from inner-city hoops, skating at the Arlington Roller Rink on Crenshaw, cruisin' Westwood, the Fox Hills Mall, Magic Burger or Fatburger; all certainly do merit such skill-sets!

Iron Sharpens Iron: My Uncle & the 'Big O'

As a kid, my moms brother, my Uncle Mike, honed his game alongside Oscar Robertson in Cincinnati, where my parents met at Walnut Hills High School. As a student of the game, I strived to emulate the blueprint of the Big 'O': Averaging a Triple-Double! Wow!

My Uncle Mike's Phonebook Pals:
***Willie Stargell & *Bernie Casey!!!**

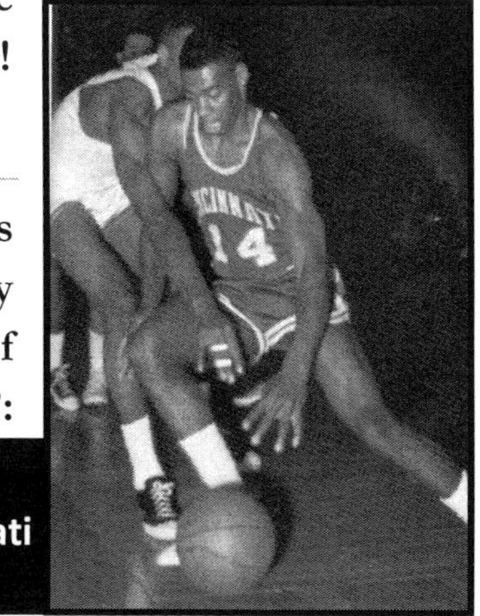

Oscar Robertson
University of Cincinnati
NBA Hall of Fame

MOM QUOTE: "ALL YOU GOTTA DO IS SHUT YOUR MOUTH AND READ."

IF...

A B C D E F G H I J K L M N O P Q R S T U V W X Y Z

EQUALS...

1 2 3 4 5 6 7 8 9 10 11 12 13 14 15 16 17 18 19 20 21 22 23 24 25 26

Coincidence OR Not???

If...

ABCDEFGHIJKLMNOPQRSTUVWXYZ

Equals...

1 2 3 4 5 6 7 8 9 10 11 12 13 14 15 16 17 18 19 20 21 22 23 24 25 26

Then

K•N•O•W•L•E•D•G•E
11•14•15•23•12•5•4•7•5 = 96%

H•A•R•D•W•O•R•K
8•1•18•4•23•15•18•11 = 98%

Both are important, but fall just short of 100%

But

A•T•T•I•T•U•D•E
1•20•20•9•20•21•4•5 = 100%

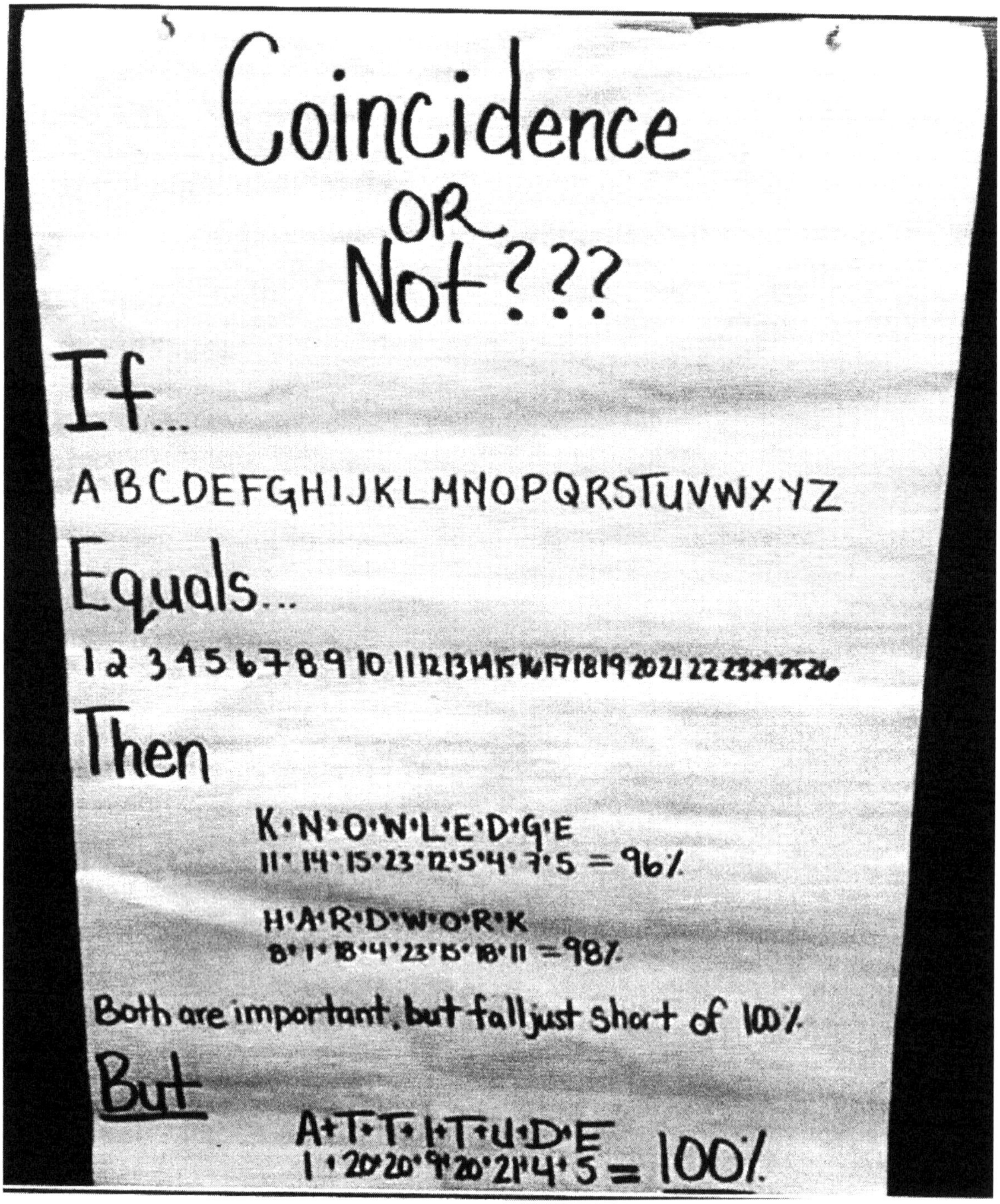

40-year Lineage: Mindfulness Conditioning **First Printing, 1974**

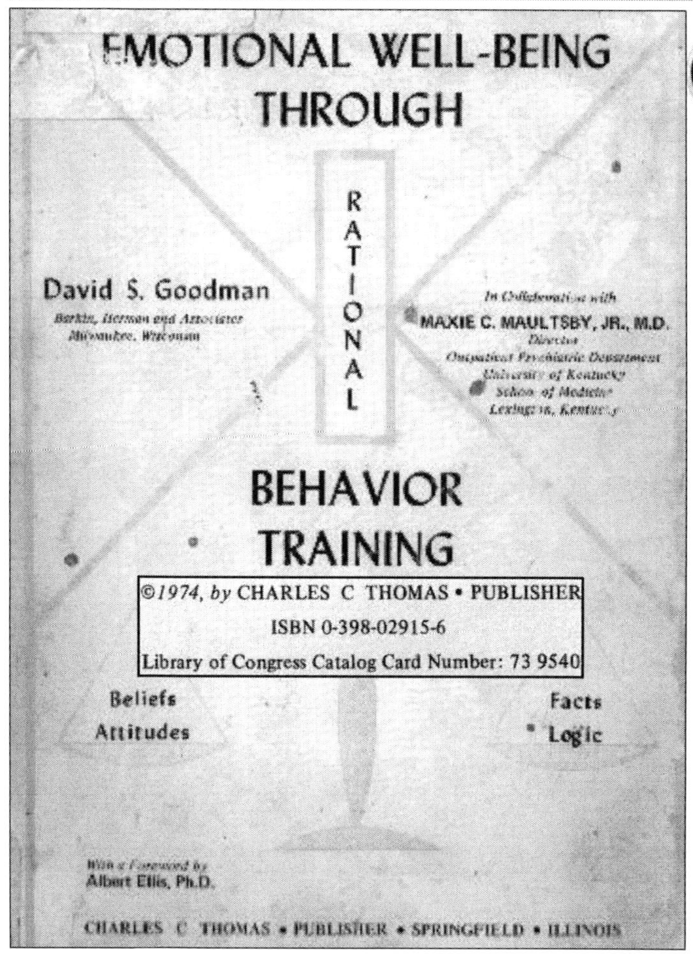

EMOTIONAL WELL-BEING
THROUGH
RATIONAL
BEHAVIOR
TRAINING
David S. Goodman
MAXIE C. MAULTSBY, JR., M.D.
©1974, by CHARLES C THOMAS • PUBLISHER
ISBN 0-398-02915-6
Library of Congress Catalog Card Number: 73 9540
Beliefs
Attitudes
Facts
Logic
Albert Ellis, Ph.D.
CHARLES C THOMAS • PUBLISHER • SPRINGFIELD • ILLINOIS

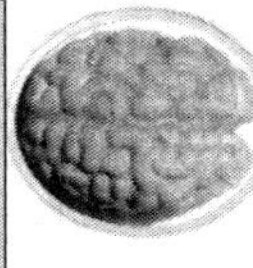

Emotional Well-Being Through Rational Behavior Training

Based on how the mind receives, absorbs and acts upon the specific and repetitive information we feed it: **'Tell It What to Do, Not What to Avoid.'** Mute the word "Don't". GHMBS blitzes you with targeted quotes, keen theories and thought processes designed to engrain them to the point that they become your empowering default mindsets and prudent baseline personality traits. This is not from 'The Department of Redundancy Department', nor fluff or filler. It is simply cultivating change via my purposeful emersion. Conditioning is like grooming. You work at it daily. Conditioning, good or bad, takes time. And, quite often we are reconditioning faulty traits, 'data', habits and mindsets that have taken root over time. So, rebooting so to speak, with the consistent saturation and application of the new or corrected 'data' is critical so that the preferred belief systems are able to have a full and lasting effect. Consider my form of mental conditioning for our psyche as being similar to how we apply lotion to moisturize our skin. When it is first applied to dry or damaged skin it's very quickly absorbed, requiring saturation and reapplication on a given timetable. Furthermore, we all have varying skin types, unique pigmentations, sensitivities, allergies, oily areas, dry, irritable and/or rough patches that require we use multiple types or brands of lotions or potions for various needs. Likewise, with our psyches, we all have our own unsavory personality traits, quirks, sensitivities, pet peeves and periodic rash reactions. Right? **Human Conditions**, yet, solely unique to us. We must be as dutiful and diligent in identifying and addressing our psyche issues as we are with our grooming rituals. Especially the hidden flaws that we try to camouflage and keep to ourselves. **In sports, our psyche flaws will surely be unveiled.** Just like a pimple. C'mon! As our bodies change over time, likewise our attitudes, temperaments, maturity levels and knowledge-base, all must evolve.

My Mind & Body Conditioning: A Universal Elixir for all Ailments and Endeavors.

YOU DON'T HAVE TO BE SICK TO GET BETTER!

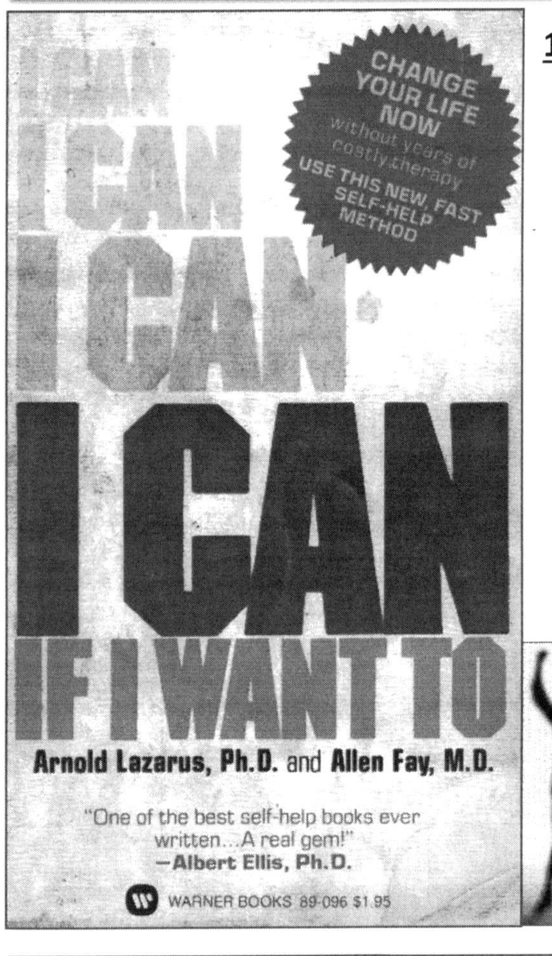

1975

DO YOU BELIEVE

—that you are a victim of circumstances?
—that you must <u>earn</u> your happiness?
—that pleasing other people is the only way to get along in this world?

This kind of thinking can make you neurotic and can ruin your life. Begin now to combat this defeatist, defeating attitude with this easy-to-follow, step-by-step program. Learn how to assert yourself and control your future.

Change your thinking,
Change your behavior,
Change your life.

"This is a little book, but it packs a lot of common sense. It is a how-to-do-it manual, and it must be taken seriously."
—Kansas City Star

WARNER BOOKS 89-096 $1.95

WARNER BOOKS EDITION

We firmly believe that therapy is education rather than healing; that it is growth rather than treatment.

Once people realize that overcoming emotional problems is an educational process, the concept of *self-education* is easily understood. In the same way as it is possible to teach oneself gourmet cooking, a foreign language, or how to type, psychological self-help is entirely feasible. In fact in the professional literature of late, there has been an enormous amount of data confirming the value of self-management and self-help procedures.

At the early age of ten, I was conditioned with what would become my 'Branding Philosophy' upon purchasing this $1.95 book, which I still have today. Beyond the content, I embraced the presentation format of:

BELIEF Identification

RETHINKING

Behavioral CHANGE

I CAN IF I WANT TO

MISTAKE # 9: BE RIGHT. SHOW OTHERS THAT YOUR OPINIONS ARE BETTER THAN THEIRS

1. I *think* I know, therefore I do know.
2. My opinion is not just my opinion but a fact.
3. It is important that my opinion be right. Otherwise I look like a fool.
4. When I present my views, if I don't act as if I'm right, people won't respect me.

DO *YOU* BELIEVE ANY OF THIS?

Judge, Not! ~ Live & Let Live!

Gab Dad Quote:

'Opinions are like butt-holes, everyone has one; some emit very unsavory content.'

English as a Strange Language

'YOU MUST REFUSE TO BELIEVE IT WHEN ANY COACH VIEWS YOUR GAME AS REFUSE.'

G' Hoops: 'One Coach's Trash Is Another Coach's Treasure!'

Whether it's MaryAnn vs. Ginger, Miracle Whip vs. Mayonnaise, or Porsche vs. Corvette; we all must learn to hone the ability to agree to disagree.

ARNOLD LAZARUS/ALLEN FAY

HOW TO CHANGE

A. Rethinking

1. There is a big difference between fact and truth on the one hand, and belief, opinion, taste, and preference on the other.
2. A fact can be tested or checked: Lincoln was born in 1809. A belief, opinion, taste, or preference cannot: corn tastes better than peas, long hair is more attractive than short hair.
3. Every person has the right to express his opinion without being ridiculed or shouted down.
4. Differences of opinion and one's tolerance of these differences lead to growth.
5. It is important to avoid attacking or labeling those who disagree with us. There is a significant difference between what is wrong and what we dislike or disapprove of. There is no such thing as wrong or immoral thinking or behavior unless it can be shown that it results in harm to other people.

Corrective Behavior

1. When not dealing with clear-cut facts, practice saying "It seems to me, it is my impression, I think, I believe, it is my opinion . . ." rather than "I know, it is a fact, it is certain," etc.
2. Monitor this trait in others as well as in yourself. Record with a check mark in the notebook every dogmatic statement you make: "You are wrong, I

65

I CAN IF I WANT TO

am right, you have no taste, you don't know what's good, you have no brains."
3. Politely correct this type of communication in others. For example, if someone says "You have no taste," you respond nicely with "You mean you disagree with what I said."
4. Practice disagreeing constructively with others: "This may be a great painting but I don't particularly like it."
5. If you are not accustomed to thinking about the difference between fact and belief, make a mental note each time you have a discussion or dispute as to whether the issue is an "f" issue (fact) or a "b" issue (belief).

WE ARE PRODUCTS OF OUR CONDITIONING

While practice bowling at age 11, he said, "If you join the Blazers you'll get a knowledge of the game of basketball that will last a lifetime."
Weldon Lafluer, Father of Andre Lafluer

IRON SHARPENS IRON

Training with superior 'mates makes you better!

At L.A.'s West Pico Bowl, two blocks from my home, Mr. Lafluer approached me after repeatedly seeing me practicing after school. I emulated the (late) great Earl Anthony and bowled left-handed with his trademark Orange Ebonite ball. Mr. Lafluer noted seeing me also bowl right-handed, with different balls. Yes, sir. I throw with both, but I write only left-handed. Enticed, he asked if I played basketball what hand did I dribble with? Both. Shoot with? Both. Hit a baseball? Both sides, equally. In sum: Athletically Ambidextrous. Lastly, he inquired about my grades. Solid, nothing ever below a B, or I wouldn't be here. Thus, my Blazer recruitment and bond with Andre arose with a promise. **Basketball IQ!**

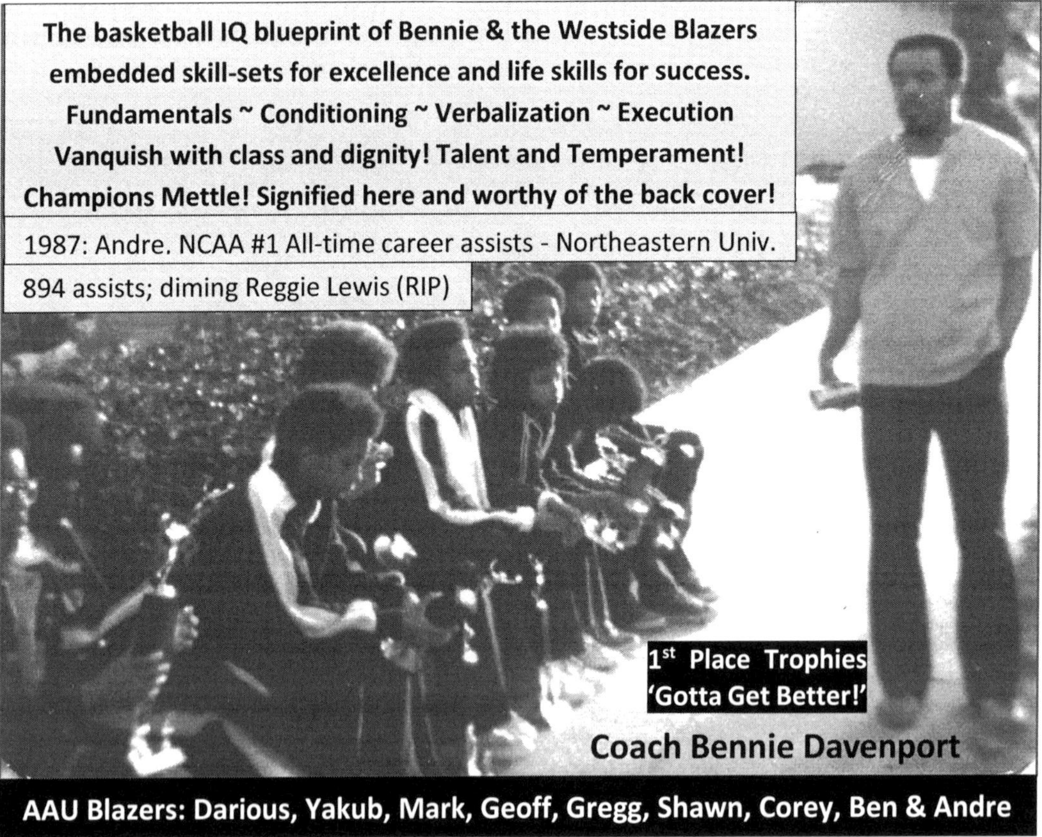

The basketball IQ blueprint of Bennie & the Westside Blazers embedded skill-sets for excellence and life skills for success.
Fundamentals ~ Conditioning ~ Verbalization ~ Execution
Vanquish with class and dignity! Talent and Temperament!
Champions Mettle! Signified here and worthy of the back cover!
1987: Andre. NCAA #1 All-time career assists - Northeastern Univ.
894 assists; diming Reggie Lewis (RIP)
1st Place Trophies
'Gotta Get Better!'
Coach Bennie Davenport

AAU Blazers: Darious, Yakub, Mark, Geoff, Gregg, Shawn, Corey, Ben & Andre

Corey Gaines played for Loyola Marymount's killer squad, Riley's Knicks, and won rings coaching the WNBA's Phoenix Mercury. G' Hoops embodies the drills, core techniques, verbiage, fundamentals, and commitment to **'lock-up'** defense, engrained within me and my band of brothers by Bennie & Yakub's dad, Wooden Pupil, Olympian; Walt Hazzard.

The Blazer's selection process was unique. There was no physical tryout. They wanted raw moldable talent with good attitudes and good grades that could be cultivated into a cream of the crop basketball squad, in ability and behavior. Our diet and nutrition was monitored as intensely as our report cards. We had prepared meals and on-staff academic advisors. Also, a 'Parental Participation & Code of Conduct Agreement' ensured that all our players could compete without any pressure, anxiety, negativity or counter-productive input from our parents. A rarity in youth sports then and now. Core of G'$! I played just two years with the Blazers, but, Andre Lefluer and I became very close friends spending much time together on and off the court for many years to come. **'Dre and Mr. Lafluer Honed ME!**

NATURE & NURTURE

The weekend after I signed to play with the Blazers my Uncle Mike swooped me up in his sweet Triumph TR-6 drop-top convertible for a Hoop Intervention trip. It was the intro to a G'$ Brand Venture!

My dad took great pride in his German Volkswagon Squareback, sharing the translated definition (Hitler's demand) "A car for all the people." ~ Volkswagon

First Stop: Fedco, the original Costco-like one-stop membership store which sold EVERYTHING! Uncle Mike took me to the suits department and had my waist measured, then on to the sporting goods section where he studied and carefully chose two items of '*underwear*'? We paid and rolled out to his house on 64th Street, off La Brea; ten minutes of top down joy. Having two younger daughters, as did his best friend and neighbor, Carl Henderson, we enjoyed many such outings as they equally embraced my gregarious personality which also filled a void. Upon arrival at his house, I waved to Uncle Carl across the street, polishing his car.

Uncle Mike & Uncle Carl: My intro to the 'Jock Strap' & Porsche

Inside, Uncle Mike gave me my first 'jock straps' as a serious conversation ensued about my transition and commitment to playing competitive basketball; not playground or rec! Hoop was his realm by way of example and, from this day on, it would be my venture of a lifetime. I'd aspire to emulate and employ the 'game' and genetic potential he bestowed. I was shy putting on my '*athletic supporter*'. Uncle Mike, "Boy, I've changed your diapers!" Then, he educated me on anatomy and the virtues of this critical 'contraption'; as a must!

Later, I went to visit with Uncle Carl. A visit that would impact my life and my hoop vision. Uncle Carl would put a new spin on the term: To Vanquish! A Brand & Man I'd Emulate.

G'hoops Brand Emulation: Ferdinand Porsche 9/3 ~ 'Vanquish'

Uncle Carl was tinkering with his beautiful black sports car. I noted the engine was in the back just like my Dads Volkswagon Squareback. He told me both cars were made by the same man. Dads car was for all people but the Black Beauty was designed for a select few.

Uncle Carl: "This is a high performance automobile designed to compete. The Brand is named after a Man who persevered through severe trials and tribulations to engineer and create a race car with one vision: To Vanquish! It comes from the same country as you do. Germany. Land of the Autobahn. Where there is no speed limit. Young G, this is a Porsche. The pinnacle 911S. The engine placement gives a competitive racing performance advantage. She's made for speed, not comfort. She's designed to be pushed to the limit. In fact, if you don't push a Porsche with regularity they break down on you. It's the ultimate driving experience. Proper maintainance is most essential. Judge for yourself. Let's take a ride. And, read this book on Herr Porsche."

That was the type of Brand Vision I wanted to emulate in my hoop quest. G' PORSCHE! I read the Porche book while he called Uncle Mike, who shared our 'First Jock Strap Chat.' We got into the tiny plush cockpit. He said, 'Buckle Up'. **As he started the engine: OMG!** This was a true thrill! On the open road the 911 roared it's approval. Fast, tight and nimble. We stopped for gas and Lesson One: Only Top-Grade Fuel for this Machine. Got it! Then, Uncle Carl took me to visit his good friend, L.A. Laker Happy Harriston. Memorable Day! My Porsche kinship is organic in nature, void of arrogance. **Mr. Porsche & G'$: Sept 3rd!**

#1 L.A. RADIO: 1580 K-DAY
Before Swoosh: We wore Converse!
Before Levis: We wore Toughskins!!
You can't do
pic s with
asic people.

Yakub, Ben, G' (w/ cast), Geoff & Coach Bennie

Pasteur Jr. High ~ P.E. Teacher, Mentor & Coach Ron Kiino

Back then we went to 'Jr. High', which is called Middle School today in the 7th grade and High School in the 10th grade. I attended Louis Pasteur Jr. High where I was molded by a life-changing P.E. teacher/mentor, Coach Ron Kiino. He made me expand my comfort zone and strive for more than I thought I was capable of. Words cannot duly express his impact on me at such a critical stage in my life. We reconnected in 2012. I was humbled by his excitement to hear from me. The sincerity in his words was chilling, knowing that his teachings were never forgotten and remain as pillars for my life and my 'Mental Athlete Pedigree'. Unbeknown to me, Coach Kiino had broken rigid ethnicity barriers in baseball with college stardom at USC, followed by a distinguished pro career. A truly humble hero.

SWAS: School Within A School (AVID-type) Class Curriculum

At Pasteur, I was in a curriculum named SWAS that met for Periods One thru Four. There were two adjoning classrooms with 30 students each. My teacher was Mr. Joe Zell and in the other was Mr. George Woods. A superiorly diverse and demanding academic platform.

Noble Mentors ~ Role Models ~ Tough Positive Sports Examples

During my formative years. I enjoyed being social. I went to house parties, pool parties, roller rinks and BBQ's where alcohol was present. My parents hosted parties rampant with libations. But, I had my noble elder role models (Mark, Dave Lewis & Marvin Mensies) to emulate. So, I easily abstained from alcohol until I went off to college. **Bless My 3 'Bros'!**

Perfect First Job: '31' Flavors...Vested My 1st 'Cycle

My Dad had an affinity for good ice cream. Baskin Robbins was only a block away. I went so often the Manager, Tony, offered me a **Sweet Job!**

2 Blocks N/W: La Cieniga Park on Gregory Way in Beverly Hills

Huge public pool! Baseball fields, tennis courts, outdoor lighted basketball courts where I first learned to play 'Shirts & Skins'. Also, I met my good friend, Marc Copage, who was a child actor on the popular and barrier-breaking TV show, Julia. He played the role of Corey, son of Julia, who was played by African-American actress, Diahann Carroll. We often played baseball at Roxbury Park!

Marc Copage

"The main ingredient of a player's stardom is the rest of the team."

John Wooden

MY PERSONAL 'PYRAMID' FROM JOHN WOODEN

July 1977: I attended the UCLA Summer Sports Camp, a choice that would forever alter my destiny. Four weeks of learning various sports, in pristine facilities, while being coached by some of the best college athletes and coaches at one of the top universities in the nation. One week each of Swimming, Track & Field, Tennis and Basketball with fundamentals and college-level progressive training techniques being taught by UCLA athletes of each sport. Beyond, being on-time every day-without fail, attentive, focused and enthusiastic to learn and get better, I wanted to be coachable and soak up as much knowledge as possible. Seemingly abstract curiosities were creating a vision of my future; from navigating a college campus, choices of what to eat in the cafeteria, to probing each coach about their path to becoming a top-tier student-athlete on a D-1 collegiate level. Each one had personal stories of perseverance that was unique and inspirational, and I was a sponge taking mental notes.

On the final day I was excited as I took my seat at the farewell awards ceremony. Beyond the *participation swag* all athletes would receive, and the effort, morale and hustle awards for those of lesser athletic abilities, my focus was on the special certificates to be awarded to the few who excelled in each individual sport. I had worked so hard that it was difficult to throttle my competent expectation. This camp had hosted over 200 athletes and since we rotated weekly I didn't get to see most of the others perform in person. How was the competition, I wondered? As each award was presented and my name went uncalled, I became more and more disappointed, while maintaining my composure. As the final certificate was given, I was devastated on the inside but I kept my emotions in check. Then, Coach John Wooden stepped forward to address us. He spoke of the coaches' excitement in recalling one talented athlete who, beyond great skill, was highly coachable and humble enough to accept and immediately apply their direction with enthusiasm and zeal. He excelled and improved noticeably in every sport. "A special athlete merits a special award". Then, he called my name, and presented me with a personally autographed and inscribed glossed plaque of his 'Pyramid of Success' that read: 'Most Improved Athlete & Best All-Around Performer'. As he shook my hand he said to me, "Consider this a 'Most Likely to Succeed Award', you have a bright future ahead of you in whatever sport you choose to pursue. Take and apply these principles, always." Awe-inspiring; the 40 year-old Wizard of Westwood, a true legend, giving me his seal of approval. Humbling! This priceless plaque would be posted above my bed for many years to come as a constant source of my quest.

Trivia time

Who was the first three-time consensus All-America basketball player?

What's On Your Wall??? ~ G'$ 1984: University of Hawaii-Hilo

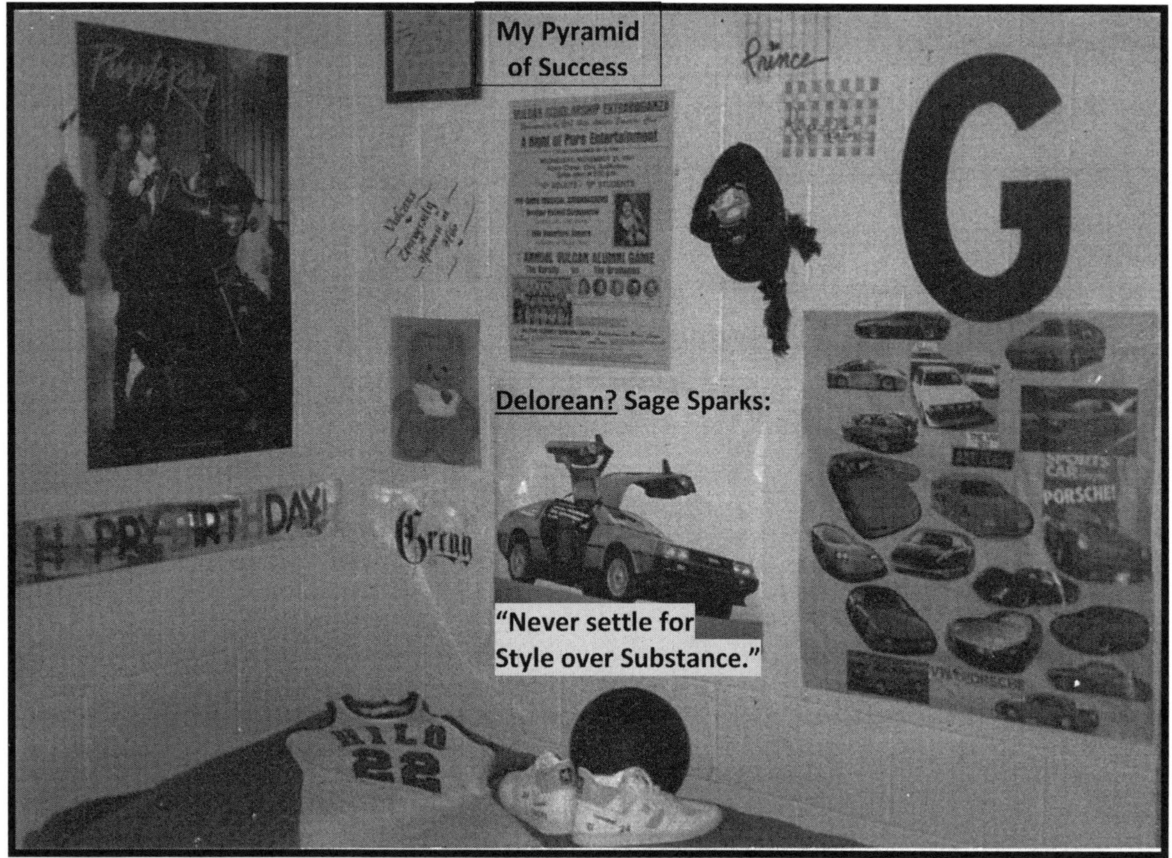

- My age 12, Wooden inscribed 'Pyramid of Success' Award Plaque!
- 'G' placard: Most coveted, as Sparks has a matching 'D' in his lair!
- Porsche: Collage personally created! Brand athletically embodied!
- Delorean Sports Car Poster: Sage Sparks' Quote Applies to Sports!
- Jersey: Rep the Name on the front ~ Brand the Name on the back!
- The Ball is my Best Friend. And, two or more are ALWAYS at-hand!
- Shoes? Not Just Footwear; G' Flight Take-off & Landing Apparatus!
- Prince! Music Can Uniquely Soothe The Soul And Ignite The Spirit!

Trivia answer

John Wooden of Purdue (1930-32)

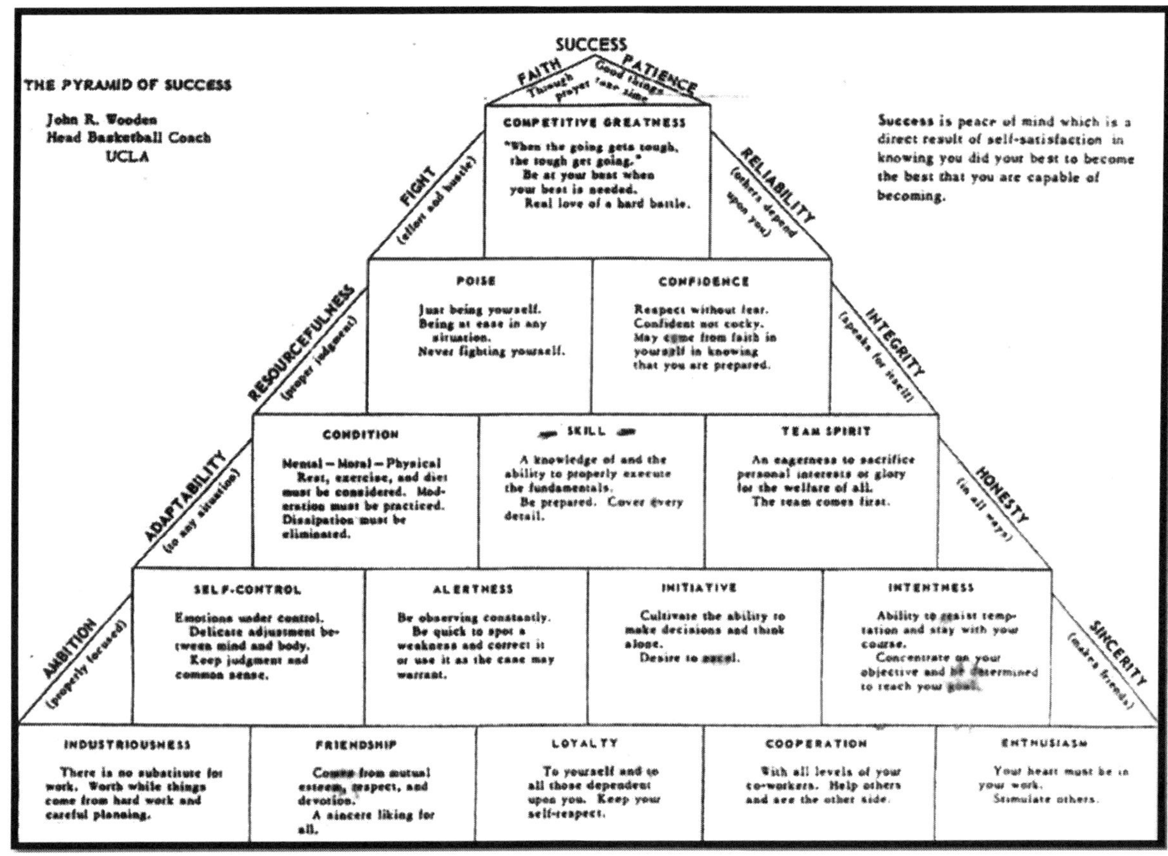

Compare & Contrast: As a true Wooden disciple, discrepancies and omissions from my bestowed Pyramid of Success to the 2013 'CoachJohnWooden.com' version must be identified and RECTIFIED!

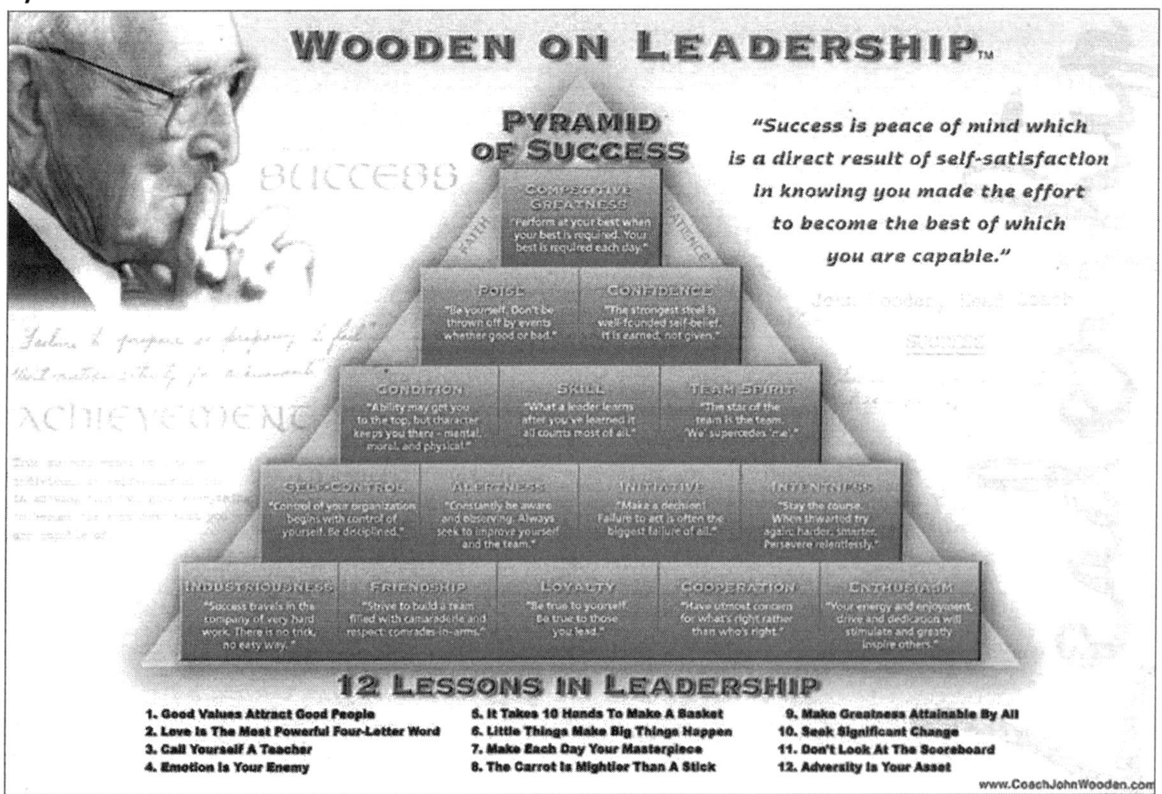

Industriousness	**There is no subsitute for hard work. Worthwile things come from hard work and careful planning.**
2013 Pyramid	**Success travels in the company of very hard work. There is no trick. No easy way.**
The Difference	**"No Substitute For": Leave No Wiggle Room. Traveling in the company of is vague. Worthwile Things: All Universal. "Careful Planning": A must-have trait! Not in '13 Pyramid!**
Friendship	**Comes from mutual esteem, respect and devotion. A sincere liking for all.**
2013 Pyramid	**Strive to build a team filled with camaraderie and respect; comerade at-arms.**
The Difference	**Mutual...: Three Critial Components! Not in '13 Pyramid!? Sincere liking...: Being good natured as a personality trait.**
Loyalty	**To yourself and all those dependent upon you. Keep your self-respect.**
2013 Pyramid	**Be true to yourself. Be true to those you lead.**
The Difference	**Factually, I don't lead my coaches, agents or my sponsors. Yet, they all 'depend' upon me and deserve 'true' loyalty. Self-respect: A must-have trait; absent in the '13 Pyramid.**
Cooperation	**With all levels of your co-workers. Help others and see the other side.**
2013 Pyramid	**Have utmost concern for what's right rather than who's right.**
The Difference	**All levels...: Teammates, Ball Boys, Equipment Managers, Trainers, Office Secretaries and, for me, even the Janitors! Help Them to Help You! Maintain a two-way perspective.**
Enthusiasm	**Your heart must be in your work. Stimulate others.**
2013 Pyramid	**Your energy and enjoyment, drive and dedication will stimulate and greatly inspire others.**
The Difference	**"MUST": Emphasizes a Required Prerequisite for Success. Inner SPIRIT is where contagious passions are ignited and fueled. "IN YOUR WORK": Critical Mindset for any Quest!**

◆ Missing 2013 Pyramid ~ Sidebar: Ambition (Properly focused)

Self-Control	**Emotions under control. Delicate adjustment between mind and body. Keep judgement and commons sense.**
2013 Pyramid	**Control of your organization begins with control of yourself. Be disciplined.**
The Difference	**'Control of Emotions': Critical. Mind and Body Awareness. Judgement!! Common Sense!! BOTH VOID in '13 Pyramid!**
Alertness	**Be observing constantly. Be quick to spot a weakness and correct it or use it as the case may warrant.**
2013 Pyramid	**Always be aware and observing. Always seek to improve yourself and the team.**
The Difference	**Spot a weakness and correct it or use it: Within Yourself or Your Opponent. Awareness & Analysis & Application!**
Initiative	**Cultivate the ability to make decisions and think alone. A desire to excel.**
2013 Pyramid	**Make a decision! Failure to act is often the biggest failure of all.**
The Difference	**Cultivate Speaks to an Introspective Learning Process! Independant Thinking is a Highly Valuable Personal Trait. Desire to Excel! Desire to Excel! Desire to Excel! NO TYPO!**
Intentness	**Ability to resist temptation and stay with your course. Concentrate on your objective and be determined to reach your goal.**
2013 Pyramid	**Stay the course. When thwarted try again, harder, smarter. Persevere relentlessly.**
The Difference	**"The Ability to Resist Temptation": CRITICAL VERBIAGE! GS PASSION: A FOCUSED & DETERMINED 'GOAL GETTER'! GS PROMO: A 'MENTAL ATHLETE' HAS 'POSITIVE INTENT'!**

◆ Missing 2013 Pyramid (r) Sidebar: Sincerity (makes friends)

◆ Missing 2013 Pyramid (l) Sidebar: Adaptability (To any situation) sole

Condition	**Mental ~ Moral ~ Pyhsical** **Rest, diet and exercise must be considered. Moderation must be practiced. Dissipation must be eliminated.**
2013 Pyramid	**Ability may get you to the top. But, character keeps you there - mental, moral, and physical**
The Difference	**Integration of Rest, Diet & Excercise: As a Must! Balance! Moderation: Must Practice! Abstain! Void in '13 Pyramid! G'$: Excel & Sustain! You Must Be FIT, AGILE & DURABLE!**

Skill	**A knowledge of and the ability to properly execute the fundamentals. Be prepared. Cover every detail.**
The Center of the Pyramid 2013 Pyramid	**What a leader learns after you have learned it all counts the most.**
The Difference	**Whatda...? A Wooden Pyramid void of his sole trademark term, "Fundamentals", is Blasphemy! Knowledge! Ability! Proper Execution! Preparation! Details! As a Disciple, it is my duty to forever tell the Teachings of the True Pyramid!**

Team Spirit	**An eagerness to sacrifice personal interests or glory for the welfare of all. The team comes first.**
2013 Pyramid	**The star of the team is the team. We supercedes 'me'.**
The Difference	**"Eagerness to Sacrifice": Compassion and Redirection for our noble personal goals and our true selfish motivations.**

Alertness	**Be observing constantly. Be quick to spot a weakness and correct it or use it as the case may warrant.**
2013 Pyramid	**Always be aware and observing. Always seek to improve yourself and the team.**
The Difference	**Spot a Weakness and Correct It Or Use It: Within Yourself or Your Opponent. G': Awareness ~ Analysis ~ Application**

◆ Missing 2013 Pyramid (r) Sidebar: Honesty (In all ways) cultivate

◆ Missing 2013 Pyramid (l) Sidebar: Resourcefulness (Proper judgement)

Poise	**Just being yourself. Being at ease in any situation. Never fighting yourself.**
2013 Pyramid	**Be yourself. Don't be thrown off by events whether good or bad.**
<u>The Difference</u>	**GS: THE MOST CRITICAL PERSONALITY TRAIT TO POSSESS! "Being at Ease": A CULTIVATED TRAIT! Not in '13 Pyramid! 'Never Fighting Yourself': KEEN PSYCHE & TEMPERAMENT.**

Confidence	**Respect without fear. Confident not cocky. May come from faith in yourself in knowing that you are prepared.**
2013 Pyramid	**The strongest steel is well-founded self-belief! It is earned, not given.**
<u>The Difference</u>	**3 Sage Vital Mental Mantras Linking Psyche & Demeanor! Inner Faith via Preparation. Competence keys Confidence. The Most Potent Emotion All Elite Athletes Must Possess!**

◆ Missing 2013 Pyramid (r) Sidebar: Integrity (Speaks for itself)

◆ Missing 2013 Pyramid (l) Sidebar: Fight (Effort and Hustle)

Competitive Greatness	**When the going gets tough, the tough get going. Be at your best when your best is needed. <u>Real love of a hard battle.</u>**
2013 Pyramid	**Perform at your best when your best is required. Your best is required each day.**
<u>The Difference</u>	**POWERFUL! Awareness of Self & Situation! Tough Times Inspire Inner Grit Toughness! 'Real Love of a Hard Battle'! <u>Intestinal Fortitude and Crunchtime Clutch Performances!</u>**

◆ Missing 2013 Pyramid (r) Sidebar: Reliability (Others depend upon you)

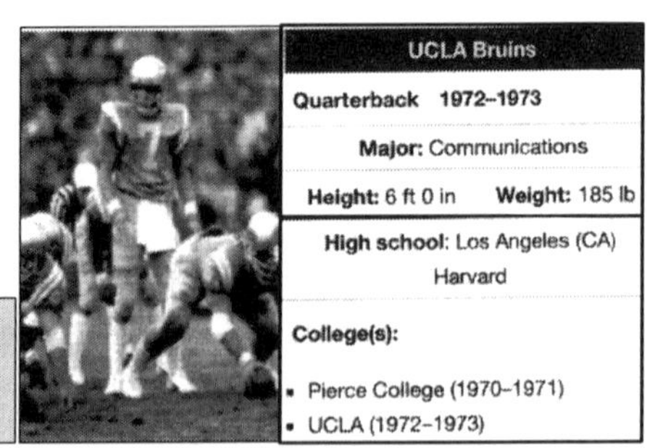

UCLA Bruins
Quarterback 1972–1973
Major: Communications
Height: 6 ft 0 in Weight: 185 lb
High school: Los Angeles (CA) Harvard
College(s):
Pierce College (1970–1971)
UCLA (1972–1973)

UCLA Quarterback Mark Harmon aka Special Agent Jethro Gibbs on N.C.I.S!

◆ **(l) Sidebar: Faith ~ Missing Quote (through prayer)**

SUCCESS	**Success is peace of mind which is a direct result of self-satisfaction in knowing you did your best to become the best you are capable of becoming.**
2013 Pyramid	**Success is peace of mind which is a direct result of self-satisfaction in knowing you made the effort to become the best of which you are capable.**
<u>The Difference</u>	**GS: Knowing you DID your BEST and DOING your BEST set the bar for my realm of success. Clearly, Making the Effort pales if compared to 'Doing your Best'. It Lowers The Bar. Effort Isn't Enough! My Plaque Embodies a Higher Calling!**

◆ **(r) Sidebar: Patience ~ Missing Quote: (Good things take time)**

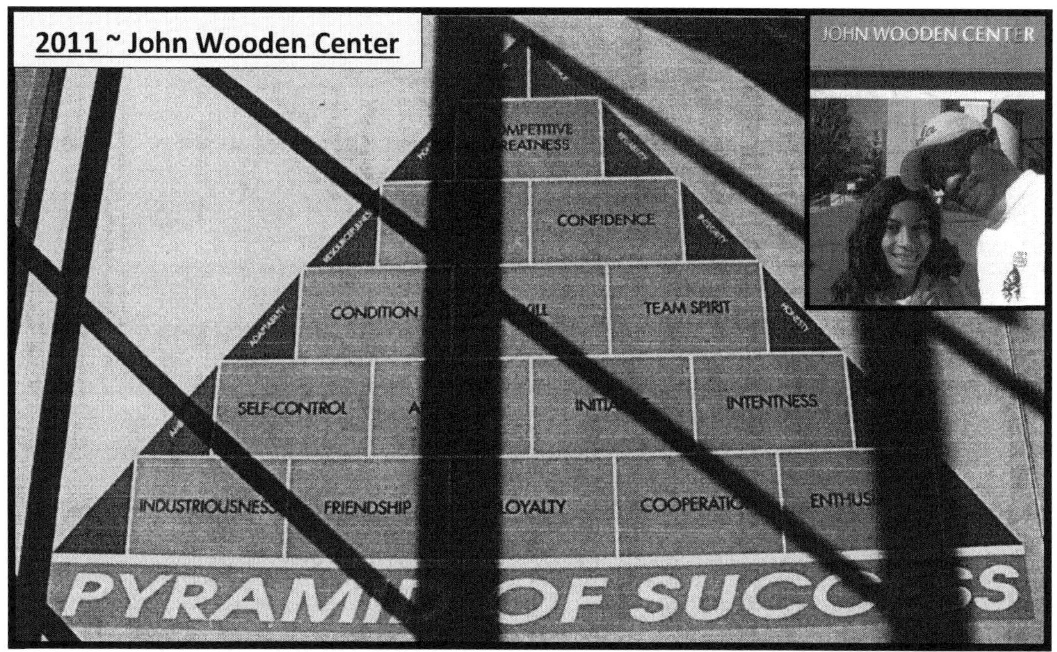

Solo & Duo vs. Team Sports ~ 'Etiquette' vs. 'Gladiator' ~ Static vs. Fluid Sports

✎ Etiquette Sports: Rivals can't dictate your ability to compete.

- Not Competing Against an Opponent ~ Limited Interaction with Competitors.
- Bowlers: Compete against and adapt to the lane conditions; not contestants.
- Golfers: Compete against and adapt to the course and climate; not contenders.
- Gymnasts: Compete for points based on the execution of routines; not rivals.
- Net Sports: Compete against rival(s) in full sight. ~ Taunting! But, No Touching!

✎ Gladiator Sports: Survival & Schematics ~ Self-Starter & Synergy

COMPETE: 'To achieve mastery of or to strive for a prize'

I interprete being multi-talented or possessing a diverse skill-set as pale semi-compliments. Recognition Proceeds Application of Skill. What skill to apply when, **and** how to apply it.

Cerebral & Versatile: Adaptable Aptitudes & Skill-sets ~ Awareness & Ability

Awareness: Self Awareness ~ Court Awarenss ~ Situational Awareness Teammate Awareness (make them better!) ~ 'Crunch Time' Awareness

When and How to: Dictate & Direct ~ Delegate & Defer ~ Dominate & Destroy

I wanted to be great! I trained harder! I studied my craft! I had great mentors!

Individual Training: 'GottaWanna' Pay the Cost to Be the Boss

The difference maker. Hour by Hour. 'To Achieve Mastery Of.' I knew my competition practiced hard, had private coaches and suitable skills. But, my solo training system was something they were not duplicating. I fixated on cultivating a clear competitive advantage beyond skill, technique and cardio. Psyche! While others played video games, I was on my G'$ Grind for merit in multiple sports, and on a hunt for elite supremacy in one: Basketball. **Covet fatigue and push beyond it!** Through the pain, doubt and despair! Pay your dues!

Every Damn Day! 'It's not the hours you put in. It's what you put into the hours!'

Cross Training: Fit, Flexible, Agile & Durable ~ G'$ 'FlexAgility'

Primed by my biological bro, Mark, his BFF, Marvin Mensies & my 2nd bro, Dave Lewis!

- Jumped rope 1000 reps with precision and a scheme. Minus 5 per miss! Ouch!
- Got on my bike/Lifecycle with focus, drive, and a predetermined, timed route!
- Went to the Santa Monica Pier for 3 mile sand runs to Venice Beach **and** back!
- Laced up my skates, soon Nike rollerblades, to train. Not just at the roller rink!
- Dove into the pool strictly to do laps. Not once did I play 'Marco Polo'. **Cardio!**
- Stretched with Cognizance & Consistency. G' Hoops Pre-Flight Elasticity System

Dave Lewis: "I always said 'Little Gregg' got his hops from our typical 10-mile bike rides to La Brea Tar Pits and Farmers Market (pre-Grove) and our monthly 30-mile trips to Santa Monica, Venice, Marina Del Ray, then south to the old Orange Julius in Manhattan Beach. Mark and I had sweet Schwinn 10-speeds. Gregg rode a heavy steel metal single-speed dirt bike from Fedco. We'd be at the top of a steep hill as Little G' trailed behind, never stopping. When he was 15 and I was 18½, we were playing 1-on-1 in his backyard and Gregg took one dribble at me, went up and dunked right over me! In close quarters. Nasty! And, I never played him 1-on-1 again. Ever. He had mad game and sic boosties."

A gift to myself on my 13th birthday that was a mind and body roadmap in my quest for excellence, as a student of the game.

VIA CASSETTE TAPES AND MY SONY WALKMAN; THE FOUNDATION WAS LAID FOR MIND & BODY CONDITIONING, THE 'MENTAL ATHLETE' AND GLOBAL HOOPS.

By: Stan Kellner, 1977

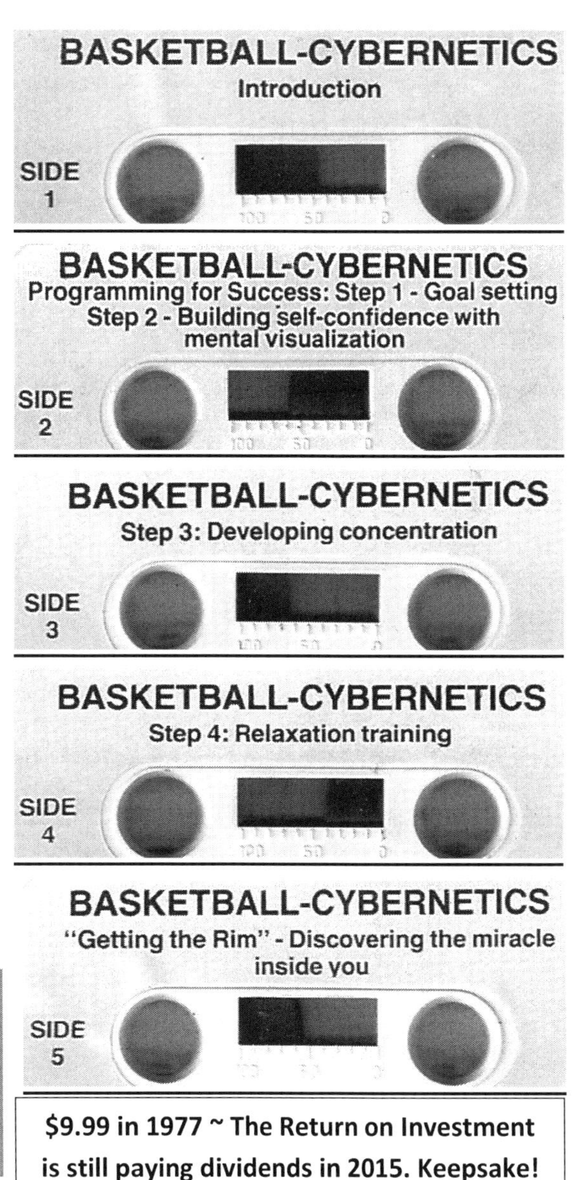

$9.99 in 1977 ~ The Return on Investment is still paying dividends in 2015. Keepsake!

BASKETBALL-CYBERNETICS

Becoming the clutch performer and developing your own personal tradition of winning

SIDE 6

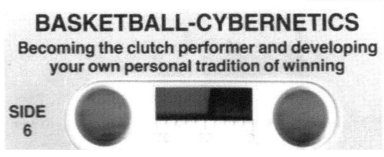

We are measured by performance, victory and, yes, championships. My G'$ Axiom: To Vanquish

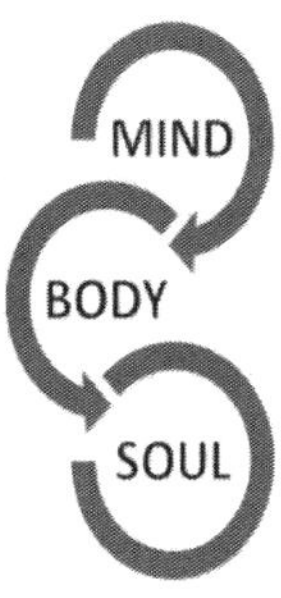

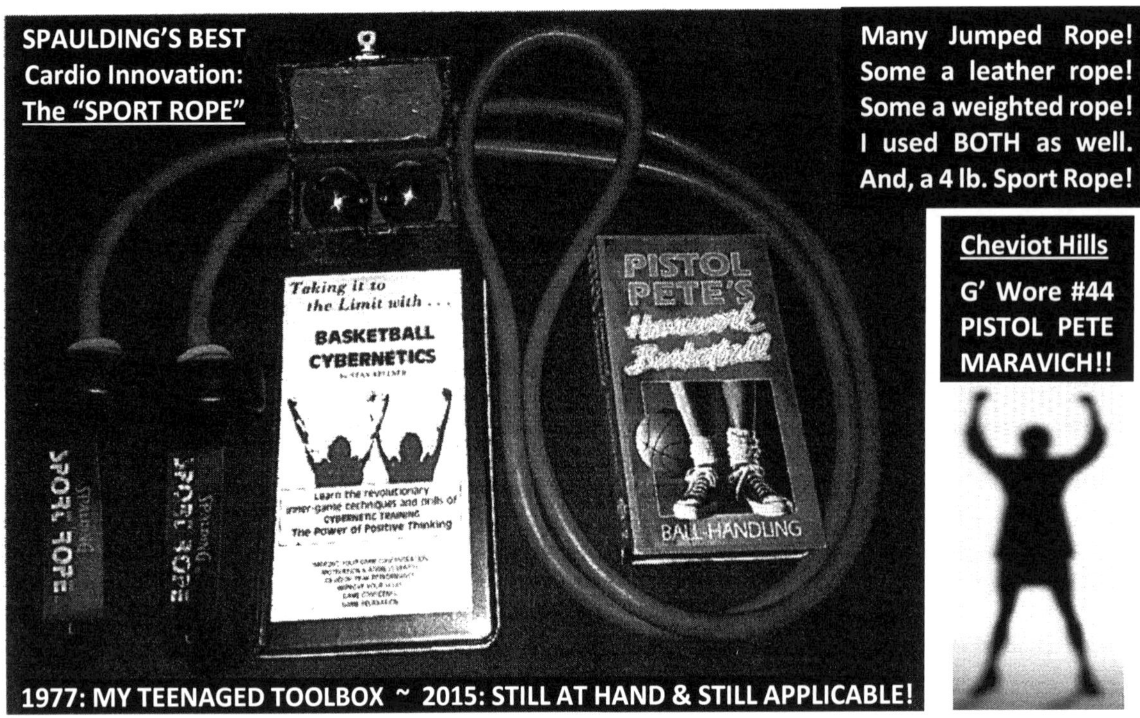

During my eighth grade year I had my first experience playing for two basketball teams simultaneously; 'Play Ball' (Culver City AAU) and Cheviot Hills Rec.! Cultivating the acute awareness and ability to play different roles in different systems with different teams and teammates; sometimes on the same day, was a foundational **G' Hoops Trait: Versatility!**

❖ PlayBall: G'$ Future Impact: Asst. Coach Al Quote:

> **"G', I'm going call you Pure! It's a perfect description of your jump shot. PURE!"**

- ✎ **Arch Visualization 'Hoop Hands' Drill**
- ✎ Bank Shot: Awareness ~ Angles ~ Fractional Aquity ~ Proficiency Drills
- ✎ Timed Cardio Sand Runs: **Deep Sand 1½ miles ~ Shore Line 1½ miles!**

❖ Cheviot Hills Pre-draft Tryouts: Dribbling drill and five open shots. **I missed ALL 5!** Mom Quote: "Don't fret, they see it." Coach Mike:

> **"I drafted him in Round One! I knew Gregg could lead my team to a championship."**

First Pre-season Game: Final possession down by one point and I passed the ball to an open teammate who missed the shot. We lost. I consoled my 'mate. Coach Mike met with my mom. She waited until we got to the car. **Rule One:** 'Don't Critique Your Kid in Public!' "Coach needs you to be more selfish. Not every player is equipped to take and make that shot. You're at your best in the clutch. Gotta be willing to be the hero or the goat." 'Gotcha Mom!' Coach Mike inspired me to 'Be The Man' and Cultivate 'Killer Instinct'!

Coach Mike, in tears, at our 'Champions Banquet': "Gregg is the best player I've ever had the pleasure to coach. A Warrior. A Champion. And, our MVP!"

The Wilshire Cobras **Junior Thurman** **Home Field: Fairfax High School**

Football? Mom said, "Oh No!" Pops said, "Heck yes!" My Dad took off from work to attend the registration!!

#87: As a so-called tight-end, I'd use this season as a learning experience of how to suit-up, train, hit and be hit in a violent sport where proper form and technique is literally life-saving. I was a sponge in studying and learning the terminology, drills and schemes; and getting to know and later emulate our star QB (#10) Junior Thurman. Like his brother, Dennis, (then) a stalwart defensive back with the Dallas Cowboys, Junior was also very smart, athletic and tough, yet extremly humble, easy-going, and was often smiling. He was a natural leader, a solid QB, a great teammate and a good personal friend. It was a prophetic blessing to have had his blueprint to emulate in my own QB quest. Coach Ferguson was a great teacher of the game with a humble cool swagger. **My love of the gridiron game and my QB Quest would trump all my Hoop Dreams!**

QB QUANDRY! G' "THE NEXT WARREN MOON!"

One Jr. High P.E. teacher, Coach Lertzman, was also the Head Varsity fooootball coach at Hamilton High. He resorted to soliciting my brother, Mark, to recruit me to Hamilton where Mark was in his senior year. **My bro' came home and gave me Lertzman's pitch:**

"If your brother comes to play quarterback for me, I will make him the next Warren Moon", referring to the NFL Houston Oiler (HOF) QB who was a star at Hamilton. My QB Spot: Guaranteed!!

But, my favorite P.E. teacher, Coach Ron Kiino sat me down in the middle of my senior year and inquired about a voluntary high school intergration program called the 'PWT', (Permit with Transportation). This would be an impactful life and athletic career altering chat. The PWT program would have me out the door every morning at 6:45 commuting one hour by bus to El Camino Real High, in Woodland Hills. A gamble on the unknown.

COACH RON KIINO: 'MR. MIYAGI' PROPHESY

"Gregg, sometimes it's better to be a big fish in a small bowl."
"Integration programs like this need student-athletes like you."

Pasteur Jr. High: 'Most Athletic'

"I knew Gregg had a very bright future. He always had a good head on his shoulders. In my 20-plus years, two of my all-time Top 5 student–athletes were from Pasteur Jr. High. Marvin Menzies and Gregg Scott, the prodigy kid brother of Marvin's best friend, Mark. But, Gregg was very special. A multi-sport marvel. The guy could've been a World Class gymnast. He was voted 'Most Athletic' by his Sr. Class! That speaks to his talent and fame." Ron Kiino

Nothing is more important to me than the mutual respect and admiration of my peers. Being voted 'Most Athletic' by my Sr. Class and featured in the yearbook was humbling.

One of my good friends at Pasteur was the best and fastest reciever I ever played with. Stephen Baker ('The Touchdown Maker'). He was going to Hamiilton and we had planned to make a great tandem at the next level. **Stephen Baker was an All-Star wide receiver who went on to Fresno State and won a Super Bowl with the N.Y. Giants!**

Stephen Baker

Mentor Dave Lewis: Quarterback & Recievers Camp Manual

'Bro' Dave Lewis

Dave Lewis provided many blessings and memories! From his Pacific Palisades High football games to his graduation. He played the sax! At Pali's Holiday Music Fest his band put us all in a frenzy jamming a 1974 KC & The Sunshine Band Masterpiece, **"That's the way I like it"**, to start the show!

Two Gifts: QB/Receivers Manual & Gifting his time training with me instead of his team. Dave signed to play WR at Cal State Long Beach, but spent his summer at La Cieniga Park. Working out with me! Running routes and teaching me the nuances of a good quarterback. QB Recivers Camp Manual: Diagrams, illustrations, sets, and drills was my first Workbook. A merged format of footwork, timing, reads and routes. Visualization Propels Execution.

Talent is God given. Be humble. Fame is man-given. Be grateful. Conceit is self-given. Be careful.

John Wooden

EL CAMINO REAL HIGH

BEE QB: Utilize Varsity Pro System

The Valley Circle Blvd. exit off the Ventura Fwy is the byway to ECR in Woodland Hills and also to Calabasas (KardasianVille) & Westlake Village. The upper crust of the West Valley. Yet, void of any racial issues. Classy!

ECR was a legit football school with only Varsity and a BEE team. Both had senior QB's! Six weeks of conditioning with the Varsity and Hell Week. Coach Nishimoto, "G' is QB."

Verbalization: An art and a required trait that requires a different voice based on the specific sport and the specific positions within that sport. My Varsity mentor, John Mazur!

- **As a quarterback: confident, calm, clear 'communication skills' are critical.**
  - **Know every players assignment on each play in the entire playbook.**
  - **Verbiage ~ Volume ~ Clarity ~ Tone ~ Voice Inflection ~ Tempo**
  - **'Command the Huddle' ~ Inspire ~ Leadership Without Criticism**
  - **Audible & Cadence at line of scrimmage. Poise under fire & duress!**
  - **Oxymoron: Simultaneous Execution of Progressions and Check-downs.**

Pre-Season Home Debut: Friday Night Lights at Pierce College!

Our 'home' games were road trips as our home field was nearby plush Pierce College First game vs. Fremont. First possenssion I was amazed at the speed of the game. Coach Nish' called a time-out. "Relax, Breathe, You're well prepared." Mental Game!. No X's and O's. 'Mr. Miyagi' worked wonders. By the 3rd quarter we wer up 17-7 after I threw my first TD. Next possession the Fremont band echoes a "Grapevine" as I'm at the line of scrimmage.

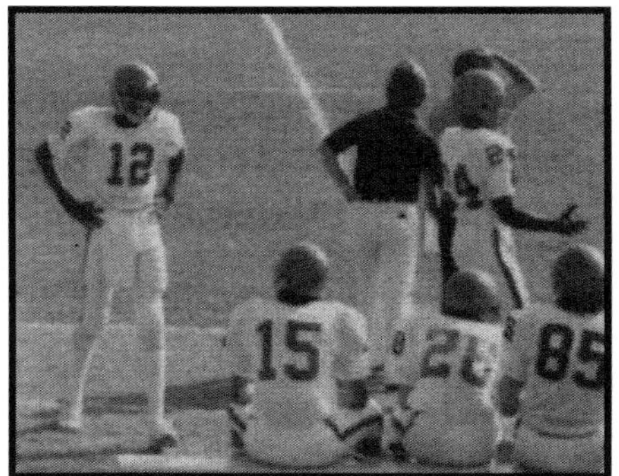

I look back at DT smiling., disregarding the play clock. Coach Nish callls a time-out for a sideline rant! "Keep Your Head in the Game!" The Varsity bus had arrived! The players were all lined up behind the end zone as I entered the huddle. 'QB Draw'. My 'mates got geeked! Fake back, follow my pulling guard, hit the hole, freeze the on-coming DB, recall Dave's Imminent Contact tip "Deliver a blow. See what you hit." Smack! Scott Score!

First QB TD 'Celebration' Coach Kiino "ACT LIKE YOU'VE BEEN THERE BEFORE."

The DB didn't expect that goal-line head-up collision from a QB. I was so excited as the Varsity boys erupted and the crowd roared insanely. I immediately handed the football to the ref (my spike in practice bounced up and hit me in the gut!). *Kiino* I dapped the V' hearing shrieks of folly as my linemen engulfed me in bliss.

ECR at Monroe High: It Never Rains In Southern California??

Freezing rain, driving wind and muddy conditions was the setting for **my five mishandled snaps in the First Half!** Coach Nishimoto spoke a truism in the lockerroom. "Our **playbook doesn't mean a thing** without the QB/Center exchange. We can't run our offense if we can't execute a **QB snap**." We solved that issue. But, I got smacked on a blitz, fumble, and they scooped and scored. **We Lost: 6-0**! I had failed my team! Yet, Coach Nish' ordered us all to take a quick shower: **"Wash off the loss and leave it here."**

Protectors of G'12: LT Derrick Brooks ~ LG Joel Feinstein ~ C Mark Gallasso ~ RG Greg Warlick ~ RT Mark Pullen ~

Next Week: A day game at Granada Hills High. Field of a Varsity QB: **John Elway.**

I threw three TD's, scored one TD, had 260 yards in the air, and no turnovers! Sweet Victory Happy Coach!

G's Playbook Mixture and Play-Changing Mischievousness

Inverted Slot Left. X Motion. 56 Blast Pass. Stick 64. Z Post. Snap: Reverse Pivot. Fake Hand-off. Drop Back. 70 Yards of Air!

In practice our D' was reading our plays and shutting us down so I changed a basic 15 yard curl into my **'Home Run'** play. Same basic play, except I swap receiver sets, added motion and a play-action fake hand-off culminating with a curl as the bait and a HR backside post!

Coach Nish' was also my 4th period teacher. Next day, "Mr. Scott please see me after class." "Show me that play in this playbook." 'No disrespect, Coach. It's a combo of your plays.' I opened my playbook to show him the pages of combo plays I'd created. He was amazed. Coach reviewed my work and asked the name of the play. 'The Home Run'. "Ok, go eat." Homecoming Game at Pierce College. The Varsity was watching. Three minutes left in a tie game. **Coach calls the 'Home Run'.** Touchdown! Nish' comes jumping into my arms!

'MentalAthlete' Facebook: Jim Wagoner Chat Conversation August 28, 2014

Jim Wag': "I'll never forget the 4th quarter 60-yard bomb you threw against Kennedy that enabled us to win our Homecoming game at Pierce College!"

G': 'I'll never forget how cool you were to me when I got the job. I do recall you were a 1st Team All-league DB on our team of champs! Be well QB. Ciao.'

1979 ALL VALLEY "AAAA" LEAGUE

BEE FOOTBALL TEAM

FIRST TEAM OFFENSE	
Mike Galasso — El Camino Real	Line
Ed Spurling — Cleveland	Line
Kavin Williams — San Fernando	Line
Todd Haines — Taft	Back
Jim Bubek — Monroe	Back
Greg Moser — El Camino Real	Back
Randy Bernstein — Granada Hills	Back
James Sneed — Monroe	Back
Rickey Carter — San Fernando	Back
Matt Hubert — Kennedy	Back
Gary Manuel — Kennedy	Back
*Barry Blonsky — Taft	Back
Kevin Lee — Monroe	Back
Charles Zaebik — Kennedy	Kicker

SECOND TEAM OFFENSE	
• Greg Scott — El Camino Real	Back
Chris Schoen — Taft	Back
Rick Bailey — San Fernando	Back
Ray Gonzalez — San Fernando	Back
Troy Robinson — Cleveland	Back
David Baldini — Cleveland	Back
Alden Clark — Granada Hills	Back
Tom Ruby — El Camino Real	Kicker
Greg Warlick — El Camino Real	Line
Dan Glogatch — Taft	Line
Scott Gibson — Kennedy	Line
Steve Price — Monroe	Line

FIRST TEAM DEFENSE	
*Mark Pullen — El Camino Real	Line
Kirk Kennedy — El Camino Real	Line
George Murphy — Monroe	LB
Henry Boyd — Kennedy	LB
Dave Pistotnik — El Camino Real	LB
Jeff Billie — Taft	LB
Troy Christman — El Camino Real	LB
Scott Cook — Cleveland	DB
Jim Wagoner — El Camino Real	DB
Mario Broughton — Monroe	DB
Michael Pugmire — Kennedy	DB
Arthur Ramsey — San Fernando	DB

SECOND TEAM DEFENSE	
Dave Walker — El Camino Real	DB
Gary Urie — El Camino Real	DB
Gerry Atkins — Taft	DB
Sam Tellez — Kennedy	DB
Steve Huerta — Kennedy	DB
Dan Augino — Kennedy	LB
John Quiroz — Monroe	LB
Delvin Akins — San Fernando	LB
Frank Romie — Taft	Line
Rene Flores — San Fernando	Line
Ricky Neil — Cleveland	Line
Mark Fluent — Taft	Line
Reginald Hill — Granada Hills	Line
Roy Close — Kennedy	Line

ECR: 4A League Champions & 12 All-League Players!

Politics in Sports...no Varsity or JV

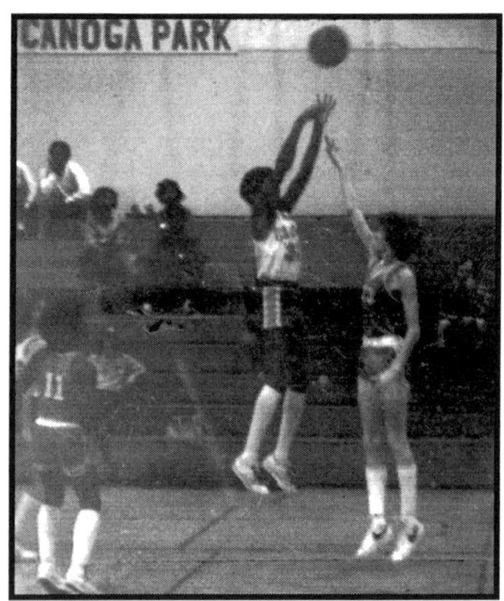

My gridiron accolades became a double-edge sword. They thought I was a QB hoping to play basketball, unaware that I was a hoopster moonliting at football. Since basketball season began before football ended, I wasn't allowed to try-out for the J.V. or Varsity teams.

I, along with my super-athletic wide receiver, Richard 'Kurt' Austin, was banished to the lowly 'BEE' team. **My Mom Urged: Channel my frustration into fuel!**

"Prove them wrong on the court. Game Speaks!"

Will do! My first game, at Cleveland, I came off the bench and promptly went to work. I hit the game winner at the buzzer to earn my starting spot and was in *G'$ mode* thereafter. In mid-season we traveled to our arch-rival, Taft High. Since the JV/Varsity games were being played at ECR later that evening the gym was packed with fans. Before the game I had a great court-side reunion with my Taft LB #55 homie. It was bitter-sweet, as I was a bit ashamed at being on the 'BEE' team. Aptly, I served Taft for 43 points and a dunk fest!

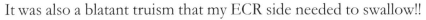

Taft fans cheered later in our gym: "ECR varsity? Without the QB who scored 43? From what WE SEE AND WHAT WE'VE SEEN. Your BEST PLAYER PLAYS on your 'B' TEAM!"

WEST VALLEY LEAGUE "BEE" BASKETBALL
ALL LEAGUE TEAMS 1979 - 1980

1st Team

NAME	GRADE
Bill Streeter (Taft)	12
Brad Gore (Taft)	12
Alex Gates (Chatsworth)	12
* Greg Scott (El Camino Real)	10
Jeff Perry (Cleveland)	12

2nd Team

NAME	GRADE
Rick Yep (Canoga Park)	12
Mike DeLange (Canoga Park	11
Gary Golnick (Canoga Park)	12
Perry Griffith (Taft)	11
Alonzo Maloy (Taft)	11
Victor Stewart (Chatsworth)	12
Alex Massengale (Chatsworth)	11
Richard Austin (El Camino Real)	10

As our arch-rival chanted in unison, I was astounded by the creativity of the acknowledgement. Taft LB#55 props! It was also a blatant truism that my ECR side needed to swallow!!

Politics in Sports: As the only non-senior to be selected **First Team All-League**, I was pissed off as I was chosen **Co-MVP** at our team banquet in front of all the Varsity coaches and players. My teammate, Dale, played 3 years on the BEE team, never made All-League. Honor him and soil my MVP status with 'Co'! **What?** My mom allowed me to leave the banquet early! She made me wait to trash my trophy. **Next Day: I smashed it with my bat!**

MY SOLE ADVOCATE AND SAVIOR was Varsity Asst. Coach, JEFF DAVIS!!

Hoop Vengance Plot: I skipped my summer QB 7-on-7 passing league at Granada Hills with John Elway to 'prove myself' in a BCI basketball league. A good and bad CHOICE!

BCI: Basketball Congress Int'l. Summer League All-Star Game

The top 16 players from the BCI Summer League in the Valley were selected to play in the All-Star game at Cal State Northridge. We were also competing for 10 spots on a BCI team heading to the Sports Festival at the Olympic Training Center in Colorado Springs. At 22 points per game, **I was the only non-Varsity player chosen to play** in the All-Star game!

G'$ GAMESPEAK: IT'S A TEAM SPORT, BUT IT'S NOT!

My family would be there but I rode with 'da homie', Kenski, who was on me the entire way. "Turn this Shiznit out!" The packed gym had all the hype and hoopla worthy of the many D-1 coaches, clipboards in hand, sporting polo shirts adorned with school logos. In pre-game warm-up I was surprised that this was 'the cream of the crop'. Compared to L.A. I wasn't impressed at the so-called 'Top Varsity Talent' in the San Fernando Valley! While they dunked in warm-ups I shot jumpers. Kenski was down-right insulted and he strolled to the baseline literally growling, "Yo Ott, whatcha waitin' for? Flight G' Mode! Get busy!" Honestly, I had never practiced dunks, dunked in warm-ups or cherry-picked for dunks. On my next lay-up I showcased an ambidextrous G'Flight sample. Crafted in my backyard.

I bounced the ball off the floor, off the backboard, took off of two feet, caught it above the square with my right hand, turned mid-air, switched hands and flushed it with my left! It's the first time I ever made a crowd go silent. Only a few affirmative giggles from Kenski.

As the game started I focused on harnessing my adrenalin and exhibiting my will on D', facilitating, and 'boarding at both ends of the floor to sway the tone and tempo. I shot well and had a few G'Flight plays early, and didn't let up one bit. I did work, in dynamic fashion! **I was on the radar. The elated hug from my ECR Asst. Coach, Jeff Davis: Prideful!**

Ken Custis: "G'man put in WORK in every phase of the game! Stellar Defense! He hit the boards at both ends! Flawless ball-handling and passing. Efficient shooting! And, he also had a few nasty highlight poster dunks that silenced the entire crowd!"

I received the game MOP award and was approached by Coach Fred 'The Fox' Snowden from the University of Arizona. He commended me and was looking forward to seeing me at the Sports Festival. I confided to him that I wouldn't be available to compete due to my varsity football conditioning program commitment. **Coach Snowden inspired me!**

Then, my dad led me outside to see a VIP Guest and #1 Fan, 'Mr. Don'. Hint: Soul Train!

ECR Varsity Football

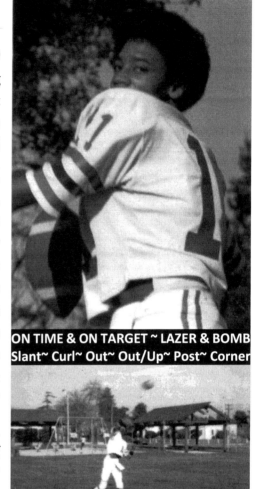

FAILURE TO TRAIN IS TRAINING TO FAIL!
ON TIME & ON TARGET ~ LAZER & BOMB
Slant~ Curl~ Out~ Out/Up~ Post~ Corner

From the Ground, Up! QB = FOOTWORK
Strong Arm! Critical Element = CONTROL
IQ! PLAYBOOK MEMORIZED = CEREBRAL

Going into the three weeks of conditioning in 100 degree heat prior to 'hell week' limited throwing sessions to evenings at home throwing to the light post. When 2-a-days came, my arm was not up to the task. Sore, Sore, Sore. Sit! Sit! Sit! **Ice! Ice! Ice!**

After hell week our starting QB was chosen and I had not even made a single pass yet. Altie Schmit, a solid lefty senior won the position. By the week before our first game I was completely healed! My arm was strong and my spiral was tight. Then, in our 'live' defensive scrimmage the scout team QB's were getting crushed by our nasty D'. They were flinching, fumbling and frightened. Coach G' was beyond angry and barked out to me, **"Scott, can you throw yet?" 'Yes, coach!' "Put on a vest, get in there and run the darn scout team." 'Yes sir.'**

I put on the red QB vest as taunts and jeers from teammates were blatantly chanted. The unveiling of the champion BEE QB on the Varsity level. 'Meat!'

A Blatent Varsity QB Initiation Loomed! First Play: Pro right. Fake 32 dive, read option right. Simple!

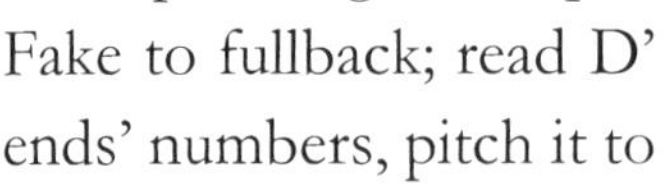

Fake to fullback; read D' ends' numbers, pitch it to my tailback (DT) or turn up-field and go. Nope: I get the snap, take a step and BOOM. I'm hit hard, lifted up, driven back and slammed to the grass as, NFL-bound, Elston Riddell crashed down on top of me. **"Welcome to the Varsity, Prettyboy G'!"** Bedlam: 'Glad to have ya' 'It's a new level'. Coach G' reprimands.

Derrick Traylor: "G'man got up, took the vest off, came into the huddle; pissed off. 'WTF is that BS? Show some @#$% pride. Same play! Pro right, read option right. Do your job!' He kept it, turned up field for a touchdown! First pass play: G' got smacked, was going down as he slung a left-handed spiral for another TD." Coach G': "Glad he's on our team!"

Post Game on-field TV Interview replayed in homeroom & articled in our ECR Student News

ELSTON RIDDELL: ON ECR'S DEFENSIVE DOMINATION AS LEAGUE CHAMPS, WITH PLAY-OFFS LOOMING

"Collective Preparation has been at the core of our defensive dominance this entire season. Every year the coaches do a masterful job of scouting and breaking down game film of our opponents to prepare us. And, I believe we watch much more film than most teams. But, what makes this years' team uniquely special and defensively dominant is simple. We have highly talented skill players you may not see much of on Fridays, who take abundant pride in their vital role in our teams collective preparation,

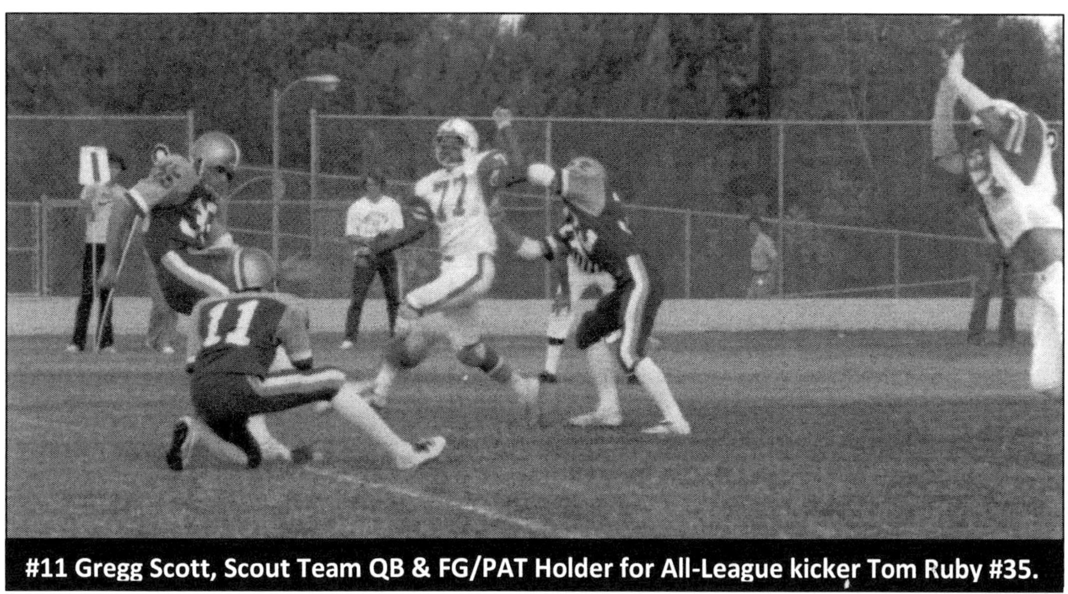

#11 Gregg Scott, Scout Team QB & FG/PAT Holder for All-League kicker Tom Ruby #35.

Monday through Thursday. Our offensive scout team is our difference-maker. Look, week after week, their role is to watch film of a different teams' offensive system; to study it, digest it, and then execute it against us on the practice field. They have the intelligence and the ability to adapt our system to our upcoming opponents' system, or, most often, duplicate opponent systems from 'scratch'. Every day in practice, week after week, the varying systems, schemes, sets, plays and tempos were ran, not just soundly, but also successfully. Their priceless contribution to our collective preparation got us as a defense to a point that on certain nights, and I mean no disrespect to any of our opponents, but, we actually had an easier time stopping our opponents' offense in the actual games, than we did in practice the week before. We're a team of tough, talented players, all with a champions will to prepare and get better every single day. Tonight is simply the net result. Still, while we briefly celebrate this league title, we still remain focused on our ultimate goal of walking out of the Coliseum tunnel in three weeks. So, come Monday, we're back to work towards that ultimate goal. Thank you."

Friday, 12/19/80: L.A. Coliseum, L.A. City 4A Title Game: ECR vs. Banning

4-A Championship Friday!

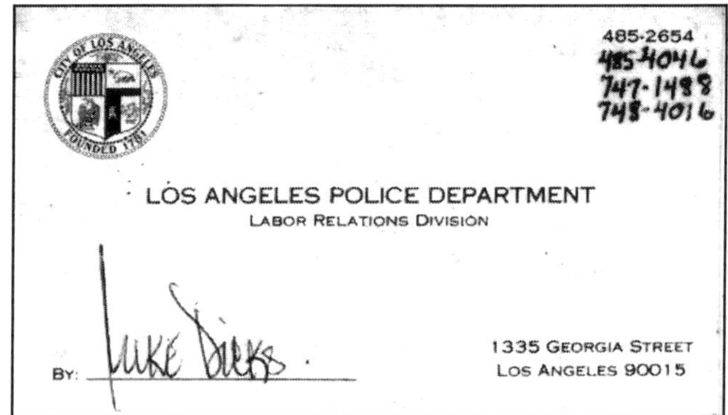

485-2654
LOS ANGELES POLICE DEPARTMENT
LABOR RELATIONS DIVISION
BY:
1335 GEORGIA STREET
LOS ANGELES 90015

With a frenzied pep rally complete, we boarded the luxury buses with a police escort for the 2-hour trip downtown. We arrived at the legendary Coliseum all geeked up, and all ready to rumble. Finally, dressed in the tunnel, goals and dreams had been realized. **Gametime!** As we hit the field to warm-up, I scanned to the section on the tickets ECR gave my family. I saw my dad and my brother, but, not my mom. I assumed she was in the restroom. No. She wouldn't miss one second of this game. Something was up. I worried the whole game. It was a blur. We lost 35-17. Afterwards on the field, my dad told me why mom was absent.

MICHAEL THOMAS DICKS
PASSED AWAY
DECEMBER 19, 1980
MASS OF CHRISTIAN BURIAL
DECEMBER 24, 1980 - 9:00 A.M.
ST. JEROME CATHOLIC CHURCH

I dedicated my basketball season to my Uncle Mike!

Uncle Mike had suffered a fatal heart-attack while driving on-duty that day.

Mom had been grieving with family at his house. I was 100% heartbroken. Coach G' announced my familial loss to our team and I left immediately to go to my Uncle's house to see my mom. Words can not express the deep sorrow of Championship Friday. **King of Sorrow!**

G. Scott #23 ~ ECR Starting Guard ~ The Fruit of my BCI Labor

~ TGIF ~
ECR's gym is packed! The music is rockin'! The aroma of popcorn fills the air! Butterflies! At long last I'm on the hoop court and in the starting line-up! 'Get Busy'!!

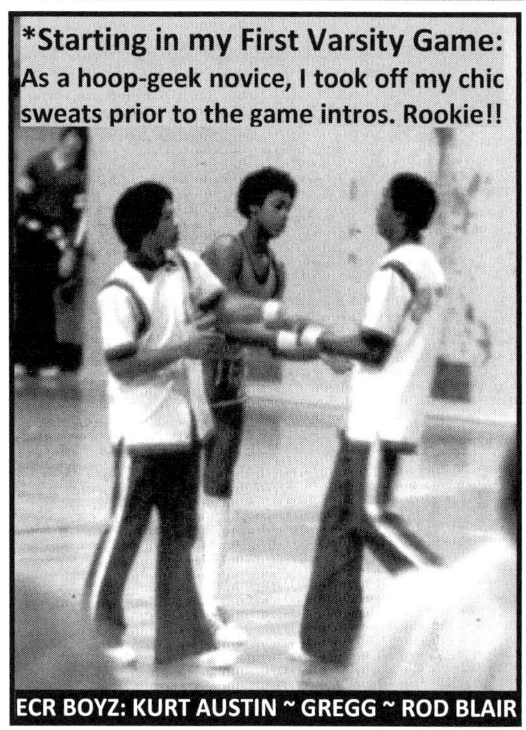

***Starting in my First Varsity Game:** As a hoop-geek novice, I took off my chic sweats prior to the game intros. Rookie!!

ECR BOYZ: KURT AUSTIN ~ GREGG ~ ROD BLAIR

GameSpeak: I relished it. Did Work! Earned my Stripes! Performance-Based Merit!

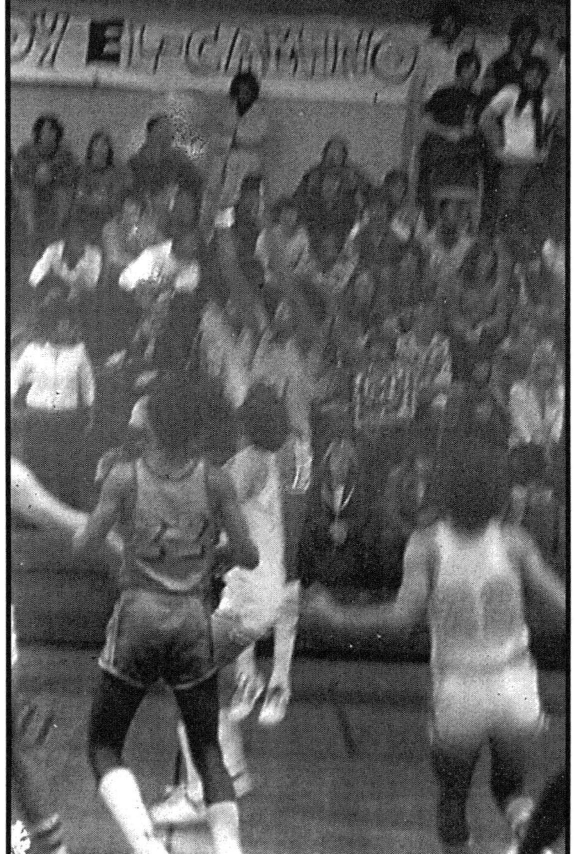

Jeff Davis: "Gregg Scott is one of my all-time favorite athletes. His gridiron greatness led to his hoop heartache due to the disdain of our Head Coach. I witnessed Coach demote him prior to our final game. G' was so shattered."

@MentalAthlete

It's not so important who starts the game, but who finishes it.

John Wooden

To me, being a starter matters! It's a status symbol. It's earned! Coach Al Bennett brought up two JV players and put them in the starting line-up over me and Kurt as a clear punishment for our football unavailability.

ECR NEWS HEADLINE: G' HOOPS PURGATORY!!

Page 4
'YOU GOTTA BE WILLING TO BE THE HERO OR THE GOAT!'

Final game in our gym, versus arch rival Taft, for a playoff bid. Fouled on the shot. 0:03 on the clock. No Fear. Two (perfect) missed free throws. First crunch-time failure ever! Postgame, Coach Bennett told me, "If you're unwilling to quit football next season and commit to my program, then we don't need you." Purgatory! No Sr. Year for G' Hoops!

Total of 18 Varsity games! Zero pre-season, holiday tourneys or summer league games.

Purgatory: Agony ~ Anguish ~ Torment ~ Suffering ~ Despair ~ To Purge and to Cleanse. The next morning my dad picked me up for a visit to a "client's" home. Mr. Don, a Savior!

Sr. Yr.: DB & QB, NO BB

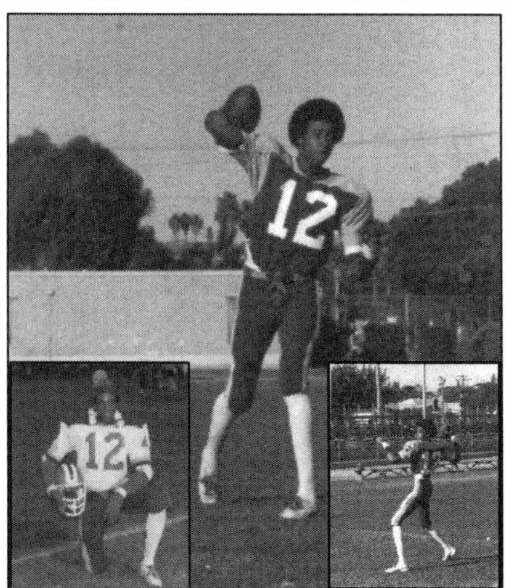

#12: I studied Jack Tatum's, 'They Call Me Assassin'! Rover-back: I counted Stick Marks and Snot-Bubbles!

No Sport Compares to Friday Night Lights!

BFF: #12 QB/DB G' & #41 RB Derrick Traylor

6/82: The University H.S. gym was closed. As I was leaving a sweet new brown Pontiac Firebird with T-tops rolled up. The familiar man said, "Their ballin' at Beverly Hills High. Do you know how to get there?" 'Yes Sir. It's on my way home'. L. A. Laker Michael Cooper followed me, then invited me to play. Coop' vocally inspired a G'$ show, head-up against 'Stormin Norman' Nixon!

Michael Cooper

My defense was stellar, but Coop' demanded more. He chanted, "Don't just D' him up, 'Youngster'. Go at him and work him out!"

After the solid workout Coop' invited me to a workout at the UCLA Men's Gym later that week. He told me where to park and to get a campus map. Upon arrival, I knew this was: MEN AT WORK! There, I earned an invite to the Hoops Mecca: Pauley Pavilion Wooden's Lair. With the UCLA Men's players.

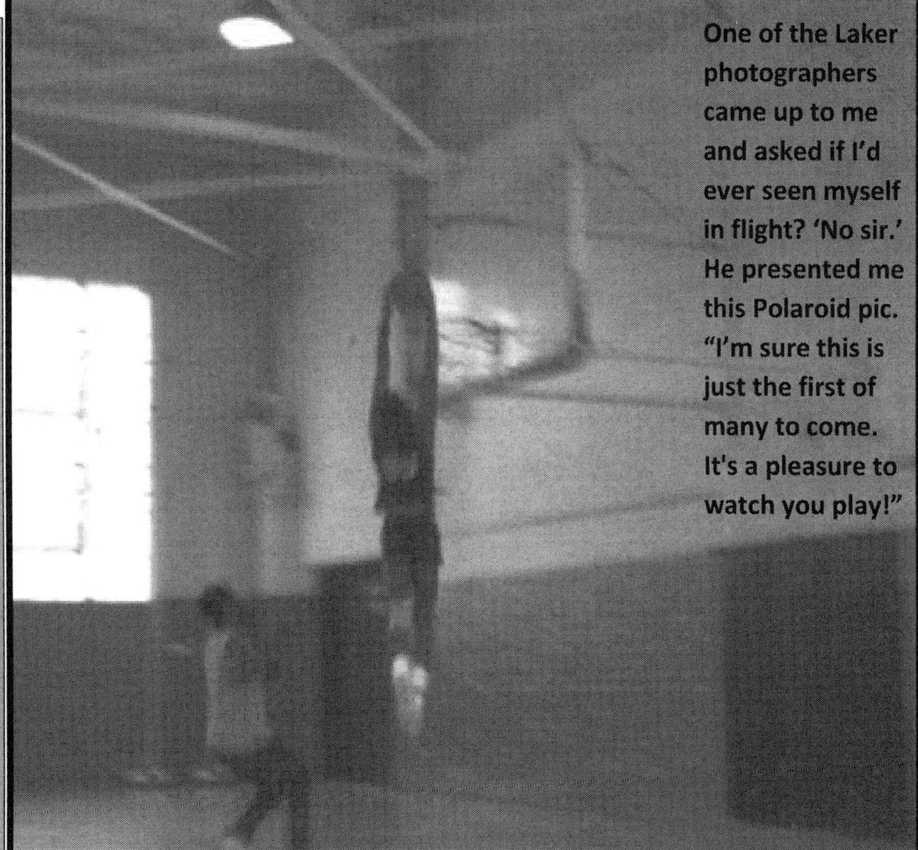

One of the Laker photographers came up to me and asked if I'd ever seen myself in flight? 'No sir.' He presented me this Polaroid pic. "I'm sure this is just the first of many to come. It's a pleasure to watch you play!"

MOMS $17,505 WAGER: U OF A 2-SPORT WALK-ON

QB Or Not QB at UNLV? Hoop Redemption? Baseball Rebirth?

Football? Basketball? Baseball? I had one scholarship offer to play QB at UNLV, on the heels of Randall Cunningham. The star ECR tailback from my junior year, Tony Lewis, was playing at UNLV. I was recruited based his 'Scout QB' input But, my dad adamently squashed that notion for his reasons While in the ECR coaches offices I found a U of A football brochure with a pic of Fred Snowden in McKale Arena. I pondered our convo at the BCI All-Star game. Seed Planted!

> **"Gregg Scott has the talent to play at the D-1 level at multiple positions, IF football is the sport that he ultimately chooses to play. He's that good."**
>
> **Skip Giancanelli**
> **ECR Varsity Coach**

Coach Snowden Announces Retirement!

I got in touch with Coach Snowden although I knew had retired. He was very embracing. He told me of the new coach, and, "due to his resignation two players were transferring." Inside Info!! It'd be a quest that no Frosh had ever accomplished. **As a paying walk-on!**

My mom funded a trip to visit the U of A campus and to meet new coach, Ben Lindsey. I'll never forget mom and me standing in McKale Arena as I said, 'I want it!. I can do it!' I also met with legendary UA baseball coach, Jerry Kendall. He offered a Fall Ball tryout.

Peril of Divorce & A Blessing in Disguise: $17,505 'The Forum'

$17,505! A very special and prophetic number for me! Hint: Primed in 'Showtime'!

- University of Arizona: One semester of Tuition, Room & Board, Books & Travel
- The Great Western Forum: **Chick Hearn, "Lakers sell-out crowd of 17,505!"**

As a result of my parents divorce gone was the family unit and the family home. Out of the ashes my mom vested $17,505 in me. **Over 30% of her profits from the home sale.**

My 'Bro' Dave Lewis was with me when I bought my first car and my Bro Mark drove with me and dropped me at my UA dorm. 'Either way this won't be for long.'

Rush Week Sage Sparks Intro: "G' articulated his goals. I asked his age. 17 Sir."

Moms wager: $17,505 for <u>one</u> semester. **My Quest:** 'walk-on' for baseball & basketball, simultaneously! School, baseball practice, then to McKale Arena. Cleats off. Hoop Shoes!

U of A Baseball Coach Jerry Kendall: "You're too talented for me to cut you. But, for now just focus on the basketball. I'll still be here for you." Yes, Sir!

Shelby Brooks

There was one guy, another 2-sport phenom walk-on player I was close friends with. In fact, this guy was the best pure all-around athlete that I've ever encounterd. Bar None. Shelby Brooks from Peoria, IL. I was an eyewitness. Baseball and Basketball. He signed up with Meadowlark Lemon's Bucketeers!

Rush Week Intro to Sparks

I got no locker and no real love from the team prior to try-outs. Just my gym bag and gear! Oh, I brought my GAME too! Daily. Then, fooling around with my bud from the womens team, Heather, I casually dribbled to my right and rolled my right ankle!Sprained ligaments!

> Scott suffered a sprained right ankle two weeks ago — he said "things were looking bad for me there for a while" — but UA basketball trainer Rick Mendini said Scott is "doing fine now."

I cried like a baby in the ice whirlpool! But, UA trainer, Rick Mendidi, told me "You're impressing people. It's rehab! I'll get you ready." He did!

ECR grad Scott wins place on Arizona Team

sports — **Lindsey cuts 7 walk-ons at 1st practice**

Tuesday, October 19, 1982 — **ARIZONA DAILY WILDCAT**

Mom's $18K check was mailed!

Walk-ons catch Lindsey's eye to eam final spots on roster

By MIKE CHESNICK
Arizona Daily Wildcat

The waiting is over for walk-ons Greg Taylor and Greg Scott, but the pressure still remains for the two newest additions to the University of Arizona basketball team.

Taylor, Scott and Duane Twine were named finalists for the two walk-on spots Friday, but Wildcat coach Ben Lindsey held off until yesterday's 3 p.m. practice to give Taylor and Scott the good news.

"I picked Taylor and Scott because I think they can be a help to us," Lindsey said. "Both are capable of contributing to the team this season."

Lindsey has 13 players on scholarship but decided to select two walk-ons to fill the roster after forwards Kevin Roundfield and Ernest Taylor-Harris left the team.

Although Taylor and Scott said they were worried about making the team, both expressed even more concern about living up to Lindsey's expectations in practice this season.

"I'm pretty excited, but I was nervous before today's practice," Taylor said. "I didn't know if I would make it. But about 30 minutes before practice, coach said, 'Go get fitted for shoes,' and I guess that meant I made it."

Taylor, a 6-foot-6, 200-pound junior forward, came to Arizona from Mesa Community College via the University of San Diego.

"I knew coach Lindsey from junior college," he said. "I'd love to play some this season and help the team, but I know I've got to work my hardest to get to play."

Taylor, who played his high-school basketball at Brophy Prep in Phoenix, said he transferred to Mesa because "I wasn't getting to play much at San Diego."

Scott, a 6-foot-3, 165-pound guard, comes to the UA from El Camino Real High School in Woodland Hills, Calif. The freshman said he has "been working for this since my senior year in high school."

"I was confident about my chances, but still worried," Scott said. "We (the walk-ons) were under a lot of pressure and all I could do was work hard and hope for the best.

"I'm looking forward to helping the team. I hope I can play some, but I've still got three years to play after this season," he said.

Scott suffered a sprained right ankle two weeks ago — he said "things were looking bad for me there for a while" — but UA basketball trainer Rick Mendini said Scott is "doing fine now."

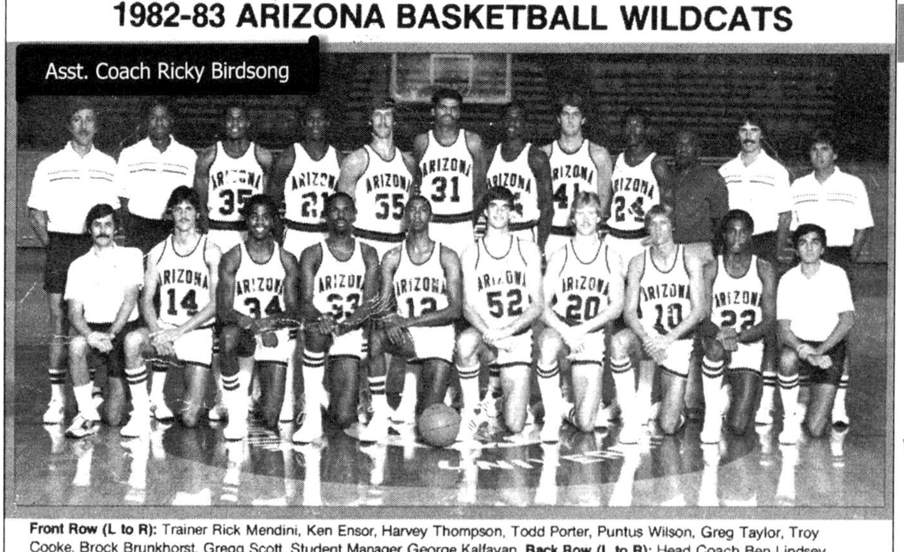

1982-83 ARIZONA BASKETBALL WILDCATS
Asst. Coach Ricky Birdsong

Front Row (L to R): Trainer Rick Mendini, Ken Ensor, Harvey Thompson, Todd Porter, Puntus Wilson, Greg Taylor, Troy Cooke, Brock Brunkhorst, Gregg Scott, Student Manager George Kalfayan. **Back Row (L to R):** Head Coach Ben Lindsey, Assistant Coach Ricky Byrdsong, Donald Mellon, Keith Jackson, John Belobraydic, Frank Smith, Morgan Taylor, Jack Magno, David Haskin, Equipment Supervisor Phil Gaines, Graduate Assistant Coach Mike Haddow, Assistant Coach Jerry Holmes.

Sage Sparks

"Never allow one defender to deny you the basketball."

"Never kill your dribble near the mid-court line."

"Never take a one-bounce dribble while standing still."

"You may have bad moments, but, never a bad game."

Business First...Where to live?

Sage Sparks

Sparks' input was crucial. Most athletes lived at the Babcock Apts. A party spot off campus. I was excited that the only unit available was a single room sharing a bathroom with the infamous Vance Johnson, who was then a star running back and track champion; and a future *'3 Amigos'* Denver Bronco. Sparks squashed that! "Wrong environment for you G'."

On the Roster! Not Always on the Team!

Randy Robbins

Our season debut was on the road at the Houston Kettle Classic hosted by the Drexler led 'Phi Slamma Jamma' Houston Cougers. Yet, sadly, I was not even allowed to travel. Alone at training table, UA football player, Randy Robbins, invited me over to eat in their lair. Sharing my high school QB/DB pedigree with the verbiage of his position, we cemented a bond. "Hey y'all, we got a football player here perpetrating as a hoopster." Randy rapport!

I dined with the Footballers even after my team returned!

Rickey Hundley

G' Gridiron Perk: U of A Football Players Game Tickets!

Sage Sparks: 'Prudent Partying 101' ~ Mindfulness Mentoring

- **Tolerance Levels ~ Public Behavior ~ Self Awareness ~ Exit Strategies**

Party Purging at Bear Down gym! Each 'morning after' he'd wake me up early **by throwing pebbles at my window** from the parking lot below. "Sweat it out now G', not in practice." "Coaches know which players party on the weekends by how they perform on Mondays."

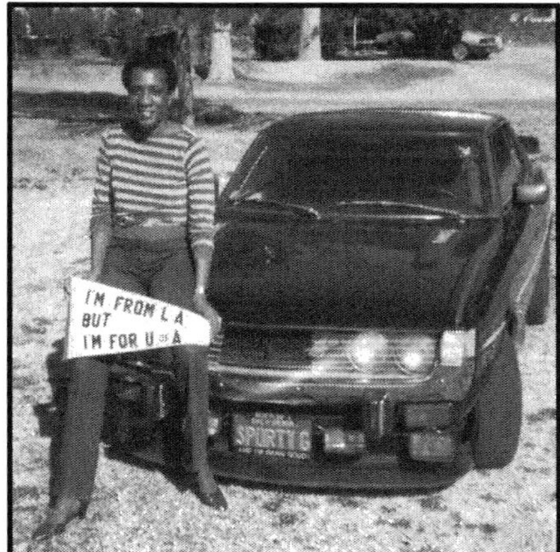

Mom: #1 fan

Strange! My Mom flew in from LAX for our game vs. UCLA on the very same flight as the entire Bruin squad. They knew me! In pre-game we had a midcourt reunion.

ARIZONA

1982-1983 Basketball

Arizona vs.
Athletes In Action

Monday,
January 3,
7:35 p.m.

In This Issue:

- Meet UA Walk-Ons Greg(g)s Scott & Taylor
- What's Coming Up In UA Athletics
- Lady Netters Looking For Top 10 Finish

$1.00

Cover drawing of Gregg Scott & Greg Taylor compliments of The Wildcat Club

One would think that a player who has not seen a minute of playing time through his team's first eight games would be frustrated, down and ready to cut the net. Especially since that team, the Arizona Wildcats, had won just twice during the eight-game period.

Not freshman Gregg Scott. Oh sure, he would love to see a little action, and most likely will before season's end. But realistically, Gregg is just happy to be a part of the team. His value in practice sessions cannot be measured.

You see, Gregg was one of 13 other Arizona students who attempted to walk on the Wildcat cage team last October—to fill two spots on the roster. "Gregg showed us some pretty good ball handling and shooting during our two day tryout," said head coach Ben Lindsey. "It is difficult for a walk-on to

Gregg Scott

come in and make a big contribution. But we think he can make a contribution to the program, otherwise he wouldn't have been selected."

Scott prepped at El Camino Real High School in Southern California where he lettered in both football and basketball. He was selected All-Conference twice in football and once in basketball, and set the school passing record as a sophomore and led his football squad in interceptions as a senior.

Music Master G'

Stacey Snowden

Randy Robbins invited me to an off-campus 'party'. I was in the company of the 'upper-crust' of the UA hierarchy. Ricky Hundley, (track star) Kim Gallagher, Stacey Snowden (daughter of Coach Fred). Smitten! I played DJ all night while they played Spades. Stacey soon asked me to DJ her house party. MC Sporty G'!

Game Day vs. Arizona State & Byron Scott

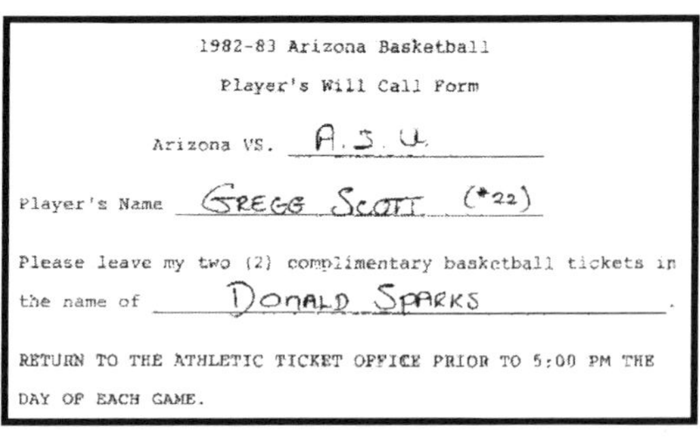

1982-83 Arizona Basketball

Player's Will Call Form

Arizona VS. A.S.U.

Player's Name Gregg Scott (#22)

Please leave my two (2) complimentary basketball tickets in the name of Donald Sparks.

RETURN TO THE ATHLETIC TICKET OFFICE PRIOR TO 5:00 PM THE DAY OF EACH GAME.

The local papers ran a nice article about the two Scott ballers from Los Angeles playing in the UA vs. ASU rivalry. Byron was a star! I had yet to play in a game!

22

GREGG SCOTT
Guard
6-2, 170, Freshman, HS
Los Angeles, California
Born: 9-3-64

Donald Sparks: My 'Mental Athlete' Guru! **Sage Sparks: My Global Hoops Cultivator!**

Game Time: G' gets the call for court time

At halftime the game was close and Byron wasn't playing very well. Six minutes into the second half Coach Lindsey made his familiar stroll down our bench; a bit farther down into my area. He kneeled down in front of me and said, "Son, are you ready to play some basketball?" I replied quickly, "Yes, sir!" My intro to college hoops would be as the first substitute of the half in a tight game; far from the typical walk-on 'garbage time' minutes. As I stood up and, at long last, cooly unsnapped my warm-up pants, I heard the crowd react with premature applause as I walked to the scorers table to sub into the game. I spun around and sat to stretch facing in the direction of Sparks' seat behind our basket. We made eye contact and he pointed to his head and then he softly pounded his chest. The simple translation was to play smart and compete with heart. Amen! At hand was the moment I'd dreamed of and worked so hard for. A moment to cease the pain of my 'ECR Purgatory'. My self-talk was all positive. **Breathe! Poise! Perform! GameSpeak!**

"Ladies and gentlemen, checking into the game for the University of Arizona, and making his Wildcat debut, let's give a warm welcome to the 6' 2" freshman from West Los Angeles, Californina, number 22; Gregg Scott."

ASU's ball: 'Who I got? #4 Byron Scott'

TRUE LIFE TALES

As the fans greeted me with an animated applause, I matched-up with #4. Before the ball was inbounded his teammates on their bench began yelling and yapping, "Yo B', you got a Freshman on you!" Repeatedly. I was unphased and embraced the test. I defend one way, regardless of who I'm guarding; with fundamental soundness!

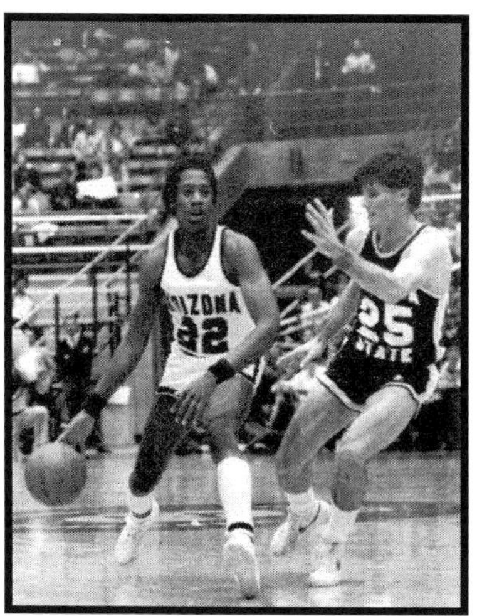

So, this dude submits to their verbal peer pressure and walks me into the post area. I bodied-up in a half-denial stance on the (inbounding) ball side; between man and basket. More instigating chants echoed from their bench. Woefully, B.S. gave me some *BS* in the form of a blatant elbow to my chest. He sent a message; I'm obligated to send a reply. He made a statement; ok, I have a rebuttal.

I absorbed his elbow without flinching. Note to self: *When retribution is cleary in order, make it count. No weak fouls!* Ok, based on my position and his anatomy, I quickly had his ribcage in my crosshairs and gave an upward thrust forearm that I knew would briefly debilitate him but surely not injure him. Mission Accomplished! As his posture returned to an upright position, he turned and glared. **Undaunted, I whispered a G'$ TRUISM:**

Sage Sparks: "G'man got his first official game statistic within five seconds; while on defense. Byron Scott gave G' an initiation to college hoops with a swift elbow to the chest. And, I'm proud to say that without any hesitation at all, my boy G' shot Byron a forearm to his ribcage that made him buckle and pissed him off. As G' was called for the foul, Byron spun around as if to confront him. But, G' didn't budge as he calmly said something to Byron that clearly made him pause. I couldn't wait to ask."

'Being a Freshman doesn't make me a PUNK. So, whatcha wanna do?'

Not false bravado; just G'. I maintained a calm demeanor, a straight face and rigid eye contact. My words seemed to squash the situation. He and his 'mates went silent. The ref told me, "Well said, Young Man." Byron relaxed, as the horn blew. He was substituted to the bench, prompting a memorable rouse from UA fans.

Knowing I had limited minutes to get in the 'books', my plot was to value possession, run the offense and attack the rim on the ASU back-up guard. Our third possesion! Sage Sparks: Separation Dribble & J'. I blew by him from 'left wing to baseline', measured the help-side defender, and I exploded straight up and lofted a soft sweet jumper arching high over the on-coming big man. Then, **SWAT!**

Sage Sparks: "G's first basket came on a tough baseline drive into a 5 FOOT baseline 'J' that got swatted 5 ROWS into the crowd. Goaltending!"

Highlight of the Game

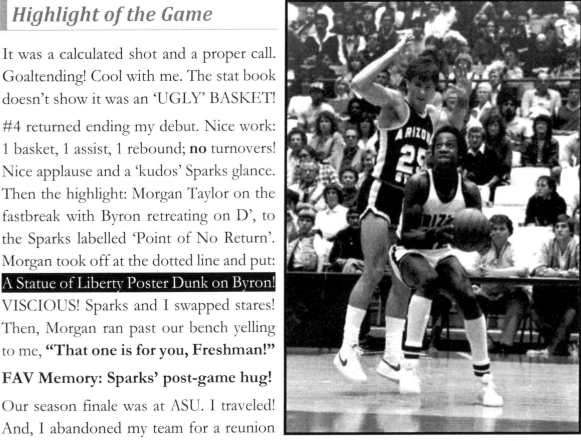

It was a calculated shot and a proper call. Goaltending! Cool with me. The stat book doesn't show it was an 'UGLY' BASKET!

#4 returned ending my debut. Nice work: 1 basket, 1 assist, 1 rebound; **no** turnovers! Nice applause and a 'kudos' Sparks glance. Then the highlight: Morgan Taylor on the fastbreak with Byron retreating on D', to the Sparks labelled 'Point of No Return'. Morgan took off at the dotted line and put: A Statue of Liberty Poster Dunk on Byron! VISCIOUS! Sparks and I swapped stares! Then, Morgan ran past our bench yelling to me, **"That one is for you, Freshman!"**

FAV Memory: Sparks' post-game hug!

Our season finale was at ASU. I traveled! And, I abandoned my team for a reunion with my ex-ECR football teammate Keith Rosenberg and his Samoan ASU gridiron crew!

Mutiny Meeting: Players met with UA AD, Cedric Dempsey. Lindsey got fired; Lute hired! A season void of UA lore! Fact: UA owes a debt of gratitue to our futility. If not, no Lute!

Bear Down Gym: Sparks 101~ Post Game ~ 10's full-court drill

- **"You have the potential to be the best conditioned player on the court." Remember: "POTENTIAL is an ugly word!" ~ "Supreme Condition: Calling Card"**
- **"Showing up in peak condition sends a message that you respect this one opportunity enough to show up in prime shape. Symbolize your Brand."**
- **"You must recognize the emotions of others, and cultivate the skill-sets to get each one of your teammates a quality scoring opportunity in their comfort zone, on cue."**
- **"Don't be content scoring 25 points and allowing your man to score 20."**
- **G'$ Mantra: 'If you're playing me even then you're out-playing me.'**

Sage Sparks: "Gregory, be versitile enough to play multiple positions! Starting 2-guard and back-up point guard, or vice-versa. The coaching substitution patterns then turn in your favor."

Back Home in L.A.! GHMBS 'No Pleasure Cruise'

The day I sadly arrived at my moms condo she gave me a **Great Western** Bank passbook with a note attached. On the paper was a copy of my **$18,000 check** and my letter. She said, "I'm so proud of you. You accomplished your goal. You did what no other had done. That's all I ever wished for. That's why **I paid $17,505**. Belief. I was vesting in your dream. And, you repaid me in full, **plus interest?** Baby, your hoop dreams are my best dividends." The passbook was for a checking account in my name with a $495 balance. **Simple Math.**

Sparks: "G', being ambidextrous requires you to workout 30% longer. Capitalize & Cultivate!"

"When I dropped Gregg off at the U of A, he was a kid brother. A freshman. When he returned just nine months later, he had transformed himself. He raved about the impact of his mentor. A guy named Donald Sparks. The first time we went to hoop was at Fairfax High. I saw the impact." ~Mark Scott~

I wanted the best pick-up game possible. Mark advised Fairfax High. Beyond Coincidence:

Of all the Gym Joints, Parks & Playgrounds: Retribution Ricky!

<u>Retribution:</u> Vengence ~ Revenge ~ Pay-Back ~ Reprisal ~ Reckoning ~ Justice

If you'll recall back when I was six and lived on Pointview street, Ricky Wilson lived in the same apartment building as us. Unlike my mentors, Dave Lewis and Marvin Mensies, who were nurturing, Ricky was a bully to me. He'd constantly call me "Little Punk" and try to intimidate. Dave once interceeded and told Ricky to "chill out". I then told Ricky that, 'I'm not the punk here and I won't always be little'. Dave smiled proudly, while Ricky smirked. Also, Ricky was the only person I ever saw make my brother literally 'Fighting Mad'. Well, Tussling Mad, actually. They were playing with Aqua Man in our bathroom tub and argued to the point that both of them ended up in the tub tussling. It was hilarious. My dad broke it up and asked, "Why are you two fighting?" I had to interrupt! 'Dad, they weren't fighting. When you fight you throw punches. They threw Sissy Fits.' Mark and Ricky leered at me. Pops had Mark go with Ricky to his apartment and apologize to his parents. Soaking Wet!

They were all 3½ years older and bigger than me and Ricky was tall for his age. Not today! The age difference remained. But, Wretched Ricky Wilson was just 5'11", while I was 6'2". At last, my prophecy was reality. In his high school gym, on his turf, in front of his peeps.

Mark and I warmed up as Ricky's team won two straight games. As we came on the court, Mark may have exchanged pleasentries with him, but I didn't. Don't break bread with foes. It didn't take long. I get the ball, a fastbreak with only Ricky back on defense. It's 1-on-1. I bow outwards to get an angle, I take off, he goes up, and I bashed on him so nastily while tossing him to the floor. I then stood over him and said, **'Who's The Little Punk Now?!'**

THE DRIVE—Under the ever watchful eyes of his teammates and coaches, Gregg Scott, a sophomore guard, drives toward the basket. Behind Scott, from left, are Greg McCaffrey, assistant coach; Jon Jayet, forward; Frank Carbajal, head coach; Eddie Mitchell, forward; Matt Ruiz, assistant coach; Chris Abreu, guard, and Ted Heinrichs, forward.

SANTA BARBARA CITY COLLEGE: BAMBOOZLED!

U of A football player, Steve Couch, was from Carpenteria, via Santa Barbara City College. I promised him I'd visit after we left Arizona. Steve took me the home of his cool SBCC friend, George Schnackenberg. It 'broke barriers', but his family treated me like a cherished son of their own from day one. Geroge had signed at UHH via SBCC. We all went out and played on campus. I did my work and Schnack' was legit, too. I was later recruited by Coach Frank Carbajal who had a true 'Drill Instructor' reputation. **Worst yet, 6 a.m. and 3 p.m. practices; for the entire season**! **Anti-Porsche:** He ran a slow 'tempo offense' delay game. His teams won while scoring in the 20's. Total! Carbajal's sole fame was Ron Anderson, whom he hyped (PTI 'slurped') quite often. Ron was in the NBA via Fresno State.Yay. I had contracted a viral nfection, Cytomegala, and wasn't cleared to play until December. I played in one 2-game tourney, the Moorpark Classic, in which we won the championship. The next morning, a Monday, I was five minutes late to our 6:00 a.m. practice. Overslept! Coach Carbajal ordered me to run five miles for the 5 minutes I was late, out on the track, in the frezzing cold of the ocean across the street. I get my Arizona lettermans and a beenie and hit the track. Motivated by my new plan, I trudged for 20 grueling laps. As I returned to the gym I rejoined practice without any negative emotion, only pondering my new plan. At the end, as the team was seated, Carbajal began a rant with, "One may truly be the most talented player who ever walked through that door….." Then the disparagement flowed. I honestly muted every word that followed. Envisioning my new plan. Practice adjourned.

It's winterbreak. I went to admissions to drop all my pending classes! Got transcript copies. Met with Carbajal out of respect. My mindset was, 'I'm not going to quit to avoid running 5 miles. I'll run the 5 miles, then I'll quit.' And, so I did. Next, roll to my condo and pack. A brief stop at the leasing offfice and the Schnackenberg home, before hitting the Pacific Coast Hwy. In 3 hours I was at Tito's Tacos in Culver City getting lunch for mom and me.

SANTA MONICA COLLEGE

Anthony 'Budda' Fredricks RIP

Sterling Forbes

At Santa Monica College, I was soon on the court with their two star players, 6'10" Anthony 'Budda' Fredricks and 6'7" Sterling Forbes, in an intense pick-up game. They chose me at the urging of an old friend. Oddly, the gym was packed with rabid fans. It's game point as I get a rebound and start a 3-on-1 fast break. On my left was the future Indiana Pacer, Budda. On my right, a future Harlem Globetrotter, Sterling. On defense was 6'5" Walt, who was both buff and tough. Alas, he lacked the fundamental: **'Stop Ball'!** Hence, Sparks' U of A vs. ASU scenario of a retreating defender, at the point of no return, dotted line Statue of Liberty, defender grasping my forearm, poster dunk; came oh so true. I honorably implemented Sage Sparks' G'$ scheme and the gym exploded in utter hysteria. Instant hoop fame and credibility, as well as instant hoop friends and incredible kinships.

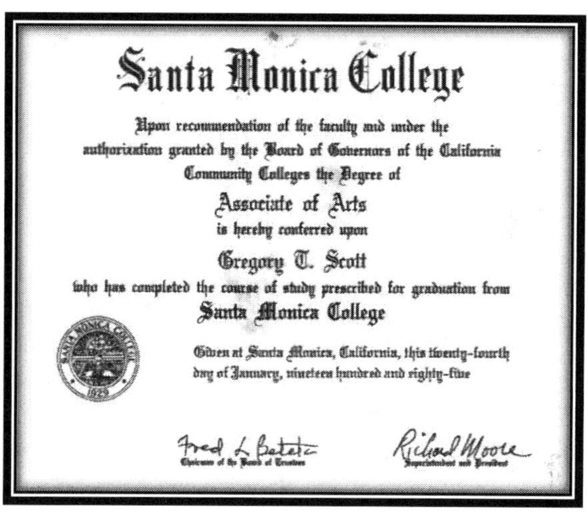
Santa Monica College

Upon recommendation of the faculty and under the authorization granted by the Board of Governors of the California Community Colleges the Degree of

Associate of Arts

is hereby conferred upon

Gregory T. Scott

who has completed the course of study prescribed for graduation from

Santa Monica College

Given at Santa Monica, California, this twenty-fourth day of January, nineteen hundred and eighty-five

Budda: "G' has total game and stupid hops. That dunk was sic! He victimized Walt."

One Summer Love: Pepperdine Scrimmages

Dwayne Polee

Budda had signed to play for Coach Jim Harrick at lavish Pepperdine University in Malibu. Coach Harrick invited Budda and Sterling to play in spring scrimmages against the team. Budda told him about me. Hook Up! We roll up the PCH in Budda's canary yellow Toyota Corolla Squareback to the posh PU pavillion on the hillside campus overlooking the ocean. Budda reunited with his long-time friend who is the 'Man' on the squad. Dwayne Polee, a legend in L.A. from his stardom at famed Crenshaw High. **The 'Shaw Dogs!** Polee played at UNLV before transfering to Pepperdine. I knew of his rep.! Polee gave Sterling dap, as Budda put his arm around my shoulders and introduced, "D' meet my G'man. He can go!" Game Recognizes Game! We met. We bonded. He insited on playing with us against the PU squad. OMG! We four, all thin-framed Porsches. **Polee was a 6'5" Wonder Guard. For six weeks I ran with the best hoop crew I've ever had: Me, Budda, Sterl', Polee!**

UH-HILO COACH & MRS. YAGI PAY A HOME VISIT

ALOHA G'! UH-HILO COACH YAGI SIGNS SCOTT!

"Next season I've scheduled ranked D-1 schools like LSU, Louisville, Creighton and the defending national champion Georgtown Hoyas, and I want to be competitve. That's why I'm here recruiting you. If what I have heard about you is true, that schedule will entice you, not frighten you. Also, I do care about your future, Gregg! So, if you come to UHH with your A.A. degree completed, I'll give you three years of scholarship for your two years of eligibility. And, play U of A in Hilo and Tucson!"

COUNTY OF HAWAII · STATE OF HAWAII

HERBERT T. MATAYOSHI
MAYOR

Office of the Mayor

I so wrongfully assumed that this was a SWAG letter sent to every new recruit from the Mayor.

When I arrived in Hilo, I went to his office to deliver a care package. A buzz of gawking arose as I sat. The Mayor came to greet me in person and took me on a tour of the Kuhio Plaza Mall adjacent to his offices. Mayor Matayoshi and I had an *ono* lunch & Shaved Ice.

May 30, 1984

Mr. Gregory T. Scott
2023 Pruess Road Apt 2
Los Angeles, CA 90034

ALOHA FROM THE BIG ISLAND OF HAWAII

I understand from Coach Jimmy Yagi that you are planning to come to the Big Island of Hawaii in August.

On behalf of the people of the County of Hawaii, I would like to welcome you as you continue your undergraduate college career at the University of Hawaii at Hilo.

We are very pleased with the growth of the UH-Hilo and its contribution to the life of our community. You should know too that the Vulcan tradition has been firmly and proudly established here on the Big Island. We certainly look forward to your joining us here.

Enclosed for you are a few pieces of information about our Island County. I hope that they will help to familiarize you with Hilo and the Big Island of Hawaii.

We are happy to learn of your decision, and I wish you much success and happiness in your college career.

Aloha.

HERBERT T. MATAYOSHI
MAYOR

Later, when the team was together, I asked about their 'Mayoral Letters'. They had no clue. I showed them my copy. Embarrassingly, I was the only player who received one. Yikes!

GREGG SCOTT
No. 24 / Guard
Junior / 6'2" / 175 lbs.
West Los Angeles, California

A guard with outstanding jumping ability, Gregg transfers to UHH from Santa Monica College (CA) . . . played freshman year at University of Arizona after making the team as a walk-on . . . former outstanding basketball and football performer at El Camino Real High School where he earned All-West Valley League honors in both sports . . . once scored 43 points while in high school . . . contemplates a profession in marketing . . . enjoys spaghetti and listening to the music of Rodney Franklin . . . plays the piano and enjoys swimming and bowling . . . biggest thrill in sports was playing in the LA Coliseum for the LA City 4A football championship . . . mother has been inspiration in sports . . . nickname is "Morris" . . . birthdate is September 3, 1964 . . . son of Henry T. and Janet K. Scott of West Los Angeles, California.

Yagi on Scott: *Gregg possesses "Jay (Bartholomew) the Bird-like" leaping ability and great quickness that adds immeasurably to our pressure defense and offensive transition. Exciting performer who is in control. Just what we need!*

The Media Hype of a New Regime

George Schnakenberg, from SBCC, had referred Coach Yagi to me. Schnack' was a great teammate and one of my roommates. Cool dude! I embraced his Guts, Grit and 'GameSpeak'!

He was one of the five seniors on the 'V' team, while I was one of the five new Yagi recruits. A truly epic mix!

More about Vulcan mania

Scott is a super jumper who has a consistent outside shot to compliment an explosive drive to the basket. He played at the University of Arizona as a walk-on freshman.

Ex-Vulcan & Mentor James Bradley lived across from Richardson's Beach at the end of '4-mile'

"No one comes to Hawaii, especially Hilo, thinking they're a bad-ass. No matter if you're a star ball player in 1984 or Dog the Bounty Hunter in 2014. Before the G'man arrived, the Vulcan hoop players had spats with the baseball team and a rep for being cocky and of bad character. So, they wisely stayed in their tiny bubble to avoid taking any lickings. Then, you heard about a dude rollin' solo in a sweet tinted-out VW Scirrocco with Cali' plates chanting 'Sporty G'; playing pick-up ball with the locals at Wainaku gym or the Hilo Armory. Shooting with the kids after school at the Boys & Girls Club and playing HORSE with 'da Boyz' on the portable basket at Richardson's Beach. Word traveled fast about the cool humble ballplayer who was being embraced because he never spoke of basketball. When I first met him we bonded instantly. Sporty G' is a rare breed with an Aloha Spirit. But, when he's on the court; that's when we witness the true G'man!" **Darrell Pakele**

James Bradley: "I warned Gregg of *O'Rear Backlash*. Bill and I were teammates and enemies on Yagi's first championship team. He despised G'man based on our close friendship. O'Rear did sabotage him, but Gregg remained a loyal friend and protégée. G'man preferred to train, swim, study and chill off-campus, away from all the hoopla."

Michael Coleman: "Bill O'Rear picked on Gregg from day one in our first team meeting, going on a rant about our off-campus associations and activities. "We know where you guys go. We hear about what you do and with whom. We don't want any players getting hurt playing pick-up ball off-campus. We want you to pick your friends wisely."

"G' asked, 'Who is 'we'??' Bill replied, "We, the coaching staff." G', 'Well your 'we' isn't the 'WE' who recruited me. The 'WE' who signed my scholarship papers know it has an addendum contrary to your 'we' babble. So, please do your homework, Coach We.' Bill, stunned and silent, looked at Coach Yagi, who nodded his validation. Checkmate!"

GameSpeak: Sporty G was a Moniker! Never entered the Gym!

Michael Coleman: "First open gym workout, G' hit the hardwood and was all business. You only had to see him once and you didn't have to see him long. He was truly legit."

UHH Vulcan Women's Volleyball defending NAIA National Champs ~ Cora & Celyn!

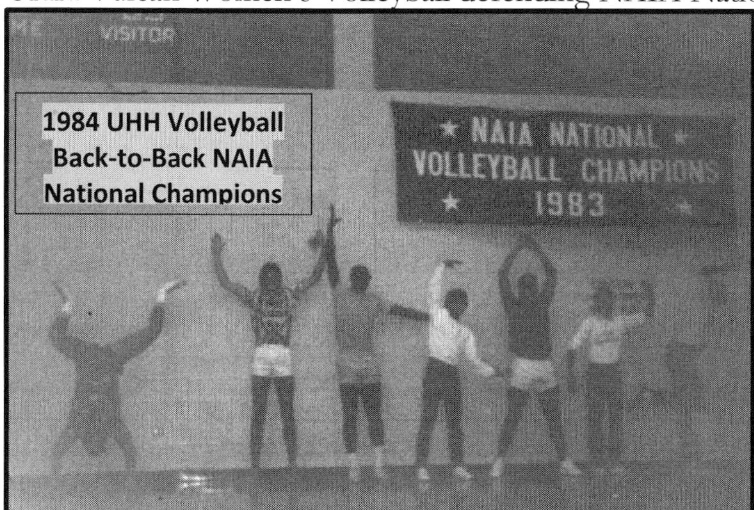

My 20th B'day party: Q, G', Schnack & Mike ~ G' & Hilo Hula Goddess, Lori Lei.

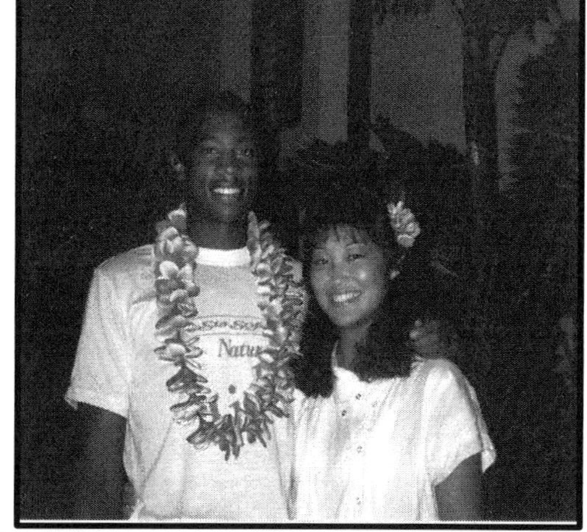

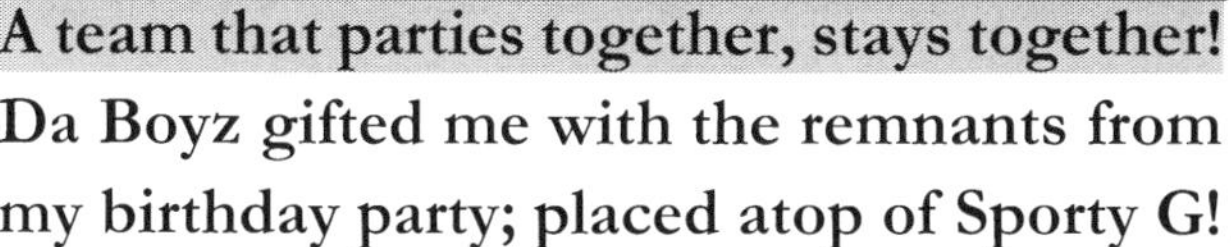

A team that parties together, stays together! Da Boyz gifted me with the remnants from my birthday party; placed atop of Sporty G!

<u>Michael Coleman:</u> "G' was a Lightweight! So, we'd buy BEER for the team AND a 4-pack of Wine Coolers for him."

Mother Nature

October 1984 11 p.m.: Mother Nature Roars! The earth around us roared from Kilauea to Hilo as the distant sky turned a bright orange. We drove to the volcano. No barriers or safeguards to prevent me from getting this picture.

The AMAZING Big Island!

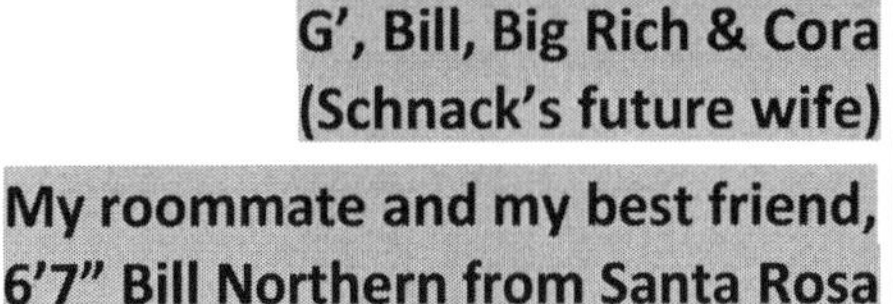

G', Bill, Big Rich & Cora (Schnack's future wife)

My roommate and my best friend, 6'7" Bill Northern from Santa Rosa

Michael Coleman: O'Rear verbally sparred with Gregg during our 3-week conditioning. "Okay, we've got five final suicides, then we're done." G', 'I'll take the 1st, 3rd and 5th.' G' wins the first suicide easily, then finishes 2nd in the second suicide. O'Rear, "If you can win every sprint, you should win every sprint." G' wins the third sprint and says, 'I don't need to shoot every shot, get every rebound or win every sprint. I'm unselfish.' G' finishes 2nd in the fourth suicide. O'Rear chants, "You run these suicides to get in shape for the season." G' snaps, 'For me there is no off-season! I stay in superior shape.' G' wins the final suicide, quite easily. Then, he curtly whispers, 'Your conditioning doesn't fatigue me and your criticizing doesn't faze me. I don't need anyone to get me in shape. Who here questions my fitness?!' Hushed!"

DEFENSIVE DRILL — Nineteen UHH Vulcan basketball prospects are currently participating in a three-week conditioning program at the old UHH Gym. Vulcan head coach Jimmy Yagi will pick the 1984-85 team and begin regular practice next month. The list of prospects includes eight returnees, five recruits and six walk-ons. Here, players go through a defensive drill of containing the offensive player.

In the final days of conditioning, Bill O'Rear went too far. A new G' régime was instilled.

A New Regime Coach Bill! Live Drill "Transition on Change..."

The next to last day of three weeks of conditioning in the humid Old Gym. We'd had no live scrimmaging at all. We were competing for starting spots! Near the end of practice in a rare live 5-on-5 half-court drill. "D' transitions to offense on change of possession."

James Bradley: "Do not be fooled, G' talked so much 'trash' on the court, but only the players could hear it! Still, he did back it up with his game. Cold-blooded!"

Mike Coleman: "I'll say this. G' never started it and he spoke only the truth; on-court, campus and in da club"

G'$: "You can't allow another man to taunt, injure or punk you! <u>Don't start none and there won't be none!"</u>

Mike Coleman: "It's a live drill! The offense initiates at midcourt and G' is on defense at the point, guarding 6'3" Bobby Warden. A horrible mis-match. G' plays lock-down D' without fail, and Bobby lacked any type of handles. Five straight possessions and Bobby didn't get a single pass completed. G' steal. G' kickball, reset. G' rips Bobby. G' deflection, turnover. G' rips Bobby again! A live drill, but on each "change of possession" Bil O'Rear blew his whistle. Four fundamentally sound steals, and four times Bill stopped G's fastbreak. G's irked; threw the ball hard off the backboard in Bill's direction.

Bill had us switch from Offense to Defense as he rants about execution and then, he goes overboard. "And, NO reaching!" G', holding the ball on his hip, glares at Bill's insinuation of his previous defense on Bobby. We all froze. It was a tense moment as G' held his stare. So, Bobby 'took the fuse' as he jokingly and blatantly slapped the ball out of G's hand and laughingly went to get it in his frontcourt. Everyone stared at O'Rear who then 'lit the fuse'! "Play It!" Now, Bobby is at the free throw line and G' is still in the backcourt. Bobby takes a dribble, slowly gathers and goes up to dunk! The amazing thing is that G' even caught up to the play. He's both quick and fast. Bobby rises above the rim as G' took flight, pinned the ball to the square with his right hand, and with his left arm he tossed Bobby off the court, tumbling out the door, over 4 steps and landing on the grass outside; 20 feet away. A loud uproar was heard from a few voices as I yelled, "I got him". To shield. G' pronounced, 'Oh no! I want to know who has a problem with how I deal with the bullshiznit that's going on here? Let every man speak for himself.' Silence! All roaring voices chose to remain anonymous. Yagi ended practice. He had been in a fog, but realized his Boy G' was at wits end. Team meeting! Bobby limps back into the gym as G' was the first to check on him. 'You ok?' Yagi praised our tenacity as if all was well and announced we'd have only one practice at the new gym the next day, as a reward for all our hard work. He asked if anyone had questions. Then, he explicitly asked G'. Epic G' rant."

'29 days and 25 practices until we compete against the best in the country, and I am not going to get embarrassed. Yagi didn't bring me or us here to repeat what's gone on before. It's a new regime. This is a place of business and I'm not down with BS or headgames in the workplace. A live drill with transition means a live drill with transition; without a whistle. Don't reach means don't reach. A reach and no whistle? Get punished. So I ask, who's here for biz and who's here to BS. Let every man speak; Coaches Included!!'

Mike: "John Q. Jones and G' had a Special Kinship. I repeatedly warned G' of crossing the line with Q! Every Practice! During F/T phase, guards and bigs shot separately. Q had a singing ritual that irked G', as O'Rear was compliant. So, G' sang a Billy Paul jam! Q Got Pissed! 'ME AND MRS. JONES'. G'?"
"G' Jam: 'Me and Mrs. Jones. We've got a thing goin' on. We both know that is wrong but it's much too strong to let it go now'...."

Front row (sitting l-r): Gordon Santos, Sean Francisco, Bob Warden, Bradley Estabilio, Andy Ground, and Rene Sanchez. *Back row (standing l-r):* Linda Rowan (Athletic Trainer), Jimmy Yagi (Head Coach), George Schnackenberg, Gene Arceñeaux, Michael Coleman, John Jones, Bill Northen, Carl Moose, Gregg Scott, and Bill O'Rear (Assistant Coach).

"G didn't just pick on the meek. The next day in the New Gym we were in a live 4-on-4 shell rotation drill with the wing attacking the basket. Q was lagging. G' cut to the front of the line. G' got the ball, attacked the rim, went up and dunked right in Q's face. Silence. Then, Q cried, 'Did he just dunk on me?' We All Laughed."

BOYZ! Q and I had ZERO residue from my 'Me and Mrs. Jones' Jam! TIGHT LIKE THAT!
I ONLY sang it during our F/T Practice! Every Day!

The Vulcans

GREGG SCOTT — One of five newcomers on the team, Scott appears headed for a starting off-guard position. The 6-foot-2 junior transfer from Santa Monica Junior College played his freshman year at University of Arizona as a walk-on. He is quick and a jumper who earned All-West Valley League honors in football and basketball at El Camino Real High School in Los Angeles. He plans a career in marketing.

G'$ Mindset D-1 Foes: Barometer

Yagi recruited me in to be a difference-maker against D-1 teams and win a conference title! And, to graduate. I was conditioned to always view my opponents with due respect, and, as a baller, with ZERO awe-factor. **My psyche is founded upon one G'$ Mantra: 'Resumes, Rankings and Reputations Don't Suit Up!'** This goes both ways. Where I've been, what I've done in the past, likewise, is irrelevant. Game Speaks! As a G', I relish every single chance to compete against the best, to be tested by the best and, in turn, to put the best to my own G'$ test. Also, they didn't earn their 'rep' against me and my crew. They've got to prove it; as do I/We. **UHH: Legit Crew of Ballers!**

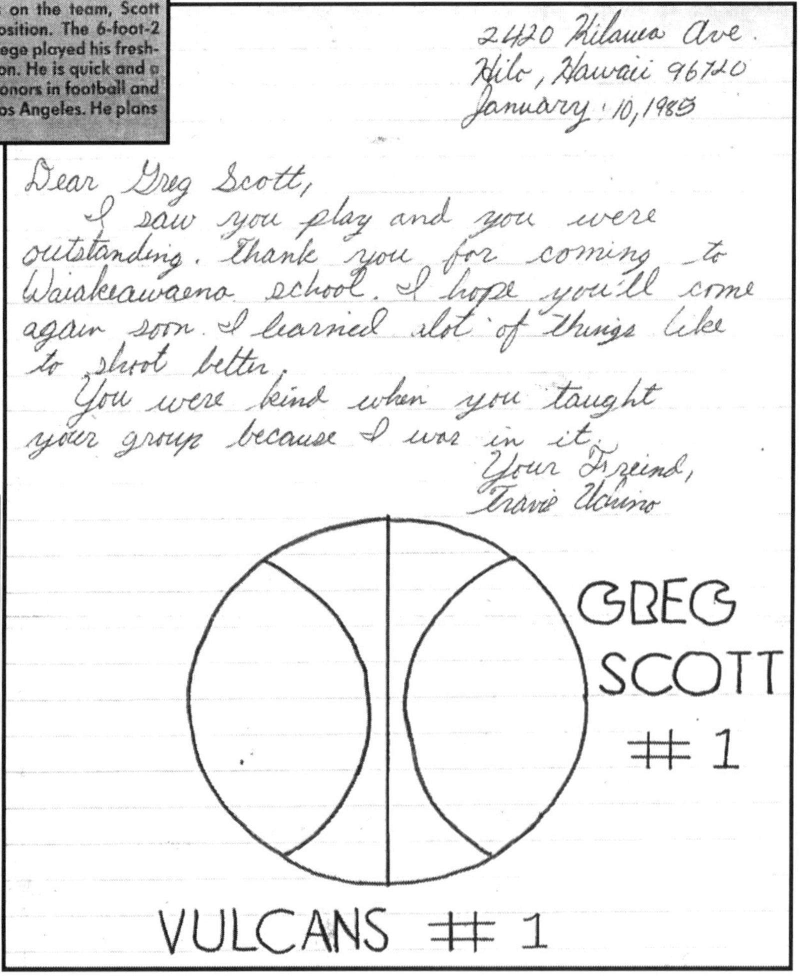

2420 Kilauea Ave.
Hilo, Hawaii 96720
January 10, 1985

Dear Greg Scott,
I saw you play and you were outstanding. Thank you for coming to Waiakeawaena school. I hope you'll come again soon. I learned alot of things like to shoot better.
You were kind when you taught your group because I was in it.
Your Friend,
Travis Uwino

GREG
SCOTT
1

VULCANS # 1

I'd played in five games since my Jr. Year in High School! G'$: primed and ready to go.

Media accolades are nice, yet I draw more inspiration and motivation from life memory letters written by loyal fans.

By: LeeAnn 'Tubby' Garcia

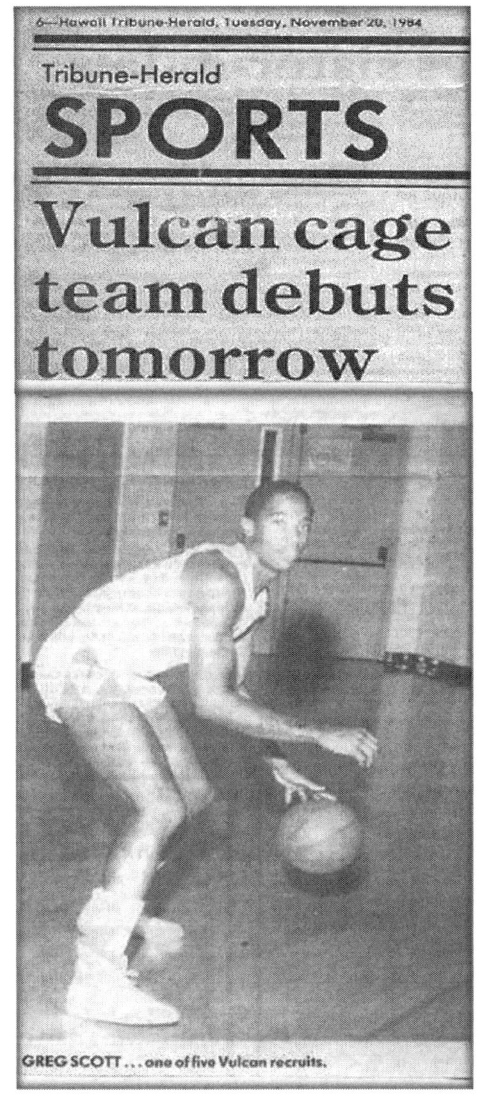
6—Hawaii Tribune-Herald, Tuesday, November 20, 1984

Tribune-Herald

SPORTS

Vulcan cage team debuts tomorrow

GREG SCOTT . . . one of five Vulcan recruits.

The Defending National Champion Georgetown Hoyas and famed coach, John Thompson, were our first opponent. One convo with 'Sage Sparks' gave me a game plan to navigate; attack mode. His prophetic advice was a true 'Sage' Godsend.

We discussed an apt cerebral approach to recognizing and attacking their full-court and ¾-court man press versus their half-court trapping press. Their Mission:

✎ Alter, increase or dictate the pace, rhythm and tempo of the game. Note: <u>Defense Creates Offense!</u>
✎ Disrupt your offensive flow and to create premature, ill-advised or rushed shots. Note: Poise!
✎ Funnel you to the 'added defenders': endline and sidelines; mid-court line and Ewing. Note: Coy!
✎ Create turnovers and blocked shots fueling transition lay-ups, scoring spurts and domination.

Also, with no false hubris, I was relieved that their talented volatile forward, Michael Graham, had just been suspended from the team and would not be a potential 'issue' for me. **Humble Self-Preservation!**

Sparks' Hoop IQ is off the charts! Thus, my Sage Sparks game plan was devised: Attack Pressure! "Lead By Example to Establish Belief Within your Teammates!" Recall those Carbajal drills inwhich he had you going 1 vs. 2 at 6 a.m. and saying, "You won't need these skills here, but one day you'll thank me." That day and opportunity is at hand. **Sage Sparks' G'town checklist:**

- ✓ **Inbounder role. Run the baseline, be coy, make sure passes; step in!**
- ✓ **Forbid denial of the ball by a single defender! Make yourelf available!**
- ✓ **Stay out of the corners! ~ Be strong with the ball! ~ Protect Your Space!**
- ✓ **Use ball-fakes and explode! ~ Disallow the trap to close in! Be Clever!**
- ✓ **Utilize & 'Coach' your big men to flash to the ball hard and on balance!**
- ✓ **'Pass and cut hard! Fill the Gaps!' ~ 'Get the ball back in my hands asap!'**

Most critical: Once you break the press, set up the offense, and make them play D! "They back-court press or half-court trap, not both. Once broken, they go zone D."

Let me be clear, survival would take a team effort and our squad was a tight crew of tough men going into this D-1tilt as united warriors on a quest to slay the Goliath. **So, game on!** Yes, the pre-game introductions were daunting. **Yikes! I'm Human! Now, Go To Work!**

UHH vs. '84 NCAA Nat'l Champions

Georgetown's famed coach John Thompson was a man I admired greatly. G'$ Navigation: attack mode!

G'$ vs. Horace Broadneaux

Billy Martin
Mark Jackson
David Wingate
Reggie Williams

Then, in the second half, one sole G'$ play had our 2,400 fans cheering and shouting; as I was pissed at myself and internally pouting. A made basket and missed opportunity. G'$ poster dunk on Pat! I drove baseline strong as Pat came late to help; within my cross-hairs. I got to my launchpoint, exploded, then second-guessed myself and put the ball high off of the backboard and in. Only my hoop mentor James Bradley knew my angst; "G'man, you had him!"

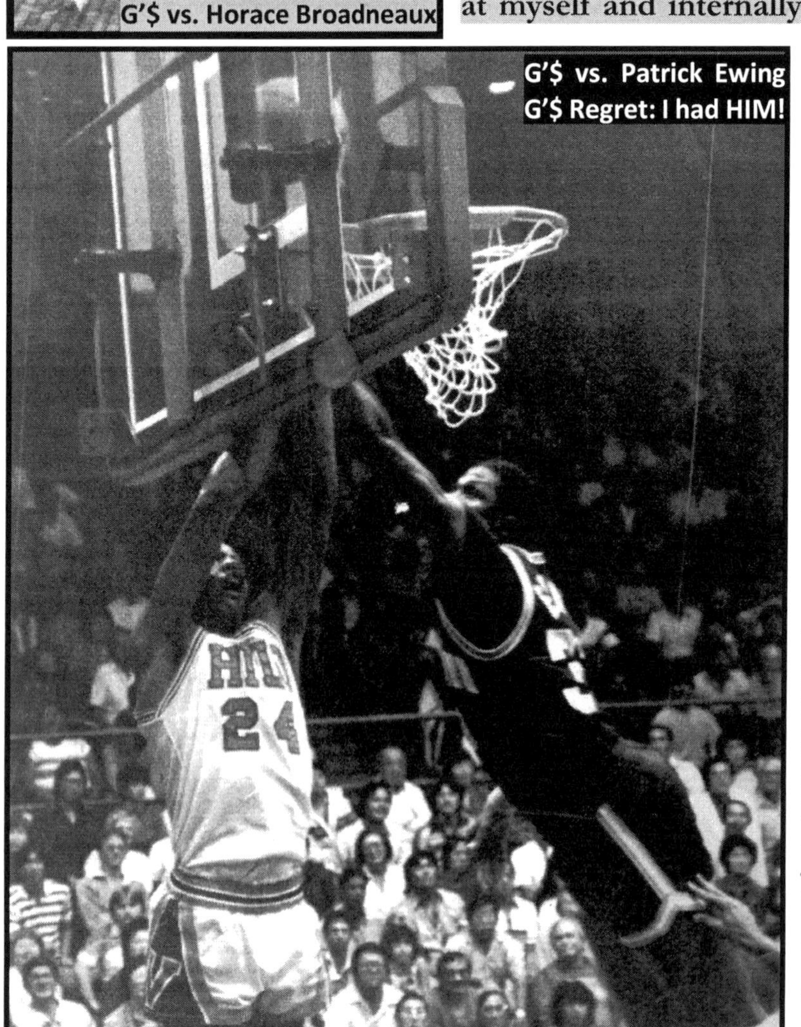

G'$ vs. Patrick Ewing
G'$ Regret: I had HIM!

My fav memory was as the game ended, Coach Thompson shook my lil' hand and said, "You're a fine player young man."

JB's apt tongue-lashing in our recap that night: "Promise me that you'll exploit every opportunity to bash on D-1 players."

Balderdash! One Coach, O'Rear & One Ref, Iggy: Sole 'Mental Game' Challenges!

Although Scott has a 42-inch vertical jump and a good jump shot, he has not had a sound mental game, Hawaii-Hilo assistant coach Bill O'Rear said last week.

"We lost to Louisville by five (80-75) but everyone remembers one thing," O'Rear said. "Gregg took an alley-oop pass and slammed over Louisville's Billy Thompson. Our home crowd of 2,400 exploded.

"He's got the necessary physical tools. He just has to get his mental game together."

"I know that's been my problem," Scott said. "I'm trying to be more consistent in my thinking."

GREGG SCOTT.

B. Thompson: 14 of Louisville's 38 Turnovers!

GREAT SCOTT!!

Final Four familiar?

And the NAIA Vulcans gave their highly - ranked Division One foes fits in both games.

LSU edged Hilo 80-71 on Dec. 3 at the Civic, with the Vulcans playing the Tigers even in the second half.

In the first weeks of UHH's 1984-85 season, coach Denny Crum's Louisville team struggled to an 80-75 win over a sky - high Vulcan crew. The Cardinals turned the ball over astounding 38 times, as d Rene Sanchez led a ng Hilo defense.

uisville forward Billy suffered 14 turnis own, the highest game individual total cal basketball observan recall.

The muscular, 6-foot-7 Thompson was also burned on one of the most spectacular plays a Vulcan has managed in recent seasons.

During a first - half UHH rally, 6-3 guard Gregg Scott soared and dunked two - handed on a lob pass, right in Thompson's face.

At shoot-around before the Louisville game, in a half-speed drill, Carl Moose and Gene got into a war for a rebound. They wrestled from the key, out of bounds to the padded baseline wall, towards our team bench on the sideline. Then viciously scrambled, intertwined and growling, to the ball, crashed into FIVE chairs and somehow simultaneously possessed it! Draw! We were all mortified. Then I chanted, "Oh yeah, fellas! We're gonna get that ass tonight!" And, we surly did!

Sage Sparks: "It's a sign of DISRESPECT if your defender looks or goes to help."

G'$: Thompson lacked 'see man and ball', 'pistols', D'. Mike: "Only Gordon 'Dino' Santos could have made that pass. It wasn't in our system or ever practiced." I told Dino, 'If I show a fist as a target look for the backdoor *Coop-a-loop.*' Yup! BT turned his head; FIST! Dino threw it Up, Up!! I cut backdoor, Billy Jumped...Above The Rim! I sealed him with my left arm and caught a perfect lob pass with my right hand. A foot to the right of the rim and a foot above the rim...and I was still climbing. So I released my seal, added my left hand to the ball, turned my hips and flushed a two-handed poster dunk on Bad Billy Thompson that had his team bench horrified. The first thing I did was acknowledge the pass; as I heard JB, "Yo, that's what I'm talking about, G'man!"

G'$: 'Resumes, Rankings and Reputations Don't Suit Up!'

James Bradley made me promise to capitalize on the rare opportunity to compete against and posterize the best in the nation. "Have No Regrets G'man! Take Flight!"

T-H Photo by Larry Kadooka

CHALLENGES THE BIG MAN — UHH Vulcan gurd Gregg Scott (24) goes up against Creighton's 7-foot center Benoit Benjamin (00) for a rebound in Sunday's night's clash at the Civic. The Blue Jays defeated the Vulcans 76-71. UH-Hilo faces Occidental College at 7:30 p.m. tonight at the Civic.

Pure Sparks: Full vertical thrust, squared-up jumper with a hand in my face. Recognition & Competence! Bank Shot: The Backboard Is Your Best Friend!

FAV PIC! Note: My 'guide hand' is AT Rim Level! You ever seen such a feat?

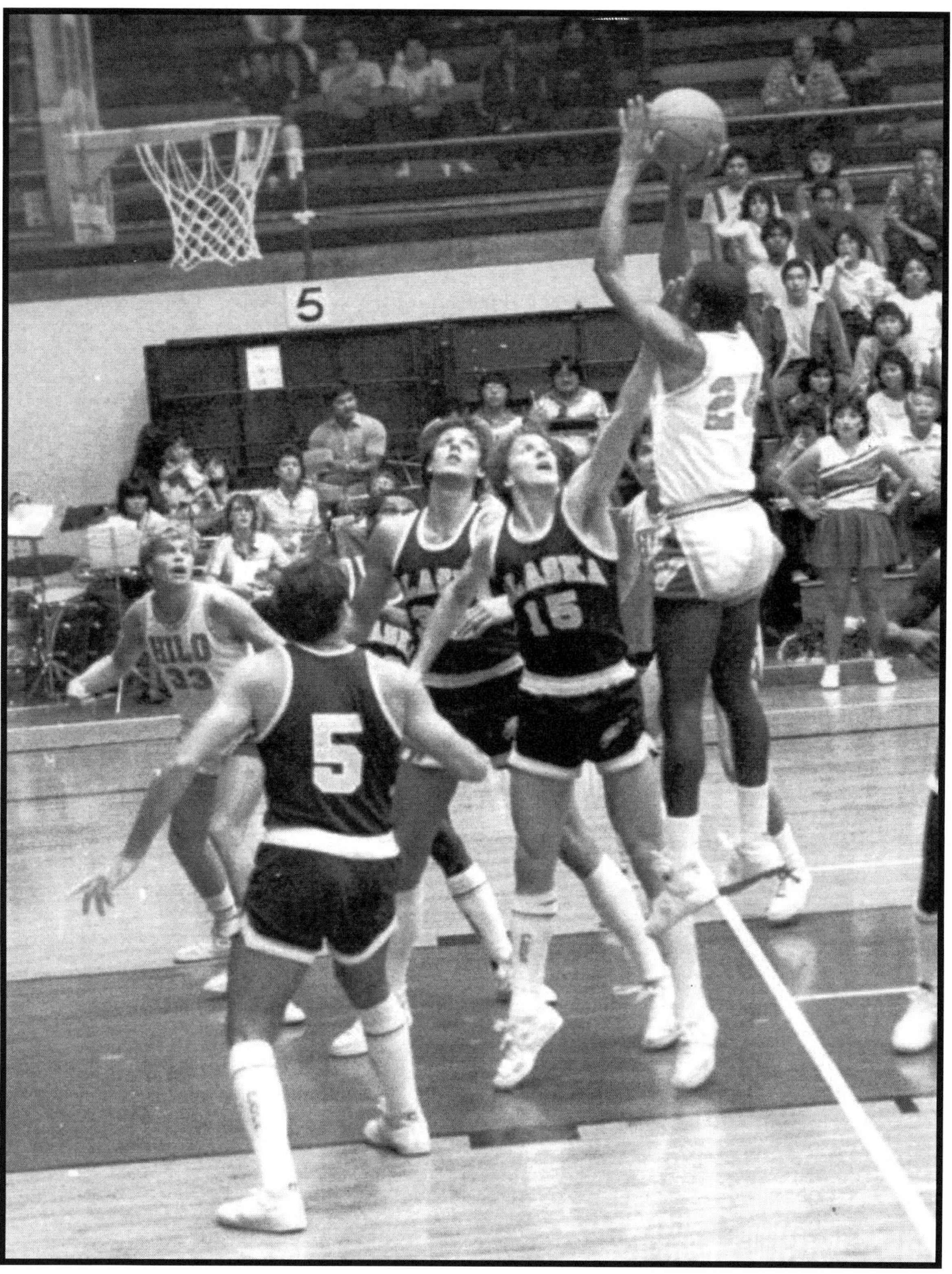

<u>Have Some:</u> **I gave this Cal State L.A. player ample opportunity to meet me above the rim and be a poster on my wall, or stand in to take a charge and surely taste the salty perspiration of my jock strap as I punched it over him.**

He Aptly Chose To 'Exit Stage Left'!

G' Flight: Aerial Artistry
Naughty ~ Nice ~ Nasty

—T-H photo by Larry Kadooka

TO THE HOOP — UHH Vulcan Greg Scott (24) goes high off the ground for a layin in a recent game against Cal State - Los Angeles at the Civic. UH-Hilo returns to action tonight against Division I University of Arizona. Tip-off is set for 7:30 p.m.

DECEMBER 11, 1984

Former Wildcat guard to start against UA

UH-Hilo vs. U of Arizona

HILO, Hawaii — Gregg Scott said on Monday he has "something to prove" tonight when Arizona is to play Hawaii-Hilo in a non-conference basketball game.

Scott, Hawaii-Hilo's starting 6-foot-2 junior point guard, was an Arizona basketball walk-on in 1982-83, under former UA coach Ben Lindsey.

"I'm trying not to get overexcited," Scott said. "But this is something special. I had always thought I'd stay at Arizona.

"Now, I want to show all those people I can play. I have something to prove."

Scott said UA coach Lute Olson, who was hired after Lindsey was fired after the 1982-83 season, didn't invite him back.

"He (Olson) said they needed help quickly and had to get some players immediately," Scott said. "He was nice about it. I like him. He never made me feel like an outcast, but I was hoping they wouldn't take my scholarship. I wanted to stay at Arizona."

Yagi's Retirement Announcement Stung Me!

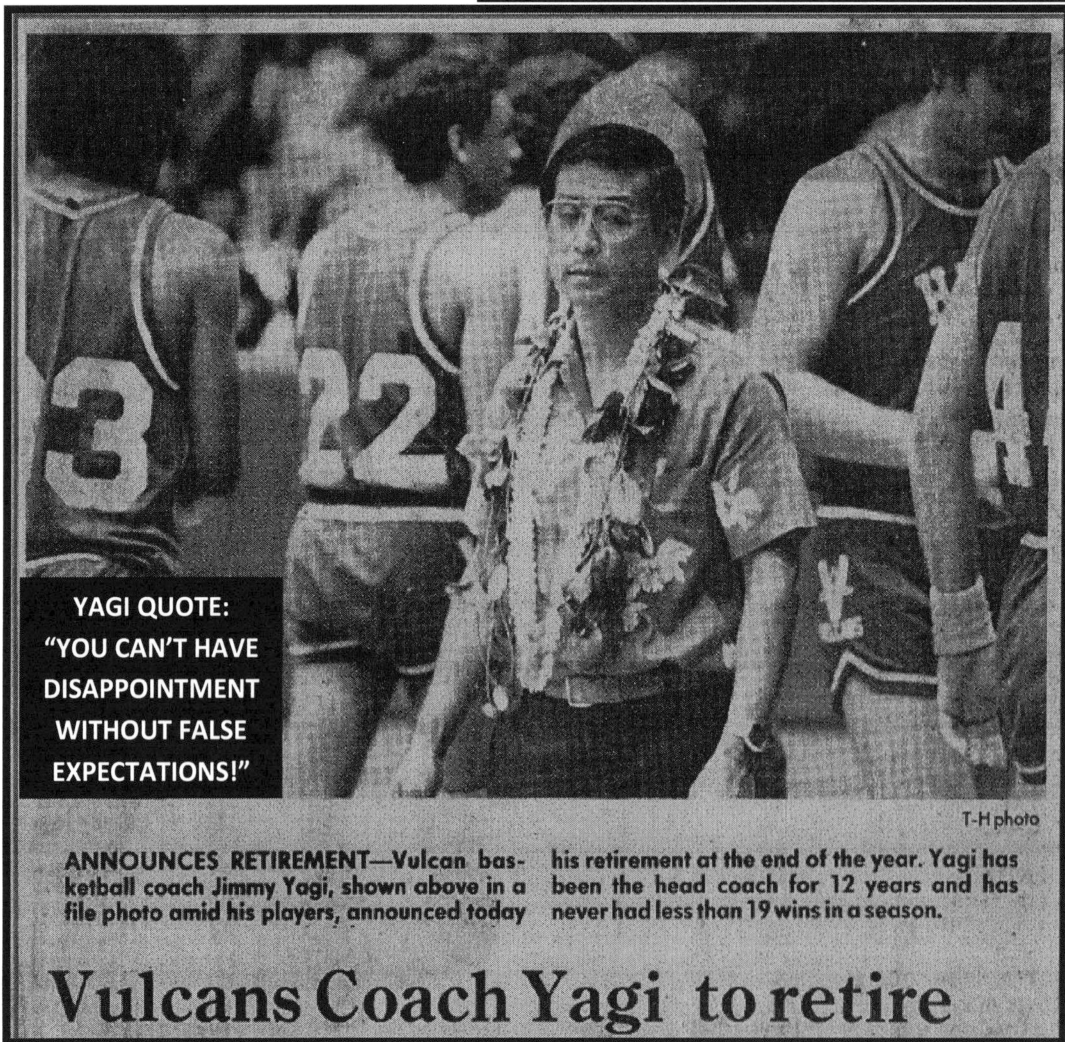

YAGI QUOTE: "YOU CAN'T HAVE DISAPPOINTMENT WITHOUT FALSE EXPECTATIONS!"

T-H photo

ANNOUNCES RETIREMENT—Vulcan basketball coach Jimmy Yagi, shown above in a file photo amid his players, announced today his retirement at the end of the year. Yagi has been the head coach for 12 years and has never had less than 19 wins in a season.

Vulcans Coach Yagi to retire

Scott seeks to prove self

Olson, last week, seemed surprised when he heard Scott was starter.

"Is that the same guy?" Olson asked.

Scott said sometimes he finds it strange the twists his life has taken. Yagi has said he is to resign after this year.

"That will mean four coaches in four years," Scott said.

"I've been through a lot since Arizona. I've matured. I want to show them that now."

Scott, 20, later was awarded a scholarship. But he didn't travel. He played guard in three of 28 UA games and scored six points. The UA went 4-24.

"Sporty, controlled aggression will see you through." Mark Lovelace

My mom flew in for the game and I performed and represented; indeed!

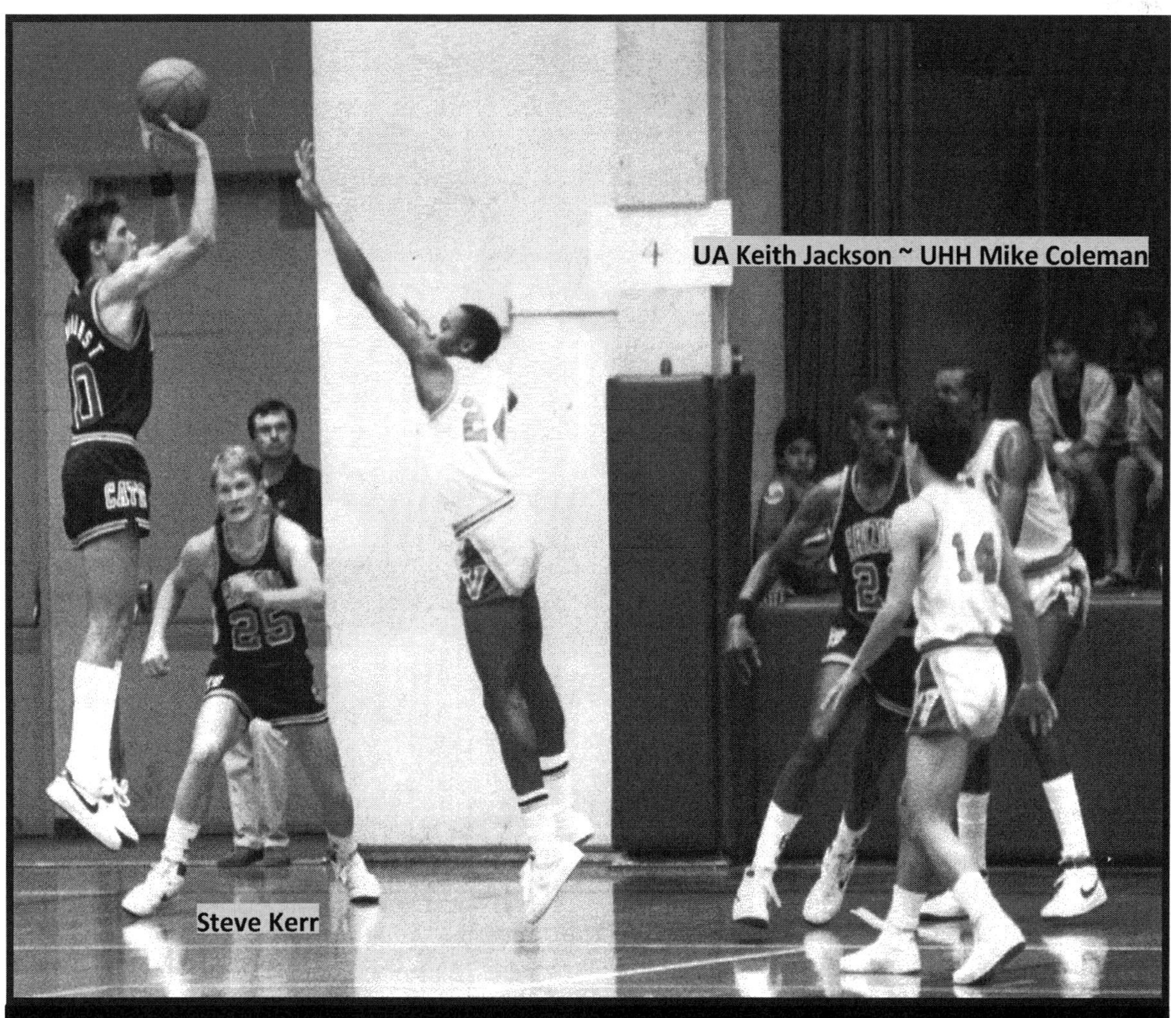

G' Scott: Fundamental 'Close-Out' on Brock. And, my intro to #25, Steve Kerr. A Prophetic Night!

ABOVE THE RIM: MIDAIR MYSTIC!

ABOVE ALL: PROSPEROUS PURE JUMPERS GOT ME PAID!

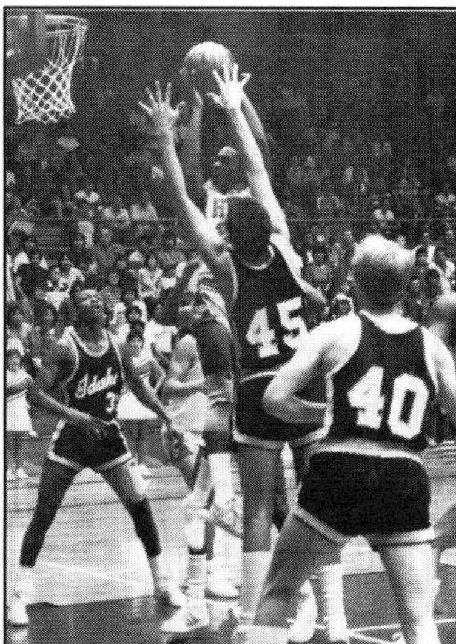

COACH YAGI TO RETIRE!

UH-HILO 1984-'85 NAIA

HAWAII CONFERENCE

CHAMPIONS

Tom Hawkins of Chaminade finds his path to the basket blocked by Hilo's Greg Scott. A foul was called on Sean

Overtime, in Hilo with a league title to be had! A true battle of will and a test of pride fueled our gritty Champions Mettle.

Bedlam Yagi Hug "I brought you here for this. Mahalo!"

I contemplated a Pro gig utilizing my dual citizinship status in Germany.

Mom vetoed that without hesitation!

Honor thy Mother! Student-Athlete & College Graduate!

GENE LOORAM

Vermittler von Basketball-Spielern
Basketball Player Agent

Kiefernweg 27 Tel. 09276-632
D8583 BISCHOFSGRÜN, Germany
Bankkonten - Bank Accounts:
Raiffeisenbank Gefrees Nr. 315133 (BLZ 77069749)
Postscheck Nürnberg Nr. 19073-851 (BLZ 76010085)

SWEET VICTORY — A Vulcan basketball player raises his arms in triumph last night as the team defeated Hawai'i Pacific College by one point in overtime. See story page

Summer Jobs in West L.A.: G'$ Avia Personal Shoe Sponsorship!

Front Runners **was a privately owned upscale athletic shoe store located in plush Brentwood in an era when O.J. Simpson and Nicole were their VIPs!**

My 2nd Job: <u>Culver City Parks & Recreation!!!</u> Sr. Rec. Leader 4 at legendary Fox Hills Park. My boss gave me a key to a tiny hidden gym inside of the Veterans Memorial Auditorium with a wood floor and a single basket. 24/7!

July 3, 1985

Gregg Scott
2023 Preuss St.
L.A. Calif. 90034

The grand opening of the Westside Pavilion Mall would be the venue for *Front Runners II*. The Mandatory Tech Rep Promo Presentations every other Saturday lead to a noble Avia intro! Kenn Rasmussen was keen on sponsoring me!!

Dear Gregg:

I would be very much interested in your wearing Avia basketball shoes. As you may know, the easiest thing in the world is to give away shoes. Many times it turns out like, "flushing them down the toilet." Once, in a while it turns out to be a tremendous investment.

What I need to know is your shoe size. Phone it in to me or mail it to me as soon as possible. I will put you in touch with our Hawaii salesman, Brian Kawakami. I have inserted his number.

I would like you to wear the shoe during Vulcan games, and talk it up among the players and with your coach. We have a special deal for college teams. The shoes can be colored to look supersonic!

Avia, HQ in Beaverton, OR, was primarily an aerobic and fitness shoe brand with a unique <u>concave sole</u> system. As a true student of my game my Q & A with their rep afterwards led to a sponsorship that evolved over a decade!!

Best regards,

Kenn Rasmussen

Kenn Rasmussen

cc/kawakami
cc/saltsberg

Summer Grind: Memorial Gym, Santa Monica

Leon Wood

The gym was crowded and the pick-up ball was intense. I noticed a familiar figure working out solo at the far basket on the middle court. I knew this dude was the real deal. His jump rope routine impressed me, so I grabbed mine and inquired. For the next half-hour I was mentored by a Team USA Pan-Am Games gold medalist! Leon Wood tutored many topics: Pick-up ball Perils! Skills! Drills! G' Jump Rope Schemes!

SR. YEAR: G' FLIGHT NETS AVIA SHOE CONTRACT

Coach Bob Wilson was a 'Good old' Boy' from Enid, Oklahoma. He had overt disdain for me from our first convo. "You're lucky to be here, son." Similarly, I had overt disregard for his disdain. 'My scholarship is guaranteed, sir.' His Asst. Coach, Tim Lovejoy, was a cool former NAIA All-American who served as a coveted buffer

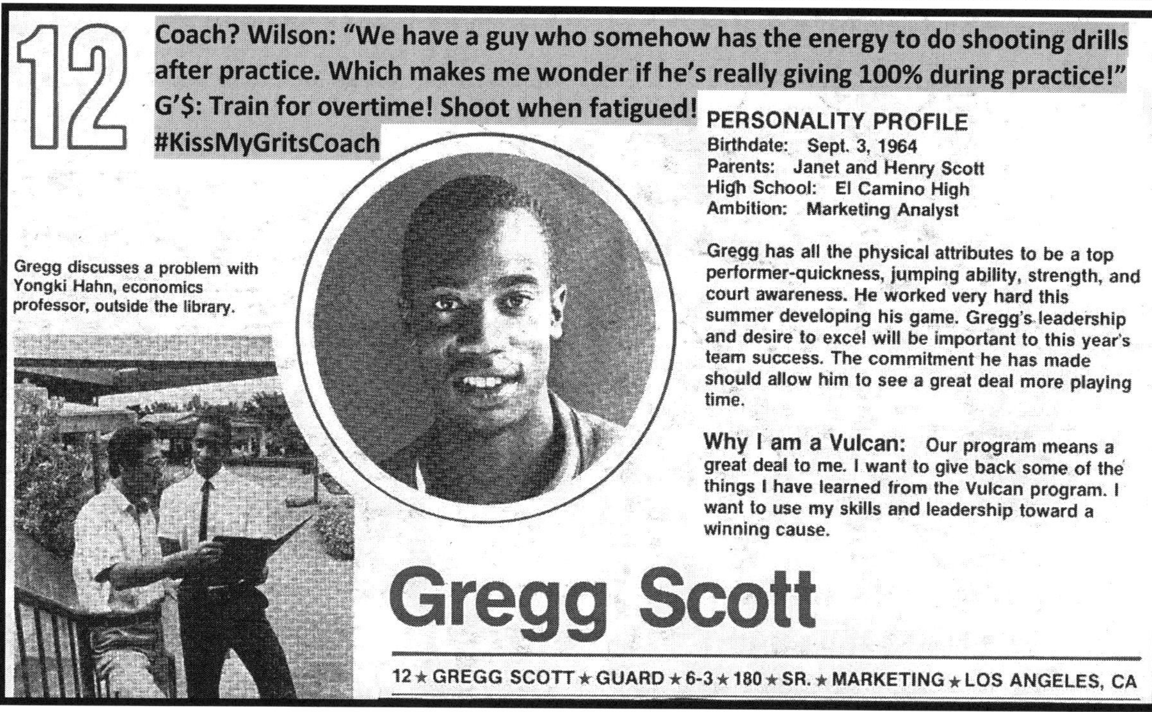

12

Coach? Wilson: "We have a guy who somehow has the energy to do shooting drills after practice. Which makes me wonder if he's really giving 100% during practice!"
G'$: Train for overtime! Shoot when fatigued!
#KissMyGritsCoach

PERSONALITY PROFILE
Birthdate: Sept. 3, 1964
Parents: Janet and Henry Scott
High School: El Camino High
Ambition: Marketing Analyst

Gregg has all the physical attributes to be a top performer-quickness, jumping ability, strength, and court awareness. He worked very hard this summer developing his game. Gregg's leadership and desire to excel will be important to this year's team success. The commitment he has made should allow him to see a great deal more playing time.

Why I am a Vulcan: Our program means a great deal to me. I want to give back some of the things I have learned from the Vulcan program. I want to use my skills and leadership toward a winning cause.

Gregg discusses a problem with Yongki Hahn, economics professor, outside the library.

Gregg Scott

12 ★ GREGG SCOTT ★ GUARD ★ 6-3 ★ 180 ★ SR. ★ MARKETING ★ LOS ANGELES, CA

Coach Wilson axed Mike Coleman and brought in some weak players who truly didn't deserve to be on a full hoop ride. I bristled out loud about the '6' 10" wimp he brought with him from sorry Phillips Univ., and a few busters he recruited onto our defending League Champion UHH roster. So, I punished them all in practice! And, I put in WORK against Georgetown!

SURE TWO — University of Hawaii - Hilo's Gregg Scott wanted to make sure he scored two points after stealing the ball and racing down court during Tuesday night's game against Louisiana State University. Scott dunked the ball on the play, but the Vulcans still dropped a 70-61 decision to the 11th ranked Tigers. UHH has eight days off before

'GameSpeak' vs. LSU

A G'$ Performance #11 LSU!
G': 'Resumes, Rankings and Reputations Don't Suit Up!'
You Show Me! I'll Show You!
Even as a Sub off the Bench!

YouTube*.com/MentalAthlete*

Scott, a 6-3 senior, hit six of nine from the field and added a free throw for 13 points. He also had three rebounds, four assists and helped the Vulcans effectively bring the ball up against LSU's full - court press. He played 27 minutes.

ZERO TURNOVERS & ONE G'$ ASCENT on LSU 7' Jose Vargas

This fine basic baseline jam wasn't even a Top 100 dunk; except for the Special Victim. A 7-footer is highly coveted pray to posterize for G' Flight.

Jose Vargas: Now You Know!

"G' Flight is Clear for Takeoff: Jump Only at Your Own Risk!"

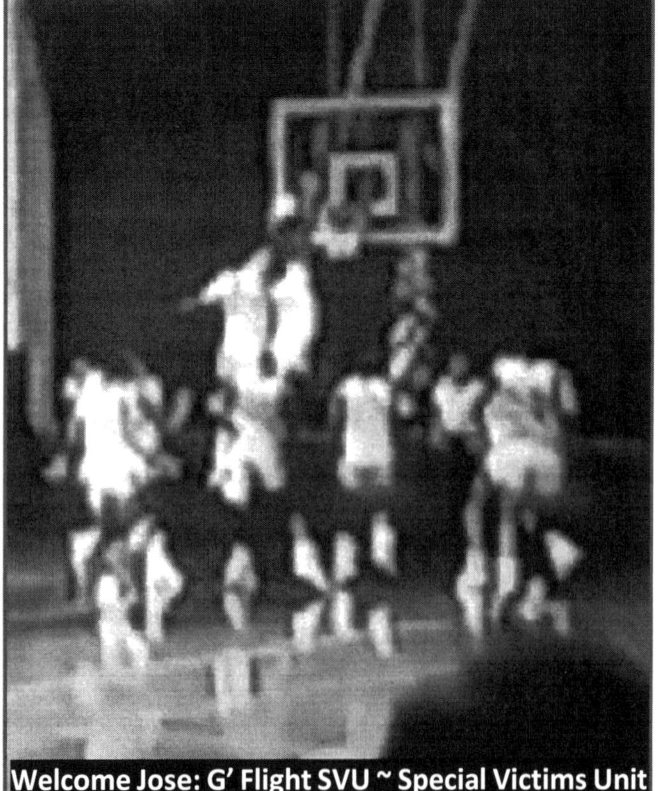

Welcome Jose: G' Flight SVU ~ Special Victims Unit

Scott helps Hilo stop Warner Pacific, 80-79

By Hugh Clark
Advertiser Big Island Bureau

KEALAKEKUA, Hawaii — Gregg Scott made three throws in the final 1:15 last night to help the University of Hawaii-Hilo gain an 80-79 basketball victory over Warner Pacific College.

Wilson was pleased with Scott, who had a season-high 16 points and six assists in addition to two free throws with 31 seconds to give the Vulcans an 80-76 lead.

Larry Kadooka

VULCANS REBOUND—Hilo posted its first two wins of the season Thursday and Friday night against Warner Pacific College. Above, senior guard Gregg Scott launches a 10-foot baseline jump shot Thursday at the Civic. Scott averaged 14 points and 6.5 assists in the victories.

Great Scott: Senior Guard Leads Hilo Past Anchorage

A complimentary article!? Yet, a dis' to my true love for Coach Yagi with blatant fibs of facts, stats and my "laments", that I didn't appreciate! Oahu Media: Don't assume! Just interview me!!

James Bradley: "Only Bill O'Rear would say that *BS*; as a Hilo Tribune sports reporter and ex-Asst. Coach."

By Chris Reed
Special to the Star-Bulletin

HILO—You will have to excuse Hawaii-Hilo senior Gregg Scott if he failed to lament longtime Vulcan's Coach Jimmy Yagi's decision to resign last spring.

Under Yagi, Scott lost his starting post in mid-season and ended the 1984-85 year as Hilo's fifth guard. The rap on the 6-foot-3 Los Angeles native was that he had a bad attitude and often played out of control.

But under new UHH Coach Bob Wilson, Scott has blossomed into one of the Vulcans top players. Last night, he continued his comeback, leading Hilo to a 72-66 win over Alaska-Anchorage before 1,650 fans at Afook-Chinen Civic Auditorium..

"Gregg is playing very well for us," said Wilson, whose team improved to 6-6 (6-2 against small college teams) after an 0-5 start.

The Vulcans meets Division I South Alabama tonight at 7:30 at the Civic while Anchorage (7-7) plays Hawaii Pacific College next Tuesday at McKinley Gym.

Scott had a career high 11 assists, 10 points, eight rebounds and just one turnover bringing the ball up against the Seawolves' press. His two free throws in a one-and-one situation with 47 seconds to play put Hilo up, 70-62. It took the steam out of a late Anchorage rally that made the game seem much closer than it actually was.

Stats Don't Lie! Clutch Free Throws!

Too Late: A Pure G'$ 'J' Over a 7-footer!

Scott's greatness is a product of persistence and perspective

ROAD TRIP NIGHTMARE: HEARTACHE & JAW BREAK!

After a red-eye flight from Oahu, we arrive at our hotel in Tucson, got our room keys, and told to get rest until we get a wake up call for practice. Mario and I slept in our room, **224**, and we got no calls. We woke up hearing the team arrive after practice! Summoned to the coaches' room we learn that they told the entire team and UA peeps that we were being sent back to Hilo ASAP for leaving our hotel. Utter embarrasment. Except, Coach Bob had us in room **221**, not **224**! **Expunged! Still very shameful. No apology given! He did let us go to MeKale Arena with Coach Lovejoy to shoot and explain. New Years Eve! No curfew? See ya! Sparks' adobe crib vistas: Perfect for a Happy New Years!**

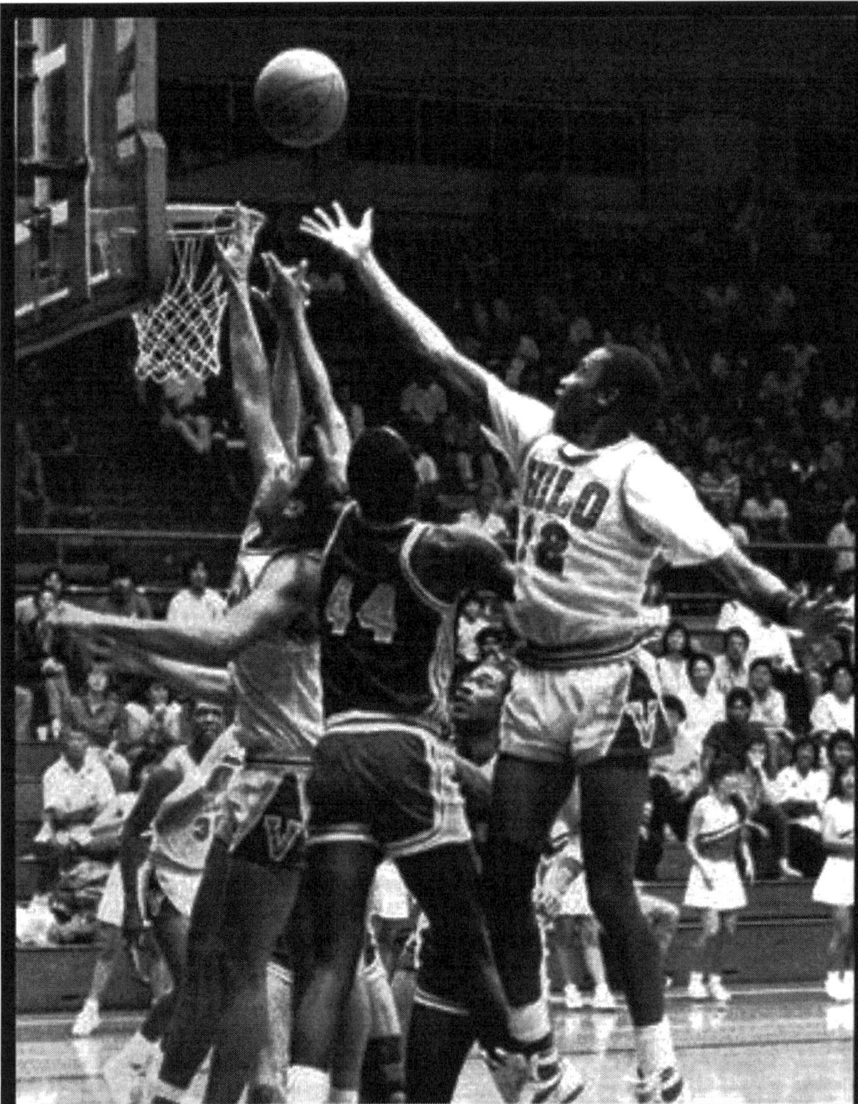

ON THE ROAD — The University of Hawaii - Hilo Vulcans open a four-game mainland road trip with a game at the University of Arizona tonight. The Wildcats will be the Vulcans sixth and final NCAA Division I opponent. Six - foot - seven forward Bill Northen will not suit up for today's game due to pending eligibility requirements. UHH takes on Grand Canyon in Phoenix Saturday night and Cal-Poly at Pomona, Calif. Sunday afternoon. None of the road games will be broadcast, although KHILO radio station does plan to report halftime and final scores. Here, UHH's Carl Moose (nearest the basket) and Gregg Scott (12) battle for a rebound during the Vulcans' win last month over Point Loma of California.

Arizona vs. Hawaii-Hilo
January 2, 1986

Game Night Funk: A player is late! We all are in the vans!

<u>G' Funk Net Stats:</u>
0-for-5 in shooting!
5 pts 5 rbs 6 dimes.

1/4 vs. Grand Canyon: 2nd half Blindsided from behind, outside of the key, after the whistle; rendered unconscious!! No memory of the elbow or who hit me, or the brawl, or the ejections. As the fog lifted, I felt no pain. Then, I was handed my tooth! My teammates had tears in their eyes as they told me what happened and viewed my dangling two front teeth and the pinkish bony fragments of my broken jaw. Whatda....? I assessed my damage in the coaches' office as I heard the ejected players in an adjacent locker-room laughing. I put my tooth in a cup of my saliva, grabbed a wood bat, then prayed; "Lord forgive me and be with me." G' mode*

*Coach Lovejoy had alerted them to "get some police protection". They intervened just in time. As I was rushed to the hospital I still had no recollection and, at that point, no severe pain. Only a minor discomfort of my 3-inch tooth in my mouth was a horrid reminder of the gravity of my injury. As the sun sets we arrived at the hospital. I could only listen in horror to Linda recounting the ugly incident. When the triage doctor asks how long was I unconscious, I was stunned at her reply, "over a minute". After an MRI, CAT scan and x-rays, I was told that beyond my dental woes, I had sustained a broken jaw near my right nostril. Sadly, in a span of six hours I went to three different facilities for extensive surgical and major dental treatment. Being a Sunday evening, the offices were all closed so each surgeon, dentist and staff members, all were summoned to work in my regard. Humbling! Alas, the dental office aroma and vibrations of reclining chairs echoed by, "going back, open wide", would be my 'new normal' for many years. <u>I Hate GCU Commercials!</u>

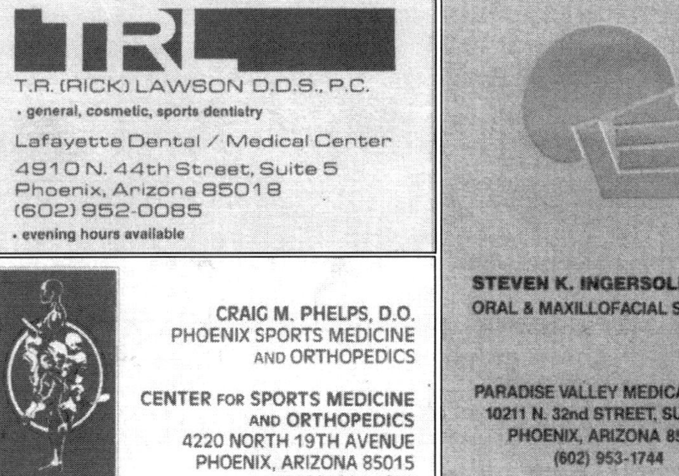

Dear Mr. Ely:

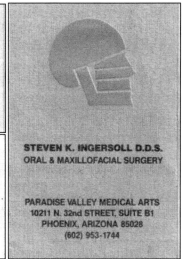

This office has been approached by Mr. Greg Scott, a basketball player with the University of Hawaii at Hilo. Mr. Scott was injured in a basketball game which was played in Phoenix, Arizona on or about January 4, 1986. This was in a game between the University of Hawaii at Hilo and Grand Canyon College. My understanding is that the game was played at Antelope Gymnasium in Phoenix.

My further understanding is the Mr. Scott was injured when a player from the opposing team, after the ball had been whistled dead, intentionally and without provocation hit Mr. Scott in the mouth with an elbow dislodging several teeth and causing severe orthodontic damages. A dentist who subsequently worked on his teeth in Phoenix was a witness to the incident. The other player was ejected from the game. Mr. Scott missed some subsequent games and has continued to undergo surgical and other orthodontic treatment. The basketball player involved in

Coaches Media Fibs: "Undercut"

To add salt to the loss, Wilson also said starting senior guard Gregg Scott was undercut late in the game and lost two teeth in the fall. The senior was taken to the dentist after the game for stitches and may not play until Wednesday against Cal Lutheran in Hilo's final mainland game.

After midnight, my team trainer, Linda, and I arrived at the Phoenix Airport for a 6 a.m. flight to Ontario. My upper jaw wired, yet, all teeth in place! Medicated and soley tormented by being blindsided and my utter lack of due retribution! Emotionally drained and physically disfigured! Sad, somber and sedated as the reality of my broken hoop dreams began to set in along with the swelling of my broken jaw. Through it all, **Linda was my Savior!** While so keenly handling all the related treatment paperwork, phone updates to my mom, logistics and travel plans, she chatted with me just enough so I didn't dwell too much. Bless Dr. Rowan! We went directly from the airport to Cal-Poly Pomona where my mom was awaiting my arrival at the gym. She gave me two boxes with fresh Avia shoes and a very much-needed hug!

Hilo got some good news before the Cal Poly game, however, when Wilson learned senior guard Gregg Scott could play. Scott was undercut in the Grand Canyon contest and suffered a broken jaw and loss of two teeth.

"Gregg played today (last night)," Wilson said. "His front lip was about triple its size. But the broken jaw doesn't effect his eating or talking. It's high up."

"Undercut": Balderdash!

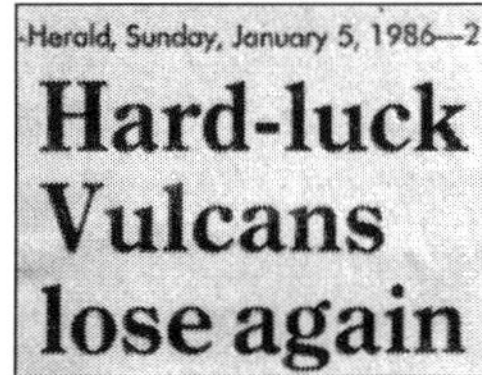
Herald, Sunday, January 5, 1986—2

Hard-luck Vulcans lose again

I was told that, "if the true story was printed in Hilo, someone may have gotten on a plane seeking revenge for him." "The love we have for G'man is fanatical ."

Insult to Injury: A $435 bill via mail!

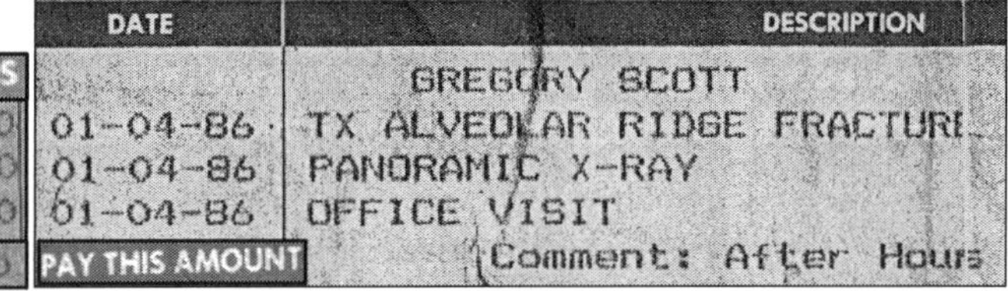
STEVEN K. INGERSOLL, DDS,PC
10211 N. 32ND STREET #B1
PHOENIX, AZ 85028

GREGORY SCOTT
39 W. LANIKAUA
HILO, HAWAII 96720

CHARGES	DATE	DESCRIPTION
		GREGORY SCOTT
$350.00	01-04-86	TX ALVEOLAR RIDGE FRACTURE
$35.00	01-04-86	PANORAMIC X-RAY
$50.00	01-04-86	OFFICE VISIT
$435.00	PAY THIS AMOUNT	Comment: After Hours

UHH vs. Cal Poly Pomona

G' on D'

At our practice my mouthpiece let cold air hit my nerve, twice! I went down to the floor in pain and briefly lost consciousness. Luckily, my Pops was there and he drove me to the hotel early.

UHH vs. Cal Lutheran

Hilo plays BYUH tonight

I was a hoop celebrity on Oahu, too. Local fans always treated me well. On defense vs. BYU-Hawaii, I took a shoulder to the mouth and heard my wiring stretch before the pain put me on my back. The next thing I saw was Linda gazing down at me. Once again, I had gone unconscious! Going to the bench my tears flowed as did the tears of many of the fans!

Greg Scott, who missed the HPC game, has been struggling because of painful root canal work. He lost two teeth and sustained a broken jaw in a collision in a game against Grand Canyon.

WALLACE F. CHONG, JR., D.D.S., INC.
74 PONAHAWAI STREET
HILO, HAWAII 96720
Telephone 935-5651

SADE Trio of G'$ TALES:
G'$: "Smooth Operator"!
G'$: "KING OF SORROW"!
G' Hoops: "Is it a Crime"?!

February 7, 1986

Three long Jr. High School years of orthodontic appointments, wearing braces and an obnoxious over-the-head harness headgear: WASTED!

University of Hawaii-Hilo
1400 Kapiolani Street
Hilo, HI 96720
Attn: Athletic Department
Re: Mr. Gregory Scott

To Whom It May Concern:

Thank you for your inquiry regarding the long term prognosis for Mr. Gregory Scott. He presented himself with a history of orthodontic treatment, fracture of the maxillary area and stabilization of the area. In regards to the fracture, it is my understanding that the right lateral (tooth #7) was completely luxated and the right central (#8) was partially luxated; both teeth were reimplanted, repositioned and stabilized. At the present moment, root canal fillings are done (not completed because teeth are tender to pressure) on #7,8 and 9. The prognosis for the retention of #7 and #8 is questionable (resorption of the roots) and a number or combination of sequelae are possible:

The dental re-wiring, multiple root canals and pulp tests were agonizing. The visits to UHH booster, Dr. Murasaki, to get braces (again) as a Senior in college; DEPRESSING!

M Greg
HAS AN APPOINTMENT WITH
Dr. Milton M. Murasaki, D.D.S., Inc.
280 Ponahawai Street
Hilo, Hawaii 96720
Telephone 935-5488

MON. ______ AT ______
TUES. ______ AT ______
WED. ______ AT ______
THURS. 3/6 AT 9:00
FRI. ______ AT ______
SAT. ______ AT ______

IF UNABLE TO KEEP THIS APPOINTMENT PLEASE GIVE US 24 HOURS NOTICE.

My Shattered Graduation Quest: 4 years & 4 schools! I was taking 18 units in school and on par to graduate in June of 1986. Yet, the pain and trauma of constant dental and surgical treatments, plus the medications, took a real toll. I had to drop one class and opt for an incomplete in another. Therefore, I'd have to return to UHH for the Fall semester to complete those two classes; just 6 measly units to earn my B.A. degree.

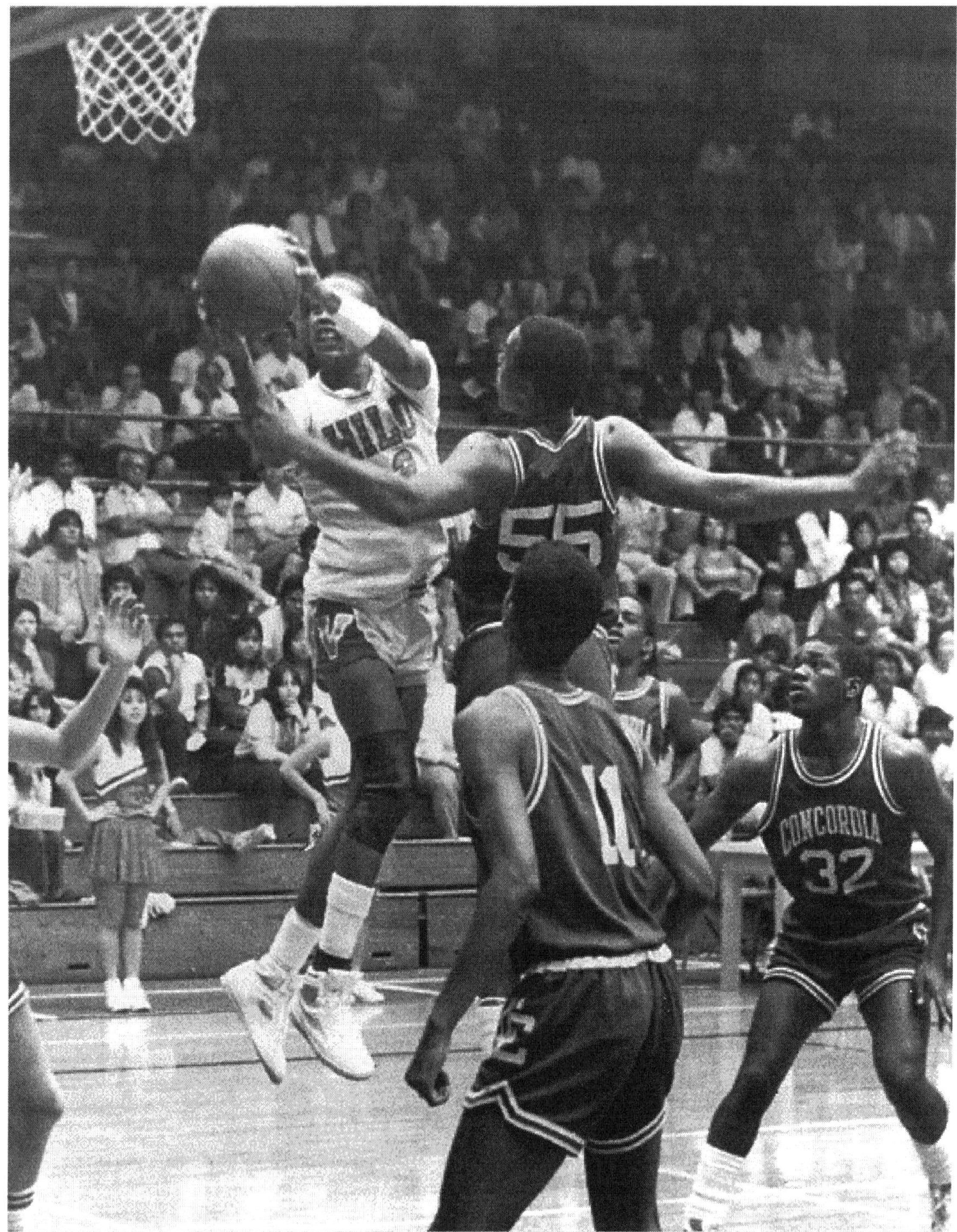

—Photo by Larry Kadooka

TOUGH TWO — University of Hawaii - Hilo's Gregg Scott double clutches before laying in two points in a game against Concordia earlier this season. The Vulcans (1-3 in conference, 11-13 overall) host Hawaii Loa at 7:30 p.m. tomorrow at Afook - Chinen Civic Auditorium. Hilo needs a win and also Sunday against Chaminade at the civic to keep its playoff hopes alive.

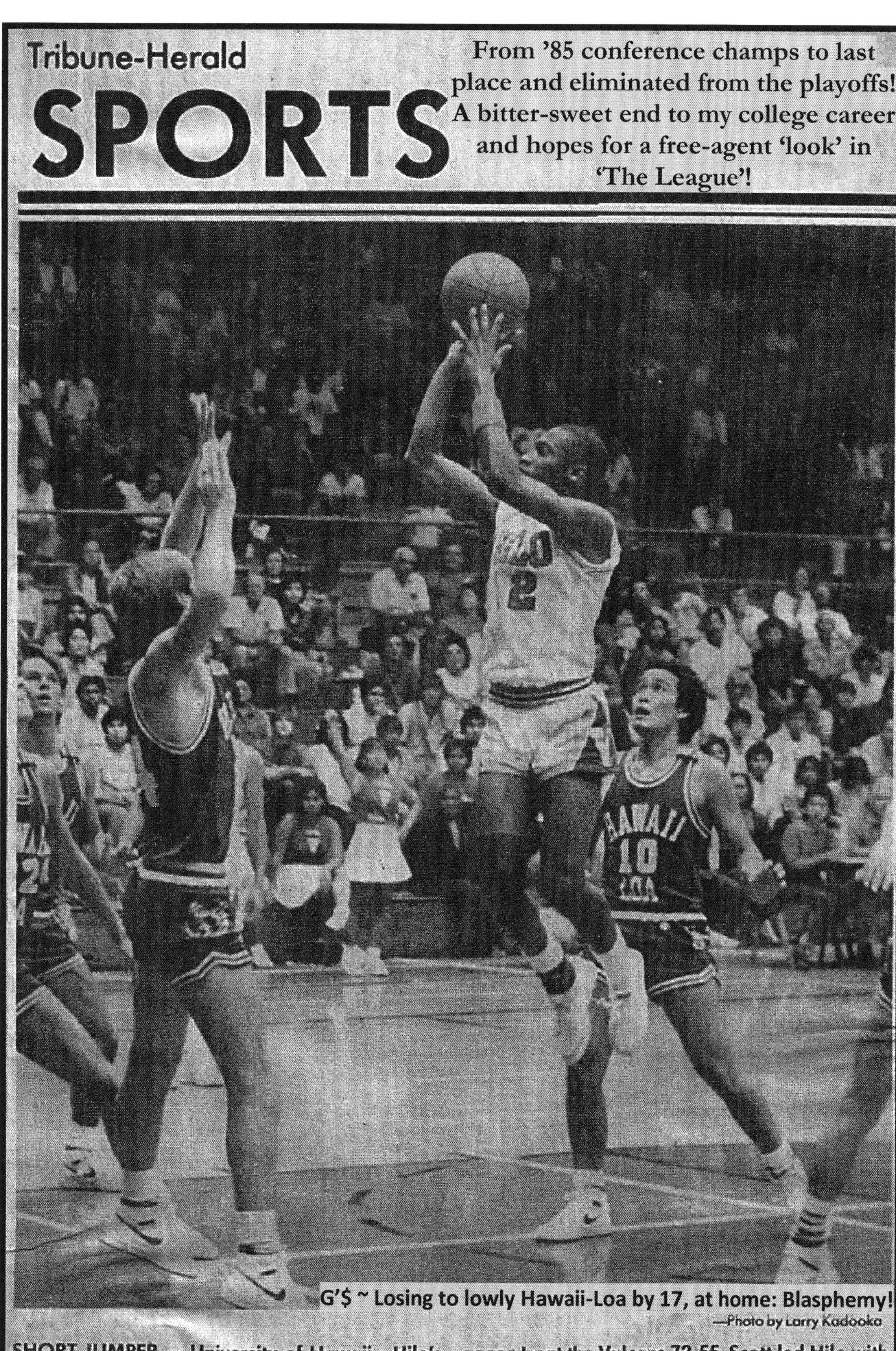

Tribune-Herald

SPORTS

From '85 conference champs to last place and eliminated from the playoffs! A bitter-sweet end to my college career and hopes for a free-agent 'look' in 'The League'!

G'$ ~ Losing to lowly Hawaii-Loa by 17, at home: Blasphemy!

—Photo by Larry Kadooka

SHORT JUMPER — University of Hawaii - Hilo's Gregg Scott scores on a short jump shot against Hawaii Loa during last night's game. The Mongoose beat the Vulcans 72-55. Scott led Hilo with 14 points.

MVP Praise: I Do Not Covet Moral Victories!

"I've paid my dues, time after time. I done my sentence, but committed no crime. And bad mistakes; I've made a few. I've had my share of sand kicked in my face, but I've come through!" ~ Queen

WE ARE THE CHAMPIONS

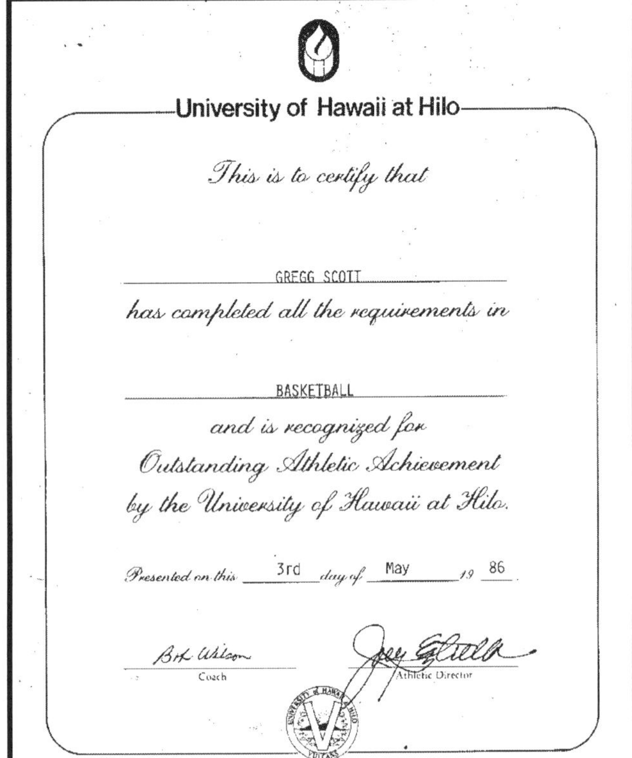

University of Hawaii at Hilo

This is to certify that

GREGG SCOTT

has completed all the requirements in

BASKETBALL

and is recognized for
Outstanding Athletic Achievement
by the University of Hawaii at Hilo.

Presented on this 3rd *day of* May *19* 86

Coach

Athletic Director

My Most Coveted Award: Bachelor's Degree Diploma

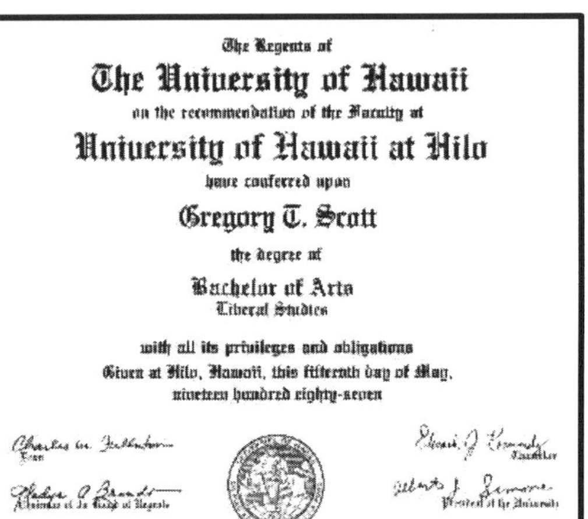

The Regents of
The University of Hawaii
on the recommendation of the Faculty at
University of Hawaii at Hilo
have conferred upon
Gregory T. Scott
the degree of
Bachelor of Arts
Liberal Studies
with all its privileges and obligations
Given at Hilo, Hawaii, this fifteenth day of May,
nineteen hundred eighty-seven

Kannapali Shores Beach Resort ~ Lahina, Maui

Summer Job: Initially a doorman and greeter at this 5-star resort. An occasional valet task and twice daily I drove the shuttle to nearby Lahina. Soon, I was given the coveted **Pool Lifeguard Gig!**

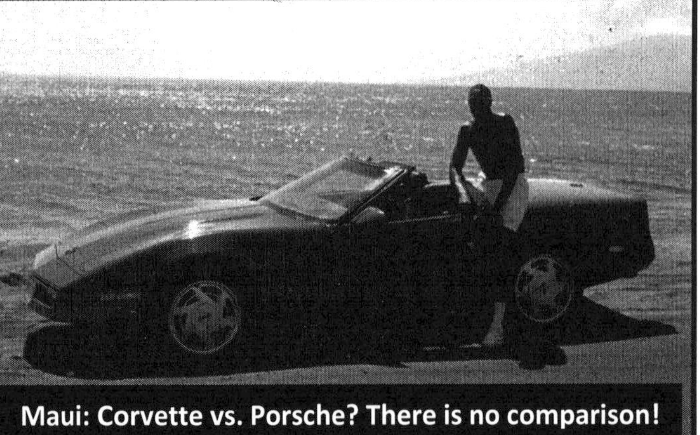

Maui: Corvette vs. Porsche? There is no comparison!

Maui: Issac 'Bud' Stallworth 3-point Shot Coach

Issac 'Bud' Stallworth: G3

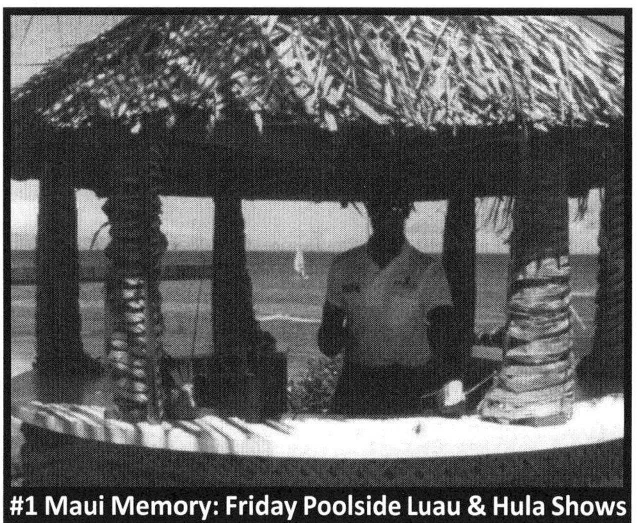

#1 Maui Memory: Friday Poolside Luau & Hula Shows

He was a 6'5" and 190 lb. shooting guard and played at the University of Kansas (KU) where he was named 1972 All-Big Eight Player of the Year. Also in 1972, Stallworth scored 50 points in a KU win vs. Missouri. Stallworth was selected 7th overall by the Seattle Supersonics in the 1972 NB Draft, and also by the Denver Rockets in the '72 ABA draft. After two seasons with the SuperSonics, he was made available in the 1974 expansion draft to be selected by the New Orleans Jazz for whom he played for three seasons. He played in the NBA from 1972-1977. His playing career was cut short due to a back injury sustained in an automobile accident in 1977. **Maui:**

Bud had VIP status which allowed us to train at the Lahaina Civic Center, the future site of the now renowned Maui Invitational. His personal training and savvy shooting drills added infinite range and enhanced my game. Bud's impact is still coveted. Great NBA 'stick-um' use stories!

FACEBOOK: Monday May 4, 2015: 9:39 a.m. Issac Stallworth:

"Man, you have brought back some great memories. Those games will always be a part of my favorite activities while living on Maui. Thank you!"

Isaac "Bud" Stallworth

Along came the Ice Man: G'man props!

From the public beach behind my lifeguard hut, up walks NBA HOF George Gervin and his kids. He asked if I knew Bud. 'On speed-dial, Sir.' I called him, 'Yo, Bud, the Ice Man is here.' George Gervin came to visit and shared stories with me for the next four days. Autograph:

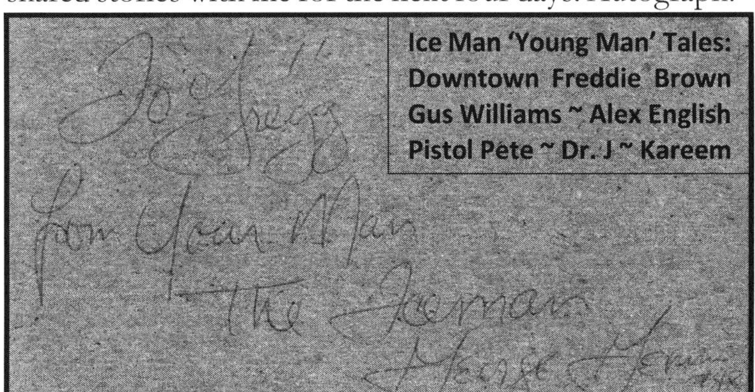

Graduation:
12/86~Mission Accomplished! G': 4 schools in 4½ years.

Global Hoops:
Mission in full motion as a Biz Entity. G'$!

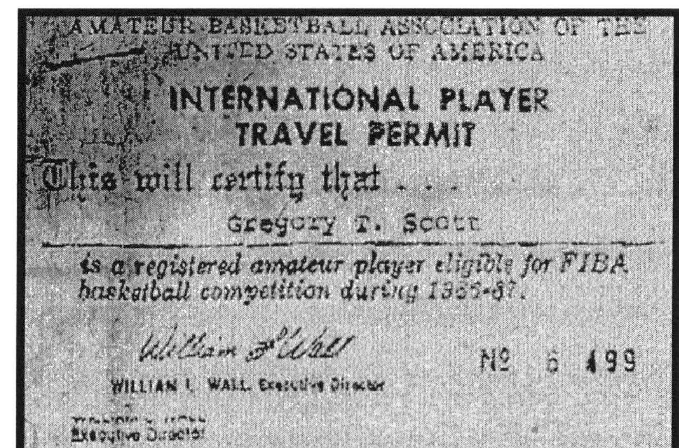

AMATEUR BASKETBALL ASSOCIATION OF THE UNITED STATES OF AMERICA

INTERNATIONAL PLAYER TRAVEL PERMIT

This will certify that . . .

Gregory T. Scott

is a registered amateur player eligible for FIBA basketball competition during 1986-87.

William L. Wall

WILLIAM L. WALL, Executive Director

Nº 6 499

1750 EAST BOULDER STREET, COLORADO SPRINGS, CO 80909-5777 USA TELEPHONE (303) 632-7687

GLOBAL HOOPS BIZ: ABAUSA PERMIT!

The Biz of International Amateur Basketball

You are a commodity of varying value to be signed, traded or cut at the clubs discretion. In my case, I was traded before I left the USA.

AMATEUR BASKETBALL ASSOCIATION UNITED STATES OF AMERICA

WILLIAM L. WALL
Executive Director

OFFICERS:

President
BRICE B. DURBIN
NFSHSA
(816) 464-5400

Vice President (Men)
DAVID R. GAVITT
Big East Conference
(401) 272-9108

Vice President (Women)
PAT HEAD SUMMITT
University of Tennessee
(615) 974-4275

Secretary
BETTY JO GRABER
Weatherford College
(817) 594-5471

Treasurer
C.M. NEWTON
Vanderbilt University
(615) 322-4610

COUNCIL:

TOM APKE
NCAA

QUINN BUCKNER
Athlete

DONNA DEVLIN
At-Large

SONJA HOGG
At-Large

TOM JERNSTEDT
NCAA

GEORGE E. KILLIAN
NJCAA

BEN LEWIS
Armed Forces

CHARLES MORRIS
NAIA

JOE O'BRIEN
At Large

JOHN PARISEAU
AAU

GEORGE RAVELING
At-Large

EDWARD S. STEITZ
Past President

HOLLY WARLICK
Athlete

LYNETTE WOODARD
Athlete

BANK
First National Bank of Colorado Springs, Colorado
Account No. 159818110

FIBA Member For USA
National Governing Body
(NGB)

TWX 910-920-4960
CABLE: ABAUSA

M E M O R A N D U M

TO: International Basketball Player

FROM: Bill Wall

SUBJECT: ABAUSA Letter of Clearance

Please find enclosed your ABAUSA Letter of Clearance, which certifies your amateur status and eligibility to play basketball in a foreign league.

Your Letter of Clearance remains valid as long as you play consecutive seasons in the same country. Once you receive a FIBA license to play in a foreign country, you are under the control of the country you are licensed to and must receive their release if you choose to play in another country.

If you should return to the United States, it is your responsibility to notify the ABAUSA office.

Best wishes.

WLW:dd

Enclosures: Letter of Clearance
Insurance Information

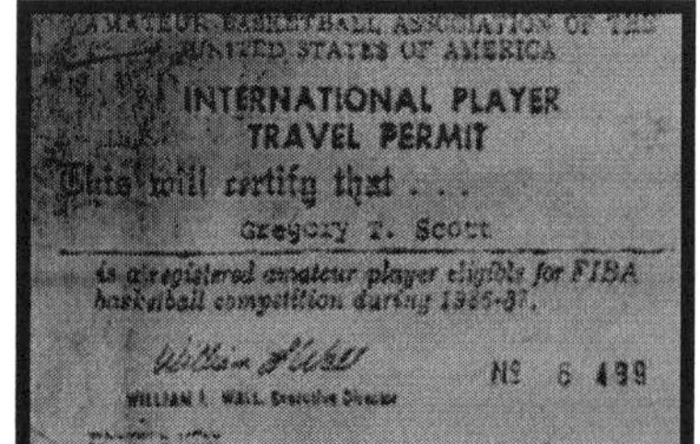
AMATEUR BASKETBALL ASSOCIATION OF THE UNITED STATES OF AMERICA

INTERNATIONAL PLAYER TRAVEL PERMIT

This will certify that . . .

Gregory T. Scott

is a registered amateur player eligible for FIBA basketball competition during 1986-87.

Nº 6 499

Class A Member

May 1987: The AVIA HQ in Beaverton, Oregon. Prior to departing for Argentina, the product development techs and I brainstormed on a blended combination of basketball and aerobic models that I'd worn and tested. A custom concept: AVIA G' Flight 7 Prototype! Logos on a ¾ mid-cut with cast-molded gel orthotics. Personal Signature Model!

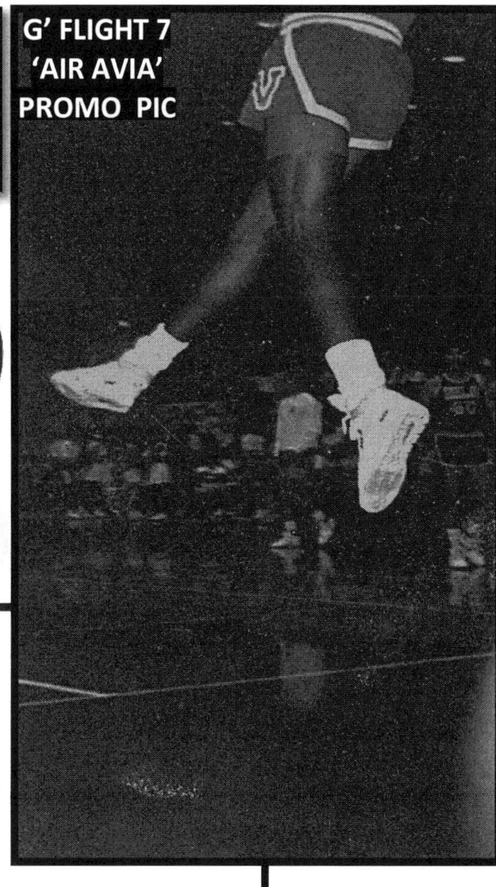

A Group International, Inc.

The Avia Brand has a unique <u>concave sole</u> system. Prudent G' Flight Gear is the most critical element.

August 22, 1995

TO WHOM IT MAY CONCERN,

Gregg Scott has been associated with Avia since 1984 when we sponsored him as a basketball player at the University of Hawaii at Hilo. During his early years professionally we remained his sponsor, until he went to play in some markets where we did not have shoes available in South America. At that point he became involved in our Wear Test program. His input has helped us with our Product Development and Promotions. We have had a good relationship with Gregg and recommend him for any opportunity that he seeks.

Sincerely Bruce Potts,

Bruce Potts

Wear Test Coordinator

Two-handed Reverse Jam!

On the break or back-door; from the dotted line or the baseline. Taking off of the left or right foot; or both. Up and over, going forward, backwards or sideways, with one hand, two hands; or even switching hands; mid-flight. G'$: Sponsor worthy!

Student of your Game

- Know and Respect the history, predecessors and legacies of your sport
- Know the Rules: Written & Unwritten
- Know the 'CODE' & Enforce your 'CODE'
- Know and respect the local 'CULTURE'
- Know the Fundamentals & Basic Principles
- Engage wise mentors to 'show you the ropes'
- Etiquette and Behavioral 'Expectations:
    - Team & Club Functions
    - Locker-room & Club Facilities
    - Weight Room & Training Facilities
    - Training: Team & Individual
    - Travel & Road Trips ~ Touring Teams
- Rituals, Traditions & Rites of Passage
- Verbiage ~ Lingo ~ Cultural Divides
- Engage in building rapport at every level.
- Employ a professional work ethic with pride!
- Maintain proper care of your 'working' gear, equipment and supplies.

Michael Coleman

"Our moms had stayed in touch and told me G' got his jaw broken in a game. I asked her what did G' do to the other guy. "G', blindsided from behind. Knocked Out." I said, ok, otherwise...! I gave them info for my U.S. agent, Roy Wooden. Roy's Argentina agent, Edwardo Patrini told me G' signed to play in B.A."

Global Hoops

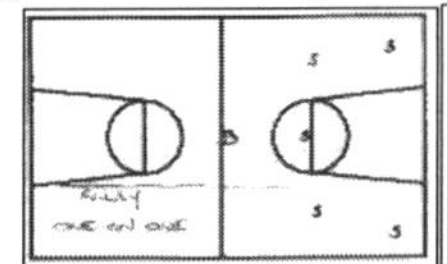

Commodity: At LAX my plane ticket was "Cancelled." My 'new' club reinstated it the next day as I depart LAX. 18 hours later I met Patrini. "Stay at my home tonight."

- ✓ Disregard jetlag & travel fatigue: You're a commodity! Investor unveiling is Day One!
- ✓ Different court dimension: FIBA court is 91 feet! The key widens f/t line to baseline!
- ✓ Varying court surfaces: Tiled with Caulking ~ Cement-like Tarten ~ Nice Hardwood
- ✓ Sub-par gyms and world-class venus! Humble accomodations and high class resorts.
- ✓ Late-night training and games, high pitched whisltes, and relentlessly chanting fans.
- ✓ **FIBA refs: <u>Horrible officiating</u>! Missed calls; Bad calls and FANTOM calls! Shenanigans that are Performance Blocker #1; and permit PB #2: <u>'Poachers'!!!</u> You MUST compete & defend without fouling, <u>and</u> without appearing to foul!**

G'$ 6'3" 175 lbs.: Svelte Little Fella! Mike: "Don't Let The Smooth Taste Fool You."

Hola Argentina: Coleman Gets G'$ Traded

Mike: "If Gregg Scott is available you've got to get him. Or, pray that you don't play against him. 'But Mike, this guy is 6'5...' Size don't matter! What matters is the size of the Chest Cavity and G' has more heart and game than any man I know. 'But, so and so played at...' College hype doesn't translate here. This is a different animal. It's how you train, not how you play. G' had his jaw broken his senior year, otherwise he'd be paid! So, make it happen."

3 DE JULIO DE 1987 PAGINA NUEVE

Básquet: Todo el Fervor se Traslada a Santa Rosa

Coleman y Scott, pivot y base de «los trotamundos»

Scott, un base para Estudiantes

El Club Estudiantes incorporó anoche a su plantel de basquetbol al jugador norteamericano Gregory Thomas Scott, completando el grupo con vistas al campeonato Provincial que se iniciará este fin de semana.

Scott es un base de 1,94 de estatura y cubrirá el vacante lugar en el equipo que dejó el tucumano Daniel Coronel, que se alejó días atrás de la entidad.

Estudiantes habría buscado un jugador para ese puesto, logrando ahora un importante refuerzo. El basquetbolista ya practicó anoche con sus nuevos compañeros.

La presencia de un nuevo base en el equipo había sido señalada por varios in-

SCOTT

tegrantes del plantel y del cuerpo técnico, considerándolo imprescindible para aspirar a lograr la clasificación para el regional.

My first night at Edwardo Patrini's home his wife was animated, "Greggorio, your trade created much publicity and took so much work that I just had to meet you."

Mike Coleman: "At UHH, G' and I were not nessesarily tight off of the court. But, on the hardwood we were cohesive business partners. And, his work ethic is irresistible. The trade wasn't about sentiment. It was all about hoop business and winning! So I vested my rep and much Club $$$ in my G'man."

The International Hoops Game is a very unique sub-species of basketball.
A Job With Distinct Occupational Hazards. Adapt; Train; Survive; Thrive!

BASQUET

SCOTT-COLEMAN NUEVO DESTINO?

Mike Coleman was an All-Star on the famous Boca Juniors Club team prior to 'El Estudiantes'.

Foreign agents and domestic sponsors.
Passports, visas and embassy locations.
Int'l. flights, airports and train navigation.
Customs clearances and border crossings.
Language barriers and currency exchange $$;
Taxes and insurance;
Contract Negotiations!

Actualmente están Gregory Scott y Michael Coleman; dos jugadores de buenas condiciones, que seguramente con la eliminación de Estudiantes —al no poder clasificar para la Primera Regional—, tendrán que buscar nuevos horizontes, porque lógicamente ellos son profesionales y sin competencia y las arcs de cualquier club que realice un esfuerzo económico como el de Estudiantes, comienzan a tener déficit.

Podemos coincidir en que generalmente la presencia de un jugador extranjero en un equipo de basquet ayuda mucho al rendimiento del conjunto y pasa a ser uno de los protagonistas más importantes de la

Santa Rosa, La Pampa. Club Estudiantes

Club Estudiantes' Home Court: Brutal, Slick Black Tile & Grout!

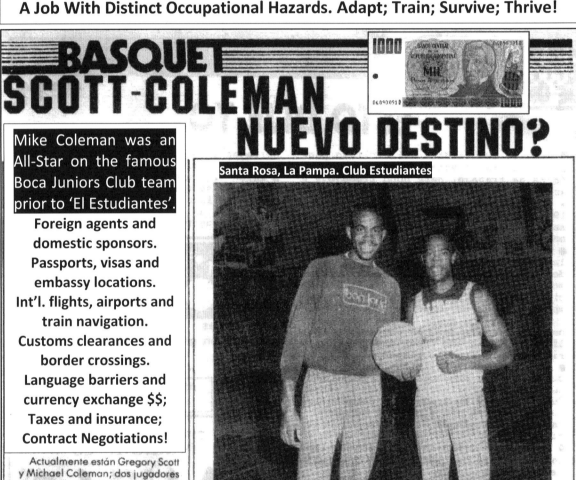

Minister of Encroachment Enforcement

Poachers Will Be Punished

True life tales of 'The Minister' are inherently unsavory. Self-preservation & Retribution! Not Intended for Emulation!

Judge, Jury & Executioner

Protect & defend yourself; your space, on the floor and in flight, without fail!

Noble Vigilante: There's no justice or 'just us'. There's just me!

A six-shooter of Clint Eastwood movies describe the true PGH. As a 'High Plains Drifter' competing on foreign soil, in a quest to earn 'A Fist-full of Dollars', you must digest 'The Good, the Bad & the Ugly' of Pro Global Hoops. The reality of your unsung role in the eyes of your opponents as 'The Outlaw Josey Wales' with a target on your back and, literally, a bounty on your head. Consequently, in order to survive before you can thrive, noble vigilante justice is not only a required trait, it must serve as your steadfast strong-suit; requisites of coy covert tactics and/or cunning and overt acts, based on severity and situation. Then, in the aftermath of the application of your valiant retribution, you transition into 'Dirty Harry' mode, as you must look the big bully or little punk, in his eyes; take a peek deep into his 'chest cavity', and back your play with "Now what?!" And, that exact phrase must be spoken in their language (yes, I had cue cards), to avoid any misinterpretation. Sending a Ministers Memo to him, his team, the refs, and everyone else watching. 'ClintSix' sum! When I train my 'Million Dollar Baby' in any team gladiator sport, since in boxing your opponent is in front of you, these two survival mindsets must be chisled within: Keep your head on a swivel and protect your space at all times!!

Forgive me, Dr. Martin Luther King*

*Poetic Vigilante Justice: Kareem vs. Kent Benson
Dr. J vs. Larry Bird ~ Nolan Ryan vs. Robin Ventura

- A peaceful resolution is not an option; as determined by The Minister!

Yes & No, Malcolm X: True, *"It's not paranoia if they really are out to get you."*

- You can not seek retrobution by any means necessary! Job #1: Win!!!

Poise Under Fire! Reprisal; yet never at the cost of winning. Eyes are on you! Still: Don't Be Like Blake! Passive Acceptance: You're part of the solution or you meekly are part of your own problem. Barkley: "I'm all about Get-Back and Retribution!"

***G' Minister never punched, fought or got ejected; but never ever had a repeat offender!**

Mike Coleman: "After a WIN! G' went into the other teams' locker-room to get Pay Back!"

G'$ tapped & Mike swatted the shot! D'!
#6 Mike 6'7" SKILLS: On the Hoop Court, a Tennis Court; AND on the Dance Floor!

Coleman, Scott y Moreno en todo el fragor de la lucha bajo las tablas, donde ganará el pivot de Estudiantes con su oportuno bloqueo. Asisten a la

Mike had me in a 20 degree gym every morning at 8! It was so cold we wore gloves in all our ballhandling drills!

First Pro Memory

As I jogged onto the court for our first game I ran past a policeman in full riot gear with a shield in one hand and a leash to a dog seated alertly beside him. Also, a cop with a dog was on each corner of the court. **4!** My only thought: Where am I? So this is my HOME court!

GameSpeak Debut

Mike was a top-tier player! He facilitated for me with ease and eagerness by using his superior basketball IQ **He was a great teammate as well as a homie for life!**

SINTESIS DEL PARTIDO

ESTUDIANTES 84 — Primer Tiempo:
PICO F. BALL.... 86 — Estudiantes 40
Jugado en Estudiantes. Pico F.Ball 37
Juez: Carlos Etchart - Arbitro: A. Alanís.
ESTUDIANTES: Darío Requejo (8), Michael Cóleman (18), Raúl Carrizo (8), Gregory Scott (39), Marcos Aguerrido (5) fi.

One memory of my debut was Helman Griffin got an offensive rebound, elevated facing away from the rim as I went up to contest. He quickly put a one-handed dunk right over me. Mike: "First time G' got got!"

G'$ 39 Points! Bitter Loss by 2

I aptly renegotiated my contract the next day! G'$

G'$ Targeted & Tackled! ~ Retribution? Winning Comes First!

Mike: "After his 39 point debut, I knew it would not take long before G' got introduced to the extreme measures opponents employ to stop a scorer. In the second half of our second game there was a loose ball near the sideline and the midcourt. As G' went up high to grasp the ball, his defender ran right underneath his legs and barrel-rolled him into an ugly 1½ cartwheel in which he narrowly missed the scorers table as he landed upside down slamming his head, neck and shoulders on the large tray of white chalk beside the table, rolled underneath the scorers table and was motionless."

"I went after the player immediately. By the time I was restrained I recall them disconnecting the scoreboard and moving the scorers table as the paramedics and doctors were surrounding him with a back-board and neck brace nearby. Two people were putting bandages on both of his bleeding shins that got cut in his tumble under the table. Others wiped his face and flushed his eyes from the white chalk that covered him from head-to-toe."

I remember bits and pieces of that dirty play. I got to the spot first and exploded up strong, secured the ball, got hit and was upside-down, twice, before it took an eternity for me to land, luckily on that chalk tray. I was focused on the ball and don't recall much else. Soon, people were around me and I told them, 'I'm WEDGED, I can't move.' They panicked. I was bloody and bruised, had several lumps and cuts, but, I was ok. Pinned due to the ball. **They thought I was paralyzed, not 'wedged'.** I had to convince them to let me get up. As I stood up I instantly saw that EVERYONE in the gym was standing in stunned silence. Men, women and children, in tears. I was covered in the chalk, bood stained my socks and bandages told the tale, but the emotional exhale of the fans was tangible and memorable. I walked over to Mike, who was standing alone at the far end of the court. 'What was that?'

Mike: "I was astounded as he approached me. Are you ok? Seriously G', are you ok? He said, 'I'm a QB! The ball had me wedged. Yo, where were you?' Honestly G', I think he was trying to get you. So, I was trying to get at him. But, right now we need to put that aside and get this win. It's crunch time. To his credit he compartmentalized, went to work and led us to a gritty win. He cemented his Estudiantes superstar status. In the lockerroom G'man got dressed fast, without a word. It's 20 degrees outside and we all were to eat dinner together. Then, he says, 'I'll be back.' I asked where he was going. He said, 'You told me that guy was trying to get me, right? So, I'm going to go into his lockerroom and ask him face to face.' I told him I'd go with him. He said, 'You don't have to.' I told him, Oh Yes I Do! 'Suit yourself.' We went into the lions den of the enemy. His perpetrator was contrite. Thank God!!"

The next morning I was (Quarterback) **sore** from my shins all the way up to my shoulders!

Our third game was a road-trip for a late 8 pm tilt. However, the other team broke the backboard in pre-game warm-ups, so we had an hour delay. It was a long tough regrettable game. I was having fits guarding their 6'5" stud who was dominating me in the low post.

Mike: "Winston Morgan was the first guy ever to have his way with G'! He used his big butt to seal him, again and again. They kept on feeding him. At one point G' fouled him and I told G', 'We may have to take this dude out.' G' was silent. After the first free throw I went to G' to apologize. 'My bad.' After the game was the unfortunate lowlight of the trip. It was past midnite as we showered, dressed and loaded onto the bus. Hurting and hungry. At the all-night restaurant a teammate who was ill with the flu wanted a sip of my drink. Oh no, you're sick. G' offered his drink. I warned him...TWICE! The next morning G' is crying out for me. He's curled up in his bed sweating and panting then shivering and chattering his teeth. G' had contracted pnumonia, bronchitis, and a viral infection. For the next week I seriously had to consider how I would tell his mom that I let her son die in La Pampa."

It was in a dire situation as I walked through the hospital with patuents lining the halls wailing and pacing as passed through a real life 'Coocos's Nest movie set. My condition and my cloudy chest x-rays required I be admitted. No way! Being in this place could kill me! Luckily,the Club Estudiantes liaison, Susanna, was marrie to a well0 renowned doctor who came to treat me twice a day at the Hotel Calfacura. Painful penicillin injections ith an 8" needle left me bruised and in tears each time. I was feeble and at His mercy. We moved into our plush apartment two weeks later. By His grace, I was on the mend but still, bedridden. The team went into a tailspin.

Mike: "We got eliminated from the classification and I got a contract to play in Paraguay, so I had to leave G' as he was just resuming a training mode."

The club stood by me while nurturing me back to health. They fed me so well. Steak and eggs for breakfast! They paid my medical bills, paid for my apartment, and paid my salary! They said, I couldn't leave until I was fit in my Mind and Body. "You have blessed us all."

23rd Birthday Gift: Petrini Plea 'All-Star Game in Buenos Aires'

Mike: "By default, G's gonna get: 25+ points; 7-8 assists; 7-8 boards (half being offensive), a few steals and a couple of blocked shots. Plus, he's going to lock-up their best guard. Guaranteed! But, Don't Let The Smooth Taste Fool You. There are 3 areas to be very wary of in order to limit the collateral damage. 1) G' Flight: Don't Get Caught Slippin'! Don't' Jump! 2) Flossers & Trash-talkers: He'll hit 40+ on cue! 3) Dirty Players: Try It!"

All-Star Showcase: ♥ARGENTINA

Mike: "G' never saw a shot he didn't like. Any shot from any spot from any distance. 50% on 3's! 55%+ on 2's! 90% at the line!! Efficient Clutch Facilitating Scoring Guard!"

BASQUET

TRES EN LA PORFIA PARA LLEGAR AL TITULO

Mrs. Petrini: "Gregg, this city is so excited to see you perform." An article told of the guy I was traded for: **9 Point Debut vs. G' 39! Debates swirled of a trade gone bad. He was sent home six weeks later. The Buenos Aires media had hyped all of my 3 game stats: 39, 33 and 30 points, prior to my PNEUMONIA.**

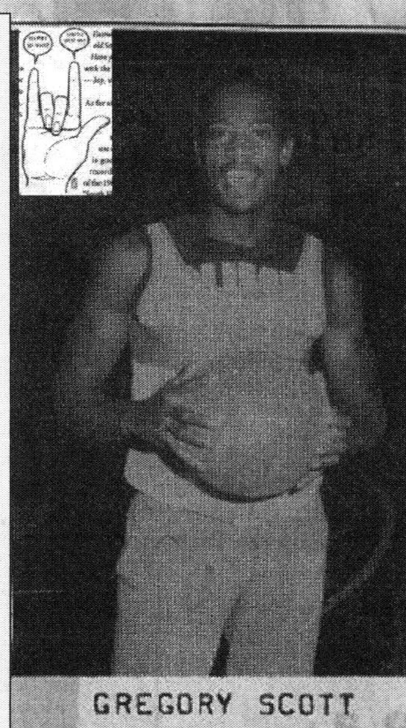

Logo: G' Flight 7
Avia Prototype HQ Customized Name & 7 logo! White and Grey with laces and a G' Velcro Strap & Gel Orthotics!
True Flight Gear
Two pair of nice socks, towels, wristbands and a few caps, too.
True Baller Gear
G'$ GameSpeak

Avia G' Flight 7's Propulsion Apparatus with Shock Absorbing Pillows!

I had gotten back into shape by myself and I felt fit and ready as I boarded the midnite bus for an 8 hour trip. Petrini met me at the depo and gave me an Avia package with my Customized G' Flight Prototype shoes and some sweet gear. He took me shopping to get matching sweats. "Tonight you shine!" We went to his home and his wife had food and fruit prepared for a "Showcase Game!" **Then, I took a nap.** We arrived at the venue to rabid fandom and a swarming media as we drove into the underground parking area. Petrini was a 'VIP' with his prized possession as in tow as we walked to the lockerroom. I could faintly hear the crowd and feel muted vibrations of chanting fans. In the lockrroom I met my teammates. All were very cool and embracing. I geared up noticing glances to my G' Flight 7's as I stretched in my #7 jersey. Game Time! As I ran thru the tunnel onto the shiny hardwood the fans were fanatic. Futball Fanatics! Chanting!!!. Normally, I don't dunk in warm-ups. But, this bouncy floor and eager crowd was too enticing and I needed a barometer of my boosties. Two hand lefty jam! Oh my….! From that point on the fans fueled a G'$ performance that provided life memories for all. Awarded the MVP award in an on-court post game live interview I addressed the crowd 'Mucho Gusto Buenos Aries' to a thunderous roar as I shared the mike with the interpreter. First, I thanked my competitors and my teammates. I thanked Petrini next. I told them I was a bit was sad because my I would be leaving my beloved town of Santa Rosa, La Pampa and Club Estudiates who all had sacrificed so much for me when I was stricken with pneumonia, then nurtured me back to health and told me I would not leave until I was fit in "Mind and Body". Tonight, I proved to myself that I'm fit in my Mind and Body! But, tonight I performed for you! I could feel your passion, love and energy from the start.

You didn't let up so I couldn't let up. So, moslty, I want to thank you Buenos Aires because tonight your have impacted my Soul. And, someday, I'm going to write a book about my Global Hoops: Mind, Body & Soul epics, and I promise that no matter where this game takes me I will always remember this game and this very moment! Viva Argentina. Gracias!'

As I embeded the emotions so evident in their final chanting applause, I turned to salute each section of the audience, embraceing the life memory, and pondering my promise of writing Global Hoops as a testament of my perseverance through trials and tribulations.

Then, my agent, Eduardo Patrini was summoned away. He came to the lockerroom and simply said. "I need you to sign an autograph." I asked if he had a pen. He laughed and said "your presence has been requested and you must sign in person." No problem! He handed me a 7-up! It was so good! Petrini was giddy. We walked underneath the arena and entered a huge office that led to a small private conference room with a half-dozen member entourage surrounding a lone sole sitting at a table. They abruptly cleared the room for us.

Toyko Open: *ガブリエラ・サバティーニ GABRIELA SABATINI 1987*

GABRIELA SABATINI

Gaby had just returned from the U.S. Open. She and Steffi: Semi-Final Injury 'Withdrew' Team Gaby had a midnight flight to Tokyo!

I entered the room and was introduced to this beautiful bright-eyed 17 year-old who said::

"I love basketball and I've seen many players. I watch you. And for me, you are truly the best player I've ever seen. You play hard and smart. That is what I seek to do in my sport of tennis."

For the next half-hour we shared what I consider as my first mini-Mental Athlete Workshop with an eager and talented pupil. She spoke of her nemisis and doubles partner, Steffi Graf. And, her looming red-eye flight to Tokyo for a tournament. 'Disregard Jet Lag!' She was annimated and articulate recounting my plays in detail. **My Autograph:** 'To Gabriela, Play Hard & Play Smart! Your Future is Bright. Best Wishes! Gregorio Scott #7'

Then, I made my second declaration of the eve. I told this beautiful bright spirit, 'If I ever have a daughter, I'm going to name her after you and I pray that she will emulate your spirit and your psyche.' Gabriela was absolutely delighted. As I left, her 'Mom' thanked me for brighting her mood prior to her trip. "Bless you! She's our country's greatest hope in sports since Diego Maradonna. You've inspired her." I instantly became a G' Sabatini fan!!

G' Sabatini 'GameSpeak': #1 Seed WTA Tokyo Indoor Tourney

G': 27-hour Flight ~ 1st Rd. Bye ~ 6-1 6-0 Debut ~ Tourney Champ vs. #2 Seed ~ Never Lost a Set!

Tokyo Indoor Japan
Women's Singles - Main Draw
32 DRAW

14 Sep - 20 Sep 1987
Tokyo
Japan

Grade : Main Draw
Prize money : $ 250000
Surface : Carpet (I) Spuckturf

1st Round

1 SABATINI, G (ARG) 1
2 BYE
3 NA, H (USA)
4 GERKEN, B (USA)
5 BOWES, B (USA)
6 BENJAMIN, C (USA)
7 INOUE, E (JPN)
8 KELESI, H (CAN) 7
9 MALEEVA, K (BUL) 4
10 BYE
11 WHITE, A (USA)
12 LL PROVIS, N (AUS)
13 KIJIMUTA, A (JPN)
14 HERR, B (USA)
15 Q DIAS, N (BRA)
16 BALESTRAT, D (AUS) 6
17 LINDQVIST, C (SWE) 5
18 Q OKAMOTO, K (JPN)
19 BURGIN, E (USA)
20 WHITE, W (USA)
21 MOULTON, A (USA)
22 Q MASCARIN, S (USA)
23 BYE
24 POTTER, B (USA) 3
25 FERNANDEZ, G (USA) 8
26 WHITE, R (USA)
27 WERDEL, M (USA)
28 HENRICKSSON, A (USA)
29 Q MOCHIZUKI, T (USA)
30 VAN NOSTRAND, M (USA)
31 BYE
32 MALEEVA, M (BUL) 2

2nd Round

SABATINI, G (ARG) 1
6-4 6-4 GERKEN, B (USA)
6-4 6-7 6-3 BOWES, B (USA)
6-2 6-2 INOUE, E (JPN)
MALEEVA, K (BUL) 4
6-2 7-6 PROVIS, N (AUS)
6-3 6-2 HERR, B (USA)
4-6 6-3 6-3 BALESTRAT, D (AUS) 6
6-2 6-4 LINDQVIST […]
6-3 6-3 WHITE, W […]

Quarterfinal

6-1 6-0 SABATINI, G (ARG) 1
6-3 6-4 INOUE, E (JPN)
6-4 6-2 MALEEVA, K (BUL) 4
6-3 6-3 BALESTRAT, D (AUS) 6

Semifinal

6-2 6-3 SABATINI, G (ARG) 1
6-2 6-0 MALEEVA, K (BUL) 4
7-5 5-7 6-4 LINDQVIST, C (SWE) 5

Final

7-6 6-4 SABATINI, G (ARG) 1

Winner

6-4 7-6 SABATINI, G (ARG) 1

PARAGUAY: G' HOOPS' SEASON OF REDEMPTION

As my plane smoothly departed Buenos Aires I was in great spirits, feeling very blessed and thankful for His grace. I was seated next to a knowledgeable and distinguished hoop fan from Asuncion who excitedly and repeatedly chanted the name "Marvaliso", aka Frank Jackson. He considered "Marvaliso" to be the top player on the top team, Libertad, with a "Legendary" reputation. His teammate from Auburn, Carey Holland, was a beast in the middle and Frank was a flamboyant crowd favorite, as a less-than six-foot guard! I had to employ my muzzle. We exchanged cards and I jotted down a few motivation notes as we prepared to land. I invited him to our game. As we parted ways I pondered, **'Ok, who the heck is Frank Jackson?'**

Paraguay under Military Rule by 'Dictator' Alfredo Stroessner

Clearing customs in any country is always discomforting. But, this was truly intimidating as there were young Uzi-toting soldiers posted throughout the airport. The driver sent to meet me with a sign, "Senor Scott", spoke very good English. The first thing I noticed as we departed the airport was the continued highly visible military presence. Literally, teenagers with automatic weapons strapped across their bodies, pistols in their holsters and blank stares on their faces, were on guard seemingly at every major intersection in the capital city of a country under 'military rule' by Strossner. Intense! I asked for a drive by: The U.S. Embassy. It's better to know it and not need it, than to need it and not know it!

My teammate was awaiting my arrival at a nice hostel we stayed in for our first few days. Cary Brooks, also from L.A., was my age and in his first season of pro hoops. While he was upfront about his casual approach view of basketball being a vehicle for him to see the world on someone else's dime, we hit it off from Day One. He was 6'5", tough, with Mad Hops! The first order of business was meeting the owner of the club, Marcelo Bedoya, who was a wealthy real estate tycoon and also owned a T.V. station. These two biz ventures would provide us with unique perks such as superior living arrangements and having many of our games televised live and re-played later (in the club). While there was no Club San Jose, Marcelo bought his way into the pro league and team practices were at the Palacia, our home court and a neutral court. As we arrived at his gated home in a neighborhood that would be considered ritzy in any country. Quite clearly, this was an affluent and highly successful business man. A bright smile proceeded a warm handshake and fatherly embrace with each of us. He was a five-foot tall, three-hundred pound man with a well manicured beard and a jovial disposition. His elegant home was impressive in size, setting and décor. After a brief tour he said he had a 'regalo' (gift) for us. He returned with a Paraguay National Team jersey for each of us. Mine was #15. I still have it! Then, Marcelo smiled as he said he had a surprise for me at a scrimmage that night, after which we would negotiate our contracts. A light-hearted moment that went to the root of business. Suddenly, I knew that my negotiations would be based upon performance at the scrimage, regardless of the gifts, good will and his surprise. My 'Fist Full of Dollars' were in the balance and at hand. And, Marcelo had signed the National Teams 6' 5" star point guard, Santiago Ochipinti. So, I'd be employed soley as a shooting guard! The perfect situation for both professional and personal redemption!!

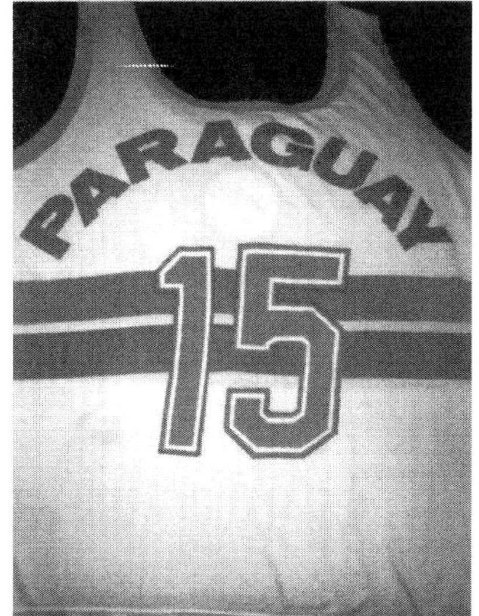

1st Night, 1st Scrimmage, 1st Impression

Our driver took us to our hostel and returned in the evening to courier us to the 'try-outs'. We arrive at the huge AFEMOT facility with lodging and a large dome style arena. As our courier leads the way to an entry door to the gym, Cary enters and I hear the clicking of cameras and all attention sways our way. I was impressed by the size and quality to this clubs gym, as I heard**, "Oh by God, is that G'?"**. That familiar voice was Mike**,** who had last seen me in my recovery mode in Argentina. His reaction and our genuine embrace was a main attraction for all to witness; the media to swoon over, and my soon-to-be teammates and coach to take note of. Cary and Mike were friends from L.A., so it was all good. I was estatic to see him and he was gratified to see that I was not only healthy, but ballin' again. Meeting the team and the coach; awkward. A quick warm-up and we start the scrimmage.

Mike Draws a Line Between Boyz and Business. It Still Stings!

Our initial possesions were set offense in the half-court. Then, I got a defensive rebound and dribbled the ball up the court with no defender on me as Mike starts yelling franticly. "Defensa de el…media linea." As I crossed half court Mike stopped the scrimmage and openly admonished my defender, in Spanish. I understood 'defend him at the mid-court.'

Mike Coleman: "The first time-out of the scrimmage, as we cross paths, G' comes up to me and says, 'Yo Mike, you know contracts will be negotiated based on this.' G', you know I love you. You know we'll go out tonight and the first round is on me. But yo, what you need to understand is that right here and right now you're on the other side partner. The truth hurt him. G' came out, did his work, got a max contract; and we hit La City that night."

Getting Paid

Marcello signed me to a nice contract to which we added a few incentives. A bonus for me finishing in the top 5 in scoring. Another for top 3 in scoring. And, a major bonus if we made the classification. Finally, a bonus for finishing in the top 3 scoring in the playoffs. He asked why I didn't ask for a bonus for finishing first in scoring? 'I don't need that goal.' The teams best interest always comes first! I prefer victory over money. He respected that.

Home Sweet Home with a live-in Maid! Affluent Neighborhood!

Marcello's Real Estate company provided Cary and I with the best lodging situation of all the American players. Bedoya Propidades gave us a plush 3-bedroom home on a half-acre lot in an upscale area (by U.S. standards) with a patio separating the 'Maids Quarters' that housed our maid and houseman couple. The home had luxurious furniture including an elegant 8-person formal dining table with high-back chairs and an expensive chandalier above it. We had a big, rarely used, living room and a TV room where we spent the majority of our time at home. The maid cooked all of our meals and did our laundry daily. She often was squeezing sacks of oranges by hand for our fresh juice. Food was dropped off every few days and she was a great cook. We had a driver. We got paid twice a month in U.S. $$!

Day 1 Homie Cary Brooks: Teammate, Friend & Noble Warrior

Cary Brooks was from Los Angeles and "just here for the traveling experience", as he put it to me on the day we first met. I respected that honesty. Still, from Day 1 we were tight! We shared many spectacular great times on the court and many more unspeakable great times off of the court. Enough Said!!! And, we still share our 'Baller Love' in the year 2015!

Unmentionable Great Times with Mike Coleman: Phase 2 Boyz

Mike and I enjoyed many memorable outings together; and unmentionable antics!

Meeting Frank "Marvallisio" Jackson and other American Pros

Mike, Cary Brooks, Frank, Alexander Hamilton and Calvin Haynes were all from L.A and were baller buddies. Frank shared a high-rise apartment with his teammate, Carey Holland, from Auburn. Carey chant: "I played with Chuck & Charles", i.e. C. Person and C. Barkley! Frank and I were Day 1 Homies. He was really cool. Their crib was the daily meeting spot. We went out together often to eat and shop. Marvallisio was as advertised. We were Boyz!

Debut: Coaching Woes & A Heartless 6'10" Big Man/'Tin Man'!

San Jose vs. Rowing

The Palacia, San Jose's home arena. Crunchtime. I've put in 30. The game is tied 85-85 with 7 seconds left. It's our ball at the midcourt line. Coach wants Tin Man to inbound!? I object!

Gag! Turnover, layup! Ball Game!

ROWING 87 (47)
SAN JOSE 85 (42)

Jugado en el Palacio de los Deportes. Arbitros: Luis Vera Yegros y Narciso Alcaraz. ROWING: Edgar Barrios 13 (1 triple, 4 dobles y 2 simples en 2 intentos), Steven Hill 25 (0-8-9/9), Craig Stephens 16 (0-8-0/2), Esteban Cabrera 20 (0-8-4/4) y Oscar Bécker, formación inicial; luego Luis Gamarra 13 (0-5-3/4) y Jorge Da Silva. D.T.: Edgar Cordero. SAN JOSE: Santiago Ochipinti 12 (2-3-0), Cary Brooks 24 (1-7-7/9), Gregory Scott 30 (3-8-4/5), Albert Araújo 6 (0-3-0) y Manuel Giménez 1 (0-0-1/2), f.i.; luego Aldo Kabbout 10 (0-2-6/6), Humberto Arce 2 (0-0-2/2) y José Sánchez. D.T.: Miguel González Arca.

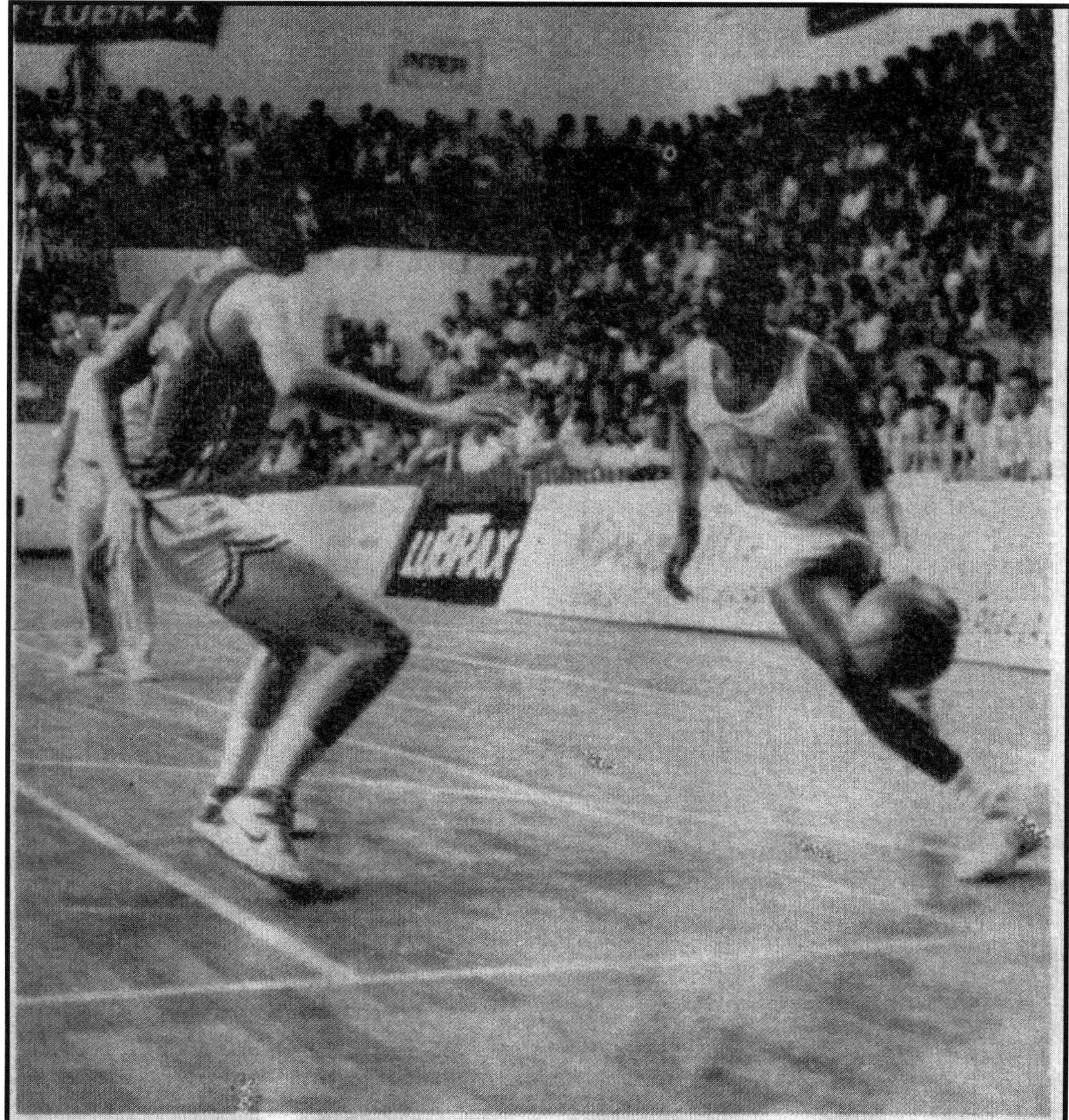

Gregori Scott, del equipo santo, arremete hacia el aro del Rowing, ante la marcación de Esteban Cabrera. Scott fue figura importante en el conjunto de San José, que cayó derrotado por 87 a 85.

San Jose vs. Libertad ~ G'$ vs. Frank Jackson aka 'Marvallisio'

Michael Coleman: "G' was relishing the *Showdown* with Frank because he's always taken much pride in locking-down the opponents' top scoring guard. Legendary Marvallisio, a packed house, and on TV; G' was surely salivating. But, 'Ochi' was their star point guard and initially was guarding Frank which was a bad mis-match. G' switched onto Frank for a few possesions, to the clear dismay of his coach who called a time-out. Ochi guarded Frank the entire game and got served for 45. G' was irked and grinded for 42. 4 point loss! So, the question was, does Frank score 45 with G' defending him; and does G' score 42 with Frank matched-up on him? I'll say this, Frank openly admited that he hated it when G' guarded him. And, G' is gonna get his 40+ regardless of who is on him, because one man can't guard him. Factually."

Coach offended me: "Ochi's the Point Guard. Save your energy."

Salto en el aire de González Galli que hace un intento por tratar de sacar el balón que se dirige al cesto de su equipo. Ganó Libertad por 93 a 89 a San José en la apertura del campeonato de la liguilla del básquetbol. (Fotos de Jorge González).

G'$ Benched by his Coach! For Guarding the Top Scoring Foe!?

I didn't complain to Marcello about my coach! In the next game all was well until the second half when our opponnt sub'd in a young stud who was giving Ochi' fits. I swithced onto him and my Coach lost his mind and took **ME** out of the game! He chastized overtly!

Mike: "G' got so mad he put on his sweat top, left the bench, went up the aisles to the public concession stand. Ordered a beer (he hates beer). Tells them to put it on Marcello's tab. Drinks it all in one swig. Walks back down the aisle to the bench, barks at his Coach and he sub'd back into the game."

Cary: "I saw that G'man wasn't on our bench. Then, he came back in with beer on his breath. G' put in work! We won our very first game of the season, by 10 points, and G' played great at both ends of the court. Buzzed or not! The fans loved it. Coach was pissed! G'$'s Game Spoke!"

I had a terrible headache later! But, NOT The Agony of Defeat!!!

Luis Gamarra se dispone a realizar un amague ante la marcación de Gregory Scott,pero éste bajará su brazo y golpeará el balón,tirándola para afuera. Gran partido cumplieron ambos jugadores dentro de sus respectivas escuadras.

Asunción, sábado 21 de noviembre de 1987 HOY

AGONICO TRIUNFO TUVO INTER ANTE SAN JOSE

Gran figura en Inter fue el norteamericano Hamilton, quien se convirtió en el cerebro del equipo. Por su parte, el yanqui de San José, Gregori Scott, estuvo muy individualista, pese a que en los tramos finales del enfrentamiento estuvo muy certero en los lanzamientos de tres puntos.

Gregori Scott, en una arremetida por el corredor final del elenco de Inter, ante la marcación del otro norteamericano, de Inter, Alexander Hamilton, la jugada culminará en un doble para San José.

BELIEVE THE HYPE! I TAKE MUCH PRIDE SEEING MY 'WORK' TOUTED BY MEDIA EVEN IN DEFEAT!

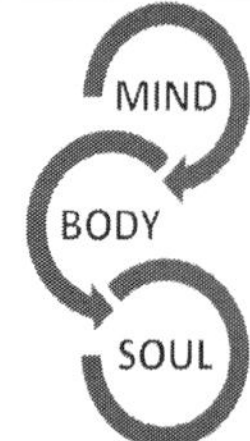

Win or Lose: After every game, Cary and I always had a fine meal at choice restaurants chosen by Marcelo Bedoya who loved to flaunt his Prized Trophies No Team. Just Us 3.

We arrived at one game 2 hours early. No Foes. No Fans. The gym was next to a casino. Oh yes! In our game sweats I went in with Cary and our interpreter to play Blackjack 21 as the pit boss got excited. I was at a table playing solo with the dealer. Single Deck! I was playing two hands at a time using the Basic Strategy and I was counting cards. In just a half-hour I killed them! Really! G'$: 30 pts. & Won!

Basketball is a TEAM SPORT! But, it's NOT!

G'$ Hits 29 vs. Inter

THE AGONY OF DEFEAT

The next week we sat in our lockerroom before practice as Marcelo informed the team that he fired the Coach! I felt every eye staring at me. I had nothing to do with it and no inside info. It was as much a surprise to me as it was to anybody. Some might have thought it was me. So what! As long as he's gone. The new coach and I got along great! We went on a winning streak and got back into the Classification Hunt.

Bonus $$$ within sight!

INTERNACIONAL 103

Víctor Ljubetich (13), Alexander Hamilton (21), Carlos Sosa, Calvin Heynes (37), Carlos Cabral (14), formación inicial. También jugaron: Héctor Torres (5), Igor de Mello (5) y Kike

Manuel Jiménez (20), Gregori Scott (29), Santiago Ochipinti (12), Aldo Kabout (16), Carey Broock (20), formación inicial. También jugó: Alberto Araujo (2).

SAN JOSE 99

Gregory Scott realiza un amague en la bomba del Inter ante la atenta mirada de su compañero Aldo Kabout y de sus adversarios Calvin Haynes e Igor de Mello. El jugador santo posteriormente se elevará y convertirá el doble.

Caption Translation:

"Gregory Scott realizes a pump for the threat from Inter under the watchful eye of teammate Aldo Kabout and his adversaries Calvin Haynes and Igor de Mello. The saintly player subsequently elevated and converted the two points."

Mike Coleman & G'$

Mike club, AFEMOT, was the National Telephone company. Big $$$ and some big players. Two 7-footers allowed Mike to play GUARD! His Dream Job! I knew he was giving his crew apt plots to stop me. FUTILE!

AFEMOT 116 SAN JOSE 94

Jugado en el estadio del Consejo Nacional de Deportes. Arbitros: Guido Bobadilla y Julio Rafael Vera. AFEMOT: Inicial: Lee Bates 40 (3 triples, 15 dobles y 1 simple en 3 intentos), Michael Coleman 20 (1-7-3/4), Arnoldo Penzkofer 28 (1-11-3/6), Hugo Sosa 9 (1-3-0) y Ronald Emmart 9 (0-4-1/1); luego Andrés Gómez 6 (2-0-0) y Juan Carlos Barán 4 (0-1-2/2). DT: Julio César Ré. SAN JOSE: Inicial: Aldo Kabbout 4 (0-2-0/4), Gregory Scott 41 (2-14-7/9), Cary Brooks 19 (0-9-1/6), Santiago Ochipinti 9 (1-3-0) y Manuel Giménez 10 (3-0-1/2); luego Albert Araújo 8 (0-4-0), Humberto Arce 3 (0-1-1/2), Daniel Páez Coll y José Sánchez. DT: Miguel González Arca. Resultado parcial: AFEMOT 60-San José 45. Salieron por 5 faltas: Emmart (A) y Giménez (SJ).

Mike: "We knew G' was a star and would get his. But, he was really geeked up for us when he finished a fastbreak with a 360 degree dunk; that was actually more of a 280, but, very nice regardless. He wasn't one to flaunt a solo fastbreak. I'd never seen him floss one like that! Later, he pressed his luck and tested my patience. We were on offense and G' somehow, gets switched to play D' on me, in the post! I said, "What you doing down here?", as I called for the ball. G' latches onto and pins my arm, at an angle the ref can't see. I said, 'Let go G'...G' LET GO!' Just as he was about to get it, he let go! We still laugh about it! We won. G' Did 40+ Work."

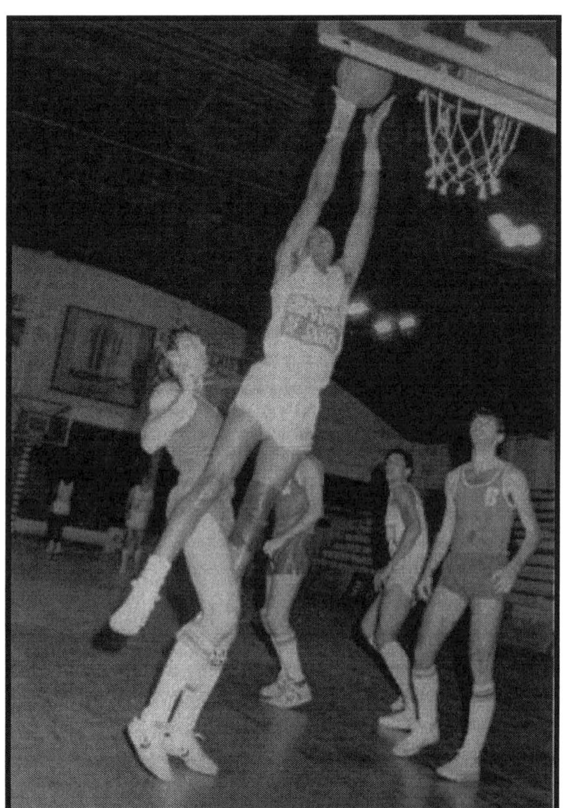

YouTube*.com/MentalAthlete*

'Global Hoops Montage' Video

We had a must-win road game at Feliz Perez to qualify for a one-game playoff to classify. This game was perhaps my best performance! The 'tube video shows legit 1st half highlights. But, not my 2nd half G'$ crunch-time heroics. Stay Tuned: Film Don't Lie. We Vanquished!

Final Classification Spot Playoff

Olympic Hall: San Jose vs. Cuidad Nueva
Paraguay's finest hoop venue was jam packed. Cuidad was a dirty team with no Americans! With pride, playoffs and 'paper' $ on the line we kicked that ass. And, a player tapped mine. 2nd half during a free throw a player put his finger up my butt. **I was appalled and irate.**

I stalked him as he back-peddalled and said, "Hit me so you get ejected." Then, I heard:

Mike: "Don't do it G'! Think of the MONEY!" So, I chilled. We got the 'W'. Classified!

Cary and I were at a playoff game in the concession area and he saw the guy who sodomized me. We went to him. I inquired. He denied. I wasn't sure. Then, SMACK! Cary hit dude flush in his jaw. And, down he went! I looked at Cary, 'Why you do that?' **Cary: "You were taking too long!"**

Tabla de posiciones

Hexagonal de básquet

Equipos	Pj.	Pg.	Pp.	Tf.	Tc.	Bon.	Pts.	Dif.
Rówing	5	3	2	469	472	2	10	-3
Internacional	5	4	1	521	491	-	9	30
Afemot	5	3	2	498	473	-	8	25
Libertad	5	2	3	483	499	1	8	-16
Sol de América	5	3	2	512	508	-	8	4
San José	5	0	5	449	489	-	5	-40

GOLEADORES (Del hexagonal)

Frank Jackson (Libertad) .... 171 puntos
Calvin Haynes (Inter) .... 159 puntos
Gregory Scott (San José) .... 155 puntos
Lee Bates (Afemot) .... 149 puntos
Alexander Hamilton (Inter) .... 148 puntos
Ronald Woods (Sol) .... 109 puntos
Steven Hill (Rówing) .... 103 puntos
José Velázquez (Sol) .... 101 puntos
Arnoldo Penzkofer (Afemot) .... 101 puntos
Gary Alan Hook (Sol) .... 99 puntos
Craig Stephens (Rówing) .... 98 puntos
Carey Holland (Libertad) .... 98 puntos
Esteban Cabrera (Rówing) .... 96 puntos
Francisco Velázquez (Sol) .... 95 puntos
Cary Brooks (San José) .... 92 puntos

We made the HEX playoffs and I got my bonus. G'$: I was #3 scorer at 31 ppg!

Cha Ching

Da BOYZ! Chillin' in the Club! "La City"!

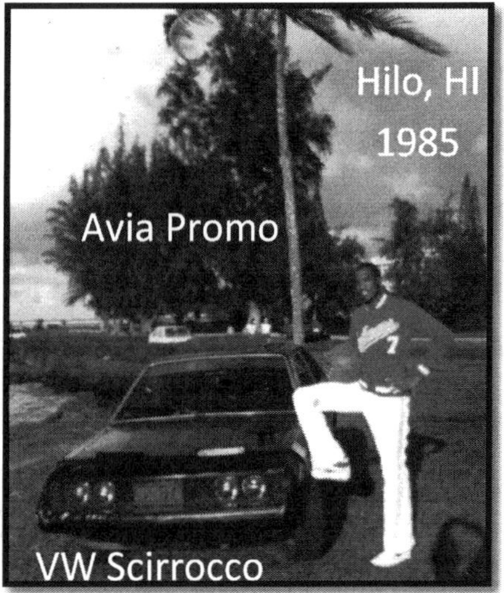

Why I Wear Jersey #7

- 7 letters make up the name bestowed upon me by my parents:

  Gregory

- 7th letter of the alphabet:

  'G'

- 7 letters name the performance brand (& man) I embody athletically:

  PORSCHE: Born in Stuttgart ~ G' Hoops: Born in Landstuhl

  Ferdinand Porsche & I was born on September 3rd; & Charlie Sheen!?

- 7 words on my Pyramid of Success plaque John Wooden awarded me:

  "Most Improved Athlete & Best All~Around Performer"

- 7 words of the 1st sentence in my all-time favorite song and mantra:

  <u>Hints: Sung by Queen ~ The 1st word of the title is "WE":</u>

  "I've Paid My Dues Time After Time"

"WE GET KNOCKED DOWN SOMETIMES. BUT WE GET UP. BECAUSE THE GROUND IS NO PLACE FOR A CHAMPION."

REV. JESSE JACKSON, JR.

THE MIND OF A CHAMPION

'SAGE SPARKS' QUOTE:
THE TANGIBLE EMBODIMENT OF GLOBAL HOOPS

"What makes a champion ~ I mean the legends.
The top percentile who consistently dominate their opponents,
perform at their highest levels at the most crucial times,
and ultimately distance themselves from the
near-greats and the also-rans?

The champion's true edge exists solely in the mind.

He has a profound sense of dissatisfaction with his accomplishments.

He is always coming from behind,
even when the score indicates he is destroying his opponent.

He never believes he is performing as well as he is."

Mark McCormack

GHMBS: 'Champions Mettle' Mantras:

You've gotta have your heart broken before you can be a Champion!

The Champion Doesn't Always Take Home the Prize!

PAT RILEY QUOTES FOR GLORY

> Each warrior wants to leave the mark of his will, his signature, on the important acts he touches. This is not the voice of ego but of the human spirit, rising up and declaring that it has something to contribute. In every contest, there comes a moment that separates winning from losing. The true warrior understands and seizes that moment by giving an effort so intense and so intuitive that it could only be called from the heart.
> Pat Riley (page 121)

"The only thing that I've ever known in my life about the game is hard work. That hard work and concentration and dedication is not going to guarantee you anything. But, without it, you don't stand a chance." Pat Riley, Showtime Lakers

"Pat Riley is about business; and the business is winning championships."
Jim Hill

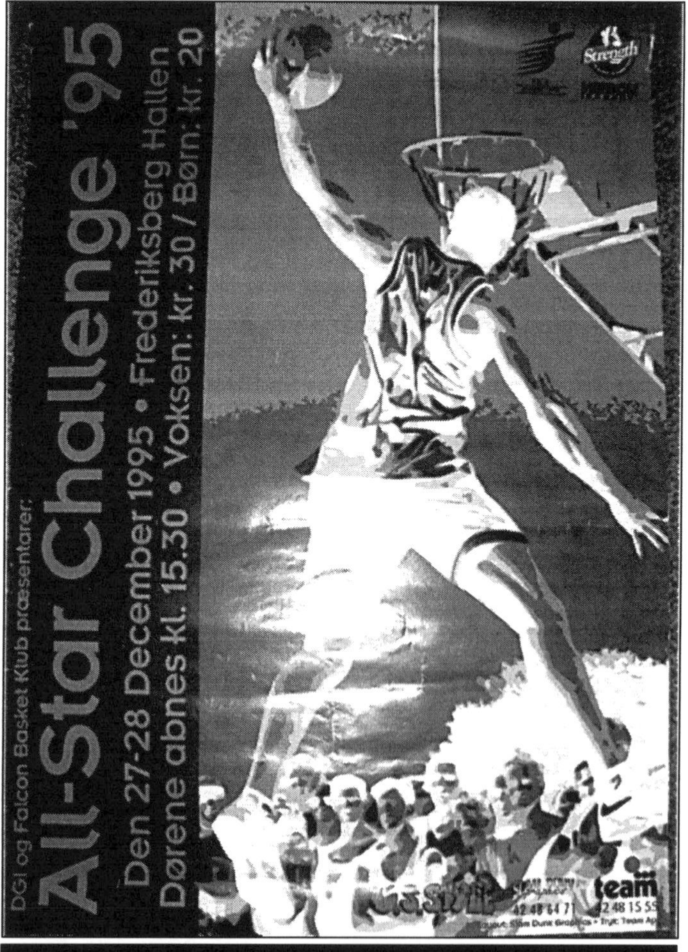

G'$ POSTER: '95 European All-Star 'Lefty' Jam!

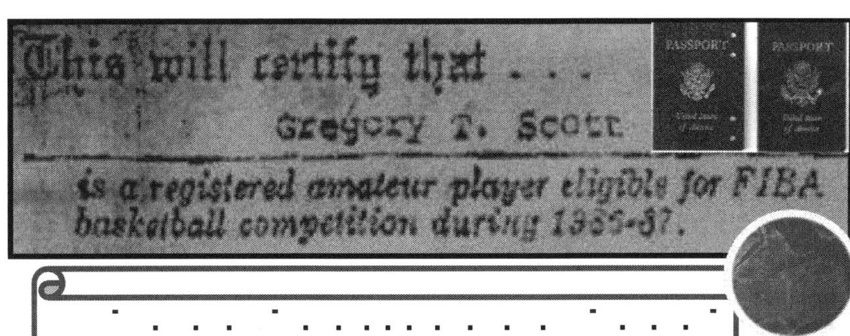

This will certify that . . .
Gregory T. Scott
is a registered amateur player eligible for FIBA basketball competition during 1986-87.

MOMS PERSISTENT PLEA:

"PROMISE ME. TELL YOUR STORY!"

Asuncion, Paraguay '87

SPORTSFREUNDE: GREG SCOTT (BASKETBALLER) SAMSTAG, 7. FEBRUAR 1998

All-Star sagt im Sommer Bye-Bye

TVK-Amerikaner arbeitet als Promoter bei den großen Sportartiklern

1987 ~ 1998

Argentina ~ Paraguay ~ Mexico ~ High Five America Germany ~ France Austria ~ Holland Switzerland Denmark ~ Spain Greece ~ Italy Indonesia

GLOBAL HOOPS

Over 1M miles of Peak Performance provided a platform to impact 1M young minds and lives with the tools and traits of the 'Mental Athlete'. Think, Train, Fuel & Compete with the Mind of a Champion.

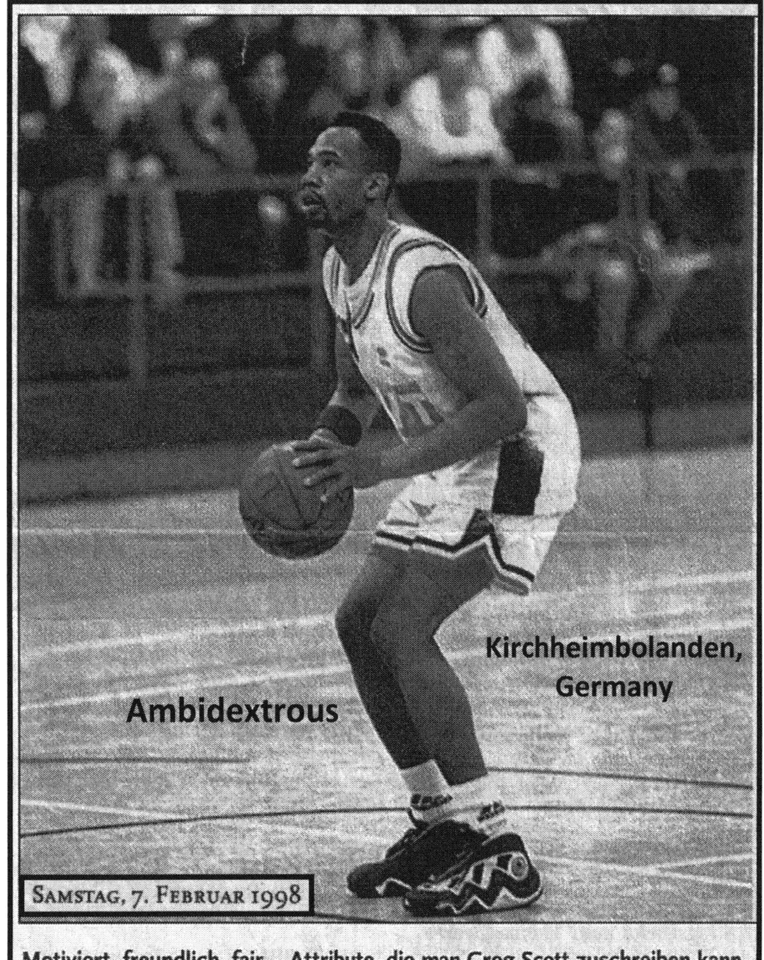

Motiviert, freundlich, fair – Attribute, die man Greg Scott zuschreiben kann. Über mentales Training hat er sogar ein Buch geschrieben. —FOTO: STEPAN

THE ONE WILL GO FURTHER.

THE ONE WILL DIG DEEPER.

THE ONE WILL CHANGE EVERYTHING.

The Legacy of Jordan Brand & 'Air Jordan'

A BLUEPRINT NEVER TO BE FORGOTTEN!

WILL YOU BE THE ONE?

NO Fine Print: GHMBS is Primed & Proven to be 'THE ONE'!

Trustworthy	RELIABLE, TRUTHFUL, UPRIGHT, AUTHENTIC
Human	UNIVERSAL CHARACTERISTIC OF MANKIND
Essential	IMPERATIVE, ESSENCE, FUNDAMENTAL, VITAL, INDISPENSABLE ELEMENT
Of	TO
Nurturing	FEED, NOURISH, REAR, EDUCATE, TRAIN, BOLSTER
Excellence	VALUE, WORTH, MERIT, VIRTUE, DISTINCTION, SUPERIORITY

Excellence: G' Hoops 'I Train, Compete & Perform in a Quest to VANQUISH!'

Empowerment: See It 2 Be It...The Mental Athlete Workshop Manifesto

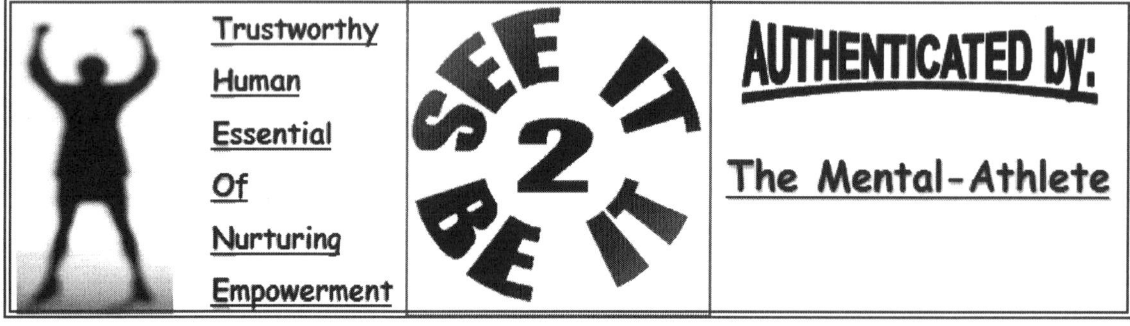

Give a man a fish and you feed him for a day.
Teach him how to fish and you feed him for a lifetime.

Mom Quote

"Beware of your thoughts;
As your thoughts become your words.

Beware of your words;
As your words become your actions.

Beware of your actions;
As your actions become your habits.

Beware of your habits;
As your habits become your character.

Beware of your character;
As your character becomes your destiny."

VIRGO (Aug. 23-Sept. 22). Whether it's a box, a bun or a system of belief, this is the time to think outside it.

CUTTING EDGE CONDITIONING AT AGE 13 & CORE OF MY GAB 13

THE KEY OPERATING PRINCIPLES OF THE SUBCONSCIOUS

There are certain natural laws for operating the subconscious as a success mechanism. Study them carefully. They will be a key to developing into the best person you can be.

1. **Your success mechanism needs a clear-cut purpose to activate its powers. The purpose can be in the form of a goal, a problem to be solved, a skill to be mastered, or a habit or attitude to be acquired. Winning starts at the beginning…set goals.**
2. **Write the goal down on a 'goal card' and carry it around with you at all times.**
3. **The goal must be something you want and desire, not something someone has told you that you need. Wanting is essential.**
4. **Start to visualize the goal as an "accomplished fact". Think in terms of the end result. What you want must be put into image form. Your mechanism works best on mental pictures. A mental picture is worth a thousand words. Imagination is your success mechanism's most powerful ally.**
5. **Never worry or be afraid of making mistakes. Errors are temporary failures as long as the end-result picture is kept in mind. Skill learning is accomplished by trial and error. Forget the misses, remember the successes. You must not forget that one step short of success is failure!**
6. **Trust your subconscious to do its magic. You'll only jam it if you try too hard. Easy does it. Let it work rather than make it work. Trust thyself means trust your subconscious.**
7. **Keep your subconscious mind busy with expectations of success. The best way to eliminate negative thoughts is by focusing your thinking on a positive expectation. You'll get what you expect!**

8. **Never use the words "I can't"; "I can't" really means "I won't". Your subconscious takes you at your word. Overcome this tendency by saying, "I CAN!"**
9. **Your subconscious will accept any thought it believes to be true. This law of belief is the law of your success mechanism. Start to believe in what is best for you. Whatever your conscious mind assumes to be true, your subconscious will bring to pass.**
10. **Your subconscious does not know the difference between a real experience and a vividly imagined one. Learn the power of visualization and employ it continuously.**
11. **The more often you repeat the visualization process, the greater will be its impact on your subconscious.**
12. **Your mechanism works below the conscious level. When your mind and body are relaxed and you are in a sleepy state, the influence of the conscious mind is submerged. Interfering negative thoughts in the conscious mind are neutralized. Your subconscious mind accepts positive visualization more willingly.**
13. **Your subconscious works 24 hours a day. During sleep it's especially susceptible to suggestion. Awaiting sleep, present your success mechanism with a problem to solve or a skill that you want to master. Start the mental wheels moving before you go to sleep and in the morning you'll have a solution or an improved skill.**
14. **Never become overly concerned about the outcome of your performance. You'll strain your mechanism. Visualize the goal. Never become anxious over attaining it. You will.**

<u>The Key Operating Principles of the Subconscious: Included in the original 1991 Workshop Manual</u>

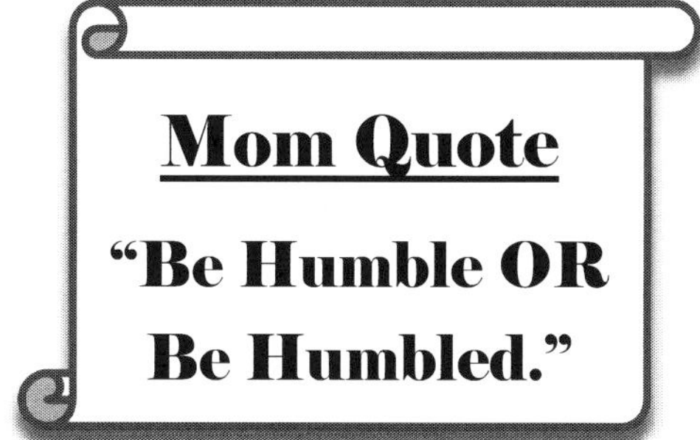
Mom Quote
"Be Humble OR
Be Humbled."

The Basketball Cybernetics kit was a life and game changer for me from the age of lucky 13, and I still have it in hand as I finish this book. Yet, the risk of my analysis paralysis taking effect precludes me from reviewing it often. I revisited the tapes while creating the original 1990 Mental Athlete Workshop Manual. Trust in these sage, timely and timeless tidbits to unleash your magic from within. Not only What to Think but How to Think! Volkswagen Ventures & Porsche Pursuits!

MY APT & EMPOWERING 'LIST TO LIVE BY'

The world's most incredible computer……………..The Brain

The most destructive habit…………………………..Worry

The greatest joy..……………………………………Giving

The greatest loss……………………..…Loss of Self-Respect

The most satisfying work…...……………….……Helping Others

The ugliest personality trait…...............................Selfishness

The most endangered species…………......Dedicated Leaders

Our greatest natural resource…………………..…...Our Youth

The greatest 'shot in the arm'…...……………...Encouragement

The greatest challenge to overcome...…………………......Fear

The most effective sleeping pill…………………....Peace of Mind

The most crippling failure disease……………………Excuses

The most powerful force in life……………………..……..Love

The most dangerous pariah………………………...A Gossiper

The worst thing to be without……………….……………Hope

The deadliest weapon……….……………………The Tongue

The two most power-filled words…..………………..…"I Can"

The greatest asset…………………………………………Faith

The most worthless emotion……………..…………Self-Pity

The most beautiful attire…………………..…………..A SMILE!

The most prized possession… **…...Integrity**

The most contagious spirit. **.Enthusiasm**

You Are
What You
Think!

"Make not your thoughts your prisons." William Shakespeare

THE POWER OF HABIT

- I am your constant companion.
- I am your greatest helper or your heaviest burden.
- I will push you onward or drag you down to failure.
- I am completely at your command.
- Half of the things you do, you might as well turn over to me;
- And I will be able to do them quickly and correctly.
- I am easily managed; you must merely be firm with me.
- Show me exactly how you want something done;
- And after a few lessons, I will do it automatically.
- I am the servant of all great individuals.
- And, alas, of all failures as well.
- Those who are great; I have made great.
- Those who are failures; I have made failures.
- I am not a machine, though I work with all the precision of a machine.
- Plus, the intelligence of a human being.
- You may run me for profit or run me for ruin;
- It makes no difference to me.
- Take me, train me, be firm with me;
- And I will put the world at your feet.
- Be easy with me, and I will destroy you.
- Who am I?
- I am HABIT!

Author Unknown

The Book: 21 Day Habit

@MentalAthlete

"We are what we repeatedly do. Excellence then, is not an act, but a habit."

Aristotle

The Mental Athlete Workshop

Time Tested & Globally Proven

Transcending typical sports psychology, The Mental Athlete Workshops have meshed my 'Pursuit of Peak Performance' with proven International philosophies and techniques, and topped it off with a global education specializing in Sports Performance Enhancement in a personal quest for Excellence.

SEE IT TO BE IT™

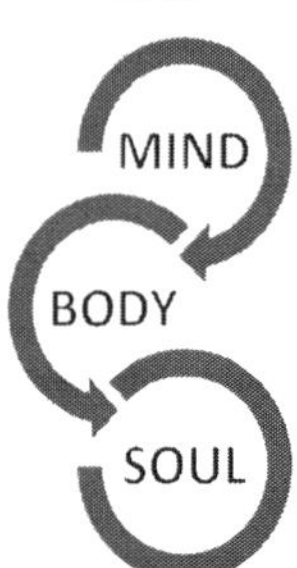

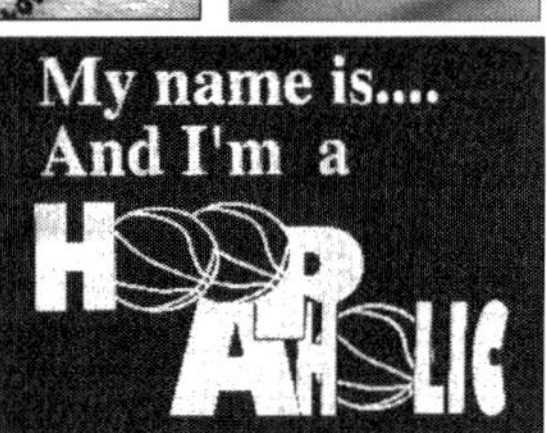

THE MENTAL ATHLETE WORKSHOP

25 years of Tangible Global Evolution

Workshop Creation
'The Club' ~ Kona, HI
Home of the Ironman

See It 2 Be It
'The Mental Athlete'

Multimedia Workshop Presentations

25th Anniversary

Social Media Branding

twitter

Adidas ABC Euro Camps
Germany, France, Italy, Greece, Spain & The UK

Mental Athlete Workshop Live on Radio Show
Kaliedescope Radio Magazine

Global Hoops: Mind, Body & Soul
Trafford Publishing

1990	1995	2000	2003	2007	2012	2015
•.Mind & Body Conditioning for Peak Performance •Personal Trainer: Club members & Ironman triathletes	•Translated into German & French •FIBA Recognized •Co-wrote Players & Coaches Manuals Coached Jr Nat'l Tms	•Company Launch •Peak Performance •Website & Logos • U.S. target market Club / Travel / AAU Olympic Train'g Ctrs	•1-hour Live via KTST 89.5 FM & seeit2beit.com •Media Credential •Retaind all radio show copyrights	•Custom Workbooks •Custom Powerpt. Applications •Peak Performance & Elite Athlete Platforms	•Trafford.com •Non-fiction •Peak Performance •Self-Help •Workshop Infused •BB IQ Blueprint	•Branding via MentalAthlete •Twitter/Facebook •Youtube/Instagrm •Seeit2beit.com •Ghoops.com
•San Diego~Mental Athlete Workshops •Launched 'The Competitive Edge' •UCSD Instructor Wt. Trn'g & Fitness	•Gregg's European Hoopaholics Camps •Wiesbaden DoDs •Frankfurt Int'l Sch. • Brechenheim Club Surabaya, Indonesia	•The TEAM Concept Tools, Education, Application & Motivation •Demographically Universal	•Infused radio show content into Workshop Presentations •First Baskeball Refereeing Cert.	•Bball Officiating: •CIF High School •Cal State Games •Club & AAU @ AIU •Intertribal Sports ITS	"True Life Tales, Tools, Teachings and Testimonials of an Int'l. Pro Ballplayer & Mentor"	•Resurrection of the Workshop~Globally •Brand'g Gear Line •Int'l Hoop Camps •2015 Global Hoops Book Publish'g Tour

THE MENTAL ATHLETE & GLOBAL HOOPS MIX

"A business has to be evolving, it has to be fun and it has to exercise your creative interests."
~ Sir Richard Branson ~

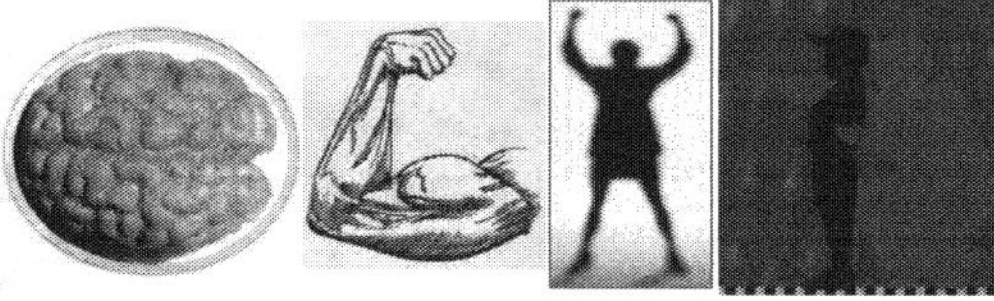

@MentalAthlete

"It is foolish to expect an athlete to follow your advice and to ignore your example."

Gregg Scott ~ Global Hoops

A Champions Pedigree

Fan & Namesake: Gabriela Sabatini

1987: "Play Hard & Play Smart"

1998: Gabriela Sabatini Induction ~ Pro Tennis Hall of Fame*

*Honored by her HOF nemesis & doubles partner, Steffi Graff.

Mom Quote: "To Thy Own Self Be True."

"Always remember Gabriela Sabatini's first words to you: 'I really love basketball and have watched many players. And for me, you are truly the best player I have ever seen.' Son, your core impact is your gift of great performances."

GHMBS
BUILT TO VANQUISH.
BORN in Argentina.
BRED IN PARAGUAY.
BONAFIDE IN EUROPE.

"Excel at both ends of the court...
And everywhere in between."

Gregg Scott
Euro Pro.

*BLUEPRINT TO EMULATE

A bitter pill of being out-muscled in ONE Argentina game festered past Paraguay!

Winston Morgan A fit 6'5" 215 lb. big-butt Adrian Dantley/Barkley hybrid played for Bobby Knight's IU Hoosiers fed me a slice of Pro Hoop Humble Pie!

Physiques Gym ~ Hilo

February 11, 1988

Two Rec Leader stints for the Culver City Parks & Rec as a teen qualified me for a unique government job as Recreation Coordinator at the Hawaii Job Corps in Hilo.

Physiques
29 Shipman, Suite 104
Hilo, HI 96720

Physiques Gym allowed me to bring groups of my Job Corps kids to workout in their Hilo facility. Their sage owner, Herbert Kobiyashi, said, "You'd make a great trainer." Later, he offered me a Personal Trainer job.

Dear Sir:

Recently I took advantage of your 2-for-1 offer and joined your organization--the first time in my life I have ever belonged to a spa or gym.

When the day came for my initial evaluation, I made a special trip into Hilo from our home nearly 30 miles from town only to discover that through an appointment mix-up, I could not be seen. Needless to say, I was less than happy.

The main point of this letter, however, is to let you know that when I did receive my initial evaluation, it was handled by Greg--and he more than made up for the initial disappointment. His genuine interest in me as an individual was apparent and coupled with his desire to tailor a program which would accomplish what I wanted to accomplish made it an unbeatable combination. His encouragement and enthusiasm in showing the various machines and routines left me feeling great--not only about myself but about the fitness program he designed.

You have a valuable employee in Greg and I look forward to working with him in the months to come.

Yours truly,

Pat Merrill

Patricia E. Merrill
15-2678 Welea St.
Pahoa, HI 96778

I vowed to resurrect my physique into NBA Quality! Size, Strength and Durability!

James Bradley

On a Ninja roadtrip to Kona I met Marlina Lee. She and husband Jeff were opening a posh fit gym 'The Club'. Bingo!

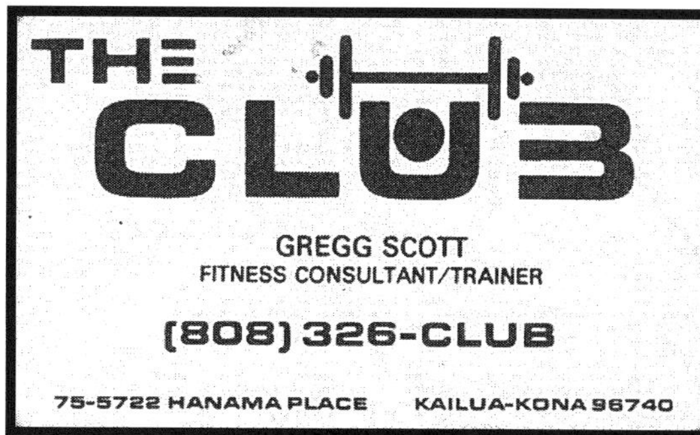
THE CLUB

GREGG SCOTT
FITNESS CONSULTANT/TRAINER

(808) 326-CLUB

75-5722 HANAMA PLACE KAILUA-KONA 96740

2nd Gig: A Pool Lifeguard at the Kona Surf Hotel. Gig PERK: A 24/7 BUFFET!

LAMBERT K. LEE LOY, M.D.
KEAUHOU BEACH HOTEL
78-6740 ALII DRIVE
KAILUA-KONA, HAWAII 96740

TELEPHONE (808) 322-2750

The 'Mr. Atlantis' Competition!

The Mind & Body Conditioning pedigree of the 'Mental Athlete' is founded upon my years of study, education and application as a Fitness Trainer & Performance Coach. Transcending G' Hoops!

November 9, 1989

Knowledge & Bedside Manner: Honing the skills to listen, probe, counsel, motivate, inspire and rehabilitate; athletes and non-athletes, alike!

To Whom It May Concern:

It gives me a great deal of pleasure to recommend Mr. Gregg Scott to you. He has, during the last several years, been an integral part of our community and the Keauhou Medical Clinic. His roles have been varied and challenging but nevertheless always completely successful.

Mr. Scott has been a consultant, lecturer, fitness trainer, has handled the challenges of working with groups of patients and athletes as well as on a one to one basis. He has mastered all of the skills necessary for effective patient counselling.

Mr. Scott is indeed an intelligent dedicated individual who would be an asset to any organization. I unequivocally recommend him to anyone fortunate enough to have him as a member of the team.

Sincerely,

Lambert K. Lee Loy, M.D.

3rd Gig: DJ on Thursday Nights jamming R&B at a "Rock & Roll" Pub Bar & Grill.

GS: 'You Can't Out-Train a Bad Diet!'

G'$: 71 point game!

SHORTHOPS

Scott tanks 71 for win

Former University of Hawaii at Hilo basketball player Gregg

Regretably, my memories of this game are indistinct. It was one of those special nights when my teammates who were relishing their roles in getting me off fueled my 'Kill Mode'. The NBA-sized court in Konawaena was a gym I had played in for UHH and performed quite well. Every shot was an entity and my shooting range was rediculous. I had 30 points at halftime. Efficiently! My crew kept me in the zone and I stayed focused and relentless at both ends of the floor while scoring 41 in the second half. 18 3's! A life memory for my 'mates!! Prophetically, My 71 point game earned a hoop intervention from a few mentors on my 'BOD'. "Aloha!"

Bobby Dudley, Tom Ward, Frank Gipson and Don Tomfor, my trusted elders, sat me down and convinced me to take my game to the pro level. The time was now. **"G'man, we all love you Brah. Don't get complacent in the Aloha lifestyle and waste your God-given talents here in Hawaii. You've got special gifts that can get you paid!"**

Dan Fast's Belief $ponsorship ~ C.B.A. San Jose Jammers Camp

Back when I arrived in Hilo I used to train at the the Boys & Girls Club after the Biz Mens Noon Ball pick-up games. Dan owned several car dealerships in Hawaii so he would hang out and watch me grind. He knew my work ethic up close and in person. He also sold me my TR-7, my Ninja motorcycle, and my Jeep. Beyond that, he mentored me on establishing credit and even had me join the Big Island Credit Union. He sponsored my Bay Area trip.

San Jose Jammers CBA Try-out 'Cattle Call' Camp ~ No Thanks!

I arrived one day before the 2-DAY 'try-out camp'. 75 players vying for only 3 spots Nah! This isn't for me! A 'Cattle Call'! For what they were paying? **I'm Hungry, Not Starving!**

1989
SOUTHERN CALIFORNIA
SUMMER PRO LEAGUE
July 21 – August 13
Loyola Marymount University
Los Angeles, California
IN COOPERATION WITH THE NBA
Tryouts July 7–11 & July 14–18
at St. Bernard High School

First Game: A man gave me a biz card for the NBA Summer Pro League!

Last Game: I hit a deep '3' at the buzzer to end the camp. SJ Coach: "Well done."

Eric Williams: San Jose State and the #1 pick of the Jammers

We bonded on Day One. Eric shared stories of growing up in Oakland with Ballers: Kevin Johnson, Brian Shaw, Jason Kidd and Gary Payton. All KILLER BAY AREA GUARDS!

Intro to Streetball…

Scott also scored the most points in the open with 43 and had the most two-point shots with nine.

Isle hoopsters compete at Ghetto Blast

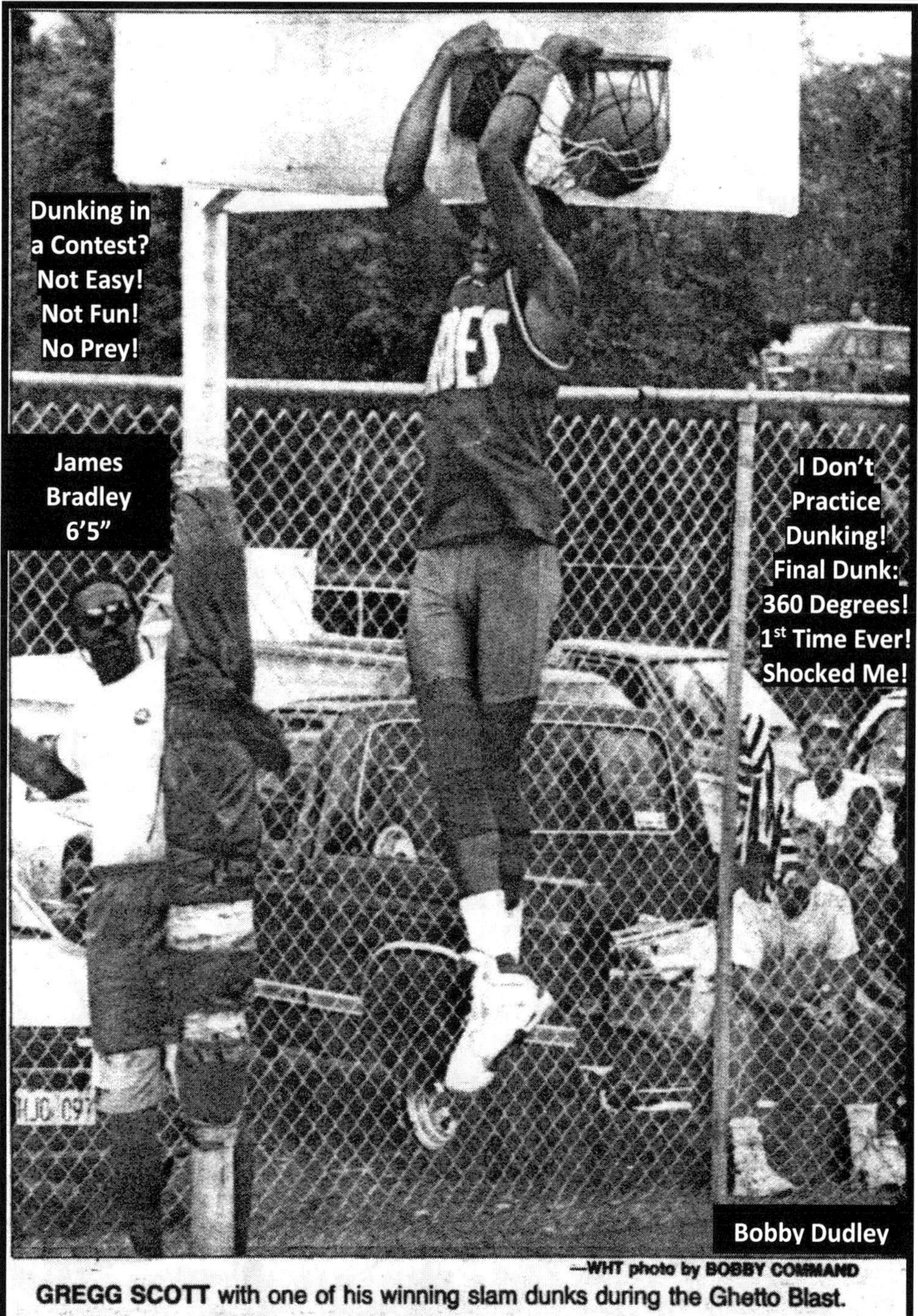

Dunking in a Contest? Not Easy! Not Fun! No Prey!
James Bradley 6'5"
I Don't Practice Dunking! Final Dunk: 360 Degrees! 1st Time Ever! Shocked Me!
Bobby Dudley

—WHT photo by BOBBY COMMAND

GREGG SCOTT with one of his winning slam dunks during the Ghetto Blast.

Probably the single-most impressive part of the tournament was the slam-dunk contest, which was near NBA quality.

Gregg Scott was the winner despite quality performances by Lovejoy, Long, Ray, Robbie Shropshire and Thomas Falcinella.

Mentor Dan Fast G' Pro $ponsorship!

Dan Fast put his money and trust in me BIG TIME!

Sparks and Patricia offered me their couch and a car!

1989
SOUTHERN CALIFORNIA
SUMMER PRO LEAGUE
July 21 – August 13
Loyola Marymount University
Los Angeles, California
IN COOPERATION WITH THE NBA
Tryouts July 7–11 & July 14–18
at St. Bernard High School

Club Paradise 24: Reunion with Mike

"Yes, I'm too old to go. But, that doesn't mean I'm too old to know where to go." My Pops!

My dad urged me to fly in on a Wednesday. "I've got a spot you need to hit up on Thursday night." **'24'** was the premier Thursday night 'hotspot' for VIP's, pro athletes, entertainers and music moguls.

Mike Coleman: "Thousands of people in this wharehouse-like venue with multiple sectors, multiple levels, and amazingly I see G' cut thru the crowd. In one hand he holds his familiar clear cocktail with no ice, and in the other he holds the hand of an exotic '10'; by anyones standards. What a moment! Brotherly love. He told me he was in L.A. for the summer pro league and he wanted to get a run in ASAP. Since G'man was now looking more like a bodybuilder than a ballplayer, I asked him what type of a run did he want? He got offended. 'Yo Mike, whatcha tryin' to say? I want the best possible!' I was amused at his annoyance. Okay, G'! Rodgers Park, Saturday at 8:30."

"Saturday at 8:20, G' rolls up ready to ball. This was the top spot so I'd be able to see his game get tested. He's 21st on the list. It was over two hours, during which I'd played twice (and won), by the time G' got onto the court. He's miffed at the long wait and goes out and puts in work from the start. He wasn't as good as before, he was better; and buffer. G' took his team to the brink of victory and they had game point at 14-10. Then, his teammates each took a turn trying to be the hero. Bad shots, decisions and turnovers. Soon it was tied at 14 and catcalls from the sidelines chanted of their choke. G' got the ball on the baseline and started to dribble up the left side of the court. I'm sitting at midcourt on the left sideline opposite of the scoreboard. G' is in a slow left-handed trot coming right by me as the chants continued. 'They don't want it!' 'Get one more stop!' His defender intensly guards him. As he coyly dribbles by me at the half court, I stand up and begin walking onto the court. Why? Beacause, I knew one thing: This Shiznit is now over! G' takes one dribble in the front court, pulls up from 35' and releases his pure jump shot, as I yell out for all to hear, 'Ass Hole!'. G' lands, steps back, I put my arm around his shoulders, we walked and watched. SWISH! G'$!"

Drazen Petrovic

Petro'

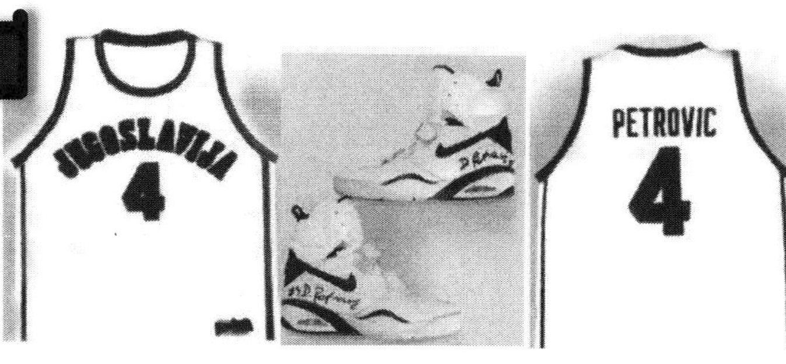

A week before the summer league began, I went to train at LMU early in the morning when it was empty. But, it wasn't. I befriended and also trained with a European Superstar named Drazen Petrovic from Yugoslavia. We were very good friends and shared shooting drills, insights, and we had great shooting competitions. Drazen trained early and often to prepare for his debut with the Portland Trailblazers, and to take his mind off of the tales of war in his homeland as told to him daily by his family. The gym was his refuge. One subject that brightened his spirits was our shared love of the Porsche Brand. I believe I was the first to give him the moniker of Petro' as I related the Spanish translation of fuel or gas. His scoring ability: **High Octane Petro'. Combustible!** On the last day, the floor was being cleaned and we couldn't workout. Blessing! So, I drove Drazen to my Dads office in Century City to introduce them and ask a favor of his clout. He made a call and set an afternoon appointment for Petro' and me. It was almost noon so I took Drazen to my spots. First, we hit up Tito's Tacos in Culver City and got grub to go. Next, intro him to the famed Venice Beach hoop mecca to eat, people-watch and chill. Lastly, to our appointment in Marina Del Rey. Test driving a new Porsche! Thanks, Pops! Drazen noted the difference between his German specs Porsche and this U.S. 'Imposter'! I will always remember that day and my week with Petro', and I would wear his #4 jersey.

1989 Summer Pro League

ORIGINAL

Lawyer Mike Arias was a new agent with NO clients! Mike signed ME and Fred Jones to launch his agency!

STANDARD PLAYER AGENT CONTRACT
(NON-NBA)

AGREEMENT made this __ day of July, 1989, by and between MICKEL M. ARIAS, ESQ. (hereinafter the "Agent") and GREGORY T. SCOTT (hereinafter the "Player").

G'$ Vision: Euro Pro Hoops!

WITNESSETH:

We met often in his Westwood HQ of 'Artists & Athletes International'.

In consideration of the mutual promises hereinafter contained, the parties hereto promise and agree as follows:

1. Contract Services

Mike: G'$ 'Marketability' merited a move back to Cali.

Commencing on the date of this Agreement, the Agent agrees to represent the Player -- to the extent requested by the Player -- in conducting individual compensation negotiations for the performance of the Player's services as a professional basketball player for pay anywhere in the world, except in the National Basketball Association.

Playing as a Free Agent put me on a team with a **high-flying 5'8" Baller!**

MVP Craig Johnson!

The brother of NBA's Dennis J.

We had a kinship!

The Club became, and remains, the premier training facility in Kona; home of the Ironman Triathlon. The triathletes' input spawned my Mental Athlete Workshop.

Club Mates: G' & Kraig Hill

JB & G'

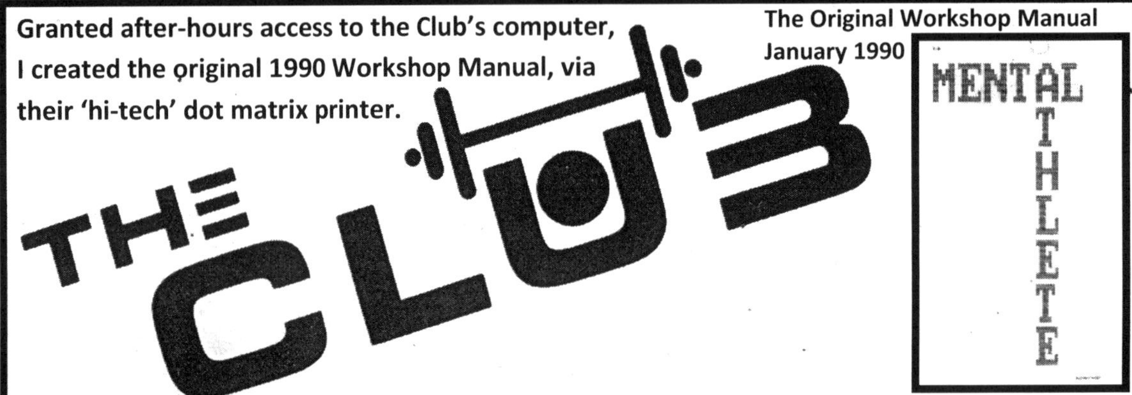

Granted after-hours access to the Club's computer, I created the original 1990 Workshop Manual, via their 'hi-tech' dot matrix printer.

The Original Workshop Manual January 1990

The Club's owners funded our ACSM Fitness Training Certifications. Educational Expertise: Anatomy ~ Diet & Nutrition ~ Supplementation

June 24, 1990

To Whom it May Concern,

This letter is in reference to Gregg Scott and his outstanding qualifications in the Health and Fitness, Business and Public Relations fields.

We had the opportunity to work with Gregg during our first year in business. It was a crucial time for setting high standards and a good reputation among our athletic club members and the community at large. Gregg definitely helped us to do this. His professionalism, friendliness and overall concern for our members was obvious in his job performance.

I feel that whatever path Gregg chooses he will devote himself to it 110%. We here at The Club in Kona feel fortunate to have been able to work with him and hope that our paths cross again in the future.

**THE CLUB coxed me into entering the 1990 Mr. Atlantis All-Natural Bodybuilding Contest! They trained me hard! I fueled and hydrated! ~Voila: 2nd Runner-up!

Sincerely,

Marlina Lee
Owner
The Club in Kona

A CLASS ACT University of California San Diego

REC CLASSES - Winter 1990-91

Learning for the fun of it is the key to RecClasses! There are no credits, grades or attendance requirements.

Most classes meet twice a week for one hour, 8 to 10 weeks each quarter. Many of the fitness programs operate on a continual basis. The majority of classes are held on campus.

Recreation classes are open to all UCSD students, faculty and staff as well as the general community. Students and RecCard holders pay the discounted price. All others pay the general price (second one listed).

To sign up, drop by our offices at Canyonview or use the mail-in registration form available in this

SPORTS & FITNESS

BEGINNING WEIGHT TRAINING (COED)

This class covers the specifics of proper weight training techniques and personal fitness programming from accomplished weight trainer and body builder, Gregg Scott.

TTh 6-7pm 1/15-3/7 $24/38

BODYBUILDING FOR WOMEN

Accomplished bodybuilder Gregg Scott, will help you develop your own personal fitness program in the weight room. Learn how to firm and strengthen those hard-to-work, but easy to see body parts as well as the facts and fallacies of nutrition and fitness.

TTh 7-8pm 1/15-3/7 $24/38

I was recruited for this position via a 'headhunter'. Creating curriculums, programs, workout cards, exercise signage, safety protocols and customized journals for co-ed and gender-specific fitness classes at a major university: **Priceless!!!**

'1st Saturday' Monthly Health & Fitness Seminars! G. Scott

- Pre/Post-Natal Fitness
- Cuircut Training Course w/ Diet & Nutrition Infusion
- **Performance Training**

WEIGHT TRAINING (COED)

This class covers the specifics of proper weight training techniques and personal fitness programming from accomplished weight trainer and body builder, Gregg Scott.

TTh 6-7pm 7/2-8/27 $28/43

BODYBUILDING FOR WOMEN

Accomplished bodybuilder Gregg Scott, will help you develop your own personal fitness program in the wieght room. Learn how to firm and strengthen those hard-to-work, but easy to see body parts, as well as the facts and fallacies of nutrition and fitness.

TTH 7-8pm 7/2-8/27 $28/43

Improving the self-image, health and well-being of each and every 'student' was my most cherished objective. To educate and inspire!

<u>'Bodybuilding' for Women Classes:</u>
"I don't want to bulk up." I hear you.
Toning & Trimming Programming
TVA Core Train'g. & Flexibility Session

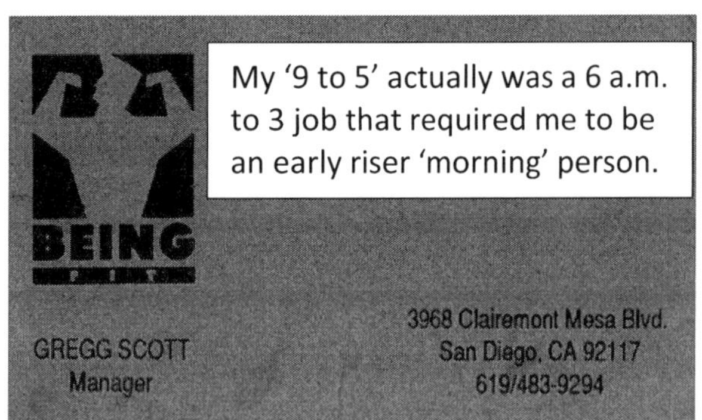

BEING
GREGG SCOTT
Manager
3968 Clairemont Mesa Blvd.
San Diego, CA 92117
619/483-9294

My '9 to 5' actually was a 6 a.m. to 3 job that required me to be an early riser 'morning' person.

Multi-tasking: Biz/Brand/Ball

My intro to Fitness Management 101! Also, Team USA volleyball player, Troy Tanner, was a VIP Being Fit member who gifted me Mizuno's and World Class Jumping Drills!!

Plyometrics Guru: Troy Tanner

The Competitve Edge Launch

Inaugural Mental Athlete Workshop 1991

The Competitive Edge, infant precursor to See It 2 Be It, was founded upon my original 'Club' Mind & Body Manifesto: The Mental Athlete Workshop Manual.

Mind & Body Conditioning

Mr. Bob McKenna:

December 19, 2007

Gregg,

I have fond memories of your conducting the mental athlete workshop for my boys many years ago at the Pacific Beach Rec Center. The boys loved it and I was most impressed by your enthusiasm and emphasis on character. Your message is as timely now as it was 20 years ago.

Bob McKenna

Entrepreneurship as a SOLE Proprietor. 'The Club' educated us on the science, our use, and marketing of supplements. Capitalizing: I got my Biz License and a State Seller's Permit. Bingo presto, a rep from Nature's Best in Irvine, strolls into Being Fit asking for the Manager. Me. Cha-Ching: An All-Natural Supplement distributer needs me!? Wholesale Co-Op! Being Fit, UCSD and monthly swap meet.

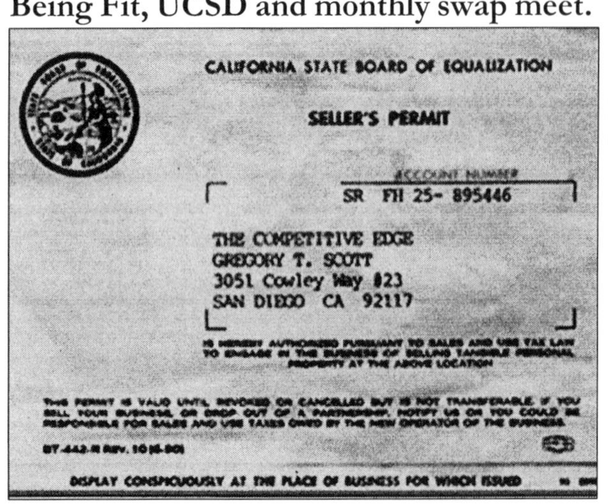

CALIFORNIA STATE BOARD OF EQUALIZATION

SELLER'S PERMIT

ACCOUNT NUMBER
SR FH 25- 895446

THE COMPETITIVE EDGE
GREGORY T. SCOTT
3051 Cowley Way #23
SAN DIEGO CA 92117

IS HEREBY AUTHORIZED PURSUANT TO SALES AND USE TAX LAW TO ENGAGE IN THE BUSINESS OF SELLING TANGIBLE PERSONAL PROPERTY AT THE ABOVE LOCATION

THIS PERMIT IS VALID UNTIL REVOKED OR CANCELLED BUT IS NOT TRANSFERABLE. IF YOU SELL YOUR BUSINESS, OR DROP OUT OF A PARTNERSHIP, NOTIFY US OR YOU COULD BE RESPONSIBLE FOR SALES AND USE TAXES OWED BY THE NEW OPERATOR OF THE BUSINESS.

BT-442-R REV. 10 (6-90)

DISPLAY CONSPICUOUSLY AT THE PLACE OF BUSINESS FOR WHICH ISSUED

I hawked and consumed a select few of their many high quality supplements. Whey Protein Powder, Amino Acids, Fish Oil, and 6-week Cybergenics Kits. I sold and spoke of what I know works for my fitness clients and works for me. Hippocratic Oath: First, Do No Harm!

PB Rec: The SD Hoop Mecca

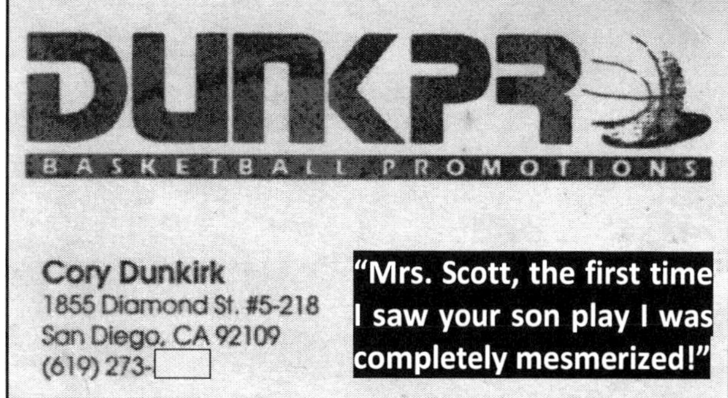

DUNKPRO
BASKETBALL PROMOTIONS
Cory Dunkirk
1855 Diamond St. #5-218
San Diego, CA 92109
(619) 273-
"Mrs. Scott, the first time I saw your son play I was completely mesmerized!"

On my summer visit I was informed that Pacific Beach Rec on Diamond St. had a reputation for being the top spot for hoops. So, I leased a condo at The Plaza on Diamond St.! **5** blocks from the gym!

Day One I reunited with Eric Williams from the San Jose Jammers. He had relocated to SD for his **Real Estate Appraisal** firm. On this day we went against Cliff Livingston and his two guards from the Atlanta Hawks. See Ya! We held down the court all day. Guard Play! E' was a 6'3" terror with mad hops! From that day on we were inseperable and Did Work at every hoop court we ventured to.

Eric Williams

A Noble 6:30a.m. Personal Training Session

I'm not at all a morning person. Yet, I dial in when necessary. In this training session I was demonstrating a squat on the Smythe Machine with no weight. As I racked the hooks onto the bar and decended, I noticed the bar was not balanced. As I rose to lift the bar it released down just an inch hard onto my shoulder. Bam! I immediately knew that I was truly injured.

G'$ Mumford Procedure Q: A Cadaver Ligament or Synthetic?

Dr. Davidson surgically made a synthetic labrum ligament, but warned me that I'd never play above the rim again. Yet, my wise 'healer' Dr. David Libs added his rehabilitation genius and the words that I needed to hear. "Gregg, I promise that you can come back. And, play better than ever!"

JULY 13, 1991

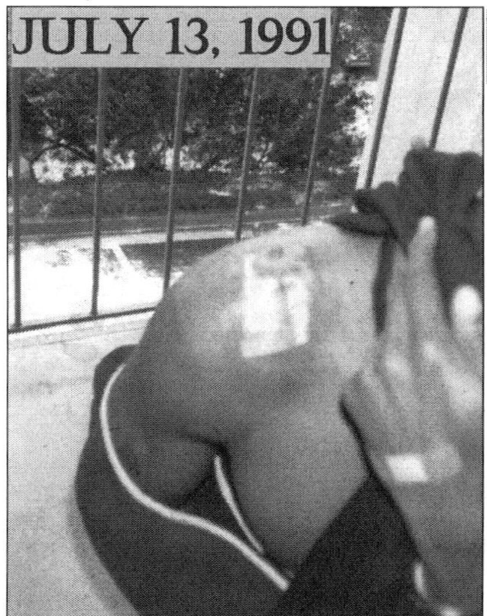

Workers Comp! A Great La Jolla Rehab Therapist: Leslie Friedle!

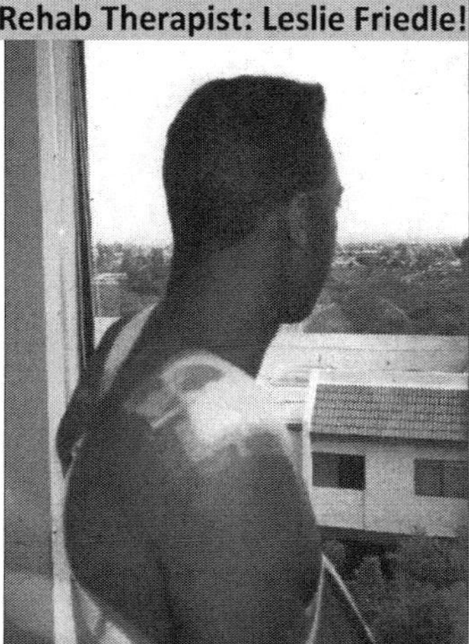

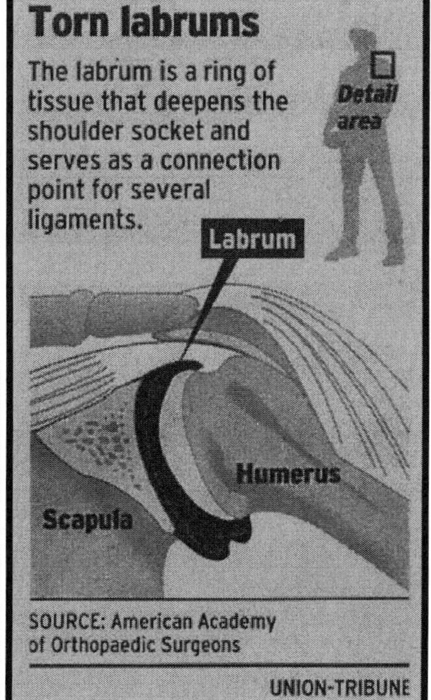

Torn labrums
The labrum is a ring of tissue that deepens the shoulder socket and serves as a connection point for several ligaments.
Detail area
Labrum
Humerus
Scapula
SOURCE: American Academy of Orthopaedic Surgeons
UNION-TRIBUNE

Scott Genetic Potential: Finance

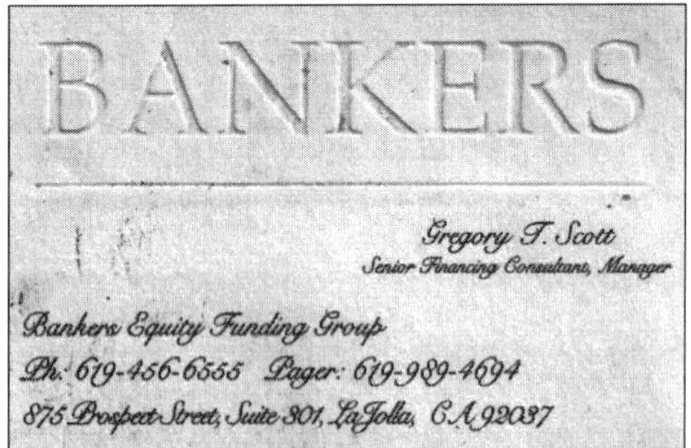
BANKERS
Gregory T. Scott
Senior Financing Consultant, Manager
Bankers Equity Funding Group
Ph: 619-456-6555 Pager: 619-989-4694
875 Prospect Street, Suite 301, La Jolla, CA 92037

MY 1ST FASHION MENTOR

Carl Ruston, a true baller in his own right, christened my novice attire as a "Sears Businessman's Starter Kit suit"; took me under his wing and taught me proper 'Biz Fashion 101' fit for La Jolla clientele. Carl changed my game:

"G', sometimes it's ***not the man in the suit***, but, ***the suit on the man***, that impresses."

And, Carl went beyond just talk. He invited me into his home on a few occasions, hooked me up with an elegant wardrobe, and schooled me on the subtle nuances of dressing for success with style and savvy. Carl's 'family' pics with Stedman & Oprah: Simply Priceless!

Miss Manners JUDITH MARTIN

Wardrobe speaks loud and clear

GREGG SCOTT
GREGG SCOTT
In a mall a lady asked me if I would like to be a model. She was 100% legit! $$$
WANTED!
$10.00 REWARD
We'll pay up to $10 for your old Levi 501s & jackets
- dead or alive!
Call the Information Line:
273-LEVI (5384)
Inspirational
Good Luck to.... From.....
102 Gregg Scott
California's Top Models Showcase 1991
-Gregg, you've got the edge.......Always had it......Always will! Good Luck, The Competitive Edge
-To our "Mr. Fitness"! Best of luck Gregg. Just do it-Being Fit
-Gregg, as usual you'll come out smelling like a rose! Love Aunt Skeet
-Best of luck Gregg-We're pulling for you....Love Dad & Doreen
-To one of my "All-Star" patients. Good Luck Gregg-Libs Chiropractice
-Eh, you one Tahreefic kid ovah deah! Have fun, no pressure. Aloha, Mom
-Yo "G" howzit? We miss ya here in Hawaii. Good luck, The Club in Kona
"CALIFORNIA'S TOP MODELS SHOWCASE '91"
Once Upon a Time...
WANTED
$10.00 REWARD

My 'Creekside' Condo: 3 rooms literally with a 'Top Gun' view!

15 freeway south; exit 14 sign 'Palomar Rd/Miramar Rd ¼ mile'. Look to the right, viola! My top floor corner end units U-shaped patio, accessible from 3 sliding doors, is unique. Each room had an unobstructed view to the exact flight paths and airspace of the **'Top Gun' Fighter Pilot School at the Miramar Naval Airbase that Tom Cruise made famous**

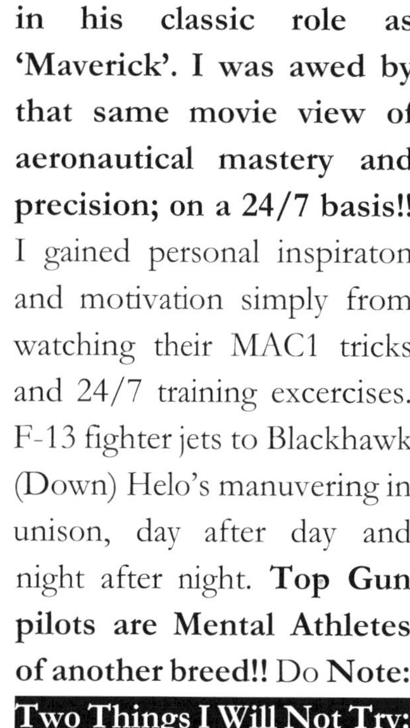

in his classic role as 'Maverick'. I was awed by that same movie view of aeronautical mastery and precision; on a 24/7 basis!! I gained personal inspiraton and motivation simply from watching their MAC1 tricks and 24/7 training excercises. F-13 fighter jets to Blackhawk (Down) Helo's manuvering in unison, day after day and night after night. **Top Gun pilots are Mental Athletes of another breed!!** Do **Note:**

Two Things I Will Not Try:

1) Pilot an airplane SOLO! Crashed 'Flight Simulator'!

2) Jump Out of a perfectly good plane for any reason! I lack the guts/sensibility!

The deal was sweet: 3% down FHA loan with a 3% commission as my own agent = zero down!
The deal-maker for my condo purchase was a tandem 2-car garage for my toys!

GREGG SCOTT
Sr. Financing Consultant

"Experience Is The Difference"

Accredited Home Lenders
A division of MSK Financial Services, Inc.
10968 Via Frontera
San Diego, California 92127

Off: (619) 451-7050
Pager: (619) 989-4694
Fax: (619) 451-7064

G' Hoops Training Regime

Miramar Lake, a mile from Creekside, is a training mecca in Scripps Ranch with a 5 mile trek of moderate slopes, dips and inclines circling a beautiful lake was my personal rollerblading and biking haven.

A Prophetic Global Hoops Revelation from a 'Psychic Reader'

I had a great job and many suggested basketball was not in my future. Desperate times call for desperate measures, so I accepted an invite from my Loan Processor, Traci, to visit her 'psychic' reader who she had raved about for months. She guided me to the home parlor, and I met a unique soul. She described the long lifelines in the palms of my hands. Said, I like speed… on four wheels or two. She 'sees' me in a white sports car. Ok, I drove my Jeep and Traci could have told her I had a White ZX and a motorcycle. Then, as she asked about my family she proved her 'psychic' gifts beyond all doubt. I told her my parents were divorced, my mom was a teacher in Hawaii, my dad was a banker in Century City, and my only brother was a finance guru like my dad, and also lived in Los Angeles. She looked confused. "You said you have just one sibling?" 'Yes, my brother, Mark.' "No, I see four Scott children" OMG: The Twins! They both passed away within days of being born. How could she possibly know that fact? I was a believer! So, I asked her about my hoop future?! "You are a man of very special talents and you also posses a very special ability to influence and impact others. Yes! You will resume your basketball career and you will perform better than ever. Live your dream! Believe it! The Best is Yet to Come!"

Mount Whitney Trek: Hubris!

What were we thinking. We're in great shape for the hoop court. The mountain is humbling. At the summit. Eric got bad altitude sickness!
Lesson Learned: Respect Mother Nature!

E' suggested that I become a Loan Officer.

My CA Real Estate Principles class at SBCC! CA Real Estate Exam: EZ Pass!

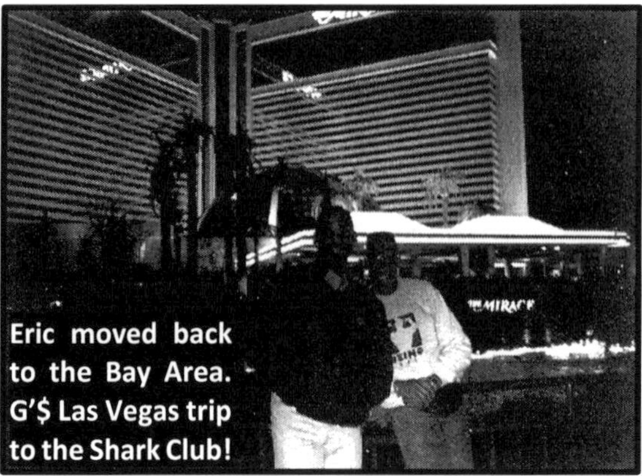

Eric moved back to the Bay Area. G'$ Las Vegas trip to the Shark Club!

October 1991 G'hoops Resurrection at P.B Rec...Hoop Mecca

PACIFIC BEACH BASKETBALL LEAGUE

Shoes, uniforms and venues vary. One Critical Constant: Kallassy Ankle Brace Supports! Part of my G' Flight Gear in every training, exhibition, Streetball event, All-Star game & professional competition I ever participated in. Bar None. I Never Needed To Be Taped!

Separate Left and Right Supports! Figure-8 Velcro System! No Laces!

HAS AN APPOINTMENT WITH
DR. ROY PHILLIPS
Podiatrist
Clairemont Medical Center
3660 Clairemont Dr., Suite 2
San Diego, CA 92117

1992 ~ San Diego: Dr. Roy Phillips
G'$ intro: Kallassy Representative

September 14, 1994

To whom it may concern:

This correspondence is being prepared as a formal letter of recommendation for Mr. Greg Scott.

As League Director of the Pacific Beach Recreation Center Men's Basketball League since 1991, I have had the fortunate opportunity to watch Mr. Scott excel on the basketball court.

Throughout San Diego County, Pacific Beach Recreation Center carries the reputation as hosting the highest caliber of play. Mr. Scott has only enhanced that reputation. In fact, as a 20 plus point per game scorer, he has more than held his own against the likes of former and current Division I and NBA players. Players such as Chris Dudley, Jud Buechler, Sean Rooks, Jeff Lamp, Bob Carrington, Zack Jones, Howard Wright, Scooter Barry, Michael Yoest and Herman Webster grace the courts of PB on a regular basis.

Greg has the respect of his peers as an excellent shooting guard and a top notch defender; an excellent all around player. His poise, leadership, athletic ability and tremendous feel for the game are a constant asset to which ever team he has decided to play for. His excellent vision and passing abilities help raise his teammates to his level. As a fan of the game, it has been a pleasure to watch Greg play.

Mr. Scott's basketball talents and his commendable off court demeanor would be an attribute to any organization. I would highly recommend Greg for any position he seeks. Please feel free to contact me at (619) 453-6627 with any questions.

Zack Jones ~ Bam Webster ~ Scooter Barry ~ Buzz Peterson

Sincerely,

Christopher Hazeltine
League Director

APR CALIFORNIA
ALL NET

OCT CALIFORNIA
N IIDEEP

Todd Gandy: "I first met G'man in Mexico when we played together in a game versus their Nat'l. Team. G' scored 45, in victory! We bonded for life!"

HIGH FIVE AMERICA INTRO 1992

Interviewed May 2002
High Five America HQ
Alliant Int'l. University

"My name is Gene Heliker, I'm a coach, and I've been coaching for an organization called High Five America for going on 15 years. In the beginning, the conception of High Five America, we are an organization with a mission statement to use the platform of athletic excellence to help young kids learn important life skills, and to teach them the fundamentals of basketball and how to take full advantage of a sports career through grade school, high school and college. Gregg had graduated from college and fit the profile of the player that we were looking for. We did a college exhibition schedule in the fall, we played in International pro tournaments in the spring and summer, and we needed graduated college basketball players that could play at an Olympic level and go out and represent High Five in the way we wanted to be represented; and Gregg fit that profile perfectly."

G' HOOPS: #22 – HIGH FIVE AMERICA '92, '93, '94

"The beginning of a program called the 'home team', or the High Five Dream Team, was a concept that I'd created and had difficulty selling to our president and founder at that point and time. Because I would travel around in Southern California and see men's leagues and these big 3-on-3's at the beach, and I would always come back and say, 'Gosh, there's some incredible talent'. Maybe not in the mainstream of the sport, but this area of Southern California has an immense amount of talent athletes. And, I went to a men's league game in La Jolla YMCA of all places, in a championship basketball game and when the game was over I found myself saying, 'there are guys here that can compete on an International or Olympic level or a Division 1 college level, and we could take these guys, create our own Home Team, and be able to go out and represent ourselves well.

Gregg played on the championship team and was as responsible as anybody in the gym that day for winning, and he just was every bit the player that normally we would go out and pay a lot of money for to play against top Division 1 colleges in the fall. Here was a guy working a full-time job and keeping in shape; right on our own doorstep."

YouTube.com/MentalAthlete

"Yes. The mentoring that we believe in for the young athlete is very important us. And we do that through mentorship programs; in other words, older players mentoring to younger athletes. The nature, the personality, the character, the integrity, the life skills that are important to become a good mentor are as important to us when we're looking for players to come play for High-Five. We need a certain type of person to represent us. All you have to do is watch players like Gregg play and compete at a high level, and how they conduct themselves, how they speak, how they perform, and how hard they work. I can watch a player for just a few minutes and tell you whether or not he's of High-Five quality. And, I was immediately very impressed. In fact, I went up to him after the game and introduced myself, and that chat was the beginning of a life-long relationship with Gregg."

THE FUTURE IMPACT BEYOND BASKETBALL

"The High Five America college program is arguably the hardest basketball venue on earth to play in. We play against everybody from small NAIA schools, to Duke, Berkley, USC. We have to go out and find guys on a moment's notice and prepare them. Every year you have a different group of players, a different set of personalities, different karma. And every year you hope that you have one or two or three of those kinds of guys that can always lead a team. They're the glue. They transcend racial lines, ethnic lines, communication lines. They can work with, speak to, and bring any group of people together and get out of them what you need. You as a coach cannot do all those things. You have to rely on a certain type of a person. Gregg was always one of those people that was the glue to the team. He could be a leader; he could not say a word. He could score 25; he could score zero. He knew what had to happen to make this team a team. So, he was a chameleon of sorts. And, if he wasn't there you struggled. Or, without someone like him, at the college level, you struggled."

"He was never out of shape. He was never late. He'd stay late. Always your best student."

1992: A ROAD TRIP WARRIOR ~ HIGH FIVE VS. NAU

"One of the reasons when I said that the High Five America college program is the toughtest in the world. The first year Gregg played for me, if I remember correctly we had 17 games in 23 days. Those are just numbers to you. But, when you're the player and you're eight or nine or ten games into this season, spending night after night after night on a plane, in a car and in a hotel; it takes on a whole different significance. And, I don't know how many games into the season we were, but I know that

two nights before we were against USC, we were at Cal State San Bernadino, and the next thing I know we're driving eight hours through the night, in the snow, to get to Northern Arizona in Flagstaff, at an atltitude of over 5,000 feet; with a crew that had been beaten up pretty good. We had our share of injuries, and we were shorthanded. And, Gregg played point guard from buzzer to buzzer. And I play this tape for young athletes now and I talk to them about commitment and hard work, because there were literally times in that game when I had people telling me, 'You gotta take that kid out or he's gonna die.' And, yet I'd stand up and say 'do you need a rest?', and he ran by the bench one time and I was sure he was about ready to pass out. And I asked him again if he needed a rest. And he took a look at the bench and realized that we didn't have anybody else that could play the point; and said, 'No, I'm ok.' That takes a lot of courage. That has nothing to do with conditioning. That has to do with heart. A very good example of the character and the kind of person Gregg is."

YouTube*.com/MentalAthlete*

Full Disclosure: High Five vs. NAU ~ Half-time Intervention

Rick Curtis: "Tell the full story G'. We're in lay-up lines and an NAU player is along the sideline next to us talking to a female in the stands. G's Man!"

I jog to the far sideline and Rick is waiting for me, pointing to the stands and yelled at ME!

"Isn't that your guy talking to that girl? The altitude has him thinking he doesn't even need to warm-up to handle you! A Sign of Disrespect, G'MAN!"

"G' taunted and tormented 'Playa' relentlessly. Once, he dribble up near our bench and said, 'Is your girl watching? I'm gonna take you over there so she can get a good look. Then, I'm takin' your weak ass straight to the hole.' And, that's exactly what he did! Gene heard G' and asked, "Whats the deal?" They all pointed to me. So, I told Gene about my halftime rant. He laughed!"

Gene summoned me, "Rick just informed me of the your situation. Don't let up. Do Him!"
Rick: "Put the NAU clips on Youtube for all to see, G'man! Film Don't Lie!"
We hit the club that night. 'Playa' and 'fan babe' were there! They left abruplty. **Good D'!**

May 1993: Moms Good Karma from the 50th state to the 49th!

Dec. 1986: My UHH B.A. degree secured, I had one free semester on scholarship. My mom insisted that I take some prudent coursework. I chose a Jr. Achievement businesss course at Waiakea High School. The course instructor was Barry Toniguchi, G.M. at KTA SuperStores Supermarket. Barry and I bonded quite well. He was a true Vulcan fan and a very astute businessman who was a fan of my game and my humility. Our J.A. venture was to create a board game similar to Monopoly with Hilo businesses as the real estate and the game cards had 'Pigeon English' translations. Our company also bartered services to create a limited production of 100 actual games. A memorable business triumph. **Mahalo Mom!**

May 1992 UHH Graduation: Janet K. Scott, (age 54) B.A., English. Mission Accomplished!

The Regents of
The University of Hawaii
on the recommendation of the Faculty at
University of Hawaii at Hilo
have conferred upon
Janet Kathryne Scott
the degree of
Bachelor of Arts
English
with all its privileges and obligations
Given at Hilo, Hawaii, this sixteenth day of May,
nineteen hundred ninety-two

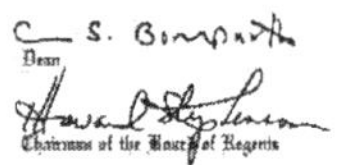

Dec. 1992: My mom had relocated to Hilo in '88. Her name was one of hundreds of entries in the KTA SuperStores 'Mega Sweepstakes' bin, with dozens of fabulous prizes to be awarded, one by one. Lastly, the Final Grand Prize was the most coveted. Someone dug into the bin and then announced, **Janet K. Scott.**

Janet K. Scott: English Teacher at Kapiolani Elem. School in Hilo.

Barry Toniguchi told me later via phone, "Gregg, hearing her name being called truly gave me 'chicken-skin'. And, I instantly thought of you. It was 100% legit, brah. I witnessed it with my own eyes. It was amazing."

The Grand Prize was a 7-day 5-Star Tour, Rail & Cruise thru Alaska!

May 1993: Scott Vacation ~ 2-day railroad tour of our 49th state to Anchorage. Visits to Juno, Denali Nat'l. Park, Iditarod Exhibitions & Salmon Hatcheries.

A 3-night cruise aboard a Holland America ship thru Glacier Bay, Sitka then to Vancouver. In Vancouver, a visit to Chinatown and an untold G' solo night out!

Moms Belief

I'd rather be lucky than good! "G', as for you in sports; be both!"

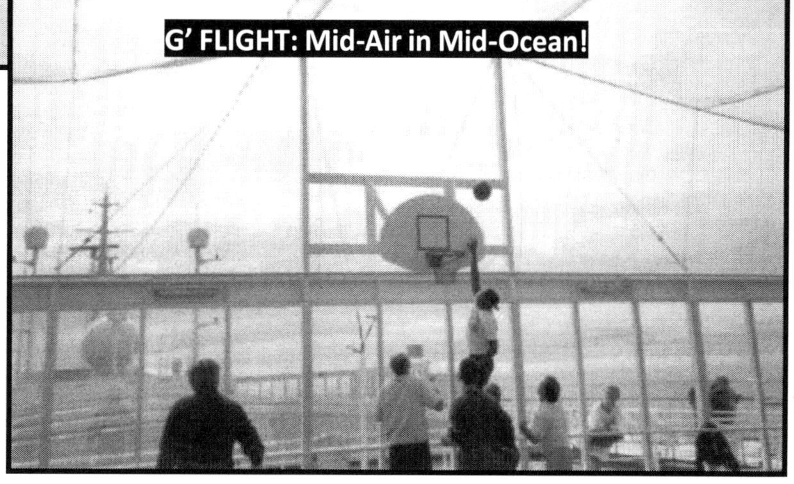

G' FLIGHT: Mid-Air in Mid-Ocean!

On Let's Make a Deal mom was chosen by Monte Hall and won a Club Med trip to Tahiti (& 7 pc. PINK luggage long before it was vogue).

On Bowling for Dollars she introduced Mark and me to host and Laker broadcaster Chick Hearn. Got a 9 spare!

When I was 9 our family went to a L.A. Kings game at the Forum. Late in the game my Dad wanted to leave early to beat the traffic. My Mom insisted we wait because there was a ticket raffle for 10 prizes at the games end. Sure enough, my ticket was the chosen! Mark and I played on that premium 4'x6' NHL HOF "Bobby Hull" Hockey Game for many years!!!

G' HOOPS: Aboard H.M.S. Rotterdam
G'$ Pure Jump Shot: On Land, Or At Sea!

1ST USA & RUSSIAN MIX COACHED BY GOMELSKY

A Collection of Ballers!!!

HIGH FIVE AMERICA

Winning what counts…a drug free America

We lost by 9 against Cal
***Jason Kidd: DNP (knee)**

NO	NAME	POS	HT	WT	LAST SCHOOL
1	Dennis Churavlev	F	6-9	234	Ukraine (Russia)
2	Igor Molchnov	C	6-10	249	Ukraine (Russia)
3	Demetrius Laffitte	G	6-5	202	Long Beach State
4	Shaun Manning	G	6-2	179	Universtiy of Laverne
5	Deshang Weaver	F	6-7	195	California State - San Bernadino
21	Steven Rousseau	G	6-5	200	Ferris State University
22	Greg Scott	F	6-4	185	University of Arizona/University of Hawaii-Hilo
23	David Fulmer	F	6-7	210	University of Californi-San Diego
24	Matt Hancock	G	6-2	190	Colby College
25	Mark Miller	C	6-10	220	San Diego State University
31	Tim Kareen	C	6-11	229	Kentucky Wesleyan
33	Rick Curtis	F	6-9	275	Brigham Young University

Head Coach: Gene Heliker   Asst. Coach: Alexander Gomelsky

High Five vs. Cal Berkley: I closed-out on Lemond Murray and he beat me to the middle. I yelled help. Igor, our Russian center, contested him. OMG! Murray put his 'sac in Igor's mouth with a sic poster dunk as poor Igor slide into the cheerleaders. His bewildered look made me feel so sorry.

"In the early nineties a gentleman showed up on our doorstep named Alexander Gomelsky, after the political and social structure changed in Russia, and he coached here for quite some time. And, it didn't take long for me to realize that in Russia they embrace their young athletes. That's why they had been so successful in the Olympics for so many years and had won so many Gold medals. We had a complete misinterpretation of how they treat young athletes. They mentor and they nurture. Their understanding of child psychology and sports psychology in the development the young athlete is mega-years ahead of us. And, myself, and the players that were around, Gregg included, we were all just drawn to this man like a moth to the flame, because of his ability to nurture and teach young athletes. That's also what lit the fire in Gregg in terms of his program, 'The Mental Athlete'. Gomelsky's influence on both of us, we were like kids,

we would sit around the campfire and listen to this guy talk for hours. It had nothing to do with 'boxing out', the profile of a shot or a motion offense. It had to do with nurturing the athlete. Gomelsky once said to me, 'In America we look for a God-gifted, talented athlete, and we don't care what's in his head or in his heart. If he represents dollars and can sell shoes, we're ready to rush him through the system just as hard as we can go'. Gregg's goal is to change that. It's an honorable goal and Gomelsky had a lot to do with that. To be perfectly honest with you, Gomelsky loved Gregg very uniquely, as a great player, and just like a son."

YouTube*.com/MentalAthlete* ~ 'Gomelsky Impact'

THE PEDIGREE OF A COMPLETE PLAYER

"I've had a lot of people ask me about Gregg Scott as a player. And, I've had some of those players who can just wow a crowd time after time after time. It's very easy for me to answer the question about Gregg Scott as a player. When he's on the floor you win. When he's on the bench anything can happen. He's played everything from point guard to power forward. He's played hurt. He's stepped onto a court, because of other things going on in his life, without having had a lot of practice time with us, and you would never know it. He's the kind of player that at the end of a game I would always find myself looking at the stats going Gregg had 18; how did that happen. His man only had 4. There were just things about the complete game that you always found in Gregg. And every basketball team that goes to a championship has one or two or three; hopefully as many of those players as you can get on it. Everybody loves the dunker. Everybody loves the 'stroker'. But, without those complete players on your basketball team you prabably don't get through the conference and you certainly don't get through the playoffs."

"He's gifted, coachable, a great teammate; above all a WINNER."

ALOHA HIGH FIVE: 3 GAMES & 9 DAYS IN HAWAII

Hawaii Pacific University ~ University of Hawaii ~ UH-Hilo

Gene Heliker gave me the ultimate gift in scheduling our long (vacation) road-trip. The opportunity to play agianst HPU and D-1 UH in the Blaisdale Arena was great! But, returning to my alma-mater UHH representing High Five America: Blessing!

Gomelsky and two Russian players were traveling with Rle, so Gene invited Mike Coleman to play with us, per my personal request. Dual Retribution! Sadly, Mike had work conflicts.

HIGH FIVE AMERICA

Winning what counts...a drug free America

NO	NAME	POS	HT	WT	LAST SCHOOL
3	Demetrius Laffitte	G	6-5	202	Long Beach State
4	Shaun Manning	G	6-2	179	Universtiy of Laverne
5	Deshang Weaver	F	6-7	195	California State - San Bernadino
21	Steven Rousseau	G	6-5	200	Ferris State University
22	Greg Scott	F	6-4	185	University of Arizona/University of Hawaii-Hilo
23	David Fulmer	F	6-7	210	University of Californi-San Diego
24	Matt Hancock	G	6-2	190	Colby College
25	Mark Miller	C	6-10	220	San Diego State University
31	Tim Kareen	C	6-11	229	Kentucky Wesleyan
33	Rick Curtis	F	6-9	275	Brigham Young University

Head Coach: Gene Heliker

Hawaiian Air: "Welcome High Five America & UHH Alum G.S.!"

We arrived, acclimated and conquered HPU by 12 two nights later. Off day. Next, we had the Rainbow Warriors with all my peeps in the house. It was ON! I was ballin' well and in a legit shoot-out with their star guard. Crunch Time: 3 frigin' 100% phantom calls in a row! On Me! I'd only fouled out of ONE game ever (Paraguay). Dismissed! I had to walk out into the tunnel for a few minutes to calm myself down. Refs Won! We lost by five. Mahalo!

Return to the Big Island ~ Bobby's Kona Crib ~ Moms Potluck

With three days "off", I took the team around the entire island. Hilo, to Waikoloa, Hapuna Beach, Mauna Lani Hotel, Hyatt Waikoloa, and Kona. I called Bobby Dudley to say hello. **Bobby: "Greggo', we're on Oahu. You know where a key is. Stay over, Brah."** My team and I stayed at Bobby's (then) $1M+ custom oceanview home. **Sent A Bouquet!**

Two nights later, Mom hosted a potluck and we trounced UHH! **MOM was SO PROUD!**

3 ON 3 STREETBALL HYSTERIA

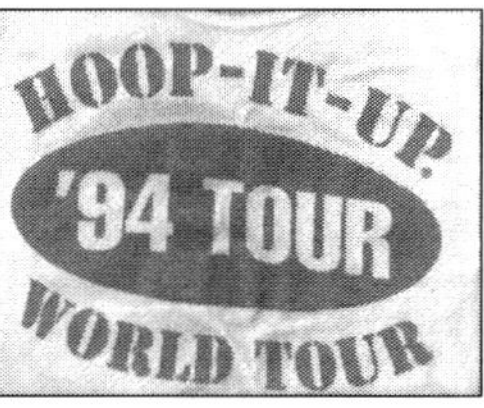

Gus Macker Tourney ~ Hoops at the Beach ~ Hoop-It-Up

This is another animal: Playing on the blacktop, just like at the park back in the day. Not all players can transition to the 3-on-3 bump and grind. This is a realm of hoops that will test your intestinal fortitude. Guts and Nuts (in a Sac, not a Shell). The meek, weak or faint of heart will be exposed and exploited. Ditto that for finesse players! **It's STREETBALL!**

"Still Got It': 1994 Gus Macker CHAMPIONS!

Qualcomm Stadium

Zach Jones & G'$ ~ Gus Macker Finals!

There was no celebration, just ultimate relief and an embrace only teammates can comprehend. Mike had sacrificed his body, absorbed back-to-back games of punishment in our apt scheme to double-team Zack. A man approached us and introduced himself and his U12 son, Matt. **Matt: "My Dad saw you score 50 points in a game at the La Jolla JCC. 50!"** Dad: "So, I was very surprised to see you out here. I told Matt about your skills and to watch how you work. We stalked you all day yesterday. Last night, he asked if we could skip church to watch you today. We never do that. But, Matt reminded me it was my idea in the first place. So, we came early this morning. I must tell you, he was heartbroken when you guys lost the first game. I told him its double-elimination. Let's see how they respond. The way you three battled and competed today will never be forgotten! Classy Champions!"

CLUTCH: G' $avior Free Throw!

Victory Hug: G' & Mike - Dave

Mike: "We are 3; no sub. **Semi-finals: I fouled out. 2-on-3!** It's game point! G' stole their inbound pass, took 2 guys, got fouled and hit a **Saviors** free throw!"

G'$: SAAB 930S Turbo

CHAMPIONS HARDWARE

MARCH 1994 ~ INDEPENDENCIA, MEXICO

YouTube*.com/MentalAthlete:* Global Hoops Montage

CLUTCH: Film Don't Lie!

In the video the first half clips are a nice dunk, nice dime, nice trey! Misleading, as I was in a funk of my own creation. Why? Fouled in the act of shooting, I was at the free throw line where I'm $! Went through my routine three-bounce dribble and on the third bounce it hit a 'dead spot' on the court and I mishandled the ball briefly. As I hesitated, I pondered taking an additional dribble. Nope. Idiot! I missed it and was so furious that I missed the second shot as well! Blasphemy that I carried forward. I had not missed two free throws since my Purgatory Jr year at ECR! Then, with the clock winding down I raise up to shoot a 3, get hit, you hear the whistle blow followed by the horn. Film Don't Lie. The 'home' referees ruled no foul. Halftime. I slammed the ball to the floor and walked to the bench as the cameras zoomed in on us. Fuming at myself, the refs and the fact that the score was tied. We had a legit foe to slay.

> **"Gregg Scott scored 45 points in the last ballgame here and he comes into tonight's contest shooting over 50% from the field. He's just having an uncharacteristic night. And, just as I say it, he puts it in. Nothing but oxygen for Gregg Scott." ~ Mike Benson ~**

Film Don't Lie: G'$ Tourney Champion & MVP! ~ Prelude: Magic

Magical: The next day while leaving our hotel, a man from **Pro Serve** sports agency was waiting for me in the lobby. He gave me his card, took my info and said he'd be in touch.

MAGIC! A FORUM SCRIMMAGE INVITE FROM EARVIN!

Pro Serve Agent: "Earvin is having a formal scrimmage at the Forum and I told him about you. Magic has personally invited you to come and workout."

Yes, the 'Pro Serve agent was true to his word. Magic's Travelling All-Star team was his pride and joy at that time and he wanted a select group to have a live scrimmage against. He got me Magic's invite based on my gritty MVP performance in a game in Mexico. Prophetic.

The Fabulous Forum

I gushed with pride as I gave my name to the guard who directed me to the players parking, underground in the belly of the **Showtime** Mecca. The Forum! Unforgettable! An empty arena was buzzing with activity. I did gawk at the championship banners and HOF jerseys that adorned the rafters above. I was a 'B' grade baller in heaven. Then, I got into G' Mode and focused on the task at hand as I walked out onto the court. I met the organiser who was the same 'Surfer Baller' who ran the show at Pauley Pavillion whom Michael Cooper had introduced me to. He remembered me, which gave me clout. The All-Stars warmed up at one end and our 'scout team' at the other. Then, Magic appeared! What a special moment that was for me. I recall being in the parking structure of Bankers Equity, in tears, listening to 'The Announcement' of his retirement years ago. He looked GREAT! Blessed!

Game Time: Magic Elated Puig, "Would you be Timekeeper?"

Four 10 minute quarters. The All-Stars on Magics squad were all legit ex-pros. We start ballin'. I was dialed in and playing well. I hit one real deep '3' from the corner and stumbled off the arena court as Magic stopped the game to make sure I was ok. Very Cool. Later, Reggie Theus and I matched up tor awhile and had memorable convos of our mutual love of tennis and my lament not to play QB at his alma mater UNLV. Prophetically, it was a convo we would revisit in 2015; in Las Vegas! By the 4th quarter I was a one-man show as my team got fatigued. Magic ended the scrimmage. **Magic: "Thank you, Gentlemen. It appears that only ONE of you is truly in supreme condition. That's what it takes." They had a '3' point contest. As one of his 'Stars?' shot 2 ugly 'bricks', Magic stated, "It's never gonna happen." His initials: D.B. His name rhymes with: Neon Frown! DB had trash-talked Mike prior to playing us in the Gus Macker! <u>Mike Served Him!</u>**

As I left the Forum, my cell phone rang. Pro Serve Agent: "You're invited to return!"

G'$ SHOE PROMO TRIP: SAN FRANCISCO, MEXICO??!!

My MVP performance in Independencia, Mexico had led to two hookups. The Pro Serve Sports Agent…Magic connection was the next morning. Yet, immediately after the game, I met a lady named Priscilla who offered me a 5-day 'gig' to rep a basketball shoe branded by a company named "Runners" who had a (knockoff) model, The Bump (Rebook Pump). They would pay me to fly deep into Mexico for an annual "Zappataria", major shoe bazzar that lasted three days, just for me to walk around in their shoes and meet people. That's it!

Skeptical G'$: All Money Ain't Good Money ~ Sounds Too Good!

The details of the trip were worrysome. I would leave my car at Priscilla's gated home in Chula Vista, be driven across the U.S. Border to the Tijuana Airport, fly several hours and meet her cousin, Cesear, upon arrival. **Sounded like a movie plot to me!** I trusted in her.

As I depatrted TJ airport, all was well. I was blessed by whom I randomly sat next to. A 20-year old kid wearing a surgically implanted 'halo' screwed into his skull. He had survived a horrible car accident. "Lucky to be alive." The most amazing LIFE convo I've ever had!

Once in S.F., Mexico, I met Cesear and everything went just as proimised. Cuz was great. **The shoe was great as well.** It pumped up via a Bump Ball on the tongue just above a hidden spot for a 9V battery to power **lightbulbs** around the heels! **Very Cool Kicks!**

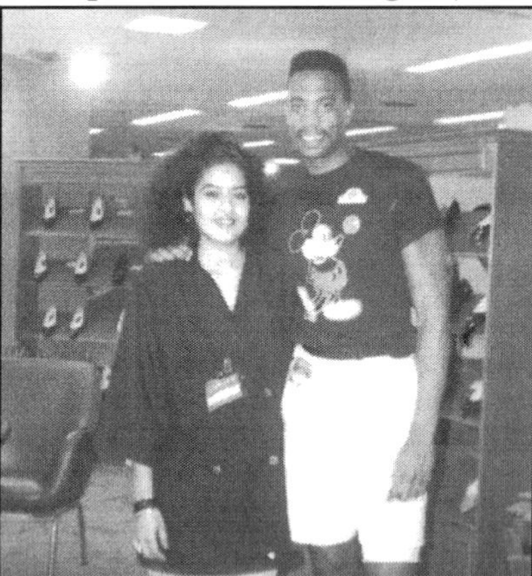

With a 5-star hotel and treated to fine fare & FAV tacos! **All Premium and Better Than I Imagined.**

They also had a huge MJ #23 poster with Jordan in a RUNNS jersey. **Copyright???**

My pay was correct. My return was safe. And, my car was ok!

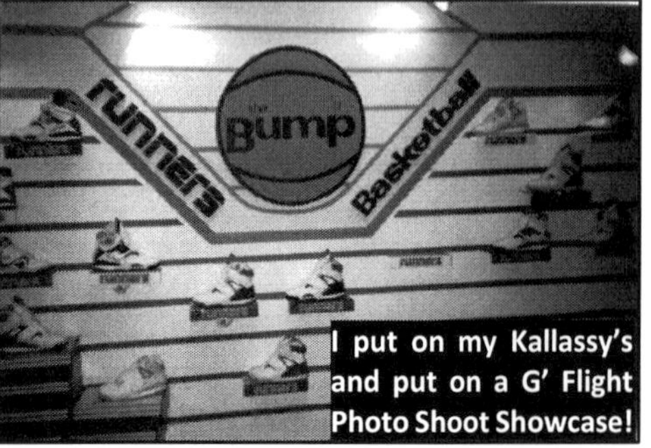

I put on my Kallassy's and put on a G' Flight Photo Shoot Showcase!

Black Mickey T': '96 Controversy

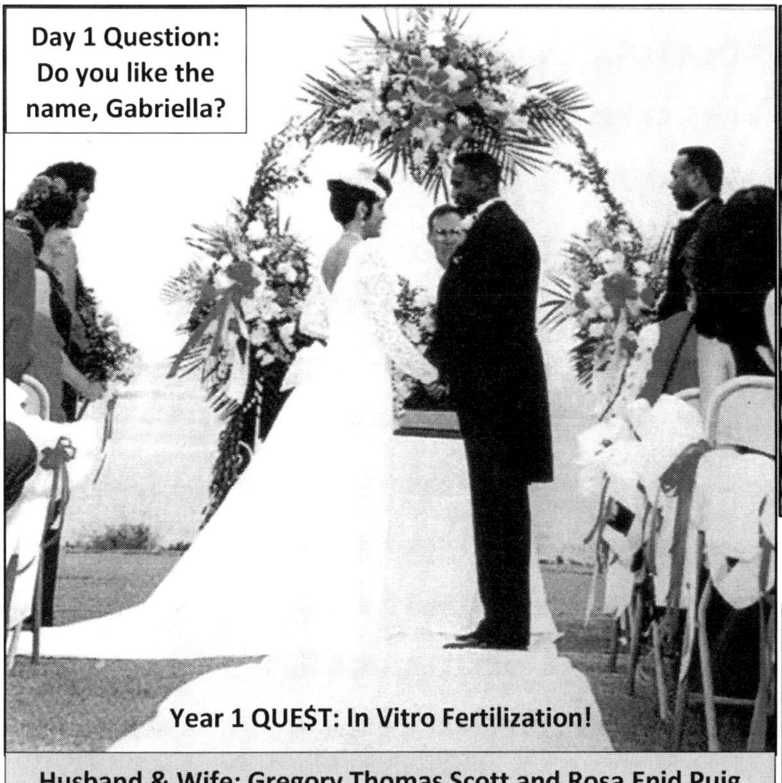

Day 1 Question:
Do you like the
name, Gabriella?
Year 1 QUE$T: In Vitro Fertilization!

Husband & Wife: Gregory Thomas Scott and Rosa Enid Puig

Sparks put his movie on a 24 hour hiatus to be my Best Man!

Proud Groom & Lovely Bride

HOLY MATRIMONY ~ 1994

Sept. '93 TGIF The Red Lion Hotel. Voila! Rosa Puig, an engineer from Puerto Rico, was a civilian GPS Navigation guru for SPAWAR under the U.S. Navy command in S.D.

I called her 'Puig' from day one, and throughout this book.

Best G' Men: Michael Coleman and Don Sparks

Mark, Mom, G', (Aunt) Peggy & Dave Lewis

ABOVE THE RIM: BRAND & PIONEER

Bobby Capener requested my G' Hoops Quotes for ATR Gear:

The fans can make you famous
A contract can make you rich
The press can make you a superstar
But only the LOVE can make you a player!

Somewhere, someone is practicing and when you meet him in head to head competition...

He'll Beat You.

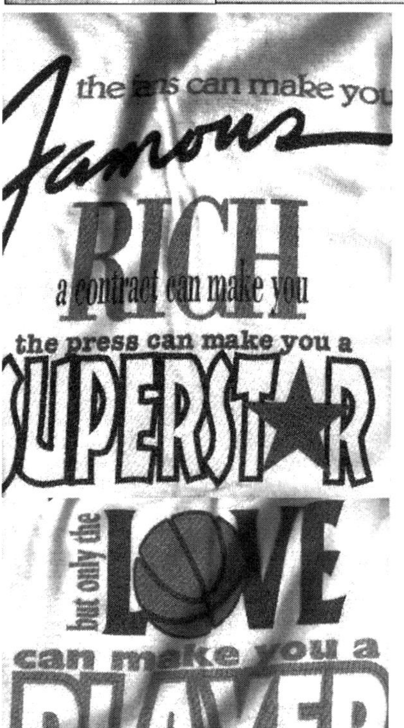

Two Mantra T-shirts! Still in my possession, and still the core of my G' Hoops <u>obsession!</u>

<u>Untold True Tale!</u>
Bobby's ATR Brand was sold to Reebok for Million$. Soon mis-managed; gifted back to him. 'All Net': More Million$!

'94 Hoop-It-Up 3 on 3 Palm Springs

G' Sporting ATR Hoopwear & Nikes!

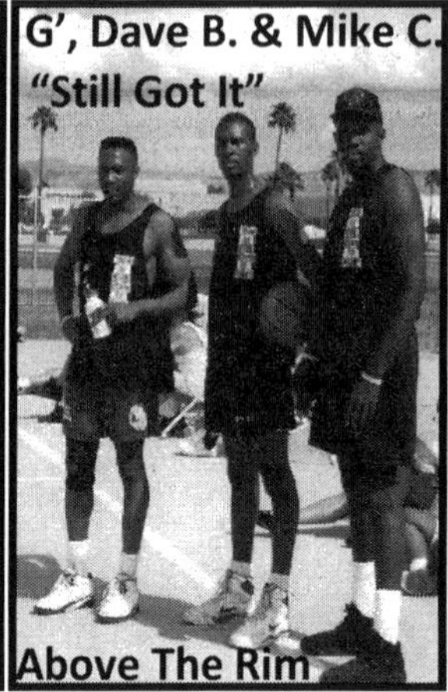
G', Dave B. & Mike C. "Still Got It"

Above The Rim

Bobby Capener: High 5 America teammate! My close friend, sponsor, and a legit baller! ATR: A precursor to And1 & Under Armour!

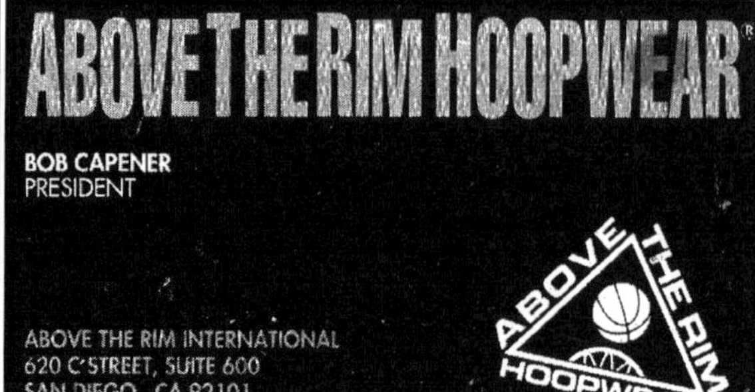

Dishonorable & Hilarious
YOUR GAME'S AS UGLY AS YOUR GIRL
"YOUR GAME'S AS UGLY AS YOUR GIRL"
AND 1
YOU'RE JUST LIKE YOUR GIRL
EASY TO SCORE ON.
AND 1
WHEN SHIRTS TALK
See It 2 Be It... The Mental-Athlete
Note to All: G'$ does not wear, chant nor endorse Trash Talk!
I bought this T-shirt & Cap decades ago! Never worn!
I wore my brother's gift of a poster dunk T-shirt that chanted: "Ya Better Ask Somebody" (front) "Get Paid" (back)
Mark's Gift: GameSpeak G'$ TRUISM

PROTOTYPE

"Well I don't want there to be a contradiction here. When I said 'when he's on the floor we win, when he's not...' Everybody wants to win. So, if you ask me what first interested me about Gregg Scott, I'm going to tell you that; I was asked to go compete against major universities, and to play international tournaments against some of the best players in the world. And, never on a home court. Not with my team of choice, usually. And, to be quite honest with you, I wanted him there because when he was on the floor we had a pretty good chance. But after spending time with him, and seeing the sacrifices that he made; getting off of his job and traveling, and giving up his pay while donating his time. And sitting in the back of the bus talking to a young kid who had a temper problem, and relating to him. Or had parental problems. And, the timing was perfect as it was at the same time that Alexander Gomelsky showed up. I began realizing that Gregg was the prototype of the product that I wanted to come out of my program. If I'd worked with a young athlete from 7th grade through high school and through college. And, he had been through all the struggles that we know young athletes do. And he had grasped it, grabbed it and run with it. Did his very best and turned out to be one of those people that you just loved and admired. Here was somebody that had already struggled through there and had somehow made that happen for himself. Here was a prototype handed to me, and I knew that I could turn to any mother or father and say, 'I'm going to have your child work with Gregg Scott', and feel that mission would be accomplished. Whether that kid ever played on a winning basketball team or not. The character, the integrity, the commitment, the conviction; I soon knew that I was on to something very, very special. From that point in time I knew that I'd be glad to beat USC, and happy that Gregg helped us to win.

But, I was more interested in Gregg's future. Because I knew that he was going to have a tremendous impact on all the kids that I'd be working with from then until the end of time. I immediately went from Gregg Scott helps me win basketball games, to Gregg Scott is the kind of person that I want to be associated with in the world of sports."

"I wouldn't agree that he was looking for somebody to dunk on. A complete player will find a way to be successful whether he scored 18 or 2. And if Gregg got into a game and was struggling you didn't have to pull him out and talk to him. Gregg could coach himself. The defensive intensity picked up. I have a saying. I tell other coaches and players. 'Give me a guard that will rebound and I can win basketball games.' Gregg would do that one little intangible all the way through the game. Rebound over a bigger player. Block the shot of bigger player. Do all those things that help you as a player to get you as back into the game. And, in reality the game never really got away from you totally. Having said that, when you least expected it, he would do something that would bring you to your feet. And, you'd find yourself saying, 'That was Gregg?' Because he always had the physical ability to do so. He used it with taste and he used it with class. There was never any arrogance about it. So, I never really felt that he was out of the game. He could tell me he was having a bad day. Yet, you got to the end of the game, you could still pick up the stat sheet and whether he had scored double-figures in points or not, there was still something on there that lead to the reason that you won, or stayed in the game."

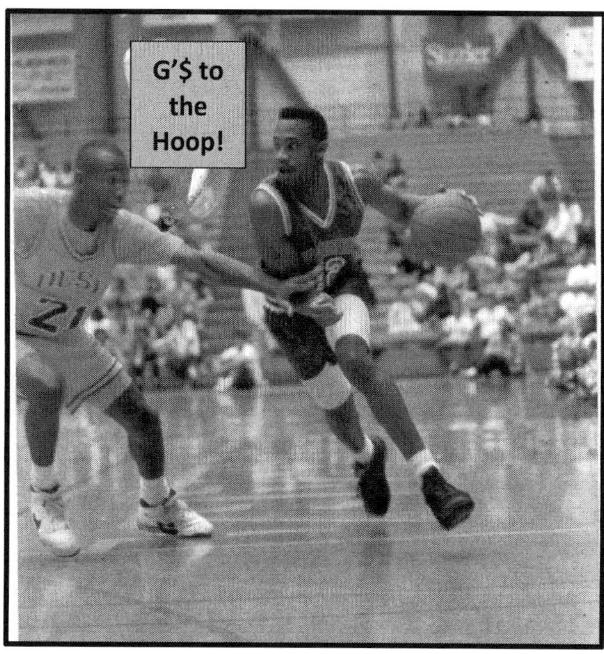

DECREE: COACH MIDNIGHT BBALL & 'POTUS'!

"We went through all the political, which were innumerable, to get to where we could host the first Midnight Basketball league here in San Diego. And at midnight in a not so nice part of San Diego in a gym were 286 kids off the streets; 17 to 25 years old. We were all nervous. I'm telling you that story because there was a certain mentality in that gym. And a nice upper middle-class Caucasian American coach like myself had some learning to do. It was an invaluable asset to be able to turn and see that standing on your right and on your left were people who had been there and done that. And could teach us how to communicate. And, out of this we created an inner society of Midnight Basketball. And, their mentors were people like Gregg Scott, who could talk to them, reason with them, motivate them, put them into a team, put them on the floor and amazingly turn this group of *'Top-Ten Most Wanted'* into surprisingly good basketball players. And, out of that over forty of those kids came up through that system, thanks to people like Gregg, went back into school, went back into the work life. We put over 40 of those kids into 4-year colleges on sports scholarships. I'd like to take a huge amount of credit for that but that would be wrong. The skill which they respected, the backgrounds which they identified to, the ability to communicate- which I'm sure was as educational for Gregg as it was for me- are all things now we draw from when talk about Mental Athletes or developing the young athlete. He, the first time in, took a group of athletes, not necessarily the best players and... ***True Tale Continued: EAGLE**

On draft day, Coach G' told us how his methodology:

***'I don't want to Coach any of the* 10 Best Players!**

***I want to Coach and Cultivate the* Best 10 Players!'**

'I Coach Like I Compete; Solely to Win Championships.'

COACH G' MEETS THE 'POTUS' SECRET SERVICE

Two weeks into the season Gene summoned me to a meeting at the High Five HQ in Rancho Bernardo to discuss a "scheduling change for a specific Midnight League game". I (silently) wondered why a 'scheduling change' would require my presence in a meeting.

I arrived at High Five HQ ten minutes early. Now, being bred in L.A., I still note 'Narco' undercover cars, CA exempt plates and on this day, the U.S. Government plated vehicles in the parking lot. Yet, given the circumstances I didn't give them a second thought. Ha!!! In the reception area Gene comes to escort me into the 'meeting'. He only said, "FYI, I was sworn to secrecy on the specifics of this meeting, okay?" Bamboozling was looming. As we enter a conference room I instantly notice the trio of well-suited clean-cut men, all standing, staring politely, yet, not smiling. Quickly linking them to the government cars, I pondered that their attire was too elegant for 'detective level'; so these 'Feds' were either the FBI or CIA. The tenor was tangibly serious for a supposedly benign schedule change.

I shake hands with High Five president and head coach, Rle Nichols, and he introduces me to the group. "Gentlemen, this is Gregg Scott." I can't contain my curiosity as I say, 'I can not think of any good reason that I'm here right now'. '*Head Fed*' then speaks, "Mr. Scott I'm Special Agent '*Joe Blow*', this is Special Agent '*Jim Blow*', and he is Special Agent '*John Blow*'. We're with the United States Secret Service." Whatda heck is going on here?? "The Midnight Basketball League is a government sponsored program and in a couple of weeks the head of our government will be in Coronado for a few days. So, we would like to confirm that you will make yourself available on (x) date/time to coach your team. On that day, President Clinton will be making an appearance at the venue and will participate briefly in the first half of an actual game; and Sir, he is going to be playing on your team." I utter, 'Well whos bright idea was that?', as Gene chuckles an 'I told ya so' type of laugh. Yes, some may consider this an honor. Not me. I wanted no part in it, honestly. "You've been previously **vetted** as a government employee in 1988 in Hawaii, and you apparently have a highly disciplined team that will pay due respect beffiting the President." Truism!

Since there was no question mark in his statements, I was being informed; not asked. So, in sensing that any rebuttal would be fruitless, I asked two pertinent questions. 'What do you suggest I name the play I'll design for Mr. President? His call sign would be proper.' The trio exchanged glances, then '*Head Fed*' uttered a resounding, "Eagle". Nice moniker! 'My final thought is to ensure Eagle is a success. I know the President writes left-handed, as do I. Yet, I'm ambidextrous. Can you confirm what hand he shoots a basketball with?' '*Head Fed*' replies, "I'll get back to you on that." Meeting adjourned. **EAGLE Tale: p. 168**

BASKETBALL I.Q. BLUEPRINT FOR EXCELLENCE

Unlike a Quarterback. The beauty of basketball is that you match-up at both ends of the court.

The Consummate Team Game of Movement, Flow, Tempo & Timing!

- **Running vs. Sprinting: Go Full Speed & 'Throttle Down'! Footwork!**
- **Change of Pace & Change of Direction on balance! Conceptualize It!**

THE GAME IS EASY. THE PLAYERS MAKE IT HARD!

Ray Mills: I was invited to tryout for High Five. At the gym and they were filming a promo shooting video with only one guy doing all of the shooting. The "G'man" was hitting deep 3's. 7 straight! Then, he casually got the ball, bounced it off the floor, off the backboard, went up and flushed a sic dunk."

THIS IS CHECKERS, NOT CHESS! NOT CHINESE CHECKERS!

Mike: "G came to L.A. to play at my spot, Icess Park. We had held down the court and G' had put in proper work. We had a point guard who kept throwing G' back-door lobs. By our fifth and final game he had atleast 15 dunks. As we scored to get to Game Point, I run back on D' as G' picked up his man with the ball in the backcourt. Then, I saw G'$ Commit Blasphemy!

I'm on D'. Mike stopped the game. "Hold Ball, Yo!" Then, he walked **angrily** towards me.

"Are you hurt, because I know you're not tired? G' said, 'I'm good, Whatup?' Whatup? G'! That man has zero 'handles'! That's WHATUP!. You just let that man lollygag with the ball in the backcourt! I'll tell you what... I turned to the other players and told them: Y'all don't need to play any defense. If that guy beats my guy then they deserve to score. I then told G': Now, get in his ass, take his candy, finish this schiznit, and lets go eat. G' was embarrassed! But, he got in his stance, stole the ball and scored the game-winning layup."

As we got to the sideline I asked Mike: 'Why'd you put that man on blast?' **Big Mistake!**

"Bleep him...! This is about you! This isn't recreation! It's your occupation! You play D' one way without fail! Every damn day! That's why you get paid!"

"We got to our cars. I went over to him and gave him a hug. G', Good Work!"

Defense as your Calling Card

'If you're playing me even then you're out-playing me!'

Defensive Transition: Sprint Back! ~ Stop the Ball! ~ 'Man-up'!

Guards job #1: 'Stop Ball'. Force Change of Direction! Good Footwork! Communicate!

MINDSET: DEFENDING THE BASKET IN A HELPING MAN-TO-MAN SYSTEM!

Know your job! Do your job! Trust your teammates to do their jobs!

Communication: Verbalize and heed verbalization from teammates!

- **Stay between your man and the basket! Keep your man in front of you at all times!**
- **Create Turnovers; not steals! Force opponents to make contested shots. No bailouts!**
- **Your Job: Disallow dribble penetration! Deny the direct entry pass! Nothing more!**

On Ball: Active Hands on a pendulum within your space. Don't reach!!

- **Stance: Bend at the knees, not at the waist. Knees behind toes. Upper body erect.**
- **You're in the woods, gotta go #2; squat and don't get heel stain. Drill: Wall Sits!**
- **Slide your feet (move feet is vague). "Step-Slide" is a verbal cue linked to physical movements, hand position and transfer of body weight in motion.**
- **Drop-Step & Recover: Cut your man off; don't ride him. No Matador Defense!**
- **Active Hands: on a pendulum out and up. Stay within your space. Not lurching.**
- **Ceased Dribble: "Stick" ball pressure w/o reaching. Trace!!! Team in full denial.**

Help-side Defense: See Man & Ball ~ Help & Recover ~ Help the Helper

- **One pass away: ¾ stance, hand in the passing lane w/ thumb down! Deny flash!**
- **Deny: Hand in the passing lane, seal arm up w/ palm on chest. Don't grasp/hold!**
- **Two + passes away: 'PISTOLS' point to ball and to man. Use peripheral vision.**
- **Recognize & Verbalize ~ Rotate & Recover ~ Ball Pressure & Court Awareness Don't foul off-ball. Don't fight for floor position. You are defending the basket!**
- **Show your hands! 'Don't put the whistle in the referee's mouth.' Be Disciplined!**

Execute The Fundamental 'Close-out' Principles & Techniques

<u>A basic fundamental principle often clouded by the 'I/Me' syndrome.</u>

<u>Close-out Principles:</u>

Objective: Neutralize the advantage of a player with the ball and unguarded.

- ***Sprint 2/3 of the way, drop butt, chatter out with hand up, under control.***
- ***Do Not leave your feet unless the shooter does. 'Keep your feet'! <u>CONTEST ONLY!</u>***
- ***Do Not try to block shots! Keep your man in front of you! Fly-by's produce 5 on 4.***
- ***Maintain Stance! Trace ball fakes. Stay down. Arms on a pendulum. Discipline!***
- ***Deny the 'direct post-entry pass'. Active hands within your space. Don't Reach!***
- ***Do Not Allow Dribble Penetration. 'Cut-off' the baseline! Funnel to the sideline!***

Contest
Hand Up
"Shot!"
DON'T FOUL
Block-out
Find the Ball
Rebound
Close-Out
Just Do Your Job

- On ball 'D'
- Stance
- Trace
- Slide Feet
- Don't Reach
- On Balance
- Ball Pressure

<u>Never</u> Foul a Jump-Shooter!!!

<u>'GameSpeak': Loud and Clear!</u>

- A constant opportunity to display fundamental awareness, discipline and skill; or not!
- Final phase of D' is rebounding. Stay between your man and the basket, without fail!
- **Simple Math:** 'Risk vs. Reward' factors dictate fewer fouls and offensive advantages.
  - **33%: 1/3** may = a **block** ~ **1/3** may = a **foul** ~ **1/3** may = **5 on 4 detriment.**
  - **So, 2/3 of the time, 'false hustle' most likely produces a negative result.**
  - **100% of the time it = a demerit for bad defense by coaches and scouts!!!**

The proper execution of the fundamental 'close-out' is a tangible element of a complete player. Gambling by reaching, overreacting to head or ball fakes and blocking jump shots is simply 'fool's gold'. It puts your team at risk and exposes you to the 'give & go' or lost rebounds. **Fact:** 'The Disease of Me' is an invite to foolishly play your way to the bench!

The 'I/Me' Syndrome: Reaching Fouls! Frustration Fouls! Compounding Errors!
<u>Off-ball Fouls:</u> "That player cannot hurt you or score if they Do Not have the Ball."

"No Rebounds, No Rings!" ~ Limit them to ONE shot!

All defensive effort is wasted if not culminated by securing the rebound!
Cerebral Mindset: I may not get it, but my man absolutely will NOT get it!

- ✓ **Block Out! Move your feet! Maintain inside position! Seal! Don't hold or grab!**
  - **'Butt to the Gut'! Get into a body before getting to the ball! Get Physical!**
- ✓ **Protect your space and move your man out! Wide base w/ arms up and out! Big!**
- ✓ **'Locate the ball'. Eyes up while feet are moving. INTESTINAL FORTITUDE!!!**
- ✓ **Anticipate where the ball is most likely to come off the rim based upon:**
  - **Where the shot originated. Does it appear to be short or long? Off glass?**
- ✓ **Maintain contact and go straight up. Verticality includes your arms straight up!**
- ✓ **Avoid senseless fouls. Discretion. Protect Self! Always use two hands if possible!**
- ✓ **Secure the ball. 'Chin it' w/ elbows out. Pivot w/ hips and shoulders. Be Strong!**
- ✓ **Energy, Hustle, Desire, and Aggressiveness are necessary traits. 'Chest Cavity'!**
- ✓ **Timing is just as important as height or jumping ability. Master the jump rope!**

Transition, Fast Break and Delayed Break Principles

- Outlet the ball to a guard. Guards have head up; no automatic dribble. Be Aware!
- Get the ball to the middle of the floor. (Exception: Sideline fastbreak systems).
- **Advance the ball. The ball advnces faster via the pass than on the dribble!**
- Wings: Get wide (sideline), **SPRINT**, stay wide, basket cut at F/T line extended.
- Ball-handler: 3 strong dribbles from outlet spot to front court top of the key area.
  - Pass or jump-stop at or before F/T line. Enter the key; commit to shoot!
- Pass and Cut ~ Move the Ball and Move Your Feet ~ **Maintain Proper Spacing**
- Know what passes to make. Execute your system. Look for and reward the trailer.
- Get a few touches and swing the ball from one side of the floor to other. Critical!!
- Value Possession ~ Be Efficient ~ Meet All Passes ~ Make the Extra Pass ~ Talk

Fastbreak Beauty: Four passes by four players for a layup without any dribbling!!

Transition vs. Full-court Pressure following a made basket

- Recognition! Verbalize! Get all teammates in press-break positions; then inbound!
- Inbound: Clear the key! Run the baseline. Don't inbound under opponent basket!
- Run your press break system based on defense; zone/trapping man-to-man press.
- Guards: Stay out of the corners. Big-men flash to the middle hard; turn and face.
- The baseline and sideline are 'defenders'. Get the ball to the middle of the court.
- Attack Pressure! Run, Pass & Catch! Come to the Ball! **Be Strong With the Ball!**
- **Breaking the Press: Set up your offense and make them play half-court D'.**

Offensive Basketball

Run, Dribble, Pass & Catch ~ Cultivate Ball Handling IQ:

- ***Passing IQ on the dribble. "Don't kill your dribble on the exterior."***

Basic Passing Fundamentals

- **On time and on target: Sharp, Crisp, Accurate and CATCHABLE passes.**
- **Know and execute the correct pass for the situation. Stationary or Moving!**
  - **Chest Pass:**
    - **Forward thrust. Snap release w/ thumbs down. Finish w/ palms out.**
    - **The ball should have a reverse rotation while in flight. Strong Hands!**
  - **Bounce Pass:**
    - **To a spot two-thirds of the way to the receiver. Target is waist high.**
    - **Deliver with either or both hands as the situation dictates. Cultivate.**
  - **Skip Pass**
  - **Overhead Pass**
  - **Diagonal Pass**
  - **Post Entry Pass**
  - **Outlet Pass**

> **"As my Jr. High school coach used to tell me."**
> **'There is no such thing as a Jump Pass.'**
> **Charles Barkley**

Non-Fundamental Errors & Faulty Decision Making

- **Inbound the ball underneath the opponents' basket; I'm yelling this! NEVER!**
- **Pass the ball towards your opponents' basket against any backcourt pressure.**
- **Jump to Pass! See Barkley quote above. Disregard the current NBA example.**
- **Pass the ball <u>through</u> the key. A 'skip pass' is an overhead pass, <u>over</u> the defense!**
- **Feed the low post from above the free-throw line extended. Bad Passing Angle!**
- **Pass to your big men on the move, needing to dribble. Know Your Personnel.**
- **Telegraph passes! Make constant use of head & ball fakes and peripheral vision.**
- **Pass to a teammate going away from you; unless it's a lead pass to your basket.**

Be Smart! ~ Be Strong! ~ Recognize Overplay! ~ Don't Force It! ~ Value Possession!

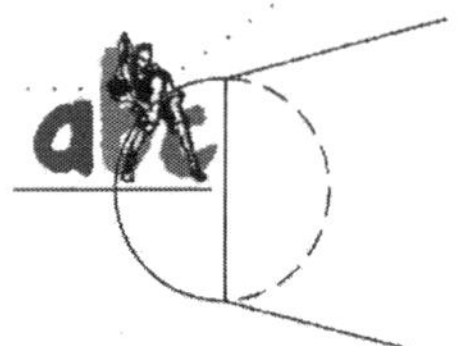

Drills:

- **3-man weave full court. Chest pass or bounce pass. No Dribble**
- **5-man weave full court: Touch Pass. No Dribble. Add 1 Dribble**
- **5-Star Passing- Half-court. Lay-up or shot. Best Interactive Drill.**

OFFENSIVE WITHOUT THE BALL (off-ball O') - EXECUTION

Mental Fundamentals: SPACING ~ TIMING ~ TEMPO ~ SYSTEMS ~ STRATEGY

Know your System! Make the Defense Work. Swing the Ball from Side to Side.

Ball Movement and Player Movement with Purpose! 3 or more passes; swing the ball!

Study the moves of your opponent and the habits of other defensive players who might shift to you in order to decoy them or set them up for your own moves. Be Cerebral.

Ability to fake direction of movement is as important as faking shot or pass. Make your defensive man constantly be adjusting and turn his head away from the ball. Be Coy.

Work for the ball, do not stand and call for it. One man mustn't be able to deny you the ball! 'Step to the Ball': Meet all passes. Secure the ball on balance with good footwork!

Physical Fundamentals: VISION ~ STANCE ~ FOOTWORK ~ BALANCE ~ POWER

If you want to get open set a screen. The screener is always open. Don't fake it. Solid pick.

Move with a specific purpose. Each movement should result in a screen, a passing angle or reception, good rebounding position, or exploiting an opportunity to score. Timing!

Screens: Set (execute) 'solid' screens w/ proper footwork and court position awareness.

- **Set up side screens as close to opponent as possible *without initiating contact*. Erect!**
- **On back (blind) screens, allow the opponent one step backwards. Stay Straight Up!**
- **On ball screens allow the dribbler to rub his man off of you. Stay In Your Space!**
- **ALL SCREENS: Set your feet wide with anticipation of your next movement. Sly!**
    - Pick & Roll: body weight on inside foot, pivot wide, roll, seal, show target hand.
    - Pick and Pop / Pick & Re-pick / Pick and Open Up: body weight on outside foot.
    - Down Screen: body weight on inside foot, get low, pivot strong, seal, show target.

- **Protect yourself setting ALL screens: wide base; erect torso; arms up; across chest.**

Be prepared for a defensive 'Switch'. Recognize and expose the mis-match. Be decisive!

Run your defensive man into and/or off of screens. It's your responsibility. Do Your Job!

'Back Door': Only when defense takes eyes off you, or over-plays on the exterior. Flash!

Seal vs. over-play/fronting defender: Protect space. Release seal when ball is above head!

Move the Ball and Move Your Feet ~ Be a Scoring Threat ~ Square-up ~ Triple Threat!

Shooting ~ Scoring ~ Free-Throws

Triple-threat

Anatomy of a Shot

Concentrated Repitition

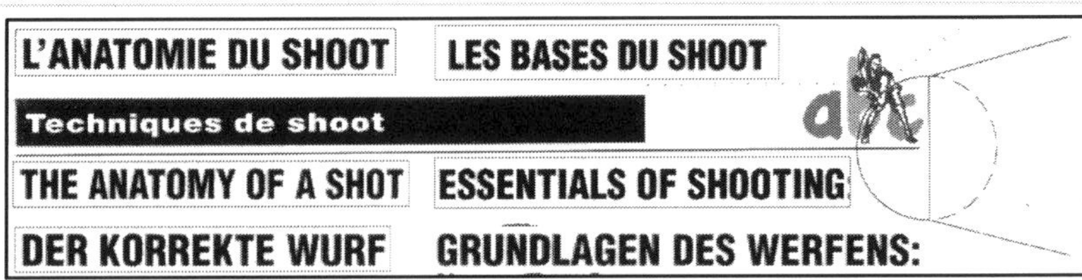

- **It Starts from the Ground, up! Foundation! Wide base. Feet hip-width apart!**
- **Square Your Hips to the Target! 'All around the world; Same Song'. Same shot!**
  - The Target is Not Always the Basket: **The Backboard is Your Best Friend!**
  - **Disregard Squaring Shoulders…! Shooting shoulder is slighty forward.**
  - **Stay in Your Space! Straight Up; Don't Fade/Lean 'Give up Real Estate'**
- **You Shoot with your Legs! Seated Shot Drill ~ Upward Thrust: Feet, Toes, Legs!**
- **Shoot It; Don't Throw It! ~ Shooting Hand Positioning Exercise ~ G'$ Creation!**
  - **Cradle Position: Hold the ball at your side w/ shooting hand underneath.**
  - **Shooting Position: Bring ball up to S/P. Arm parallel to floor. Elbow fwd. Ball is in same hand/grip position with gap between palm. Laces across!**
  - **Return to Cradle Position and back to Shooting Position a few times. Rest**
  - **Shooting Position to Release Point. All energy trajectory and focus is UP! The Ball & Elbow rise several inches UP to the Release Point culminating with the Wrist Flick (up & forward forearm snap). Trajectory: up not at!**
- **Shoot Up, Not At! Hand/Rim Arch application ~ Energy Rising: toes, legs, torso!**
- **Eye the Target! THE RIM IS NEVER THE TARGET! Swish It, Don't Brick It!**
  - **Varies by shot and court location. The far inner net ring of the rim.**
  - **Bank-Shots target a specific spot on the backboard. "Find the Square"**
- **Wrist Flicks Intro: 3 Spots ~ One hand ~ Lace Rotation ~ Arch ~ "No Rim"**
- **Intregrate Guide Hand ~ Bank Shot Intro ~ Shot Selection ~ Mid-Range Game**
- **Astute Footwork: Baseline ~ Pinch Post ~ Inside Post Play ~ Ball & Head Fakes**

Situational Shooting & Shot Selection

"Gregg Scott never saw a shot that he didn't like"
Michael Coleman

- You can shoot 10 variations from 1 spot. Master them All!
- **Both sides of the court. Both near and far!**
- **Pure Sparks: 'Separation Dribble'**

G' Scott can teach ANYONE to shoot!

adidas abc Basketball Camp

I Don't Shoot: Blind Hope Shots ~ Blatant Heat Checks ~ Buzzer-Beater Heaves

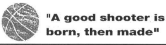

"A good shooter is born, then made"

"Ein guter Schütze wurde zuerst geboren, dann gemacht"

"On ne naît pas bon shooter, on le devient"

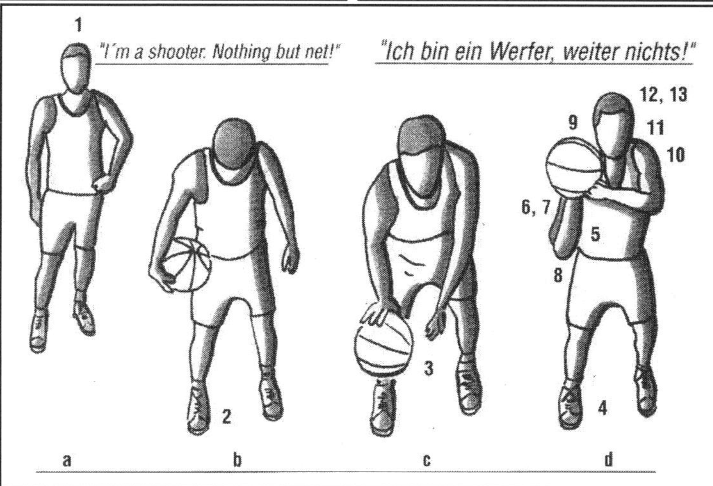

Shooting Techniques Global Hoops

POSITION DE LA MAIN QUI SHOOTE

SHOOTING HAND POSITION

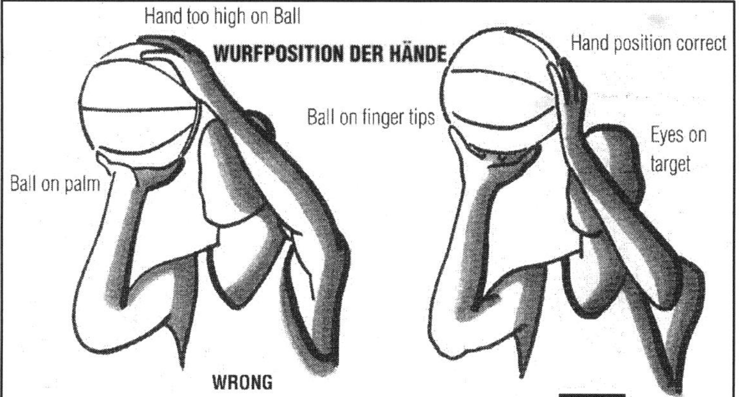

Offensive Rebounding

Mental Fundamentals: Exhibit Your Will

- **GET IN THERE! Don't concede possession. Crash the Boards Hard & Smart!**
- **Allowing a rebound with fewer than 3 offensive players in the key is a sin. Amen.**
- **Be cerebral, with effort and foot movement towards the rim. No 'False Hustle'!**
- **Most teams shoot less than fifty percent; assume that every shot will be missed.**
- **Think of a shot as a loose ball that's in the air. We scrap for ALL loose balls!!!**
- **It's found money! Pads your stats. Increases your court time. Champions mettle!**
- **Provides your team with additional energy and creates 'added possessions'.**
- **The team that controls the boards usually controls the game. Numbers don't lie.**
- **Second and third efforts are imperative. This gritty labor produces much fruit.**

Physical Fundamentals: Intestinal Fortitude

- ✓ **Move your feet to get into rebounding position. Be Hungry!**
- ✓ **Protect your space with arms up and out. Be Aggressive!**
- ✓ **Use purposeful fakes to get inside of or around defensive players.**
- ✓ **'Locate the ball'. Eyes up while feet are moving! Be Active! Be Smart!**
- ✓ **Anticipate where the ball is most likely to come off the rim based upon:**
    - **Where the shot originated.**
    - **The arch of the shot; does it appear to be short or long?**
    - **Is it a bank shot? Anticipate the carom and stay active.**
    - **Intelligence; scan your database of thousands of similar shots; go there.**
- ✓ **Make contact and go straight up. Verticality dictates your arms be straight up!**
- ✓ **Avoid senseless fouls by going over the back of defensive players. Use Discretion!**
- ✓ **If you can't control it, tip it; keep it alive. Be Rational & Be Relentless!**
    - **Note: back-taps can start a break the other way. Be wise.**
- ✓ **Energy, Hustle, Desire, and Aggressiveness are necessary traits. 'Chest Cavity'!**
- ✓ **Timing is just as important as height or jumping ability. Get on your jump rope!**
- ✓ **Be able to tap with either hand around (above) the basket. Convert all easy ones!**

G'$: Offensive rebounding was an engrained fundamental. Heart, a 42" vertical mixed with an ambidextrous 80" wingspan dictates better stats, poster dunks and a fist full of dollar$.

If the Offensive Rebound is Earned: VALUE POSSESSION

- **DON'T think you've earned the right to immediately shoot the ball. Be Smart!**
- **SITUATIONAL AWARENESS**
  - **Cleary, a put-back is correct on an air-ball with an expiring shot clock.**
  - **Just as clearly, down by three with time running out, don't shoot a two.**
  - **If you're within range, with the ability to score, get paid! Finish Strong!**
  - **Depending on skill-set, dribble out or make a smart pass; exit the key.**
  - **Reset and make the defense work. This demoralizes your opponent.**

No Rebound: TRANSITION D! Don't Reach-Don't Foul-SPRINT!

- **Communicate ~ Stop the Ball ~ 'Man-up' ~ Get into your Stance ~ Play Defense**

Dwayne Texas ~ Grambling Univ. ~ Int'l. Pro

Dwayne Texas

"I've said it for two decades. G'$ Scott was a basketball legend in multiple countries on multiple continents long before he exploded in Europe. Great players are hyped and remembered after the game. Legends are hyped and remembered long after they've left the game. Legends perform to give fans memories for life. And, their opponents too! I was in Chile when G' was in Argentina. I got to Buenos Aries and hear about Greggorio Scott. I get to Paraguay and hear about Gregory Scott from fans and the G'man from the players. Including Marvallisio. "Tex, you should have seen this cat named G'!" I fly into Mexico for an All-Star game, their raving about Seneor Scott. Finally, Coach Gene Heliker from High Five America is recruiting me to play. He noted his best player, Gregg Scott. 'Oh! Say no more. Where do I sign?" Day 1 Homies: "I met G'! So cool and humble. On the court he was All That!!"

~ PATRIOT GEAR FIT FOR COACHING POTUS ~

G' COACH: POTUS & HYBRID 'EAGLE'

MBL Draft Round 1: 11th pick! **G' Motto:** Don't Need **The 10 Best**. I Have **The Best 10!**

I wasn't an X's & O's guy. I didn't create schemes and plays just for pleasure. I ran what I was coached. Having spent so many hours on the road in gyms, hotels, planes and cars with Gene, delving deeper into his playbook database, beyond our apt High Five systems, I had a bevay of offenses at my disposal. And, only ONE way to play D'! Fundamentally! My Squad: All cerebral players with discipline. No Stars or Gunners! Worthy of POTUS!!

'Eagle' Game Night: Midnight Hoover High School, San Diego

I had three POTUS security and logistics briefings leading up to Game Night. I also created a special play named **'Eagle'** that was a hybrid of our existing motion offense that would be a perfect misdiretion ploy to guarantee an easy open lay-up for the left-handed POTUS!

Such a night even motivated, early-bird, Puig to come watch me coach President Clinton. As we got close to the school on El Cajon Blvd the Secret Service and police presence was absurd. Helicopters in the air, police cars, SUV's and various law enforcement agencies everywhere. I had proper credentials. Still, the high-tech metal detectors at the entrance to the gym was unnerving to me. **The POTUS Plot**: A first half arrival and a 5 minute cameo.

Patriot Gear: My IXSPA Hoop Tour Jacket! Back: A U.S Flag "Proud to be an American"!

I told my crew to expect POTUS midway through the half. We ran our motion offense to set the table for 'Eagle'. We were playing well and full of anticipation. As the half dwindled down I was bewildered. The half ended without an appearance by the President. When we came out from the lockerroom to start the second half, all of the Secret Service, and all of the security personnel, and the metal dectectors had vanished. Like they had never even been there**. Poof! Presto! Buzzkill!**

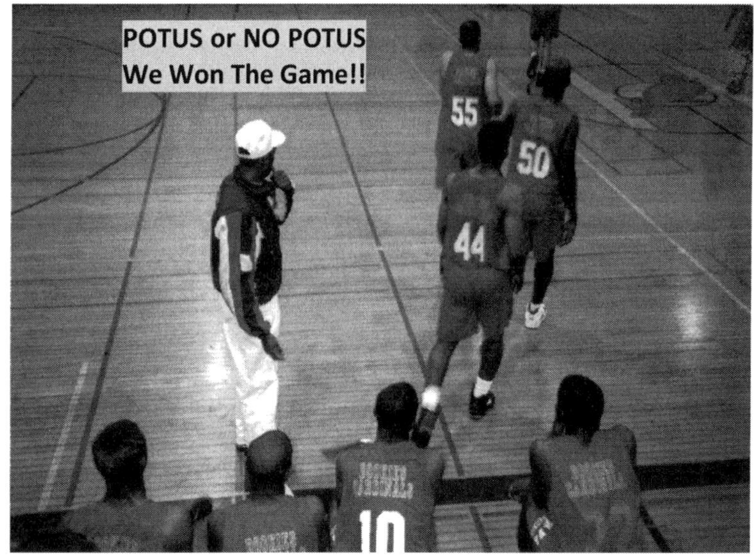
POTUS or NO POTUS
We Won The Game!!
55
50
44
10

I was only told that POTUS was a no-show due to some BS **'Security Trepidation' crap!**

To aliviate my deflated soul, I ran the hybrid motion offense and I chose my own POTUS! **'Run Eagle!' It worked! EZ!**

With the playoffs looming we were in third place going into our final game of the season against the fifth-place team. A good match-up with bracket seedings on the line. In the second half the game got a bit testy and we suffered several bad calls which had my team whining and in an irreversible funk. We lost a very winnable game. I wasn't going to vent on them in front of the fans. But, in the lockerroom I said, **'I hope you all lose sleep tonight! I know that I will. Perform like that again and your season will be over! Your goals and dreams will end in self-inflicted failure! The True Agony of Defeat!'**

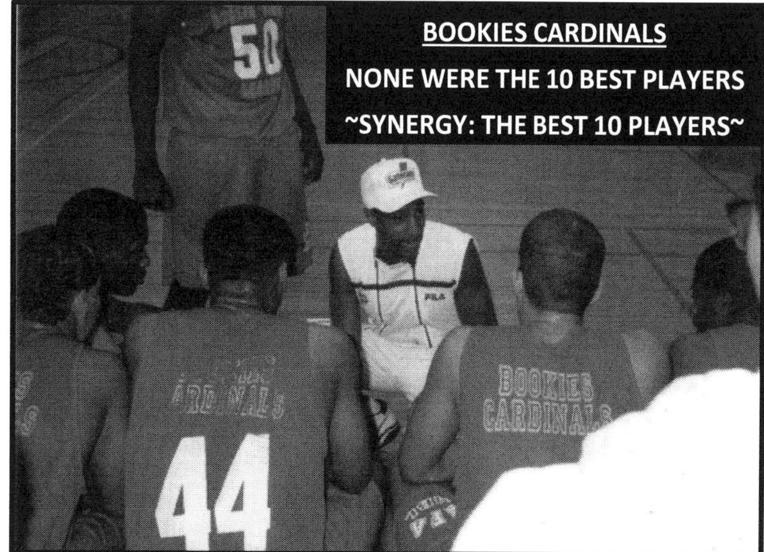

We dominated the playoffs!

The Championship

My crew was all business! In the final minute we're up by 8. I called for Hybrid 'Eagle'! Basket! 'Timeout!' 'Gather in here close men. Breathe very deeply! DNA! You're all breathing in the Air of Champions! Best 10!'

JOSTENS
JOSTENS CHAMPIONSHIP RING
OF THE NBA ~ NFL ~ MLB ~ NHL~
CHAMPIONS

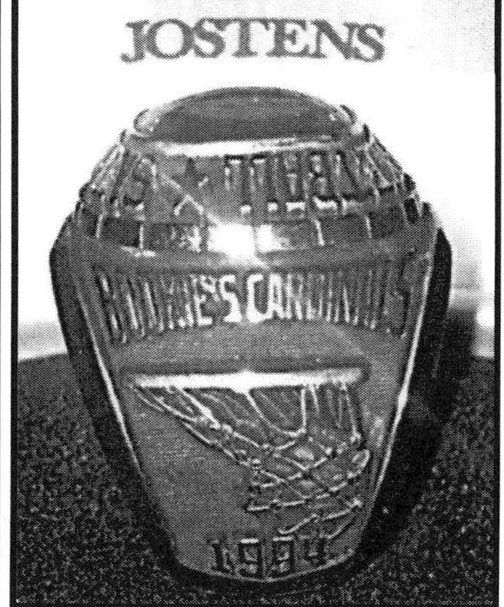

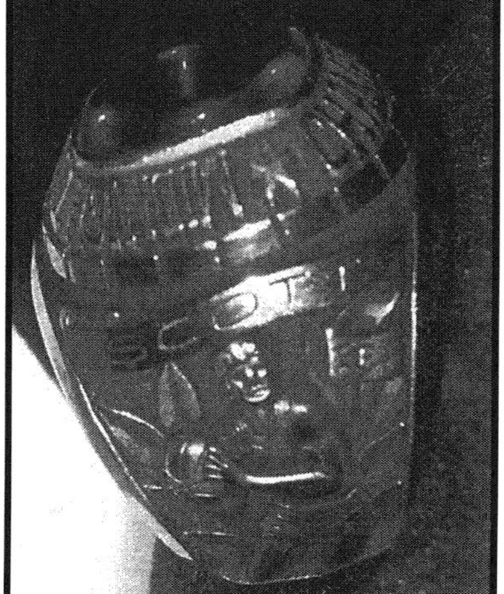

High Five America vs. Cal State Northridge: A Tainted Victory!

Gene scheduled the CSUN game with me in mind. It was in the San Fernando Valley near ECR and close to where my dad lived in North Hills. My brother graduated from CSUN, so Mark, Pops, Don Sparks, Mike Coleman, their wives and all my L.A. peeps were there to see me. A rarity! I performed well in a victory. Yet, overshadowed by one 2nd half play:

I sprint back in transition D' as the bottom defender in the key as a 3-on-2 fastbreak is coming at me. I'm stationed in the middle of the key as their point guard lobs a high pass to their left side of the basket. I instantly knew I couldn't get to it and walked calmly out of the key without even looking back at the ball. All I heard was the crowd go wild. As I looked to where my peeps were sitting I immediately saw Sparks and Mike stand up and walk out of the gym arm-in-arm, giggling. Factually, I had exited the area, I didn't see the finish, and I certainly didn't jump. I was told the dunk was by Keith Gibbs*. *Movie Actor*

Postgame: Sparks and Mike regally gifted me a **"Certificate of G'$ Being Dunked On!"** Signed and dated by my two 'Best Men'. Keith and I bonded at the '94 Hoop-It-Up in OC.

***Keith Gibbs: Blue Chips ~ Celtic Pride ~ The Cable Guy ~ BASEketball** **KG Gift G'$: Upper Deck Cap!**

Hoop It Up 3-on-3 Palm Springs: Keith Gibbs

STILL GOT IT

Championship Sunday 9 am Game: Playing against CSUN's Keith Gibbs, teamed with a solid guard from Hawaii Pacific and another shooter. We're on D' and up 14-13. **First team to score 15 wins!!** We didn't need a stop, just NO 2's. Keith Gibbs squares-up Mike on the left wing far beyond the '2-pt' line. Studder-step, jumpshot: Bang! Game Over. Banished to the losers bracket; won 3 straight games to claw our way into a Winner Takes All Finals. A Rematch! Gibbs' Squad! Same Scenario: On D' up 14-13! Gibbs: Same Spot! Same Shot! Bang! Tourney over! Mike was **INCONSOLABLE!** Win or lose: Baller Love!

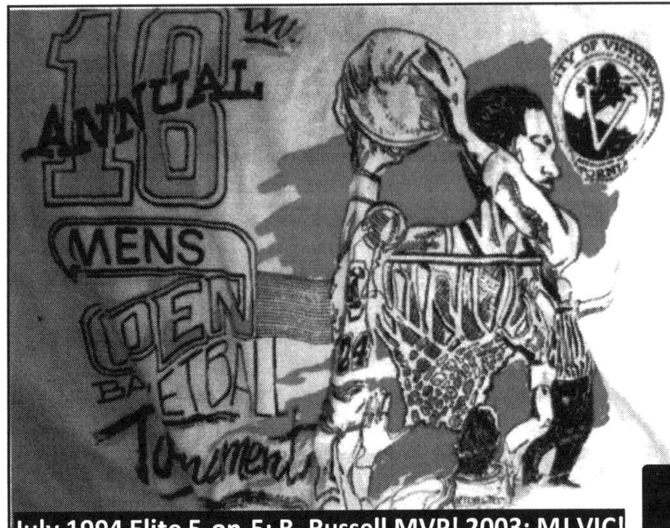

July 1994 Elite 5-on-5: B. Russell MVP! 2003: MJ VIC!

Victorville Prophecy: 'D.J.'

Mike: "We lost early on Sunday. Grind on! Won the semis in O/T. The finals we beat the #1 team by 3. Rematch: Tied, one minute left. We ran out of gas. Lost by 3. Sat in the lockerroom an hour; silent."

Dave DJ Jones: "Yo Dog. Be proud! This is an unforgettable event for me. Why? Because today I went up against the real damn deal. G'!"

Bryon Russell | Dave Jones

High Five Bay Area Road Trip: G'$ Coached Like a 'Step-Child'

This two game road-trip to play San Jose State and Cal Berkley was originally on our 'Home Team' schedule with Gene and Gomelsky coaching. But, Rle took the game and replaced 8 of my boys on the roster! Worse, he and his son would be coaching with Gene and Alex. I was a 'step-child' substitute. Against San Jose State I was ballin'. Then, I got a rebound, Rle yelled slow it up, just as Gomelsky uttered "Go" in Russian. I took his heed and put on a Maravich inspired ambidextrous fastbreak dribbling exhibition that culminated with a left hand behind the back bounce pass between the defenders legs for a dunk and a foul.

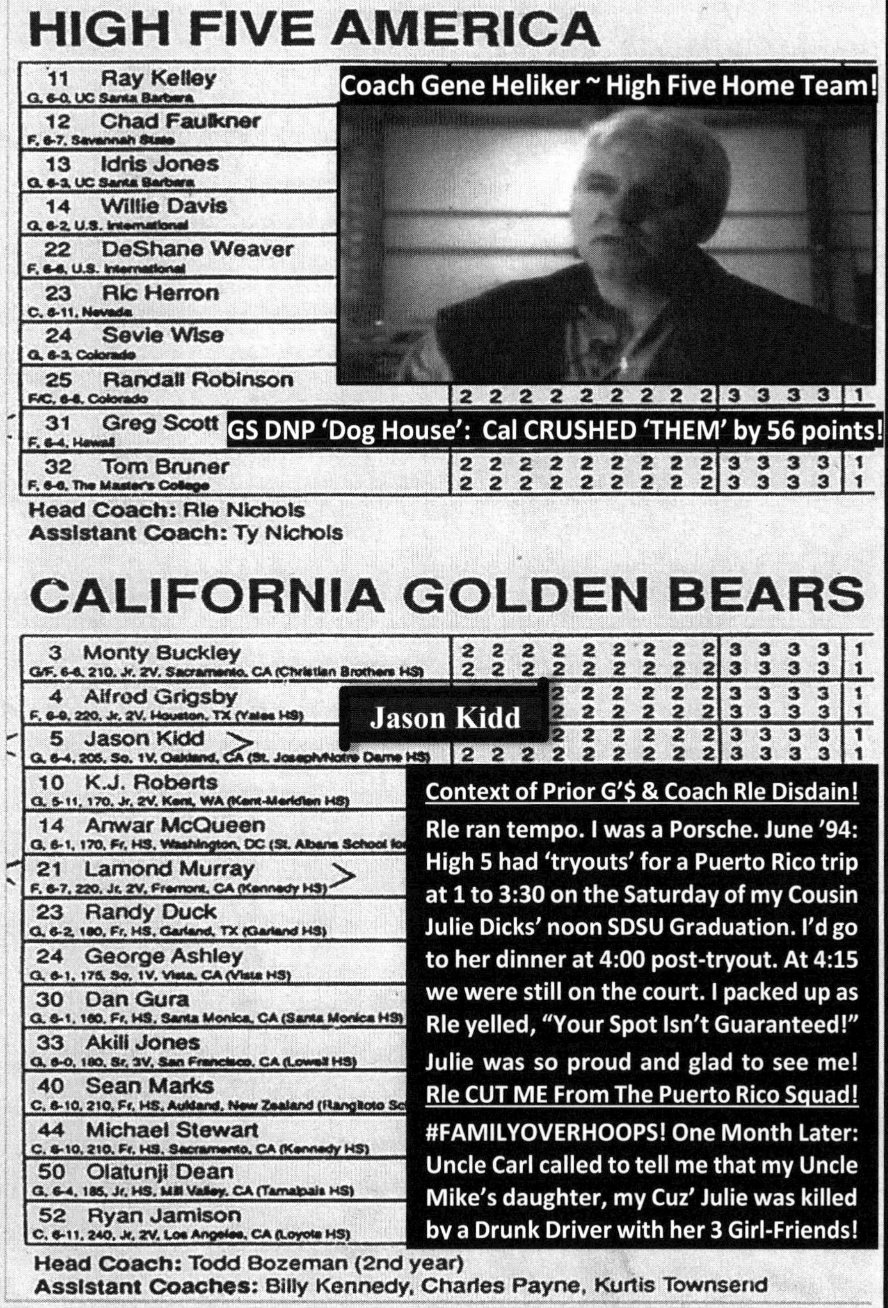

HIGH FIVE AMERICA

11 Ray Kelley — G, 6-0, UC Santa Barbara
12 Chad Faulkner — F, 6-7, Savannah State
13 Idris Jones — G, 6-3, UC Santa Barbara
14 Willie Davis — G, 6-2, U.S. International
22 DeShane Weaver — F, 6-6, U.S. International
23 Ric Herron — C, 6-11, Nevada
24 Sevie Wise — G, 6-3, Colorado
25 Randall Robinson — F/C, 6-6, Colorado
31 Greg Scott — F, 6-4, Hawaii
32 Tom Bruner — F, 6-6, The Master's College

Head Coach: Rle Nichols
Assistant Coach: Ty Nichols

CALIFORNIA GOLDEN BEARS

3 Monty Buckley — G/F, 6-6, 210, Jr, 2V, Sacramento, CA (Christian Brothers HS)
4 Alfrod Grigsby — F, 6-9, 220, Jr, 2V, Houston, TX (Yates HS)
5 Jason Kidd — G, 6-4, 205, So, 1V, Oakland, CA (St. Joseph/Notre Dame HS)
10 K.J. Roberts — G, 5-11, 170, Jr, 2V, Kent, WA (Kent-Meridian HS)
14 Anwar McQueen — G, 6-1, 170, Fr, HS, Washington, DC (St. Albans School
21 Lamond Murray — F, 6-7, 220, Jr, 2V, Fremont, CA (Kennedy HS)
23 Randy Duck — G, 6-2, 180, Fr, HS, Garland, TX (Garland HS)
24 George Ashley — G, 6-1, 175, So, 1V, Vista, CA (Vista HS)
30 Dan Gura — G, 6-1, 180, Fr, HS, Santa Monica, CA (Santa Monica HS)
33 Akili Jones — G, 6-0, 180, Sr, 3V, San Francisco, CA (Lowell HS)
40 Sean Marks — C, 6-10, 210, Fr, HS, Aukland, New Zealand (Rangitoto Sc
44 Michael Stewart — C, 6-10, 210, Fr, HS, Sacramento, CA (Kennedy HS)
50 Olatunji Dean — G, 6-4, 185, Jr, HS, Mill Valley, CA (Tamalpais HS)
52 Ryan Jamison — C, 6-11, 240, Jr, 2V, Los Angeles, CA (Loyola HS)

Head Coach: Todd Bozeman (2nd year)
Assistant Coaches: Billy Kennedy, Charles Payne, Kurtis Townsend

Coach Gene Heliker ~ High Five Home Team!
GS DNP 'Dog House': Cal CRUSHED 'THEM' by 56 points!
Jason Kidd
Context of Prior G'$ & Coach Rle Disdain!
Rle ran tempo. I was a Porsche. June '94: High 5 had 'tryouts' for a Puerto Rico trip at 1 to 3:30 on the Saturday of my Cousin Julie Dicks' noon SDSU Graduation. I'd go to her dinner at 4:00 post-tryout. At 4:15 we were still on the court. I packed up as Rle yelled, "Your Spot Isn't Guaranteed!" Julie was so proud and glad to see me!
Rle CUT ME From The Puerto Rico Squad!
#FAMILYOVERHOOPS! One Month Later: Uncle Carl called to tell me that my Uncle Mike's daughter, my Cuz' Julie was killed bv a Drunk Driver with her 3 Girl-Friends!

Chick Hearn Quip: **'The mustard is off the hotdog!"** Rle had a hissy fit. He sub'd me out as punishment. Then, Coach Gomelsky came to sit with me and gave me props. "Well done, son." That soothed me!!

G'$ PROUD STAT LINE: DNP COACHES DECISION

Cal blitzed us from the start. Kidd was the 'Schiznit'! They were up 20 at half.

It got much worse. We're down by 52 with 3 minutes left. Rle came to me!? No, Thanks! DNP!

1994: GOMELSKY COACHES CAMP ~ PRAISING G'

Coach Gomelsky hosted a 2-day coaching camp for top high school and college coaches at Rancho Bernardo High featuring five of his best Russian players and five choice U.S. players demonstrating his systems and drills. My most challenging hoop experience ever! Russian guard, baller and friend, Sasha, and I were captains and showcased throughout the camp. Seeing Gomelsky feed the pivoting postman with a drop-kick pass from the sideline hashmark, on target and on time every single time, to multiple players: **Priceless! I was excused from the Early Morning TRACK Conditioning Session on Day Two. He respected my mantra; 'I sprint 94 feet, that's it and that's all. Baseline to baseline.'** In the final cool-down session Gomelsky kneeled next to me and taught me a personal relaxation technique of tensing and relaxing specific muscle regions, as he mentored me.

San Diego North County Times article excerpt: Gomelsky

"As coaches, we are nothing without the players. Many of you have especially asked about one. So, allow me to share my story. Two years ago, I came to the USA and a High Five America training, I awed at one player amongst the many that very first night. Perfect supremely conditioned basketball physique; strong, fit, tough and durable. Fundamentally sound in all phases of the game with far superior athleticism, physical skills, and one-of-a-kind even-handed dexterity. A superb psyche and competitive temperament along with a brilliant basketball IQ. His focus and work-ethic in the drills impressed me. But, his performance in the scrimmage had me in awe. I admit to you, for the first time I became a 'fan' of an American player. Since then, I've had the unique pleasure to coach and befriend a great player, and a great young man. This camp has provided us just a glimpse of his rare aptitude to flawlessly execute any drill, master any system, adapt to any coaching style, lead and improve any teammate. I introduce, Gregg Scott."

Riveted and shocked as I stood up. As he shook my hand, I asked if I could quote him in my book. Placing his hand on my chest, "Listen to me my son**, the best is yet to come.** You posses all elements of my friend Coach Wooden's Pyramid, that you covet so much. You've been my prized pupil from day one. Very soon you will have the opportunity to show your talents to the world, and the responsibility to share our teachings. When that chapter is done and the seeds you planted have bloomed, quote me amongst the many."

Chris Carter, A.D. and Varsity Coach at R.B., was impressed. He facilitated my first Hoop specific Mental Athlete Workshop Manuals for my presentations his teams. A springboard. The same weekend, Puig facilitated a 90-day stint in Frankfurt with the Corps of Engineers Puig was loaned to the CoE by, Efrain, a division director who was also from Puerto Rico.

MARCH '95: PROPHETIC DEUTSCHLAND

We were living in the turnkey Frankfurt Consulate Housing complex for U.S. Embassy and DoD civilians. It was adjacent to the base and Frankfurt DoD Schools where Coach Snyder sent me to TV Langen.

TV Langen Club

Markus Hallgrimson

TV Langen was a 1st Bundesliga club and only a 20 minute train ride from Frankfurt. The club allowed me to workout and train with their players, one of whom was quite special. The first baller since Petrovic who could match me shot for shot in my 3-point shooting drills. Markus Hallgrimson was a friendly skinny 19 year-old 6'3" shooting guard who had played one year of college ball in Oregon. He was uninvited to return due to his off-court antics and choices. Still, I really liked this kid, so I gifted him a G' Hoops Mental Athlete Workbook with a promise. That night his Adidas exec dad, Paul, called. He signed me to a 3-year 3-stripes gig to coach abc camps and infuse my Workbook!

Heidelberg Food Court

Victorville to Heidelberg to the Xanthus All-Star Tour
5 weeks ~ 4 Countries ~ 3 International Tournaments

I'm with Puig, her cousin Frank, who was stationed in Heidelberg with his wife and kids. As I scan the plethera of junk-food options I notice a somewhat familiar face staring at me from a distance. He comes over and we figured out how we knew each other. It was DJ from the Victoville Tourney. Baller Love! I noted a Coach Burton who's phone was disconnected. DJ takes out his cell. "Joe, there's a guy with your old number named Gregg Scott. Yeah, I'm with him right now. Yo, I can play with him. So, you need to sign him up right now. Yup, like that. I'll tell you what I told him back when we first met. He's the real damn deal. Put it this way, pay him exactly what you're paying me. And, here's the best part. You don't need to pay for a point guard from the States to fill-in while I'm gone. G' can play point guard, too. Oh, he's living with wifey in Frankfurt so you give him my ticket for a 48-hour visit home during the break. You'll thank me later." DJ hands me his cell. **Xanthus Tour!!**

Oberaching: X' Tour 3-day Training Camp

The ten players all met at a Lodge with a restaurant and rooms in very close proximity to Joe's former club where we trained. Joe did get some solid young ex-college players from the States. We 'smelled' each other in our first workout to establish an apt hierarchy. Who's who! Who Can Do What! **DJ & I Reigned!**

First "X' All-Stars?" Scrimmage vs. 'Deutch'

Joe wanted to see what the Young Bucks had and started 5 of his most Hubris Hoopsters. DJ and I chilled in our sweatsuits on the bench for the first half as the Youngsters showed they weren't ready for Prime Time. Like deer in the headlights. At halftime the game was tied against a team void of Americans. Joe got us in the locker-room and spit out a speech:

Joe Burton: "DJ has a contract! G'man will get one! So, I kept them on the bench to give you all a look. Opportunity! You let 10 Germans play you even! If you're only as good as they are then why would they pay you. Be Better! They want Jordan. They want special. This Is All About Paper! Getting Paid!"

Joe started me and DJ. We trounced that 1st Bundesliga Club team by 15. A Killer Tandem!

Xanthus Tour Debut vs. BV Rheinhessen

'Big John' Bolden

We hit the road for our debut in Rheinhessen. This venue was packed with fans, had a live legit DJ jamming and a nice shiny hardwood floor! Joe told DJ and me to got to work immediately. Green Light. 'Yes Sir!' When we started the game, DJ complained about the DJ playing music. The refs, coaches and captains huddled. I said, 'Yo, lets play like we're ballin' at the park on a Sunday afternoon. Bball, BBQ, Babes & Beats.' Captain 'Big John': " Now, that's what I'm talkin', baby! I like this guy!" I went to the DJ and said, 'Do your thing. Do it Proper.' **And, he did!**

DJ and I Did Much WORK!!! From start to finish! A Showcase! Then, I went to holla at John Bolden.

John Bolden: Intro to Nike's 'Le Runners' Streetball Tour & Wiesbaden Military Hoops!

Our first Xanthus game in Germany, Joe gave DJ and me the 'Green Light'. **Yup!** 70 points; both scoring 35. 'Big John' and I bonded in their locker-room, post-game.

LE RUNNERS

Ayyub „Andy" Anderson, Alter: 28, Geburtsort: Muskegon/Michigan; College: University of Ozarks/Arkansas

John „Baby" Bolden, Alter: 28, Geburtsort: Jacksonville/Florida; College: Junior College Jacksonville

Michael „Mike" Witte, Alter: 26; Geburtsort: Limburg; High School: Beaver/Utah

Dan Mooney, Alter: 34, Geburtsort: New York; spielte in der NBA einige Partien für Phoenix, Sacramento und Atlanta, in der CBA für Albeny.

BASKET 7-8 95

John Bolden of Le Runners

BASKET

5 95

Charles Barkley

Charles Barkley will endlich den Titel. Doch ob's für die Suns in diesem Jahr reicht? Denn auch die Konkurrenz ist für die Play-offs bestens gerüstet. Seite 34

Erst in seinem zweiten Jahr in der NBA, doch schon ein ganz Großer – Penny Hardaway von Orlando Magic. Seite 96

Le Runners

Die Jungens von „Le Runners" mögen's hart aber herzlich. Mit diesem Motto waren sie die Stars der Streetball-Szene '94. Seite 74

16 Seiten Michael Jordan

Alles über sein Leben, seine größten Erfolge, sein Comeback und seine neuen Ziele. Dazu die besten Jordan-Fotos, ein großes Gewinnspiel – und: Jordan [illegible]

TITELFOTO: NATHANIEL S. BUTLER

"I will never forget the call from 'Big John' after his game against the Xanthus All-Stars. John was thrilled in the fact that he had a player who I simply had to have. 'The total package!' I signed him to a Le Runners gig sight unseen. G', was better than advertised!"
Jack Sussmann, Le Runners CEO

Lorraine, France: All-Time FAV Global Hoops Pic ~ G' Defense!

Samedi 6 mai 1995

SPORTS lorraine

Samedi 6 mai 1995

s'est bien amusé

une Sélection américaine, l'équipe nancéienne hier soir, à Fléville.

#7 G. Scott

Xanthus Euro Touring

Paris & Champagne, France
Dusseldorf, Hilden &
Langen, Germany

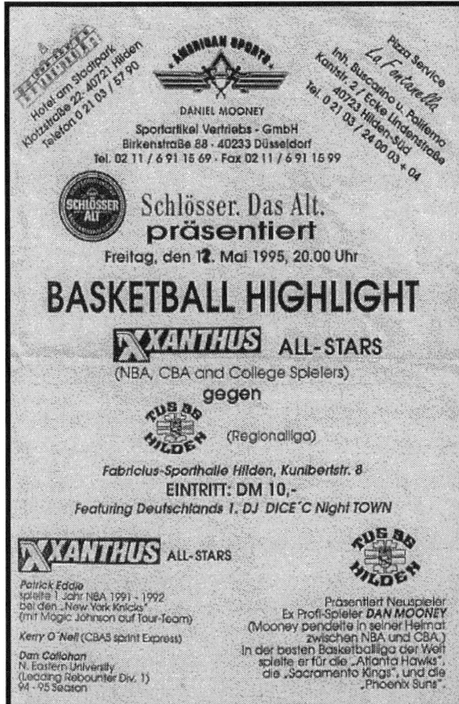

The Louvre Museum ~ 'Mona Lisa' ~ Paris, France

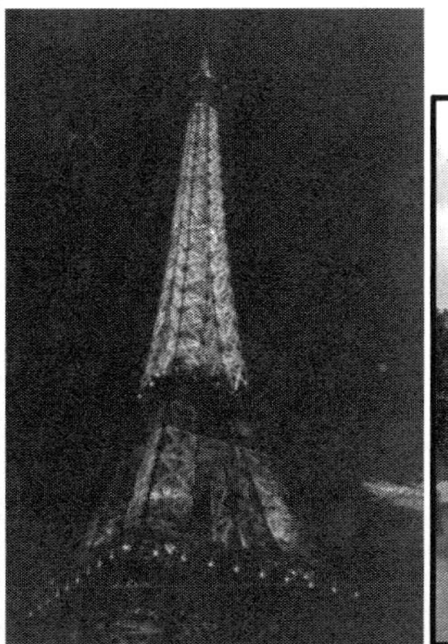

The Arch de' Triumph ~ Paris

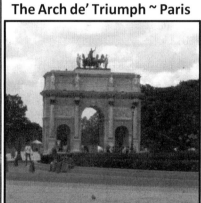

Chalons sur Marne ~ Champagne, France

Xanthus Post-Game Victory ~ France
Daniel Hallgrimson, John Blake, G' & Lo' Williams

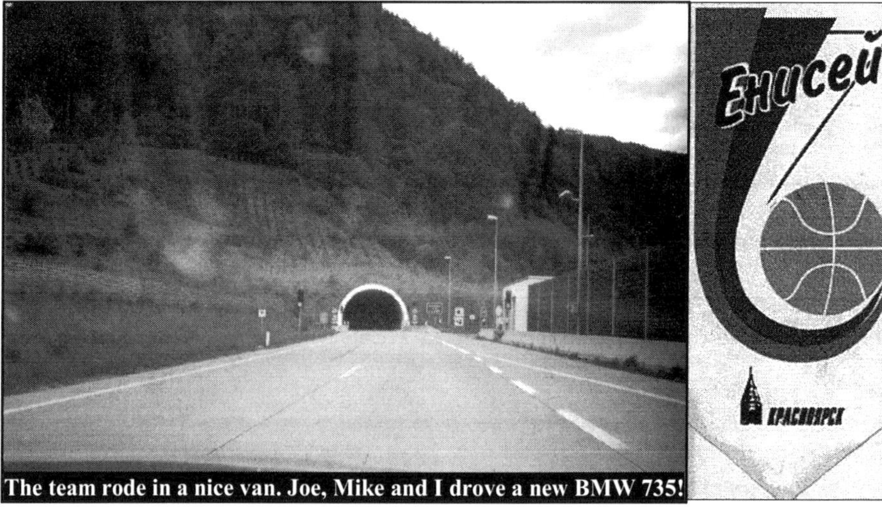

The team rode in a nice van. Joe, Mike and I drove a new BMW 735!

Vienna, Austria

After a long drive thru creepy 40 km tunnels within the Swiss Alps, we got to the famous town, and birthplace of Arnold Swartzenager. Debut: Beat a savvy Croatia team 96-88 as we incorporated 6' 9" Mike Moten into our squad with great effectiveness. In the championship game we faced a massive Russian National Team of seasoned pro players. In the second half we lost our poise and our 10 point lead cut to 3. **The refs made horrible calls and the game turned dirty. 2:05 left to go. 99-102.** Coach Joe got fed up and called a timeout. In the huddle he told us, "Gregg, I recall that you've played for a Russian coach before. So, I need you to run this huddle while I talk with the referees." 'Spit some vet-speak G'man':

I signed to play 2-guard with DJ; *and* point guard in his absence.

- ✎ We can only lose if we beat ourselves!
- ✎ We must stay unified and show poise!
- ✎ Leave the ref's alone; don't get baited!
- ✎ Show your hands on D' and Verbalize!
- ✎ Have No Fear Fellas! I got this! On D'!
- ✎ My man is the weak link. He'll cough it up. Run the floor; delay break. Clock is our friend! Lay-ups & F/T's! Be clutch!
- ✎ **This is USA vs. RUSSIA! Represent!**

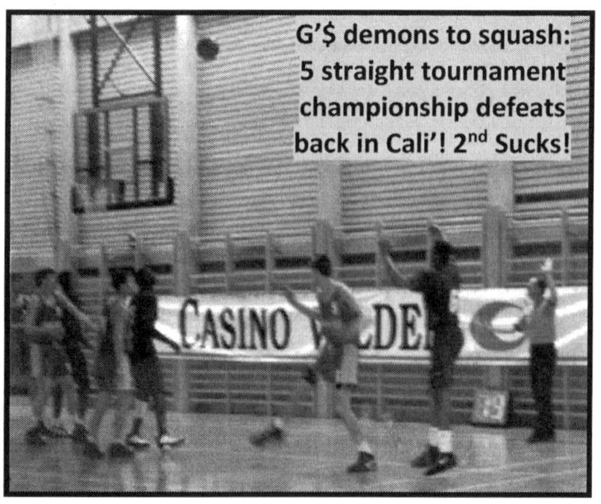

G'$ demons to squash: 5 straight tournament championship defeats back in Cali'! 2nd Sucks!

Vanquish! Leave no doubt

I got a steal and scored on an easy dunk. Ripped him clean again and got fouled.

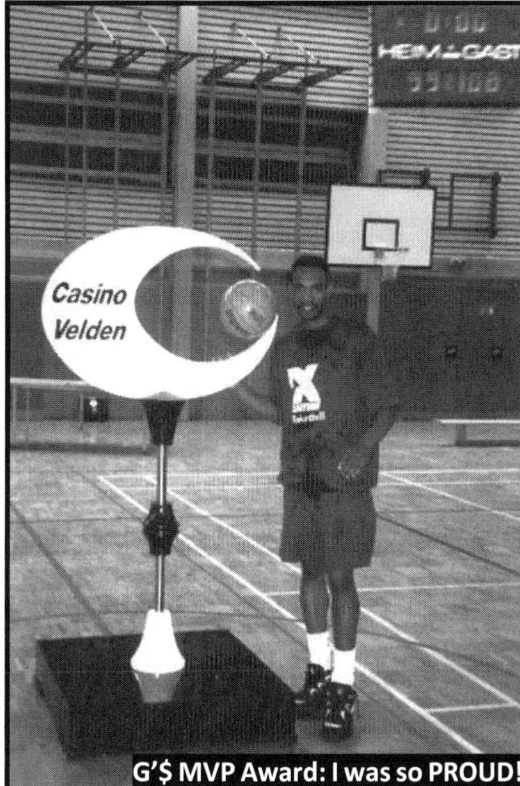

G'$ MVP Award: I was so PROUD!

Hit 2 *'Doug Collins'* F/T's. Steal #3 and dimed Mike on the delay break. Game!

99-108 G'$: MVP!

Xanthus All-Stars: Casino Velden Tourney Champions! Defeating Russia 99-108
M. Moten ~ D. Crocker ~ G. Devon ~ D. Callahan ~ J. Leahy ~ J. Blake ~ G. Scott

Une sélection de joueurs américains
en tournée européenne
XANTHUS
ALL STAR
TEAM
RENCONTRE
GENEVA
TEAM
SOIRÉE EXCEPTIONNELLE
DE BASKET
BERNEX • Salle en Vailly
Vendredi 19 mai 95 à 20 h 00
TRIBUNE DE GENÈVE

5/19 ~ GENEVA, SWITZERLAND

We departed Vienna late and we arrived an hour late at the plush, packed arena in ritsy Geneva, Switzzerland. We rushed into the lockerroms, got dressed and hit the court! This two-tier venue had a nice floor and fanatical fans. Chanting loudly during our ten minute warmups.

4-Team Euro Tourney: Host vs. X'

We came out flat against the host, Geneva Team. They were fueled by their fans and our lethargy. Just three minutes in, we we're in a tie game. Joe put me it on me. "Yo G', you're being **tentative!**" That stung! **Coachable!** 'G'$ Vanquish Geneva!'

Tourney Finals!

X': Tourney Champs!

Xanthus All Star Team			The Geneva Team			
Lawrence	**Williams**	201 cm	4	Sevag	**Keucheyan**	173 cm
Dwight	**Crocker**	193 cm	5	J-Louis	**Ngabonziza**	189 cm
Craig	**Scott**	182 cm	7	André	**Ceesay**	188 cm
Daniel	**Halgromson**	183 cm	8	Stéphane	**Baillif**	195 cm
David	**Jones**	186 cm	9	Matthias	**Kautzor**	196 cm
George	**Duvon**	206 cm	10	Carlos	**Diez**	187 cm
John	**Blake**	203 cm	12	Frédéric	**Baillif**	178 cm
Dan	**Callahan**	203 cm	13	Matthieu	**Baillif**	179 cm
John	**Leahy**	201 cm	14	Samuel	**Bourquin**	202 cm
Mike	**Moten**	206 cm	15	Amadou	**Romero**	194 cm
			16	David	**Dar-Ziv**	195 cm
			18	Deo	**Djossou** *USA*	201 cm
Coach:	Joe **Burton**		Coach:		Nicsa **Bavcevic**	

CHAMPIONS METTLE

CHAMPIONS MEDAL

ALBERTVILLE, FRANCE SITE OF THE 1990 WINTER OLYMPICS

Visiting a 'ghost-town' of sports history!

5/21/95 Albertville. France

Albertville, France ~ Olympique Centre '95

X' Day Off: R & R in Albertville, France

The Swiss Alps ~ Modane, France

MODANE, FRANCE

8-team Int'l Select Tournament in a venue that views the Alps.

Xanthus: Tourney Champs!

Modane, France

CHAMPIONS METTLE

CHAMPIONS MEDAL

MID-TOUR BREAK: G'$ 24-HOUR FRANKFURT TRIP

VIA STUTTGART!

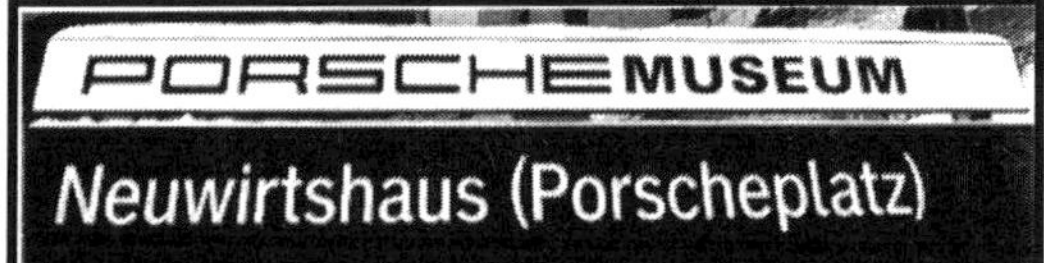

Back in Germany Joe had me stay with him the night before my train to Frankfurt. His travel agent amended my plans: Porsche HQ!

Joe's Clout: She called to Porsche HQ and faxed an intro letter with my game pic in the Lorraine, France article. I received a VIP tour while signing autographs for Porsche Peeps & Execs!

SPORTS
Lorraine
s'est bien amusé
une Sélection américaine, l'équipe nancéienne hier soir, à Fléville.

The night I stayed with Joe, I asked him about his term: "Tentative" He mused as he said, "It worked!"

METZ ~ NANCY ~ NANTES ~ PARIS

G' Hoops Euro Racing: Porsche 993 GT3 Pace Car

DJ was back and the vanquishing continued!

LE MANS, FRANCE

G'$ in a Porsche pace car on the '24-hours of Le Mans' race track.

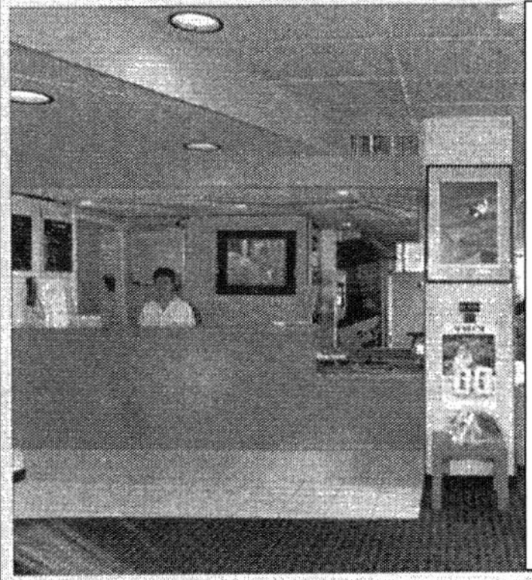

We were in Le Mans for 3 days. The town was transformed by the racing track. **I had the Hotel Concierge call my Porsche HQ guys** and I gave her their biz cards. Instant hook-up: G'$ Pace Car!

Responsable :
Dominique MOUTON
Quai Ledru-Rollin - 72000 LE MANS
Tél. 43.23.18.23 - Fax : 43.24.00.72
Ouvert toute l'année.

☞ **Description générale :**

La réception de l'hôtel est à votre disposition 24 h sur 24 h. L'hôtel est situé en centre ville, face à la vieille ville, à 10 minutes de la gare SNCF - TGV et du Palais des Congrès.

☞ **Accès :**

❑ De l'autoroute A 11, par la sortie n° 7, Le Mans nord puis centre ville.

❑ En venant de Tours, Angers ou Chartres, prendre direction Alençon.

❑ En venant de Rennes et Laval, suivre les indications centre ville.

XANTHUS TOUR: 25-1

Metz, France: At our pre-game meal the restaurant had carafes of red wine on each table. Several players took full advantage before Joe busted them. In the game we swallowed humble pie and our sole defeat of the tour. 25-1 record and 3 tourney championships!

Fav Memory of the X Tour:

Mike Moten's club in Hannover, Germany, was north of Frankfurt. Joe was heading 3 hours south of Frankfurt. So, I had to be a proper teammate, albeit an inconsiderate husband. 'Honey, I'm home. Oh, we have a guest on the couch.'

Mike Moten

The bond shared by teammates! The next morning we had a huge breakfast in the cafeteria and had a rare chance to exhale and watch the Oprah Winfrey Show on AFN. We joyfully reminisced about the exploits and the antics of the tour.

Celebrity All-Star Game Live on Jammin' Z 90 FM

Kevin Bloomfield knew I was back in town only long enough to pack up our household goods before relocating to play in Germany. He pleaded with me to consider playing in a celebrity game to be broadcast live on San Diego's premier hip-hop station, Jammin' Z90. The risk of injury never entered my mind. This is what I do. Still, I needed to assure myself that I'd have cohesive players alongside me to do what I do. So, I had to review the rosters! I checked two names to play with and two names to play against. I had to have Zack Jones and Carl Rushton on my squad and I also wanted to go against my 'big bro' Demond 'Bam' Webster and the ex-NBA star, Phil Smith. Lastly, it was East vs. West. I rep the 'Westside'!

G'$: Z90 Game Day Venue Acclimation and Solo Shoot-Around

Wes Atkins: "Kevin asked me to meet with Gregg at noon to give him the layout of the venue and the format of the event. The custodian would meet us there to turn on the lights and lower the baskets. G' arrived and we discussed setup details."

Z'90 Rep, G' & Wes Atkins: Game Day

Kevin, aka Juice, was the game MC announcing courtside with the DJ!

Z'90 broadcasting live from the far sideline opposite of the fans and the team benches.

"G' elected the West bench; 2nd half basket! Then, he put on his ankle braces, laced up his Nike's and hit the court with two balls. He dribbled up and down the court as if surveying the floor; each and every spot. At times he paused, detected and took mental notes of audible dead-spots on the court."

G'$ Game Gambit: Purposeful and Prophetic!!

GAME NIGHT & 'GAMESPEAK

Bam: "I admit that I perpetrated the 'incident', so to speak. It was late in the second half of a close game that was intense and physical. G' beat his man off the dribble, got into the key, I came to help and G' shot me a quick sly shove, that got me off-balance, as he pulled up for a short jumper. So, I put a hard foul on him and also got in his face a bit. He's so coy! We're boys! G's my little brother! Regardless of that, as G' was at the free throw line I was in his face woofing at him. G' said, 'Don't Get Mad. Get Better!' So cold!"

1 G'$ JAM: Cold-Blooded...Hard Core...Nasty...Sic...Str8 Vicious!

G'$ Pre-Game | Zack Jones | Carl Rushton | Wes Atkins

Kevin 'Juice': "Jammin' Z'90 made that sold-out event SPECIAL! With A Great DJ! And, I was courtside hyping up a Great Game."

Wes: "I could tell G' didn't appreciate Bam fronting him off like that. Nope!"

Juice: "Oh yes ladies and gentlemen as we approach crunch time it's getting chippy. Bam and G' Money are the best of friends off the court but all that goes by the wayside in the heat of battle. And, Bam let G' know it. It's On!"

Bam: "G' makes his first free throw and steps forward into the key and says, 'We're in a dog fight fellas, no doubt. Now, we're about to see who the real DAWGS are. And, I'm gonna get it started.' Uhh ohh! My teammates may have viewed G'$ as a lil' 6'3" guard talking BIG trash. I knew better. G'man doesn't talk trash. So, I knew he was gonna get busy for real. Yo! Beware!"

Wes: "G' hit his free throw, went on D' and steered his man to a dead-spot, created a turnover, and saved the ball in the corner with a blind pass to Z'."

Bam: G' forced a turnover and saved the ball before going out of bounds in the corner with a behind the back pass to Zach at the top of the key and Z' started a 2-on-2 fastbreak with Carl on the right wing, one defender on him and Phil Smith backpedaling as Zach crosses midcourt towards him. G' is a blur along the left sideline sprinting to catch up to the play. As Zack gets to the top of the key he ball-fakes to Carl and throws G' a soft bounce pass."

G' Pre-Flight

SPRINT on the sideline to the free throw line extended! Cut to the basket!

Juice: "Here we go! This is what you paid for folks. Zack passes as G' cuts..."

As I was taught: SPRINT up the sideline. Stay wide! Cut at the free throw line extended! For 20 years many rave about the culmination of the play. I rave about the pass from Zack! He threw a perfect forward rotating bounce pass that I gloved with my left hand, in stride!

Bam: G' got the pass far out on the wing as Phil slide down into the key. G'man looked Phil in his eyes and nodded his head, TWICE! Cold Blooded!"

Wes: Zack's pass enabled G' to throttle down, eye Phil, nod his head and..."

Bam: "G'man was so far from the rim that I didn't know what he was doing. He took one dribble with his left hand and went into a low two-footed squat at a launch pad that was *Beyond where Zack stands in the picture below!* G' exploded up and curled his knees up to his chest as he cocked the ball behind his head with both hands. Phil got to his own launch pad just inside the lane line and directly in the path of the on-coming G'man. Phil got up high, his hand was a foot over the rim. But, G'man got up, up, up, and was cocking the ball a foot over Phil's hand; and G' was still ascending! Nasty."

Wes: The first contact was G's knees to Phil's gut which caused him to slap and grasp onto G's forearm as their bodies collided, both above the rim. The whistle blew as G'man continued Up, Over and Through Phil, and The Foul."

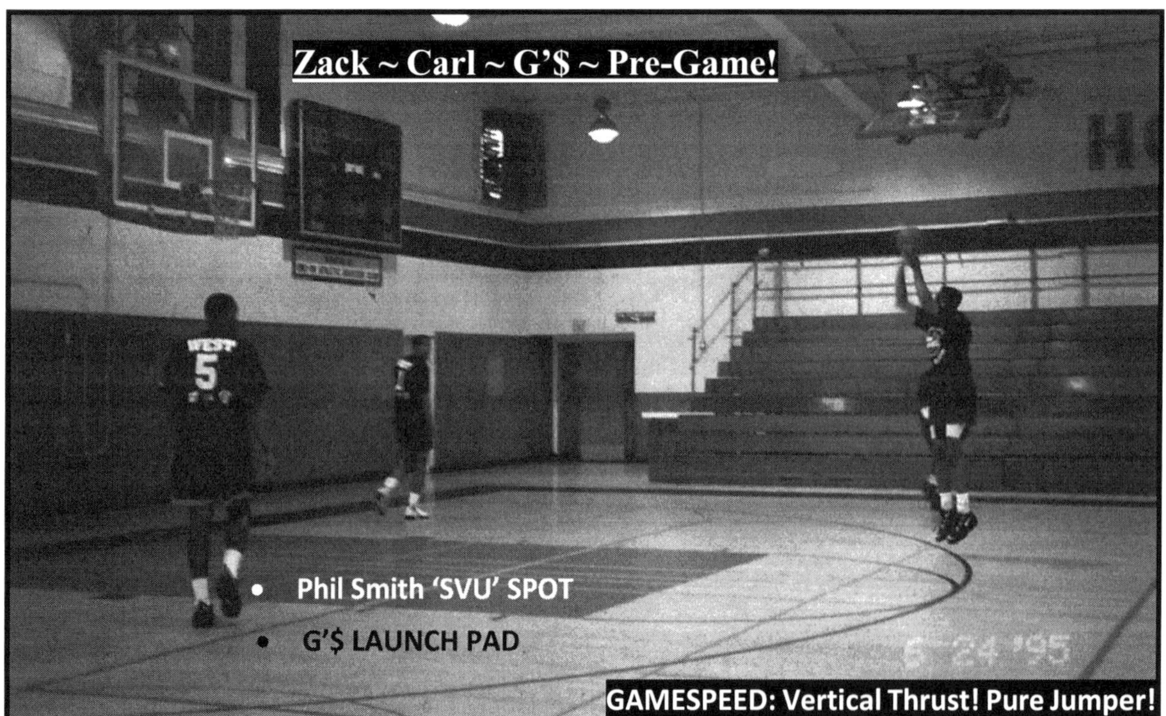

Bam: " G' gutted him and had Phil underneath him as he stretched out with Phil still clutching onto his right forearm, and at his mercy. G' was virtually parallel to the floor, released his right hand from the ball and flushed a sic left-handed dunk as he visciously tossed Phil to the floor with his right arm!" The gym exploded as Phil crashed down on his back. TRUE MAYHEM!"

Wes: "G' stretched out in midair and no part of his body was below the net! The lefty bash was rediculous. Then, he overtly shed Phil with his right arm. That was simply a hoop assualt with the intent to do dunking bodily harm. The most amazing play I've ever witnessed in person or ever seen on film! And, the first thing he did as he landed by Phil? No taunting. No celebrating. The first thing he did was point at Zach, go to Z' and acknowledge his pass!"

Juice: "G' goes up, Phil contests, they collide, a foul is called and oh my God! No he didn't. Oh my God, he dunked on Phil...Oh my God, for those of you listening, the gym is in total bedlam after witnessing the most incredible dunk ever by Gregg Scott. Wait, Phil Smith is hurt. Wow! Oh my God folks."

From where I took off, and with Phil pulling on me, I simply needed to clear landing space! So, I had to dispatch of him for self-preservation. As I landed softly and safely I glanced at Phil. He was in bad shape. I turned, pointed at Zack and walked to him. 'Sweet pass Z!'

Zack: "I wondered what you were gonna do. Now he knows! G', that was so nasty."

Standing next to him, my proud big brother who created the play, was a very cool moment.

Bam: "Teammate be dammed. I went up to my Boy G', and we celebrated. 'Way to posterize him, G' DAWG.' He said, 'You know you owe that man an apology for putting me in mode.' I told him, 'I was thinking the same thing.' 'Yo G', we're going to dinner after the game so we can reminisce!' We Did!"

There was a long delay as Phil was being tended to. Juice took a radio break. I went to him.

Juice: "I told you, you're a million dollar player, G'. Thank you for playing!"

Finally, they carted Phil off and he seemed ok. I checked on him but he was not all there. Still yet, I had a free throw to make, work to do and a victory to get! **Yes, We Vanquished!**

I was soon Euro Bound and Juice had an NBA HOF friend call me: George Gervin!

Chauncey: "G'man I can't even have this conversation with 95% of players! I'm from Detroit, not 'Diego. I know basketball! And, I love your G'$ game." "Don't just Play Great. Be a Great Player. You have the tools, skills and the psyche to be famous on a Global level. What I respect most is Consistency!"

"You DO WORK every single time you take the floor. G', that's GREATNESS!"

G'$ ADIDAS EUROPEAN STREETBALL INTRO 1995

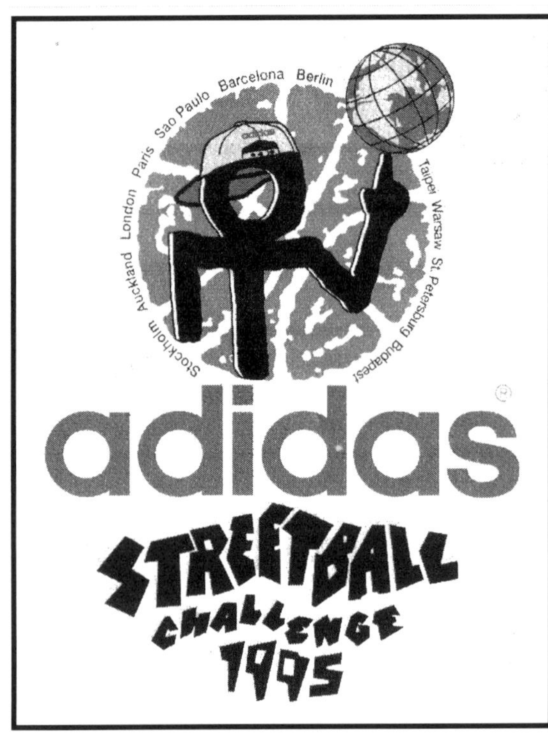

July 9th ~ Frankfurt, Germany
2 hours after landing at the Frankfurt Airport, Paul Hallgrimson presented G'$ to 'Streetball'.

'Game Dunks' Only!

360 Degrees!

Sporting my High Five America shorts, Kallassy ankle braces and *Nike Air Flights*!

'Disregard Jet Lag'
G' Flight Lefty Jam!

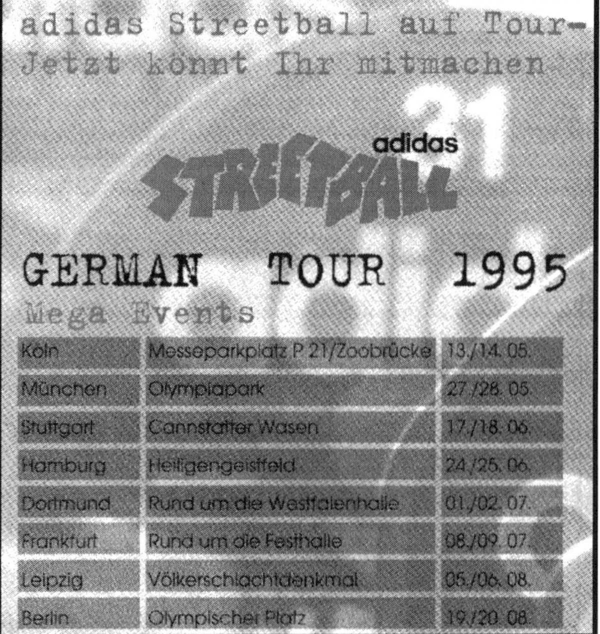

adidas Streetball auf Tour-
Jetzt könnt Ihr mitmachen

adidas
STREETBALL

GERMAN TOUR 1995
Mega Events

Köln	Messeparkplatz P 21/Zoobrücke	13./14. 05.
München	Olympiapark	27./28. 05.
Stuttgart	Cannstatter Wasen	17./18. 06.
Hamburg	Heiligengeistfeld	24./25. 06.
Dortmund	Rund um die Westfalenhalle	01./02. 07.
Frankfurt	Rund um die Festhalle	08./09. 07.
Leipzig	Völkerschlachtdenkmal	05./06. 08.
Berlin	Olympischer Platz	19./20. 08.

G' Flight: 45" VERTICAL

Launch off of my left foot, or right foot; or both. Going forward or sideways, or rotating backwards. Left or right hand or two hands or switching hands; mid-flight!

G'$: Frankfurt Slam Dunk Finals Champion!

Paul Hallgrimson:
"Gregg amazed us all.
His Streetball Stardom
was clear on Day One!"

YouTube*.com/MentalAthlete*

SPORTSHULE, Munchen-Oberhaching, Germany
Training home of the German Nat'l. Futbol Team & Boris Becker. The Mecca for Detlef's abc camps.

G'$ in Paris '95 at INSEF National Institute for Sports and Physical Education. Tony Parker!

G' & Markus with French Jr. National Team Players

Dikembe Mutombo abc All-Star Camp- Paris, France

EURO TESTIMONIAL

I met Gregg in Germany in 1995. He gave me a workbook and promised results "beyond my wildest dreams". I worked 3 camps in Europe with him and I learned about his Mental Athlete Workshop. We trained together for the next 2 years, and he personally mentored me at critical stages when I was in college. Amazingly, his promise to me has come true. His Mind & Body training has helped me in so many different ways. From proper nutrition and training habits, to game preparation, being a sincere teammate and mentally tough. Above all, he instilled his own mentality of a champion within me. Gregg and his unique peak performance workshop helped me go from an average player to a coachable athlete, an All-American, NCAA 3-point record holder, and now a paid pro. It helps me on and off the court, especially now that I'm a proud father of twin daughters. I very confidently recommend this to any athlete. It will bring you sure success in sports and life. Thanks, Gregg!

Markus Hallgrimson
Wurzburg, Germany ~ 2003

Terry Schofield was a John Wooden disciple (UCLA 1964-67)

Terry Schofield abc Camp Bayern Leverkusen, Germany

Terry Schofield abc Camp-Bayern Leverkusen, Germany

ADIDAS ABC EURO CAMPS: MUTOMBO ~ SCHOFIELD ~ HABEGGER

adidas

DIKEMBE MUTOMBO ABC CAMP

abc CAMPS adidas

Programme mercredi 9 août
1er jour de stage

HORAIRE	ACTIVITES	LIEU	RESPONSABLE
7h30	Réveil	Hôtel Campanile	Entraîneurs
8h00	Petit déjeuner	Hôtel Campanile	Entraîneurs
8h30	Transfert vers le Palais des Sports	Palais des Sports	Entraîneurs
9h00	Proprioception (travail des articulations) + stretching	Terrain central	Kiné Entraîneurs

adidas-abc-Camp mit Les Habegger

Stationseinteilung

Defense
Ernie Woods Markus Wierzoch Bernd Uhlemann Sabrina Müller Kristina Davis Marc Zimmer

Shooting
Gregg Scott Marcus Hallgrimson Thomas Blechner Kirsten Albracht Malte Arndtz

G', Kay, Markus, Ernie Woods & Les Habegger

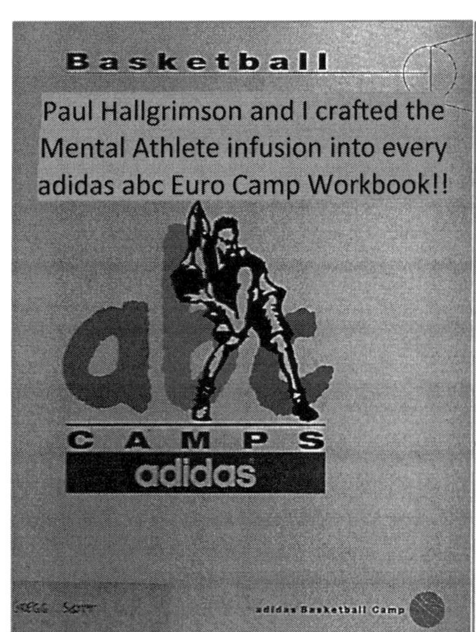

Paul Hallgrimson and I crafted the Mental Athlete infusion into every adidas abc Euro Camp Workbook!!

The Mental Athlete
MENTAL
ATHLETE
An athlete to athlete guide to improved mental preparation in the pursuit of peak performance.
Dr. Gregg Scott
adidas

My genuine kinship with Detlef, both on and off the court, boosted me from premier camps to...

Euro $treetball fame, $hoe commercials & Dassler

adidas Detlef Schrempf-Camp 1995

Staff für München 22. - 28.07.

Boris B

Nr	Name	Str.	PLZ	Wohnort	Tel:	Anzug	Shorts	Shirt	Schuhe
1.	Schrempf, Detlef								
2.	Blümel, Kay	Burgstraße 17	35418	Buseck	06408/1367 0641/32566 0641/9750415 (Mo - Fr 15-17h)	7	L	XL	9½
3.	Casey, Sean					8	L	XXL	11½
4.	Janzen, Sascha	Müllerstraße 98e	13349	Berlin	030/4524920	6	M	XL	9½
5.	Schädlich, Wolfgang	Gunzostraße 2	61352	Bad Homburg	06172/456165	9	L	XL	9
6.	Scott, Greg	Affinity Court	92131	San Diego Ca.		9	XL	XL	11

adidas

Detlef-Schrempf-All-Star-Camp

Gyms for Positioning-training

Forwards

Gym 2
Pure Radomirovic

Centers — Detlef Schrempf — Gym 1 — **Guards** — Gregg Scott

Die Formel zum Erfolg

German

DAS MENTALE SPIEL

Du bist , was und wie Du zu sein glaubst!

A) ZIELSETZUNGEN

"Wenn ich es mir vorstellen kann, kann ich es auch erreichen. Wenn

Denk daran: es ist das intensive Verlangen, Deine Ziele zu erreichen,

Une formule pour réussir

French

LE MENTAL

Vous êtes ce que vous pensez être !

A. FIXER LES OBJECTIFS:

"Si je peux me l'imaginer, c'est que

Certains objectifs semblent

A Formula for success

THE MENTAL GAME

A. GOAL SETTING

You are what you think!

"If I can imagine it, I can achieve it.

Your goals must be your own . . .

What we believe to be true about ourselves ultimately determines our successes, our failures, our ability to risk, and our strength to handle any situation.

The pictures we see in our minds are very powerful. These mental images, both positive and negative, affect our performance over a long period of time. They determine our experiences and create our reality.

The first trait we must develop is called "positive intent". We have "positive intent" when we create an atmosphere where we feel calm and confident. We expect good things to happen and success to come.

With positive intent comes the ability to DREAM. By dreaming it, you make it possible. Anything worth having begins with a dream. It is from here that we begin the process of mental training.

Wie wir uns selbst sehen, bestimmen letztlich unsere Erfolge, unsere Risikobereitschaft und unsere Fähigkeit, mit jeder Situation fertig zu werden.

Unsere gedanklichen Vorstellungen sind sehr mächtig. Positive wie negative Selbstbilder beeinflussen unser Verhalten sehr nachhaltig. Sie bestimmen unsere Erfahrungsmöglichkeiten und schaffen unsere Realität.

Was wir zuallererst entwickeln müssen, nennt man "guten Vorsatz" oder "positive Absicht". Wir folgen einem guten Vorsatz, wenn wir für eine Athmosphäre sorgen, in der wir uns ruhig und sicher fühlen, in der Erwartung, daß positive Dinge geschehen werden und der Erfolg kommen wird.

Mit den guten Vorsätzen entsteht die Fähigkeit zu "träumen". Durch das Träumen wird alles möglich. Alles, was es wert ist, zu haben oder zu sein, fängt mit dem Traum an. Hier beginnt das mentale Spiel!

Ce que ne croyons être valable pour nous est ce qui détermine nos succès, nos échecs, notre capacité à prendre des risques et à faire face à toutes les situations.

Les images que nous voyons dans notre tête sont très fortes. Ces images mentales, à la fois positives et négatives, affectent nos capacités lorsque nous exerçons une activité depuis longtemps. Elles déterminent nos expériences et créent le sentiment que nous existons.

Le premier aspect à développer est appelé: "l'intention positive". Nous sommes en face d'une "intention positive", dès que nous créons un environnement dans lequel nous nous sentons en confiance. Nous espérons que les choses agréables vont arriver et que le succès sera au rendez-vous.

L'intention positive est intimement liée à la capacité à REVER. C'est en rêvant les choses que vous les rendrez possibles. Tout ce qui vaut la peine d'être possédé commence par un rêve. C'est à partir de ce point que nous commençons à travailler notre mental.

~ English ~ German ~ ~ French ~

Planted seeds that changed the NBA!

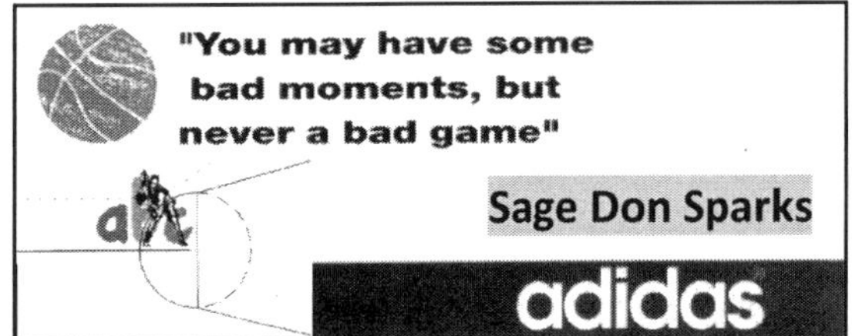

"You may have some bad moments, but never a bad game"
Sage Don Sparks
adidas

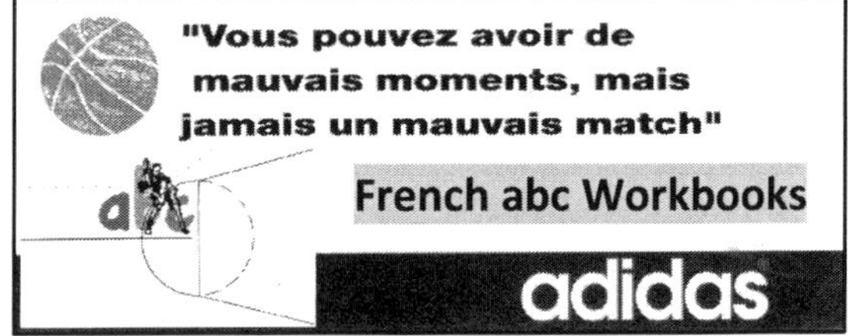

"Vous pouvez avoir de mauvais moments, mais jamais un mauvais match"
French abc Workbooks
adidas

"Prost": adidas night at a Munchen Bier Garten
Detlef, G' & Det's friend, Jeff

As a high school senior in Centralia, he led his team to the state title. At the University of Washington, the Huskies won Pac-10 championships in 1984 and 1985. With Schrempf as the team's leading scorer, the team advanced to the NCAA tournament's Sweet Sixteen in 1984. Part of a wave of tall players (he's 6-foot-9) who could handle a ball and shoot like guards, Schrempf's skills translated to 16 years in the NBA, mostly with the Indiana Pacers and the Seattle SuperSonics. Originally selected as the eighth pick in the NBA draft, Schrempf lived up to his promise. He was named to three All-Star Games and was the 1994 NBA Sixth Man of the the Year. In the 1995-'96 season he played the NBA finals series with Gary Payton and Shawn Kemp against Michael Jordan's Bulls. The Supersonics lost in five. At Detlef's camp in Munich, I purchased my prized German specs Porsche 944S. My first drive was to a road-side **Car Crash Memorial for Petro'** just 10 kms outside of Munchen.

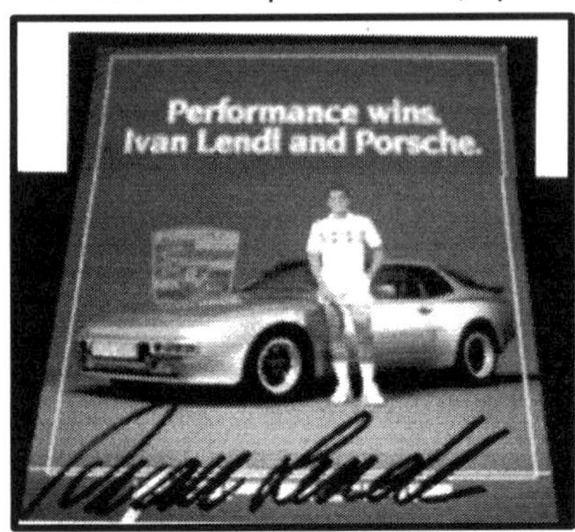

RIP Drazen

DETLEF SCHREMPF ALL-STAR CAMP ~ MUNICH

Sportshule Indoor Tennis Courts

Boris Becker

WTA Hall of Fame

Faces in the crowd

Former tennis great **Boris Becker,** who is something of a basketball junkie, showed up to do the pregame show on Premiere Television of Germany.

Boris invited me to play tennis with him. Detlef advised, "You better wear a cup!"

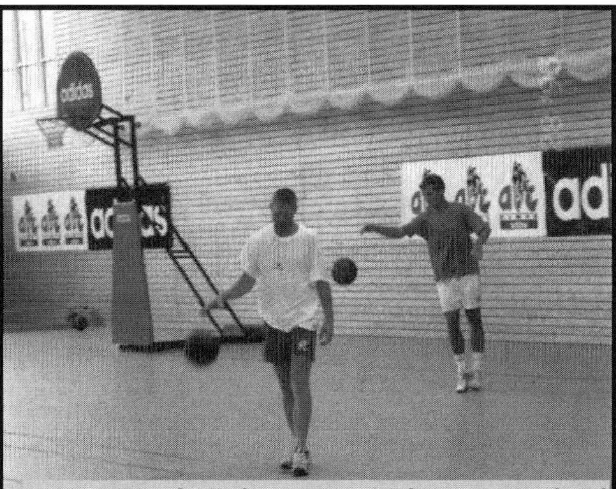

Boris was a legit hoopster with a sweet shot! He made my uber H.O.R.S.E. shots look easy!

Detlef and Boris treated me like a brother from another mother!

August 20th ~ G' & Mutombo Berlin Reunion

G'$ Intro

Streetball Challenge

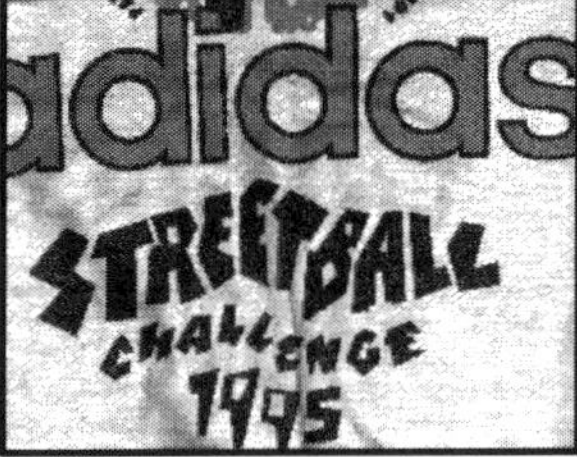

Center Court ~ VIP's G'$ & D. Mutombo!

VIP's Backstage G'$ & Dikembe

Center Court Interview

Berlin, Germany

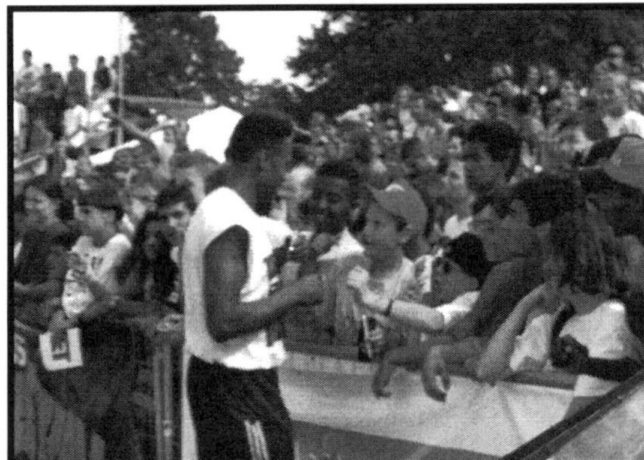

Fan Fav

G' Flight Dunk Exhibit

Warm-up

Visualize

G' Flight Mode

G' Flight...Baseline 180 Degree Corkscrew

Take a baseline dribble to my launch-point underneath the backboard, facing the crowd, explode up-up off of two feet, mid-air 180 degree spin, facing opposite crowd, eye the rim, cock back, spread legs; Flush & Floss!

Nuthin' But a G' Thang

G' Scott Signs with 0-7 TG Hanau Pro Club

LE RUNNERS BASKET 7-8 95

Ayyub „Andy" Anderson, Alter: 28, Geburtsort: Muskegon/Michigan; College: University of Ozarks/Arkansas

John „Baby" Bolden, Alter: 28, Geburtsort: Jacksonville/Florida; College: Junior College Jacksonville

Club TG-Hanau manager, Jans, called me at home with a clear intent of signing me! Jans negotiated with me and told me that their Yugoslavian coach was resistant to replacing their foreiner and was not told of my signing. Worse, the foreigner was Andy Anderson from Le Runners!! I was invited to practice where I'd be introduced to the media and match-up with Andy!! It's all about business!

This is my Occupation! G'hoops: Performance-based Business

SPORT **November 3, 1995** Jahrgang 270 / Nummer 263

Das Siegen als Lernprozeß

Gregg Scott: Sport-Psychologe und excellenter Distanzwerfer

Ein bekannter Fußballer hat einmal gesagt: Erst hatten wir kein Glück, dann kam auch noch Pech dazu. Unter diesem Aspekt stand bislang die Saison bei den Regionalliga-Basketballern der TG Hanau: Kaum ein spektakulärer Neuzugang, dafür entscheidende Abgänge. „Es ist Zeit für eine Kehrtwende, eine neue Haltung", sagt Co-Trainer Sven Witt. Und diese Kehrtwende soll nach sieben Niederlagen in Folge Gregg Scott, der neue US-Amerikaner, bewirken.

Am Donnerstag trainierte der 31jährige Forward erstmals mit dem Team. Heute abend, 20.15 Uhr, wird er in der Jahnhalle voraussichtlich gegen Aufsteiger Wittlich sein Debüt geben. Zur Begrüßung „nagelte" Scott im Training erst einmal einen Wurf von Rückkehrer Martin Boos an das Brett, schoß „Dreier" von weit jenseits der Dreipunktelinie und dunkte den Ball mehrfach elegant durch den Ring.

Gregg Scott wurde in der Pfalz geboren, wuchs in Los Angeles auf und machte an der Universität von Hawaii seinen Abschluß in Marketing und Sport-Psychologie. „Ich möchte dem Team beibringen, wie man gewinnt, denn manchmal ist das Siegen nur ein Lernprozeß", sagt er. Scott weiß, wovon er redet. Im Sommer arbeitete er als Trainer bei Basketball-Camps – in München gemeinsam mit Deutschlands NBA-Profi Detlef Schrempf, in Paris mit NBA-Center Dikembe Mutombo (Denver Nuggets). Das Spezialgebiet: die mentale Einstellung, mentales Training.

Sein Wissen über Sport-Psychologie hat Gregg Scott, der im September zu einem Free-Agent-Camp des neuen US-Profi-Teams Toronto Raptors eingeladen wurde, in einem Buch mit dem Titel „The mental athlete Workshop" zusammengefaßt. In der Jahnhalle möchte er nun praktischen Anschauungsunterricht geben und ganz nebenbei Hanaus Wurfschwäche aus der Distanz beheben. Das Selbstvertrauen dazu hat er: „Ich bin ein 25-Punkte-und-mehr-Spieler." top

Fingerspitzengefühl: Gregg Scott, neuer Basketball-Entwicklungshelfer des Regionalligisten TG Hanau. Foto: top

#CoachDisdain

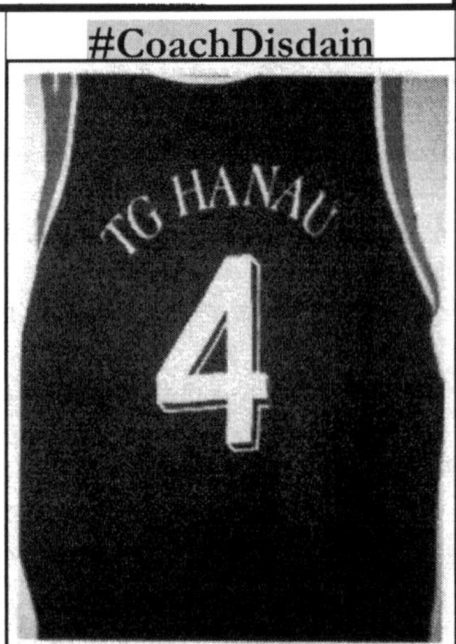

I went to training, met the aloof coach, was introduced to the team, club hierarchy, local medial and my interpreter. Doing my job dictates that I disallow you to do your job. So, suffice it to say that I did my work, put Andy on lock, bonded with my teammates and Jans upped his initial contract offer. **I took Andy out for cocktails afterwards. That's just G'!**

I wore jersey number 4 as a tribute to Drazen Petrovic and I so wrongfully thought my coach would embrace my gesture as they both were Yugoslavian. Bad Move! #4: A noble tribute that would have G'$ consequences!

TG Hanau Debut: Foreign Encroachment; 'The Minister' Reply

The entire game versus Darmstadt, I was manhandled by their 6'5" 215 lb. American player who was a tough buff redhead dude from Boston. The refs were mute to his physicality. He 'held' me to just 10 points in a close game as we got to Crunch Time. With two minutes to go, a shot went up and he was blocking me out under the basket. The ball went in the basket and as I tried to disengage, he continued, and backed me off the baseline. The play was over and he was exhibiting 'false hustle'. As I was losing my balance, I planted, got my arm under his shoulder, lifted and tossed him over the first row into the stands. There was beer, popcorn and pretzels flying everywhere as he landed in the laps of the courtside fans. No call was made, just a long delay to clean the floor. I had cleaned him up! G'$ Gutcheck! At that point his machismo was soft as tissue paper. Hence, I got the game winning tip-in.

Im entscheidenden Moment mit Fingerspitzengefühl: Gregg Scott, der mit einem Tip-In Hanaus ersten Saisonsieg perfekt machte. Foto: top

Bann gebrochen: Scott biegt im Herzschlagfinale das Spiel um

Erster Sieg für Basketball-Regionalligist TG Hanau – 80:79 über Darmstadt

Am Samstag abend um 21.47 Uhr war der Bann gebrochen: Hanau „Herren der Ringe" sprangen im kollektiven Ringelreihen durch die Jahnhalle, lagen sich in den Armen, jubelten, schrieen sich den Frust von der Seele. Der Aneinanderreihung von Pleiten, Pech und Pannen wurde ein Ende gesetzt, weil gegen den BC Darmstadt das Gesetz der Serie bestand hielt. Mit 80:79 (43:41) feierte die TG Hanau am elften Spieltag ihren ersten Sieg in der Basketball-Regionalliga, und für die Südhessen gibt es in der Jahnhalle unverändert nichts zu gewinnen.

Die Entscheidung fiel in einem Herzschlagfinale. Drei Sekunden vor der Schlußsirene spitzelte Gregg Scott per Tip-In einen Dreipunkteversuch von Mirko Witt in den Ring. Die Turngemeinde hatte den einzigen Rückstand der zweiten Halbzeit noch zum 80:79 umgedreht und damit eine neuerliche Niederlage abgewendet, weil Scott zum rechten Zeitpunkt Fingerspitzengefühl bewies.

Die TGH hatte den 31jährigen US-Amerikaner als Scorer verpflichtet. Doch der „25-Punkte-und-mehr-Spieler" konnte seinem Ruf als trefflicher Distanzschütze erneut nicht unter Beweis stellen, blieb bei sieben Dreipunkteversuche ohne Erfolg. In der Schlußminute war der farbige Forward aber der von Hanau gesuchte „Go-to-Guy", der Spieler, der die Verantwortung übernimmt. Nach einem Foul verwandelte er beide Freiwürfe zum 78:79, kurz darauf war er nach Witts Distanzwurf rechtzeitig in der Luft und als erster am Ball.

Seine stärksten Momente hatte Scott jedoch in der Verteidigung, als er nach Seitenwechsel, gemeinsam mit Witt, Darmstadts US-Amerikaner Kevin Smith abmeldete. Smith erzielte bis zur Pause 20 Punkte, danach nur noch deren drei. Scott war nicht der erwünschte Scorer, aber Jons Bauer sprang für den US-Amerikaner in die Bresche und avancierte mit 27 Punkten zum Topscorer.

Nach anfangs wechselnden Führungen übernahm der Tabellenletzte das Kommando, führte durchweg. Auch nach Wiederbeginn konnte sich die Turngemeinde nicht entscheidend absetzen. 74:68 hieß es sechs Minuten vor Schluß, als das Team von Coach Ignatovic erkannte, daß der erste Sieg greifbar nahe ist. Statt Zuversicht offenbarte Hanau erneut Unentschlossenheit, agierte auf einmal ängstlich. Vier Ballverluste, dazu der Ausschluß von Bedarf (36.) und Möhn (39.) wegen Überschreitens des Foulkontos sowie die Auswechslung von Bauer (38.), der einen Schlag ins Gesicht erhielt, ließen die Siegchancen sinken und Darmstadt auf 79:76 davonziehen. Doch der „Got-to-Guy" Scott war letztlich im rechten Moment zur Stelle.

TG Hanau: Jons Bauer (27 Punkte/4 „Dreier"), Tobias Löw (13), Sven Unruh (5), Gregg Scott (12), Jens Schneider, Michael Möhn (6), Mirko Witt (6), Roland Bedarf (11). top

Pure Pandemonium: A buzzer-beater and TG Hanau had its first win of the season!

Unscheduled, Unpaid, Unfriendly Friendly Game in Darmstadt

All are true. As is this rediculous tale of being battered, twice bloodied; Unpaid!??

Unscheduled, Unpaid, Unfriendly Friendly Game in Darmstadt

We had a week off in our schedule so I was told we'd play a "Friendly" game in Darmstadt. **Gratis!**

It was a snowy night as I arrived solo at the venue. The first thing I noticed was all the cars and the huge crowd as I was led to my designated underground spot.

An escort takes me upstairs through the main level of the arena where I noted that they were taking tickets and selling concessions! Hundreds of fans roared. Then, I saw several adidas Streeball posters of ME on the walls. G'$ on display.

We were to arrive dressed in our uniforms and meet on the court, not in the locker-room. As we began to warm-up a young Darmstat ballboy came to me for an autograph. He spoke perfect English and became my personal rebounder and confidant. He told me the game was a near sell-out and many fans came to watch me. But, macho Big Red was absent.

These players were beyond physical. They blatantly held, grabbed, pushed and prodded me at will from the opening tap. The 'unofficial' referees, dressed in sweats and untucked striped shirts were inept. Clearly, I was being punished for our triumph over them or my treatment of macho 'Big Red' in the previous game, or both. Midway through the first half I took a shoulder to the mouth that cut my lip. No call! I'm pissed. But, we're playing well. Just before halftime I got hit with an elbow that cut me on the opposite side of my mouth. Again, no call. I went up to the ref, pointed to my bloody mouth and asked, 'What's this?' He said, "That's nothing." I put some blood on my fingers and wiped it on his shirt. 'Then that's nothing on your shirt.' My coach chastized me at halftime. "Gregg this is a friendly." **'I pointed to my bloody mouth and snapped does this look like I'm their friend?'** Early second half, I drove into the key and exploded up as a Darmstadt player fouled me and held me to keep me from falling. No Call. I went to our bench, took off my wet jersey, put on my jacket, grabbed my bag and signed autographs as I walked out. No pay! No play!

TG Hanau vs. Kirchheimbolanden: Xanthus 'mate Lo Williams

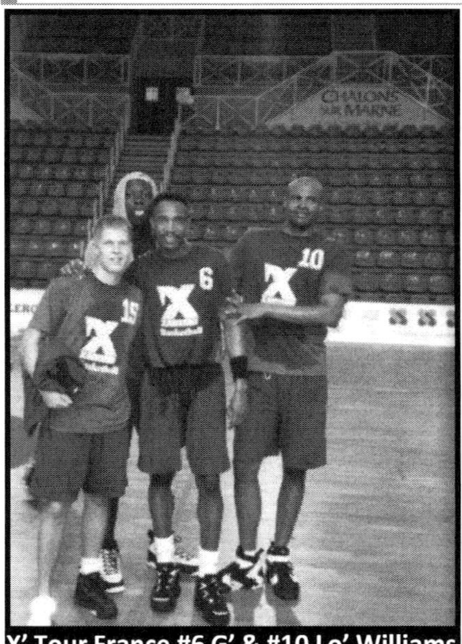
X' Tour France #6 G' & #10 Lo' Williams

I had a great pre-game reunion with Xanthus' Lawrence Lo' Williams. At midcourt we chatted and he introduced me to his uber cool coach, Holger Hanndermann. Then, he warned me of his teammate, #5, who was chatting with my coach near our bench. **"He's dirty G'man!" 'Gotcha! Crucial 411.'**

Xanthus All Star Team

Lawrence	**Williams**	201 cm
Dwight	**Crocker**	193 cm
Craig	**Scott**	182 cm
Daniel	**Halgromson**	183 cm
David	**Jones**	186 cm
George	**Duvon**	206 cm
John	**Blake**	203 cm
Dan	**Callahan**	203 cm
John	**Leahy**	201 cm
Mike	**Moten**	206 cm
Coach:	Joe **Burton**	

It didn't take long for #5 to show his filthiness. I got off to a great start scoring 15 in the first 15 minutes and we were up by 7. Then #5 got dirty. Loose ball near halfcourt. I race to it first and this dude pushes me in the back with two hands, sending me sprawling off the court out of control and towards a glass door near the sideline. I pushed the bar to release the door as I fell onto a gymnastics mat inside the chamber. There was mayhem on the court as my team came to my defense. Lo' came to check on me. My coach showed no emotion. His disdain: Drazen's #4 jersey. Croatia v Serb!

Auch Kibo Absteiger

*Do Not Emulate

Nach dem 16. Spieltag steht neben der TG Hanau auch der TV Kirchheimbolanden als Absteiger fest. Die 86:102 (48:48)-Niederlage bei der TG Hanau nahm den Pfälzern die letzte theoretische Chance. Scott (37) und Bauer (23/3) waren bei der TG Hanau nicht zu bremsen. Erfolgreichster beim TV Kibo war Williams (23). Umstritten bleibt Rang acht, der im Falle des Nichtaufstiegs des Meisters und beim Bundesliga-abstieg der TGS Ober-Ramstadt die Viertklassigkeit bedeutet.

2 minutes later **Serb #5** came to set an off-ball screen on me. **Crack!** Down and out. **No Call!** My coach was irate. He swiftly sub'd me out! I asked why. He yelled in English, **'Sit down and shut up.'** His first words ever in English to me! I went right up to him and looked into his eyes. I softly sternly whispered, 'Spreken ze English? F'bomb you! Understand. F'bomb you!' **Blink!! Punked!** I went and sat down. Our lead, gone! Halftime, he cosigned his rant, "I'm the coach." Middle Finger, 'Coach!' The team giggled. The one reason I kept my job? My second half work! **GameSpeak: 22 points, 37 total and victory.**

Lo: "G'man, I told Holger you'd kill us!"

NIKE'S LE RUNNERS HOOP TOUR: NUREMBERG

Das ist die Geschichte eines Streetball-Teams.
Zwei Amerikaner, ein Kroate, ein Deutscher.
Sie waren die Besten auf der Straße, doch nun
sind sie ausgeschieden. Nicht weil sie Schluß
gemacht haben. „Le Runners" spielen nun für
Kohle. Und doch, ihren Spirit haben
sie noch nicht verloren.

<u>Jack Sussmann:</u> "Our Le Runners tour schedule was made to fit Gregg Scott's availability." Next Showcase: Giessen!

LE RUNNERS

Ayyub „Andy" Anderson, Alter: 28, Geburtsort: Muskegon/Michigan; College: University of Ozarks/Arkansas

John „Baby" Bolden, Alter: 28, Geburtsort: Jacksonville/Florida; College: Junior College Jacksonville

Michael „Mike" Witte, Alter: 26; Geburtsort: Limburg; High School: Beaver/Utah

Dan Mooney, Alter: 34, Geburtsort: New York; spielte in der NBA einige Partien für Phoenix, Sacramento und Atlanta, in der CBA für Albeny.

BASKET 7-8 95

My G'$ Xanthus locker-room chat with John Bolden: Intro to Le Runners' Jack Sussmann!

Gregg was better than advertised!

And, all his teammates loved him!

Big John was right: The Total Package!

A Class Pro

A Smooth Operator

Jack Sussmann

Andy was Hanau's foreign player before I was signed. Still, we had a bond through Le Runners and socially! His gift to me of a huge Basket Magazine Air Jordan mural shows brotherly love!

G'$ Jump Shot: Just as my brother taught me!
G'$ Jam Southpaw: Just as I taught myself!

WIESBADEN DEBUT DELAYED

WIESBADEN COMMUNITY SPORTS DIRECTOR
WILLIE EVANS

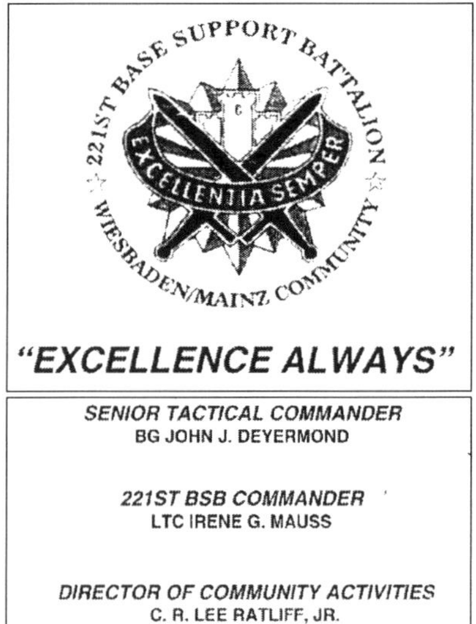

"EXCELLENCE ALWAYS"

SENIOR TACTICAL COMMANDER
BG JOHN J. DEYERMOND

221ST BSB COMMANDER
LTC IRENE G. MAUSS

DIRECTOR OF COMMUNITY ACTIVITIES
C. R. LEE RATLIFF, JR.

CHIEF, COMMUNITY RECREATION DIVISION
ANN BURSKI.

WIESBADEN COMMUNITY SPORTS DIRECTOR
WILLIE EVANS

Mr. Willie Evans

W.A.B. Sports Director:

"Back in April 'Big John' Bolden rushed into my office eagerly telling me of a game he played in versus Xanthus All-Stars and the two guards who dominated. The pair put in 70 points combined. "

John Bolden: "Mr. E, the guards blew us out! A Killer Combo! Each scored 35! You know Dave Jones, the scoring point guard from Heidleberg. But, their 2-guard was 100% the Schiznit! A tough 6'3" cool cat who could do it all at both ends of the court. The Total Package. Yo, he's moving to Wiesbaden! Gregg Scott. The G'man!"

Mr. Evans: "One morning in August as I'm in my office above the gym, I hear the sounds of basketballs bouncing in rythym and the basket snapping loudly as if a ball was dunked. I go to investigate. I saw one sweaty player dribbling two balls up and down the court and instantly knew who it was. Gregg Scott, training alone! I introduced myself and that was the creation of a union that would impact our community."

"Gregg came into my office to visit before his gym workout. Darmstadt's A.D./BB Coach was there. He told Gregg, "Son, Wiesbaden's never won anything. Ever!" Scott paused and replied, 'Well, Wiesbaden has never had me.' Silence."

"In November, Gregg came to tell me his wife demanded a vacation, so he'd be absent for our home Thanksgiving Tourney. Son, happy wife, happy life."

Holiday SKI TRIP to Garmish Pasketgurtem ~ The Alps

By Liz Moore
221st BSB sports coordinator

The Rhein Main Area USO hosted the Invitational Thanksgiving Tip-Off Basketball Tournament Nov. 24 through 26 at the Tony Bass Fitness Center. The game brought in six women's and six men's teams from various outside communities—to include our own.

With these games being pre-season, everyone wanted to see what the other teams looked like. The one team to watch was Wiesbaden's own. The gym was filled to its capacity and all the fans were loyal from the very beginning. The home team crowd watched their players run up and down the court to

I was skiing in the Alps of Bavaria as my team played.

Sunday was to be on slopes.

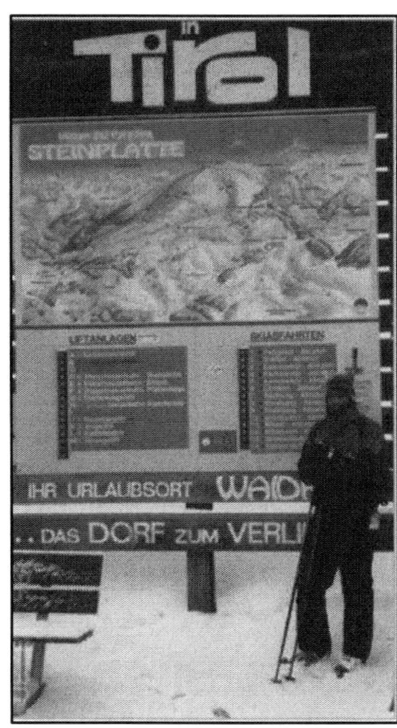

At breakfast we decided not to ski and to roll home early. We departed at 9:03 and hit the Autobahn. An amazing Porsche trip: 310 miles in 3 hours. Home by noon!!

<u>Mr. E':</u> "Gregg came into the gym in ski clothes, early 1st half of Game One as we're down by 20. I went down to Coach Brown and told him Scott was here for game 2. Coach called a time-out, summoned Gregg and spoke to him. Everyone gazed."

Coach Brown asked me how my trip was and how did I feel. I told him. 'I'm good, not too sore.' He said, "We've spit our wad and we're overmatched here so I need you to play the championship game." I rushed home to prep my gear and tell Puig.

Wiesbaden men defeat K-town 85-83

She was thrilled. "Yes. I gotta see this G'$ SHOW!"

Both teams gave so much during their first game that everyone wondered what the outcome of the forced IF game would be. K-town exploded again despite the help of Wiesbaden's Orlando Wesley's nine points, and Andre James and Rhondie Ross's four points. The first half ended at 48-40.

Bets were made on how the second half would end, and a prettier picture could not have been painted. With three minutes left on the clock and the ball in Wiesbaden's possession, the score was tied. The ball was passed back and forth, the clock was ticking down. With five seconds left, Wiesbaden's Craig Scott put the ball through the net to wrap up the win for Wiesbaden, 85-83.

SPORTS | THE STARS AND STRIPES

Wiesbaden wins tourney

WIESBADEN AB, Germany — Wiesbaden beat Kaiserslautern 85-83 Sunday night in the men's title game of the Thanksgiving Tip-off Tournament.

Craig Scott hit the winning shot with 8 seconds left.

WIESBADEN/MAINZ EAGLES

ALL-STAR CHALLENGE '95: COPENHAGEN, DENMARK

After a gritty home victory in Hanau, I drove four hours to Hamburg, arriving at Mark Gustin's home after midnight. Mark was a player and our manager. He saw me 'work' in a game in Karlsruhl. I slept a few hours before driving us to the train station to meet our European All-Star teammates.

EUROPEAN ALL-STARS	
~~TOM SEWELL~~	HOLLAND
~~MIKE FREEMAN~~	LUXEM.
~~EARL WRIGHT~~	LUXEM.
3 KEN SMITH	LUXEM. ✓
3 MARK GUSTIN	GERMANY ✓
7 GREG SCOTT	GERMANY
NENAD BRISVAC	YUGOSLAV

G'$: #7 European All-Stars

December 1995

DGI OG FALCON BASKET PRÆSENTERER

ALL-STAR CHALLENGE 95

VELKOMMEN

DGI byder velkommen til årets basketball begivenhed -

ALL-STAR CHALLENGE 1995

Spillerne er amerikanske All-Star spillere fra USA, Danmark, mange med en fortid I NBA, NCAA og CBA, hvorfor vi kan forvente at se meget spændende basket på topplan.

Vor turnering er inspireret af de amerikanske turneringer:
Her spiller hvert hold en kamp og vindere spiller i finalen.
Derudover spilles der en trøstkamp mellem de to tabende hold.

ONE WINNER TAKES ALL!!!

Vi ønsker deltagerne held og lykke og publikum en rigtig god fornøjelse. NB! Da DGI har tænkt sig at lave denne jule/nytårsturnering til en årlig tradition, kan vi kun sige - "På gensyn".

PROGRAMOVERSIGT

ONSDAG

16.30	Kørestolbasket Challenge
18.00	DGI All-Stars vs. US Style All-Stars
	Lodtrækning - 3 point shoot-out
19.30	European All-Stars vs. Vertical Sports All-Stars

TORSDAG

15.00	Finale Ynglinge Dame
	Finale Ynglinge Herre
16.45	Consolation Final
19.00	Pause - Dunk konkurrence - Lodtrækning
19.45	All-Star Challenge Final

27-28 DECEMBER · KL. 16.30
BÜLOWVEJ HALLEN &
FREDERIKSBERG HALLEN
VOKSEN: KR. 30,- PR.DAG * BØRN: KR. 20,- PR.DAG

We rendezvous, board a train and departed the depot; ferry-bound. Comatose, I only wanted to sleep.

I wake up in a panic. I'm all alone on the train and it's now inside of a humongous cargo area with cars, trucks, even 18-wheelers in sight. Whatda…? I feel a subtle motion of the ocean below me which only increased my angst. As I exited the train to view the embedded tracks underneath I was perplexed. How can this freakin' ferry stay afloat?? I finally get the gumption to go up to the passenger area and reunite with my team. To my surprise and delight, the vessel was quite plush. I'd traveled on many cruise ships, yet this was my first ferry venture. It was a very smooth trip, indeed. Hours later we board the train as the ferry enters the harbor. The engines rev as the train slowly backs out of the ferry's hull and takes us to the underground station in Copenhagen.

VINCENT RAYE
G'$ & Vince: UHH & L.A. Boyz Reunite 'Aloha Style'!

U.S. STYLE ALL-STARS	
STEVE BRUMFIELD	–
3 VINCENT RAYE	13
3 MATT TROMBLEY	10
DERON DANCY	8
DAVID JAMES	14
MARK COLLINS	12
LAVON BROWN	

It was freezing cold. We taxi to our hotel and then to the gym. As we entered the packed gym, all eyes were on us. In the awe, one voice shouts out above all, **"Oh my God, is that G'man?"**

Copenhagen UHH Reunion

Vincent Raye was my homie from UH-Hilo and he was bred in the L.A. Valley. A Baller! He arrived at UHH after my senior season. Game recognized Game and Vince took my mantle both on and off the hoop court. We were boyz! V' paid a proud homage to me.

1988 UH-Hilo Alumni Game

Gregg 1984 - '86 and #22 Vince 1986 - '88

Copenhagen G'$ & Vince! The Reunion

Vince was Famous! On Posters & Billboards!

Unbeknownst to me, Vince was not merely another All-Star. The crowd awed at our true sincere embrace because this guy was the Top Dog! The most popular, most marketed and the highest paid player in Denmark. V' was the reigning league champion and MVP! Giving reverence to me for everyone to see, was truly a magical moment! Still cherished! **Our teams didn't have to play each other!**

V' played at 6 and I played at 7:30. We were together 24/7, hanging out! I called Puig and extended my stay! **VIP Gift: The Show CD!**

RUSSELL SIMMONS Presents THE SHOW The Soundtrack

G'$: A 1½ day extended stay!

V': Tourney Champs & MVP
G'$: Consolation Champions & 1st Team All-Tournament!!!

January 19-20, 1996
~ Le Runners Tour ~
Luxembourg & Trier

THE SHOW CD:

HYPE BEATS TO FUEL G'$!

MUST BE THE MUSIC

dant Gregg Scott mit einem Dunk brillierten. Scott zeigte sich gegenüber seinem Premierenspiel gegen Wittlich deutlich verbessert, benötigte für seine 28 Punkte deutlich weniger Würfe als für seine 22 Zähler gegen Wittlich. Center Löw sammelte 16 seiner 18 Punkte im zweiten Spielabschnitt, wurde dabei mehrfach schön von Fechter in Szene gesetzt. Und Witt zeigte eine gute Partie auf der Aufbauposition.

TG Hanau: Tobias Löw (18 Punkte), Sven Unruh (6/1 „Dreier"), Gregg Scott (28/3), Mirko Witt (6), Roland Bedarf (15), Thomas Fechter (10), Michael Möhn. top

Hanau G'$ Barrage

Bester TGH-Akteur war Gregg Scott, der in den Kategorien Punkten und Rebounds zweistellige Werte erreichte, dazu auf sechs Steals kam. Der US-Amerikaner erzielte auch den spektakulärsten Korb, als er das Leder, nach einem hohen Anspiel von Bauer, direkt aus der Luft –

Bei der TGH mußte dagegen zu oft einer für alle spielen. Gregg Scott war mit 33 Punkten erfolgreichster Punktesammler der Partie. Der US-Amerikaner traf aus der Distanz so gut wie nichts, war aber unter dem Korb nicht zu stoppen, zählte

TG Hanau: Gregg Scott (33 Punkte), Ral Mosler, Jons Bauer (2), Tobias Löw (2), Mar tin Boos (10), Sven Unruh (2), Mirko Wit (16/1 „Dreier"), Roland Bedarf (9), Fran Mosler, Michael Möhn. to

TG Hanau: Jons Bauer (30 Punkte/vier „Dreier"), Tobias Löw (14), Martin Boos (11), Sven Unruh (4), Mirko Witt (4), Roland Bedarf (7), Frank Mosler (2), Gregg Scott (34/4). top

US-Amerikaner Scott stellte mit 37 Punkte eine persönliche Bestmarke auf. Forward Bauer kam auf eine 66prozentige Trefferquote. Die Center Boos und Löw schnappten sich jeweils zehn Rebounds. Mit Bedarf präsentierte sich der zweitlängste Hanauer als bester Vorlagengeber (acht Assists). Spielmacher Witt erlaubte sich lediglich zwei Ballverluste und traf drei von fünf „Dreiern". Und Youngster Frank Mosler fügte sich nahtlos ein.

TG Hanau: Gregg Scott (37 Punkte/2 „Dreier"), Jons Bauer (23/3), Tobias Löw (9), Martin Boos (16), Mirko Witt (11/3), Roland Bedarf (4), Frank Mosler (2). top

THE SHOW

Im Angriff setzte erneut Gregg Scott mit 31 Punkten die Glanzpunkte. Center Tobias Löw zeigte aufsteigende Tendenz, steuerte acht Punkte bei und schnappte sich ein Dutzend Rebounds.

TG Hanau: Gregg Scott (31 Punkte/3 „Dreier"), Jens Schneider (4), Tobias Löw (8), Martin Boos (10), Ralf Mosler (8), Mirko Witt (2), Roland Bedarf (2), Frank Mosler

March 3, 1996

KORBJÄGERLISTE

Gregg Scott verteidigte mit 32 Punkten seine Position als Korbjäger Nummer eins der Liga und beendete seine trefflichen Dienste mit einem spektakulären Dunking. Auf der Gegenseite brachte sein Landsmann Samuel Graham-Godden (29 Punkte) gleich mehrfach den Ring zum Glühen, als er viermal, einmal davon per Alley-Hoop, den Ball mit brachialer Gewalt durch den Ring „stopfte".

TG Hanau: Jons Bauer (22 Punkte/2 „Dreier"), Tobias Löw (13), Sven Unruh (11/2), Mirko Witt (13/3), Roland Bedarf (1), Frank Mosler (4), Gregg Scott (32/3). top

G'$ vs. Sam Graham-Godden!
Great Friends in Competition!
G' #1: "Nummer eins der Liga"

Punkte gegen den Abstieg sicherten sich der TSV Grünberg (112:91/54:33) beim TV Kirchheimbolanden und der Wittlicher TV (116:106/57:53). Nach gutem Start (22:8, 6.) gelang der TG um Scott (34/4) und Bauer (30/4) in der 19. Minute der 48:48-Ausgleich, nachdem Klein (31/4) und Devone (25) pausierten. Ein 13:0-Spurt des WTV bis zur 25.

Regionalliga Südwest/Nord, Herren

1. Scott (Hanau)	287	11	26,09
2. Colan (Koblenz)	456	18	25,33
3. Williams (K'bolanden)	430	17	25,29
4. Neuber (Saarlouis)	445	18	24,72
5. Smith (Saarlouis)	440	18	24,44
6. Godden-Graham (VfB Gießen)	431	18	23,94
7. Klein (Wittlich)	399	17	23,47
8. Condon (Limburg)	354	18	19,67
9. Bosnjak (Wittlich)	340	18	18,89
10. Smith (Darmstadt)	319	17	18,76

Lahnstädter die Chance zum Testen, so daß die Hanauer um Scott (28) und Bauer (18) herankamen. 20 der Zähler erzielte Scott in den fünf Schlußminuten.

G'$ English Translation:
20 wonderful points of Scott came in the FIRST FIVE minutes of the game.

WIESBADEN

Military tourneys set for 'March Madness'

Story by Janet Scott via 1997 Meeting & Interview with Mr. Evans

WIESBADEN
COMMUNITY
SPORTS
"EAGLE
EXCELLENCE"
USAREUR
SEMI-FINAL
PLAYOFFS
WIESBADEN, GERMANY

Mr. Evans: "Hosting the USAREUR Semi-Final Tourney in Wiesbaden was a tribute to our winning record as a team, and a unique source of pride for our community. With teams and fans from all over Europe invading our gym in a festival-like atmosphere and with a finals bid at stake, March Madness was on full display. And, for this tournament we had both Scott and John Bolden."

As fate would have it, the brackets were set-up with a looming Wiesbaden vs. Darmstadt game in the finals. A high-noon Sunday Showdown for the championship, and ShowTime for Gregg vs. their Coach/AD; at last." "Before the finals, Darmstadt's coach said, 'I got a surprise for your boy'."

I had a tough victory with Hanau in Trier on Thursday and was fit for our Friday debut in the military tourney. It was my pleasure! We rolled through and qualified for the final game.

Pregame Intros: "At shooting guard, from San Diego, California, #23, Gregg Scott."

Ultimate FAV Memory: Singing the Star Spangled Banner!

We snatched off our sweet gold and blue tear-away sweats and came out for the tip. As we took the court for the opening jump ball, the Darmstadt coach called the refs over to show them a booklet. They called my coach over and they all huddled. Soon they pointed at me. Coach Brown is irritated as he calls me over to him. I'm dressed in our Gold uniform and all black: shoes, socks, sweat band and sleeve-less undershirt (hid my scar). Rule infraction!

Mr. Evans: Everyone wondered what the issue was and the timing of it. Then, Coach Brown told Gregg that the rules dictate "any garment worn under the uniform jersey must match the majority color of the uniform." So, Scott takes of his jersey and we all notice that his black muscle shirt is a Mickey Mouse T'. Nothing bravado about that. But, as he took off the shirt all eyes and lots of uuu's and ahhh's were on his svelt muscular upper-body. I could've sworn he flexed his pecs at the Coach. But, G' never said a word."

Big John spoke for me, "Yo, you wanna play head games with my G'man! Ya gonna pay!" I was lazer focused on controlling my emotions and my adrenalin. I got Big J' going early, then, I broke my #1 Rule. 'Never take a 3-pointer on my first shot!' It wasn't by my design.

Mr. E': "Scott hit his first shot! A deep '3' right next to the Darmstadt Coach. Swish! I hoped he'd peek at the coach right beside him. G' turned his back."

"Gregg's second shot, a 3-pointer from the corner in front of Darmstadt's team bench hit nothing but net. His third shot was a long '3-ball' from the opposite corner. Bang. After a brief rest on the bench, he hit his fourth shot, another '3', as he was closely guarded far beyond the top of the key. Facial! Then, with two minutes left in the half, he retrieved a deflected pass at the sideline near the midcourt. He picked up the ball and faced the defender who was ten feet away waiting for him to dribble. Scott, looked at him, held his arms and the ball out and taunted, 'Yo, are you gonna play D' or what?' The player didn't move. Scott nodded his approval, took a quick left-handed dribble forward, planted and exploded, up up up, releasing a picture perfect high-arching jump shot from at least 35 feet that took forever to hit All Net! Splash! And, the fans from both sides went wild. As, the half ended, I yelled to Brown, 'Turn him loose Sgt. Major, you'll never have this chance again."

Surely, I heard him. Everyone heard him. Also, as I went to Puig to get a gold undershirt (she had cut off the sleeves), her first words were, "Great job! Don't rest and don't let up." So, I took off my jersey and put on my black Mickey T', got some water and went to shoot on the court, by myself. Then, Sgt. Major Brown came out onto the court to coach me up!

Coach Brown: "I guess I don't need to ask you how you feel. That guy made a bad mistake with the stunt he pulled right before the game. But, I respect how you responded. When you knew the eyes were on you, you let your game speak. Now, we have a very unique situation at hand. An opportunity so special that I'm going to do somethng I've never done before. I've never had a player who could handle the responsibility. A player who'd garnered the complete respect and support of each of his teammates; until right here and right now. So, look here, I'm gonna turn you loose. I'm gonna let you do your thing. The fans want to see it, your team has your back, and mostly, he needs to know of his big mistake. There is still one half to play and he has not even seen half of your total game. I want you to show him your WHOLE PACKAGE! G', have no mercy and leave no damn doubt. Huu Wah."

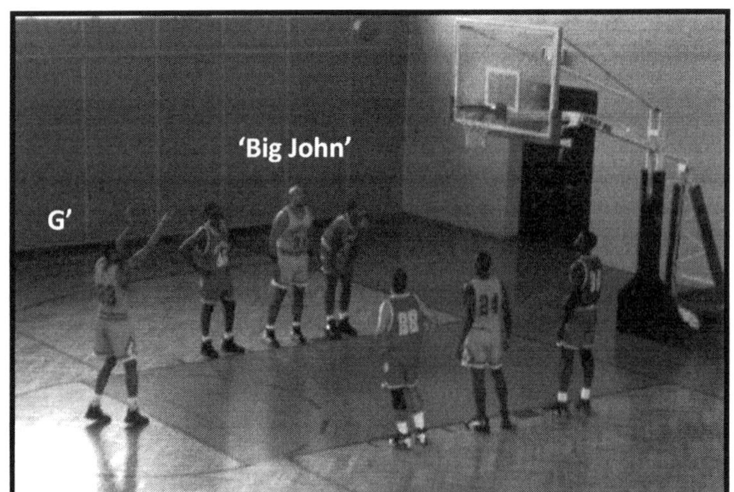

'Yes, Coach! I hear you loud and clear.' Seek & Destroy!!

G' Mode: Turn this shiz out!

Mr. E': "Scott came out with his hardhat and lunch pail. No threes at all. He was dominant at both ends of the court and facilitated for every one of his teammates. At one point he called a play for Morris, ran a pick and roll with Big John, got the ball to Morris open on the wing. His shot hit the front of the rim and Scott soared up, grabbed the rebound right above the rim; an easy follow-up. Instead, he switched hands and passed the ball right back to Morris and said, 'That's a bank-shot, Mo'. Hit the square.' Morris got the pass and lined up for the shot. He banked it off the square and in! As Morris ran back on D' he was truly thrilled as they exchanged a high five. The game was very well played and there were few fouls until one innocent foul on Gregg as he drove to the basket from the wing. The ref blew the whistle. Then, a Darmstadt player bumped hard into Gregg swiping at the ball and backing him up. Both of them were grasping the ball as some other players intervened. Then, Gregg planted his foot, lifted the ball and the player, turned him and body-slammed him hard, and then landed on top of him. Chaos! The refs only called a delay of game against Darmstadt. Sgt. Major wanted to sub Scott. There was only three minutes left and we were up by 15 points. He let #23 draw up his last play. They came out of the huddle. G's inbound pass goes to the guard, 'Big John' flashed to the high post as Gregg sprinted backdoor! A D'stadt defender deflected the pass high over the corner of the backboard. As the fans groaned, his hand with fingers extending above the corner of the board gloved the ball. Scott desended and flushed it with thunder as the gym went silent, in horror!!!"

G'$: Vanquishing Darmstadt & Tourney MVP!

Mr. Evans:

"G' autographed my stat sheet"

29 points: 5/5 on 2's ~ 5/5 on 3's ~ 4/4 on F/T's
12 assists ~ 13 rebounds ~ 3 blocks ~ 5 steals!!

The Wiesbaden Eagles, led by Greg Scott and James Bolden swept the Division I tournament Sunday and have even higher aspirations in the USAREUR tournament when they meet the Würzburg Rattlers at 2 p.m. Friday.

Mr. E: "Beyond his legacy, Gregg earned respect and honor as a true warrior by teammates who know what true war is."

USAREUR Finals: Hanau, Germany

Round 1: Fri. 2:00 Wiesbaden vs. Wurzburg

Fatefully, the USAREUR Finals tourney was held in the same town as my pro club, Hanau. I was available only on Friday due to a Saturday night TG Hanau road game in Speyer. And, John Bolden was keeping stats on Friday, not playing due to his pro club game. Compensating for his absence, I'd be playing at the 3-spot instead of my 2-guard position. I wore MJ's #45, instead of MJ's #23! **Divide & Conquer**: Merited a teary-eyed Coach Brown!

MEN	**WIESBADEN/MAINZ EAGLES**		
Damen Diggs	#53	77th MAINT CO	Pittsburg, PA
Edward Morris	#52	19th MMC	Alexandria, LA
Reginald Jones	#43	C CO 123rd MSB	Jackson, MS
Nickie Speight	#51	77th MAINT CO	Kingston, NC
Chester Brown	#32	HHS, 205th MI	New Orleans, LA
Ronnell Ashlock	#31	48th IS	Williamsburg, VA
Andre James	#42	HHC, 12th AVN	St. Louis, MO
Eric Bell	#33	E CO 5/158th AVN	Los Angeles, CA
Tirese Jones	#35	HHC, 12th AVN	Colorado Spring, CO
Jeremy Inigham	#34	3d COSCOM	Tampa, FL
Matt Stuck	#55	AAFES	Manton, MI
Gregg Scott	#45	Dependent	San Diego, CA
COACH: Eric Brown		HHC, 12th AVN	Monticello, MS
ASST COACH: Jerry Maddox		Dental Clinic	Port Gibson, MS
STATISTICIAN: John Bolton		Legal Clinic	Jacksonville, FL

Wuerzburg had a **6'** point guard with 'All-Army' status, who was a 'commentator' on the court. As he muscled his way, he taunted my boys. That's cool. But then, he yapped at my coach! Halftime:

WUERZBURG/KITZINGEN RATTLERS		
MEN	**Story by Janet Scott via 1997 Meeting & Interview with Mr. Evans**	
Derrick Canty	B CO 701st	Manning, SC
Ronald Smith	147th Maint	Prichard, AL
Kaylon Green	B CO 701st	Memphis, TN
Timothy Stephens	D CO 701st	Springfield, OH
Linwood Biddick	C CO 17th Sig	Norfolk, VA
Ray Rucker	N/A	Salma, AL
Carl Blakely	DISCOM	Laurel, MS
Monty Cummings	A CO 5/159 AVN	Miami, FL
Lawrence Springs	DENTAC	Norfolk, VA
Paul Goldsmith	HHC 121 Sig	Pensacola, FL
Marvin Potts	HHC 1TD	Stanford, CT
Eric Curtis	B CO 701st	Mobile, AL
COACH: Edward Gaines	D 4/3 ADA	Sterling, VA
ASST CH: Craig Brown	HHC 1TD	Milwaukee, WS
STAT.: Jennifer Goldsmith	HHC 98th ASG	Decatur, GA

I ask SM Brown if he was friends with the Mouth? "No, that's his M.O. But, don't worry about it." Oh, no. Hell no! 'Just give me 3 minutes on him Coach. I assure you 'Mouth' will be a non-factor for the rest of the game.' EPIC

Collateral Damage Element #2: Trash-talkers

I peeped the stat sheet and set my 'Art of War' scheme in motion!

Mr Evans: "As they matched up to start the second half, Scott went right up to 'All-Army', stood over him and queitly spoke. 'AA' steped backwards, looking to the referee for intervention. Scott calmly spoke to the referee and gestured towards the Wiesbaden team bench. The referee seemed to empathize with him. It mystified the crowd."

At mid-court, I went up to 'Mouth' and peered into his soul, **'Let's see if I'm too small.'** He moaned to the ref as if HE was offended. I pleaded my case. 'Ref, this guy talked and taunted the entire first half, unchecked. Trash-talking my teammates is NOT my problem. But, talking trash to my coach, IS. Telling my coach, ***he's too small*** and ***get a sub***, offends me! That's MY Coach, and he is to be respected! So, I'm going to teach him a lesson as a tribute to my Coach. ***Mouth*** has flaws and weaknesses in his game, psyche and physique.'

My Toolbox: Sage Sparks Post Move ~ Westside Blazers D' ~ Mike C. 'toss' ~ G'$ Bait

"Scott passed to the wing, cut to the rim, and posted-up on the right block. He gets the ball, *head fakes to the baseline* and passed the ball back out. He directs off-side player screens, as he re-posts . Wing passed him the ball.

"As he got the ball he gave an instant *head, ball and shoulder fake* to the baseline, took a one-dribble spin move into the key, low and on balance, with a quick *eyes and ball bounce-pass fake* to freeze the helper and allow 'Mouth' to recover. Then, a nifty *head and ball up-fake* to get him in the air. Scott exploded up strong with two hands, sent a stiff blow to the airborne defender, absorbed the contact, hung, and as the whistle blew, he swithced to his left hand and softly banked the ball in off of the square. Spectacular!"

Free throw line: 'Now let's see you cross-over left-to-right, at full speed, with ball pressure!' Phase II: Make the f/t! D' full court. Force his initial dribble to his left towards the sideline. Step-sliding. Count 1,2,3. Cut him off. Turn him, stay on his hip, force him to the sideline, Count 4,5,6. Cut him off, and anticipate his superior right-to-left cross. Plant on his cross, step-slide hard, keep him in front! Force him left angled to the sideline at the mid-court. Step-slide, plant, sprint to beat him to the spot. Plant, square-up, arm-lock toss. **Charging!**

Mr Evans: "As the inbound goes to Scott deep in the backcourt, he unveils an ambidexterous dribbling show right in the guy's face like '3-card Monte'. 'He's gonna reach ref' 'He can't help it' 'Hubris!' On cue, he reached, just as Scott pulled the ball back, shielded, spun, shot him a bow; the whistle blew. Foul. 5th! Scott Scoff: '3 plays, 48 seconds, DQ! Go apologize to my Coach!'"

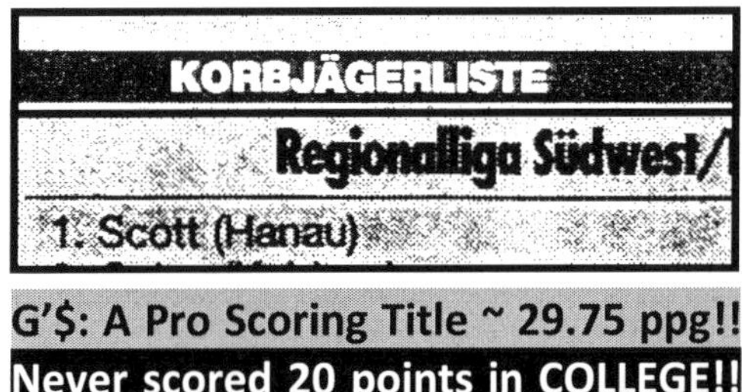
KORBJÄGERLISTE
Regionalliga Südwest/
1. Scott (Hanau)

G'$: A Pro Scoring Title ~ 29.75 ppg!!
Never scored 20 points in COLLEGE!!
TG Hanau 5th Place +.500 W/L Record!

"ALL EYES ON ME!"
MY MOM SENT ME THE 1996 2PAC CD!

programme

30 juillet au 02 Août
Stage Préolympique Equipe de France
à Sarreguemines

Du 02 au 04 Août
Tournoi INTERNATIONAL

02 Août Knutange
17 heures : Suède/Allemagne,
20 heures : Allemagne/France
03 Août Sarreguemines
15 heures : Suède/Allemagne, à Rohrbach les Bitche **à 20 heures** : France/Suède
04 Août Saint-Avold
15 heures : Suède/France

04 Août Sarreguemines 18 heures 30 match valide

Darmstadt

19 heures 45 : concours paniers à 3 points

Sarreguemines 20 heures 30 :
France/Allemagne

A la mi-temps, grand tirage au sort de la tombola avec un voyage en Italie et de nombreux prix de valeur à gagner

TECNOL

1992 ~ San Diego: Dr. Roy Phillips, G'$ intro to Kallassy representative

Orthopedic Products

HAS AN APPOINTMENT WITH
DR. ROY PHILLIPS
Podiatrist
Clairemont Medical Center
3660 Clairemont Dr., Suite 2
San Diego, CA 92117

April 15, 1996

Gregg Scott
USAEDE CETAE PM-A
CMR 410, BOX 402
APO AE 09096

Dear Mr. Scott,

Enclosed are samples of the Kallassy Ankle Support for you to wear during your practices and games. I'm sorry to hear that you've encountered difficulty in obtaining our product.

Tecnol's channel of distribution is through medical distributors. In order to keep that relationship secure, we can not sell our products directly to the end user. Nea Tec is our medical distributor in Neu-Ulm, Germany. Belen Placencio-Romer is the representative at Nea Tec and can be reached at 49 731 9807891.

Good luck to you in your professional career. Please let me know of your accomplishments.

Sincerely,

Kim Douglas
Product Manger

Separate Left and Right Supports! Figure-8 Velcro system! No Laces!

Shoes, uniforms and venues vary. One critical constant: The Kallassy Ankle Brace Supports were a part of my gear in every training, exhibition, Streetball event, All-Star game and professional competition I ever participated in. Bar None. I never needed to be taped by any trainer.

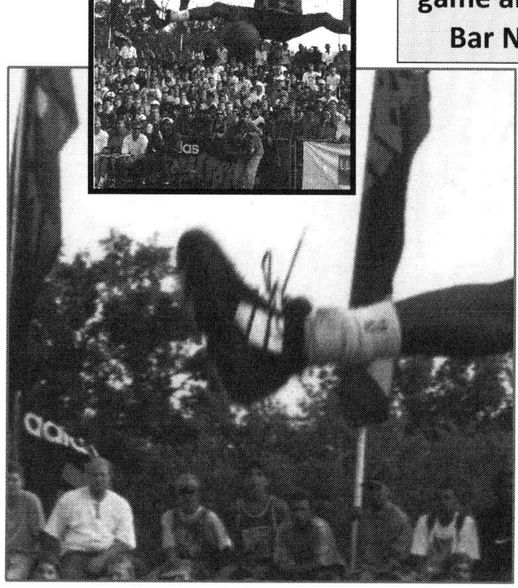

1995 Berlin

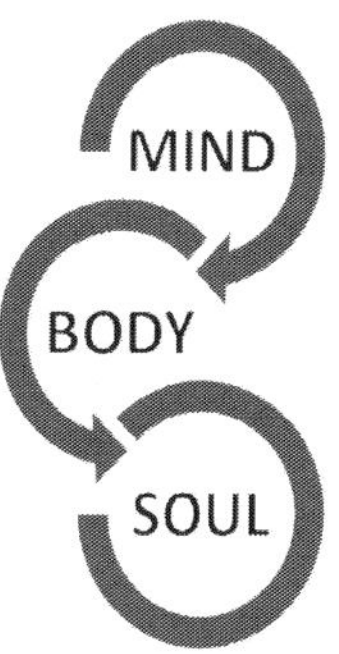

1994 Mexico

MCI ALL-STAR GAME MVP ~ KAISERSLAUTERN

Joe Burton made good on his Xanthus tour promise to get me paid outside of Germany! He got me an MCI All-Star game invite to showcase me against the top 1st Bundesliga players on a grand stage. My chance to shine with Joe and his Euro scouts there. Yup, I turned that 'ish' out! Top scorer, a 'triple-double' and the MVP!

Net: A $1.2M Spain gig or $1.5M in Italy.

G'$ vs. 1st Bundesliga All-Stars ~ G'$: MCI All-Star Game MVP!

"Gregg Scott's MCI performance was an amazing display of a multi-talented superstar! The best player I've ever seen." Steven Clauss

Steven Clauss
Diplom-Trainer
Gold Medal Group
Basketball-Service

Gold Medal Group
EINEN SPRUNG VORAUS

Am Mertenshof 36
50859 Köln
Privat 02 21/5 00 11 61

G'$ Spain Contract: My Pay Day

I chose the Spain deal. 2 years with a player option for the 3rd year, and a $igning Bonu$. **Italy's Offer: All money ain't good money!** The club was in a province where La Costra Nostra was alive and well. Hint: Point Spread! No, thanks. I preferred the **ethos** of Spain.

Family Planning

I would go to Spain solo while Puig was off to Yugoslavia for a six-month DoD assignment that required her to get immunized. Precaution: Don't get Pregnant.

Olympic Halle Barcelona Spain: Site of 1992 Dream Team Glory

MAY 11TH 1996 ~ LORRAINE, FRANCE

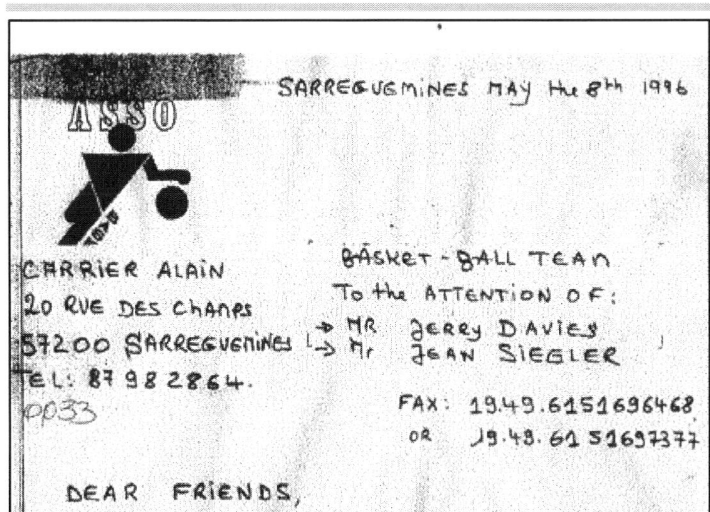

SARREGUEMINES MAY the 8th 1996

ASSO

CARRIER ALAIN
20 RUE DES CHAMPS
57200 SARREGUEMINES
TEL: 87 98 2864.

BASKET-BALL TEAM
To the ATTENTION OF:
→ MR JERRY DAVIES
→ Mr JEAN SIEGLER

FAX: 19.49.6151696468
OR 19.49.61 51697377

DEAR FRIENDS,

ALL my thanks for the participation of your team to the "4th charity game for Emilie's ill friends." The game takes place SATURDAY the 11th of may 1996 at 8.30. in the evening, in the usual gymnasium. I also send you a copy of the program and a map to help you find the way.

ASSO Charity U.S. Star Game

May 11, 1996
Lorraine France
G'$: 'Star of Stars' Award

FAMILY PLAN IN FLUX

Our family plan was in motion. I was signed and prepping for Spain and Puig had gotten her TDY departure date for Yugoslavia, and honor her tenure committments to her boss.

May 1996 TVL Club in Langen, Germany: A Godly 'Gift of Gab'!

A Scary Sight: Your spouse entering the Langen gym, 30 miles from home, unannounced and hysterical in the midst of her honored workday and my hoop workout. Ok! Who died? **Puig: (in tears) "I'm Pregnant"-**Her words confused my German 'mates. She was so distraught due to her immunization Rx not to conceive! Chill. **'My seed shall be blessed!'**

Wiesbaden American Middle School
European Region
Unit 29674
APO, AE 09096

May 16, 1996

Mr. Gregg Scott
CMR 410 Box 402
APO, AE 09096

Dear Mr. Scott,

On behalf of the AVID students in the sixth, seventh , and eighth grade classes, I would like to thank you for taking the time to speak to them.. Your message was clear and forthright concerning choices, goals, and sacrifices. Many students need to be told this from a variety of sources before it becomes a conscious decision on their own. Your message has reinforced what we have been teaching the entire school year. I think the students benefit when they have the opportunity to see and hear someone who has used these principles to achieve in their personal life.

Thank you again for taking the time to speak with us.

Sincerely,

Susan Dillard

Susan Dillard
AVID Coordinator

"I challenge you to make your life a masterpiece. Join the ranks of those who live what they teach . . . who walk their talk!"

ANTHONY ROBBINS

DEPARTMENT OF DEFENSE
DEPENDENTS SCHOOLS
OFFICE OF THE PRINCIPAL

Wiesbaden American Middle School
Building 07778
Texas Strasse
65189 Wiesbaden
June 12, 1996

Mr. Paul Hallgrimson
Adidas
Anna Strasse 7
63225 Langen

Mom Quote

"Idle hands are the devils' tools."

Dear Mr. Hallgrimson

Your company has a truly outstanding representative in Mr. Gregg Scott. Mr. Scott volunteered to speak to several of the A.V.I.D. (Advancement Via Individual Determination) classes at Wiesbaden American Middle School. As a professional athlete, he was a perfect speaker for our classes and had their attention immediately.

Mr. Scott did far more than just discuss sports with our students. He talked at length about the importance of school, about character, hard work, and sacrifice. He showed the students that there is more to sports than just athletic ability. His quiet, confident, and polite manner was also a welcome contrast to the loud bravado that so many of our students associate with sports figures.

Of the many speakers we have had this year, Mr. Scott certainly ranks as the students' favorite. Adidas is very lucky to have such a fine representative.

Sincerely

Charles L. McCarter

Charles L. McCarter
A.V.I.D. Teacher
Wiesbaden Middle School

KOLN JUNE 1-2, 1996

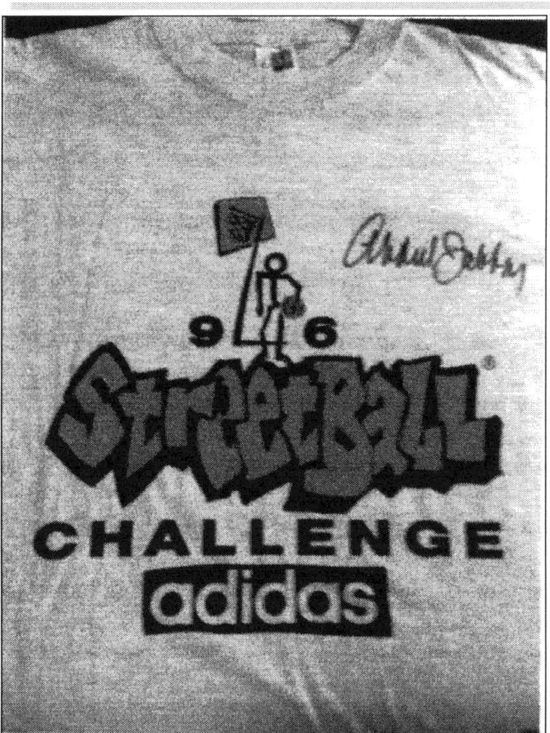

YouTube*.com/MentalAthlete* ~ **G' & Kareem 'Fundamentals'**

I was summoned to Court #13 with five German Pro players to film a promo video of the fundamental execution of offensive plays that Kareem narrated in an interview. I was the point-guard tasked to orchestrate the words of the NBA HOF Laker legend! I studied the interview carefully to prepare.

Pick & Roll ~ Give & Go ~ Penetration
We filmed one take of each play! Perfectly!

The director gazed as I infused my G'$ flair in the Dribble Penetration clip. Film don't lie!

Later, I entered the VIP area and was introduced to Kareem for the first time. His assistant asked if I knew Zach Jones when I told them I came from San Diego. Zach told me later that her name was Maria. Our convo put me at ease as Kareem engaged genuinely with us. Chatting with 'The Captain' and NBA HOF: Priceless!

My adidas liaison returned, "Gregg you're to be on Court 9 in 30 minutes to shoot the Streetball '96 promo video. You need to go to wardrobe and gear up." G' Money!

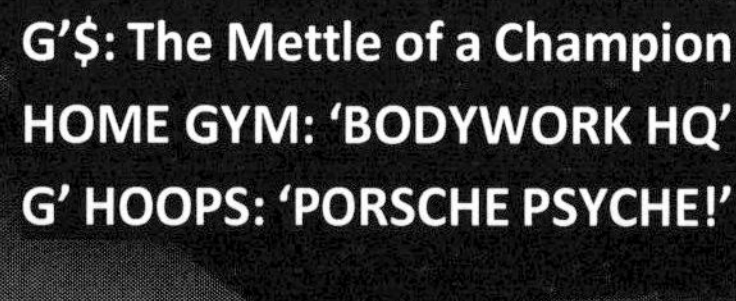

G'$: The Mettle of a Champion
HOME GYM: 'BODYWORK HQ'
G' HOOPS: 'PORSCHE PSYCHE!'

G' HOOPS STATS: 6' 3" 178 lbs.

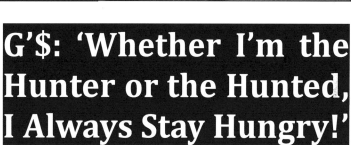

G'$: 'Whether I'm the Hunter or the Hunted, I Always Stay Hungry!'

YouTube.com/MentalAthlete

Markus & G'
~Leverkusen~

~ Paul's plea to me ~
"Please train my son in Mind and Body!!"

Paul & G'
~Munich~

Greg Scott
Berlinerstr. 31

D-65189 Wiesbaden

Langen, 6 June 1996

Subj: adidas abc Camps in Europe

Dear Greg,

I´m sending you a packet today with information about the camps that you will be attending this summer. The Camp dates are:

1. **adidas abc Camp in Bologna, Italy; 16-22 June**
2. **adidas abc All-Star Camp in Munich, Germany; 7-12 July**
3. **adidas abc Camp in Cholet, France; 15-20 July**
4. **adidas abc Camp in Sables d´Olonne, France; 21-27 July**

You need to arrive on the day before the official camp starts as the coaches arrive the day before the kids. Please fill-out the attached Coaches Form and return to me via fax as soon as possible.

Please get back to me if you have any questions. I´m sure that this will again be a great experience for you as well as for all the kids that you will be coaching this summer.

Thanks and

Warm regards,

Paul Hallgrimson

Annastraße 7
D-63225 Langen
Germany

Tel: (011-49) 6103 - 555 06
Fax: (011-49) 6103 - 92 81 42

Shoe Promotion Expo, France

Paul catapulted my Mental Athlete Brand to European Eminence!

The Sportshule, Munich, Germany

Global Name Recognition:
~ 'The Mental Athlete' ~
G' Hoops: Mind, Body & Soul

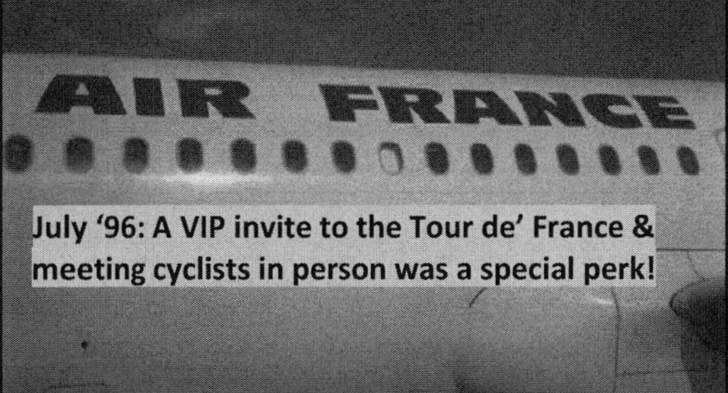

July '96: A VIP invite to the Tour de' France & meeting cyclists in person was a special perk!

Levallois, France

Cholet, France

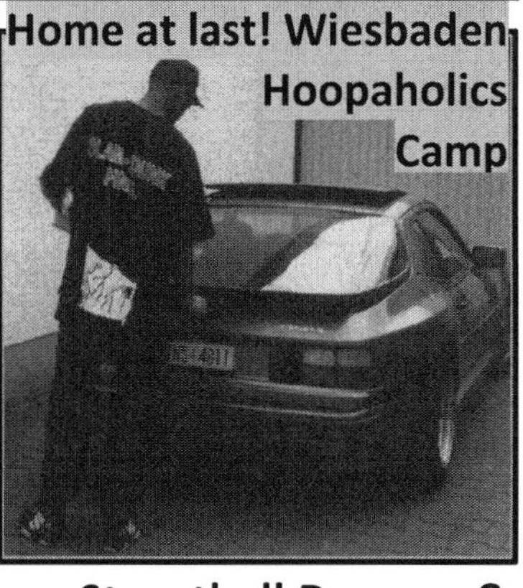
Home at last! Wiesbaden Hoopaholics Camp

Sables d' Olonne, France

G' HOOPS: Euro Streetball Promos & Tours ~ Abba Berlin & Wendell Alexis Donovan Bailey ~ Mutombo ~ Kareem ~ Joe 'Jellybean' & Kobe Bryant ~

GS HOOPAHOLICS EURO CAMPS

My mom insisted I find a way to impact the DoD kids! Gotcha!

SPORTS — THE STARS AND STRIPES

'Hoopaholics' b-ball camp held

A Hoopaholics Basketball Camp for students age 11 to 18 will be offered June 25 to 28 in the Wiesbaden High School and Middle School gyms.

The camp features Gregg Scott, an international professional player and author of *The Mental Athlete Workshop*.

In addition to focusing on the basic fundamentals, "this camp will emphasize the importance of goal setting and having a vision," Scott said. "Athletics is simply an extension of life. And, for the young athlete, the work ethic, commitment, failure and perseverance that are part of athletics truly prepare them for the game of life."

The cost is $85, and preregistering at Youth Services is required. Call YS for details at 337-

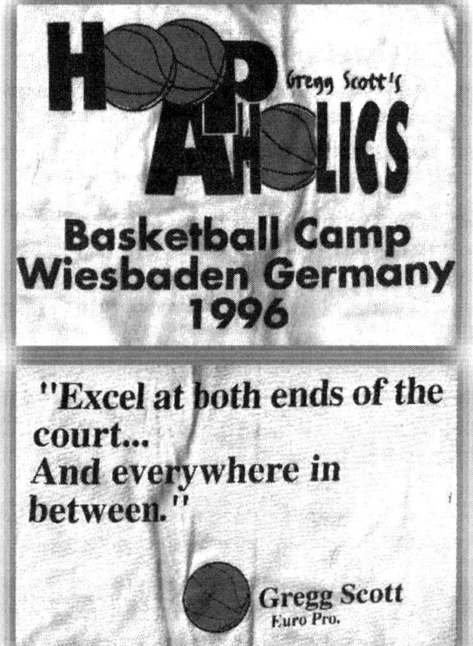

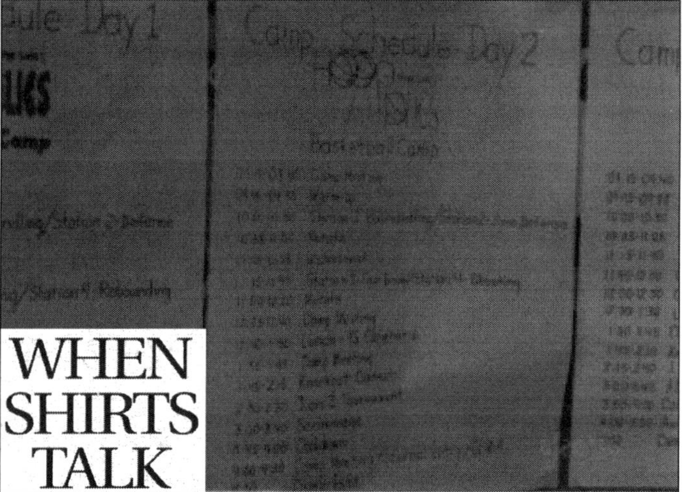

Camp T-shirts: GS Mantra to Engrain a Relentless Quest for Excellence!

Camp Schedule

Coaching as I was coached works best!

Campers Personal Hoopaholics 'Mental Athlete' Workbooks

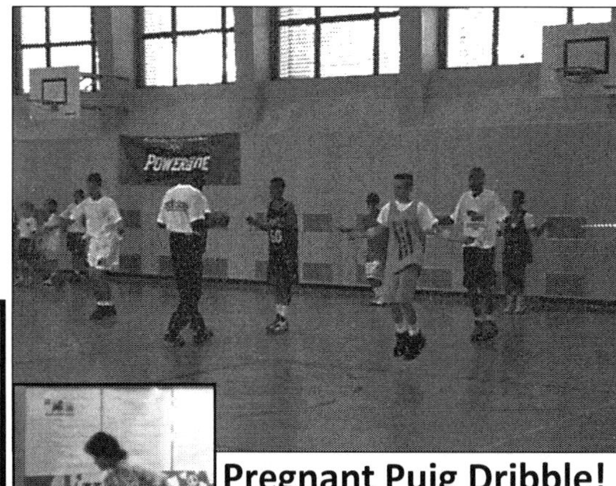

My name is....
And I'm a
HOOPAHOLIC

Nice Shot Mom!

Pregnant Puig Dribble!

Note from Mom

Hoopaholics Camp – Daily Schedule

Day 1 9-9:15 Camp Mtg.
↓

Journal note

a memorable moment: prelunch approx 9:55 am.

....his tone of voice
and the way he shook
his head from side to side

as he said,
with awe, "You have
no idea what he [Gregg]
has done for our
community!" He continued
with "and WHATEVER I can
do to help, at any time, just
let me know."

Russell,
The chef of the Camp
Program

P.S. I can't believe
I found both
paper and pen!
:)

G'$ Pure Free Throw!
Yes, I won Knock-Out!

Chef Russell Fueled My Hoopaholics Honorably!

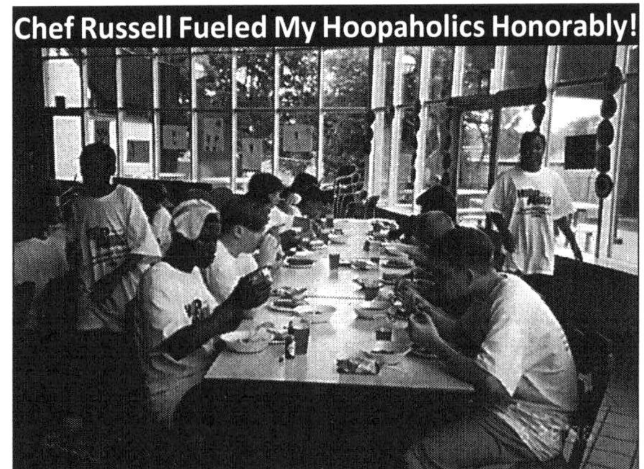

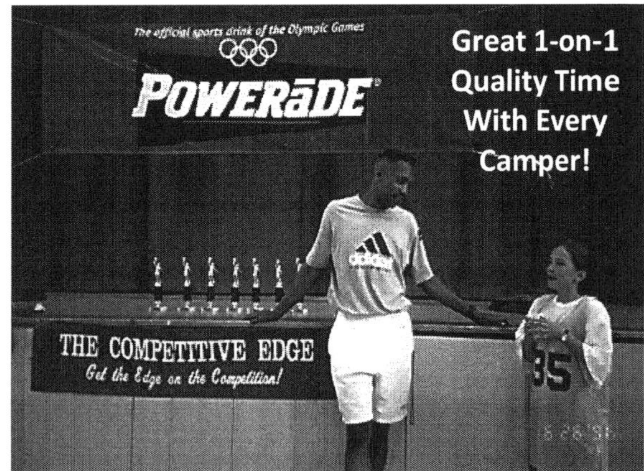

Great 1-on-1 Quality Time With Every Camper!

Gatorade: No sponsorship love. **Powerade!**

Mr. Evans secured great facilities and great coaches for my Hoopaholics Camp. Shout out to coaches Upshure, Lewis and Jessica from a grateful Hoopaholic!

Paul Hallgrimson provided enough adidas gear for every player & staff member to be awarded gear!

Life Memories

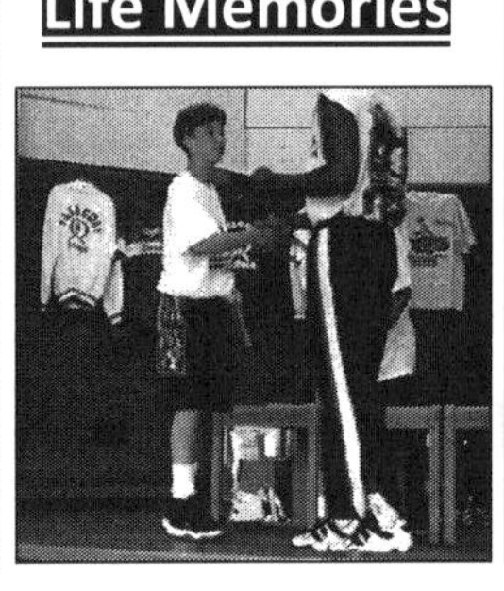

GREGG SCOTT'S HOOPAHOLICS EURO CAMPS
CREATING A BRAND BEYOND BASKETBALL

8 The 53rd Area Support Group Post-Union
July 5, 1996

WIESBADEN/MAINZ SPO

Kids learn more than basketball

By Beth Reece-Troth
221st BSB staff writer

Kids who participated in the Youth Services three-day Hoopaholics Basketball Camp last month learned just as much about imagination as they did about handling the ball.

"Picture it in your head. Imagine the real competition, the workouts you've done to get to the competition. Imagine what the actual competition will look like and what it will feel like," Gregg Scott urges young athletes. "The mind can't distinguish between what's real and what's imagined. So if you go through the imagining process and can put yourself there, then you've already been there. That will help you feel less anxious, and to relax easier."

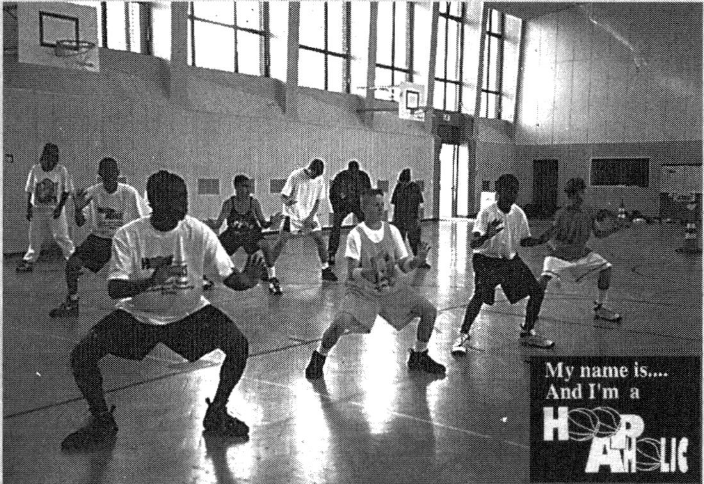

Young athletes practice the fundamentals of basketball during the Youth Services Hoopaholics Basketball Camp.

The camp was divided into two "leagues"— the CBA, made up of kids ages 11 through 14, and the NBA, with kids age 15 through 18. Each group learned the fundamentals of basketball, such as footwork, shooting, dribbling, rebounding, passing and catching, moving with and without the ball, and defending. Drills and various exercises were used to give kids hands-on, personal and competitive practice.

According to Scott, an international professional basketball player and author of *The Mental Athlete*, the camp was tailored to teach kids the fundamentals of the game of basketball, as well as the game of life.

"Athletics is simply an extension of life. And, for the young athlete, the work ethic, commitment, failure and perseverance that are part of athletics truly prepare them for the game of life," he said. "This camp emphasizes the importance of goal setting and having a vision. Young people must dare to dream."

Scott believes mental training is equally as important as physical training for athletes, since failing or losing a game is a mental process. By keeping a positive attitude and setting goals, he said, athletes can stay motivated and focused toward the ultimate objective—success.

If athletes do not develop what he calls "positive intent," then goals become lost.

"We endure so much failure because there's only one prize. Only one person, one team can win," he said. "But positive intent restores our confidence. Negativity takes up energy.

"If you miss a free throw, go ahead and grieve. Get over it and bounce back. You've got to remember all the hard practice and remind yourself that you really can do this. Everybody makes mistakes."

Without confidence, he added, no athlete can improve.

"Confidence is a state of mind. That is what this camp is all about. I try to teach kids to be a 'mental athlete,' to maintain focus and concentration despite distractions," he said. "Mental athletes know the powerful ability of the mind. Having a strong will, determination, and heart are all characteristics of the mental athlete."

Scott steadily blurts out praise to kids as they practice everything from footwork to defensive moves. He pushes them to be intelligent players, continually aware of where they are, where they should be and how to recover.

Once players master the fundamentals of basketball, they improve by competing against other players and practicing individually. While practicing, Scott said, players need to focus on weaknesses and make them strengths,.

Chris Wallace said he attended the camp to do just that.

"I knew there would be something to gain in coming to this camp. Defense is where I need most work," he said on the first day. "So far the instruction is well rounded, giving those of all age groups the chance to develop.

"Basketball is all I do. It's the passion in my life. I love the competition. It's you and somebody else seeing what you can do."

All players were asked to keep a journal during the camp in which they recorded thoughts, goals, obstacles, weaknesses and any other thing they felt were worth remembering. This, Scott said, will give them something to reflect on while they continue striving to be better players.

While kids look up to Scott for his experience, he reminds them that the life of an athlete isn't all great. There are often setbacks.

"I believe in myself and the skills I have — that's what counts," he said. "That's what I want for these kids. If they can accomplish the fundamental skills in the game of basketball they can achieve the fundamental skills in the game of life."

YouTube.com/MentalAthlete: 1996 adidas abc Camps ~ Germany ~ France ~ Greece ~ Italy ~ Spain ~ The UK ~

ADIDAS DETLEF SCHREMPF CAMP

MÜNICH. On 9th July 1996, Patrick Baumann, Deputy Secretary General of FIBA, Mr. Aldo Vitale, Managing Director of FBP, Daniel Becker, Head of FBP's Marketing Department, and Florian Wanninger, Head of the Communications Department, visited the Detlef Schrempf Basketball Camp organised by adidas in Münich. Both companies are currently in the process of building up a friendship that will be beneficial to the growth of basketball.

150 of the most talented young male and female players from Europe attended the Camp, as well as some athletes competing at college level in the USA. Detlef Schrempf not only showed the youngsters how to improve their skills on court, he also taught them how to set themselves personal goals and gave them some guidance as to how to achieve them. About 70 journalists, who attended the open day for the media, witnessed an enthusiastic atmosphere.

Le 9 juillet 1996, Patrick Baumann, Secrétaire Général Délégué de la FIBA, Aldo Vitale, Gérant de FBP, Daniel Becker, Responsable du Service de Marketing de FBP, et Florian Wanninger, Responsable du Service de Communications, se sont rendus au Camp de Basketball de Detlef Schrempf, organisé par Adidas à Münich. Les deux compagnies sont en train de consolider une amitié dont le monde du basketball pourra bénéficier.

150 des jeunes joueurs de basketball les plus talentueux d'Europe ont assisté à ce Camp, ainsi qu'un certain nombre d'athlètes jouant au niveau des collèges aux USA. Detlef Schrempf a montré aux jeunes comment améliorer leurs aptitudes sur le terrain de jeu. Il leur a aussi enseigné comment se fixer des buts bien précis et leur a donné quelques indications pour les atteindre. 70 journalistes ont témoigné de l'atmosphère entousiaste qui reignait ce jour ouvert aux médias.

FIBA BASKETBALL PROMOTION NEWS

FIBA Recognition of my Mental Athlete Infusion and Camp Presentations: PRICELESS!

adidas-Detlef-Schrempf-All-Star-Camp 1996

Dayplan

München-Oberhaching July 07th-12th 1996

Day 1:	Sunday July 07th 1996	where?	for whom?	who?
'til 09.00 h	Breakfeast	Mensa	Coaches	
09.15 - 10.00 h	Coaches-meeting, dayplan, resposibilities of each Coach	Seminarroom 2	Coaches	Head-Coaches
10.15 - 12.00 h	Stations-meeting	Gym 2	Coaches	Station-Coaches
12.00 - 13.00 h	Lunch	Mensa	Coaches	
11.00 - 14.30 h	Camper Check-in	Foyer	Camper	adidas
14.30 - 15.30 h	Camp-opening Welcome Campers Introduction of the Coaches Introduction of the Crew Contents and goals of the Camp	Gym 2	Camper	adidas Head-Coaches
15.30 - 15.50 h	Contents and organisation of the Try-outs	Gym 2	Camper	Head-Coaches
15.50 - 18.00 h	Warm-up / Try-outs into five leagues of four teams	Gymns 1 / 2	Camper	del. Coaches
18.15 - 19.00 h	Dinner	Mensa	Camp	
19.00 - 19.30 h	Free-Time			
19.30 - 20.00 h	Detlef Schrempf: Goals of the Camp and how to get there „What do we want?", „How do we get there?", „How should that look like?"	Gym 2	Camper	Detlef Schrempf
20.00 - 20.30 h	Greg Scott: „Motivation" / „Goalsetting" **GS Pedigree!**	Gym 2	Camper	Gregg Scott
20.30 - 21.30 h	Open Gym	Gymns 1 / 2	Camper	del. Coaches
21.30 - 23.00 h	Shower / Free-time	Sportschule	Camp	
23.00 h	Bedtime, Coaches-meeting	Sportschule	Camper	Crew

Detlef, Kay & the players truly humbled me with this keepsake at the awards ceremony!

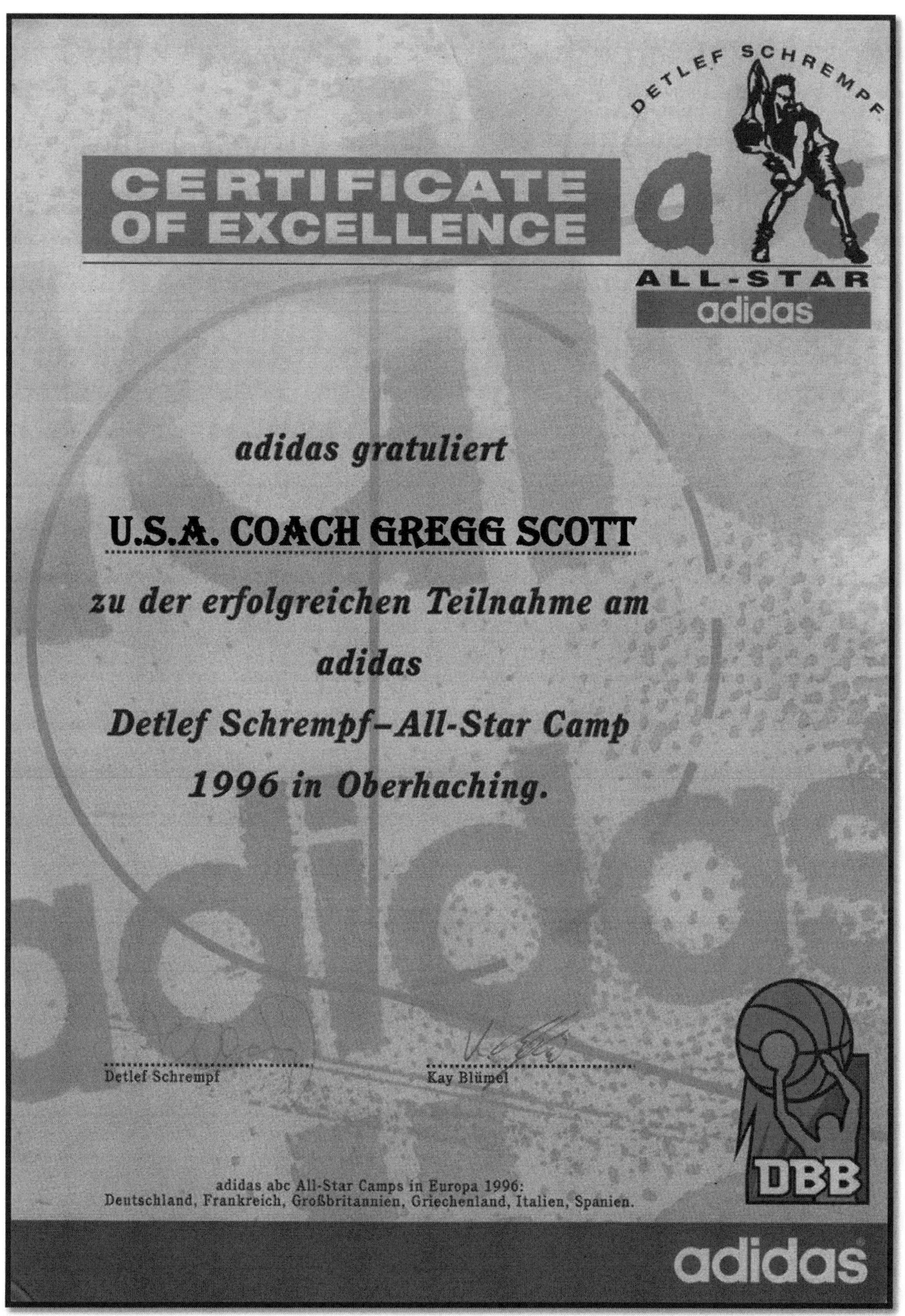

I first met Joe Bryant (below, background) at Detlef's '96 All-Star Camp. It was after lunch and raining, so I offered to drive him to his hotel. We truly bonded instantly. 'Jellybean' shared many stories and insights with me, including their covert strategy for Kobe to bypass college and declare for the NBA draft. Yup!

We'd reunite in Budapest at the Streetball World Championships, where I'd play in an exhibition with Kareem and a 3-point contest with John Starks. Ha!

Munich: Inaugural Adidas "Feet You Wear" Shoe Commercial

Mr: Evans: "Scott drove from Munich to Maheim to play in an Int'l. Tourney. He led us to a championship win over Chechoslavakia's Nat'l. Team. MVP!!"

'Big John' Bolden: "I hit G' with a backdoor pass, he rose up, the defender jumped! G'$ Poster Jam!"

FRANCE

adidas

Siège Social
adidas sarragan France
Route de Saessolsheim
67700 LANDERSHEIM France
Adresse postale
B.P.67 67702 SAVERNE Cedex
Tél. 33 / 88 87 88 00
Télex 870 974
Fax 33 / 88 69 97 25

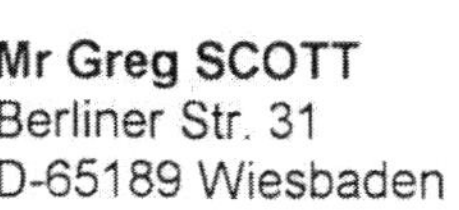

Mr Greg SCOTT
Berliner Str. 31
D-65189 Wiesbaden

N/Réf. FD/al V/Réf. Ligne directe 88 87 88 39 Fax direct 88 87 89 90 Date 26/09/96

Greg,

I hope that everything is fine for you since the French abc All-Star Camp. I'm sure that you're hardly preparing the next season.

I want to thank you very much again for the work you did during the abc Camps program. You really add value to these Camps and I think that kids will never forget that.

Concerning your salary, I really want to apologise for the delay. I hope that you will forgive us even if it's not excusable. But don't worry, it will be sent to you by October 4th.

Thanks again for your work and see you perhaps next year at the French abc Camps.

Franck DENGLOS
B.U.M. Basketball

FRANCK

G' & Colin Irish Cholet, France

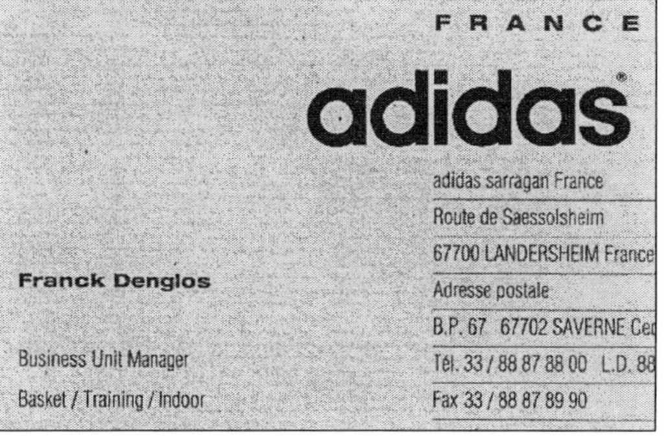
FRANCE

adidas

Franck Denglos

Business Unit Manager
Basket / Training / Indoor

adidas sarragan France
Route de Saessolsheim
67700 LANDERSHEIM France
Adresse postale
B.P. 67 67702 SAVERNE Ce
Tél. 33 / 88 87 88 00 L.D. 88
Fax 33 / 88 87 89 90

A Dassler Bros Feud led adidas France to a 'cast off' biz entity!

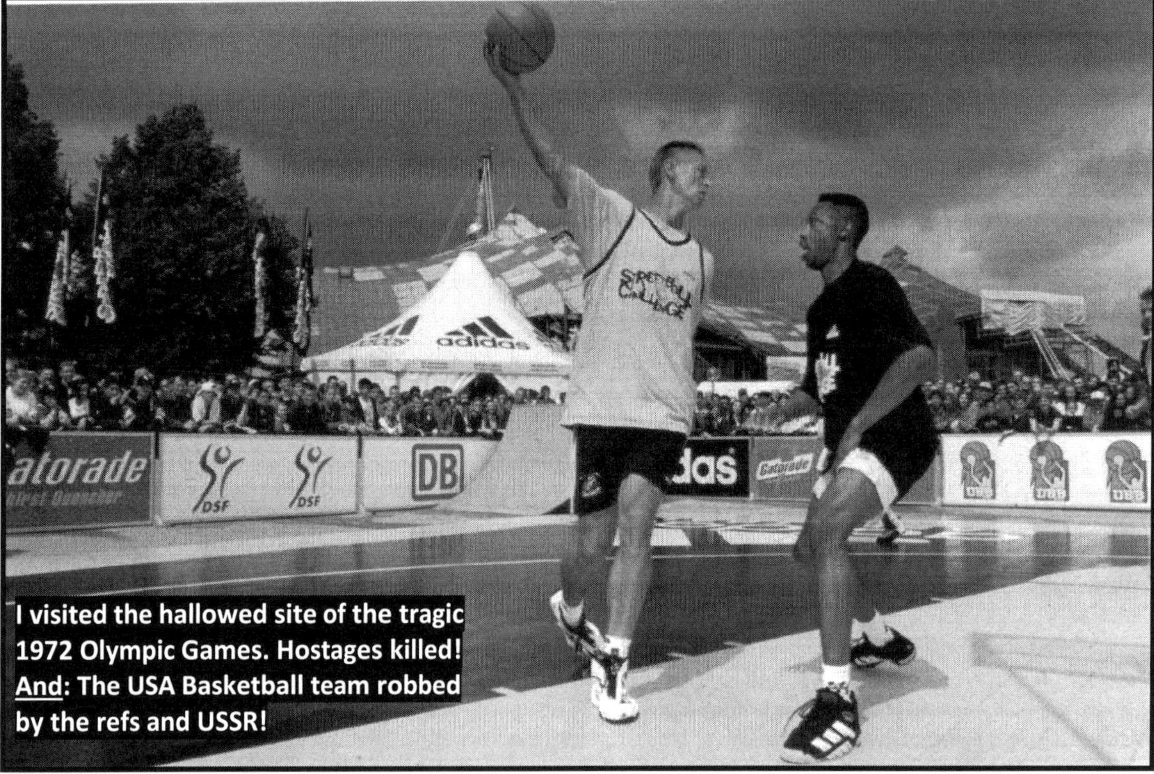

I visited the hallowed site of the tragic 1972 Olympic Games. Hostages killed! <u>And</u>: The USA Basketball team robbed by the refs and USSR!

G'$ HERZOGENAURACH 'DASSLER BROS.' HQ VAULT!

In July 1996, I was at adidas HQ for promo meetings and to do a voiceover for the Euro abc camp video in their on-site sound studios.

"Gregg, you're now our most highly marketed basketball player in Europe. We at adidas also want your voice to be heard introducing our camp video."

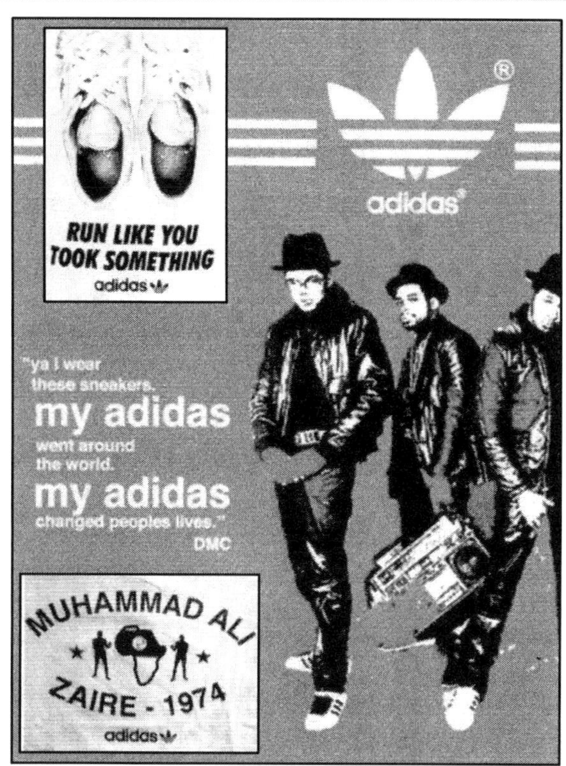

As I peeked at the compensation page in my promo info packet and script. Cha Ching $$$! All of my 3-Stripes work was extremely well compensated! Barometer of my Brand Value! Coaching or appearance fees, travel expenses, and per diem; although all events had a buffet. Most important was my **'Performance Fee'**. Anytime I had to lace 'em up to demonstrate, dunk, play or do anything besides just talk. $$$

Historical Tour of the Dassler Family Villa with Herr Dassler!

Toward the end of the promo meeting I noted some hubbub in the offices outside of our glass conference room, as an elderly man with two assistants was warmly greeted. He enters our meeting which had all the HQ VIP's I knew of. But, this man clearly had **uber clout.** He was greeted with esteem and honor by all. He said, "I heard Gregg Scott was here." I'm stunned. I was introduced to a true historical heir to the throne. **Herr (Mr.) Dassler.** He was in his 70's but very spry and energetic. "It is my pleasure to meet you Mr. Scott. May I take you on a tour? We can talk and have lunch together before your promo video!"

Dassler Bros. Feud a 'Town of the Bent Necks': adidas & Puma

A direct decendant of the Dassler Brothers, Adi and Rudy, this man was a 10 year old at the 1936 Berlin Olympics. He shared the true Dassler history with me. Jesse Owens, Hitler and a feud that had the company, the family and the entire town of Hertzogenaurach in a total divide. Adi founded adidas on the Dassler site and Rudy moved across the R.R. tracks (in full view) and founded Puma. You were either adidas or Puma .The family split with either Adi or Rudy. Bent Necks: Townspeople all looking down at shoes. adidas or Puma. There was NO Frratenizing between brands! Schools, shopping, socializing and marriage. Elders Adi and Rudy reconciled; but, are buried in opposite corners of the towns cemetary.

|1926|

First Adidas running shoe
with leader sole and hand-forged spikes

Dassler Brothers Shoe Factory

adidas

Adolf "Adi" Dassler started to produce his own sports shoes in his mother's wash kitchen in Herzogenaurach, Bavaria after his return from World War I. On 1 July 1924, his brother Rudolf "Rudi" Dassler joined the business, which became *Gebrüder Dassler Schuhfabrik* (Dassler Brothers Shoe Factory)

G'$: 1996 adidas HQ Tour

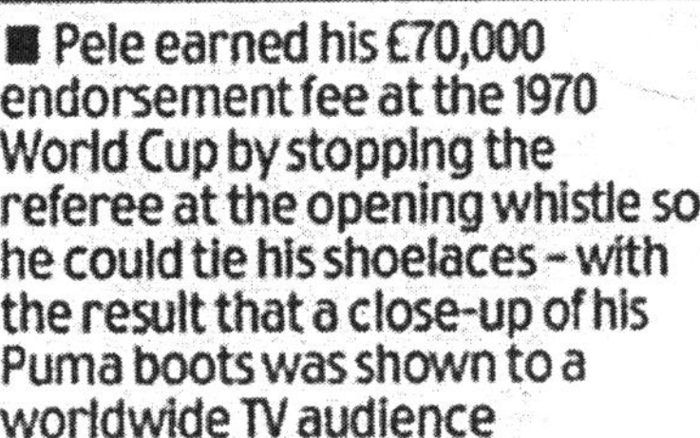

SHOES OF GLORY

■ Pele earned his £70,000 endorsement fee at the 1970 World Cup by stopping the referee at the opening whistle so he could tie his shoelaces – with the result that a close-up of his Puma boots was shown to a worldwide TV audience

■ Adidas tried flavoured laces in a desperate attempt to reverse falling sales in the 1990s

■ David Beckham's Adidas boots are still made by hand in the little town of Herzogenaurach, where the Dassler brothers, Rudolf (pictured during his days as an amateur boxer) and Adi, grew up

■ When U.S. sprinter Jesse Owens arrived at the Berlin Olympics in 1936, Adi persuaded him to try a pair of the company's spikes. The American won four gold medals in Dassler shoes, much to Adolf Hitler's annoyance

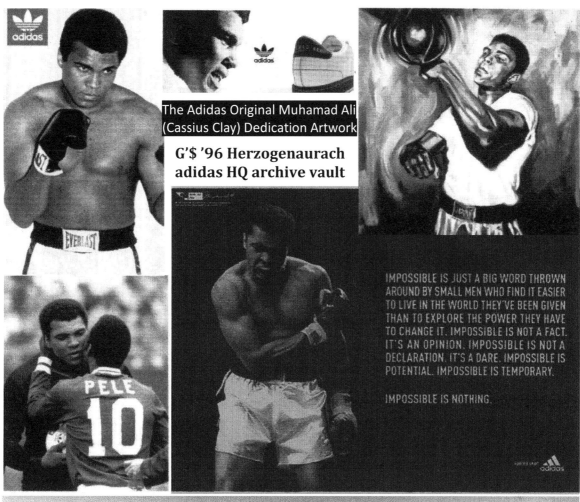

The Adidas Original Muhamad Ali (Cassius Clay) Dedication Artwork

G'$ '96 Herzogenaurach adidas HQ archive vault

IMPOSSIBLE IS JUST A BIG WORD THROWN AROUND BY SMALL MEN WHO FIND IT EASIER TO LIVE IN THE WORLD THEY'VE BEEN GIVEN THAN TO EXPLORE THE POWER THEY HAVE TO CHANGE IT. IMPOSSIBLE IS NOT A FACT. IT'S AN OPINION. IMPOSSIBLE IS NOT A DECLARATION. IT'S A DARE. IMPOSSIBLE IS POTENTIAL. IMPOSSIBLE IS TEMPORARY.

IMPOSSIBLE IS NOTHING.

Olympia Stadia Berlin: Streetball Finals

Adidas paid me to 'Showcase' with Detlef & Donovan vs. Abba; **and** play in the tourney!

Mr. E: "G' took 5'6" Diggs and 6'5" Sully with him."

'Both fit, durable and tough.'

Cool Donovan Bailey

At dinner Donovan used a foreign term: Paparazzi! We 3 hit the Club!

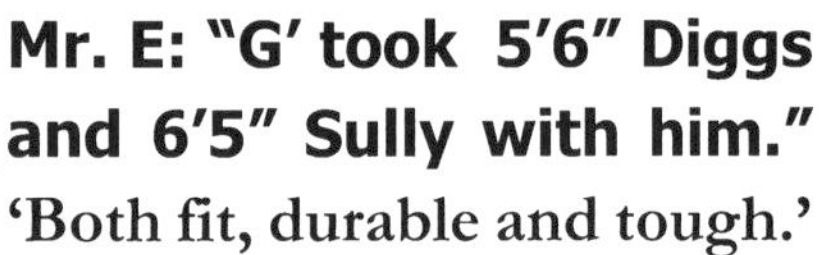

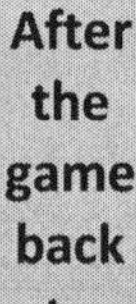

After the game back to Work

Donovan Bailey ~ Canadian 100m Olympic Gold Medalist!

Adidas Deutschland Streetball Day 2!

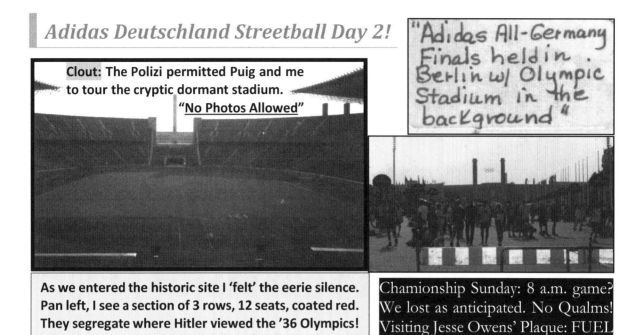

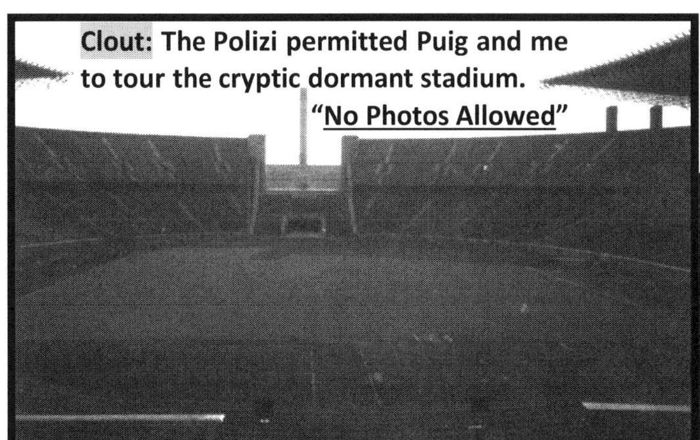

Clout: The Polizi permitted Puig and me
to tour the cryptic dormant stadium.
"No Photos Allowed"

As we entered the historic site I 'felt' the eerie silence. Pan left, I see a section of 3 rows, 12 seats, coated red. They segregate where Hitler viewed the '36 Olympics!

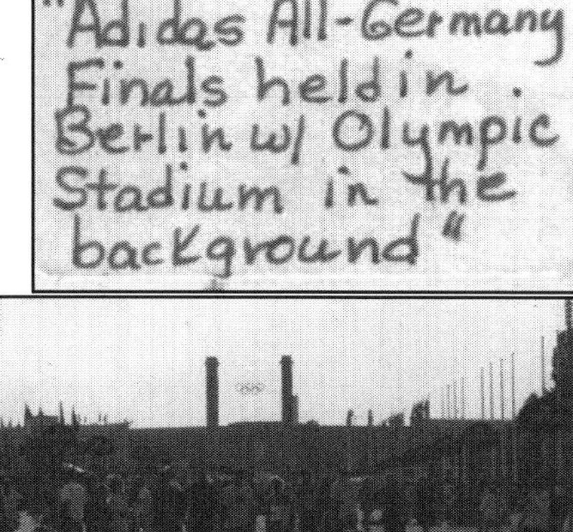

"Adidas All-Germany Finals held in Berlin w/ Olympic Stadium in the background"

Chamionship Sunday: 8 a.m. game? We lost as anticipated. No Qualms! Visiting Jesse Owens' Plaque: FUEL

Banished to the outer courts of the double-elimination **losers bracket** for two games vs. conceited foes with hostile fans; butt-hurt as we dispatched both teams to get to the Semis.

Tourney Semi-Finals: Pure G'$

We faced a very tough and fit squad of Euros, none German, and they were up by 3 with a minute to play. We didn't wilt. I hit a deep '2'! And, I stole the inbound. Go to the hole? No! Only a hard foul or a non-call awaits. No Tie! I took a Markus Hallgrimson move out of my toolbox. Head-fake, a sly one dribble lateral side-step, plant my right foot, get on balance, go vertical, eye the square, cast off a smooth pure jumper, and called 'glass'! Dagger. Game!

Finals adidas 1 vs. GS's adidas II: G'$ Tourney Champ & MVP!

"We Are the Champions" was played with Olympic Stadium in view for my TV interview. G'$ MVP: 'I did amaze myself!'

Awards Ceremony: Volumes of 'sic' MVP Gear!

G'$ Cap to the back & Hoopaholics Brand Gear!

G' & KAREEM: SKYHOOK & STREETBALL ~ BUDAPEST

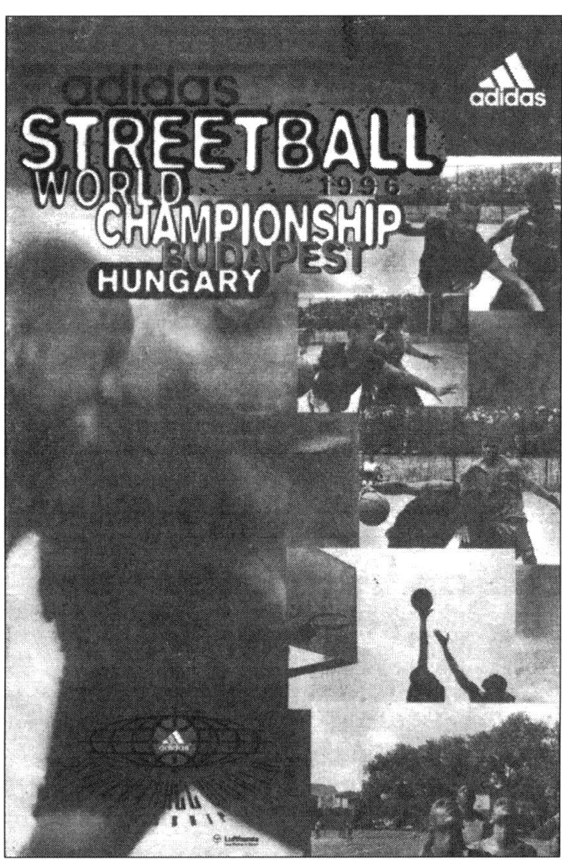

A covert, vague invite: Confirmed my itinerary, travel docs and event ID. Then, "BRING PLAYING GEAR." Contradicting my ID title, 'ORGANISING'!?

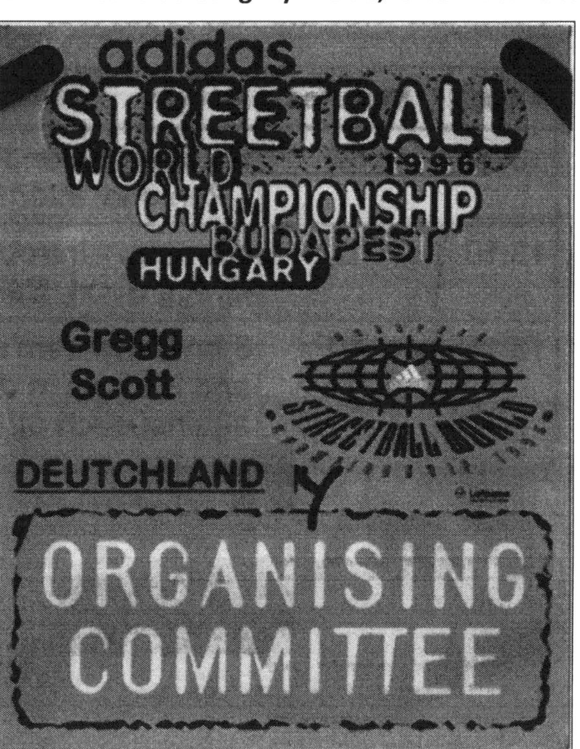

September 10, 1996 Mission Destination: Budapest, Hungary

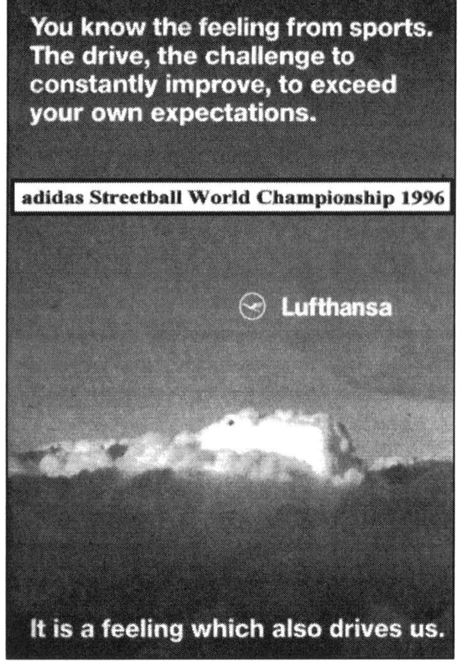

You know the feeling from sports. The drive, the challenge to constantly improve, to exceed your own expectations.
adidas Streetball World Championship 1996
Lufthansa
It is a feeling which also drives us.

Frankfurt Airport: As I entered the Lufthansa Air VIP area it was strange to see myself on their TV monitors in multiple adidas streetball commercials and promos. One had me spinning a ball from an overhead view, and my first thought was, 'I didn't get paid for that.' I giggled. Fact: adidas always paid me rediculously well!

Upon my arrival in Budapest I met my adidas liaison, Dietre, a cool Euro who worked full-time for adidas. His task was to inform me of, and escort me to, all of my vaguely stated *Organising* duties. First was a brief check-in at our hotel. Then to an awaitng water-taxi for an unknown destination on the famous Danube River, which separates the two cities; Buda and Pest! We soon arrived at a beautiful castle right on the river.

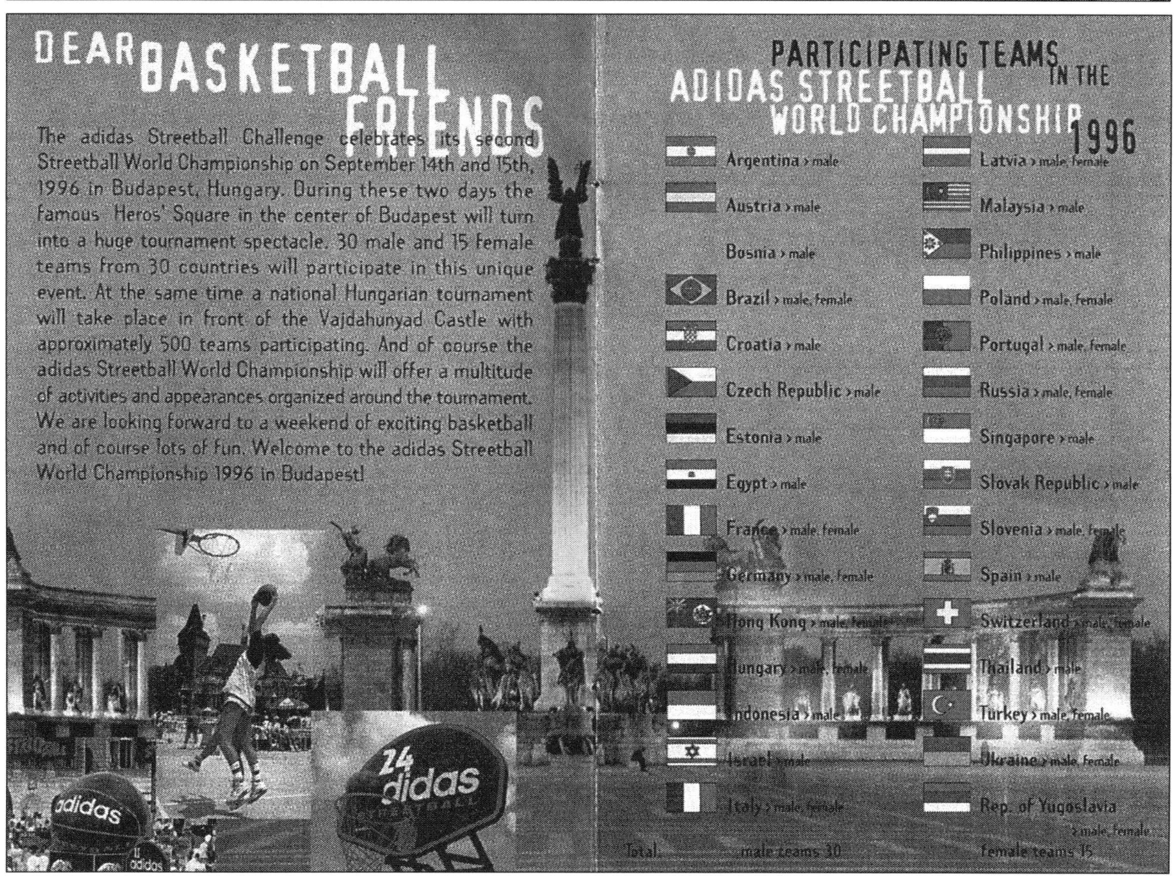

DEAR BASKETBALL FRIENDS

The adidas Streetball Challenge celebrates its second Streetball World Championship on September 14th and 15th, 1996 in Budapest, Hungary. During these two days the famous Heros' Square in the center of Budapest will turn into a huge tournament spectacle. 30 male and 15 female teams from 30 countries will participate in this unique event. At the same time a national Hungarian tournament will take place in front of the Vajdahunyad Castle with approximately 500 teams participating. And of course the adidas Streetball World Championship will offer a multitude of activities and appearances organized around the tournament. We are looking forward to a weekend of exciting basketball and of course lots of fun. Welcome to the adidas Streetball World Championship 1996 in Budapest!

PARTICIPATING TEAMS IN THE ADIDAS STREETBALL WORLD CHAMPIONSHIP 1996

Argentina > male
Austria > male
Bosnia > male
Brazil > male, female
Croatia > male
Czech Republic > male
Estonia > male
Egypt > male
France > male, female
Germany > male, female
Hong Kong > male, female
Hungary > male, female
Indonesia > male
Israel > male
Italy > male, female
Latvia > male, female
Malaysia > male
Philippines > male
Poland > male, female
Portugal > male, female
Russia > male, female
Singapore > male
Slovak Republic > male
Slovenia > male, female
Spain > male
Switzerland > male, female
Thailand > male
Turkey > male, female
Ukraine > male, female
Rep. of Yugoslavia > male, female

Total. male teams 30 female teams 15

G'$ in Buda & Pest! "Cussunnem Sapen" or Cuss at 'em Sapen: Thank you Very Much

G' on Defense: Back Cover of '96 Streetball World Championships Official Program

G' on Defense: '96 Koln, Germany ~ Streetball Promo. Note: The director requested I "not" contest the shot!

Exiting the water taxi and walking into this majestic castle was epic. An enchanting maze of pathways to a mecca for healing and therapy. Multiple caves, pools, hotsprings, whirlpools and a dreadful hot/cold therapy that felt like BB gun pellets; all carved into the amazing castle. Two hours of heavenly pampering. We enter a small room with two long metal platforms that were similar to a coroner's room, with two huge hairy Hungarian men with a white brick of soap to apply and a green garden hose to rinse. Massage Time! We grunted and groaned as they twisted, prodded and went 'deep tissue', head to calves.

Next, the crème de la crème! We strolled along the paths of the castle into a salon of sorts. I sat back in the lounge chair and extended my feet into the healing hands a therapy guru! Reflexology! Goodness Gracious. Deitre gave me a booklet. The adidas official program. "You're going to be playing with Kareem; and against John Starks. Kareem must prevail."

PROGRAMME

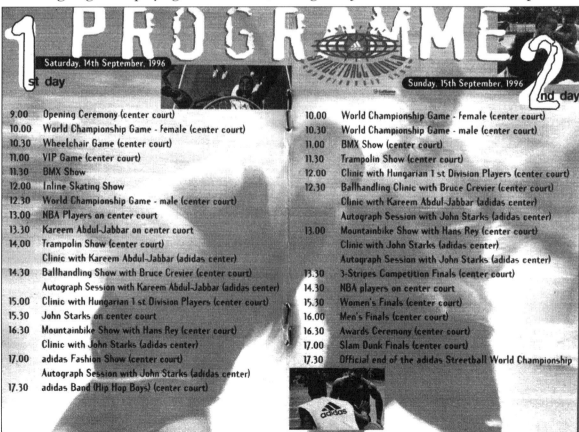

1st day — Saturday, 14th September, 1996

9.00	Opening Ceremony (center court)
10.00	World Championship Game - female (center court)
10.30	Wheelchair Game (center court)
11.00	VIP Game (center court)
11.30	BMX Show
12.00	Inline Skating Show
12.30	World Championship Game - male (center court)
13.00	NBA Players on center court
13.30	Kareem Abdul-Jabbar on center cuort
14.00	Trampolin Show (center court)
	Clinic with Kareem Abdul-Jabbar (adidas center)
14.30	Ballhandling Show with Bruce Crevier (center court)
	Autograph Session with Kareem Abdul-Jabbar (adidas center)
15.00	Clinic with Hungarian 1 st Division Players (center court)
15.30	John Starks on center court
16.30	Mountainbike Show with Hans Rey (center court)
	Clinic with John Starks (adidas center)
17.00	adidas Fashion Show (center court)
	Autograph Session with John Starks (adidas center)
17.30	adidas Band (Hip Hop Boys) (center court)

2nd day — Sunday, 15th September, 1996

10.00	World Championship Game - female (center court)
10.30	World Championship Game - male (center court)
11.00	BMX Show (center court)
11.30	Trampolin Show (center court)
12.00	Clinic with Hungarian 1 st Division Players (center court)
12.30	Ballhandling Clinic with Bruce Crevier (center court)
	Clinic with Kareem Abdul-Jabbar (adidas center)
	Autograph Session with John Starks (adidas center)
13.00	Mountainbike Show with Hans Rey (center court)
	Clinic with John Starks (adidas center)
	Autograph Session with John Starks (adidas center)
13.30	3-Stripes Competition Finals (center court)
14.30	NBA players on center court
15.30	Women's Finals (center court)
16.00	Men's Finals (center court)
16.30	Awards Ceremony (center court)
17.00	Slam Dunk Finals (center court)
17.30	Official end of the adidas Streetball World Championship

"Oh, you'll also be in a 3-point shooting contest with John and 3 tourney All-Stars."

Statistically Speaking: I'm not impressed! 1995-'96 SHOOTING FG: 44% 3-Pt. 36%
Sage Sparks: JS '94 Knicks vs. MJ's Bulls ~ "Gregory! That could so easily be you!!"

A '3' point contest! Oh Yes! We soon departed to an adidas all-hands meeting at the hotel. At the meeting, I was so pleased to see the itenerary for Joe Bryant as Starks' adidas liaison.

Time schedule forJohn Starks

Date:	Time:	Location:	Programme:	contact:	comments:
Wednesday, 11th	8.50 h	airport, Hotel Hyatt	arrival in Budapest with flight Delta 91C from New York to Budapest (operated by Malev), check-in at hotel	Todd Lazlow, Michael Kalman	pick up and welcome at the airport, check-in at hotel
Joe Bryant Info	morning	Hotel Hyatt	briefing of Joe Bryant with the previewed event schedule	Todd, Joe Bryant	explain schedule to Joe, discuss his role
	15.00 h	Hotel Hyatt	National press conference	Todd	

The next morning, I enter the VIP tent and reunite with Joe Bryant. It was so cool Then, he said, "Let me introduce you to John in the back room." We get to the exclusive VIP, sitting solo reading a USA Today newspaper. Joe introduces me. Starks doesn't even take his eyes off of his newspaper, just a meek dismissive reply. Joe, "Gregg's here..."- I point to my badge- Joe gets my hint. "He's on the Organizing Committee from Germany." Not a peep. "So, you're on the court with Kareem tomorrow?" 'No big deal'? I'd heard enough. I said, 'Well, I have some organizing to do. I look forward to seeing you play up close and in person tomorrow, John. I'll see you later, Joe. Thanks alot.' The Nerve! I've been around hoop royalty and this dude is rude? I went and had shoot-around on center court by myself.

Game Time Intro

Joe heard my European hoop pedigree first-hand. 9 Euro Tourneys! 9 Titles! Scoring Title! Dunk Title! Streetball Champ & MVP I came onto the court and peeped John. Yup it's me!

Program with the NBA-Players: **The G'$ Intro Clip: Surprised ME!**

Time	Minutes	Action
13:00	10	Introduction and welcome of Kareem and John - Personal information about their careers
13:10	5	warm-up - Introduction of the other players Gregg Scott, Balogh, Németh
13:15	10	3 on 3: Kareem's team vs John's team - John and Kareem in different teams, but not playing against each other **G'$ vs. John Starks!**

G'$ Intro Clip: "Basket Magazine hailed Gregg Scott is **The Premier U.S. Import Pro,** whose dynamic performances and European impact reign uber supreme."

'There's no Charles Oakley or Anthony Mason setting picks for you today, Bro! I'm going through all screens and your teammates know it. Full denial sticky D'! No help! You & Me!'

I'm playing with a Legend!

Get Big Fella his Skyhook

Run the Pick & Roll

Create the Give & Go

Hit All Open Jumpers

Exploit the Back-Door

Cerebral & Versatile:

When and How to
Dictate & Direct
Delegate & Defer
Dominate & Destroy

Skyhook Streetball ~ Mission Accomplished!

G'$ 'GameSpeak':

Kareem was Glorious!
Starks was Scoreless!
They added five extra minutes of game time.

G' Hero! Starks Zero!

Joe Post-Game: "G', I admire your humility."
Props from Jellybean!

Plain & Simple: 'Doing my job dictates that I disallow you to do your job!'

To the Victor go the Spoils; Burger King Reward from Kareem

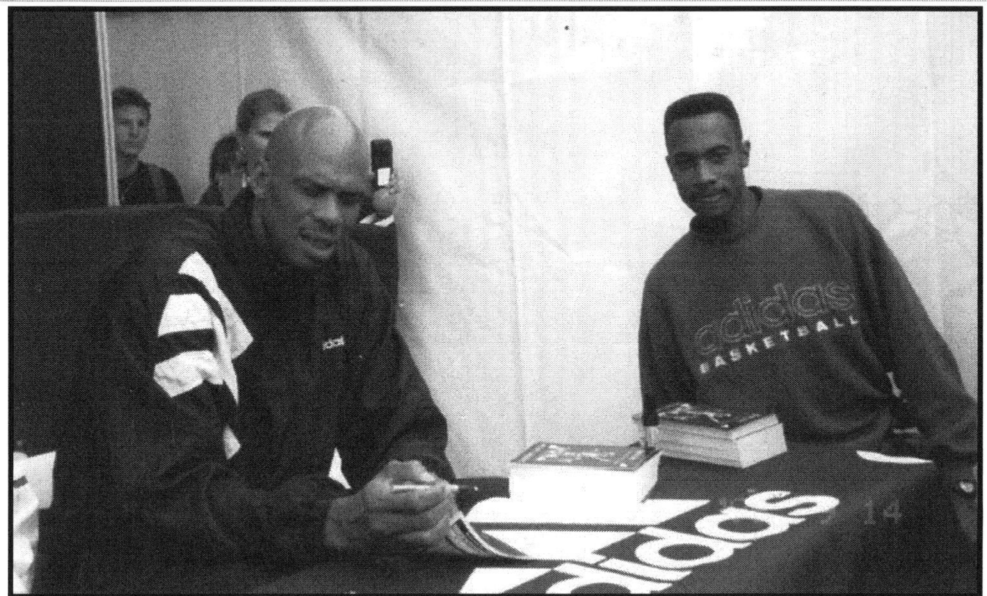

Post Game: Kareem and I were alone in a staging area waiting for him to sign 100's of autographs. He praised a fondness for yoga as a key to longevity. Kareem had a Burger King bag handed to him with six hamburgers. He handed me two. I declined at first. Professionalism concern. Kareem squashed that. "I'm sure nobody will mind if you share a couple of burgers with me. Besides, you did good work out there. You made it easy for me. So, consider the food to be well earned fruit for your well done labor."

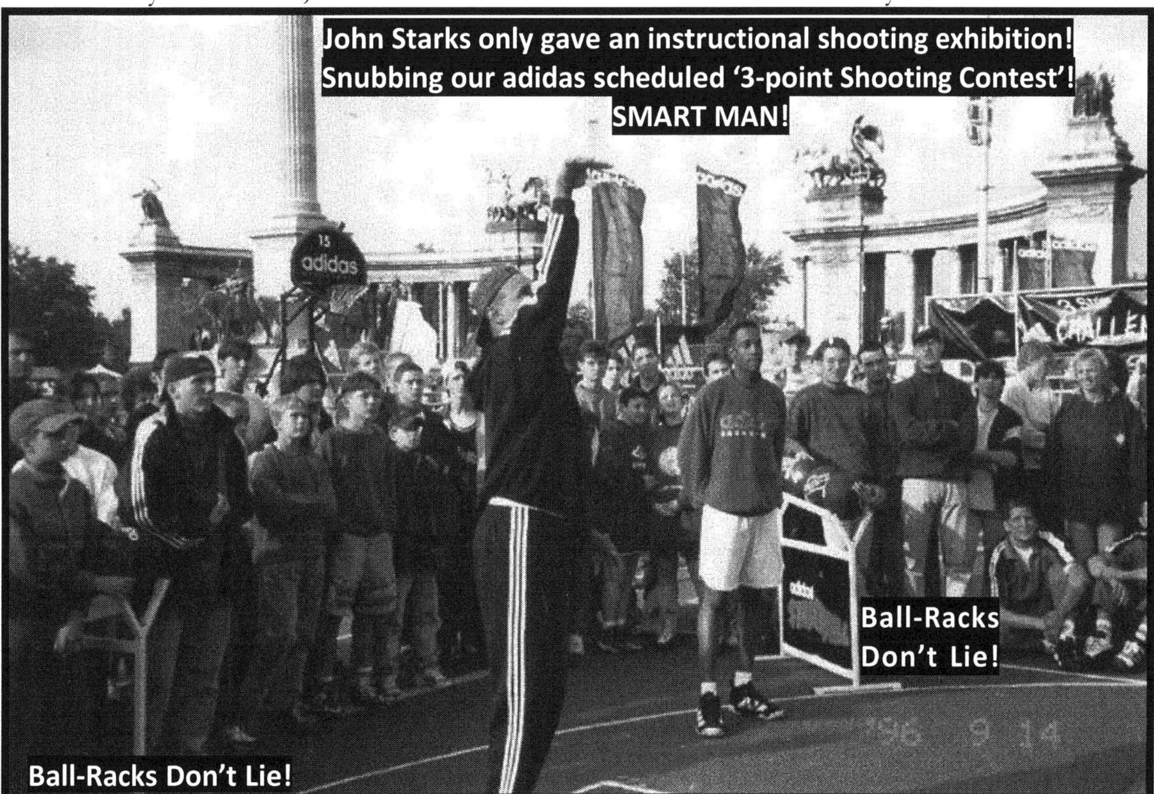

John Starks only gave an instructional shooting exhibition!
Snubbing our adidas scheduled '3-point Shooting Contest'!
SMART MAN!
adidas
Ball-Racks Don't Lie!
Ball-Racks Don't Lie!

G' Hoops Signs with ASC Mainz

I signed with Mainz for 15% of my Spain contract; and the 15 minute proximity to Wiesbaden. I made more $$$ 'off the court' than on it.

Mainz had 20 players at an open tryout for 1 Pro Import contract. I Turned That S... Out. DID SO MUCH WORK!

G'$: Premadonna

Hans Beth was a young arrogant coach who had a training camp retreat scheduled for three days. I had an adidas shoe promo set for the second day of the camp. Also, I had zero interest in his two-a-day conditioning training! Ditto, for team bonding. Sorry! Day 1 & Day 3 scrimmage only!

Coach Hans Beth and I had a stormy relationship. But, the A$C Club Manager, Ollie, loved me!

nes Heimdebut der drei TVK-Zugänge freuen. US-Boy Greg Scott begeisterte mit seiner Schnelligkeit und Treffsicherheit, war gemeinsam mit dem defensiv wie offensiv reboundstarken Rü-

"Home debut of the three TVK additions are looking forward. US-Boy Greg Scott was enthusiastic with his speed and quickness, together with his defensive and offensive strong rebounds." **~Translated~**

ASC Debut: Snatching Defeat from the Jaws of Victory!

I scored to 'seal the deal'! With 10 seconds left we're up by 4. **Hans calls a time-out?** Our last! 'Why?' Set up in **Zone D'!** 'What? No Ball pressure! No Rebound'g position!' **He rebuffs me. Up by 4; in DEEP Peril!** They roll the ball endline to midcourt as no time elapses, and shoot an open '3', miss, backtap, open shooter hits a '3' with only 5 seconds left. Our inbounder panics and he throws a lazy pass. Loose ball on the floor. They land on it, face down. 3,2,1... Our guy dives on top of him. The whistle blows just as the horn sounds. ASC FOUL! 1-and-1. The player hits two free throws! **AGONY!**

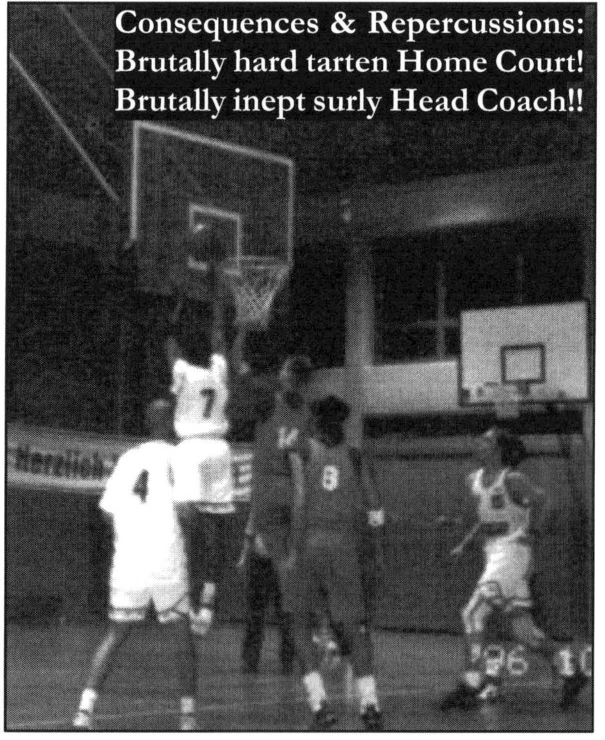

Consequences & Repercussions: Brutally hard tarten Home Court! Brutally inept surly Head Coach!!

G'$ Return to BC Darmstadt: ~ "Elf Dreier" ~ "Eleven Threes" ~

Lokalsport

MZ III

Montag, 7. Oktober 1996

Deutch "Held" English "Hero"

US-Boy Scott ist der ASC-Held

Amerikaner führt die Theresianum-Basketballer zum wichtigen Erfolg in Darmstadt

msch. – Die ersten Punkte sind unter Dach und Fach. Am dritten Spieltag der Basketball-Regionalliga Südwest brachte der ASC Theresianum Mainz im Derby der sieglosen Teams vom BC Darmstadt ein 76:67 mit. Der Aufsteiger aus Mainz stürzte damit den letztjährigen Tabellensechsten mit dem Ziel „obere Tabellenhälfte" in eine sportliche Krise.

Entsprechend der Ausgangslage begannen die Akteure äußerst nervös und lieferten sich ein körperbetontes, aber faires Spiel. Mainz machte mit zwei Dreiern von Scott und Langen auf, hatte aber nur kurze Freude am 6:2. Der BCD konterte

Furios der Mainzer Einstieg nach dem Kabinengang. Innerhalb von sechs Minuten knallte der explodierende Gregg Scott vier Dreiwürfer ins Netz und wendete das Blatt zum 50:42. Ein Durchhänger bis zum 60:60 (33.), als Uli Mediger mit fünf Fouls vom Feld mußte, konnte am Mainzer Selbstbewußtsein nicht kratzen.

Und selbst als mit Jens Bastian fünf Minuten vor dem Ende mit einer Platzwunde ausfiel, war die zum Schluß gespielte Zone dicht. Ein 69:60-Vorsprung wurde sicher über die Zeit gebracht. Held des Tages war US-Boy Scott, der bei elf Dreierversuchen siebenmal traf und insgesamt 36 Punkte erzielte.

ASC Theresianum Mainz: Langen (11), Bastian (4), Faßhauer, Koltai (4), Wedel (4), Kreh, Scott (36), Rähmer (3), Braun (6), Mediger (8).

My first time back in Darmstadt since my mid-game friendly departure with Hanau. I'd absorbed punishment with a classy exit. The fans were again very welcoming and I had my same ball boy during my warm-up. Never could I have imagined what ensued. **I was Geeked Up! Keen G'$ Kill Mode!**

die Zeit gebracht. Held des Tages war US-Boy Scott, der bei elf Dreierversuchen siebenmal traf und insgesamt 36 Punkte erzielte. "elf" "11"

ASC Theresianum Mainz: Langen (11), Bastian (4), Faßhauer, Koltai (4), Wedel (4), Kreh, Scott (36), Rähmer (3), Braun (6), Mediger (8).

"The most complete player I've ever seen. The best shooting performance! The first play of the game, ASC won the tip, the pass went to Gregg and he drove to the basket, exploded up dunked over two guys and got fouled. The arena went dead silent! He made the free throw. And, those two shots were the only shots he would take from inside of the 3-point line the entire game. Amazing! He hit pure jump shots from unbelievable distances and angles. In the first half, Gregg made 4 of his 6 triples. At half-time he told me softly, 'The Best Is Yet To Come.' The second half was truly unforgettable. Besides rebounding and passing well, he put on a shooting exhibition that awed us. Gregg went 7-for-8 on threes and finished 11 for 14 on three pointers alone. He scored 36 POINTS on 15 SHOTS and ONE free throw. It was incredible!"

Andres ~ BC Darmstadt Ball Boy

Motor stotterte vor verhaltenem Publikum

Regionalliga-Basketballer des ASC Theresianum bezwangen GW Frankfurt 94:79 (43:32

Beam me up, Scottie: ASC-Flügelspieler Gregg Scott steigerte sich sein gesamtes Team nach der Pause. **Foto: Bernd E**

The GW Frankfurt Yugo 'import' was the leading scorer in the Regionalliga. Starcevic! So what! **I play lock-up D'! So, I held him to 15, scored 30, in a 94-79 beatdown!!!** With hundreds of Wiesbaden fans in attendance, it was a special night and I put on a G'$ show!

Wiesbaden American Middle School

Thomas W. Snyder
Gifted & Talented Specialist
AVID Coordinator

Unit 29647 Texas Strasse 07778
APO 09096 65189 Wiesbaden

0611-721182 DS N 337-6242
FAX 0611-723496 (H) 0611-721079

"Gregg and his ASC club sponsored a very special Sunday 'game night' field trip for 200 Wiesbaden DoD students to Mainz. Three luxury buses, snacks, game tickets, food and beverage vouchers, gift bags and on-court post-game autographs and pics. A memorable event and a truly mesmerizing performance by Mr. Scott." Tom Snyder

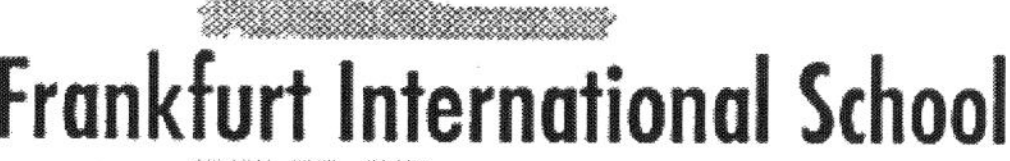

Frankfurt International School

A world of opportunities

The Frankfurt International School e.V - An der Waldlust 15 - D-61440 Oberursel

Athletic Department

The Frankfurt International School e.V
Established 1961

An Der Waldlust 15
D-61440 Oberursel - Germany
Phone +49 (0) 6171 / 202 - 171
Fax +49 (0) 6171 / 202 - 172
email ray_morgenstern@fis.cocos.de

1 December, 1996

To Whom It May Concern:

In August of 1996, I heard a presentation made to an Athletic Directors' Conference by Mr. Gregg Scott about his "Hoopaholics" Basketball Camps and his *Mental Athlete Workshop*. I was so impressed with his presentation that I decided to pursue the opportunity to have Mr. Scott come to our school and work with our basketball teams. On Saturday, 16 November 1996, The Frankfurt International School High School Basketball Teams (50 girls and boys at the varsity and junior varsity level) began their season with an all-day clinic presented by Mr. Scott.

Gregg Scott's clinic was a perfect way to launch our basketball season. The day was an ideal blend of work on skills & fundamentals, mental training & motivation, and having fun with the game. Mr. Scott's articulate style of presentation is both captivating and motivational. Goal-setting, nutrition, conditioning and positive mental tools were at the core of every aspect of the day. His emphasis on how to deal with failure and how to have a positive vision of one's self was truly inspiring to our young athletes. The tools he presented are the things that can make a difference if a player wishes to move his game to a higher level. It was ideal to have them presented and reinforced by a someone who has achieved such a high level in the game by living and using the principles he offers.

A perfect summation of the day was given to me by one of my best varsity players as we were leaving the gym at the end of the day. I asked him what he thought of the clinic and if he felt he had gained anything from it. He told me, "I walked out of there feeling like I could achieve everything I've ever wanted to in basketball. I could even be a professional player if I want to, it was so inspiring."

We are already pursuing the idea of having Gregg Scott return to our campus and do a similar program with our school's Middle School teams. Whether to begin a season on a high note or to build motivation for the off-season, I give the highest of recommendations to Gregg Scott and his "Hoopaholics" Basketball Camp.

Sincerely,

Ray Morgenstern,
Athletic Director & Varsity Boys Basketball Coach

Accredited by European Council of International Schools and Middle States Association of Colleges and Schools
The International School Wiesbaden is a branch of The Frankfurt International School e.V.

FRANKFURT INTERNATIONAL MINI-CAMP

9:00	Camp Meeting - Introduction
9:15	Warm Up
9:20	Stretch
9:30	Ball Handling Drills –
9:55	Defense/Rebounding, Shell Game, Alley Drill
10:20	Knockout
10:30	Water Break
10:35	Camp Meeting - Introduction Shooting/Getting Open
10:45	Shooting Drills –
11:00	Five Shots from Five Spots Contest
11:20	Knockout/Five Spot Final
11:45	Camp Meeting –

Evolution and Impact of a Hoopaholic!

Hoopaholics Mini-Camp: Frankfurt Int'l. School

Intro to Lucas!

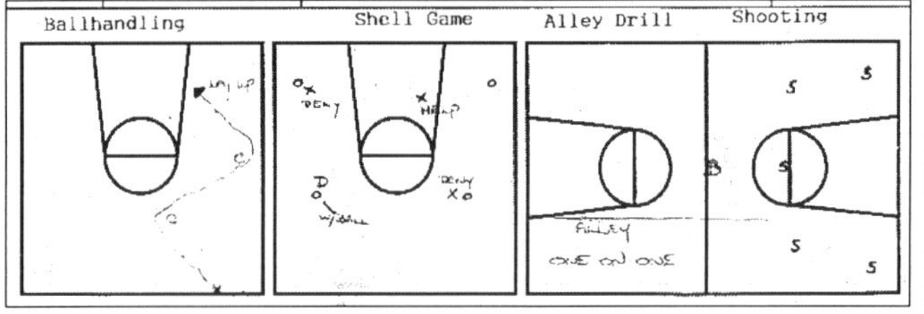

FRANKFURT INTERNATIONAL MINI-CAMP

My name is.... And I'm a HOOPAHOLIC

1:00	Camp Meeting - Introduction
1:15	Warm Up
1:20	Stretch
1:30	Group A: Ball Handling/ Group B: Knockout
1:50	Group A: Knockout/Group B: Ball handling
2:10	Water Break
2:15	Camp Meeting - Introduction to Shooting/Getting Open
2:20	Shooting - All
2:45	Group A: Defense/ Group B: Five Spot Shooting
3:05	Group A: Five Spot Shooting/ Group B: Defense
3:25	Knockout/Five Spot Final (Include coaches)
3:45	Camp Meeting

OBJECTIVES:.

To convey the fundamentals of the game in a fun and enjoyable environment.

DATE: 11/16/1996
STATION: 3 Rotations
SESSION NUMBER:

TIME	DRILL/ACTIVITY	POINTS OF EMPHASIS	GROUPING
9:30 (1:30)	Ballhandling	Basketball position w/ head up Protect ball w/ off hand Develop weak hand!	
9:55 (2:45)	Defense/Reb. Shell Game	Stance/Footwork/Verbalization Help and recover on wings Help and rotate on the baseline Helpside player must see man and ball	
	Alley Drill	Footwork and quickness Determination	
10:45 (2:20)	Shooting	Balance Shoulders square to the basket Good Legs / No fading Repitition - Same shot every time!	COACHING POINTS: Teach & Motivate

Lucas Tasa: Frankfurt Int'l School ~ G' Hoops Pupil & Protégé

It was a typical November day in Frankfurt, Germany – gloomy, gray, and somewhat rainy. It was Saturday morning and most other high school sophomores would have been sound asleep at home - but not me. My high school Athletic Director had invited all members of both girls and boys JV and Varsity basketball teams to attend a session with Gregg Scott, a former professional basketball player from the U.S. who was now in Germany playing professionally. Being a huge basketball fanatic, I was of course extremely excited about this opportunity. I attended the session and listened to what Gregg had to say about the game of basketball. I don't recall much about the session itself, other than Gregg talking about a lot about "the mental aspect of the game". It was a phrase he used a number of times that morning and being the naive, overenthusiastic teenager I was, I was unsure of what it really meant. I also recall a number of stretching exercises he showed us, along with some fundamental basketball drills, which I had never done before and felt were really good and valuable. In addition, Gregg introduced us to a number of basketball related literature, as well as his "*Hoopaholics*" line of branded t-shirts and sweatshirts. I was very impressed with the athleticism Gregg displayed as well as his insight into the game. He introduced me to a whole other dimension of the game of basketball I had never come into contact with and had never heard of from the number of coaches and basketball camps I had attended in my young life.

I purchased a white "*Hoopaholics*" sweatshirt that morning from Gregg. I believe I was one of only a few students who did purchase a shirt. I also surveyed the range of books Gregg had brought along with him. The one that stuck out to me was entitled *The Winner Within*, by legendary coach Pat Riley. Being a Chicago Bulls fan (who wasn't in the mid 90s?), I was all too familiar with Pat Riley and his New York Knicks. I remember returning home that morning after the session with Gregg and calling my Grandmother in Chicago, asking her to please order *The Winner Within* for me, as I didn't have access to many English books, living in Germany.

Soon thereafter our high school basketball season started. The previous year I had transferred to the Frankfurt International School because of their superior basketball program and because I knew I wanted to eventually attend an American university after graduating from high school. I was on the Junior Varsity team at the time and had not had a very good freshman year, having to deal with a very biased coach who seemed to have some prejudices against me, since I had come from a German school and played in local German clubs. Basketball was not a very popular sport with the German youth, although once in a while you could spot a red Michael Jordan Chicago Bulls jersey on the playground. Among the faithful at the Frankfurt International School, the German basketball scene was viewed with little respect and generally perceived to be not very disciplined and very disorganized. It would be difficult for me to argue that point – it just wasn't a popular sport, and thus finding good talent as well as good coaching was a difficult task.

But this year was going to be different, I told myself. My school had hired a new JV coach – an American who seemed to have good basketball resume and was also relatively unbiased coming into the season. I won a starting spot on the JV team that year ----

My Hoop Injury & Agony: I understood, coming off an injury that I would most likely come off the bench for the next game or two. But I would not start a single game for the rest of the season. In fact, I would hardly even play in any of the games for the rest of that season. I was crushed and started questioning my skills and even my choice to attend the Frankfurt International School. One of the main reasons I chose that school was because of the basketball program. And now my dream had been destroyed. I was very depressed and contemplated not trying out for the team the next season.

I had had a number of heart-to-heart conversations with my parents, who to this day support me through everything I have ever done in my life. My father suggested I find someone who would focus on coaching me through the off-season and helping me rehab my deteriorated basketball skills. After giving it much thought, my parents suggested I call Gregg Scott to see if he knew of anyone willing to be a personal coach to me. In the conversation I had with Gregg, he said he could not think of anyone who would be willing to do it, other than himself. I remember being shocked when he said that – not believing that someone of Gregg's status would be willing to help out a mediocre junior varsity high school basketball player regain the confidence and skills needed to continue to play basketball through high school. But at the same time, I was extremely excited. Gregg had made a lasting impression on me the first time I met him during that clinic he held at my school. I was thoroughly impressed by his demeanor, how he carried himself, his knowledge of the game and the mental aspects of the game he would always speak about.

Gregg and I met once per week for the next few months, usually early on a Saturday morning at a gym on the military base near Gregg's home in Wiesbaden, Germany. Gregg taught me how to properly warm up and stretch, how to lift weights, and of course how to practice and train certain basketball skills. But beyond the physical training Gregg provided, he taught me the mental aspect of the game. Gregg taught me that physical fatigue could be overcome with mental strength and that training the mind to overcome certain barriers was as important as, if not more important than, the physical training and the repetition of drills.

Our sessions usually began with some warming up on a treadmill, to get the muscles loose and warm. Then we would go through the 6 fundamental stretching exercises Gregg believed to be the most important stretches before playing basketball. There were days I would only do the stretching half-heartedly, and those were the days Gregg would not start the basketball portion of our session until I focused on the stretching. Then we would go into the gym and jump rope for 10-15 minutes, or however long it took me to get the exercise right.

The basketball portion started out with "the touch drill" – standing underneath the basket and focusing on holding the ball on your fingertips and shooting the perfect shot. This meant the ball was not allowed to touch the rim, only the net. We did this from each side of the hoop and then gradually moved it further into the court to make for a longer shot. From there we went into numerous other shooting drills and throughout these drills Gregg would constantly talk to me, telling me what I needed to focus on in terms of my mechanics, or telling me my mechanics look fine, but I wasn't concentrating enough – the mental aspect. He taught me to practice shooting free-throws while I was tired, how to concentrate, where to aim, and how to envision the ball going through the basket. And most importantly, he taught me to set goals for myself and to achieve them. We started with small attainable goals, such as making 6 out of ten free throws. Later, when I was consistently making 10 out of 10 free throws, we set the goal of not touching the rim on any of the shots – a much loftier goal. Each session we would conclude with a competitive shooting game, such as H.O.R.S.E or a three-point or free throw competition. In all the months Gregg and I trained together, I was only able to beat him once in a game of H.O.R.S.E. And to this day, I am convinced he let me win that game. But in doing so, I became much more competitive and much more driven and much stronger physically and most importantly, mentally. This competition ignited a fire in me to be better than the next guy I was playing against, and to do so, not by talking trash or by verbally putting someone down, but by letting my game show what I was capable of. Gregg taught me to out-smart the other player, to learn how my body reacts to certain nutrition, fatigue, how to overcome that fatigue mentally, and how to envision success before even achieving it.

While we were training, we set the goal for me to make the varsity team that next season. My high school had the most talented group of players ever that year, so I knew making the varsity was going to be nearly impossible. Gregg told me to keep that goal in front of me at all times and to work towards that goals with everything I had. And by keeping that goal in front of me, he didn't mean just mentally, he meant physically. I wrote that goal on a piece of paper and stuck it to the inside of my locker at school. I also stuck that goal on the ceiling above my bed, where it would be the last thing I would see before I went to sleep, and the first thing I would see when I woke up the next morning. I had to see it to be it. Gregg encouraged me to dream. He encouraged me to think about the next steps I wanted to take in life, such as playing basketball in college, or even professionally. He encouraged me to dream about dunking the basketball, and he encouraged me to write down all of those dreams and goals and to keep them in front of me at all times. He said I had to see it on paper, in my dreams, in my head, in order to achieve it and to be it. I had to think of myself as a varsity player and envision myself as such, in order to be one.

The following Fall I tried out for the basketball team again, as I did every year. But this year my goal was to make the varsity team. During the try-outs I concentrated on all the tools Gregg had given me throughout the last months. I thought of myself as a varsity player and envisioned playing in the gym the varsity team played their games in. (The varsity and junior varsity teams played their games in separate gyms). And I made the varsity team that year. I came off the bench, but I had achieved my goal. After finding out I made the team, I immediately called Gregg and told him the good news. He was thrilled for me and said all of my hard work has paid off. He encouraged me to find and set the next goal for myself and to take down the papers I had on my locker and on my ceiling and replace them with new ones. But also, to hold on to the papers with the past goals so that in the future, I could look back at what all I had achieved.

Für einen ersten Höhepunkt sorgte Gregg Scott in der 17. Minute, als er bei einem Fastbreak auf den Korb zog, dann aber auf den Wurf verzichtete und statt dessen Steffen Braun – den effektivsten Center – mit einem Paß hinter dem Rücken

Mainz

"Scott did return to his Marks Manship."

Vielleicht wäre es in der zweiten Halbzeit dazu gekommen. Gregg Scott hatte zu seiner Treffsicherheit zurückgefunden, das Mainzer Spiel lief merklich runder. Zwei, drei starke Grün-Weiß-Aktionen reich-

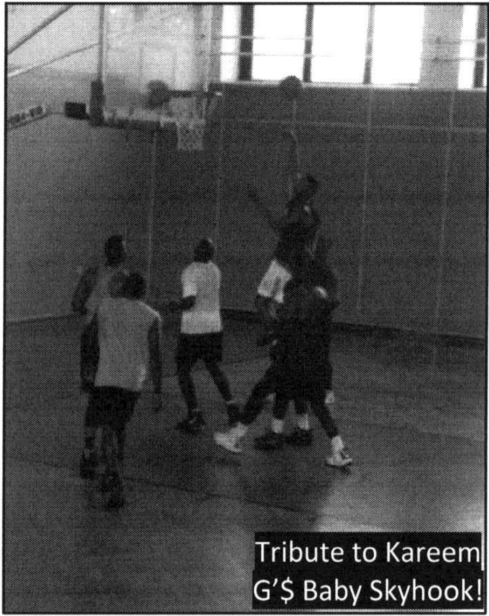

Tribute to Kareem
G'$ Baby Skyhook!

My Xanthus tour roommate, Mike Moten, called me to inform me that I was eligible to be a 'DoD' Substitute teacher based on my 'Dependent Status! And with my prior experience teaching at UCSD, and hoop stature; done deal!

DEPARTMENT OF DEFENSE
DEPENDENTS SCHOOLS
OFFICE OF THE PRINCIPAL
WIESBADEN AMERICAN MIDDLE SCHOOL
UNIT 29647
APO AE 09096

Fact: The students in the Computing class I sub'd introduced me to the Internet! My 1st www? eBay!

11 DECEMBER, 1996

MEMORANDUM FOR WHOM IT MAY CONCERN

SUBJECT: Employment Verification

Gregory T. Scott is employed by Department of Defense Dependents Schools (DoDDS) at the Wiesbaden American Middle School as a Substitute Teacher.

This is an intermittent, seasonal position which pays $68.50 per day. Mr. Scott works on an average of 3 to 4 days per week.

Point of contact is the undersigned at 0611-721182.

Lambert J. Kroon
Assistant Principal

Mom was an Elementary School Teacher in Hawaii. THE APPLE DOESN'T FALL FAR FROM THE TREE.

1996 FIBA EUROSTARS - EUROPE'S FIRST OFFICIAL ALL-STAR GAME

Basketball is booming in Europe... Silver and Bronze in Atlanta... the arrival of the new EuroLeague... the adidas Streetball Challenge is going from success to success... and now Europe's best get to showcase their skills in the first ever European All-Star Game.

FIBA EuroStars '96

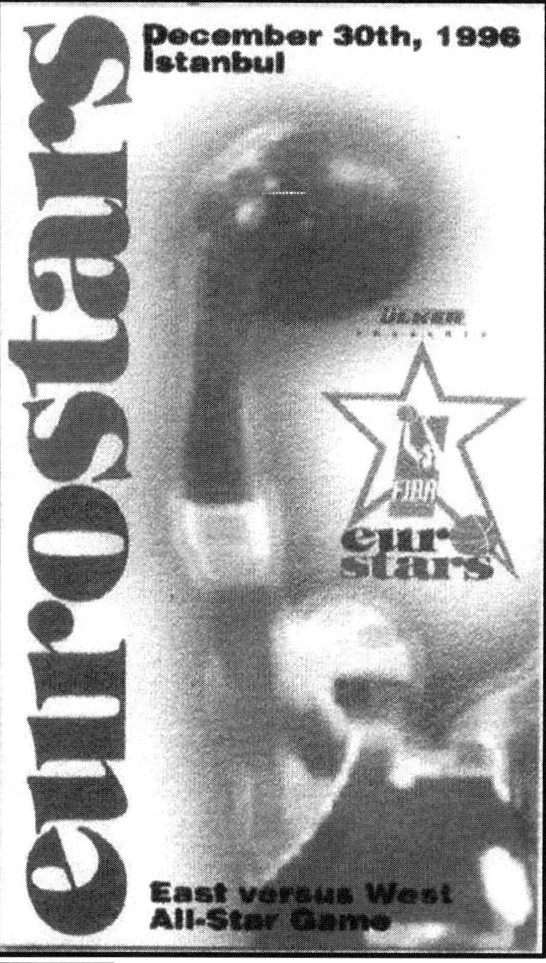

East versus West... Can the best players from the West overcome the traditional power from the East? The argument will be settled in Istanbul on December 30th 1996, when FIBA, the International Basketball Federation hosts the inaugural EuroStars.

EuroStars will be more than a game... there will be slamdunks, a three-point shoot-out, the adidas European Streetball All-Star game and big basketball party time, all in one of the world's most captivating cities - Istanbul in Turkey.

FIBA and adidas present: adidas Streetball at the FIBA EuroStars in Istanbul!

Not only the finest basketball players from the continent will meet in Istanbul on December 30th, 1996. For the adidas Streetball game, which will be the pre-game of the EuroStars Game, adidas will select a Streetball World All-Star Teamî at the adidas Streetball World Championship in Budapest on September 14th-15th, 1996. It will be invited to travel to Istanbul and play against a Turkish All-Star Team selected at the Streetball Finals in Turkey. Flight tickets, accomadations, meals and an adidas product package will be free of charge for the players.

Be a part of it!

exclusive sportswear sponsor of 1996 FIBA Eurostars

FIBA EuroStars 1996

West: Gregg Scott #13

GabDad gave up a $1M contract for a $1M bond with gs! #FAMILYOVERHOOPS

I had attended the lamanze child-birth classes, sonograph appointments and 'first-timers' parenting workshops in preparation to be an active participant during the birth of my G'.

All while G'hoopin' in All-Star games, Le Runners' tour, adidas promos and ASC Mainz. As I was making much more money outside of my Mainz contract my Coach was aloof!

January 12th, 1997. Game Night: TV Mainz vs. MCK in Kaiserslautern against my good friend, Sam Godden-Graham. As my wife goes into (false) labor that morning at home in Wiesbaden we went to the hospital only to be sent back home. Decisions on my playing status are eminent; my coach insists that I play. Nope! This would be the only game I'd ever miss in my Euro career. Ten hours of false labor was actually enough time for me to have played in the game. The baby slept well past midnight.

Jan. 13th: Born at 2:13 a.m., g' was a NIGHT-OWL like G'

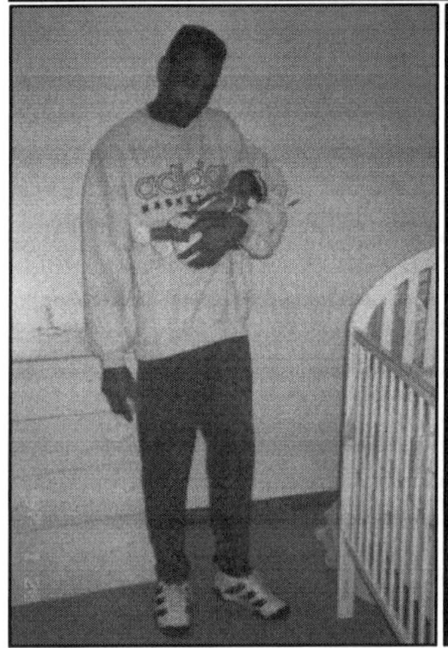

It was 2:13 a.m., January 13th: Our miracle child & my '87 Sabatini namesake promise Gabriella Renee Scott came into this world; my world! As they cleared her eyes the first thing she focused in on were my eyes as she smiled! Our bond was established. Two of my comical recollections: *Cutting the embilical cord was harder than I expected. * Don't view the after-birth! Placenta was Disconcerting.

Mainz lost the game. I won!

#GabDadDutiesReign

For whatever reason Puig could not breast-feed. Some questions are better left **unasked!** Thus, alternating overnight feeding every four hours was my REM sleep-depriving ritual. **Many late nights:** Gabby was so active I'd put her in the car and drive until she fell asleep. My sleeping habits altered. But, we shared unique bonding time. **Our nanny was a Savior!**

Girls' Sports in their formative years entail unique gender-specific dynamics & psyche sensitivities.

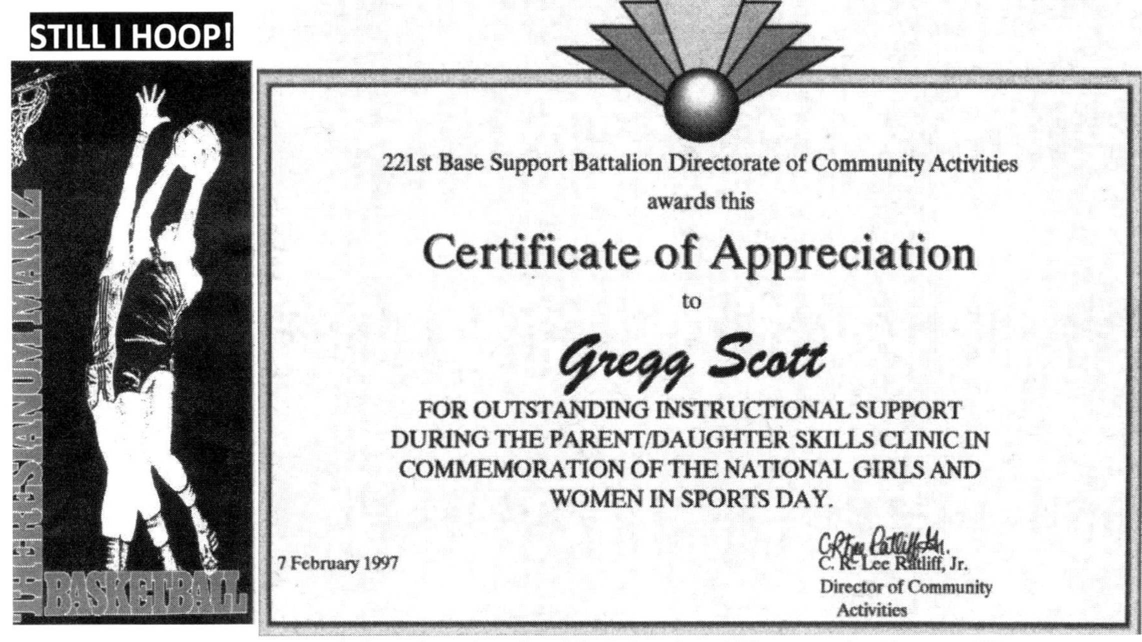

221st Base Support Battalion Directorate of Community Activities

awards this

Certificate of Appreciation

to

Gregg Scott

FOR OUTSTANDING INSTRUCTIONAL SUPPORT DURING THE PARENT/DAUGHTER SKILLS CLINIC IN COMMEMORATION OF THE NATIONAL GIRLS AND WOMEN IN SPORTS DAY.

7 February 1997

C. R. Lee Ratliff, Jr.
Director of Community Activities

I took great honor participating in the Weisbaden Women in Sports Day event.

Coaches Publiclly Posted Blatant Media Slap...After a Victory!!

It was a home game against a club that I had lit up for 33 points playing for TG Hanau! TSV Grunberg ran a triangle & two defense; 3 defender zone & 2 players guarding me! My coach was baffled so I designed an offensive scheme in which I'd be a distant decoy. A basic 4-on-3 strategy: 2 guards, big at high-post, big down low. Flash! Diagonal Pass!

I put in my work with a 15 point, 12 rebound, 10 assist stat line in a gritty 94-92 victory.

Hatte an der ASC-Sensation wenig Anteil: Der schwache Gregg Scott. Bild:Volker Oehl

Kreidebleich, aber sehr glücklich

ASC-Trainer Hans Beth nach dem 94:92-Sieg über TSV Grünberg: „Wir sind gereift"

"Wir sind gerefit" Translation "We have matured"

msch. – Marcel Rähmer setzte den Rahmen. Er war der Joker des Basketball-Regionalliga-Aufsteigers ASC Theresianum Mainz. Der Spieler „von der Bank" war der Highscorer des Tages (28 Punkte) und zerstörte vorerst einmal die Bundesliga-Aufstiegsträume des TSV Grünberg. Die Hessen erlitten zum Rückrunden-Auftakt bei den Mainzern mit 92:94 (78:78) nach Verlängerung ihre zweite Saison-Niederlage.

Kreidebleich saß ASC-Trainer Hans Beth nach der Schlußsirene auf der Bank, wie weggeblasen der hochrote Kopf. Derweil führten die Spieler vor knapp 500 Zuschauern Freudentänze auf. „Das war das i-Tüpfelchen, meiner Mannschaft ein dickes Lob", faßte Beth dann kurz und schmerzlos zusammen. „Grünberg war das erwartet routinierte Team und kam immer wieder ins Spiel zurück. Völker allein hat uns gezwungen, viermal die Abwehrstrategie zu ändern. Wir sind gereift und agieren und reagieren jetzt flexibler." Daß er in der Minute des größten Saisonerfolges kein Wort der Kritik fand, ist nachvollziehbar.

Was aber wäre gewesen, wenn der letzte Wurf der Gäste zur Verlängerung (78:78) nicht ein Zweier, sondern ein Dreier gewesen wäre. Denn der schläfrige Zeitnehmer des ASC hatte vergessen, das automatische Horn einzustellen und war von den dramatischen Schlußsekunden vom Spiel so gefesselt, daß er versäumte, die Partie manuell zu beenden.

Der ASC-Trommler mußte lange warten, bis der Funke auf die Fans übersprang. In der ersten Hälfte spielten beide Teams wenig spektakulär mehr oder weniger solides Basketball (44:40). Der grippekranke Spielmacher Nik Koltai mußte mehrfach auf die Bank. Bei einer Niederlage hätte man wohl über den smarten Amerikaner Gregg Scott reden müssen. Er bewegte sich wie ein Mannequin auf dem Laufsteg, ohne einen Tropfen Schweiß zu vergeuden. Alles andere als ein führender Kopf im Team.

Kapitän Henk Wedel wurde den Ansprüchen dagegen gerecht. Er machte mit Langen und Rähmer den nötigen Druck, der die ASC-Center in ein helles Licht stellte, auch wenn diese in der Schlußminute (73:66) in der Abwehr immer einen Tick zu spät foulten und den Gästen zu Bonuswürfen verhalfen. Taktische Brillanz in der Verlängerung: Einwurf auf Rähmer, „stop the clock" der Gäste an ihm. Die coole Antwort: sieben von acht Freiwürfe im Korb.

ASC Theresianum Mainz: Langen (9), Bastian, Faßhauer, Koltai (2), Wedel (7), Kreh (12), Scott (15), Rähmer (28), Braun (18), Mediger (3).

#Blasphemy! A day after a gutsy home win: Coach Posted a Cruel Article at Our Club!

The security guard waved me into my underground spot at ASC HQ for training. I entered a reception area with a display case where I saw an article of me prominently posted with the notable 'Club News & Highlights'. It was in German with a picture of me. Pleasing!

Scandalous Media Scorn

Hatte an der ASC-Sensation wenig Anteil: Der schwache Gregg Scott. Bild:Volker Oehl

Then a friend of mine approached with a hint of sadness. "Don't worry about that, Gregg. You performed great." I was confused, asking him to interpret the article to me. "Sorry man, I like you too much to read that BS to you."

I slid the glass open and removed the article and went to our locker-room. A bit early, only a few players lingered. Hans, at the far end drawing on his clipboard with Tim, only briefly glanced up at me. No hellos. Mutual disdain. Summoning my team interpreter to me, I handed him the article. 'Read this to me, please.' He resisted. I insisted!! 'Excuse me? You're paid to interpret. You don't need to like what you interpret. So, earn your money. Interpret.' He was stuck between a rock and a hard place for sure. Hans was glaring at us from afar and I wasn't relenting! Hans choosing to publicly post it and embarrass me. Ha! The media can tout what they want. I don't even read it! Be it good or bad, I just send it all to my mom to archive.

***Scorn: "Having no part in the ASC-Sensation. The weakening Greg Scott."**

'Man uber Smart American Greg Scott…'
'…Like a Mannequin…' I read no further.

lage hätte man wohl über den smarten Amerikaner Gregg Scott reden müssen. Er bewegte sich wie ein Mannequin auf dem Laufsteg, ohne einen Tropfen Schweiß zu vergeuden. Alles andere als ein führender Kopf im Team.

1 month old GabDad! G'$ scoring average falls below 20 points!!

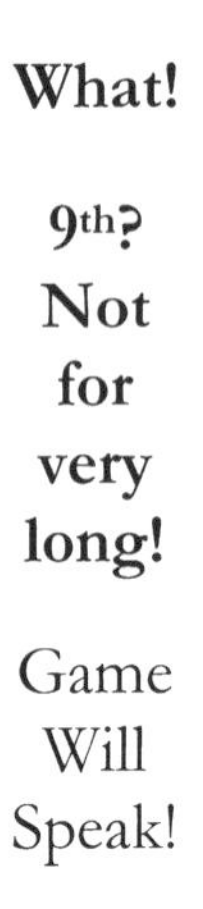

What!

9th? Not for very long!

Game Will Speak!

It Did!

KORBJÄGER

Regionalliga Südwest/Nord (Herren)

	Pkt.	Sp	Pkte/Sp
1 Starcevic (GW Frankfurt)	301	10	30,10
2 Karaffa (Ober-Ramstadt)	382	14	27,29
3 Bosnjak (Wittlich)	371	14	26,50
4 Berak (Saarlouis)	366	14	26,14
5 Neuber (Saarlouis)	353	14	25,21
6 Klein (Wittlich)	245	10	24,50
7 Bilalovic (Limburg)	338	14	24,14
8 B. Völker (Grünberg)	260	13	20,00
9 Scott (Mainz)	268	14	19,14
10 Laas (Wittlich)	246	13	18,92
11 Dinca (Ober-Ramstadt)	259	14	18,50
12 Greunke (Langen)	256	14	18,29

Stand: 13. Februar 1997

G'$: ASC in 6th Place! 9-8 Record!

Regionalliga Herren

VfB Gießen - TV Saarlouis	**78 : 79**
VfR Limburg - TSV Grünberg	97 : 78
ASC Mainz - Wittlicher TV	97 : 64
Ober-Ramstadt - BC Darmstadt	101:85
GW Frankfurt - TV Langen II	69 : 72

Early Season! Stats Don't Lie!

G'$: 44 points and a win at Wittlicher TV. **Next!**

1. VfR Limburg	17	1549:1249	28: 6
2. TSV Grünberg	17	1500:1348	24:10
3. TV Saarlouis	**17**	**1509:1449**	**22:12**
4. Ober-Ramstadt	17	1524:1431	22:12
5. VfB Gießen	17	1382:1396	20:14
6. ASC Mainz	17	1346:1350	18:16
7. TV Langen II	17	1212:1251	16:18
8. BC Darmstadt	17	1282:1373	10:24
9. GW Frankfurt	17	1278:1500	8:26
10. Wittlicher TV	17	1369:1604	2:32

Jahrgang 6 Saison 1996/97 Nr. 15

Seite 5 / Nr. 15

Mannschaftsaufstellungen

TV 1872 Saarlouis	ASC Mainz
6 Christian Neuber	4 Jens Bastian
7 Alek Zivanovic	5 Nikolaus Koltai
8 Alexander Greer	6 Oliver Kreh
9 Holger Gebhard	7 Gregory Scott
10 Mariusz Dziurdzia	9 Marcel Rähmer
11 Frank Willim	10 Henk Wedel
12 Achim Münzebrock	13 Tim Langen
13 Andreas Pink	14 Steffen Braun
14 Markus Eisenbarth	15 Ulrich Medinger
15 Igor Berak	Trainer: Herr Beth
Trainer: Hermann Paar	Co-Trainer: Herr Schoch

Sonntag, 23.03.97

16.00 h BL Damen
TVS - BG Bonn

18.00 h RL Herren
TVS - ASC Mainz

Kreissporthalle Saarlouis

ASC at TV Saarlouis: G'$ 34

A 3-hour trip in a bad snowstorm! I glanced out of the bus and felt like I was in Siberia. Just white snow on the horizon. Not one ASC fan made the trek. Our foes fans were raucous, rabid, rude and rowdy. I put in my work! In the 2nd half their 6'9" Yugo Igor hits me with a blatant elbow in my 'grill'! I hit the floor. Foul! His teammate jumps on top of me. "Gregg, please don't do it. That guy really is crazy. He does it to us in practice. Let it go." I Did! Gotta Know When to Fold 'em! I got 34 points. We got the 'W'. I 'got' him in Mainz!

TV 1872 Saarlouis - ASC Mainz

Es darf mit einem spannenden Spiel gerechnet werden. Im Hinspiel verloren unsere Herren mit einem Punkt. Die erste Revanche gelang im Halbfinale des Linksrheinpokals, welches der TVS nach spannendem und dramatischem Spiel mit 94 : 90 gewinnen konnte. Bester Mainzer war der Amerikaner Gregory Scott mit 34 Punkten (6 Dreier). **Home at 2am. Gabs Hug: Hit my injured nose. I gently put her down. I Cried!**

DREIER RAUSCH: "THREE NOISE"

Gregg Scott im Dreierrausch

Die ersten Zähler in der Regionalliga Südwest/Nord der Herren fuhr Neuling ASC Mann des Tages war dabei Gregg Scott, der 38 Punkte erzielte. Von elf Dreierversuchen fanden sieben ihr Ziel. Bei den hektisch agierenden Darmstädtern erzielten Peric (17) und Schäfer (11) die meisten Punkte.

I held their top scorer Peric to 17 points. G' DEFENSE!

Darmstadt visits ASC: Elf=11 3's Sequel

In our early-season game I hit "Elf Drierversuchen" or "eleven 3's" and 36 in Darmstadt. **Tonight The Sequel:**

Montag, 7. Oktober 1996

US-Boy Scott ist der ASC-Held

Amerikaner führt die Theresianum-Basketballer zum wichtigen Erfolg in Darmstadt

Kill Mode With Coach Disdain! Again, I served DARMSTADT for elf or eleven 3's & 38 points!!!

die Zeit gebracht. Held des Tages war US-Boy Scott, der bei elf Dreierversuchen siebenmal traf und insgesamt 36 Punkte erzielte.

ASC Theresianum Mainz: Langen (11), Bastian (4), Faßhauer, Koltai (4), Wedel (4), Kreh, Scott (36), Rähmer (3), Braun (6), Mediger (8).

G'$ GAMESPEAK SCORERS MENTALITY

Gab was my G' mate! Win or Lose: Holding Gab was my Top Triumph!

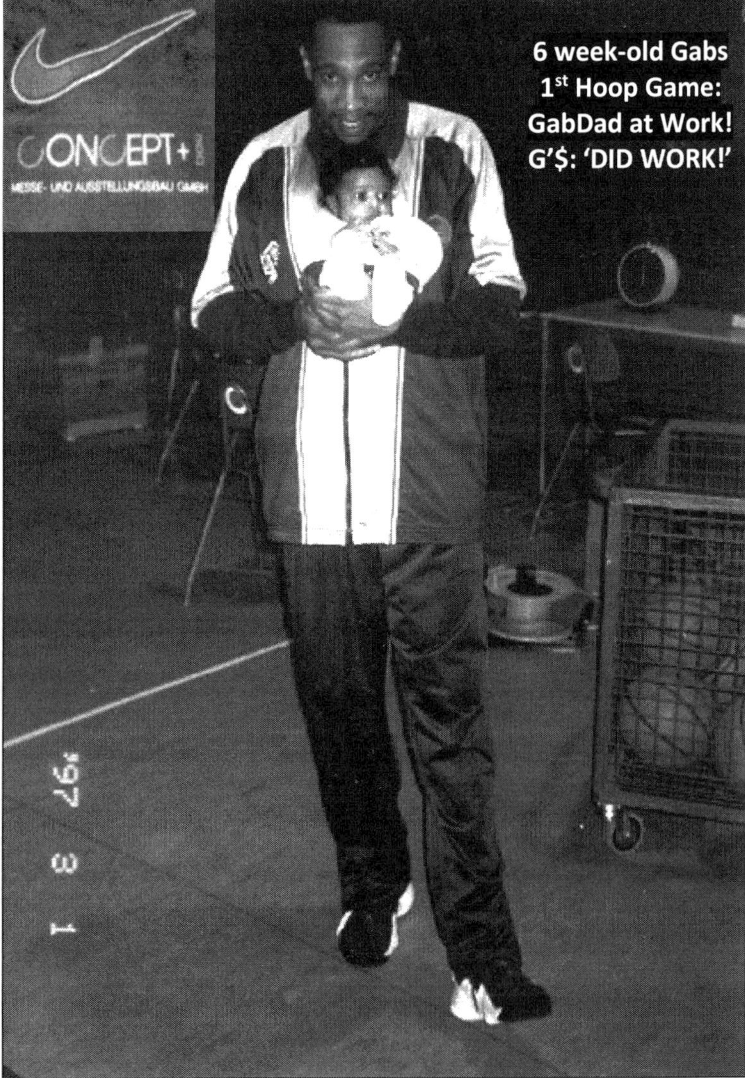

6 week-old Gabs 1st Hoop Game: GabDad at Work! G'$: 'DID WORK!'

AMERICAN BASKETBALL CAMP

FLAT 2, 166 WILLESDEN LANE, LONDON NW6 7PQ, ENGLAND PHONE: /81 451 5276
E-mail: Charles Dodson

CHAMPION & GABDAD

25 April 1997

Gregg Scott
Berlinerstr. 31
65189 Wiesbaden
Germany

Dear Gregg,

Sorry this has taken so long. I have to admit that when I received your letter in December and talked with Ray Morgenstern at FIS, I put it aside and pretty much forgot about it. December is not a time when I am working on camp business. I usually get heavily involved with camp issues once my own coaching season is over in March.

I would love to have you come to Switzerland as part of our staff or even to make a guest appearance if it can be arranged. As we begin to think about the future of our camp we recognize that we must begin to draw from Germany, Switzerland and France in particular. For several years we were content to provide a camp for American youth resident in Europe. Our players were divided equally from Dept. of Defense Schools and International American schools. With the cut back in the number of US forces in Europe our base has gradually eroded.

Your link to German clubs and youth programs might be just the connection that will help us broaden that base. For that to work, I would hope that you could come to Leysin and evaluate our teaching program, facilities and standard of operation. We believe that we provide a good camp and a unique service for American youth in Europe. I also think that German youth would benefit from the American style coaching of fundamentals not to mention the competition against American players.

I would be interested in your response to my suggestions and I hope that you are still available in some capacity to join us in Switzerland this summer. By now I hope congratulations are in order to you and your wife on becoming parents. You have many fond experiences in front of you. Congratulations and good luck.

I await your reply and apologize for the lateness of getting back to you.

Sincerely,

Chuck

Chuck Dodson
Camp Administrator

G'$: HOOPAHOLIC GOES TO SWITZERLAND!

'IF THERE'S A CURE FOR THIS, I DON'T WANT IT'!
'AND, IF THERE'S A REMEDY, I'LL RUN FROM IT!'

DEUTSCHLAND

I originally declined these two events for legit reasons. I had a vacation planned to Czechoslovakia with my mom & family during the first event. Also, Kobe's event was only a week before the first Nike Hoop Heroes event, and both being in Berlin. Ouch!

adidas AG, Postfach 1120, D-91072 Herzogenaurach

Gregg Scott

Berliner Str. 31
65189 Wiesbaden

However, the adidas USA BB V.P. informed me that Joe Bryant had again personally requested me for Kobe's event; and adidas offered to pay 'all expenses' for our entire 5-star vacation to the Czech Republic, and then on to Berlin for the first event. $old!!!

adidas AG
Adi-Dassler-Str. 1-2
D-91074 Herzogenaurach
Telefon 09132/84-0
Telefax 09132/84-2241
2865
0171-2208694
6342038

Ihre Zeichen	Ihre Nachricht vom	Unsere Zeichen	Telefon 84-/Fax 84-	Datum
			2884 / 2865	24.07.1997

Slam Dunk Contest in Berlin am 23./24. August und 3./4. September

Lieber Gregg,

wir würden Dich gerne einladen.
Am 23./24 August findet in Berlin auf dem Olympischen Platz unser adidas Streetball Challenge German Final statt. Im Rahmen dieser Veranstaltung wollen wir mit den besten Slam Dunkern einen Contest veranstalten. Neben vielen Stars aus Sport und Musik werden auch Detlef Schrempf und Randy Livingston anwesend sein.
Wir würden uns sehr freuen, wenn Du an diesem Slam Dunk teilnehmen würdest.
Der Contest findet am Samstag (ca. 17.30 Uhr) und Sonntag (ca. 18.00 Uhr) statt.
Bitte teile mir mit ob Du kommen möchtest. Selbstverständlich werde ich die Reisekosten (Bahnticket), sowie die Übernachtung organisieren und bezahlen.
Darüberhinaus wird am 3./4. September Kobe Bryant nach Berlin kommen. Im Rahmen des ersten BBL Saisonspiels ALBA - Herten werden wir in der Halbzeitpause einen Slam Dunk Contest mit Kobe Bryant organisieren. Auch dazu würden wir Dich gerne einladen und bitte Dich um Rückantwort.

Über eine kurze schriftliche Bestätigung, evtl. schon mit detaillierten Reisedaten würde ich mich freuen.
Für Rückfragen stehe ich gerne zur Verfügung.

Mit freundlichen Grüßen

Hannes Kranzfelder
Kommunikation D

Vorsitzender des Aufsichtsrats: Henri Filho
Vorstandsvorsitzender: Robert Louis-Dreyfus
Vorstand: Glenn Bennett, Herbert Hainer, Dean Hawkins, Michel Perraudin, Erich Stamminger, Christian Tourres
Sitz: 91072 Herzogenaurach, HRB 3868, Amtsgericht Fürth, UST-IDNR: DE 132490588
Bayerische Vereinsbank, Erlangen (BLZ 76320072) 4 607 112
Dresdner Bank, Erlangen (BLZ 76080040) 540 690 000

Still, the timing and proximity of both events made for an uncomfortable transition from adidas to Nike. Yes, I had fulfilled all of my three year adidas obligations with pride and distinction. My bro's new gig at Nike Sports Marketing & Entertainment: <u>G'$ PERK!</u>

Karlovy Vari, Chech Republic

GabDad & Gabriella

YouTube.com/MentalAthlete ~ Streetball

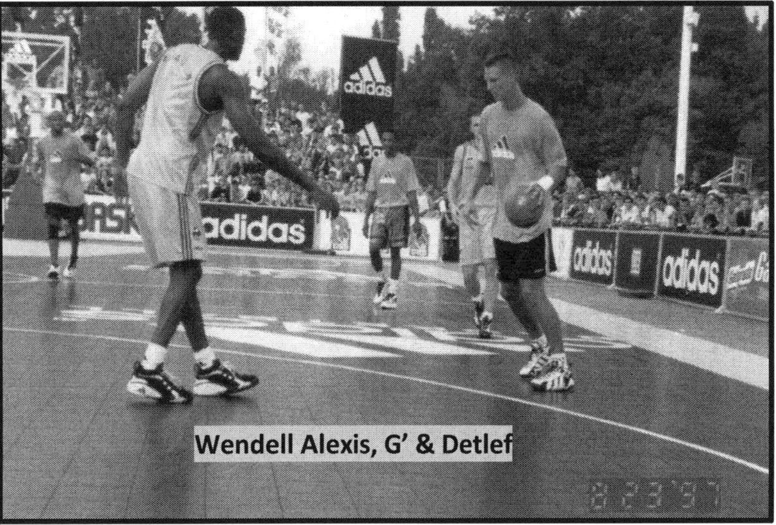

Wendell Alexis, G' & Detlef

STREETBALL
FINALS '97
BERLIN

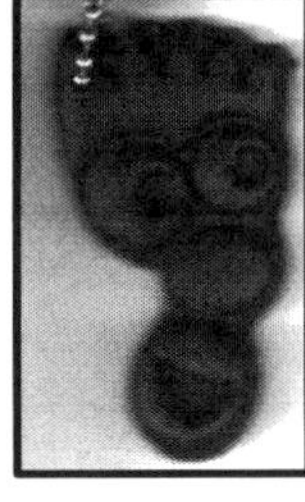

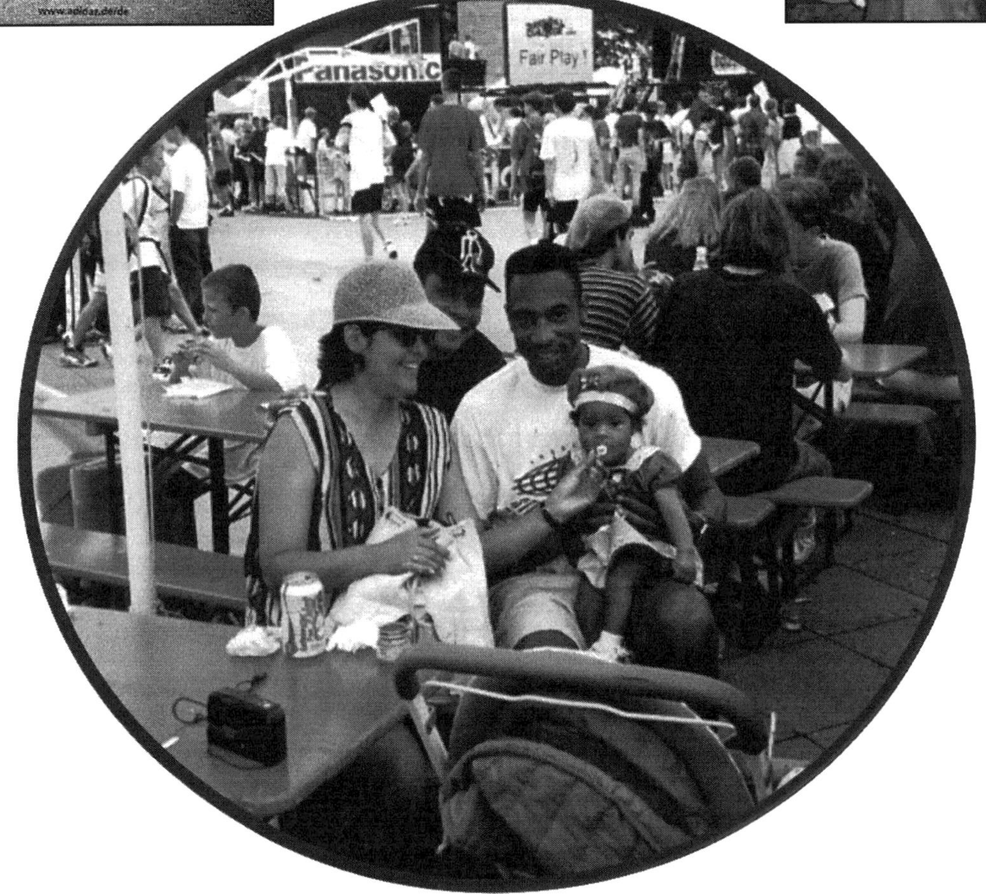

YouTube.com/MentalAthlete

kobe clinic & autogrammstunde

Kobe Bryant Exhibit Berlin

Ablaufplan 'Kobe Clinic & Autogrammstunde

I met Kobe's mom before the event. She told me, "Joe sends a sincere thank you."

Mittwoch 03.09.1997

Nr.	ZEIT	PROGRAMM	Info
	09.00 - 13.00		
0	ab 14.00	Aufbau Schule	Aufbau von Court + evtl Halle >>> Details folgen

JELLYBEAN BRYANT PLEA: G'MAN & KOBE IN BERLIN!

Donnerstag, 04.09.1997

	ZEIT	PROGRAMM	Info	
1	9.35 - 9.45	Soundcheck		
2	11.25. - 11.45	Soundcheck		
3	13.20	Schulende 'Begrüßung durch Fritz und (briefing Radio am ....)	Anmoderation, Programmablauf und Ankündigung Kobe	
4	ca. 13.30 *	Begrüßung Gregg Scott	Interview Gregg Scott durch Fritz	Kids, Gregg Scott / ALBA Bälle
5	13.35 *	3 Point Contest	Auswahl von 4-5 Teilnehmer für 3-Piont Contest; Punktevorgabe durch Gregg, Moderation Fritz	
6	13.50	Begrüßung ALBA Berlin	Interview ALBA durch Fritz	
	14.00	3 gegen 3	ALBA Spieler + 4 Kids Publikum	
7	14.15	Eintreffen/ Begrüßung Lou Richter & Vorqualifikation Slam Dunk	5 Teilnehmer aus Publikum (senior) ; 1-2 qualifizieren sich für den Slam Dunk, Moderation Lou / Fritz, Jury: ALBA Jungs, Gregg, Mike, Joe; + 1 Stimme Publikum *	
8	14.55	Anküdigung Kobe	Anmoderation von Kobe, Lifestorie etc., evtl Kobe Quiz	Lou
9	15.00 *	Kobe Kommt	Musik, Begrüßung,Moderation / Interview Lou / Fritz	Lou, Kobe, Musik
10	15.15 *	Einlauf Slam Dunker, Slam Dunk Show	Vordunk von Kobe; Slam Dunks von Mike, Joe, Henning, Kobe, 2 qulafizierte Kids Jury: Kobe, Gregg und n.n. ALBA Spieler, Junior Slam Dunker	Lou, Kids
(evtl)	15.45	Around the world mit Kobe		Teilnehmer aus Publikum
11	15.55	Letzter Talk mit Kobe, Abschied	Verabschiedung, Ankündigung Autogrammstunde	
12	16.00	Autogrammstunde		Center Court
13	16.30	Presseinfo		Klassenzimmer
14	17.00	Abfahrt Schule		
15	18.00	Autogrammstunde Karstadt		

After the event on the street outside of the venue, Kobe's transport van had a flat tire. He stepped out for a brief, coveted convo.

Gregg Scott Itinerary: Kobe Bryant Event Berlin, Germany - September 4, 1997

- *First Class ticket (will-call): Gregg Scott c/o adidas (check-in by 7:30 am)*
- *Depart: 8:00 am- Lufthansa Airlines Flt. 884, Frankfurt–Berlin; 9:05 am arrival*
- *Transport to Hotel Kipinski, Berlin (5-star): Reservation- Gregg Scott c/o adidas*
- *12:00 Transport to venue; 1 pm Gear/Shoes/Media Pics.; 1:30 GS on-court interview*
- *3:00 Kobe Live on Center Court; 3 on 3; Dunk Contest; Transport to Hotel Kipinski*
- *Return Flight: Lufthansa; Pending additional 9/5 P.R. video promo with Alba Berlin*

G' DISCOVERING DIRK

SportSchule '96 ~ G' Hoops & Deutschland's National Team

Media Day with FIBA & the German National Team

10/96: When Markus Hallgrimson asked me to drive to Wurzburg to see a young kid named Dirk Nowitzki play, I thought it was simply for the Porsche thrill.

How could Dirk be absent from our media day and on-court exhibitions at Detlef's 1996 All-Star Camp with FIBA and the German National Team??

The Battle of the Brands

Wurzburg was Nike sponsored! He wore a Swoosh; not 3 Stripes!

Dec. '96 Frankfurt Sheraton:
I first met with two Nike execs, Les Badden and Mike Golub, to interview for my Hoop Heroes gig. I told them, 'You MUST get this Nowitzki kid. He is very special.' My brother called me the very next day to confirm! NBA Altering Fact: Nike introduced Dirk to the NBA via G', Mark Scott & Hoop Heroes

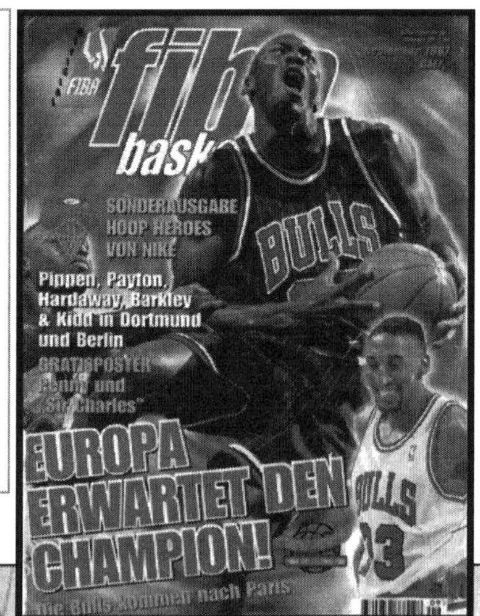

battle OF THE Brand

I informed the NIKE peeps that Nowitzki is pronounced NoVitzki.

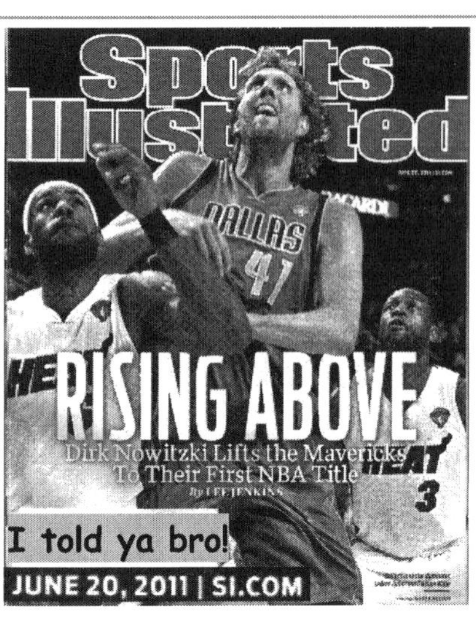

By Frank Rumpenhorst, AFP/Getty Images

Welcome home: Huge crowds turned out in Dirk Nowitzki's hometown of Wuerzburg, Germany, to celebrate the NBA star's return. Nowitzki led the Mavericks to the NBA title this month.

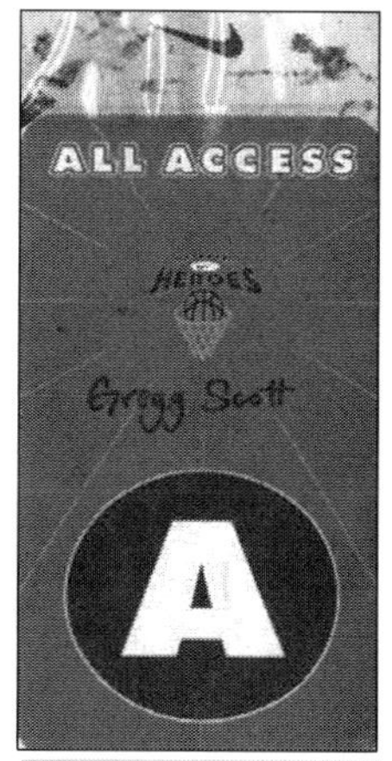

EUROSWOOSH!
'97 NIKE NBA
HOOP HEROES
BARKLEY, PIPPEN, PAYTON, MILLER & J. KIDD

Confidential and double top secret

Mr. Barkley embraced me from day 1. Invited me for cocktails; gave me his #4 jerseys in the locker-room. Both games!

Scottie DNP-foot. Still, we did share unique one-on-one time with his puppy German Rottweiler.

Dirk Nowitzki ~ Barkley

I reverently told Sir Charles that *'I've __never ever__ worn another man's jersey*, but my daughter will surely cherish it.' "That's cool. At least with her, I know they won't end up on eBay."

Pre-game in the locker-room, Nike's Coach George Raveling instantly recognized me from our High Five America games versus his Harold Minor led USC Trojans. Linking me to High Five's new HQ & multi-court facility at USIU (now AIU). Our reminiscing convo exposed G' Hoops credibility!

Reggie Miller

Dirk

SWV

Jason Kidd

Gary Payton

Untold Barkley Tale: 'LO$T & FOUND'

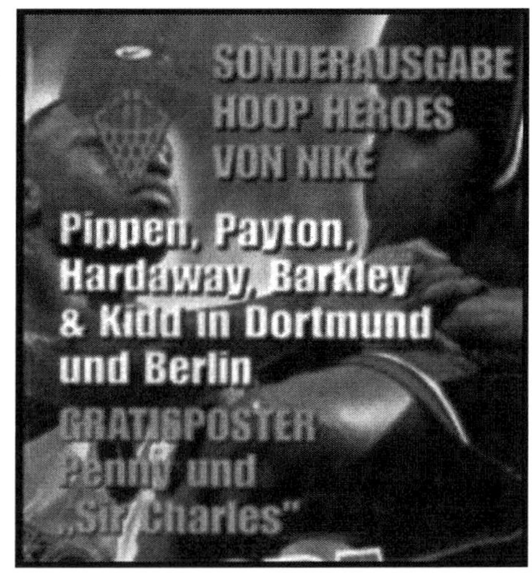

My First Task Upon Arrival at the Berlin Airport: As I emerged from my Lufthansa flight I saw the familiar "Herr Scott" sign held by a 'limo' driver. I was confused. A limo for me? No. He opens the door and I get in to find my direct boss, JoAnn Scott, on the phone and 'Big Boss', Les Badden, sitting beside her, listening to her conversation. JoAnn: "Ok, we're sending in a Nike Rep to get it now. His name is Gregg Scott." "Oh, you know of Mr. Scott? Yes, he just arrived here from Frankfurt." Les smiled. I was puzzled.

The first Hoop Heroes event was in Paris, France. Les informed me that Charles Barkley had left or lost a 'package' in a taxi that was found, flown in the cockpit to the Berlin airport, and was in the Luftstanza Corporate VIP offices. I'd been there. So, I go into the VIP office to sign for the 'package' and they hand me the manifest. OMG! Among the items I initialed: TWO Rolex watches and over $5,000 in CASH! I've never shared that story, not even with Sir Charles. Respect: I hope he approves! Hotel Kapinski: I first saw Barkley as I entered the Nike HQ room. He was upset at a guy, "You're nothing but a Puppet with a Swoosh on his chest." I said, 'Amen.'

Puppet Paid Le Runners' GIG$!

Hoop Heroes Berlin, Germany

'Puppet once replied to Mark's 1995 introduction of me, "If I didn't speak German, then Nike didn't need me." Later: Barkley, "I'm hosting in the pub later tonight, and I'd like to invite you." Gulp! 'Yes, Sir.' I called Mark to get his permission. "You gotta go. I'll email alert the bosses." G': Great Eve!

	Nike Hoop Heroes
Version: September 17, 1997 (post-Paris)	
TIME:	SEQUENCE Berlin, Germany
8:00	ANC Truck Arrives, unload Nike gear
SWV jammed! All the loud floor construction ceased! The normally rigid Germans fell into a hypnotic hip-hop trance!	
2:00	SWV Sound check Sound and Lighting Check Redo the opening light for segment #1

The next morning, I'm in a taxi with Les and Jim, Scottie's 'Personal Protection'. Jim had great stories. At the venue I directed the driver to a ramp I used as a player. As we walked in, Alba Berlin was practicing. Coach allowed them to greet me. Nike & Adidas in Bliss: As I introduced Wendell Alexis!!!

	Nike Hoop Heroes
	Dortmund
	September 18th, 1997
TIME:	**SEQUENCE**
5:00	**German Team Run through**
6:00	**Move Ball to Center Court**
6:30	**Doors Open**
7:20	**Sports Magic team begins to work the crowd**
7:40	**Players Arrive**
8:00	**Segment #1** **Event Kickoff**
8:20	**Segment #7** **Player Interview - Scottie Pippen** He also welcomes fans to the event. Explains his injury status. Answers questions about hoops and local flavor. Kid interrupts and asks to play Scottie. Scottie explains he would like to but cant due to his foot, asks if it would be okay if Jason Kidd takes his place.
Confidential and highly motivational	

In Flight: Hoop Heroes

Mark: The insurance $$$$ Nike paid protected Teams and NBA!

SWV didn't travel on our plane?

The Smoothest Flight EVER!

Nike hired an excellent magician who thrilled Scottie and Reggie. Directly across from where I sat!

Two German Polizei Helicopters landed beside us on the runway!

Hundreds of fans with candles congregated outside of our hotel for an All-Night vigil of fandom!

In the lockerrooms there is every imaginable combination of fruit, snacks, cashews, almonds, both white pistacios and red pistacios, macadamia nuts, and of course, sunflower seeds. Every gum too!

Seeing Reggie Miller shoot in the 3-point contest was very special!

Thanks to my brother, Mark, I had an unforgettable experience!

Solo with Scottie & Pup

In the final Nike meeting, Joan tells me I'm assigned to accompany Scottie Pippen, along with his purebred pup, to the airport. We chilled and chatted like we were FAM. I'll never forget it!

Zum Wohlsein Halle, Dortmund, Germany

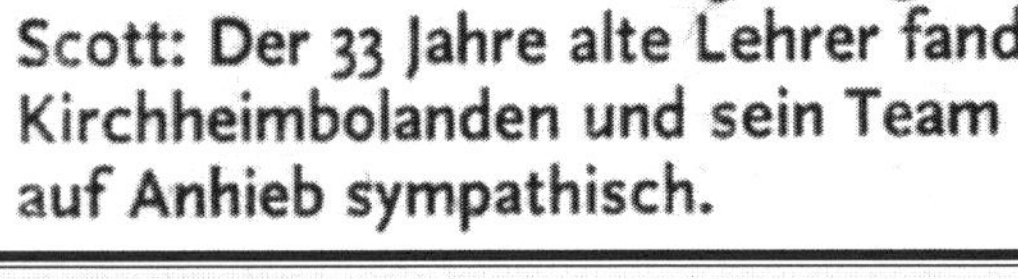

Auf Charles Caldwell folgt Greg Scott: Der 33 Jahre alte Lehrer fand Kirchheimbolanden und sein Team auf Anhieb sympathisch.

Scott Nets TVK Gig

TVK: Scott (40 Punkte)

Wenn das Kombinationsspiel im Angriff einmal ins Stocken kommt, hofft der neue TVK-Coach auf den bundesliga- und regionalligaerfahrenen Greg Scott. Der Trainer des ASC Mainz, Hans Beth, vermittelte den gerade 33 Jahre alt gewordenen US-Boy im August nach Kirchheimbolanden, nachdem die Rheinhessen die Centerposition mit einem großen Amerikaner besetzen mußten. „Greg war der Topscorer in unserem Regionalligateam und auch so ein feiner Kerl: Er fehlte so gut wie nie im Training", schwärmte Beth noch gestern in einem RHEINPFALZ-Gespräch.

„Greg ist ein guter Distanzschütze und besitzt eine enorme Sprungkraft", beschreibt Holger Handermann die Qualitäten des TVK-Neuzugangs. Neben dem hervorragenden Timing und der aggressiven Verteidigungseinstellung setzt Handermann auf weitere Tugenden: „Er ist ein intelligenter Spieler, setzt Anweisungen sofort um. Greg bringt mit seiner Erfahrung Sicherheit ins Team und versteht es, die Mannschaft zu motivieren." Scott ist darüber hinaus variabel einsetzbar. „Auch unterm Korb kann er gut arbeiten, wenn sein Gegenspieler nicht gerade arg viel größer ist", ist sich Holger Handermann sicher, mit der Verpflichtung des zur Zeit in Wiesbaden lebenden Amerikaners die richtige Entscheidung getroffen zu haben.

Greg Scott wird auf alle Fälle in Linz spielen. Die genaue Mannschaftsauf-

Serb #5 was now my teammate! So, I simply took Scottie Pippen's advice. "It's All About Winning! You Don't Have To Be Friends." Hoop Heroes Query

TVK streckt sich mit „dünner Decke"

BASKETBALL: Nur acht Spieler waren beim 91:83-Sieg über Trier dabei

TVK US-Boy Greg Scott begeisterte mit seiner Schnelligkeit und Treffsicherheit, war gemeinsam mit dem defensiv wie offensiv reboundstarken Rüdiger Fluck erfolgreichster Punktesammler.

Darauf läßt sich aufbauen: TVK gewinnt in Linz 93:70

BASKETBALL: Handermann lobt Teamleistung

Das völlig neuformierte TVK-Team startete nervös. Linz wirkte in den Anfangsminuten kompakter und auch motivierter. Dank des hervorragend aufgelegten Greg Scott konnten die nordpfälzischen Gäste die Begegnung dennoch ausgeglichen gestalten. Der neue US-Boy zeigte sich enorm variabel: Aus fast allen Positionen – von der Drei-Punkte-Linie, aus der Halbdistanz oder direkt unterm Korb – punktete Scott, steuerte alleine 23 Zähler im ersten Spielabschnitt bei.

SO SPIELTEN SIE

Scott (33 Punkte), Janneck (21), Fluck (16), Carsten Bauer (9), Vrbanic (8), Bitschnau (6), Radloff, Chr. Bauer.

In acht Minuten alles dahin

TVK überzeugt und verliert beim 1. FCK

▸ **KAISERSLAUTERN. 32 Minuten lang zeigten die „Handermänner" ihre bislang beste Saisonleistung – in den restlichen acht entschied Meisterschaftsanwärter 1. FC Kaiserslautern aber das packende Pfalzderby in der Oberliga für sich. Der TV Kirchheimbolanden hatte mit 100:86 (49:48) Punkten das Nachsehen.**

Überraschend dabei, daß der angeschlagene Greg Scott genau dort hin ging, wo es „weh tut": unter den Korb und zu den Rebounds. Was der ausgebuffte US-Boy den „FCK-Stars" Graham und Steckbauer an Rebounds vor der Nase „wegfischte", war genial. Vor-

TVK: Schulz, Wittmann (5 Punkte), Vrbanic (2), Christoph Bauer, Radloff (2), Janneck (9), Carsten Bauer (17), Schwab (14), Scott (29), Fluck (8).

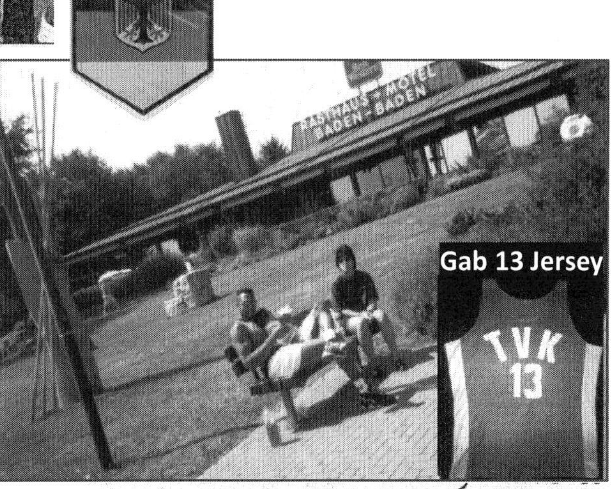

nach 15 Minuten. Und hätte nicht US-Boy Greg Scott so ein treffsicheres Händchen gehabt, dem TV St. Ingbert wäre vielleicht schon im ersten Durchgang die Vorentscheidung geglückt. Scott war mit 30 Punkten erneut erfolgreichster Korbschütze.

TVK: Scott (30 Punkte), Janneck (15), Bauer (13), Bitschnau (10), Fluck (8), Vrbanic (4), Radloff (4), Schulz (2), Schwab. (uwe)

Joe Burton, via DJ, introduced me to the 'European Game' as our coach on the 4-country Xanthus All-Star Tour in 1995.

In '96 he negotiated my $1M Spain contract. In late '97 DJ and I reunited for a 3-city German hoop tour.

FILA DEUTSCHLAND GMBH

To all FILA Coaches and Personal Contract Players

December 11, 1997

After the event, Joe took DJ (David Jones) and me to the FILA HQ gear vault and hooked us up!!! Hoop gear, tennis gear, sweat suits, parkas, sweaters, shirts, socks & caps. All sweet and plush. "Bonuses for services rendered", as Joe put it.

Invitation For a Special FILA-B'ball-Day

We will meet at the Darmstadt main train station (Darmstadt Hauptbahnhof)

at 12 o'clock
on Tuesday, December 16, 1997

The program will offer the following:

Lunch, pre-show of the 1998 collection (shoes and apparel), discussion about future activities in basketball at FILA and ... a small Christmas present from FILA.

Alas, the gift of the Grant Hill pro model hoop shoes??? Fact: He wasn't brittle or injury prone wearing Nike's at Duke! The Swoosh later saved his NBA career.

I am looking forward to seeing you all next Tuesday.

Best wishes,

FILA Deutschland GmbH
Basketball Promotion Manager

Joseph V. Burton

Pro Model Shoes? Nah!!

Any questions? Please call the following number: 01 71/750 25 66

Borsigstraße 11 · 64291 Darmstadt · Telefon 0 61 51/35 03-0 · Telefax 0 61 51/35 03-25
Amtsgericht Darmstadt · Geschäftsführer: E.D. Keppeler

SPORTSFREUNDE: GREG SCOTT (BASKETBALLER) SAMSTAG, 7. FEBRUAR 1998

All-Star sagt im Sommer Bye-Bye

TVK-Amerikaner arbeitet als Promoter bei den großen Sportartiklern

VON UNSEREM MITARBEITER
UWE EID

Motiviert, freundlich, fair – Attribute, die man Greg Scott zuschreiben kann. Über mentales Training hat er sogar ein Buch geschrieben. —FOTO: STEPAN

▸ Der sympathische US-Boy Greg Scott, seit August erfolgreicher Punktesammler bei den TVK-Basketballern, muß bald ans Kofferpacken denken. Nach dreijährigem Deutschland-Aufenthalt sucht er im Sommer in seiner Heimat eine neue berufliche Herausforderung.

„Der Abschied von Kirchheimbolanden und vom TVK wird schwer fallen. Ich hatte in den letzten Monaten eine verdammt schöne Zeit." Die Aussage von Greg Scott überrascht. So waren doch gerade die ersten beiden Jahre in Deutschland für ihn sportlich erfolgreicher und interessanter. Mit der TG Landshut spielte das Kirchheimbolander Basketball-As in der 1. Bundesliga, ein Jahr später ging er mit dem ASC Mainz erfolgreich in der Regionalliga auf Punktejagd. Nun muß er sich beim TV Kirchheimbolanden mit sehr bescheidenen Saisonerfolgen begnügen. „Sicherlich kann ich die Station Kirchheimbolanden nicht mit den anderen Engagements vergleichen", begründet Scott seine TVK-Vorliebe nicht im sportlichen Bereich. „Hier werde ich als Mensch geachtet, hier habe ich Freunde. Die Mannschaft ist einfach super und Holger ist ein erstklassiger Trainer", verteilt der Amerikaner ernstgemeinte Komplimente.

Ein „Schönwetter-Basketballer", der nach Verdienstmöglichkeiten die Vereine wechselt und Jahr für Jahr die gleichen, „seichten" Lobesworte verteilt, ist Scott auf keinen Fall. Im Gegenteil: Der Familienvater (im letzten Jahr kam seine Tochter in Deutschland zur Welt) ist ein Sportsmann der ruhigen Sorte. Daß er zum Beispiel seit drei Jahren ins Adidas-All-Star-Team gemeinsam mit dem NBA-Star Detlef Schrempf berufen wird und mehrmals gegen Deutschlands beste Vereinsmannschaft ALBA Berlin spielte, wußte in Kirchheimbolanden bisher niemand.

„Im Sommer wechseln wir wieder in die USA, dort übernehme ich Aufgaben für den Sportartikelhersteller Nike im Bereich Promotion." Daß er dann ab Herbst Events in der Frauen-NBA organisiert und dabei etwa mit Stars wie Pippen, Barcley, Miller und Payton zusammenarbeiten wird, wissen nicht mal seine Mitspieler. Greg Scott ist eben kein Typ, der auf den „Putz" klopfen muß. Seinen Einstand bei Nike gibt er übrigens im März in Stuttgart beim Fußball-Länderspiel Deutschland - Brasilien.

Ein von ihm verfaßtes Buch über mentales Training stand am Anfang der Kontakte mit der Sportartikel-Branche. „Das war für mich der Einstieg, ich kam nach Europa, bin nun seit drei Jahren für Adidas im Einsatz bei Fernsehproduktionen, Spots, Veranstaltungen, Messen oder Camps." Daß er nebenbei auf einer amerikanischen Schule in Wiesbaden 12- bis 15jährige in Sport und Computerwesen unterrichte, kam erst später. „Bei den Jungs bin ich bekannt, ich wollte mein Wissen an die Kids weitergeben. Und das macht mir wirklich sehr viel Spaß."

Nach den Sportlerstationen in Argentinien, Paraguay und Deutschland treibt es ihn nun wieder nach San Diego. Spielen wird er nicht mehr, zumindest nicht mehr ernsthaft. „Dafür habe ich keine Zeit mehr. Beruf und Familie haben für mich dann Vorrang", versichert der 33jährige, daß der TVK defintiv seine letzte aktive Basketball-Station sei. „Nach all den menschlich angenehmen Erfahrungen in Kibo fällt es mir wirklich leicht, hier einen Schlußstrich unter meine Karriere zu ziehen."

February '98: TVK Road Game at ASC Mainz: G' & Gab Return!

A highly anticipated and celebrated event. The planned pre-game visit wth my former clubs fans and staff with Gabriella in my arms was sincerely awesome. As I headed to the visitors lockerrom I lamented about the awful floor that had painfully caused my big toes to calcify. Luckily, Holger was a 'physio-therapist' and gave me therapy before training and all games. Game Time: Shook hands with all my former teammates. Didn't even glance at Hans Beth. We took an early lead and were up by 9 at halftime. The floor was more taxing than ASC. In the second half we stretched our lead and were in control. With six minutes left I scored on a layup, got fouled and an ASC player stepped on my foot as I landed. At the free throw line my sweat masked the tears of pain rolling down my face. I made the free throw. We're up by 14. Holger sub'd me out. He knew I was hurting. Job well done. Meager applause. For the first time I unlaced my shoes and took off my ankle braces as Holger manipulated my feet and toes. Suddenly, Mainz made a run, pressed, got turnovers and cut our lead to 7 with two minutes left. Holger called a timeout to settle us down. Nope, Mainz hit three straight 3's and took the lead before I could get sub'd back into the game. They won by 2!

As the final buzzer sounded the place exploded with cheers, horns, and, get this, fireworks! I recall thinking, they never did that for us last season; is that even legal? Worst of all, as I stood on the midcourt circle waiting to shake hands, the ASC team was in a dog-pile under the basket celebrating wildly. I waited…and waited, all alone. Then, Holger came over to me and put his arm around my shoulders, "C'mon Gregg. They lack the good sportsmanship. I'm so sorry for my regretable coaching decisions tonight." I whispered, 'You made the right decision, Coach. We win and lose together.' As we walked off he uttered a prophecy. "I can't wait until April!" He handed me his clip board. Highlighting: **ASC Mainz vs. TVK, in Kibo! So, I met Puig at the car. No shower. No socializing.**

April '98: ASC Mainz visits TVK ~ 40 Point Sweet G'$ Revenge

No sugar-coating! I was salavating. I'd proerly compartmentalized my ASC angst. Tonight, revenge was imminent. Gametime: I didn't shake hands or speak to them before the game. From start to finish I punked the punks! I put fear in their eyes and pushed 40 points down their throats! They weren't advasaries, they were enemies. Thus, I aloofly vanquished ASC!

Gelungene Revanche

KIRCHHEIMBOLANDEN: TVK schlägt ASC Mainz

Greg Scott, mit 40 Punkten überragender TVK-Spieler, steigt auch in dieser Szene am höchsten. —FOTO:STEPAN

May '98 Surabaya, Indonesia: Hoopaholics Pre-season Camp

Club CV Gumular: 1st Division Pro Team Sponsored by **Nike** *~ May 22-25, 1998*

Special thanks to Mike Moten, my roommate on the Xanthus European All-Star Hoop Tour, for introducing me to his Indonesian contact, Mr. Sarwoco, who facilitated a great Indo trip!

A Sign of Good Karma: Frankfurt pre-flight! On-board our plane as the flight attendant came to Mike and me and asked us to follow her. She moved us to First Class! For a 15 hour flight!

My brother got me a hook-up with a Nike Asia Marketing Manager and a sweet sponsorship. White Hoop Summit caps, Black Swoosh bags, Grey Nike T-shirts; all gratis. Thanks, Mark!

Election Time: Each day a different color party publicly campaigned. Never on the same day. Hilton Hotel Pub: Samoan Group perform 'Black Magic Woman'! Bali: Amazing! 'Sari Club'!

GHOOPS **January 2002: Mike Moten Update & Lamar Odom Prophesy**

From: "mike moten" < **Mike played college ball at U of Rhode Island**
To: <ghoops@san **with Lamar Odom and for Coach Jim Harrick.**
Sent: Friday, January 04, 2002 3:05 PM

Mike wanted to introduce me to Lamar for a 'Mental Athlete' Intervention! Beyond Basketball.

Hello Gregg and Happy New Year! Did you and the family enjoy Vegas? I have just signed a contract to play in the town of Jesi, Italy for the rest of the season. It is a good deal and I will probably be leaving in the next week or so. I have tried and tried again to reach Lamar, but nothing. I would have to see him in person when they play the Rockets and get to him, but I won't be here. I am keeping your company in mind and I will have your info. with me in Europe, my partner and I are also starting our basketball after school program in the fall of this year and it is something that you could also be a part of. I will keep you posted of everything, take care and best of luck in the New Year. Mike

2015: Mike Moten 'For Love Basketball Int'l.'

EUROPEAN FAREWELL! 'GOING BACK TO CALI'

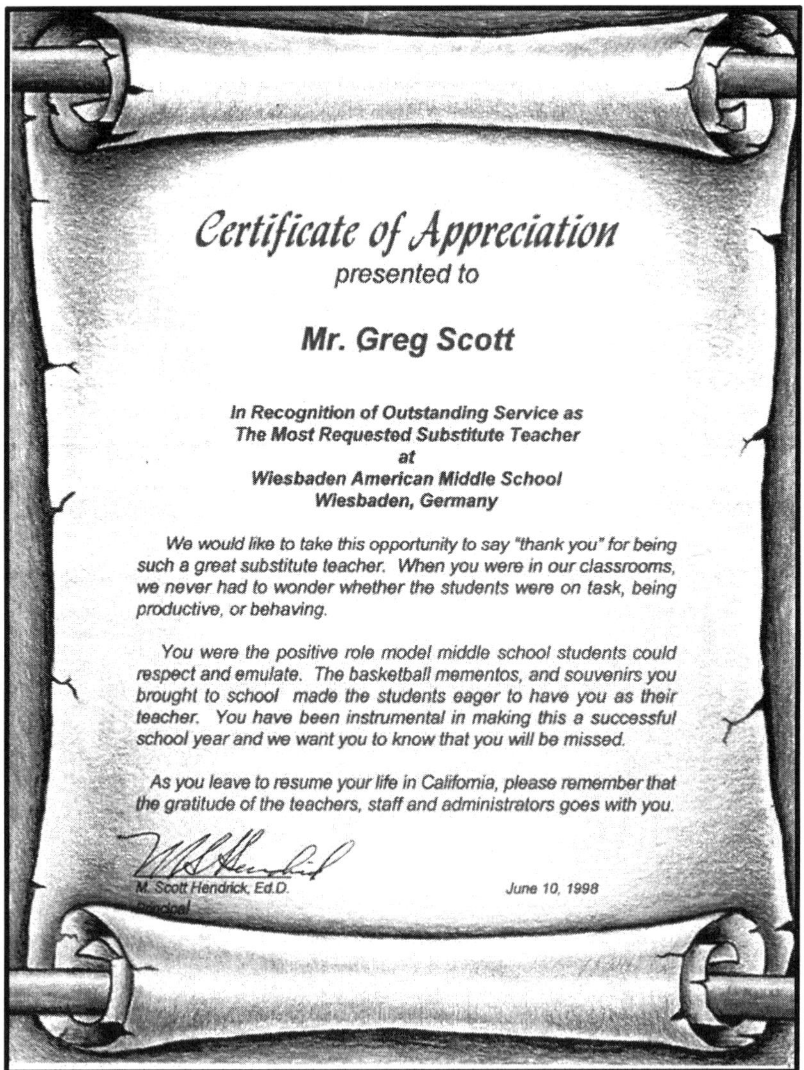

Certificate of Appreciation
presented to

Mr. Greg Scott

In Recognition of Outstanding Service as
The Most Requested Substitute Teacher
at
Wiesbaden American Middle School
Wiesbaden, Germany

We would like to take this opportunity to say "thank you" for being such a great substitute teacher. When you were in our classrooms, we never had to wonder whether the students were on task, being productive, or behaving.

You were the positive role model middle school students could respect and emulate. The basketball mementos, and souvenirs you brought to school made the students eager to have you as their teacher. You have been instrumental in making this a successful school year and we want you to know that you will be missed.

As you leave to resume your life in California, please remember that the gratitude of the teachers, staff and administrators goes with you.

M. Scott Hendrick, Ed.D.
Principal

June 10, 1998

Globetrotter Sterling Forbes: G'

The week we returned to San Dego I saw a TV commercial promoting an exhibition featuring a former Harlem Globetrotter, Sterling Forbes. In San Diego! I had to see my boy! It was an outdoor event at the Ocean Beach Rec Center. I sat in the stands as Sterl' put on a great show. While he's at midcourt speaking to the crowd, he sees me and smiles. Then, spontaneously, he beckons me onto the court and introduces me! **Words can not express that special reunion!**

UH-Hilo Alumni Game ~ November 1998

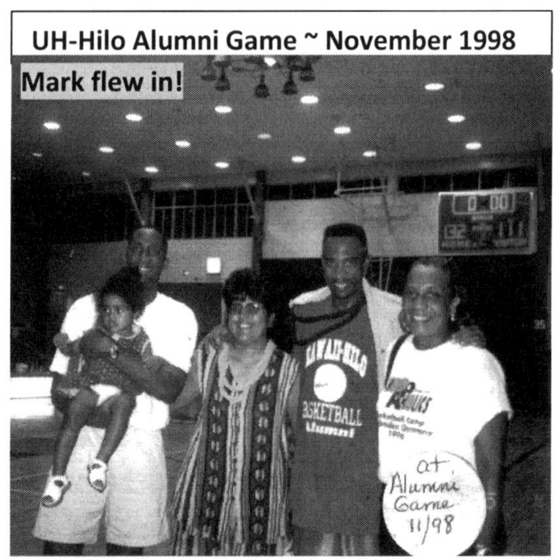

Sept. '98: Back to Cali, AHL & Branding my Biz ~ See It 2 Be It

Home: Rancho Penaquitos, 5 miles east of the Del Mar coast. Superior schools within the acclaimed Poway School District, and great proximity to AHL and High Five America's 52,000 sq. ft. Sports HQ at Alliant Int'l University (AIU). PQ was it!

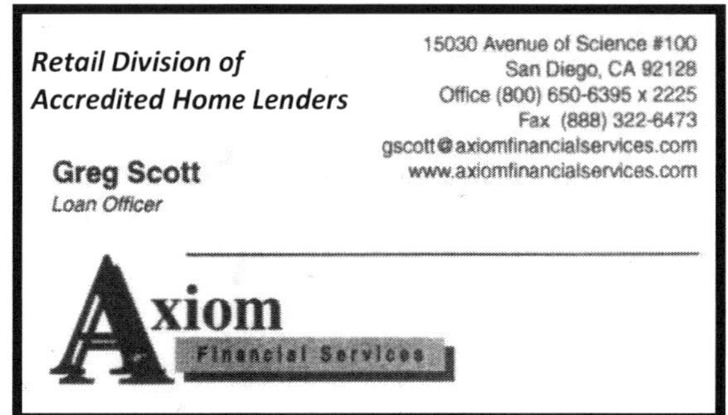

Retail Division of
Accredited Home Lenders
15030 Avenue of Science #100
San Diego, CA 92128
Office (800) 650-6395 x 2225
Fax (888) 322-6473
gscott@axiomfinancialservices.com
www.axiomfinancialservices.com
Greg Scott
Loan Officer
Axiom
Financial Services

Mind & Body Conditioning for Peak Performance
You Are
What
You Think!
SEE IT 2 BE IT
Gregg Scott
M.S., Applied Sports Psychology
Int'l Professional Basketball Player
Ph. (858) 780-2501 * Fax (858) 780-2599
Email: ghoops@san.rr.com
www.seeit2beit.com

G'$ Home Gym Wall of Fame!

Junior Seau's 'Shop with a Jock'

Gene Heliker called me franticly asking if I was available that night for a 'special event'. Junior Seau had an annual event, in which over 100 kids from disadvantaged situations gathered after-hours at a Mervyn's store in Clairemont to 'Shop with a Jock' and spend $100 for gifts as they so desired. Someone called Gene requsting a "credible athlete" to be a chapperoen. Cool, I'm in. He told me the details would provided upon arrival at the venue; "Just ask for Junior Seau. He's expecting you, and only you." Humble pie, indeed.

I was greeted by such a bright soul. "Hello Gregg, I can not thank you enough for being here tonight." He took me aside and the few minutes we chatted were simply golden. He noticed my U of Hawaii class ring and spoke of the G' Hoops pedigree as Gene decreed. Honestly, the NFL's pinnacle **#55** made me feel as if I was his MVP. Albeit a brief convo, this life memory with (the late) Mr. Seau merits inclusion here. RIP. Still, my night was made by the selfless teen Chula Vista girl assigned to me. We bonded as we shopped. She had her list, did her math, and shared the truly touching story of her life. At check-out, I asked her about her list. To my shock, every gift was for someone else, minus $5 for her school supplies. 'Oh, no no no. Excuse us, we have more shopping to do.', as we exited the line. She was resistant. Our thrifty quest netted: $25 powder blue **Seau #55** jersey, $7 capri shorts, $6 Charger cap, $12 Nike sandals and a $5 3-pk of Swoosh socks. Sum total: **Pure karma...$55; of G'$! Her tears of joy and apprection was 100% PRICELE$$!!**

Lucas Tasa, Frankfurt International School

Gregg Scott
From: lucas tasa
Sent: Monday, December 14, 1998 7:54 AM
To: gscott@accredhome.com
Subject: Re: YO YO

WAZZUUUUUUP,G

What is up, Cali connections! So good to hear from U again. Life is so good and so bad. Where do I start.... Basketball is a good place to start: Check dis, I am starting at the 3 position giving me the freedom I need to play my game. We had a preseason tournament in Munich at the end of November and of course coach waited until the huddle to announce the starting 5, but that worked out o.k. I played pretty well, scoring 25 points in four short games over the weekend, but leading the team in Rebounds. Then we got back home and played Giessen DODDS. Of course being our first home game the two hot sh o/i ts on my team (the starting point G and the 2 man) wanted to pull off their own little show and didn't pass the ball much. I did go 100% in that game only scoring 8, but that was on a jumper and 2 three's. One of the 3's was NBA range: I looked the guy in the eyes smiled and pulled up, and this was about 2 feet away from my coach.(talk about confidence) God that felt good. Then came the real #42. That weekend we played Paris at home, the team we beat in the Finals last year, scoring 12 points in two minutes to win by three. You can imagine they were out to get us, but they had to go through me first. Stats for that game: 23 points (6 of 7 Trey's) 8 rebounds, 3 steals, 4 assists. So life is good right now. Basketball is good, Girls are good, it's all good.

School is keeping me real busy, one reason why I didn't hook up with Lewis. I've been so snowed in with work I can't cope with it all. Essays, College applications, Basketball, Girlfriend(s), extra curricular activities, Exams, drivers liscense,.... just to name a few. It's really been tough this year, and there's more to come.

I went to Washington D.C. for that National Young Leaders Conference in November and I had a blast. That was increadible. We went to the house of representatives, Pentagon, FBI building,a.s.o. And the people were awesome, too. I ________________ Miss Teen Alabama 1997/98. DAAAAMN!

Otherwise all is well. Matthew's CD hits the stores in January and he is really excited about that. Dad is still working on the Vette and mom is still giving me hell. I plan to send you a Christmas letter, so look for that in the near future. That will tell you what we're all up to.

College is going well. I sent out all my applications and should be getting replies towards the end of December. Just to remind U, I applied to Illinois Wesleyan, Ohio Wesleyan, Webster University in St. Louis, Missouri, and the Univ. of Illinois. I might be looking into a few more, but I'm not sure. I'll keep you posted on that.

Well, it's time to put an end to this novel. Speaking of Novels .... what's up with your book? Let me know how that is going.

Say what's up to the Family and have a nice X-mas and new year. God bless you guys.

Much Luv,

Lucas Tasa #42

My protégé Markus Hallgrimson was in the perfect program!

Montana State Univ. was known for their 3-point oriented offense which was a textbook fit for him. He had put on weight, improved his defense and ball-handling skills to earn more minutes at both guard spots and had put up good numbers. We chatted often as he prepared for his senior season and final shot at the greatness I forecasted as we trained in Germany. As a legit Mental Athlete he was primed to break records. Appraising his 2-yr stats, 38.75% avg., I emphasized one career stat as **the benchmark** for a 3-point shooter to be elite. Calculated: Shoot 42% this year with only one-tenth of 1% as his margin for error. **Acute & Prophetic**

Markus Hallgrimson (6'2", 180 lbs.)
Junior, Guard
Langen, Germany

Year	GP/GS	FG/A	PCT.	3PT-A	PCT.	FT-A	PCT.	PTS.	AVG.	OR	DR	TR	AVG.	A/P
1997-98	28/3	99/242	40.9	78/201	38.8	25/30	83.3	301	10.8	23	38	61	2.2	30/1
1998-99	28/20	197/464	42.5	133/344	38.7	25/28	89.3	552	19.7	16	37	53	1.9	39/1

MOST 3-POINT FIELD GOALS

Already in the record books: 1998 11 for 23 & '99 12 for 18! Markus was primed for greatness! My G'$ pep talk ensued!

Markus Hallgrimson	12/18 vs. Western NM (2/18/99)
6. Danny Phillips	11/15 vs. Western NM (2/23/01)
Markus Hallgrimson	11/23 vs. Central OK (12/17/98)

Markus & G' Leverkusen '95

Terry Schofield

Markus & G'

1995 Mutombo Camp ~ Paris, France

G' Hoops in Langen, Germany

I used Sage Sparks' exact words: As a specialist you must earn the sincere support of every teammate! They must WANT to get you off and revel in it. Sparks recalled Steve Kerr at U of A as a his example. Synergy fueled him as much as his great jump shot. Solid picks, timely passes; by others for him. **'Share the Love'!**

Markus called me the week prior to a crucial late season road trip to Hawaii for a 2-game tourney at Chaminade. Our deep convo was prophetic, and I even had him taking notes.

- ✎ This must be a biz trip **void** of any Aloha novelty, distractions or Hawaii Malaise.
- ✎ Hawaii Climate Acclimation: Competitive Disadvantage! Hydrate the week prior!! Regardless of all else, if you're dehydrated you will not perform**. Moniter Weight!**
- ✎ The Chaminade tourney venue was similar to a Frankfurt H.S. gym we trained at when I first arrived in Germany in '95. Anticipate a 'shooters gym' in this tourney.
- ✎ My peeps will be in the house. Note: The locals embrace humility over talent. Stay Humble & Kill 'em Softly. Why celebrate? It's your job. Don't Gloat! **Next Play!!**
- ✎ **Bust That Ass!** No Heat Checks. **Every shot is its own entity**. Share the Love!

2/5/00 11 p.m.: Markus calls from the locker-room in tears saying, "Gregg, we did it!!!" I asked him what they did. **MH: "No, WE did it, you and I." "It was just like you said! Dude, I just went off for 51."** We reveled briefly. Our convo is sacred; yet, the core gist of it was:

- ✎ Deflect all praise to your teammates, the system, and coaches.
- ✎ **G'$ Mantra:** "Resumes, Rankings & Reputations don't suit up!"
- ✎ Rehydrate & Refuel! It's game night & the night before a game!

1995: G' & Markus in Paris

Q & A: Why do only nine of 30 teams have winning road records in the NBA?

"Because when you don't know how to play basketball, team basketball, it's hard to win on the road! Now, when you are talented, you gotta understand, when you've got home court advantage that adrenalin, that level of incentive; that extra level of incentive is given to you. But, when you're on the road in hostile confines, your talent is not enough. You have to know how to play basketball, literally understanding it from a mental position. Not only that, also knowing how to play alongside your teammates. A lot of these guys are great individual talents, but, they're still learning how to play team basketball. And when you don't know how to play team basketball; play together as a cohesive unit, you're not going to win too many games on the road. That's why San Antonio and Detroit shines above everybody else. That's why nobody in this day and era would beat Magic with the Lakers with Cooper and Norm Nixon and those boys. Or, Larry Bird and those boys of Boston."

Stephen A. Smith
'Quite Frankly', circa 2005

The Mentality of a Scorer: Shot selection first and foremost! With my personal body of work as a model, I set the bar for Markus' senior year with the same blueprint and mindset of the Pete Maravich NCAA pedigree that had served me so well.

G'$ Mantra: "You can't make shots if you don't take shots!"

To Reign Supreme; let the 3's Rain!

The Pistol never shot a 3!

1 week in February: Prelude to NCAA history!

- ✓ 2/5 - 51 pts. vs. Chaminade 13/22 on 3's
- ✓ 2/6 - 45 pts. (Biz Trip Tourney Total: 96 pts.)
- ✓ 2/12 - 50 pts. vs. Western NM ***16/28 on 3's**
  ***NCAA Division II Record**
- ✓ **Encore!!!** February 26th - 40 pts 13/28 on 3's

Scoring 10 — **Pistol Pete!**

Individual Records

POINTS
Game
100—Frank Selvy, Furman vs. Newberry, Feb. 13, 1954 (41 FGs, 18 FTs)
Season
1,381—Pete Maravich, LSU, 1970 (522 FGs, 337 FTs, 31 games)
Career
3,667—Pete Maravich, LSU, 1968-70 (1,387 FGs, 893 FTs, 83 games)

POINTS VS. DIVISION I OPPONENT
Game
72—Kevin Bradshaw, U.S. Int'l vs. Loyola Marymount, Jan. 5, 1991

AVERAGE PER GAME — **The Blueprint!**
Season
44.5—Pete Maravich, LSU, 1970 (1,381 in 31)
Career
44.2—Pete Maravich, LSU, 1968-70 (3,667 in 83)

POINTS IN FIRST CAREER GAME
Game
52—Wilt Chamberlain, Kansas vs. Northwestern, Dec. 5, 1956

COMBINED POINTS, TWO TEAMMATES
Game
125—Frank Selvy (100) and Darrell Floyd (25), Furman vs. Newberry, Feb. 13, 1954

COMBINED POINTS, TWO TEAMMATES VS. DIVISION I OPPONENT
Game
92—Kevin Bradshaw (72) and Isaac Brown (20), U.S. Int'l vs. Loyola Marymount, Jan. 5, 1991

COMBINED POINTS, TWO OPPOSING PLAYERS ON DIVISION I TEAMS
Game
115—Pete Maravich (64), LSU and Dan Issel (51), Kentucky, Feb. 21, 1970

GAMES SCORING AT LEAST 50 POINTS
Season
10—Pete Maravich, LSU, 1970 — **Sick Stats!**
Season—Consecutive Games
3—Pete Maravich, LSU, Feb. 10 to Feb. 15, 1969
Career
28—Pete Maravich, LSU, 1968-70

GAMES SCORING AT LEAST 40 POINTS
Career
56—Pete Maravich, LSU, 1968-70 — **Wow**

MOST 3-POINT FIELD GOALS

1.	Markus Hallgrimson	16/28 vs. West. NM (2/12/00) *
2.	Markus Hallgrimson	13/28 vs. Western NM (2/26/00)
	Markus Hallgrimson	13/22 vs. Chaminade (2/5/00)
4.	Reece Gliko	12/17 vs. S. Oregon (12/28/96)
	Markus Hallgrimson	12/18 vs. Western NM (2/18/99)
6.	Danny Phillips	11/15 vs. Western NM (2/23/01)
	Markus Hallgrimson	11/23 vs. Central OK (12/17/98)
8.	Danny Phillips	9/18 vs. OK Panhandle (1/13/02)
	Danny Phillips	9/14 vs. Hawaii-Hilo (1/26/01)
	Reece Gliko	9/17 vs. Willamette (11/29/96)
	Danny Phillips	9/18 vs. OK Panhandle (1/13/02)

* NCAA Division II Record

Individual Single-Game Records

MOST POINTS

1.	Reece Gliko	54 vs. S. Oregon. (12/28/96)
2.	Markus Hallgrimson	51 vs. Chaminade (2/5/00)
3.	Markus Hallgrimson	50 vs Western NM (2/12/00)
4.	Roy McPipe	48 vs. Great Falls (2/19/74)
5.	Roy McPipe	46 vs. Western MT (3/2/73)
6.	Markus Hallgrimson	45 vs. Western NM (2/6/00)

ALL-TIME INDIVIDUAL LEADERS—CAREER POINTS

THREE-POINT FIELD GOALS MADE

Player, Team	Season	G	3FG
Alex Williams, Cal St. Sacramento	1988	30	167
Markus Hallgrimson, Mont. St.-Billings	2000	26	160

ALL-TIME INDIVIDUAL LEADERS 69

All-Time Individual Leaders

***6.2 Avg.: NCAA Record for ALL Divisions**

Single-Game Records

SCORING HIGHS

Pts.	Player, Team vs. Opponent	Season
113	Clarence "Bevo" Francis, Rio Grande vs. Hillsdale	1954

Markus' Jr. Season ranked 10th All-Time
Still, our mission was to be #1 All-Time!

THREE-POINT FIELD GOALS MADE PER GAME

Player, Team	Season	G	3FG	Avg.
Markus Hallgimson, Mont. St.-Billings	†2000	26	160	*6.2
Alex Williams, Cal St. Sacramento	†1988	30	*167	5.6
Jason Garrow, Augustana (S.D.)	†1992	27	135	5.0
Eric Kline, Northern St.	†1995	30	148	4.9
Ray Gutierrez, Calif. (Pa.)	†1993	29	142	4.9
Steve Brown, West Ala.	2000	26	126	4.8
Antonio Harris, LeMoyne-Owen	†1999	26	126	4.8
Kwame Morton, Clarion	†1994	26	126	4.8
Reece Gliko, Mont. St.-Billings	†1997	28	135	4.8
Markus Hallgrimson, Mont. St.-Billings	1999	28	133	4.8

Every shot is its own unique entity. I trained him to be a 'Marksman'; not a Gunner.

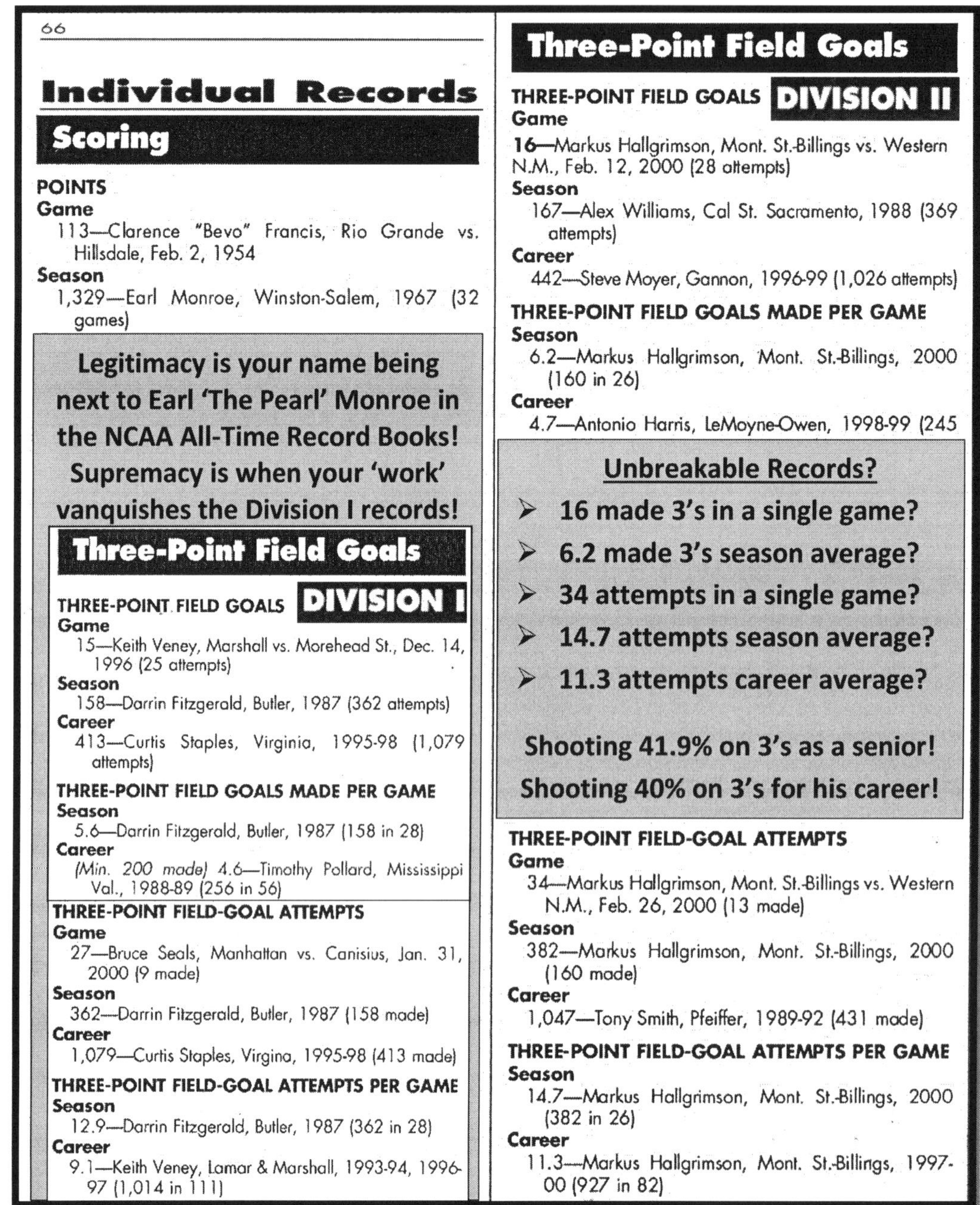

66

Individual Records

Scoring

POINTS
Game
113—Clarence "Bevo" Francis, Rio Grande vs. Hillsdale, Feb. 2, 1954
Season
1,329—Earl Monroe, Winston-Salem, 1967 (32 games)

Legitimacy is your name being next to Earl 'The Pearl' Monroe in the NCAA All-Time Record Books! Supremacy is when your 'work' vanquishes the Division I records!

Three-Point Field Goals

THREE-POINT FIELD GOALS DIVISION I
Game
15—Keith Veney, Marshall vs. Morehead St., Dec. 14, 1996 (25 attempts)
Season
158—Darrin Fitzgerald, Butler, 1987 (362 attempts)
Career
413—Curtis Staples, Virginia, 1995-98 (1,079 attempts)

THREE-POINT FIELD GOALS MADE PER GAME
Season
5.6—Darrin Fitzgerald, Butler, 1987 (158 in 28)
Career
(Min. 200 made) 4.6—Timothy Pollard, Mississippi Val., 1988-89 (256 in 56)

THREE-POINT FIELD-GOAL ATTEMPTS
Game
27—Bruce Seals, Manhattan vs. Canisius, Jan. 31, 2000 (9 made)
Season
362—Darrin Fitzgerald, Butler, 1987 (158 made)
Career
1,079—Curtis Staples, Virgina, 1995-98 (413 made)

THREE-POINT FIELD-GOAL ATTEMPTS PER GAME
Season
12.9—Darrin Fitzgerald, Butler, 1987 (362 in 28)
Career
9.1—Keith Veney, Lamar & Marshall, 1993-94, 1996-97 (1,014 in 111)

Three-Point Field Goals

THREE-POINT FIELD GOALS DIVISION II
Game
16—Markus Hallgrimson, Mont. St.-Billings vs. Western N.M., Feb. 12, 2000 (28 attempts)
Season
167—Alex Williams, Cal St. Sacramento, 1988 (369 attempts)
Career
442—Steve Moyer, Gannon, 1996-99 (1,026 attempts)

THREE-POINT FIELD GOALS MADE PER GAME
Season
6.2—Markus Hallgrimson, Mont. St.-Billings, 2000 (160 in 26)
Career
4.7—Antonio Harris, LeMoyne-Owen, 1998-99 (245

Unbreakable Records?

- 16 made 3's in a single game?
- 6.2 made 3's season average?
- 34 attempts in a single game?
- 14.7 attempts season average?
- 11.3 attempts career average?

Shooting 41.9% on 3's as a senior!
Shooting 40% on 3's for his career!

THREE-POINT FIELD-GOAL ATTEMPTS
Game
34—Markus Hallgrimson, Mont. St.-Billings vs. Western N.M., Feb. 26, 2000 (13 made)
Season
382—Markus Hallgrimson, Mont. St.-Billings, 2000 (160 made)
Career
1,047—Tony Smith, Pfeiffer, 1989-92 (431 made)

THREE-POINT FIELD-GOAL ATTEMPTS PER GAME
Season
14.7—Markus Hallgrimson, Mont. St.-Billings, 2000 (382 in 26)
Career
11.3—Markus Hallgrimson, Mont. St.-Billings, 1997-00 (927 in 82)

Markus Hallgrimson Page 2 of 3

At Mercer Island High: Markus earned four letters in basketbal and also two in tennis. His team won the state championship his junior season.

Personal: Markus is the son of Paul and Maureen Hallgrimson, born May 31, 1975 in Lorrach, Germany. He is majoring in liberal studies.

Season Wrap-up: Markus played in all 26 games, starting in 21 of those games. He started the season slowly, ending with a bang. Markus shot 43.5% from the field, 41.9% from the 3pt line and 80.3% from the free throw line. He hit a NCAA Division II and school record 16 threes on February 12th against Western New Mexico. He hit 13 threes two times in the season. He averaged 6.2 threes for the season, another NCAA Division II record. He ended his career with 371 threes, which finishes him 5th for Division II and 4th all-time for all divisions. He also hit 4.52 threes per game in his career, placing him second in Division II history and 4th all-time for all divisions. Markus scored a season high 51 points against Chaminade University on February 5th. He also scored 50 and 45 points. Markus was chosen PacWest Player of the Week, twice. Markus was, also, chosen to the 1st Team Pacific Division All-Conference Team, the NABC Division II West District 1st Team, the Daktronics Division II West All-Region 1st Team and to the Daktronics All-America 3rd Team.

School Records: 2nd for scoring in a single game with 51; 3rd for scoring in a single game with 50; 6th for scoring in a single game with 45; 1st for 3-pt field goals made in a single game with 16; 2nd for 3-pt field goals made in a single game with 13 (twice); 8th in scoring for a single season with 617; 6th in points per game in a single season with 23.7; 1st for 3-pt field goals made in a single season with 160; 5th for scoring in a career with 1,470; 10th for points per game for a career with 17.9; 5th for field goals made for a career with 500; 1st for 3-pt field goals made in a career with 371; 7th for 3-pt percentage for a career with 40.0

Sr. Year Prophecy: 41.9% Career: 40%

Hallgrimson's Career Numbers

Year	GP/GS	FG/A	PCT.	3PT-A	PCT.	FT-A	PCT.	PTS.	AVG.	OR	DR	TR	AVG.	A/P
1997-98	28/3	99/242	40.9	78/201	38.8	25/30	83.3	301	10.8	23	38	61	2.2	30/1
1998-99	28/20	197/464	42.5	133/344	38.7	25/28	89.3	552	19.7	16	37	53	1.9	39/1
1999-00	26/21	204/469	43.5	160/382	41.9	49/61	80.3	617	23.7	6	33	39	1.5	38/1

Career history

- 2000–2001 Avitos Giessen
- 2001–2002 BCJ Hamburg Tigers
- 2002 NVV Lions Mönchengladbach
- 2002–2003 Chemnitz 99
- 2003–2004 TSK Würzburg

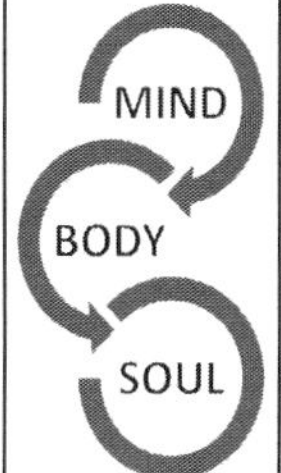

- 2004 Los Bairros
- 2004–2006 Geneve Devils
- 2006 ASC Theresianum Mainz
- 2006–2007 Mitteldeutscher BC
- 2007 Worcester Wolves
- 2007–2008 Würzburg Baskets
- 2009 SC Rasta Vechta
- 2013-present RheinStars Köln

Lend an Ear — Accredited Home Lenders
April 2000

AHL rewarded my prior tenure and loyalty with a gift; IPO stock options!

1990-2000
10 Years of Excellence

1992 ~ Accredited moves from its original site above the garage to a "new" office on Via Frontera. The new space was more than triple the size of the previous office. Accredited also does its first wholesale loan.

Production: Doubled from 1991 to 159 loans for $24.7 Million

Greg Scott

Josie Powell

Greg Scott and Josie Powell joined Accredited in 1992. At that time, Greg was a Loan Officer and Josie was his Retail Processor.

The Family Finance gene served me well.
Multi-tasking See It 2 Be It served others.

Mr. Gregg Scott
September 3, 2003
Page 2

Secondly, I have known Gregg Scott since our first contact when he was employed with Accredited Home Lenders in San Diego. I first met Gregg in 1997 when he ordered an appraisal from my company. Through working together over the past six years, I have learned that Mr. Scott is a man of high morals and integrity. He is also very personable and enjoys helping people, which is the reason he went to work for Accredited Home Lenders. I have enjoyed our professional relationship during this time.

In the past year, Gregg introduced me to his new business venture and joy: his Mental Athlete Workshop and motivational company, See-It-2-Be-It. I was so impressed by his gift for motivating children through sports that I sent my then ten year old son to a free workshop at the Scripps Ranch Library. My husband and I also attended portions of the workshop and found Mr. Scott to have a wonderful talent and ability to help children learn and handle difficult life situations through the language of sports.

This year, toward the end of the school year, my son Christopher was having difficulty in school. I turned to Gregg for assistance and he provided private consultation, working with Christopher on student/teacher relationships, building his confidence, helping him organize his school and homework, family relations, and improving his basketball skills. I am most grateful to Gregg for his vision and his assistance.

In summary, Mr. Scott is what I consider a man of the utmost Integrity. He is highly professional, honest, and caring. I would trust him with my home loan just as I have trusted him in helping train my son. Please call me if you have any questions or if I can be of further assistance.

Very truly yours,

Leeanna T. Dante
Certified General Appraiser, AG009414

Sometimes Our Greatest Blessings are Unanswered Prayers!

I had poured my heart into the **KeepWalking** grant application to catapult my brand: See It 2 Be It…The Mental Athlete. **Devastated NOT to make the cut! Fate: 9/11!**

Keepwalking.com /Features/Stories/Story_Display Page 1 of 2

KEEPWALKING.COM

ABOUT THE FUND | FEATURES | EVENTS | RESOURCES

COUNTDOWN TO GRANT PRESENTA

0 hrs 0 mins

STAY TUNED!

Hi Gregg Scott!
The Grant Finalists have been s

GRANTS AWARDED SEPTEMBE

2001 FINALISTS

On September 11, 2001, approximately twelve eligible Grant Finalists will convene in New York.

Finalists are a step away from Keep Walking Grants

After a long and exciting seven months, the first Keep Walking grant process will culminate on September 11, in New York City.

Out of more than a thousand applicants from fifty states, twelve outstanding Finalists have been selected as candidates for Grants from the Keep Walking Fund.

The long journey to this point officially began on February 12, 2001, when Keepwalking.com accepted its first Idea Plan submissions. Over the ensuing four months, we received a steady influx of excellent Idea Plans from entrepreneurs and dreamers in every state of the Union representing an incredible variety of backgrounds and interests.

Reviewing them was a pleasure; choosing Finalists was a difficult task.

On September 11, 2001, these twelve eligible Grant Finalists will convene in New York, to present their Idea Plans to the Keep Walking Board of Directors:

Malinda Allen, whose project, The Moving Laboratory, seeks to "make a lasting impact on the world through dance outreach."

Dr. Ely Brand, who plans to provide surgeons with "preferred equipment and technical data up to date for each operation and individual patient needs" through his program, Surgeon's Choice.

Deborah Gans, whose venture, Extreme Housing, will provide a "system of transitional housing for those dispossessed by natural and man-made disaster."

GHOOPS

Mark Scott: Sr. Finance Manager, Jordan Brand!

From: "Scott, Mark
To: "GLOBAL HOOPS" <ghoops@san.rr.com>
Sent: Tuesday, February 12, 2002 3:22 PM
Subject: RE: Player Relationship Manager Position

Mission: "To directly manage NIKE's relationships with the best basketball players in the world"

Looks like the hiring manager, Lynn Merritt, has been out of town last couple weeks, probably due to All-Star game. I talked to the recruiter and she said you definitely need to officially apply through the NIKEBIZ.COM website -- it looks pretty easy. They've gotten over 600 resumes and they will be shouting it down soon so I would hurry! Since I just talked to the recruiter, Cheri Fogel, go ahead and email your resume directly to her, and let her know that you had just talked to me and sent in application via the website, but wanted to put one in her hands as soon as possible. Briefly highlight that you've done some BB work in the past for NIKE and that you look forward to an opportunity to be a "full-time member of the team." Do both today before days end if you can. Her email should be cheri.fogel@nike.com. They will be sitting down in the next couple days to go through the resumes.

-mats

Nike Player Relations Manager Position

Greg,

Thank you for your interest in Nike's Player Relations Manager position. I've met with the hiring manager and reviewed your information.

I'm attaching a copy of the success profile (job description) for this position. This will provide more in-depth information concerning the scop of this role. Please review the success profile, then advise the following:

1) Are you willing to relocate. If yes, availability to relocate.
2) Are you currently under any non-compete agreements?
3) Are you willing to travel 50%+ of the time?
4) Current salary (identify base salary and bonus separately)
5) Salary expectations for this position

If you could provide this information to me via email no later than 2/26/02 it would be greatly appreciated.

Thank you.

Cheri Fogel
Recruiter
Nike, Inc.

My HR Success Profile reply regarding relocation, start date, 50% travel commitment and salary was swiftly accepted!

GHOOPS: My Dream Swoosh gig

Out of over 600 resumes I was a sole survivor by virtue of swoosh affairs and personal merit.

GHOOPS

From: "Terry, Jeannette"
To: <ghoops@san.rr.com>
Sent: Wednesday, March 06, 2002 4:02 PM
Subject: interview itinerary

Hi Greg-

This e-mail is confirming your panel interview appointment at the Nike Campus on Friday, March 8 at 1:30 pm. Listed below is your air, car and hotel information. When you arrive for your interview, check in with the receptionist at the Nolan Ryan building requesting she contact me.

Call with any questions or concerns.

NIKE TRAVEL
ISSUED: MAR 06 2002 PAGE:01
ONE BOWERMAN DRIVE MPF CUST
REF: NXX8HC
BEAVERTON OR 97006
INVOICE: ITIN
PH: 503-532-1800/800-452-4484 WTP
REF: 50100100155004

ATTN:JEANNETTE TERRY 71-3074

GREGG SCOTT 07MAR

NIKE

March 7, 2002 Plane flight, hotel & car on Nike's dime!

Panel Interview

nike

SUCCESS PROFILE

GENERIC JOB TITLE MANAGER/MKTG/ADV/II	JOB CODE	JOB BAND U
DESK TITLE Player Relationship Manager	JOB REPORTS TO (Manager's Title) Senior Director, US Basketball Development	
STATUS ☐ Exempt ☒ Full-Time ☐ Non-Exempt ☐ Part-Time	PREPARED BY Lynn Merritt APPROVED BY (Manager or Director) Ralph Greene	
DEPARTMENT US Basketball Sports Marketing	DATE PREPARED 01/01/02	REVISED ON

MISSION: *A one sentence, motivating, strategic level description of "why" the position exists. The purpose of the job.*

To directly manage NIKE's relationships with the best basketball players in the world.

CORE ACCOUNTABILITIES: *Up to ten (preferably 5-7) primary responsibilities with end results (the "what") aimed at the key dimensions of the "balanced scorecard" approach to performance management: market, financial, customer satisfaction (external delivery and quality) productivity (internal cost and speed), and innovation and flexibility. Framed in relation to the SMART model for objective setting: specific, measurable, aggressive, realistic and time-bound. List percentage weight (10% minimum) for each objective.*

% of time	(10% minimum)
40%	Serve the top tier basketball athletes. Develop the deepest, most influential relationships possible Take FULL RESPONSIBILITY for the relationship between that athlete and NIKE; Product, service, marketing, contract fulfillment, etc...
30%	Work with the Senior Director of Basketball development to assemble "THE List" of top assets. Collaborate with the elite Youth Basketball Manager to sustain effective scouting of young talent. Forecast future stars and create recruitment and negotiation strategies along with Global Sports Marketing (negotiators). Present annual draft strategy to senior management.
20%	Lead in the execution of marketing/utilization plans of leading athletes. Work with the Team/Player Marketing Manager to create plans for each player and ensure execution

While specifics of my panel interview are sacred. It was a done deal. We took a break to allow HR to finalize my 'new hire' package.

Mark and I rejoiced at lunch in the café.

Only my GabDad commitment and a 'promise' precluded my grasping hold!

Nike Founder Facts: Phil Knight & 'Blue Ribbon Sports'

NIKE FAX TRANSMITTAL MEMO FORM 2584 MAY95 | # of pages:
TO: | FROM:
Co. | Dept.

Visiting the Far East, a young Phil Knight makes an unannounced visit to a Japanese footwear company with a proposal for importing athletic shoes from Asia. When asked which company he represents, he blurts out "Blue Ribbon Sports." Knight gets his meeting and Nike's forerunner gets its name.

Lors d'une visite en Extrême-Orient, le jeune Phil Knight effectue une visite inattendue dans une compagnie japonaise de chaussures pour leur proposer une entente sur l'importation de chaussures athlétiques de l'Asie. Lorsqu'on lui demande le nom de la compagnie qu'il représente, il laisse échapper: « Blue Ribbon Sports ». On lui accorde alors une entrevue, et le précurseur de Nike acquiert son nom.

The Nike execs were fretful that I'd be relocating by myself to keep Gab in PQ schools. For weeks we tried to negotiate a plan for me to work out of the Nike offices in Marina Del Rey, yet, the position required me at HQ when not on the road. I simply couldn't say yes; and couldn't say no. But, I couldn't be an absentee father to Gab! Opportunity lost?!!

HOWARD WHITE, JORDAN VICE PRESIDENT

A LONGTIME NIKE VETERAN, HOWARD WHITE HAS BEEN A PART OF JORDAN BRAND "SINCE BEFORE IT WAS ANYTHING."

Howard White, what does Michael Jordan, Jordan brand symbolize to you?

MJ and Jordan brand, to me, symbolize excellence. [They] symbolize someone that's always ahead of the game. I know a lot of people love MJ because he's won six NBA championships, he was named the greatest player of the 20th century... I've been with Michael since he's been in the pros, and what I admire the most is that MJ always came to play; whether it was practice or a game, he [always] showed up hungry and ready to play. A lot of people say, "Well, MJ just never stood for anything." Personally, I believe that if everybody on the planet got up with the desire to do more than yesterday, the desire to give everything that they have, it'd be a heck of a place. If MJ was playing at that time...the worst team in the league, and somebody filmed it, you probably couldn't tell whether he was playing for a world championship because that's the way he showed up to play, that's the way he went to work. He would show up and play hard if it was a pickup game, he would show up and play hard if we was playing ping-pong.

...That's what I respect about MJ, that's what this brand symbolizes—what you can do if you want to work hard enough; it's something anybody can grasp, whether you're the greatest player in the world, whether you're trying to get your high school diploma or whether you've been down on your luck. That's what this is.

<u>2003:</u> Nike HQ Tour with Gab, we meet Mark's boss, Howard White. His first words, "Weren't you the 'Chosen One' for our NBA Player Relations position?"

Gulp! "I hope you know that everyone around here was highly impressed by your solid reasoning. Also, take pride in knowing that the position was never filled." Mark was so surprised! Mr. White clarified how they broadened the roles of two current Nike guys.

The origin of my radio show was pure karma. I drove up to Hollywood for an audition for voice-over work. As I entered the elevator I noticed a man in the distance scurring in the front door just as my elevator doors were closing. I hit the button to hold the elevator. He was clearly very anxious, assumably from a similar audition perhaps. Being me, I had to offer a few subtle tid-bits of inspiration, off-the-cuff; G' style. He exhaled, handed me his card and asked me to see him after my audition. His title? V.P. of Programming! When we met, he embraced my vision, 'opened a door', and a radio show was born. Voila!

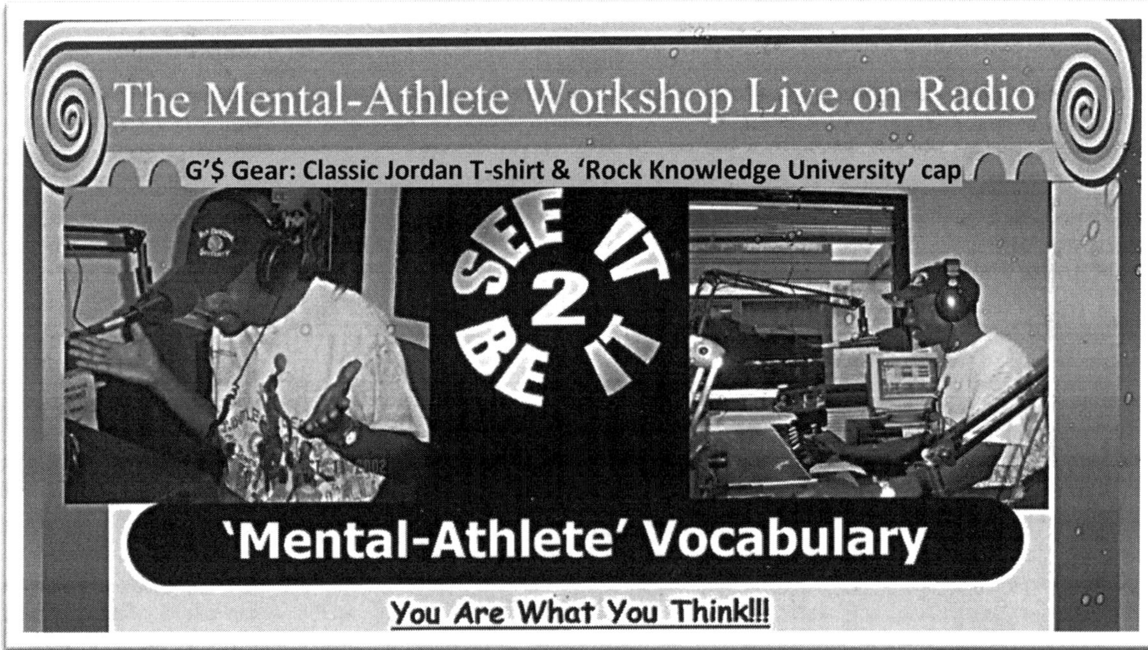

YouTube.com/MentalAthlete Broadcasting live from coast to coast and around the globe! Intro: "Nuthin' but a G' thang"! Sporty G' & The Mental Athlete Workshop Live on Radio Show!

FBN #2002032236 Details	10/22/2002
Primary Business Name	SEE IT 2 BE IT
Number of Businesses	001
Business Name	SEE IT 2 BE IT
Number of Owners	001
Owner	SCOTT GREGORY
Filing Date (CCyy/MM/DD)	20021022
Expiration Date(CCyy/MM/DD)	20071022
Business Conducted By	Individual

Music can ignite the spirit, enhance mental psyche and, in times of sorrow, soothe the soul.

KTST 89.5fm & KTSTFM.COM

Kaleidascope Magazine Radio

AMERICAN RADIO NETWORK **202 FASHION LANE SUITE#110 TUSTIN, CA. 92780 (714)** 508-0650 f-**(714)** 730-6104 **email:**ktstfm@pacbell.net

January 1, 2003

TO WHOM IT MAY CONCERN:

This letter, is written on behalf of Gregory Scott, who joined our Radio Broadcasting Program in June 2002.

Our Broadcasting Program is not a School or a Radio Station. We offer the Services of our Broadcasting Studios, to those with aspirations of entering the Radio Industry or to Produce a quality Independent broadcast that could further their career or business.

Those who are new to Radio, receive comprehensive written training materials that corresponds with training videos, which must be viewed. They are to produce a weekly Radio Broadcast, which we will air on our Cable and/or Internet radio stations, or any Radio Station that will broker time. This allows them to receive instant On-Air broadcasting credits for their Resume, aiding them in obtaining employment or syndication with us or any radio station. Studio fees are required for each broadcast, $32.00 for thirty (30) minutes or $51.00 for one (1) hour production.

Mr. Scott, clearly expressed specific goals from our Program on his first day and quickly began to masterfully accomplish each one, by one. He asked many questions and followed directions precisely. Greg, soon had learned to use the studio equipment and had watched all the videos, then he was ready to begin producing his Live one (1) hour Broadcast, which airs every Friday at 1pm. Any comments given to better the production of his Broadcast was received with one of his biggest smiles and a gracious Thank You. With his drive-time to the Studio being longer than most, he always seems to arrive early for his appointment, in fact, he still telephones letting me know that he is on the highway, always ending his call with Thank You. I view this as being very conscientious and respectful.

We all find, Greg to be very positive yet very humble, who will help anyone without being asked and always with a big smile. I am very proud of Greg and his achievements.

Sincerely,

Connie M. Torres

Connie M. Torres
President/General Manager

JUL California
SPORTY G

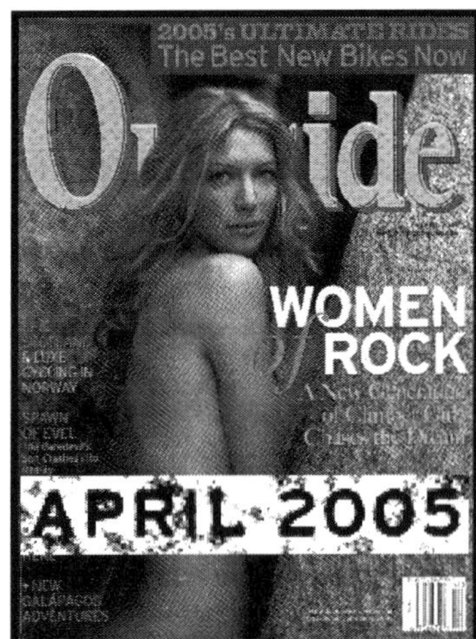

A story that almost wasn't!

My bro: Back in the Saddle.

THE OREGON CYCLIST

FOR INSTANCE, THE ONE WHO WAS SO CRAZY ABOUT RIDING AROUND IN THE BEAUTIFUL OREGON COUNTRY THAT WHEN ITS SMALL TOWNS WERE IN TROUBLE HE GATHERED UP ALL HIS CYCLING FRIENDS–1,008 OF THEM–AND SET OUT TO MAKE SURE THAT BEAUTIFUL OREGON COUNTRY STAYED BEAUTIFUL OREGON COUNTRY.

This is a story about a man who loved to ride his bicycle in Oregon. He rode through the mountains, through the valleys and desert, and when he got tired he'd rest in one of the small hospitable towns along the way. And he would have kept on riding along, except that one day on his journey he came across a woman who was weeping. She told him her town was struggling and might not survive because there weren't enough people visiting. And it wasn't just hers, but others too. Now the man was upset by this. For if the town disappeared, where would he find a nice place to rest? He had an idea. He asked all the people he knew if they wanted to join him on his next adventure, which he called Cycle Oregon. The following year he and 1,008 of his closest friends set out to experience Oregon in the best way possible—on bicycle. They toured through the dramatic landscape by day and stopped in the small towns along the way to refuel—the townspeople giving them their best welcome. The visitors were so enchanted by the whole experience that the next year it became 2,012 of his closest friends. And then 2,503. And to this day, one of the best ways to enjoy Oregon is by bike. Because after you've been taken in by the scenery, you will be just as quickly taken in by Oregonians.

Start planning your route through Oregon country. Go to traveloregon.com or call 1-800-547-7842.

2010 – Current: Category Finance Director, North America
1998 – 2010: Senior Finance Manager, Jordan Brand
1997 – '98: Financial Manager Nike Sports Entertainment
1996 – '97: Senior Financial Analyst, Nike Sports Marketing

A cool cyclist rides through Backpacker magazine, helps launch Travel Oregon bike Web site

My Bro' Mark Scott: 17+ Years of Swoosh!

By Terry Richard, The Oregonian
October 21, 2009, 3:02AM

I will be paying better attention this time when Travel Oregon launches it's brand new "everything-Oregon-cycling" Web site today at **rideoregonride.com**.

traveloregon.com

Mark Scott in Travel Oregon's cycling ad.

The Web site is already active, but the coming-out party happens this afternoon in Portland.

Earlier this year, I was blissfully unaware of how Travel Oregon had been promoting biking until I spotted one of its ads promoting bicycling in the pages of Backpacker magazine.

At first glance, I wondered who decided to spend state money (from lodging taxes) on this?

While doing time on the elliptical machine at the gym, I was paging through Backpacker magazine and turned to a two- page **Travel Oregon** ad about cycling in Oregon.

I have been a longtime reader of **Backpacker** and know the magazine rarely mentions cycling. Canoeing/kayaking once in a while, but they leave cycling to Bicycling and Mountain Bike magazines. Look at the **full ad here.**

I put in a call to Travel Oregon and got Holly Macfee on the phone. She works on brand strategy for Travel Oregon, which promotes the theme, "Oregon, We Love Dreamers."

When I raised the issue, I soon got the feeling that she wondered what planet I had been living on.

"That ad has been running for more than three years," she said, even though it was the first time I noticed it.

I also wondered who was the Lance Armstrong-look-alike in the Travel Oregon ad. He shows off a brand new bike and is outfitted in cycling duds that wouldn't look out of place on the Tour.

Mark Scott Intro

He turned out to be Mark Scott, senior financial manager for the Michael Jordan brand of products at Nike. (This guy must know how to multiply with 6, 7 and 8 zeros.)

Mark said the ad was shot back in late 2004 and began running in early spring of 2005 in Outside magazine. He has appeared in Sunset, Bicycling, Backpacker and probably more magazines he doesn't know about. He has become quite famous among his friends and, especially, his 20-plus-year-old kids.

Silly me! I thought the ad had actually been shot in 2008 during the **Cycle Oregon** tour of Hells Canyon in eastern Oregon. The ad is placed there and Mark rode the event that year. But no, it was shot in a studio at Nike and someone from Wieden+Kennedy merged the images together. And they did a good job, too. Completely fooled me.

By the way, Mark's bike was new because his old one had just been crunched by a car. The one in the photo was right out of the shop. He has put lots of miles on it since, though he voluntarily quashed the image I had of his toughness. He said he rode 2008 Cycle Oregon with a friend, while their wives followed the course with a motor home for them to sleep in each night.

I guess you've got to do what you've got to do.

Due to the notoriety of the ad, he probably would have been mobbed by the groupies, if he had camped out in a tent like the 2,000 other ride participants.

-- Terry Richard

'Jordan MotorSports'

G'$: Since the age of 15, I survived owning 5 motorcycles! Yet, too many friends did not!!

"I had to crash about 3 bikes, stunting and poppin' wheelies; before the wisdom of my 41 years said, 'You need to take a class and let's learn'!"

"It's just like basketball, if you don't know the fundamentals you can't play. You may think you can play. A street player always thinks he can play; until he gets in there with, <u>ME</u>."

Michael Jordan, *Jordan MotorSports* ~ 2003

G'$: Since the age of 33, having survived; I vowed as a 'GabDad' to never test fate on a 'cycle again!

In 2003, I created a 'scared straight' video PSA merging an ESPN story of the tragic NBA career-ending motorcycle accident of Jason Williams, and a History Channel story of novice 'Porsche Fanatic' James Dean's fatal crash.

Winslow paying stiff price for inherent brashness

Before getting a learner's permit, Kellen Winslow II purchased this Suzuki GSX-R750, a motorcycle that goes from 0 to 60 in less than 3 seconds – and looks like this after hitting a curb.
Associated Press

In the 6th grade I came home from a weekend trip, and a Honda ST90 was in our patio with a note: 'DO NOT RIDE'. Yeah, right! My mom had bought it and my brother watched her crash it in fewer than FIVE seconds on Day 1. Yes, I found the keys! A thrill like no other! I was spellbound!

I zipped across the Old Saddle Road from Hilo to Kona at 160 mph on my '87 Kawasaki Ninja XR600; the fastest crotch-rocket on the market.

Wear your helmet!!

G'$ VIP @ Porsche HQ-Stuttgart
*Raced in a Porsche pace-car on the 24-hours of Le Mans course.
*Autobahn *xtc* in my Euro-specs Porsche at legal speeds of omG!
<u>Bottom Line:</u> The Fast & Furious Shenanigans are a Death Wish!

The Autobahn: It's Not a Game

Europe G'$ missed 1 game and 1 training in 4 years. Gabriella's birth and a Spinout! *12/19/95 ~ Wiesbaden: In a very bad snowstorm, I'm heading to my training in Hanau. I throttle up onto the Autobahn onramp as it curves to the right, and my Porsche starts to spinout to the left. My Le Mans racing lessons saved me! Turn in the direction of the spin, downshift, hit the throttle and find your line. Execute it! By His Grace: A 360 Degree Spin Without Crashing! I took the next off-ramp home!!

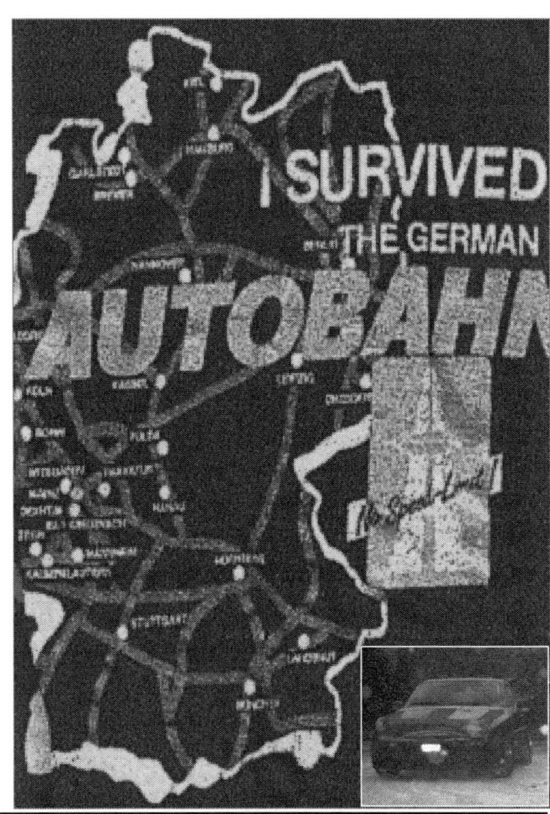

I visited Drazen's road-side memorial in Munich in my German-specs Porsche.

Petrovic no finta al destir

El genial escolta croata falleció anteayer ... ania

Drazen viajaba con dos ... en el acto tras chocar co

G'$ wore Petro' #4 Jersey in his Honor!

The net effect of this PSA?

We will never know.

R.I.P. Petro' & Pre'!

DRAŽEN PETROVIĆ
1964 - 1993

Land of the Pre

Three decades after his death, a roadside memorial in Eugene, Ore., helps keep Steve Prefontaine's legacy alive

A pair of flip-flops with the words TOM 3RD AT STATE inscribed in one sole. Racing numbers 35, 12 and 694. "Oregon Duck" lip balm. A message scrawled by a man from Malaysia: "We are what we believe."

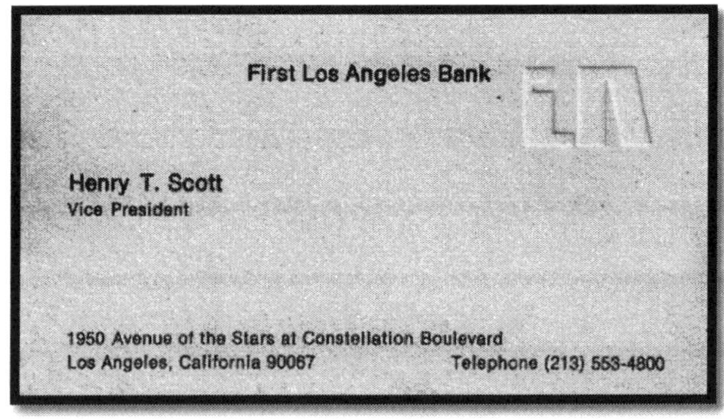
First Los Angeles Bank
Henry T. Scott
Vice President
1950 Avenue of the Stars at Constellation Boulevard
Los Angeles, California 90067 Telephone (213) 553-4800

In 1971, my brother and I were granted inside access to the business venture of, 'Mr. Don', a man from Chicago who established a banking relationship, and more importantly, a personal bond with our father that evolved over three decades. My dad, a true banking pioneer, was first a V.P. at (then) Security Pacific National Bank in Malibu, after graduating from their Sr. Executive Banking School. He ascended to First Los Angeles Bank in Century City, the entertainment financial hub of Beverly Hills and Hollywood. Pops was very humble, drove a VW, yet he took great pride in sharing his business savvy and tales of his top-shelf clientele; Jim Brown to Johnnie Cochran. He once introduced me to Wilt Chamberlain, in full volleyball gear. Fact: Neither Kareem or Mutombo compare to how massive Wilt the Stilt was! **As for 'Mr. Don', I heard his story and his personal angst of the rap and hip-hop culture, from him. As a guest in his home and at his events, I often promised 'Mr. Don' that I'd affirm his true legacy! GS**

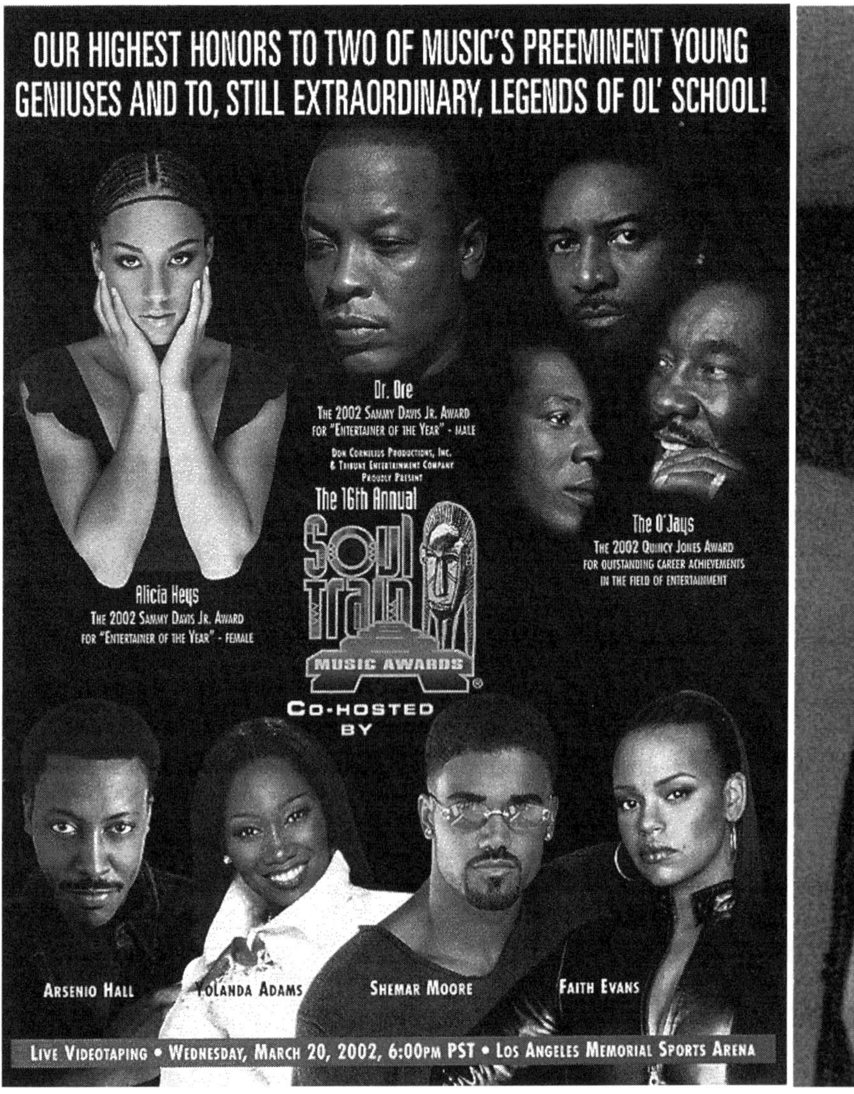

SOUL TRAIN.. & 'MR. DON': G'$ MENTOR!

http://www.soultrain.com/stweekly/story.html 1/2/2006

Soul Train - Don Cornelius Productions, Inc.

"The man has paid his dues and he deserves a shot. He's a good dude."
My Dad, Henry Scott

Soul Train Story

SOUL TRAIN Creator And Executive Producer Don Cornelius Has Been At The Cutting Edge Of Soul Music (Including Rhythm And Blues, Hip Hop, Gospel And Jazz) For Over 30 Years.

His Influence And Achievements Have Been Recognized By Hollywood And The Broadcasting Community Alike, With A STAR On The Hollywood Walk Of Fame; And His Induction Into The Broadcasting And Cable Hall Of Fame.

Ironically, The Soul Train Legacy Almost Didn't Happen. In The Spring Of 1966, Don Cornelius Took What He Considered To Be A Gamble, At Best And Enrolled In A Broadcasting School In Chicago. He Had Been Advised, During Indoctrination, That He And The Majority Of Those Enrolled In The Course Might Never Get Jobs In Broadcasting. Despite The Odds Against Success, Cornelius Decided To Give The Course A Try, Since Being A Radio Announcer Had Always Been A Dream Of His. Cornelius Attended Classes In The Morning, While Maintaining A Regular Job During The Rest Of The Day And In Three Months Had Completed The Course.

In 1967, Cornelius Was Offered A Part-Time Position As A News Announcer On Chicago Radio Station WVON, One Of Chicago's Most Popular Black-Oriented Stations. Later, He Would Set His Sights On TV And TV Production, Which Led To His Idea For A Black-Oriented Dance Show. Cornelius Pitched The Idea To WCIU-TV In Chicago And Agreed To Produce The Pilot At His Own Expense, While The Station Agreed To Provide A Small Studio.

Cornelius Completed The Pilot And Proceeded To Hold Screenings, In Search Of Advertiser/Sponsors. Initially, There Were No Takers, As Advertiser Representatives Who Would Screen The Pilot Did Not Seem Overwhelmed By Cornelius' New Idea For A Black-Targeted TV Dance Show, Which He Called Soul Train.

With A Personal Promise From Cornelius That, "Full Sponsorship Was Right Around The Corner," WCIU-TV (Channel 26) Began Airing The Original, Local Chicago Area, Version Of Soul Train In Five-Day-Per-Week, One-Hour, Afternoon Episodes, On August 17, 1970.

Soul Train Became An Instant Hit, Across Chicago TV Audiences, Which Attracted The Attention Of Johnson Products Company (Ultra Sheen/ Afro Sheen, Etc., Hair Care Products) Founder And President George Johnson, Who Proposed An Advertising Partnership That Would Involve Taking Soul Train In A Direction Toward National Syndication.

In The Summer Of 1971, Cornelius Began Commuting To Hollywood, California, In Hopes Of Locating Better Production Facilities Than Could Be Found At The Time In Chicago. After Several Trips To California, Still With Guidance And Support From Johnson Products Company, The Goals Of Securing A Good Facility And An Experienced Production Crew Were Achieved.

The Syndicated Version Went On The Air October 2, 1971. As Expected, It Was An Immediate Success In The Markets That Carried The Show.

It was at the ritzy Century Club, across the street from my dads' bank for a biz lunch. I initially called him Mr. Cornelius and he asked me to call him Don, to which I immediately said "I can't do that", as my dad interjected, "You got that right". So, we all settled on 'Mr. Don'. We bonded like we were kin. I was struck by his vibrant enthusiasm in probing my opinions of the show, and his openness in sharing his personal grassroots path and risk-taking. Also, his anguish to be the host of the looming perils of the 'Hip Hop' onslaught was openly discussed with me. Other times, I was a 'fly on the wall' as they discussed a few cunning saboteurs, such as Dick Clark, (then) host of American Bandstand. I do know what I know. Okay.

In 10th grade, at my dad's office, he was well aware of my QB quest and my hoop dream quandary. Mr. Don told me that whenever he meets with my dad the first item on their agenda is "how's the family, not business."

Pops often said, "Mr. Don really digs you, uniquely."
Then: He witnessed G'$!

After my MVP highlight performance in the BCI summer league all-star game, pops stoically took me outside to the parking lot where a long Lincoln Continental was parked far in the distance. Mr. Don exited the 'suicide doors' beaming with pride. 'Son, I'll never forget watching you today. Let me tell you somethin'. I'm from Chicago so I know great basketball when I see it. And you have a gift in this game! Someday, people will pay to see you play. You must really love footbally to deny such a gift."

The day after 'ECR Purgatory' pops picked me up for a stop at a client's home. At the door I was met by Mr. Don. He took me on a tour then to his office to view a tape. Soul Train 12/14/74 ~ Show #119 Season 4, episode 13: The Isley Bros performing, 'Holdin' On'. I cried! "Son, the best is yet to come!"

1989 Sumer Pro League: Dad calls me, "Mr. Don would like to see you before you leave." Lunch at Lawrey's Steak House was the venue for another memorable bonding session and a great meal with Mr. Don. He really reveled in my ascending hoop quest. "G'man, ballin' with the pros!" He was cushioning my dads' lament of my G'hoops "frivolous pursuit". As they discussed an upcoming special event, Mr. Don asked me about my holiday plans. I replied that I'd be in Kona preparing to move to San Diego. He opened his planner and began to write as he said, "Reconfirm Mr. Gregg's Holiday Party VIP trip w/ Scottie. Kona-LAX, hotel, car."

Treasured Perks VIP all-access to the Soul Train Events and the after-parties! From the Live Music Awards...

...the Summer Lady of Soul events, to the annual Holiday Parties; Mr. Don hooked me up! Coveted kinship!

A Request for Cooperation

Welcome to the **2002 Soul Train Music Awards.**

We greatly appreciate your presence at the **2002 Soul Train Music Awards**. Everyone involved with this show from the entertainers to the producers, thanks you in advance for all of the positive energy and genuine support you'll be giving to this production.

We want you to have a great time and express your full support, appreciation and love for the hosts, entertainers and presenters. **We do ask that you refrain from negative behavior, such as, booing or hissing** which unfairly diminishes everyone's enjoyment of the show.

If you do not appreciate the work of an artist who is mentioned or appears at this event, we ask you to simply refrain from applauding.

Your special enthusiasm is what makes the **Soul Train Music Awards** telecast more fun, more exciting and more entertaining than all the rest.

We appreciate your cooperation. Thank you very much for being here. And now let's get ready to party at the **2002 Soul Train Music Awards!**

Don Cornelius

As long as my story is told, so shall be the story of 'Mr. Don'.

Michael Coleman: "Entering the Holiday Party an ambiance of a special night was tangible. I just gave G' a hug and said, 'Thank you'. At the bar he whispered, 'Yo Mike, its *open bar* here; don't be shy.' I swiftly asked the bartender to '*make mine a double, please*'. A memorable toast ensued. As we went upstairs G' stumbled and recovered smoothly just as Mr. Scott appeared. His dad was so genuinely glad to see us. He said he needed to steal Gregg for a few minutes as he inquired about our cocktails. On cue, as they walked away, Mr. Scott chastised his mix." 'Tanqueray & 7'; no ice'. *"How can my son ruin such a fine liqueur by mixing it with 7-up? Mama's boy!"*

G': Pops took me upstairs onto the VIP level and then into the hidden VIP 'lair' (of the former owner of the venue, Prince) as I heard that famous voice bellow, "Mr. Gregg is in the house! Now we can party." With a huge hug. For the next 15 minutes I was the VIP of 'Mr. Don'. A Legend!

G' Hoops: Gets Props from Suge Knight

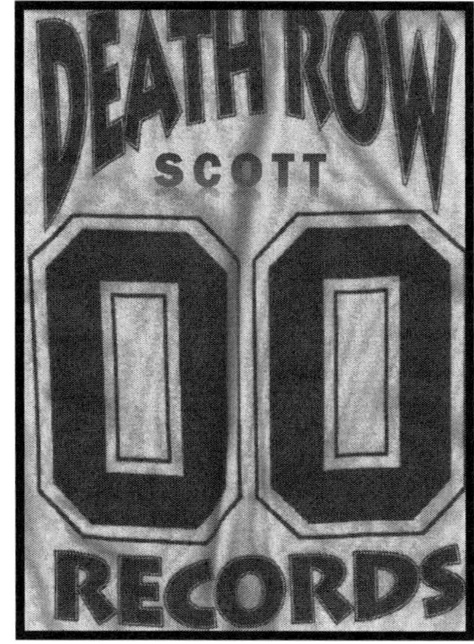

During the live taping of the '02 Music Awards at the L.A. Sports Arena, I went to the restroom on the VIP floor level, which was empty. I get to a 'stand-up' as a man enters abruptly and quickly checks each toilet stall, walks back to the entrance and opens the door. As the sound of the show roars in, I mind my business. Then, in walks the larger-than-life (6'3" 300 lbs.) image, aptly suited and 'gator booted in all red, who induced ooohs, ahhs, gasps and gulps when he first arrived at the venue, as opposed to the light applause other notables received. Indeed, Suge Knight posted up just a few feet away. He glances at me up and down. Now, I'm duly represented in my voguish charcoal and black 3-piece tux (owned, not rented) with my VIP credentials in plain view. Suge looks me in the eye, nods affirmatively and surprisingly says to me, **"What up, ballplayer?"**. That put me at ease, honestly. With bass in my voice, I replied, "How ya livin' Suge?". His acute ballplayer quip spoke volumes. I immediatley recalled a 1993 Soul Train sponsored Hip-Hop celebrity hoop game at Fairfax High in which I put on a G'$how, humility aside. I thought to ask him to sign the Def Row Records jersey I received in my post-game gift bag. Alas, I choked. 'Peace-out, Suge.'; while quickly washing my hands. His sincere reply, "Likewise Homie"; memorable. Exiting past Suge's bodyguards I ran up the unmoving escalator to call Mike! Michael Coleman: "G' called and sounded a bit shook up."

G$ Soul Train Hip-Hop Hoop Jersey

Stop The Presses! 2015 Emmy's Cued "Flashlight"!

Hip-Hop Present Day

F8

Hip-hop finds a home at Smithsonian

Soul Train pioneered the original stage show platform of the BET MTV VH1 era! Hip-Hop music is forever woven into our global society. Sports, fashion & media!

2014: San Antonio Spurs play offense with hip-hop music playing! Then the music fades, along with the opponents' adrenaline, when the Spurs transition to defense! Just mere coincidence or a coy calculated neuro-scientific home-court advantage?

2014: Pro Bowlers Tour on ESPN commercial *Background Lyrics* ~ "Baby if you give it to me, I'll give it to you, as long as you want; you know I got it." Hip-Hop!

Don Sparks: 1st A.D. Fox Studios Invite

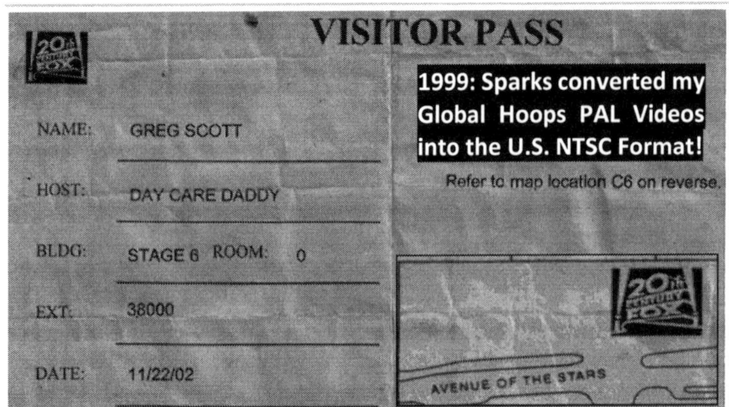

VISITOR PASS
20th Century Fox
NAME: GREG SCOTT
HOST: DAY CARE DADDY
BLDG: STAGE 6 ROOM: 0
EXT: 38000
DATE: 11/22/02
1999: Sparks converted my Global Hoops PAL Videos into the U.S. NTSC Format!
Refer to map location C6 on reverse.
AVENUE OF THE STARS

'Day Care Daddy' Preproduction

I was so blessed by his invitation. As I entered the elevator, a nice guy caught up. Producer, Dan Kolsrud, told me how much he enjoyed working with Sparks and the many exceptional attriutes he posseses and exhibits. I concurred. 'That's my Best Man!' He replies, "Well the reason I'm being so descriptive is that those are the exact same things Sparks says about you. So, I hopped on the elevator just to spend a bit of time with you." **Humbled! Surely the nicest thing anyone has ever said to me!!**

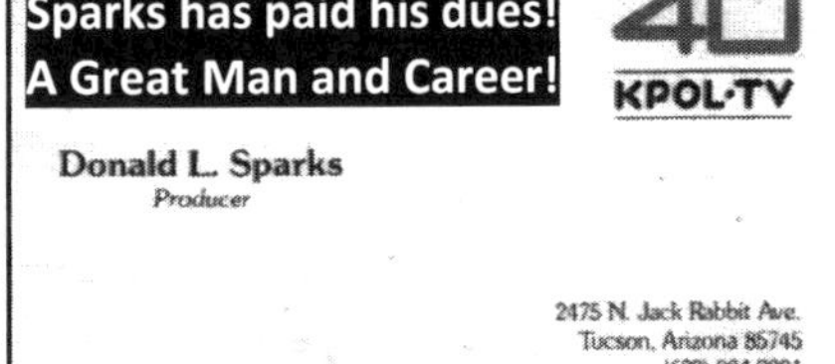

Sparks has paid his dues!
A Great Man and Career!
40
KPOL-TV
Donald L. Sparks
Producer
2475 N. Jack Rabbit Ave.
Tucson, Arizona 85745
(602) 884-9001

2002 1st AD Sparks G' Invites: Daddy Day Care Film Set

THE VIDEO TAPE COMPANY
10545 Burbank Boulevard
North Hollywood,
California 91601-2280
(818) 985-1666
TWX: 910-499-1471
Don Sparx
Video Tape Supervisor
VTC

A VIP tour of the film set and VIP intros: Priceless! I bonded with the 3-time Academy Awarded Audio Guru, David MacMillan!!

Beyond Coincidence: Blazers!

Gab and I were cruising on the bay and I saw a courtesy dock at Seaport Village. Shave Ice! We soon docked, hit the boardwalk as I saw a Blazer 'mate chatting on his phone. He took one look: "I'll call you back!" **Corey Gaines!!**

At Nike HQ Mark took us to see Geoff D!

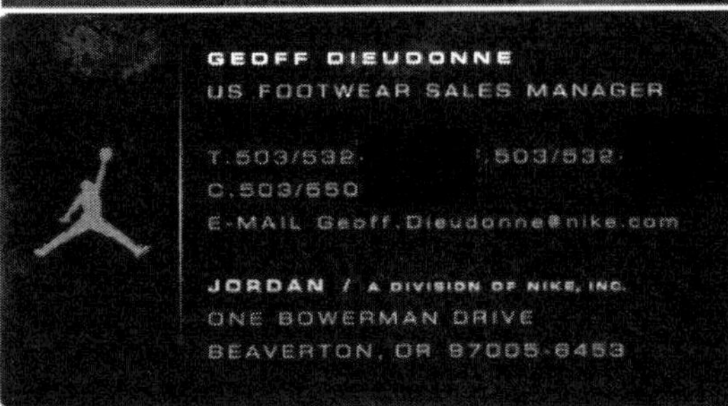

GEOFF DIEUDONNE
US FOOTWEAR SALES MANAGER
T.503/532
503/532
C.503/550
E-MAIL Geoff.Dieudonne@nike.com
JORDAN / A DIVISION OF NIKE, INC.
ONE BOWERMAN DRIVE
BEAVERTON, OR 97005-6453

Sage Sparks: While in Canada filming "Are We There Yet", reviewing the 2006 draft on NBA.com, he phoned me to note that, "The top 4 out of 5 picks were from Europe, and all cited the Adidas abc Euro Camps as major factors in their success."

Mental Athlete gets Props from Tae Bo Master Billy Blanks

The Workshop & Billy Blanks teach the same Hydration Formula: ½ your body weight in ounces!

Encino 2004: The Yellow Hummer at the gas station was driven by **Master Billy Blanks!**

Gunner Kerr Manual Gift

I summoned the gumption to approach him to ask him to autograph my 2003 Workshop Manual. **He took time to read it! "You wrote this?"** Yes, Sir. I think it's the right stuff. **B.B.: "I Don't Just Think It Is. I Know It Is! Make it happen and let me know how I can help." Then, he handed me his 2004 Tae Bo DVD!**

My '03 B.B. endorsed manual is still coveted today!!

From age 5, G'13 was raised in basketball venues watching me referee!

2003: Boss Basketball Officiating Intro, Education & Training

MOST MISUNDERSTOOD BASKETBALL RULES 2004

BOSS Officials Training Procedures

BOSS BUSINESS GUIDELINES
December 8, 2004

Officiating: A Craft! Not a Side Gig!

APPROVED BOSS SIGNALS

Every time you blow your whistle your arm goes straight up in the air.

For a FOUL, make a fist (hold up 2-3 seconds)(do not point at fouler) No other signal is needed unless to show block or charge.

Show this for any kind of foul Followed by: BLOCK CHARGE TECHNICAL FOUL COUNT IT

To stop the clock for a violation, alt/poss, timeout, or ball out of bounds, Put you arm up (open palm), indicate the reason (and verbalize it), and then point the direction.

Show this to stop clock for anything other than a foul TRAVEL DOUBLE JUMP BALL THEN POINT DIRECTION

CHOP CLOCK TIME IN 3 POINT ATTEMPT WHEN MADE FIND A GOOD BALL

ONE AND ONE TWO SHOTS FIST MEANS VIOLATION

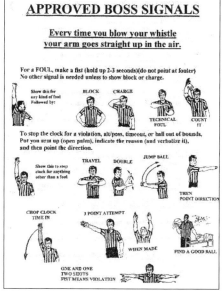

2005: AAU San Diego United Basketball Assoc. SDUBOA

2007: CIF North Coutnty Basketball Officials Assoc.

June 2015: Vegas AAU

The Camp will be held at the Alliant University - High Five America Facility with 6 courts running games all day!	***High Five America is now sponsored by Adidas and brings in elite High School teams from all over the US to compete in this major High School tournament.***

Adidas Jr. Phenom Camp --Ramping up again for 2005!

2005 Camp Dates: (GIRLS) August 4-7
2005 Camp Dates: (BOYS) August 11-14

Jr. Phenom Camp is the place to be next August! The camp will host the country's top 100 Jr. high school players in each class (2010, 2011, 2012). That's right; even bigger and better than before! Close to 300 players in all will hit the courts at the Second Annual adidas Jr. Phenom Camp.

For nearly 20 years Adidas has held the Top High School All-Star Camp in the world. The Jr. Phenom Camp will bring this great tradition to the grass roots level once again, providing valuable instruction and a launching platform for many college and NBA players of tomorrow. This prestigious camp will be held in San Diego, CA at Alliant International University in Southern California's premier multi-gym basketball facility. Alliant University is home to a state-of-the-art 52,000 Square foot gymnasium with 6 new full size wooden courts under one roof.

The adidas Jr. Phenom Camp is an "invitation only" camp that offers students/athletes a variety of mandatory classes on academics and life skills, better preparing these young men and women for success in high school, college and life. Players must attend class each day to be eligible to play in afternoon game sessions. Top college coaches and elite skills instructors will be in attendance to pass on their words of wisdom. Players will have an opportunity to test their games against other top players in their age group from across the nation throughout the weekend. The camp will culminate with championship and All-Star games on the final day under the watchful eyes of the country's top scouting services.

High Five America Hoops HQ @ AIU

Gene Heliker:

"We had a 52,000 sq. ft. facility here. I coach 365 days a year at any level. Yao Ming's first introduction to American basketball was in this gym with us." "More than any player in High Five history, this venue is a tangible result of Gregg Scott."

Here is the schedule for this weekend:

San Diego United Basketball Officials Assn. Ref G': I officiated 17 games in three days.

GAMES @ ALLIANT UNIVERSITY

FRIDAY, AUGUST 12, 2005

At an AIU AAU tourney I heard a voice utter, "Is that G'? I mean Sporty G'?"

CT 3 1:30pm for (3) G. Scott / ________ CT 3 6:00pm for (3) R. Tennant / G. Scott ✓
CT 4 1:30pm for (3) B. Devine / JJ Vroom CT 4 6:00pm for (3) B. Devine / R. Peterson

The Voice was Hilo veteran police officer Randy Apele. A good Hilo friend!

SATURDAY, AUGUST 13, 2005

Randy was with Richard Handy, a kid whom I mentored at the Hawaii Job Corps! 'Handy' had persevered! Married with two sons in the hoop tourney!

CT 6 2:30pm for (3) G. Scott / S. Glasper CT 6 7:00pm for (3) G. Scott / S. Glasper ✓

SUNDAY, AUGUST 14, 2005

G. Scott: 3 Championships plus two All-Star games!

CT 4 9:15am for (3) J. Harkrader / B. Devine CT 4 12:30pm for (3) B. Devine / J. Harkrader ✓
CT 5 9:15am for (3) T. Clark / S. Caldwell CT 5 12:30pm for (5) B. Spillane / G. Scott ✓

"In his 3-year tenure, Gregg is High Five's all-time scoring leader and the all-time leader in win %." GH

G' Hoops & G' Ref Mix: All-Star Game Coach of the "Westside"!?

I was requested to officiate the adidas Jr. Phenom All-America games, an honor indeed! Politely, I refused to wear **adidas** shoes as they requested. My G'$ ref biz gear: **Jordan!!**

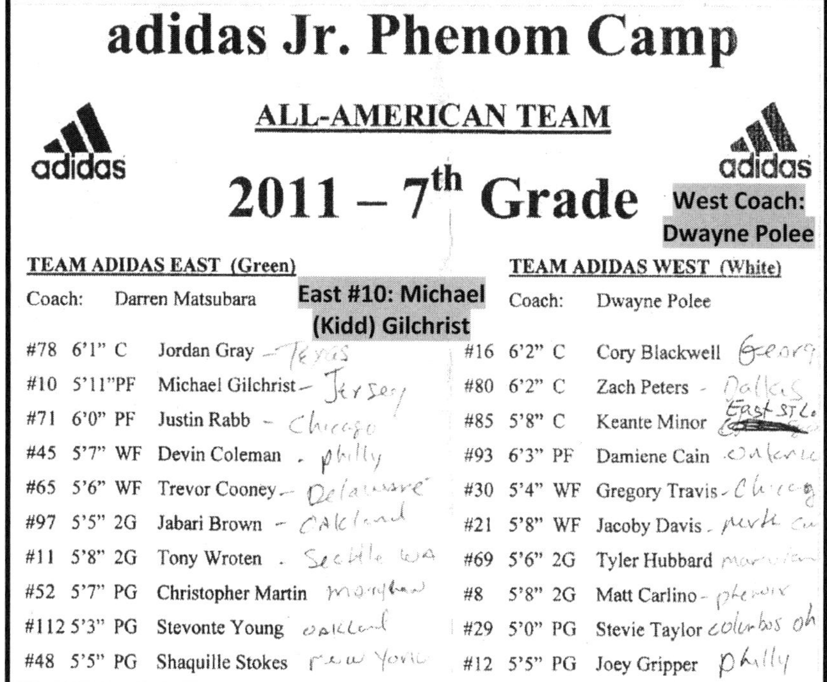

adidas Jr. Phenom Camp

ALL-AMERICAN TEAM

2011 – 7th Grade

West Coach: Dwayne Polee

East #10: Michael (Kidd) Gilchrist

TEAM ADIDAS EAST (Green)

Coach: Darren Matsubara

#	Ht	Pos	Name	
#78	6'1"	C	Jordan Gray	Texas
#10	5'11"	PF	Michael Gilchrist	Jersey
#71	6'0"	PF	Justin Rabb	Chicago
#45	5'7"	WF	Devin Coleman	philly
#65	5'6"	WF	Trevor Cooney	Delaware
#97	5'5"	2G	Jabari Brown	Oakland
#11	5'8"	2G	Tony Wroten	Seattle WA
#52	5'7"	PG	Christopher Martin	
#112	5'3"	PG	Stevonte Young	oakland
#48	5'5"	PG	Shaquille Stokes	new York

TEAM ADIDAS WEST (White)

Coach: Dwayne Polee

#	Ht	Pos	Name	
#16	6'2"	C	Cory Blackwell	
#80	6'2"	C	Zach Peters	Dallas
#85	5'8"	C	Keante Minor	East STL
#93	6'3"	PF	Damiene Cain	
#30	5'4"	WF	Gregory Travis	
#21	5'8"	WF	Jacoby Davis	
#69	5'6"	2G	Tyler Hubbard	
#8	5'8"	2G	Matt Carlino	phoenix
#29	5'0"	PG	Stevie Taylor	columbus oh
#12	5'5"	PG	Joey Gripper	philly

Beyond Coincedence: Early in the game I was the trail official passing the West teams' bench as the coach says to me, "Your partner needs to loosen up his whistle and let them play. This is an All Star game." I smiled, 'I gotcha coach'. He perks up, "I know that voice; we've balled together at some point." I was mystified as well. He looked very familiar!

Dwayne Polee

First time-out, I checked the scorebook at the table and voila. Dwayne Polee! Yes, we had truly balled and bonded. When I went and recalled our Spring 1984 days ballin' at Pepperdine with Anthony 'Budda' Fredricks and Sterling Forbes, an emotional reunion ensued right there on the sideline. A hug only bonded warriors can understand. Truism: **Iron Sharpens Iron!**

AIU: National U9 AAU Tourney Game, circa 2006

Shaquille O'Neal

Shaq "Diesel" was in the house with only a small crew, all seated along the far corner wall watching his son playing in a U9 game. As a referee, if I want to watch, I'd have more peace sitting away from fans so I had to pass by the Shaq squad. I'm wearing a grey referee shirt with black pinstripes (untucked), opposed to the game refs' 'Footlocker' shirts. Also, my black shoes, socks and long baggy shorts were <u>all</u> **Classic Jordan Brand.**

I repectfully wait for a break in the game to cross in front of Shaq. Walking by him I say, 'How ya livin', Shaq?' With his cap to the back and a bit to the side, Shaq looks at me up and down while pausing at my calves. He smirks, nods approvingly and chants, "I see ya, Baller." I was stunned and admirably replied, 'Good eye!' Shaq simply replied, "Yeah dat!"

Ahead of the Curve: G.S. Professional Health, Fitness & Nutrition Pedigree

Functional Training: Squat ~ Lunge Bend ~ Rotate ~ Push ~ Pull ~ Gait

All of our physical movements are one of, or a combination of, the 7 Fundamental Movement Patterns.

Closed Chain vs. Open Chain Exercises

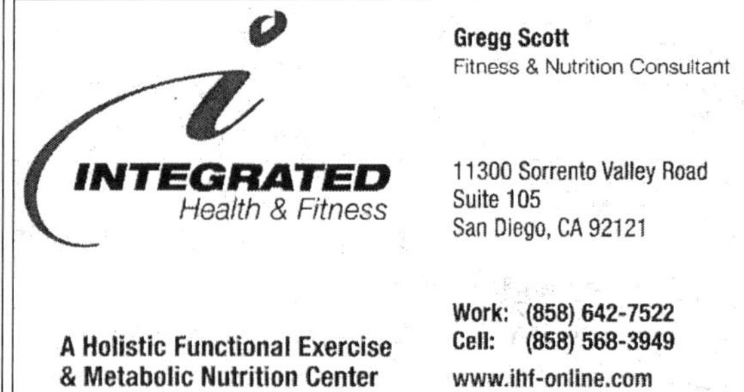

INTEGRATED
Health & Fitness
A Holistic Functional Exercise
& Metabolic Nutrition Center
Gregg Scott
Fitness & Nutrition Consultant
11300 Sorrento Valley Road
Suite 105
San Diego, CA 92121
Work: (858) 642-7522
Cell: (858) 568-3949
www.ihf-online.com

Dynamic Warm-up vs. Static Stretching ~ Metabolic Nutrition vs. Fad Dieting

To Whom It May Concern: 1/2/2008

Gregg Scott has been a contracted employee of Integrated Health and Fitness, Inc. since October 16th, 2007. For the last few months, Gregg has been dutifully performing an internship in which he has undergone an intense education and in-servicing process. This internship process has now come to a close and Gregg is as of now ready to begin working with clients. Gregg's compensation is $30 per hour for clients trained, $50 per hour for nutrition consultations performed, and $50 for health fairs attended.

Best Regards,
Craig Morgan

Owner
Integrated Health & Fitness

Individualized Functional Training Programming Protocols:

Core Stabilization Assessments ~ Flexibility Assessments Order: Largest Muscles First! Cables & Pulleys ~ Free Weights Stability Ball; No Benches! Self-Stabilization! Posture ~ Stance ~ Grip ~ Balance ~ Form ~ Core & Neck Flexor Activation ~ Neutral Spine ~ Quality Technique throughout Movement! Exhale on the Push ~ Train to Muscle Failure ~ Timed Rest!

Ashford University Monster Blitz for New Online Graduate Students

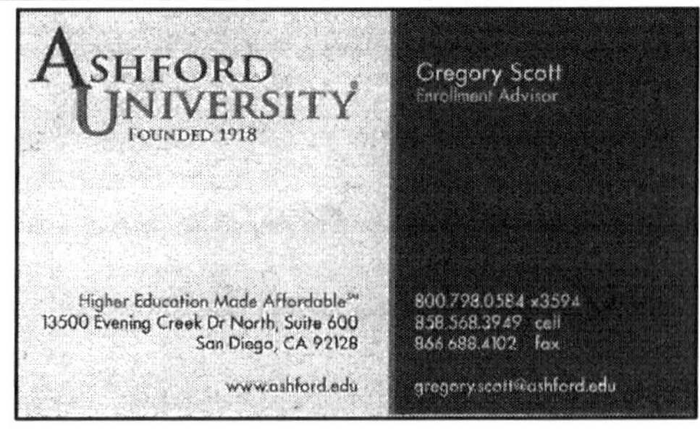

2009: For one year, exactly 365 days, I worked as a Graduate Enrollment Advisor in the seedy world of online education for Ashford University. One unsavory event was the Monster Blitz. Get us hyped up on a cooler full of Monster Energy drinks, provide us with lists of unprotected leads from other E.A. teams and allow us to poach at will. I feared energy drinks, so I emailed my bro at Nike. In homage to my mom's Fav #3, I chose a prophetic 3rd name on page 3. Mark replied swiftly, "Don't worry Bro, one won't hurt you."

I reply about my Monster peer pressure as I view the file of *Chosen Pupil,* Yvonne Mathews, a retired educator from Wilmington, North Carolina. She reminded me of my own mother. She answered the phone cheerily and a rapport flowed easily. She inquired about my family ties to which I shared my email exchange with my bro; Nike finance guru at Jordan Brand. She says, "Well, please do have your brother say a special hello to Michael from me. He will indeed remember me. MJ once quoted me in a Q & A interview for Parade Magazine."

MJ's Most Inspirational Teacher Quote: "If you make a mistake, redeem yourself." Ms. Yvonne Jacobs, 7th Grade Social Studies Teacher at MCS Noble Middle School.

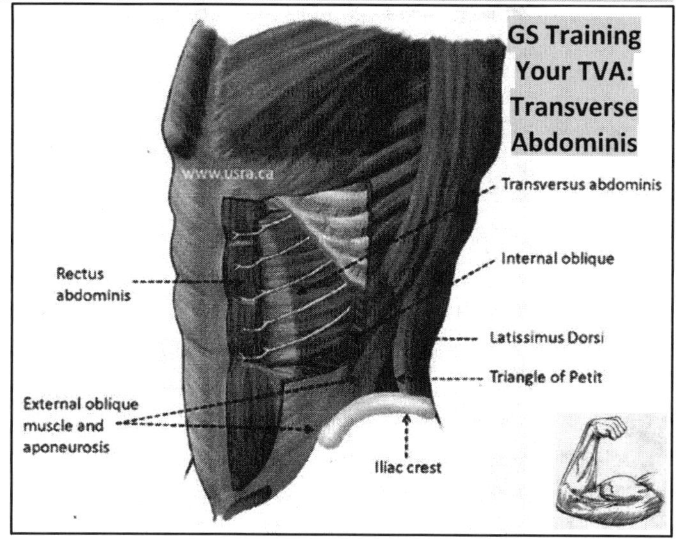

2010: A Hoop & Pelvis Parallel

Mr. James Bennett: "For years I pleaded with Gregg Scott, who is a superb referee, to coach my two kids on the court. When my son, Nate, played AAU, Gregg officiated his games often and taught Nate a neat Pete Maravich (Ricochet) ball handling drill and how to spin a ball on his finger. Nate mastered them both over time. When Nate was an incoming Frosh at West Hills High, he was cleared to play his first summer tournament after suffering chronic hamstring injuries. He was still getting rehab therapy treatments twice per week. Nate was stiff, rusty and his jump shot was simply broken. Finally, we set up a shooting session with Gregg. A customized program card detailed his 75-minute workout plan. Warm-up, physical assessment, jump rope, stretching, scoring chalk-talk, shooting intro, free throw intro, drills, rest/water breaks and cool-down. Beyond expectations, with only one rule; parents could only watch the warm-up and cool-down segments. During the initial assessment phase he came over to inform me that the workout would be 90 minutes (on his dime) to allow an extra 15 minutes to probe into and rectify a 'forward tilt' of Nate's pelvis. 'I could stretch him out for today or I can take the time to get to the root cause, teach him my prudent abdominal exercises and educate him with tools for injury prevention.' 'I can give him a fish for today or I can teach him how to fish his lifetime.' His Rx Effect: Nate's jumper was fixed and he never went to rehab again."

I probed my 'Cause & Effect' premonition. Nate had 'wash-board' abs and a six-pack. Culprit? Ab work awry! Nate's sit-up routine was done on a slant-board with feet anchored. Result: Over-active, dominant hip flexors. When the abs fatigue the hip flexors take over. Tight hip flexors initiates a foward pelvis tilt that bio-mechanically causes hamstring stress. Rx: Hip Flexor Stretches. Desgard all sit-ups. Employ my personal ab-curl program. Voila.

Dec. 2010: Hoopaholic & Hall of Famer

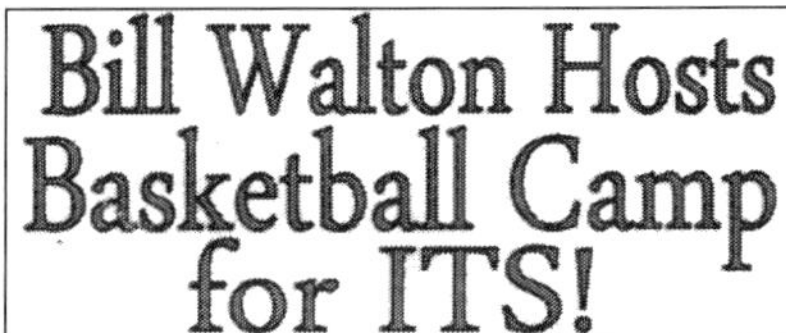
Bill Walton Hosts
Basketball Camp
for ITS!

Shane Poppen had plans & the Lakers Pachenga Palace. I added my Voice & Hoopaholic Euro Camp Templates!

ITS Bill Walton Basketball Camp

Agenda

Start	End			
		Saturday, December 4, 2010		
8:30	8:45	**Coaches Welcome: Gregg & Kevin — All Coaches & Volunteers** *Court 1*		
8:55	9:55	**Coaches Clinic: Bill Walton — All Coaches & Volunteers** Upstairs Conference Room		
10:00	10:15	**Welcome: Bill Walton — All Campers, Coaches & Volunteers** **Introduction of Camp Director, Gregg Scott** **Introduction of All Coaches** *Court 1*		
		Camp Agenda: Player Grouping (3 groups) / Station Rotation Info *Court 1*		
10:15	10:25	**Wooden Warm-up / Stretching**		
10:30	11:40	**Court : 2 Ball Handling** **Coach:** *Drills:* ***Triple-threat!!!*** *L / R around Cones*	**Court: 3 Run / Pass / Catch** **Coach:** *Drills:* *5-Star Passing* *Figure 8 Passing*	**Court 4: Shooting Fundamentals** **Coach:** *Drills:* ***Introduce bank-shot spots*** *Mindsets; Shot Selection* *Footwork; Arc; Release Point*
11:45	13:00	**Cool Down / Chalk Talk**		
11:45	12:00	**Introduction:** **Keynote Speaker: Tami Broderick from Newport Nutrition, 'Fueling Your Body'** *Court 1 ~ Audience in bleachers*		
12:00 12:45	12:40 1:15	**Lunch** **Bill Walton Address to All Campers & Coaches** *Court 1 ~ Audience in bleachers*		
1:20	1:40	***Group 1*** ***Lay-ups*** ***5-star passing***	**Group 2** **Shooting** **5 Shots-5 Spots Contest**	**Group 3** **Free Throws** **Knock-out Contest**
1:45	2:05	**Court 2: One the Ball Defense** **Coach:** *Drills:* ***Stance /Trace/Don't Reach*** *Step-slide / Drop Step* *1 pass away / Deny*	**Court 3: Rebounding** **Coach:** *Drills:* ***Principles /Timing /Desire*** *"Get a Body"* *4 on 4 Shell*	**Court 4: Team Defense** **Coach:** *Drills:* ***Man-to-Man Principles*** ***VERBALIZATION*** *5 on 5 helping 'D'!*
2:10	2:30	***Close-out Principles***	***Offensive Boards: Value Possession***	***See Man & Ball: "Pistol's"***
2:30	2:40	**Cool Down**		
2:45	22:50	**Gregg Scott Remarks:** **Sponsor Appreciation, Staff & Coach Acknowledgements**		
2:15	3:00	**Bill Walton, Closing Remarks**		

The ITS Rattle

JANUARY 2011

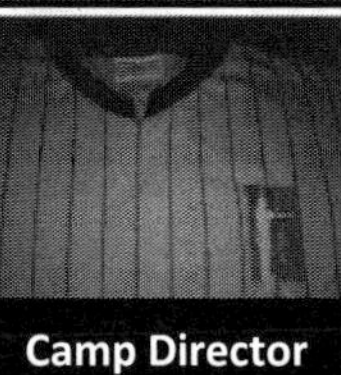

Camp Director Gregg Scott

On Saturday December 11th, 192 native youth participated in the Bill Walton Basketball Camp. The camp, which took place at the Pechanga Recreation Center from 10am-3pm, and was the largest camp ITS has held. The youth players were trained by some of the best coaches, and players in the region. While having fun and learning basketball skills, the children were also taught about proper nutrition, team work and sportsmanship by NBA legend and Hall of Famer Bill Walton. Bill made himself available to every player and parent, happily signing autographs, posing for pictures, and answering questions throughout the day.

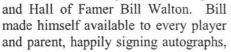

Ben Foster, ITS Sports Director "Gregg had earned the respect and admiration of our ITS kids as their favorite hoop referee. His boss, Brian Devine told us of his Euro Hoop Camp Pedigree."

With supreme and sincere appreciation, Bill Walton signed a ball for Gabby and invited us to a special ITS trip, tour & basketball game at UCLA that he was hosting.

Gregg Scott & Bill Walton

GabDad!

G. Scott ITS Officiating Venues: Pechanga, Viejas, Sycuan, Barona, Pala, La Jolla, Rincon & Cahuilla

Inter-Tribal Sports UCLA DAY 

Saturday, Feb. 12, 2011

10:00am-10:25am: Check-in, welcome, & blessing at Bruin Plaza

10:25am-10:35am: Introduce American Indian faculty/staff, programs and services

10:35am-12:00pm: AI/RAIN/AIR/AISA student interactive tour & activity

12:00pm-12:30pm: Lunch & walking over to Pauley Pavilion (30 minutes)

12:30pm-1:00pm: Check in at Pauley Pavilion

1:00pm-3:15pm: Basketball game & lunch

3:15pm-3:45pm: Basketball team meet & greet: Joe Burton, Coach Robinson, and Tyus Edney

3:45pm-4:00pm: Walking over to Mathematical Sciences 4000A and 5200

4:00pm-4:30pm: Admissions presentation

a. *Divide into two groups: 9th -12th grade + 8th grade and grade levels below*

4:30pm-4:40pm: Walking to bus & depart from campus

Joe Burton ~ Iron Sharpens Iron

Note his Club Team: The Compton Magic

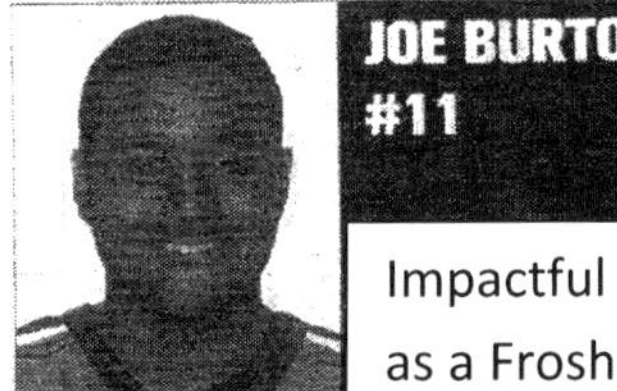

Impactful as a Frosh

1st Native American to earn a 'full ride' in men's hoops in the history of the Pac 12!?

Sophomore • Forward/Center • 6-7 • 280 • 1L • Soboba, Calif. • West Valley HS

2009-10: Played in 32 games as a freshman, starting five ... Finished the season averaging 4.7 points, 4.5 rebounds and 1.0 assists per game ... Registered six games in double figures, including a season high 15 points at Texas Tech (11/15) ... Recorded his first career double-double with 13 points and 12 rebounds at UCLA (2/25) ... Played a season-high 32 minutes against the Bruins ... Made first career start in victory at George Washington (11/28) ... Tallied 13 points in win against Cal State Bakersfield (12/6) ... Scored 12 points in win over California (2/18) ... Registered at least five rebounds in 17 contests ... Had a season-high four assists in win over Oregon (2/6). **Played club basketball with the Compton Magic.**

PERSONAL: Born in Soboba, Calif. ... Son of Dondi Silvas Nichols and Kendall Nichols ... Chose Oregon State because it's a "new, upcoming program" ... Lists golf as his hobby ... Believed to be the first Native American to receive a men's basketball scholarship in Pac-10 history ... Majoring in Ethnic Studies.

G' & Gabby: Thank you Bill Walton for inviting us to a truly special day.

JOHN WOODEN CENTER

Detour to 'The Pyramid'

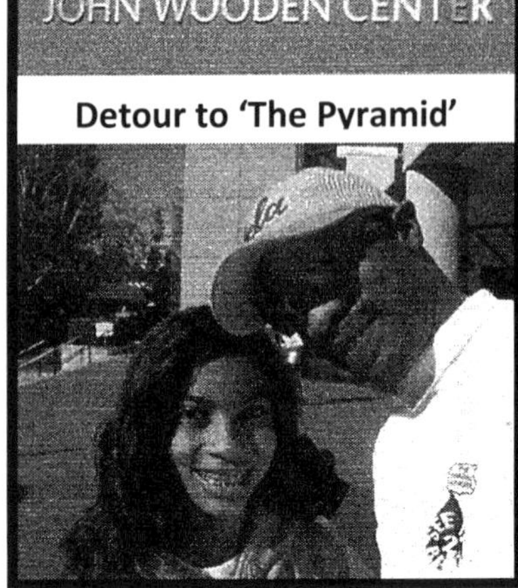

OSU Coach Robinson, brother of Michelle Obama, post-game chat.

My Agenda: To expose my daughter to UCLA as a historical tour of where I earned my stripes!

Core elements of G' Hoops & The Mental Athlete were cultivated at UCLA during my critical formative years.

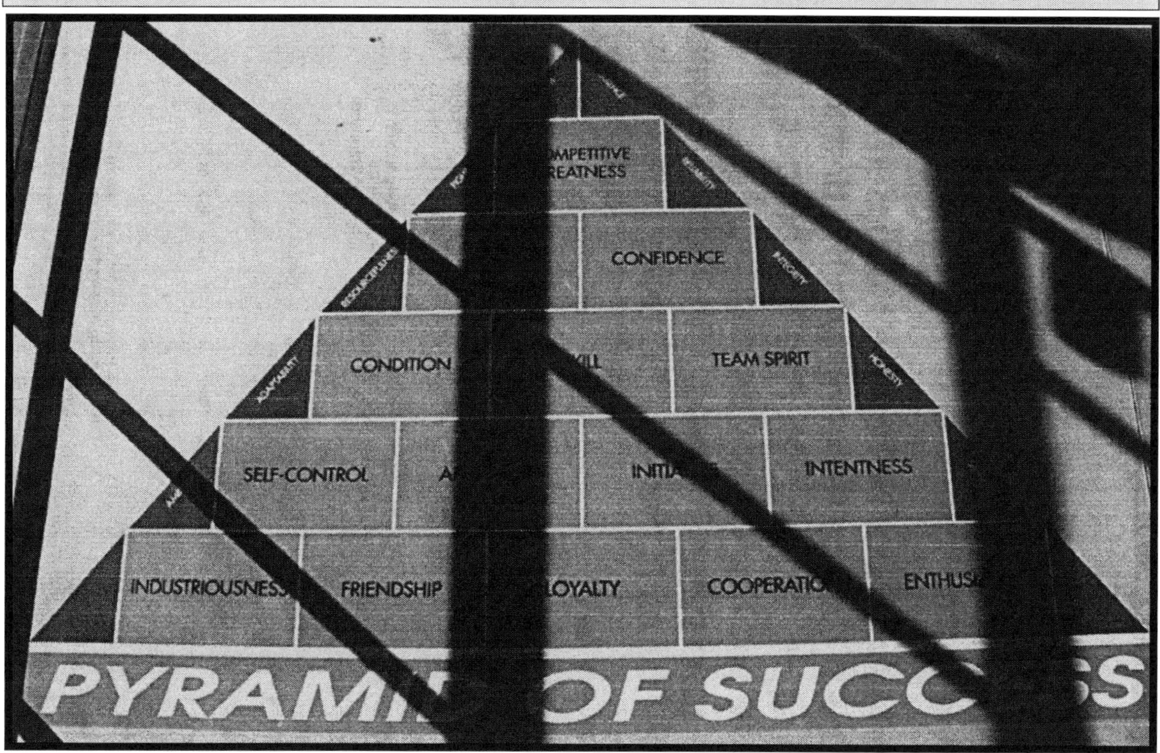

Ref Meets Hells Bells Dad: Trevor Hoffman

2003 Rancho Santa Fe Elem.: Trevor Hoffman, transforms from Hells Bells Padre into a Helicopter Parent hovering onto the court towards ME at halftime of his sons' game, questioning calls. **Game Management 101** dictated a quaint reply, 'Sir, I know who you are and what you do, but, unless you are on the coaching staff, I have zero obligation, and even less intention to explain judgment calls to you and obligate myself to explain calls to other. So, please do us both a favor and remove yourself from the court in a manner that will allow both of us to save face.' Situation extinguished with no residue and no grudges.

A decade later, I'm officiating the **2013 'War on the Floor' Varsity Summer Tourney at West Hills HS,** when I hear that same familiar voice cheering on his same son. Standing near the baseline he soon, reasonably, barked about a non-call. The next time down the court, I briefly explained my 'Verticality' reasoning. He, nodded his understanding and appreciation of my feedback. What he chanted in reply soothed my soul. "Good work, *Blue*." At halftime we enjoyed a very nice hatchet-burying chat. Mr. Hoffman: HOF Props!

2003-2013 G' Ref & 'Coach' Kerr Kids' Impact

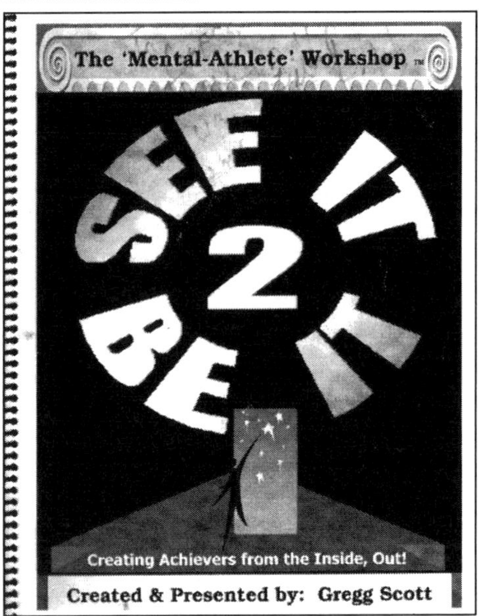

The 'Mental-Athlete' Workshop ™
SEE IT 2 BE IT
Creating Achievers from the Inside, Out!
Created & Presented by: Gregg Scott

In 2003 as I began my basketball officiating career honing my skills, one prized BOSS account was the posh **Rancho Santa Fe Elementary and Middle Schools.** I was a requested ref for their leagues and one day I gifted my new workbook to a 6-year old at RSF Elem., who was the son of an old hoop friend. 'Trust in this. Say hello to your dad for me, please.' No card, phone number or note. A sincere gesture.

In 2003: I also was expanding my geographical area, ref'g with my mentor, Mike Coleman, in Long Beach. Their ARC leagues and AAU tourneys were superior. Mike was an excellent and highly respected veteran official with the clout to get me invites. He schooled me and taught me so much! Mastering Mechanics and Mirroring Calls! Still, intense elite level hoops demand court presence, game management and a strong whistle. We worked well together; no problems. I was well received and that fan rapport would be a saving grace years later in a unique convergence of my Long Beach and RSF experiences.

2006 Escondido, CA AAU Hoop Tournament ~ Multiple Venues

I'd just worked a final 4-game set, 12th game of the 3-day tourney, as my cell phone buzzed. "We'd like you to work as the 'R' in a U12 championship game at Palomar YMCA." Sure! When I arrived at the gym the current game was at halftime. As I walked past the bleachers I noticed a few waving Long Beach peeps and then I heard a voice, "Hey, See It To Be It! How's it going Gregg." Seated on the front row in the far corner of the gym: Steve Kerr. He stood to give me 'baller love' and to give his thanks for gifting my manual to his son. As we parted, I wrongfully assumed Steve was watching the current game in parental mode.

"Coach Kerr": U12 Tourney Finals Solana Beach Cats vs. Long Beach

After a brief 'pre-game' with my partner we took the floor as the teams were warming up. I was awed by the familiar fans and teams. LBC vs. 'Cats. UA jerseys and Nikes via Coach Kerr! I utilized my 'R' designation to give pre-game with the team captains and the coaches. A rarity in AAU ball. Ref G' Laws in 33 words! 'Advantage/Disadvantage: Play the whistle. Hands off. Don't reach. Stay in your space. Maintain verticality. Respect the competition, respect the refs and respect the game. Play Hard. Play Smart. Any questions? **Good Luck!**'

A packed gym full of two divergent 'Beach' fan bases, cultures and social-economic classes; all content. Aware of my 'ref rep'. LBC fan, "Win or lose. We know we won't get screwed." Dynamic and athletic Long Beach vs. Just 7 Fundamental, gritty and sound Nike clad 'Cats. The high intensity game had a great 'ebb & flow'. Solid execution, both teams and coaches.

- ❖ Crunch Time: Coach Kerr plotted a memorable moment. LBC went into a full-court press as the Cats' guard killed his dribble near the midcourt. "Time-Out!" He asked what the count was at. 'Eight.' They huddled. I informed him that he had a re-set on the backcourt count. He paused, then said, "Let's run it anyway!" They executed some snazzy backcourt action with a neat inside handoff that created an uncontested layup; within the 2 seconds! Steve wiped his clipboard, "Thanks, Phil."

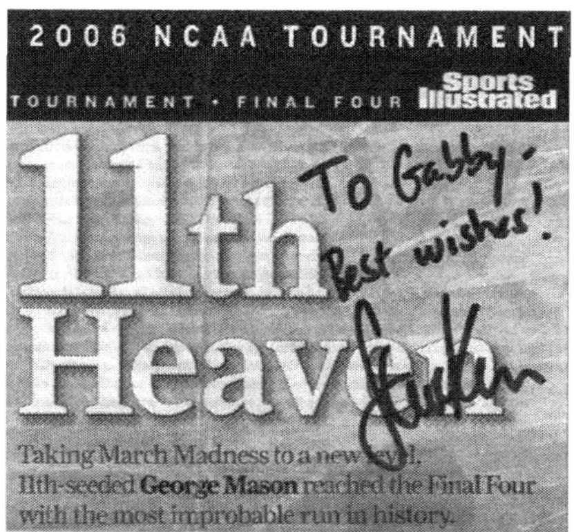

The Cat's won a clean hard-fought contest and all the fans shared in post game total harmony. For years the Kerr kids came to greet me each time they saw me officiate, without fail. Class! Steve and I met again in 2012. Torrey Pines at Westview Girls V'ball. He was with his U of A 'Cat, Judd Buchler. **3 'Cats: In Parent Mode!**

January 2012: NCBOA Speaker Leon Wood

Veteran NBA referee Leon Wood was our guest speaker. After the meeting I reminded him of the jump rope routine he gave me decades earlier at Muni Gym in Santa Monica. He perked up as we reminiced. He said, "I used to play at Muni with the L.A. Raiders' Ronnie Lott and Dennis Thurman to toughen me up." **Sage Advice: NBA Official Leon Wood: "Always Know the Consequences of Your Whistle."**

June 2012: Police & Fire Olympic Games

One week of multiple sport competitions! My legendary ref mentor, Sleep Caldwell, and I officiated 28 hoop games and the championship that was won by the LAPD squad. My Uncle Mike was smiling down!

June 2015: Ref G' 23 Games at 'The Las Vegas Classic' & 'The Fab 48' AAU National Elite Showcase Tournaments

Chris Paul had nice team! I ref'd his CP3 squad twice at the Tarkanian Academy.

Best AAU in USA! My 2nd game: Bronx New York vs. Compton Magic! I retold CSUN Coach Reggie Theus of our Forum Magic All-Star Match-up **Reggie Theus: "Thanks for that story. It truly made me smile."**

PAGE 14 BEYOND THE GAME MARCH 21-27, 1998 | SPORTS | THE STARS AND STRIPES

The Lakers can't regularly put away teams. They don't show the grit and execution to win games in the fourth quarter anymore. The precision the team displayed earlier — the screens, the cuts — is gone.

Their roster may be the fifth-youngest in the league, but that is not to be confused with inexperience. Shaquille O'Neal, Horry, Campbell and Corie Blount all have been to the Finals. Fox, Eddie Jones, Derek Fisher, Kobe Bryant and Van Exel all have been to the second round at least once. Being young is not the Lakers' problem.

Acting young is.

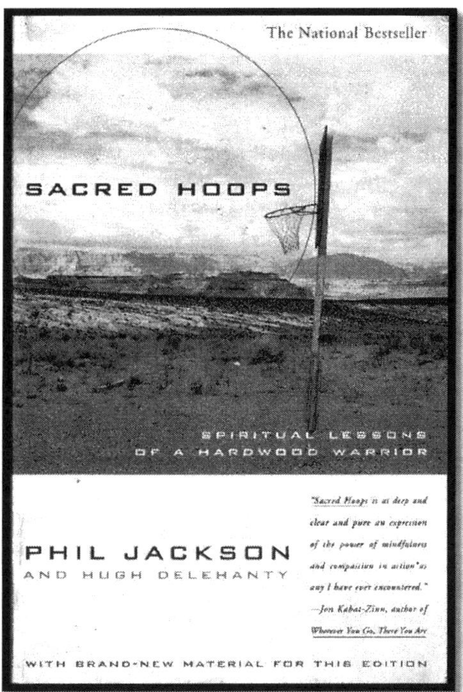

Bull coach Phil Jackson, when asked if the Lakers are the NBA's most talented team, gives an observation that is far more to the point than what Hardaway offers.

"I don't consider physical talent talent," he says. "That's athleticism. They're the most athletic team in the league."

"I don't consider physical talent talent. That's athleticism."

Bulls' Phil Jackson, 1998

Prior to coaching those young Lakers to Championships!

PHIL JACKSON ~ THE ZEN MASTER

Required Reading for The Mental Athlete ~ what is on my Bookshelf is in my Toolbox

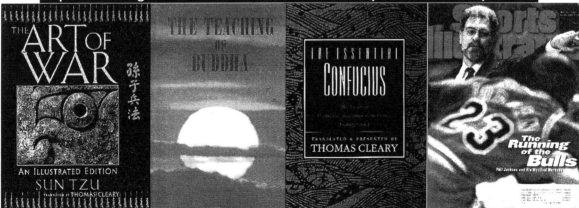

THE ART OF WAR 孫子兵法 AN ILLUSTRATED EDITION SUN TZU TRANSLATED BY THOMAS CLEARY

THE TEACHING OF BUDDHA

THE ESSENTIAL CONFUCIUS TRANSLATED & PRESENTED BY THOMAS CLEARY

Sports Illustrated — The Running of the Bulls — Phil Jackson and His Mystical Methods

The Leaders Voice

As leaders we do not grow in isolation.

Who we are and what we believe are shaped through our conversations and interactions with others.

Important people influence us more.

A little bit of each of them becomes part of us.

The height of authenticity occurs when we integrate these voices into that single voice, uniquely ours, inseparably linked with a unique self-image.

As we mature we learn to speak with a clarity that captures the attention of others.

Authenticity further demands the integration of voice and behavior.

Our ability to "walk our talk" begins with our beliefs. When we choose to lead, our voice and actions speak our intentions.

The world has changed. So has the way we communicate. Those who fail to adapt will be left behind.

But, for those who want to succeed there is only one secret: You are the message.

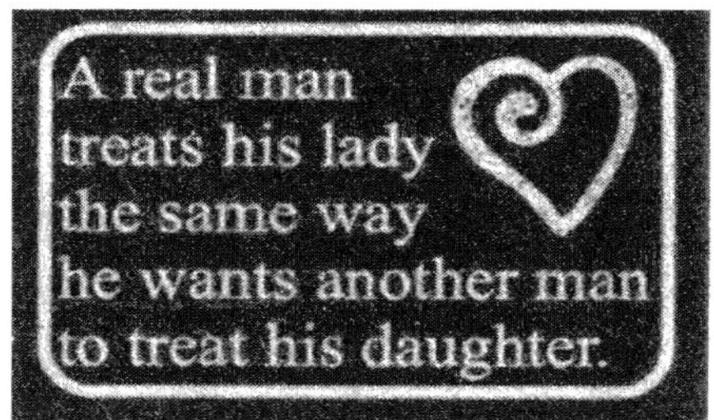

Mom Quote

"You can't tell me you want THAT if you're not willing to do THIS."

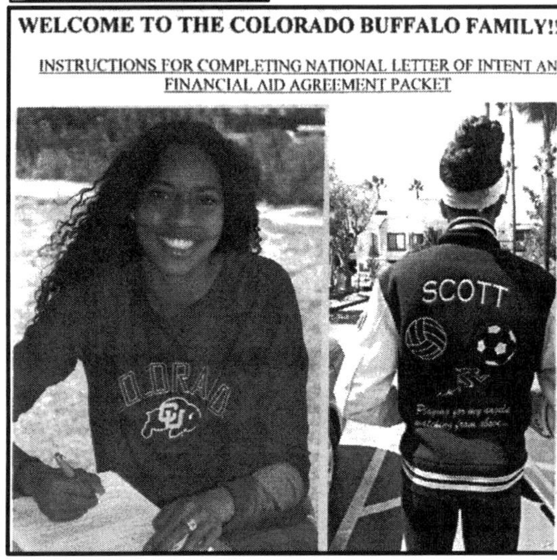

WELCOME TO THE COLORADO BUFFALO FAMILY!!
INSTRUCTIONS FOR COMPLETING NATIONAL LETTER OF INTENT AN FINANCIAL AID AGREEMENT PACKET
SCOTT

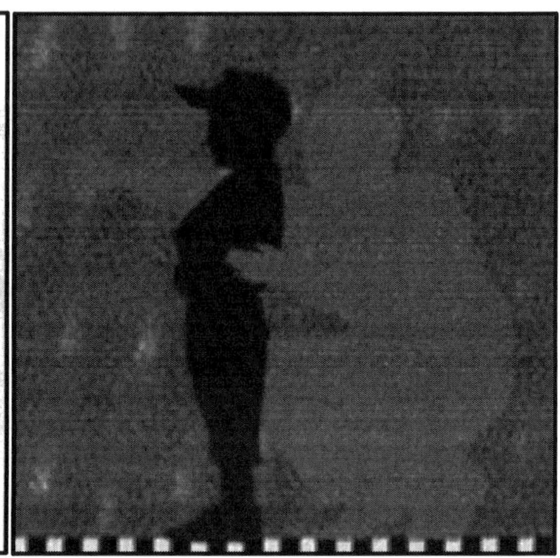

✐ **Life Skills in a Sports Context.**

✐ **Creating Achievers from the Inside, Out!**

✐ **Teaching not only 'What to Think, but How to Think!**

✐ **Prudent Coping Skills & Programming the Coping Mechanism!**

'Make your Choices with Intelligence over Impulse and with Vision instead of Instant Gratification.' GS

My Shining G$ Seed **"STUNTIN' LIKE MY DADDY"** **Gabriella Scott ~ G'13**

HOROSCOPE

VIRGO (Aug. 23-Sept. 22). Use time off to consider this: Giving of yourself in order to earn a wage is not the only way to go. Work up the steely determination you need to follow through on potentially lucrative projects of your own invention.

English as a Strange Language

"The present moment is the perfect time for me to present this present."

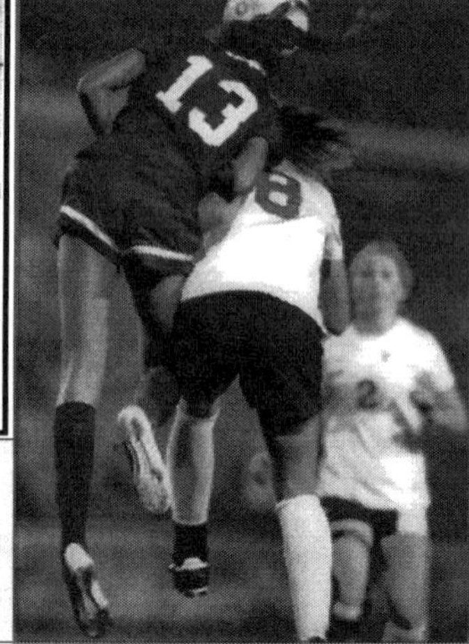

THE MENTAL ATHLETE & GLOBAL HOOPS MIX

The Evolution of the Man, the Brand, the Mentor & the 'Baller'

A Time Tested & Globally Proven Empowerment Pedigree

- ◆ Personal and Group Health & Fitness Trainer/Instructor
- ◆ Diet & Nutrition Educator
- ◆ Peak Performance Coach
- ◆ 'Mental Athlete' Guru
- ◆ 'Global Hoops' All-Star
- ◆ Euro 'adidas' Camp Coach
- ◆ Euro Streetball Champion

"It is foolish to expect an athlete to follow your advice and to ignore your example."

Gregg Scott ~ Global Hoops

- ◆ 'Hoopaholics' European Basketball Camp Creator & Cultivator
- ◆ Willing, Loyal and Committed Teammate ~ Honorable Competitor
- ◆ Coachable, Coveted and Cold-Blooded Baller ~ Champions Mettle
- ◆ Devoted Teacher, Mentor & Motivator ~ Diligent Pupil & Protégé
- ◆ CA Certified Basketball Official ~ *2003-2015: Over 10,000 games!
- ◆ Parent of a 3-sport H.S. Sr. Scholar-Athlete Pac 12 *#BoulderBound*

MIND & BODY CONDITIONING ~ LIFE CHANGING & LIFE LONG

The TEAM Concept

- ➢ TOOLS
- ➢ EDUCATION
- ➢ APPLICATION
- ➢ MOTIVATION

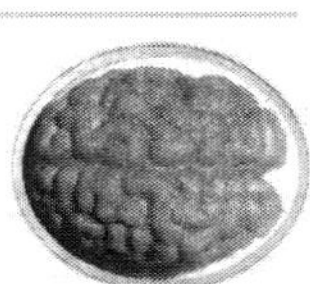

To navigate a tangible personal path to enhanced well-being, human peak performance and athletic excellence.

"Athletes, peak performance athletes, respond to challenge as long as there is respect. Ultimately, and above all, you've got to make them trust, respect and believe in you as their coach. And, that'll never happen unless you first trust, respect and believe in them."

Tony Robbins

The Mental Athlete Workshop

Time Tested & Globally Proven

Transcending typical sports psychology, The Mental Athlete Workshops have meshed my 'Pursuit of Peak Performance' with proven International philosophies and techniques, and topped it off with a global education specializing in Sports Performance Enhancement in a personal quest for Excellence.

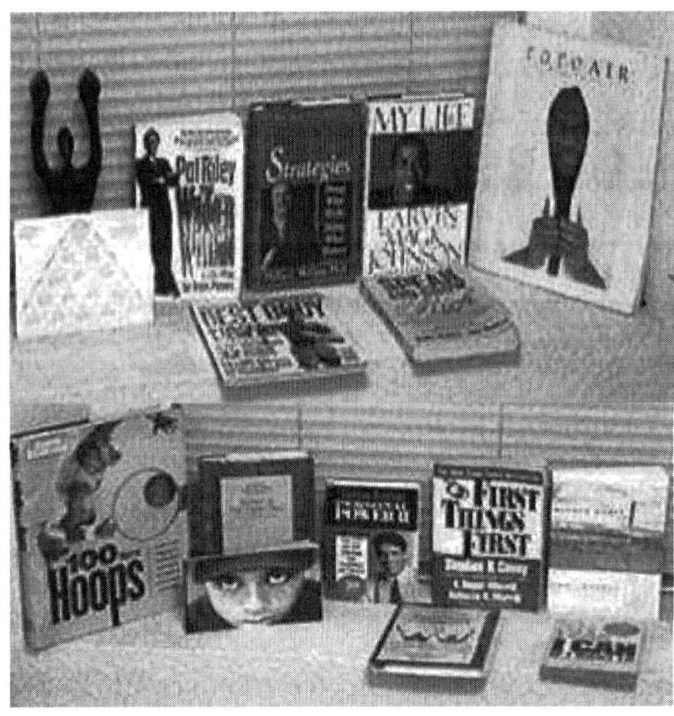

A Pedigree of Depth, Diversity & Duration of 'The Mental Athlete' Brand & Global Hoops!

THE MENTAL ATHLETE WORKSHOP

25 years of Tangible Global Evolution

Workshop Creation
'The Club' ~ Kona, HI
Home of the Ironman

See It 2 Be It
'The Mental Athlete'

Multimedia Worksnop Presentations

25th Anniversary
Social Media Branding

Adidas ABC Euro Camps
Germany, France, Italy, Greece, Spain & The UK

Mental Athlete Workshop Live on Radio Show
Kaliedescope Radio Magazine

Global Hoops: Mind, Body & Soul
Trafford Publishing

twitter

1990	1995	2000	2003	2007	2012	2015
•.Mind & Body Conditioning for Peak Performance •Personal Trainer: Club members & Ironman triathletes	•Translated into German & French •FIBA Recognized •Co-wrote Players & Coaches Manuals Coached Jr Nat'l Tms	•Company Launch •Peak Performance •Website & Logos • U.S. target market Club / Travel / AAU Olympic Train'g Ctrs	•1-hour Live via KTST 89.5 FM & seeit2beit.com •Media Credential •Retaind all radio show copyrights	•Custom Workbooks •Custom Powerpt. Applications •Peak Performance & Elite Athlete Platforms	•Trafford.com •Non-fiction •Peak Performance •Self-Help •Workshop Infused •BB IQ Blueprint	•Branding via MentalAthlete •Twitter/Facebook •Youtube/Instagrm •Seeit2beit.com •Ghoops.com
•San Diego~Mental Athlete Workshops •Launched 'The Competitive Edge' •UCSD Instructor Wt. Trn'g & Fitness	•Gregg's European Hoopaholics Camps •Wiesbaden DoDs •Frankfurt Int'l Sch. • Brechenheim Club Surabaya, Indonesia	•The TEAM Concept Tools, Education, Application & Motivation •Demographically Universal	•Infused radio show content into Workshop Presentations •First Basketball Refereeing Cert.	•Bball Officiating: •CIF High School •Cal State Games •Club & AAU @ AIU •Intertribal Sports ITS	"True Life Tales, Tools, Teachings and Testimonials of an Int'l. Pro Ballplayer & Mentor"	•Resurrection of the Workshop~Globally •Brand'g Gear Line •Int'l Hoop Camps •2015 Global Hoops Book Publish'g Tour

"YOU CAN TALK TO PLAYERS AD INFINITUM ABOUT ANY NUMBER OF SUBJECTS. AND, JUST LIKE A PARENT AND A CHILD, AT SOME POINT, SOMEONE COMING IN FROM THE OUTSIDE; GIVING THAT LITTLE BIT DIFFERENT PERSPECTIVE. COULD BE SAYING THE EXACT SAME THING YOU'VE BEEN SAYING FOR THE ENTIRE SEASON. BUT, THEY HEAR IT IN JUST A LITTLE BIT DIFFERENT WAY, FROM A SOURCE THAT THEY'RE NOT USED TO HEARING IT FROM, AND NOW THE LIGHT GOES ON A LITTLE BIT."

COACH BRIAN BILLICK

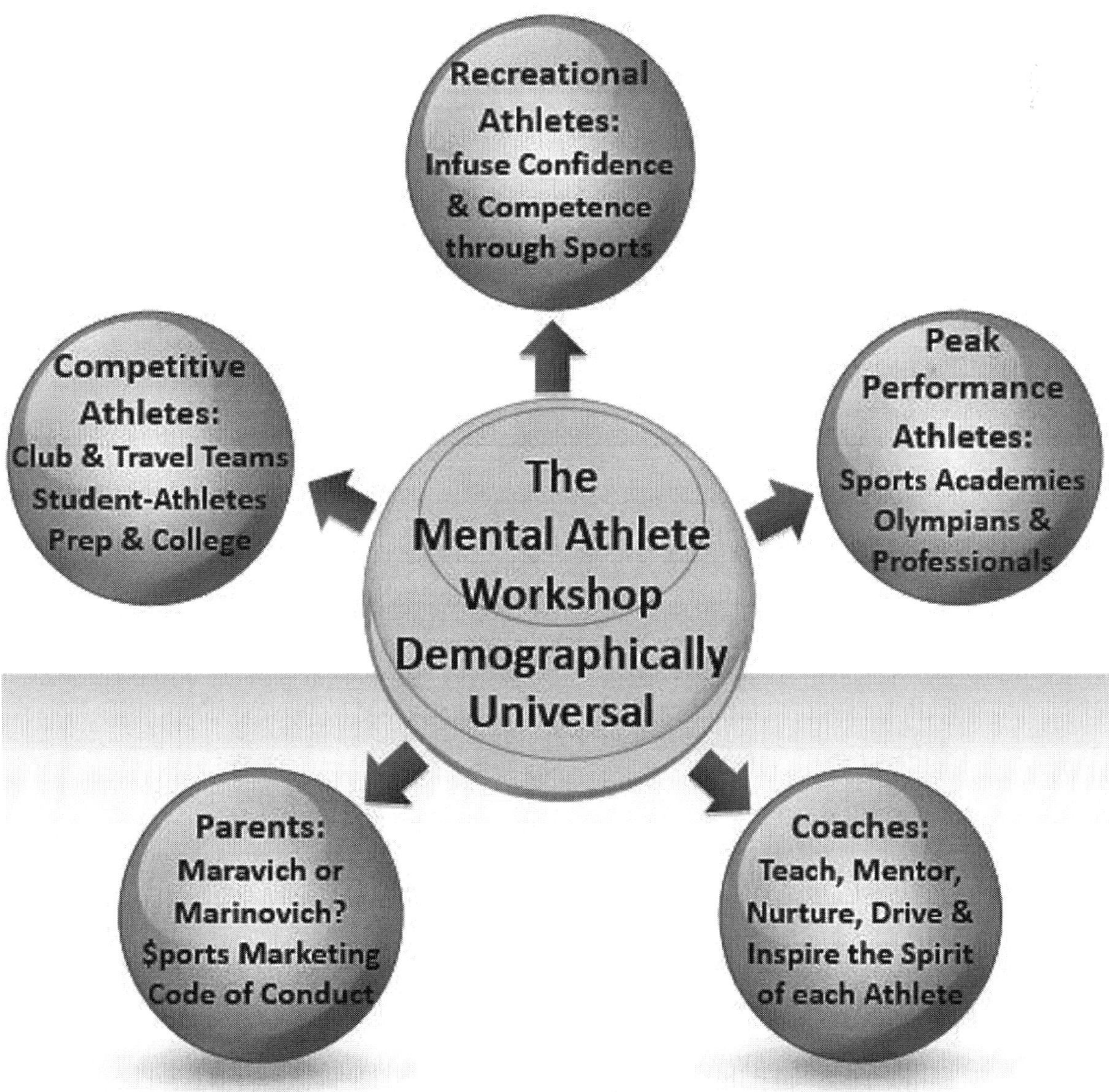

2015: The Modern Day 'Mental Athlete' Manifesto

The Mental Game
The Power of the Mind ~ Positive Intent ~ Affirmations ~ Visualizaton ~ Emulation
Goal Setting ~ Goaltending ~ Peer Pressure ~ Emotion ~ Performance Blockers

Mental Athlete Role: CEO of Brand 'YOU'
Managing Critical Ralationships ~ Your 'Board of Directors' ~ Parents ~ Mentors
Coaches ~ Trainers ~ Teammates ~ Advisors ~ (Bad) Officials ~ Fans ~ The Media

Return on Investment (ROI) ~ Student-Athlete & 'Mental Athlete' ~ Pro!
Cost vs. Benefit ~ Risk vs. Reward ~ Intrinsic Value ~ Club/AAU/Travel Team$ ~ Prep
Multi-Sport Athletes ~ $ports Marketing ~ Social Media Awareness ~ College Quest

The Physical Factors
Peak Conditioning as your Calling Card ~ Training vs. Practice ~ Team Training
Individual Training ~ Cross-Training ~ Weakness Training ~ Cardio ~ Weight Training

"Fatigue Makes Cowards of Us All" ~ John Wooden
Food or Fuel? ~ Diet & Nutrition ~ Hydration ~ $upplement$ ~ Sleep to Peak
Pain vs. Injury ~ Rehabilitation ~ Relaxation ~ Injury Prevention ~ Fit/Agile/Durable

Tangible Intangibles of a Mental Athlete
Possess The Mind of a Champion ~ Character & Commitment ~ Sincere Teammate
Coachable ~ Fundamentally Sound ~ Peak Condition ~ Competitive Zeal ~ 'Clutch'

THERE ARE LESSER PHYSICALLY TALENTED PLAYERS GETTING COVETED CLUB AND VARSITY SPOTS, COLLEGE SCHOLARSHIPS AND PRO CONTRACTS BECAUSE OF THEIR INTANGIBLES!

Your Mental Game must serve as the Foundation for your Physical Skills to Flourish and your Marketability to Shine. Mind & Body Conditioning for Peak Performance!

Balderdash Psycho-Babble: The Game is 90% Mental & Practice Makes Perfect

The Mental Game

You Think You've Got Game? How's Your Mental Game?
The Mental Athlete Approach: Harnessing Your Mental Game

YOU ARE WHAT YOU THINK!

The Power of the Mind

"Our lives gravitate towards our most dominant thoughts."
Joel Osteen

Our minds are our best friend or our worst enemy, and that can flip-flop in a heart-beat.

Hearing vs. Listening ~ Reading vs. Studying ~ Speaking vs. Articulating

Running vs. Sprinting ~ Practicing vs. Training ~ Playing vs. Competing

Holistic: Beyond the Placebo Effect

You Are What You Think!

It works if I think it works. Belief begins within us. The brain is the world's greatest computer and performs greatest when we program and nourish it with prudent and specific information, and establish a positive mindset to suitably interprete our 'life circumstances'. A glass half-full mentality is a learned trait. Be vigilant in recognizing 'interrnal viruses' based on our faulty beliefs, interpretations of external stimuli, media, and corrupt misinformation. Recogize, then Reboot & Recalibrate on cue. Ultimately, know this: What and How we Think dictates an energy flow 'cause and effect' on health, well-being, human performance, vitality, and longevity. **The Eyes Are There But See, Not.**

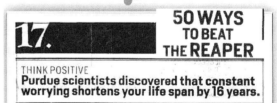

17. 50 WAYS TO BEAT THE REAPER

THINK POSITIVE
Purdue scientists discovered that constant worrying shortens your life span by 16 years.

For better or worse!

Proven by science!!!

No Angst

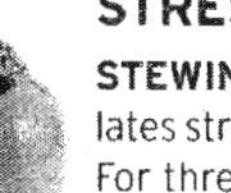

STRESS BUSTER: WHAT IF?

STEWING OVER EVERYTHING that may go wrong escalates stress, and you often end up worrying unnecessarily. For three days, jot down every "what if" that nags you. "What if I'm late for work?" Then count how many come to pass. Studies show you'll be right 10 percent of the time.

TUESDAY
January 31, 2006

THE SAN DIEGO UNION-TRIBUNE

*Energy Flows: Behind schedule; I'm concerned, but NOT stressing! **GS***

Positive Intent

Trait: distinguishing characteristic

This 'First Trait' has remained the same since my infancy. It was an engrained asset and self-serving mantra at the core of my personality, not created to be at the foundation of any future workshop, or a clever buzzword for a future brand. While this 'First Trait' evolved to become each of those, its origin was born of my personal conditioning, belief system, and as my genuine mindset.

Intent (noun: Purpose.) adj.: Committed, Resolved, Bent, Dedicated

This is not "Don't worry, be happy" psychobabble.
This is 'Don't Angst, Stay Positive' psychotherapy.

The first trait we must develop is called "positive intent". We have "positive intent" when we create an atmosphere where we feel calm and confident. We expect good things to happen and success to come.

With positive intent comes the ability to DREAM. By dreaming it, you make it possible. Anything worth having begins with a dream. It is from here that we begin the process of mental training.

Positive Intent creates miracles. Yet, we all have unique inner challenges and human limitations.

Was wir zuallererst entwickeln müssen, nennt man "guten Vorsatz" oder "positive Absicht". Wir folgen einem guten Vorsatz, wenn wir für eine Athmosphäre sorgen, in der wir uns ruhig und sicher fühlen, in der Erwartung, daß positive Dinge geschehen werden und der Erfolg kommen wird.

Mit den guten Vorsätzen entsteht die Fähigkeit zu "träumen". Durch das Träumen wird alles möglich. Alles, was es wert ist, zu haben oder zu sein, fängt mit dem Traum an. Hier beginnt das mentale Spiel!

Le premier aspect à développer est appelé: "l'intention positive". Nous sommes en face d'une "intention positive", dès que nous créons un environnement dans lequel nous nous sentons en confiance. Nous espérons que les choses agréables vont arriver et que le succès sera au rendez-vous.

L'intention positive est intimement liée à la capacité à REVER. C'est en rêvant les choses que vous les rendrez possibles. Tout ce qui vaut la peine d'être possédé commence par un rêve. C'est à partir de ce point que nous commençons à travailler notre mental.

EPICTETUS

"All philosophy lay in two words: Sustain and Abstain"

Self-Talk & Affirmations

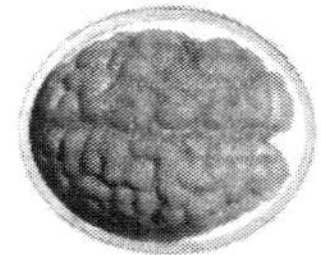

Our internal chatter, or 'self-talk', is more much more powerful than we think. Our keen minds accept our thoughts as facts! What we say to ourselves and how we say it dictates our thoughts, attitudes, interpretaions and reactions for better or worse…make or break.

- Although they may not be true at the time, affirmations must support the way we wish to view ourselves. Feed the mind properly, as our mind takes us at our word.
- "I am", "I can", "I will" statements that create a positive and supportive self-reality.
- **Affirmations must meet three basic parameters. A mainstay in your 'tool box'.**
  - **Positive: To transform negative, limiting thoughts, emotions and reactions.**
  - **Present: Dealing with the here and now. Nothing else matters so 'dial in'.**
  - **Personal: We only have control over ourselves, our energy and our harvest.**

AFFIRMATIONS FOR ATHLETIC PERFORMANCE

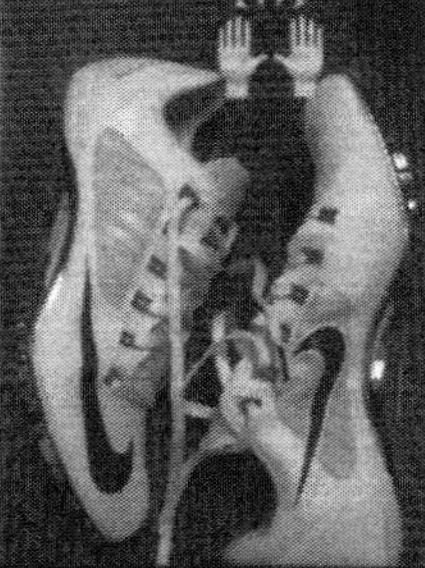

- **I am a well-trained and competent athlete.**
- **I am a strong and fluid athlete.**
- **I am relaxed and ready to go.**
- **I am reaching my goals and realizing my peak.**
- **My body is healthy and well trained.**
- **I am confident and ready.**
- **I listen to my body and it serves me well.**
- **I love and appreciate my able body.**
- **I am powerful and balanced.**
- **I am in control and focused.**
- **I am performing pain free.**
- **I am as good as any other athlete competing today.**
- **I enjoy being athletic and caring for my body.**
- **I will show poise and control my emotions.**
- **I trust my body and its durability.**
- **I will be a coachable athlete.**
- **I will be a sincere teammate.**
- **I have a winning attitude.**
- **I CAN and WILL COMPETE & CONQUER!**

Lone Survivor Quote:
**"No matter how much it hurts.
How dark it gets.
Or how far you fall.
You are never out of the fight."**

Academics ~ Sports ~ Illness & Injury Rehab ~ Social Scene ~ Relationships ~ Career

"WHAT YOU SEE IS WHAT YOU GET"
FLIP WILSON, COMEDIAN

This quote from the 'Flip Wilson Show' was chisled into my belief system from age 10. It was the Positive Intent Mantra in the original 1990 workbook and merits a reincarnation.

Teaching not only What to Think, but, How to Think, is not mearly a catch-phrase. My workshops are geared to **stir** change from within without forcefeeding. Yet, some life-altering tools, such as Positive Intent, require that I serve the info in the same manner as a James Bond martini; it must be 'shaken, not stirred'. This true strory from a supremely noble source is designed to shake you at your core and induce an instant change in your thinking habits from this day forward. **Life changing and life long.** Science based and logic based. So powerful that it needs no final thoughts or addendums from me. Ready?

"We Receive What We Believe" ~ Joel Osteen

"We receive what we believe. Unfortunately, this principle works as strongly in the negative as it does in the positive. Nick was a big, strong, tough man who worked on the railroad yards for many years. He was one of his companies' best workers. Always on time, a reliable hard worker who got along well with the other employees.

But, Nick had one major problem. His attitude was chronically negative. He perpetually feared the worst, constantly worried; fretting that something bad might happen. One summer day the crews were told that they could go home an hour early in order to celebrate the birthday of one of the foremen. All the workers left but somehow Nick accidentally locked himself inside a refrigerated box car that had been brought into the yard for maintenance. The box car was empty and not connected to any of the trains.

When Nick realized that he was locked inside the refrigerated box car, he panicked. Nick began beating on the door so hard that his arms and fists became bloodied. He screamed and screamed, but his coworkers had already gone home to get ready for the party. Nobody could hear Nick's desperate calls for help. Again and again he called out, but finally his voice was a raspy whisper. Being aware that he was in a refrigerated box car, Nick guessed that the temperature in the unit was well below freezing, maybe as low as five or ten degrees Fahrenheit. Nick feared the worst. He felt, 'what am I going do? If I don't get out of here I'm going freeze to death.' The more he thought about his circumstances, the colder he became. With the doors shut tightly and no apparent escape, he sat down to await the inevitable; death by freezing or suffocation. To pass the time he decided to chronicle his demise. He found a pen in his shirt pocket and noticed an old piece of cardboard over in the corner of the car. Shivering almost uncontrollably he scribbled a message to his family. In it, Nick noted his dire prospects. 'Getting so cold, body numb. If I don't get out soon these will probably be my last words'. And, they were.

The next morning, when the crews came to work they opened the box car and found Nick's body crumpled over in the corner. When the autopsy was completed, it revealed that Nick had indeed frozen to death.

Now here's a fascinating enigma. The investigators discovered that the refrigeration unit for the car in which Nick had been trapped was not even on. In fact, it had been out of order for some time and was not functioning at the time of the man's death. The temperature in the car that night, the night Nick froze to death, was 61 degrees. Nick froze to death in a slightly less-than-normal room temperature because he believed that he was in a freezing box car. He expected to die. For Nick, the thing he feared and expected to happen, came to pass.

Many people today are similar to Nick. They're always expecting the worst. They expect defeat. They expect failure. They expect mediocrity; and they usually get what they expect. They become what they believe. But, you can believe for good things. Drawing on the improvements you are making in your self-image, it is possible to believe for more; to see yourself performing at increasingly higher levels in every area of life. When you come into tough times don't expect to stay there. Expect to come out of that trouble. You cast the deciding vote. If you choose to stay focused on negative elements in your life. If you focus on what you can't do or what you don't have, then by your own choices you are agreeing to be defeated. Conspiring with the enemy. You are opening the door and allowing negative destructive thoughts, words, actions and attitudes to dominate your life. It's up to you. It depends on your outlook."

Joel Osteen, 'Your Best Life Now'

IMAGERY AND VISUALIZATION

"We have been endowed with the capacity and the power to create desirable pictures within, and to find them automatically printed in the outer world of our environment."

John McDonald

@MentalAthlete

"Imagination is more important than knowledge."

Albert Einstein

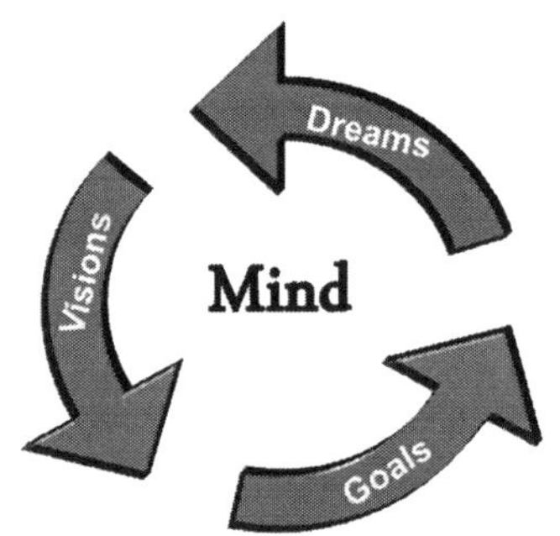

My brand of Mental Conditioning is an OPPORTUNITY to tap into, cultivate and unleash the magic of an innate human ability. We are ALL properly equipped AND equally yoked! This isn't metaphysical theory. It's the Power of the Mind. My Code!

We've all experienced awakening from a dream, or ('Jaws') nightmare, with our heart pumping, sweating, or worse yet, swinging. Let's keep it real. Some of them we wish we could revisit, while others thankfully ended. Point being, we were truly 'there'...for better or worse. Yes? Oftentimes, undesirable dreams, visions and recollections involuntarily enter our conscious (while awake) and subconscious (while sleeping) minds, which we must monitor and alter accordingly. We will cover that aspect in detail in the Emotions topic. Here, we focus on the 'voluntary'.

Imagery: 'Select Successful Situational Similes'

Imagery allows us to utilize multiple senses to create and manipulate scenarios in our minds eye with the purposeful intention of future attainment. However, 'Don't put the cart before the horse.' It is vital that we understand that visualization is the dominant component of imagery, yet, it is not the sole component. It's a subset! **See It To Be It isn't a Catch-Phrase. It's truly my life changing and life long Mantra!**

VISUALIZATION AS ANOTHER FORM OF PRACTICE

Visualization as another form of practice is a unique subset of imagery that is based on the premise of muscle memory. This is not cutting-edge information! Practiced visualization exercises are a vital part of performance preparation and anxiety reduction. In addition, its magical results are not at all limited to sports. Universal.

"Vision ~ It reaches beyond the thing that is, into the conception of what can be. Imagination gives you the picture. Vision gives you the impulse to make it your own."
Robert Collier

- The Mental Athlete is taught to experience the anticipated sights, sounds, aromas and flowing emotions in their minds eye while executing flawlessly and exuding a state of 'competent confidence'. Imagery; not just picutues. Planting seeds for future harvest.
    - Emotional Component ~ Fans ~ Refs ~ Hostile Confines ~ Pressure
    - Venue ~ Accoustics ~ Decible Levels ~ Crowd ~ Band ~ Music ~ Whistles
- Variations abound based on fluid or static situations, team sports, etiquette, contact.
- A visualization session can be for an entire event, from arrival at the venue to a locker-room routine, warm-ups, positive performance and post game. Most often we envision segmented plays, portions and scenarios targeting specific refinement to technique and sound execution of our routines, without anxiety. Again and again! Control Breathing!
- At points when your technique is flawed, timing is off, errors or mistakes are made, simply 'rewind' to moments before, 'press play', and execute the action properly. Be it.
- When the coach has drawn up a play they expect execution! Listen as you visualize your role and the role of each teammate. Have situational awareness and do your job.
- I can repeatedly visualize throwing a ball with perfect footwork, timing, release, touch, velocity and accuracy, with a changing canvas depending on if I am throwing a bowling ball to an arrow ¾ down the lane; a football into a 'window' before the receiver breaks, a basketball to a cutting teammate off the dribble, or a baseball to first base 'on a rope'!

Create a Proper Setting. Control your Breathing. Quiet your Mind. And, **See It To Be It!** We can't always be at a training venue. Visualization Creates the Venue and the Advantage.

Emulation

Beware of whom you chose to emulate and why.
From age 10, I emulated the Champions' Mettle.
Embracing the role of The Lone Ranger or Tonto;
Batman or Robin; The Cavalry or the scout team.
Goal: Vanquish via Training & Competitive Zeal

Performance & Conduct! Class & Grace! Never Opt for Style over Substance!

Ali ~ Pele ~ GG ~ Dr. J ~ 'Clyde'

Along with Jerry West, he formed one of the finest backcourts in NBA history.

Gritty
Gutsy

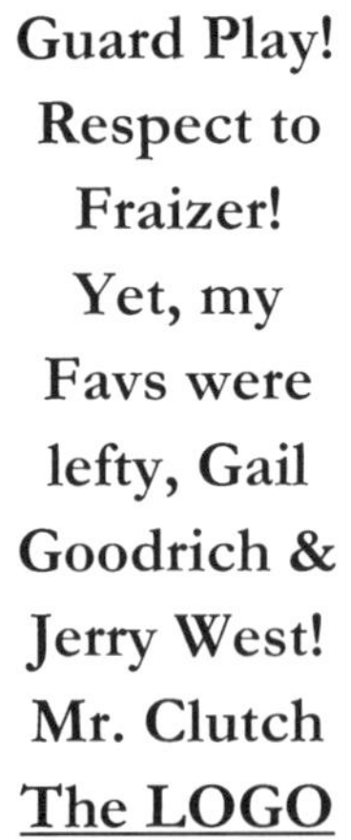

Guard Play! Respect to Fraizer! Yet, my Favs were lefty, Gail Goodrich & Jerry West! Mr. Clutch The LOGO

West's quick release made him one of the league's most dangerous jump shooters, particularly in the clutch.

Emulation

Pistol Pete Maravich: The Crux of G' Hoops

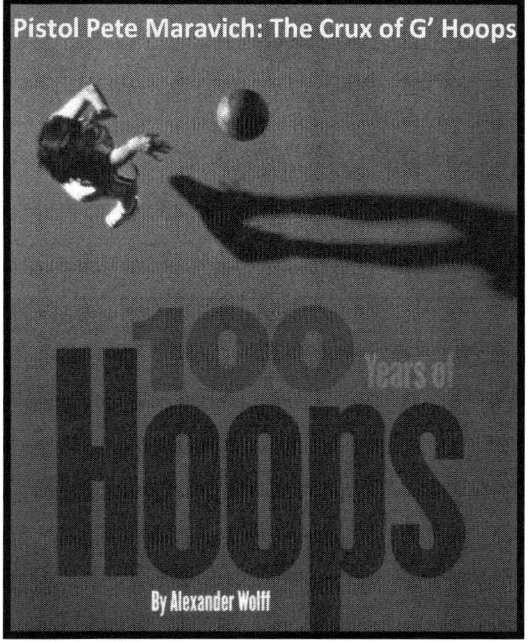

"I used to talk to Pete about conceptualizing in the game of basketball. And, you may ask what I mean by that. You've got to see one, two or three patterns ahead of time; what's going to happen." Press Maravich

'Broadway Joe' Namath: My QB BLUEPRINT

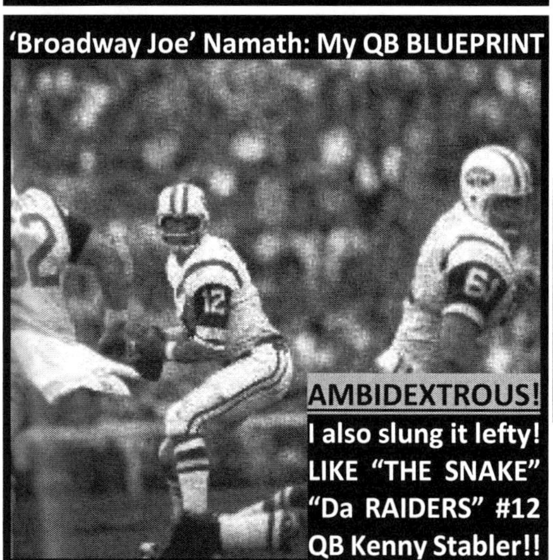

AMBIDEXTROUS!
I also slung it lefty!
LIKE "THE SNAKE"
"Da RAIDERS" #12
QB Kenny Stabler!!

Brand Emulation

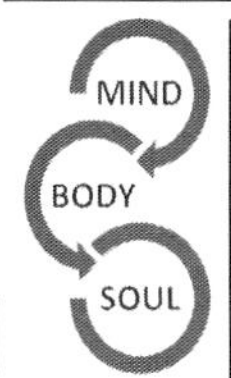

- Nike ~ Goddess of Victory!
- Gatorade ~ Win from Within!
- Porsche ~ Created to Conquer!

"We expect young athletes to emulate the best players in their sport. Unfortunately, in today's game of basketball the best players are playing for a paycheck and not for each other." Clark Kellogg ~ 2014 NBA Playoffs

MIND
BODY
SOUL

SELECTIVE EMULATION: SUBSTANCE BASED!

Style, Savvy, and the 'Champions Mettle'!! Emulate Select Skills, Psyche's & Mindsets! Don't Limit Yourself. Strong-armed QB Joe Namath had very bad knees and Pistol Pete didn't 'lock-up' on D'!

<u>Any Given Sunday: Al Pacino to J. Foxx</u>

"You're not some flash in the pan corner or receiver…you're a God damn quarterback. You know what that means? It's the top spot, Kid. It's the guy who takes the fall. It's the guy everybody's looking at first; the leader of a team. Who will support you when they understand you. Who will break their ribs and their noses and their necks for you, because they believe. Because you make them believe. That's a Quarterback!"

TOMORROW STARTS TODAY...GOT GOALS???

Qualifying Parameters for Every Goal

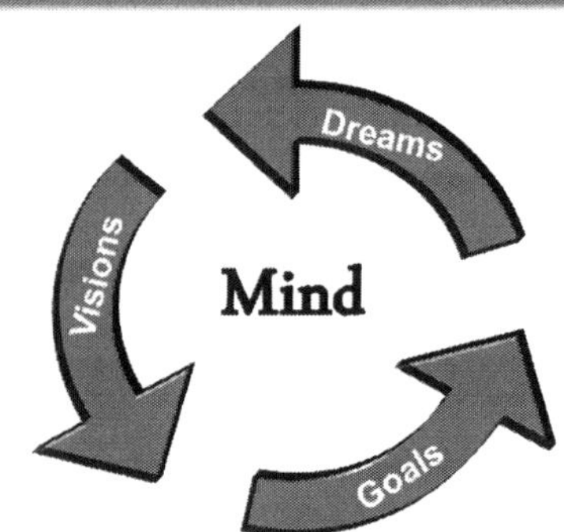

- **Measurable**
- **Within a Specific Time Frame**
- **Must Feel Realistic**

THE 5 D's TO EFFECTIVE GOAL SETTING & 'GOAL TENDING'

DREAM: **Every single quest begins with a dream. SEE IT TO BE IT!** Another word for this type of dreaming is called VISUALIZATION: High achievers and peak performers from all walks of life, master the art of transitioning what they see in their own minds-eye into a goal structuring plan, and then working that plan. We must dare to dream!

DECIDE: What do you want? To learn a new skill or improve upon existing skills? Better grades? A Club or Varsity Spot? A College Scholarship? A specific job or career pursuit? A specific sports car? Think BIG and SMALL! Be SPECIFIC! Decide today and WRITE IT DOWN!

Writing your goals down involves the application of multiple senses, which imprints a stronger, longer-lasting impression on your subconscious mind.

DEADLINE: When do you expect to achieve your goal? Some take an hour, some a day or a week. Some are a build-up over several months or even years. Set specific deadlines for achievement, as well as specific review dates to track your progress; and modify your goals.

DISCIPLINE: **A most critical trait that all successful people possess.** It establishes the true measure of commitment and desire. 'Stick-to-it-tive-ness' paves a way through doubt and over obstacles. Making prudent choices, sacrifices and changes of habit, lifestyle and schedules will require self- discipline. **Ultimately, it's about what you want and how badly!**

DAILY: Setting and Tending to goals is like good grooming; you **work** at it daily, without fail. Plug your goals and aspirations into your daily routine. Post your motivations in plain view. Constantly burn them into your subconscious mind and it will unleash its magic. **Voila**!

Goals Are Passion-Fueled! Master the verbal skills to articulate them on cue, succinctly and confidently. Humbly seek guidance and input from your 'BOD'.

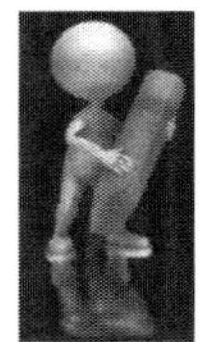

Goal Tender: 'Goal Getter'

<u>Always write down your goals.</u> List them order of priority and time frame. Place them in constant view. Consider your future educational, athletic and career aspirations and qualifications. <u>BE INTROSPECTIVE!</u> Employ Weakness Training. Classify your Goals as either Short-Term, Intermediate or Long-Term.

<u>Short-Term Goals:</u>

Very clear and specific goals aimed at being accomplished within the next month to six months. From skill attainment or improvement, training, exams, events or competitions, you still focus on the next hour, day, week and month first. Merging short-term goals is most critical, as they are often pre-requisites or building blocks to our longer-term goals.

<u>Intermediate-Term Goals:</u>

May be specific or less well-defined and require several steps to achieve. Time frame is usually within the next 6 months to a year. Fragments of these must be in your short-term.

<u>Long-Term Goals:</u>

Goals to be achieved in one year or more into the future. Dare to Dream!!!

As time goes by, our intermediate and long-term goals evolve into our short-term goals. Some are achieved, others altered or discarded. Don't worry! The main thing is that they are replaced and that we are constantly working and striving to achieve "something". Q: *What's next? Evolve-Envision-Next Level.*

<u>Goal Tending: Plan</u>

"I've had lots of players say to me, 'Coach I got this goal and that goal.' And, I ask them, 'What's your plan?' <u>A Goal Without A Plan Is a Wish!</u>"
Herman Edwards - ESPN FILMS 30 for 30 'Broke'

Next, we must create at least three 'stair-steps' or mini-goals that we deem as required prerequisites to accomplish each individual goal. These mini-goals will light a path and simplify your plan of attack towards attaining the larger goal. Place them at the foundation of your action plan and daily calendar. *<u>EVERY DAMN DAY!!!</u>*

MAKE A PLAN…NOT A WISH

"Planning"
"Bringing the future into the present,
so you can do something about it now."
Robert Klein

There is no easy path!

Thrive on Challenge

Life will challenge you regularly. Embrace that challenge with a thankful heart and a creative, resourceful mind.

Each challenge has within it great strength. Go out and meet the challenge, work your way steadily through it, and that strength becomes yours.

Challenge can be painful, inconvenient, embarrassing, tedious, and time consuming. And that same challenge also gives life much of its meaning, flavor and fulfillment.

One of the kindest things you can do for someone else is to offer a respectful meaningful challenge to that person. One of the smartest things you can do for yourself is to take on higher and higher levels of challenge.

Challenge sharpens your priorities and magnifies your performance. Lives of greatness positively thrive on challenge.

Choose to see each challenge as the opportunity for growth satisfaction and achievement that it is. The world is overflowing with challenges and inside each challenge you'll find truly immense value.

Ralph Marston

OBSTACLES: DEF. N. SOMETHING THAT STANDS IN THE WAY OF, OR OBSTRUCTS, PROGRESS.

They come in many forms. From the subtle and low key to the clear and obvious. Some are real and tangible, while others are based on perceptions or opinions; created and existing only in our minds. This is human nature. They can appear out of nowhere or be highly anticipated. In times of rest, in training, or in 'crunch time' of a competition. The demanding coach, the pressure to perform, team dysfunction, hostile crowds, officiating, injuries, and the curse of our past athletic 'clutch failures', are just a few examples of the various forms and faces obstacles may present themselves. **This is not limited to sports.**

> ***"No man can choose the cards he's dealt,***
> ***You either fold them;***
> ***Or play them as you get them."***
> **Dr. Dre**

Obstacles, in all forms, are normal inherent tests and trials on the path towards the attainment of our goals and aspirations. Remember: It's not what happens to us that is most important; it's all about how we interpret and react to it. This one therapeutic mindset perspective will change your life and well-being. We must raise our level of 'self-awareness', monitor our emotions, filter our reactions, stay positive, and manage the cards we are dealt. We have choices. Do we sulk and complain about the 'unfairness'? Or, do we suck it up, lick our wounds, get mentally tough and find a way to persevere? Again, the eyes are on us at all times, especially in times of adversity so, 'chin up'. Pay your dues, and do keep your faith!

SOME DAYS SPORTS SUCK!!!

Our athletic path, like life, will be a series of peaks and valleys. Factually, we cannot experience the peaks of significant achievement and success unless we have paid our dues and suffered through the deep valleys of underachievement, pain, injury, true heartache, embarrassment and criticism. Beyond that, we cannot truly recognize, nor appreciate, the peaks unless we have truly experienced the doubt, despair and disappointment that are an inherent byproduct of the path to becoming a high achiever, in any endeavor. Yes, the greater the challenge, the sweeter the victory. Bask in it. Yet, even in those moments of triumph and attainment, we ponder what's next? The Mental Athlete Mindset is uniquely geared to the perception: 'Win or lose, the best is yet to come; peaks are merely plateaus.'

Peer & Parental Pressure

You Can't Mute Your Parent!

2015 Las Vegas Classic AAU U15
Lady stands up and barks loudly: "I've paid too much DAMN money for you all to be playing like this!"

Every sport, every team, every clique has a few parents who simply behave badly. It's a rampant, escalating unsavory part of sports, and an inherent source of anxiety for athletes. **Negative sideline coaching & comments. Blatant verbal criticisms. High Emotion.** Those antics are impossible to simply 'Block Out' and refocus. They impact ZEAL! I have no true solutions except to keep your chin up despite the angst and embarrassment and keep your eye on the prize. Savior Psyche: The Love of Competition. No sugar-coating! **You can't mute your parents. Don't Try!** It's Fruitless! Bite Thy Tongue. **Say a Prayer!**

2015 Las Vegas Classic AAU U15
Dad tells his son on the court to tuck in his jersey. Son says, 'It is tucked in.' Dad tells coach to sub him, then orders his son to, "Get your ass outside!" PARKING LOT!

Sport Specific Parent Etiquette

In some sports you can't hear your parents. In some sports you can't help but hear them. **In some sports you wish you couldn't hear or see them. RANTS and GESTURES!**

G'13: My Teammates Loved Papa Scott's Chant of 'Go to Work!'

Gab 'Code Phrases': Sprint! Protect your Space. Head on a Swivel. Good Job!
"I loved having my Dad watch me compete. He inspired me and my teams."
"Pops expertly dug into my heart and brain to unleash the Mental Athlete."

Parents Peer Pressure & Youth Sports

THE WALL STREET JOURNAL SUNDAY
Keeping Up With the Joneses' Kid
Love & Money / *By Jeff D. Opdyke*

Noble Intent Is No Excuse! Parents surely invest huge amounts of time, money and sacrifice to give their kids the best opportunity to succeed in sports. I feel that pain! They want a Return on Investment. A scholarship! Kids: Stay Sane & Keep on Striving!!

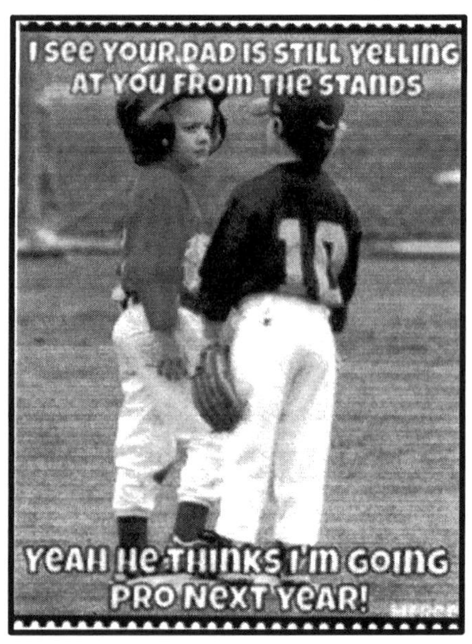

Monitoring Your Emotions

"What State Are You In?" *Anthony Robbins*

This perpetual question has nothing to do with geography or government.

We must develop a mental approach to effectively recognize, channel and combat our negative emotions and reactions that we naturally, and sometimes justifiably, want to express. To do this we must constantly and honestly 'update' ourselves of where we are (the cards), where we are headed (our goals), how badly we want to get there, and why. These are the times when we must apply our 'mental game'. It is critical to make use of our written goals, affirmations and visual aids to find direction, instill motivation and 'positive intent' to help you manage the inevitable anxiety that accompanies each and every quest, opportunity and obstacle. No Angst! Justly continue to put those positive impressions on the brain. Again, self-awareness, mental toughness and perseverance are learnable traits. Beyond that, they are all vital prerequisites for significant achievement in any endeavor or pursuit.

Mom Quote

"Don't waste $100 of emotion on a $10 problem."

The ability to throttle down our emotions, manage adrenalin and zest, is just as critical as lighting the fire within. Often we are too geeked up or overhyped. Poise: calm under fire. Again, this is a constant challenge of self-awareness; not about mastering or masking our true emotions, both impossible objectives. We're not robots. It's keenly monitoring and channeling 'valid' emotions for the greater good. The task at hand beckons. Next Play!

- Monitor your body language! Great Mom Quote: "Baby, **you pout loud**. Being silent doesn't mean you're not communicating to everyone, exactly how you feel." Truism!

- The microscope intensifies in times of adversity and the agony of defeat; victory too!

- **Sage Sparks: "G', you may have some bad moments, but never a bad game!"**

"You may have some bad moments, but never a bad game"

"Vous pouvez avoir de mauvais moments, mais jamais un mauvais match"

Performance Blockers

"Confront your fears, list them and get to know them.
And, only then will you be able to put them aside and move ahead."

Jerry Gillies

- **Negative Self-Talk ~ Body Language ~ Loss of Concentration**
- **Past Performances:** STOP LOOKING IN THE REARVIEW MIRROR!
  - **Heartbreaking Defeats ~ Costly Mental & Physical Errors**
  - **Choking ~ Panic ~ Fatigue ~ Anxiety in 'Clutch' Situations**
- **Fear of Failure & Fear of Success**
- **'Pressure' & Expectations from Outside Sources**
  - **Coaches ~ Assistant Coaches ~ Wannabe Coaches**
  - **Parents ~ Family ~ Mentors ~ Advisors ~ Agents**
  - **Peers ~ Friends ~ Fans ~ Cliques ~ 'Hangers-On'**
  - **Scouts ~ Sponsors ~ Alumni ~ Investors ~ Recruiters**
- **Focusing 'Outside the Lines'**
  - **On 'Home Turf' ~ At Neutral Sites ~ In Hostile Confines**
  - **Social Media Influence ~ Think Before You Tweet & Post!**
- **'Fools Gold' & Miscellaneous Consequences 'Inside the Lines'**
  - **Team Dysfunction, Discord and Intestinal Fortitude Level**
  - **Style over Substance ~ Celebration ~ 'Trash Talk' ~ Anger**
  - **Lack of Fundamentals ~ Lack of Fitness ~ Lack of Fuel**

◆ **BAD OFFICIATING: MY PERSONAL SELF-INFLICTED KRYPTONITE**

Performance Blockers

"Concentrate on one thing at a time and rule out all outside influences that don't have any real bearing on the task at hand."

Marty Liquori

In school, in sports or at work, when your mind inevitably wonders to outside infuences or the rear-view mirror, recognize it, dial in, and refocus. **Engage in this moment, soley!**

The Ebb & Flow of Competition

- Competing versus a superior opponent, when you're down but not out. Inspire a Comeback!
- Competing in a close back-and-forth battle of will, fortitude and crunch-time stress. Finish it.
- Competing at 'Your Speed'; intensity level, against inferior foes or lower ranked 'underdogs'.
    - Don't play down to the level of your competition. If you're better; then DOMINATE!
- **Killer Instinct: Sage Sparks,** "When you have your opponents down, you've got to be willing to step on their throats. Make it clear for next time: Any Day, Any Venue. Break their spirit!"

Compounding Errors ~ Frustration Fouls & Penalties ~ Anger

"I AM NOT CONCERNED THAT YOU HAVE FALLEN. I AM CONCERNED THAT YOU WILL RISE AGAIN."
ABRAHAM LINCOLN

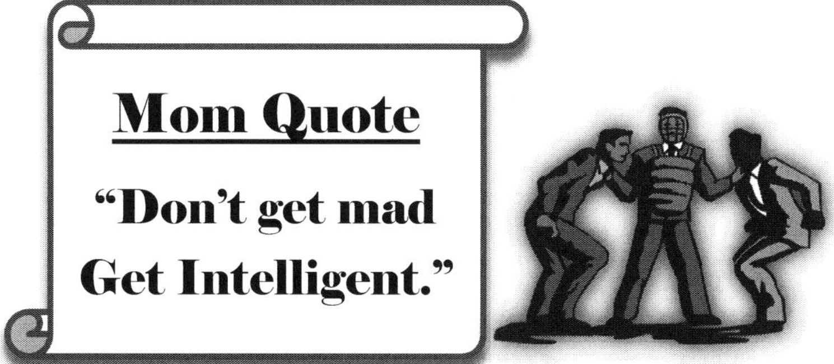
Mom Quote
"Don't get mad
Get Intelligent."

1996: At home in Wiesbaden, I was mortified as I watched a EuroSport TV clip of a pro player missing a lay-up and, in anger, he head-butts the padded basket support and then collapses to the floor; PARALYZED! True Story!!!

Perform in the Clutch: 'Be willing to be the Hero or the Goat'!

Grammar Speaks Volumes

The Declining Age & Art of Interpersonal Communication

No Red Marker: My parents were adament about our personal grammar but not anal nor overbearing. Our ettiquette, articulation and social graces were a reflection of them and was at the baseline of our core conditioning. Still, knowing the time, place and setting for 'appropriate lingo' with a refined ability to articulate well, are traits worthy of cultivating. My mom was gifted with a nurturing and informative manner of correction which was always aided by a concise quip that made it stick within your memory. I've emulated that.

Yet, I watched a TV movie in 2013 that spoke of a lady who was a mother, wife, lifelong teacher and tutor with the noblest of intents and a great following. Sullenly, she lacked any type of 'Bedside Manner', and had no regard for (pre-correction) cushioning. The movie portraid her reputation as being soiled by her judgemental reactions to, and calculatingly critical corrections of, spoken and written grammar miscues. Mostly, she was known for the blantant and offensive use of her **'Red Marker', which was her 'weapon of choice'**.

I share this story because at one point she blurted out one over-the-top correction to her own son that literally appalled me, as she went from endearing mom to 'Mommy Dearest'.

- **Son (respectfully) "I'm already done with my homework, mom."**
- **Mommy Dearest (angrily) "You're Done? Meat is Done; People are Finished!"**

I remember smiling to myself and being thankful that my mom was never so harsh or overbearing. In that very moment I had the thought that this alloof educator's toxic mix of a malicious tongue and a 'Red Marker' could drive a kid to either runaway or commit suicide. Sometimes my intuition scares me. The movie plot took a twist as the son went on a shooting rampage at his school, killed classmates, commited suicide, and left no note.

"There are three reasons we make mistakes; don't know, don't care, or not able. Ignorance, Apathy, or Ability."

Mike Davis

❖ Beware of the 'Double Negative', especially using with 'ain't'; Mom frowned on ain't!

We must adapt our communication skills, swag and verbiage to our environment and cultivate the ability to 'flip our script' in a moment's notice. From "yes" to "truedat" to "yeah brah", as the case may be. Good grammar on L.A. hoop courts or at the skating rink on Crenshaw could get your ball or your skates taken from you. Proper English in Hawaii is suspect. Fact: Ain't no party like the after party!

Mom Quote

**"Beware of Profanity.
It takes people's attention
away from your point of view,
and places their focus on your emotion."**

"Still, there is a time and a place for it!"

Double-Negative with Ain't Caveat: A Masterful Triple-Negative via the film, 'Lincoln'!

Son: 'I have to do this and I will do it, and I don't need your permission to enlist.'

Abraham Lincoln reply:

"That exact same speech has been made by so many sons to so many fathers since the war began;

'I don't need your damn permission you miserable old goat, I'm going to enlist anyhow!'

And, what would those numberless fathers have given to be able to say to their son, as I now say to mine;

I'm the Commander in Chief! So, in point of fact, without my permission, you ain't enlisting in nothing, nowhere, young man!"

SPEAKING VS. ARTICULATING

Mom Quote

"It's better to remain silent and be thought of as a fool, than to open your mouth and remove all doubt."

So many times I would regret asking my parents the correct spelling or definition of a word or term. Immediately I'd wish I could retract the question. There was no Google back then. In our family home, we had, not only multiple bibles, dictionaries and thesauruses at hand, but a wall-full of the Encyclopedia Britannica. Yes! Kids, ask your parents, or grandparents. Still, what seemed like a noble form of child abuse has paid huge lifelong dividends. In homage to my great mom, I respectfully and humbly offer you these 'Grammar Difference Makers', for your due consideration and timely application. **Rule #1: Always Consider Your Audience!!!**

"Please and Thank You should be the most-used words in your vocabulary"

- **"How are you?", "I'm well". As opposed to saying the typical, "I'm good."**
  - **Well:** positive disposition, mood or outlook. Caveat: "Blessed" also works.
  - **Good:** conduct, performance or deeds. **This is NOT a trivial difference.**
- **The "Can I?" versus "May I?" Conundrum**
  - Can I? Incorrect- Asking about the **ability** to do something. Can I go to...?
    - My Mom: "Yes, you can. But, that doesn't grant you permission."
  - May I? Correct in asking for **permission** to do something. May I go to…?
- **Mark and I vs. Mark and me: Version that allows each to correctly stand alone.**
  - **Mark and I went to the park. Mark went to the park. I went to the park.**
  - **Come with Mark and me to the park. Come with Mark. Come with me.**
- Don't say "ummm". Simply Listen, Think & Articualate ~ Gather your thoughts!
- Don't reply to a Q with, "You know…"; If they knew, they wouldn't be asking you.
- Don't be compelled to reply to (bait) statements or opinions disguised as questions.
- **Cheap is Quality ~ Inexpensive is Cost; A low price doesn't mean low quality.**

A true hot button for me. Ok, there're cable networks advertising 'more movie & less commercials', and sports drinks touting 'less calories'; that's pure hyperbole.

> **"There are less innings" -brief pause-**
> **"There are <u>fewer</u> innings, actually,**
> **in the National League because of the**
> **designated hitter rule in the American League."**
>
> **Tony Kornheiser**
>
> **PTI on ESPN**
>
> **Spring 2013 ~ Regarding (P) Stephen Strasburg**

◆ <u>Less is Volume and Fewer is Numbers!</u>

Being a 'Friend of the Program', as they chant, this "shout out" goes to Mr. Kornheiser for his sage save of this common error. I interpreted his brief pause as uttering 'less' just felt wrong, and his correction was instinctual. Similar to inbounding the basketball underneath the backboard; feels odd.

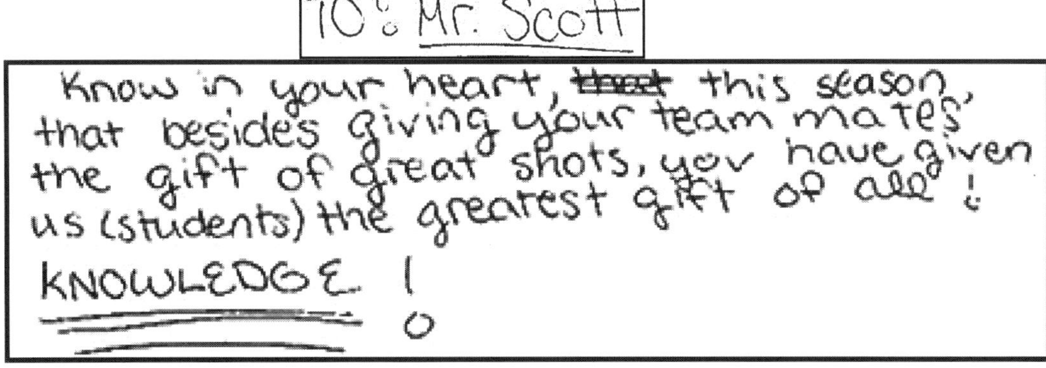

TO: Mr. Scott
Know in your heart, this season, that besides giving your team mates the gift of great shots, you have given us (students) the greatest gift of all!
KNOWLEDGE !

- ❖ **PLURAL…one or multiple: Fruit ~ Sheep ~ Deer ~ Shrimp ~ <u>FISH</u>**
- ❖ **The 'S' is Silent: Des Moines (Iowa) & (Chicago) Illinois.**

ARTICULATION HAS NO ETHNICITY

"Perception is Reality."
"Remember, it is not what you say or how you say it, but rather, what is heard that is important."

Ian Gray

The 'Silver Lining' from this unsavory true tale from Germany in '96 took seven years.

Paul Hallgrimson had arranged a try-out for me with the Head Coach (NB) for a 1st Bundeliga club named, Tus' Hurten, in northern Germany. I personally spoke with the coach TWICE at Paul's home via phone, confirming a Wednesday evening team training and my return on Friday to travel and play with the club in a tounament in Belgium. Tus' Hurten would pay my travel expenses for both the Wednesday and Friday commute at the end of the Wednesday training session. Point being, a workout and tourney commitement.

Tus' Herten Coach Hoodwinked by my Ethnicity via Telephone

Upon our arrival at the club, Puig and I were met with a shocked, yet, friendly greeting from the manager of the club. He is the coaches' boss and the money man. His first words, "Pardon my reaction, as I am a bit mortified. I understand that Coach has spoken with you several times, and you're on our roster for the Belgium tournament this weekend. Still, I must be upfront and honest with you about this coach. He does not take black players." I was dumbfounded and grateful. Does my ethnicity not come across a the telephone?

At the team training I meet an bond well with the team. Then I meet the coach. He was warm and friendly with no apparent negative vibe. Suffice it to say, I put in work to the point that in the lockerroom the team and I were celebrating in anticipation of the tourney.

As I return to the gym and get a confirming hug from Puig, we wait. The coach and Manager met with two German players. Then, only the Manager comes to us. "I'm ashamed to tell you that there is no playing opportunity for you here. Coaches decision. I'm very sorry."

Don't kill the messenger. 'Thank you.' I got paid. **Tus' got a Barry!**

Silver Lining: NBA HOF Rick Barry via Scooter!

2003: San Diego Airport Pre-flight to Honolulu for the NFL Pro Bowl Weekend fest in Hawaii. Rick next to me. 'I played in Germany and read your son Scooter was killing it with Tus' Hurten.' Instant credibility, rapport and a heartfelt convo!

Autographed Poster
"Gregg, Have Much Success with your Radio Show! Best Wishes, Rick Barry ~ HOF"

VERBALIZATION

An art and a required trait that requires a different voice based on the specific sport and specific position(s) played in that sport.

- Be a Quarterback: Confident, Calm and Clear 'Communication Skills' are Critical.
  - Verbiage ~ Volume ~ Clarity ~ Tone ~ Voice Inflection ~ Tempo
  - Inspire ~ Leadership without Criticism ~ Poise under fire & duress!
  - Know **every** players assignment on **each** play in the **entire playbook**.
  - Communication is intense, hyped-up and at times profane! Schematics!

Display Self-Awareness and Leadership!

- **Beware of emotional outbursts clouding your essence or intent.**
- **Don't Embarrass Teammates! No one like to be yelled at or belittled, especially in public.**
- **Absorb criticism without angst.**

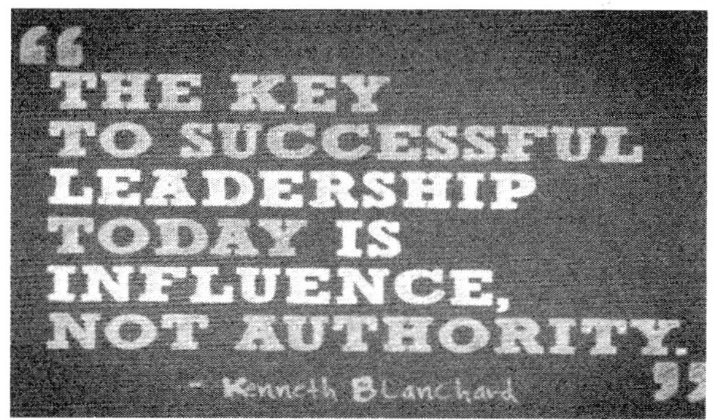

Trash-talking ~ Taunting ~ Excessive Celebration Silly Injuries

- Communicate; Don't Instigate
- Verbalize; Don't Antagonize
- Avoid Spewing Bulletin Board Material
- Don't write verbal checks that your 'game' or your teammates' 'game'/guts can't cash.
- Celebration Folly has Costly Consequences!

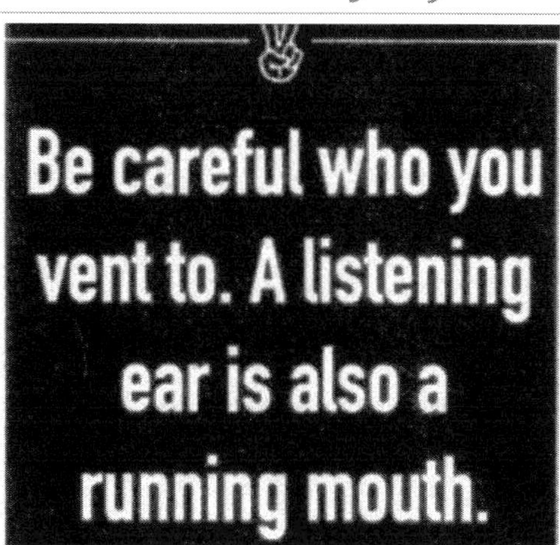

Remember: Talk is Cheap!

G$ TBoz Truism: "Don't Talk About It. Be About It!"

GAMESPEAK ~ View your Opponent as an Adversary, not an Enemy!

Mental Athlete Role:

CEO OF BRAND 'YOU'

CEO
Chief Executive Officer

Board of Directors

Parents & Family
Director(s) of:
Finance / Transportation
Nutrition / Education

Coaches & Trainers
Director(s) of:
•Playing Time and Ability
•Health & Rehabilitation

Mentors & Advisors
Director(s) of:
Sage Advice / Motivation
Academics / Marketing

Managing Critical Relationships

Coaches
- Not always 'nurturing'!
- **Be Coachable**
- Stepping Stone

Teammates
- Embrace Differences
- Build Rapport & Trust
- Understand Synergy

Officials & Referees
- Manage 'Human Failings'
- Think "Next Play"
- **Performance Blocker??**

Fans & Suitors
- Definition: Fanatics
- Recruiters / Agents
- Sponsors / Media

Return on Investment (ROI)

Student-Athlete
- Badge of Honor
- Time Management Skills
- Study Habits & Work Ethic
- **Defy Peer/Parent Pressure**

Road Trips & Gear Prep
- Master Calandar/Itinerary
- Pack Early with VISION
- Enjoy the Journey
- **Biz Trip: Compete!**

Take the helm, the cockpit or the driver's seat for the Venture of YOUR Life! Managing others begins with managing 'self'. As CEO, you are the 'Subject Matter', not the Boss. Your BOD has the Ultimate Control and VETO Power!

"Efforts and courage are not enough without purpose and direction".

John F. Kennedy

CEO of Brand 'YOU'

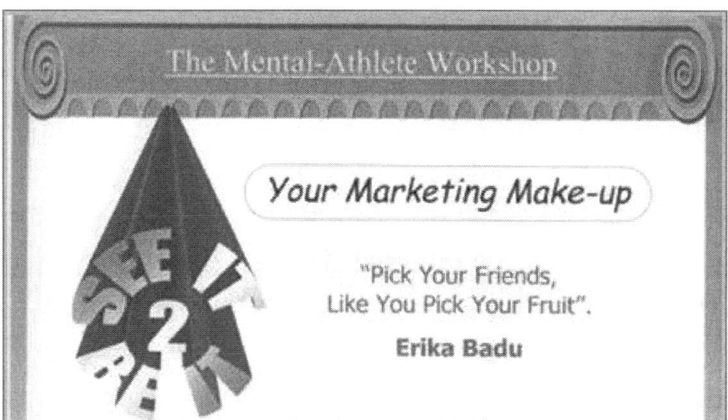

By default, you are the point person for an entity consisting of YOU, supplemented by your BOD, embarking on a venture that encapsulates your dreams, visions, goals and aspirations. Clearly, it's the role of your life, literally and figuratively, and should always be viewed from a management perspective. As CEO you will constantly make decisions and choices which chart your course, determine your marketability and, ultimately dictate whether, or to what extent, people want to do 'business' with you. Make no mistake, your social skills, behavior, and articulation, as well as what you wear and with whom you associate, on campus as well as online, is often more critical to the 'next level' decision makers than your physical talents.

- Beware: 'Freedom of Expression' in representing yourself and your 'peeps' via tweets, postings, provacative profiles, regretable tats, piercings, and profanity.
- Do consider whether or not your representation is enticing to coaches, suitors, mentors, clubs and sponsors who possess the helping hands, $$$, and contacts.

Board of Directors – BOD

My BOD definition is critical here. Some would use the term 'support system', and that is partially correct as they do provide 'support' in a multitude of ways. BOD is profound. With **Positive Intent**, your 'Mental Athlete BOD' serve to provide direction, knowledge and motivation that lights your path and your 'inner fire'. To soley give support is to give a 'hand out'. The Mental Athlete has a BOD that provide a 'hand up', as well as timely inspiration to keep your head up. They support in times of need and sorrow, yes. Still, more importantly, they inspire the eye of the tiger, set the bar, provide a platform, and they sense when you're primed and ready to be propelled forward, beyond your beliefs. Always noble and with your best interest at heart. The Mental Athlete's BOD may best be defined as a constantly evolving omnipotent springboard to your future. **Mutually Manage Well.**

Parents

Opportunities can be gained and lost via the role, attitude and behavior of parents!

Veto Power ~ Dictating your Choices!
Living Vicariously ~ Career/Absentee

Coaches

Confidence and zeal can be gained and lost via the role, attitude and behavior of coaches!

- **Head Coaches: Bennie Davenport, Jimmy Yagi, Gene Heliker, Joe Burton, Holger H.**
- **Asst. Coaches: Savior/Buffer: Jeff Davis ~ Ricky Birdsong; *OR* Saboteur: Bill O'Rear**
- **Personal Coaches ~ Specialty Mentoring: Walt Hazzard ~ Ron Kiino ~ Don Sparks**
- **Trainers & Conditioning Coaches: Rick Mendini ~ Linda Rowan ~ Jeff & Marlena Lee**
- **Private Training Coaches: Dave Lewis ~ Leon Wood ~ Isaac 'Bud' Stallworth**
- **Peripheral Coaches ~ Other Sports: Jerry Kendall UA Head Baseball Coach '82**
- **Opposing Coaches: John Thompson ~ Denny Crum ~ Dale Brown ~ George Raveling**

COACH
"A PERSON WHO INSTRUCTS OR TRAINS AN ATHLETE OR PERFORMER, ETC."

Let's not be misled by the vague 'definition' of a coach. **This title merits more clarity!**

Where do I begin? The rare breed that is at once a mentor, teacher and nurturer? Those who believe in you, challenge you, drive, guide, and motivate you while always sincerely having your best interest at heart. Or, the cold reality of those who have 'fits' and temper tantrums, play head games, utilize criticism via sarcasm, or worse; the foul-mouthed evil intimidators who literally lose their minds periodically. I will not sugar-coat anything, and my related stories in this book are truly 'better than fiction'. In all my years of playing, from the youth 'rec leagues', thru high school and college and overseas, there are only a hand-full of 'coaches' that I actually bonded with and liked. Yet, that's okay. It's more important to respect them than it is to like them. Often times it's a love-hate relationship at best. A few, I only spoke to using their first name. The coaches' job and obligation is to lead, teach, motivate and instill discipline, yet, many fall short of the mark. **Tread by aptly.**

- The Mentor ~ Teacher ~ Nurturer ~ Motivator ~ Strategist ~ Grinder ~ 'Miyagi'
- **Pedigree ~ Knowledge ~ Strategy ~ Leadership ~ Emphasis on Winning**
- **Dr. Jekyll & Mr. Hyde** ~ Temperamental ~ Profane ~ 'Psycho' ~ Intimidators
- **Recruiter-to-Coach Transformation:** Led Astray, Hoodwinked & Bamboozled
- Head Games ~ Spiteful ~ Sarcasm ~ Blatant Criticism ~ Envy ~ 'Coaches Pets'

Trainers & Health BOD:

Opportunities can be gained and lost via the role, knowledge and expertise of trainers!

Caretakers of wellness, preventative maintenance, rehabilitation, motivation, fitness education and inside information.

OASIS Sports Medical Group, Inc.
5471 Keamy Villa Road, Suite 200
San Diego, CA 92123

℞ To succeed you must work harder than those who are smartest and be smarter than those who work harder.

A wise quote for my book from my foot surgeon: KENT A. FELDMAN, DPM

Mentors & Agents ~ 'Fiduciary' Relationships

- **Power Mentors- Springboard to unimaginable opportunities. Be Loyal!**
- **Sports Agents- Initiators and Negotiators of utmost importance! Fiduciary!**
- **Travel Agents & Itineraries ~ Sports Information & Public Relations Staff**

Academic Advisors & Counselors

A key to your future that must be prioritized. Beware of trivial, non-transferable courses. Cultivate this relationship with zeal at every academic institution you attend. Matriculate!

Teachers & Professors

Manage dutifully and individually. **Don't be naïve!** Some don't embrace student-athletes! Communicate your commitment to academics and any schedule conflicts early and often.

Sponsors, Endorsements & Advisors of the Global Pro Athlete

Gear & Shoe Reps ~ Technology Advantages of Gear: **Nike reigns supreme, globally!**

Calendar Availability ~ Contracts ~ Commitments ~ Compensation ~ Commissions ~ $

Travel & Transfers ~ Meals & Accommodations ~ Weather & Climate ~ Security & $$$

Lawyers ~ Doctors ~ Financial Advisors ~ CPA's ~ Bankers ~ Realtors ~ Charities

'Brand You'! Rapport Building! Marketibility! **Based on Sustained Elite Performance!**

Fanatics: Manage your Celebrity! ~ Sparks Testament: Stalker

"G' had a stalker at the U of A when he was only 18. She called herself, **The Stranger**."

Managing Critical Relationships

Coaches

@MentalAthlete

"Players and parents need to know what a coach stands for; and what he or she won't stand for".

Gregg Scott ~ Global Hoops

Cultivating a fruitful relationship is utmost critical and challenging! Be Coachable! Covet the few who you'd run through a brick wall for!

Teammates: A bond like no other

Your comrades at arms; fellow warriors; brothers & sisters beyond genetics; **your family**. While, evey family has its dysfunctions, without a doubt the fondest memories are those shared with your teammates. The trials and tribulations, training, travel and meals shared must be coveted. Even solo sport performers must train and 'team' with others. Engage!

- Know Your Personel: Skillsets ~ Abilities ~ Physical Limitations ~ Work Ethic
- Know Your Teammate: Psyche ~ Temperament ~ Inner Fortitude ~ Clutch Play

Every family has its dysfunction. Chemistry is crucial, but being friends is not required. In 9/97, I signed with TV Kirchenbolanden. In a '95 game vs. TVK, I had to 'sanitize' a dirty player with overt vigilante justice. Now, he'd be my teammate. Analogy to Rodman:

"You don't have to love them, just manage a working relationship focusing only on winning."
Scottie Pippen ~ Nike Hoop Heroes, Dortmund '97

'Blue': Referees, Umpires & Officials...Advice via 'The Cool Ref"

Moniter your words, volume, tone, body language & eye contact. **Consequences Loom! "Call it both ways" is an insult! ~ Don't be demonstrative or touch the refs/umps!**

Fans & Suitors ~ Recruiters ~ Agents ~ Sponsors ~ Media

The eyes are always on you. Be Humble. Be Honest. Be on time! Be Marketable! Be You! It amazes me when AAU players curse on the court with college scouts in the front row.

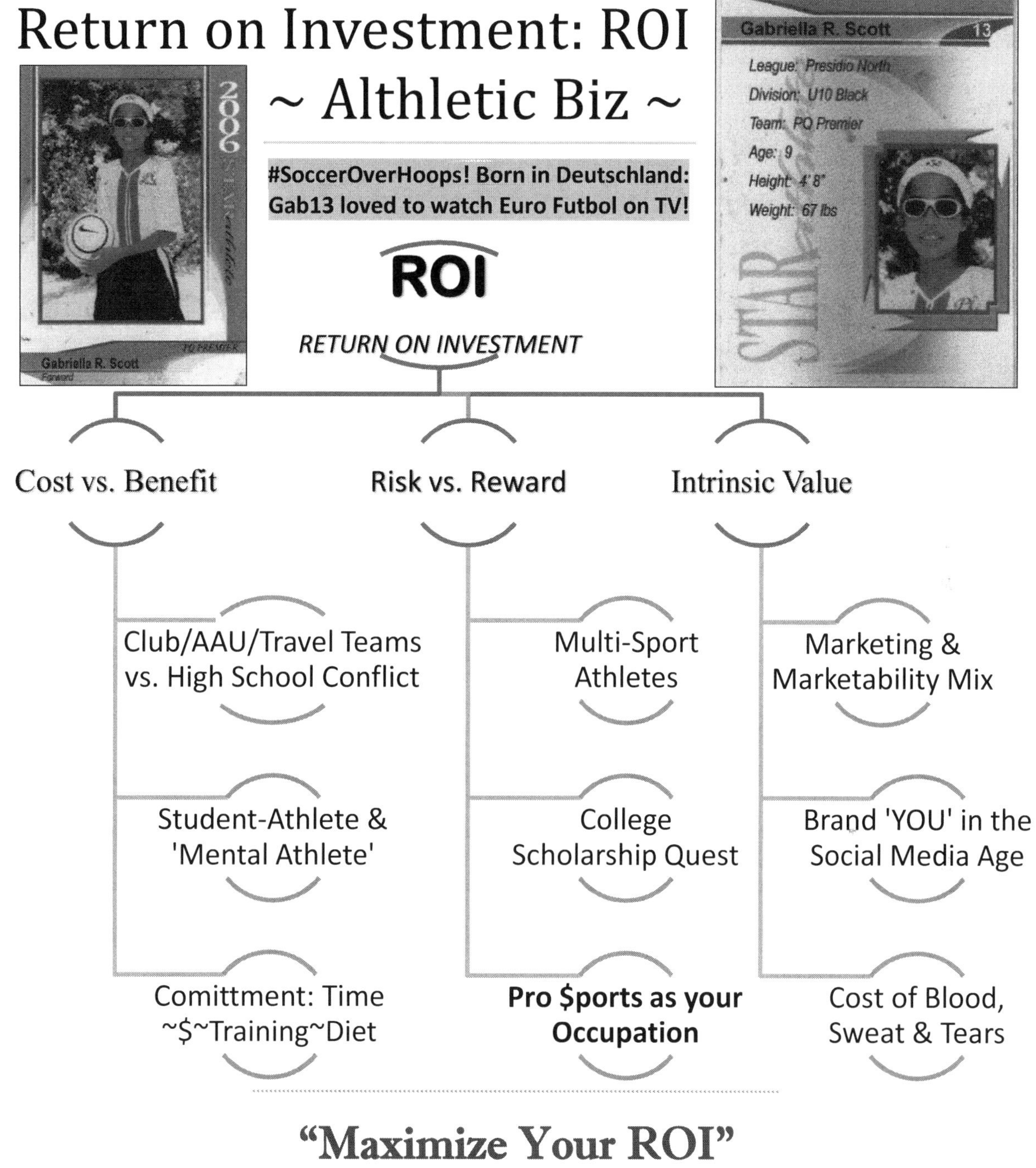

Every sports team, school or organization you compete for is a business entity with its own unique culture. All serve as 'Channels of Distribution' for exhibiting your talent and marketing 'Brand You'. Navigate your course!

Cost vs. Benefit:
Risk vs. Reward:
Intrinsic Value: Internally rewarding; Beyond dollars & sense.

Intrisic Value: 2013 Dictionary Def. 'essential' *Orig. Latin Root Def: **'Inner or Inward'**

Club/AAU/Travel Team$

The Changing Landscape

- A necessary evil in a pursuit of exposure, skill development & a collegiate quest.
  - Competitive sports at the youth level have created unsavory elements in today's ***games***.
  - Gone are the days of college scouts roaming high school campuses searching for talent.
  - Seek to train with and compete against the highest caliber of competition and tourneys.
- Your choice of club teams will provide opportunities and inherent ramifications.
  - A top-tier club may provide exposure but not necessarily a top-tier coach for your team.
  - Playing 'second string' for a top-tier club minimizes 'ROI'…'playing time' is Priority One!
  - Choosing to play for a club that your HS coach doesn't endorse could cost you a V' spot!
    - This is based on dollars and sensitivities. The majority of today's HS Varsity coaches have a Club/Travel/AAU affiliation that trumps their HS obligations financially, and skews their lens of objectivity when scorned or sensing treason.
  - Changing clubs as you evolve as an athlete can sprout from a need or an opportunity.

PLAYING FOR A CLUB/AAU/TRAVEL TEAM THAT YOUR HS VARSITY COACH DOES NOT 'ENDORSE' COULD COST YOU A VARSITY SPOT…TREASON!

- Consider club culture, costs, coaching quality, commute, practice time / facilities.
- Manage your goals and objectives within the club. Monitor conduct and 'gossip'!
  - **It's a team sport, but it's not; Team Championships & 1st Team All-Tournament.**
- Recognize the organizational hierarchy, politics, power-plays and dysfunctions.
  - Players and parents have various goals, objectives, motivations and (ulterior) motives.
  - Player selections and playing time will NOT always be based on talent and skillsets.
  - Have a voice in determining how your $$$ and time will be spent:
    - Which local & national tourneys, showcases and qualifiers will you compete in?
    - Mandatory team meals, snack bar, contributions, fundraising, carpooling, etc.
    - Road Trips: Itinerary - Travel and Accommodations costs, options & limitations!

Competing multiple times per day over multiple days requires a unique mind and body approach.

Exhausting Road Trips: 6 am wake-up calls, Win or Go Home; Champions are crowned on Sundays!

Student-Athlete & 'Mental Athlete'

Oxymoron: From grade school through college a noble title of Student-Athlete is applied. Supposedly, pursuing academic matricualtion is first and foremost, with sports considered as 'extra-curricular' activities. That naive notion surely becomes skewed as athletic pursuits often dictate or override academic motivations; and have a greater influence on self-image.

We must have balance in all that we do. Yet, merging academics and competitive sports requires a unique breed of will. A breed willing to study and **shed blood, sweat and tears.**

G'13: Del Mar Sharks

U10 thru U15 ~ Jr. High ~ Middle School

- By age 10, competitve $ports has become an 'All In' busine$$ venture for families. **Club, AAU & Travel!**
- **Daily Multi-Tasking:** School ~ Training ~ Travel ~ Compete ~ Rehab ~ Study: Textbooks/Playbooks/Film

U15 thru U18 ~ Prep ~ High School

Some nights you'll be too exhausted or too sore to study. Sleep and wake up early!

Beware: Athletes and families now move across town and across the country seeking the 'right' program, club, coach or institution soley to best leverage their athletic aspirations.

For me, the most highly coveted 'badge of honor' is a school letterman's jacket!! It's the ultimate sign of the Student-Athlete on campus and, moreso, on road trips.

- A letterman's jacket is not SWAG! It's earned, not given. Represented, not just worn.

School Spirit ~Teamwork ~Performance ~Commitment ~Sacrifice ~Discipline

- Student-Athlete: GPA ~ SAT ~ ACT ~ Honors ~ Major ~ College Prep Courses
- Mental-Athlete: Sustained Elite Performance ~ Marketibility

Gab'13 2011: *T*en years, tens of thousands of dollar$ invested and D-1 scholarships on the table! Westview High Frosh MVP and Rancho Santa Fe Attack's All-Star Phenom!! With tears in her eyes my G'13 said, "Daddy, I want to quit soccer to play club and high school volleyball and run track." 'Follow your heart, baby.'

Multi-Sport Athletes

Multiple Training Sessions, Competitions and Commitments, in the Same Day! All is in Flux for Athletes with Multi-Sport Talent!

- **Not all coaches and factions will be in harmony with your limited availability.**
- **Calendar conflicts must be recognized, communicated and managed dutifully.**

U10 thru U15 ~ Jr. High ~ Middle School ~ AAU ~ Club

- Recreation & Leisure: Find your niche. **Play and learn individual <u>and</u> team sports.**
  - **"Rec"? ~ If winning really didn't matter then they wouldn't keep score!**
- Competitive Sports demand a higher level of: **Commitment ~ 'To Pledge Oneself'**
- **Prioritize your future 'next level' potential in realistic terms, as well as passion.**
- <u>**Late Bloomers:**</u> You don't know who's going to stay hungry, who's going to stay healthy, who's going to have a growth spurt or who's going to have their growth stunted. Who's going to be a victim to burnout, or who's going to be a late bloomer!

2013: G'13 survived ten years of soccer! One solo volleyball pivot: Torn meniscus!

U15 thru U18 ~ High School vs. AAU ~ Club Travel Commitments

<u>2013:</u> I quit my job to personally rehab G'13! Bike - Jump Rope - Swim

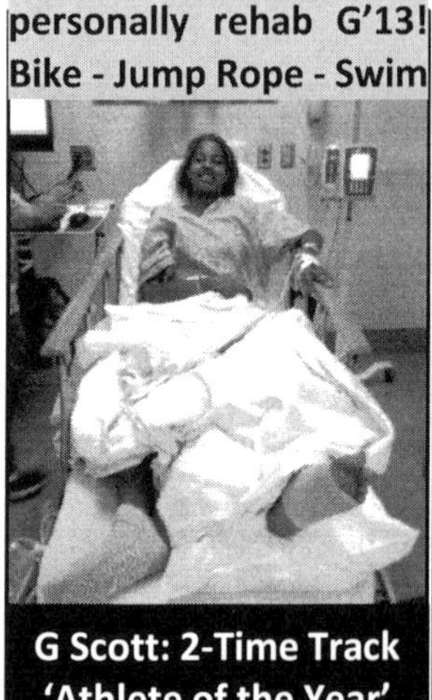

2013: Delayed Surgery: Ran SD CIF's!

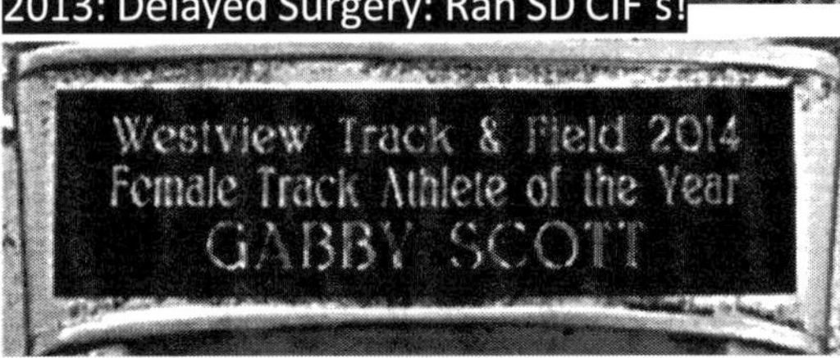

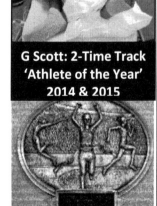

G Scott: 2-Time Track 'Athlete of the Year' 2014 & 2015

Your Marketing Mix ~ Online

CYBERSPACE: Perils & Pitfalls

~ TWEET ~ POST ~ FAVORITE ~ LIKE ~ EMAIL ~ TEXT ~

Beware of your 'Brand Presence' in your profile content and online communications. Your profile must promote your passions, visions and accomplishments in an enticing, accurate and concise manner. It's your resume! Is it full of Potential; or Prohibitive? Fact: People interpret based on sly slanted personal motives and objectives. Coaches, too! Scholarships rescinded, awards lost, career opportunities squandered, reputations soiled, and lives severely altered by online beefs, blunders, boastings and crass aberrations.

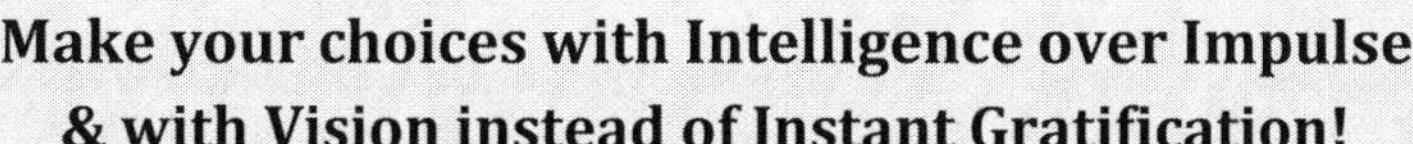

Make your choices with Intelligence over Impulse & with Vision instead of Instant Gratification!

Possibilities & Opportunities or Consequences & Repercussions?

Fair or not, what you wear speaks volumes! <u>Influence! Inferences!</u> Yes, I love San Diego, but when my own daughter came home holding a classmates Padre jersey, I DID NOT allow her to wear it. 'You're bred solely to emulate a Champions Mettle; not Hometown Moral Victories.'

Miss Manners JUDITH MARTIN

Wardrobe speaks loud and clear

Tats?

What Body Art May Say

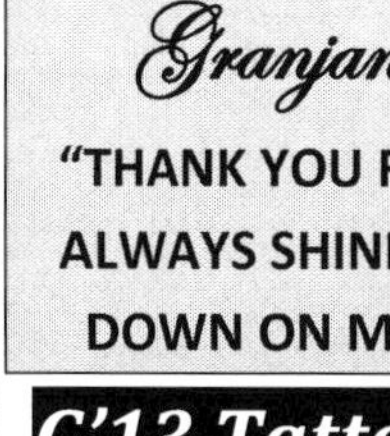

Granjan
"THANK YOU FOR ALWAYS SHINING DOWN ON ME"

G'13 Tattoo!

College Scholarship Quest

First Q of a college recruiting letter: Social Media Info!
G'13 Prospered at: <u>BeRecruited.com</u>

'The goal is to get paid to play! Compensation: An opportunity at a degree and an opportunity to compete. Academic quest for graduation & athletic quest for glory!'

Physical Factors

PEAK CONDITIONING AS YOUR CALLING CARD

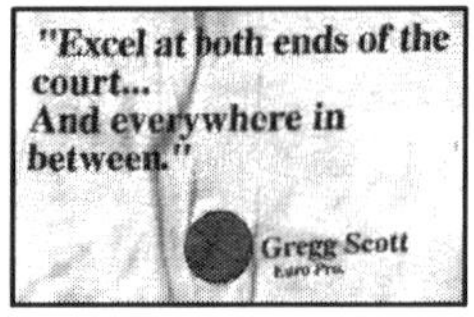

"Excel at both ends of the court...
And everywhere in between."
Gregg Scott

Training vs. Practice

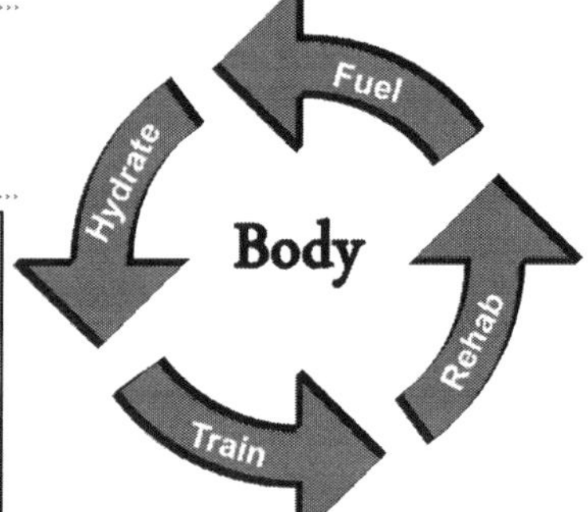

Global Techniques & Mindsets

<u>Train:</u> Work Ethic, Zeal & Pride!

Averting Injuries: Fit, Flexible, Durable & Agile

Your Best Ability is Availability!

TVA Core Training

G'13: 3-SPORTS!

<u>G'13: COAST Vball Club</u>

The TVA: Our Core Stabilization Girdle

Trusted sources often omit the most vital core muscle!
The Transverse Abdominis

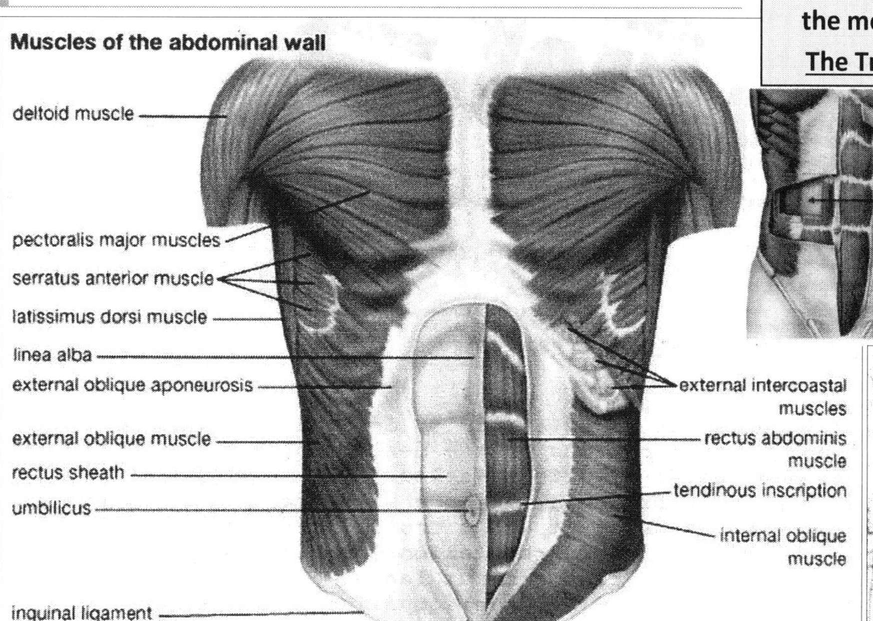

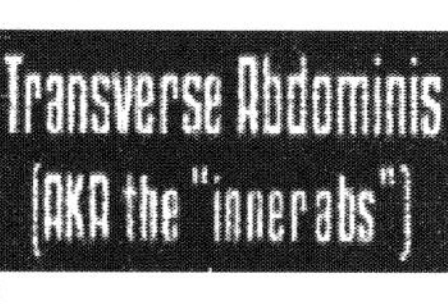

THE TVA

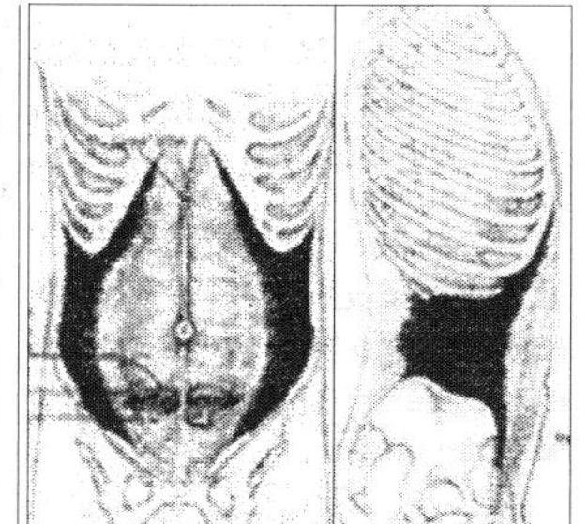

- It is the deepest muscle of the abdominal wall.
- Its fibers run horizontally. Its origins are the inguinal ligament, illiac crest and the cartiliges of the last five ribs.
- It strengthens and develops inwardly. Unlike the 'six-pack'.
- It is the critical element of core activation and stabilization.

◆ ~Press your belly-button to your Spine~

◆ Cervical Activation:
Tongue in anatomical rest position; swallow.
Hint: Above front teeth.

Transverse abdominis
Located under the obliques, it is the deepest of the abdominal muscles and wraps around your spine for protection and stability.

Internal abdominal oblique
Located under the external obliques, running in the opposite direction.

YOU DON'T KNOW
What You Don't Know!
MY CORE CONVICTIONS!

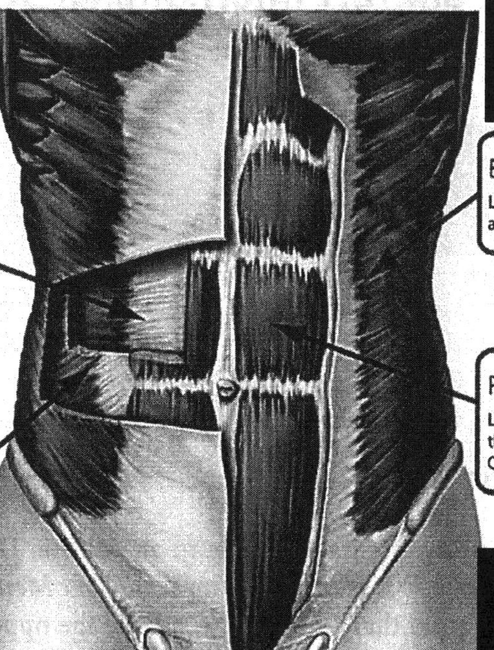

◆ TVA vs. The 6-Pack:
Grows & Trims Inwards!
NO HIP FLEXOR HELP

External abdominal oblique
Located on the side and front of the abdomen.

Rectus abdominis
Located along the front of the abdomen, this is the most well-known abdominal. Often referred to as the "six pack."

~Variations of Ab Curls~
Leg/Bent Knee Rotations
Trainer: No Sit-ups Eve!!

*G'13 2013 Soccer Reincarnation ~ *Prodded: Asst. Coach Vision*

FRIDAY HIGHLIGHTS

STREAK BUSTER: It only took 90 for Westview (San Diego, Calif.) to dent the net, and Plano West (Plano, Texas) never recovered as the California side went on to a rain-soaked 3-0 victory, ending the Texas program's undefeated streak at 42 matches. Gaby Scott scored less than 1:30 into the match as this former Top 10 squad ran its record to 2-0 at the NEPS through the morning matches. An evening tie with co-host Nolan has Westview at 2-0-1.

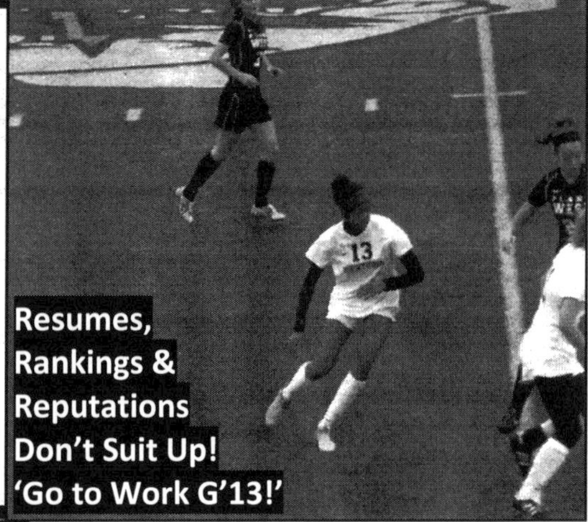

Resumes,
Rankings &
Reputations
Don't Suit Up!
'Go to Work G'13!'

MaxPreps Tour of Champions
Presented by The Army National Guard

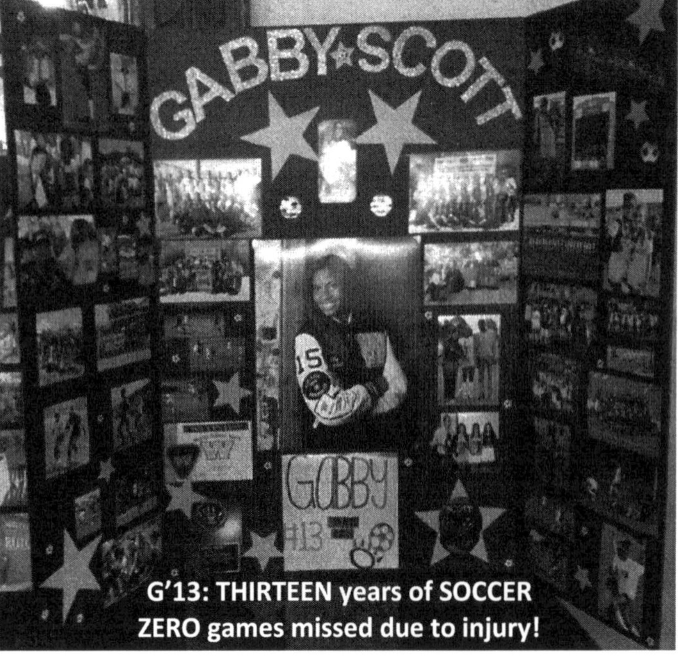

GABBY SCOTT
GABBY
#13
G'13: THIRTEEN years of SOCCER
ZERO games missed due to injury!

Purposeful Peak Performance Training

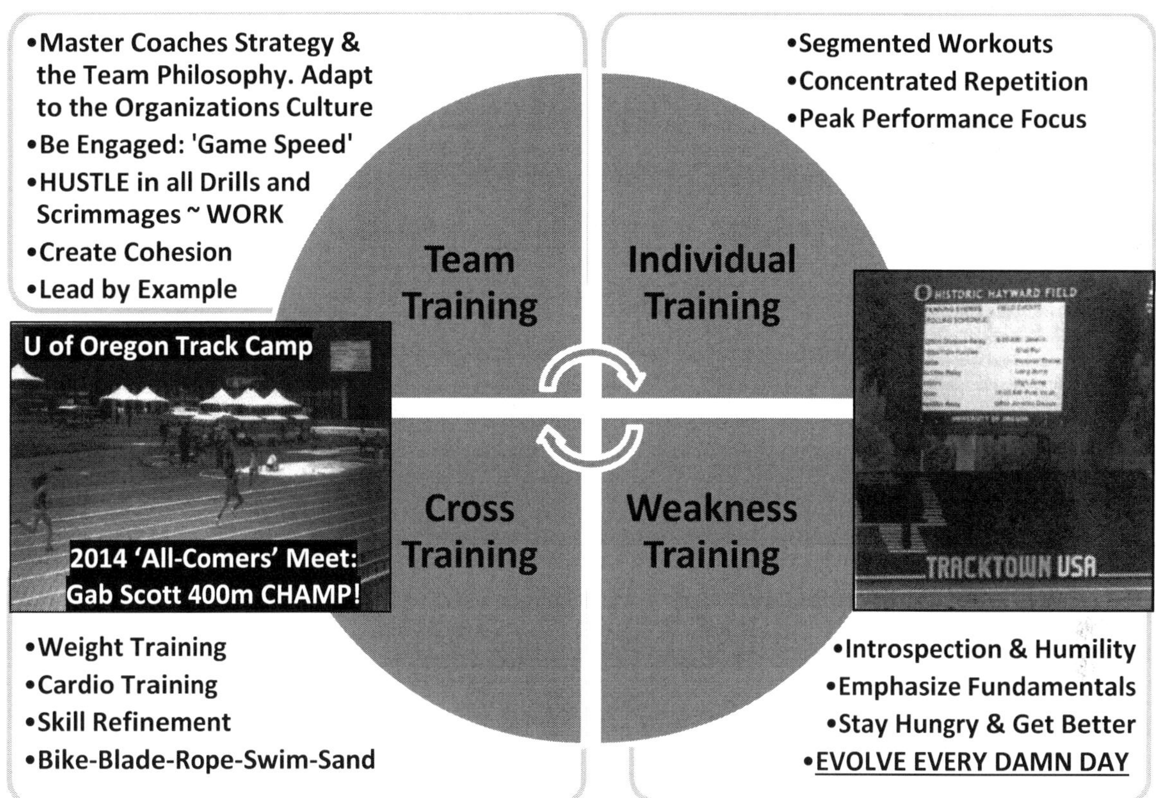

Be it talent or temperament, skill-sets or psyche, fitness or fundamentals; TRAIN!

- Cross-training is a must.
  - Adds variety, improves fitness, and gives supportive rest to the major (repetitive use) muscles that are dominate in your specific sport(s).
- Always keep a log or journal of training programs and diet/fuel provisions.
- Chart the order, duration, progress, plateaus and purpose of each training session, drill or exercise. Target times ~ Weights/Sets/Reps ~ Cool-down

Note performance variations based on the time of day that you train, and your diet. Energy levels will ebb & flow differently in your morning versus evening workouts. Quality fuel and proper hydration before, during and after training and competing.

THERE IS NO OFF-SEASON!!!

Excellence in sports is a year-round pursuit which the 'Mental Athlete' embraces!

Club ~ AAU ~ Travel Teams ~ Tours ~ Tourney's ~ Road Trips

2015 Sports Landscape Decree: College recruiters feast at U15-U18 National tournaments!

Be On Time: All team functions, meetings, meals, road trip schedules, rehab and practices. Long grueling road trips are a new normal. Manage your nutrition, hydration and recovery. It can be difficult to self-improve time-wise. You never know who's watching. Branding!

YOU NEVER GET A SECOND CHANCE TO MAKE A GOOD FIRST IMPRESSION!

Individual Training

The difference maker. Always assume your competition 'practices' hard, also has private coaches and plays against good competition. Fixate on cultivating sustaining competitive advantages beyond skill, technique or cardio. The Advantages: Strong Mind & Fit Psyche!

Coveting fatigue and pushing beyond it! When no one else is watching...GRIND!

Every Damn Day! 'It's not the hours you put in. It's what you put into the hours!'

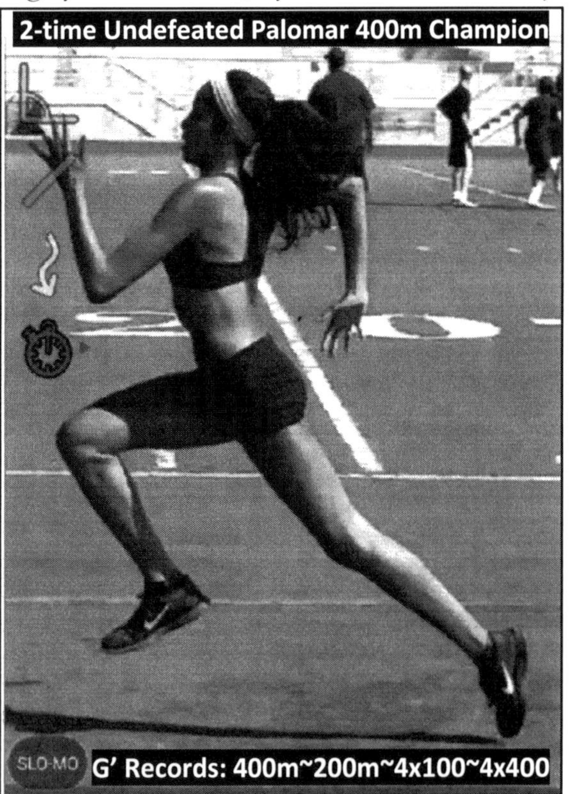

2-time Undefeated Palomar 400m Champion

G' Records: 400m~200m~4x100~4x400

GOOD IS NOT GOOD ENOUGH IF BETTER IS POSSIBLE!

Cross Training: Fit, Flexible, Agile & Durable ~ G'$ 'FlexAgility'

From my formative years, through college and Global Hoops, this was my proven personal agility and durability training system until my final pro season at age 33! The same training system is at the core of my Gab Scott tri-sport athlete pedigree. Her simultaneous scholar-athlete volleyball, soccer and track exploits tell the tale.

Sport Specific Dynamic Warm-up vs. Static Stretching System

Introspection & Weakness Training

Good athletes highlight and perfect their strong suits. The Mental Athlete knows that the opposition is highlighting our weaknesses. Stay ahead of the curve. Be proactive and evolve your game, relentlessly. Weakness Recognition is the crucial challenging process of prudent reflection, self-analysis and constructive criticism. A catalyst to evolve for the greater good.

Introspection: Self-examination ~ Analysis ~ Probing ~ Scrutiny

- "Where am I weak?"
  - ✓ Get input while not bristling at the feedback. **'Strong Mind & Fit Psyche'**
- How can I become a more complete and fundamentally sound player or athlete?
- How can I train to be a fit, flexible, agile and durable peak performance athlete?
- What purposeful moves, techniques, or situations am I uncomfortable with?
- What skills and talents do others possess that I lack? Not 'Style over Substance'.
- What drills and excercises can I do to improve in the above areas? How often?
- Application: Plan your work & work your plan. Implementation! Chart progress!

Cardio Training: Jump Rope ~ Swim ~ Bike ~ 'Blade ~ Sand

- **Goal: Get beyond the point of fatigue, only then are you actually training.**
- **No Pain, No Gain does apply! Exhaust & Push On!**

Weight Training: This is Not a Casual Pursuit

Perils of the Weight Room

HUBRIS ~ Genetic Potential ~ The Point of Deminishing Returns ~ Socializing

Gabriella Scott 2-Time Athlete of the Year 2014 & 2015

Individualized Functional Training Programming Protocols:
Core Stabilization Assessments ~ Flexibility Assessments
Order: Largest Muscles First! Cables & Pulleys ~ Free Weights
Stability Ball; No Benches! Self-Stabilization! Posture ~ Stance ~ Grip ~ Balance ~ Form ~ Core & Neck Flexor Activation ~ Neutral Spine ~ Quality Technique throughout Movement!
Exhale on the Push ~ Train to Muscle Failure ~ Timed Rest!

Fatigue Makes Cowards of Us All

This statement should be at the core of our motivation in training. When we examine this quote we understand, firstly, that 'us' means you and me, him and her, and them too. Did you follow that? Point being that none of us is immune to this quote. Fatigue via improper conditioning robs us of our ability to display our physical talents and mental skills. When fatigue sets in we play weak and off balance, lose our focus and ability to concentrate with consistency. Games, careers, and multitudes of opportunities are decided by the commitment we make to superior conditioning, which also prevents injuries. There is no worse feeling than losing to an inferior opponent due to fatigue and lack of concentration in 'crunch time'. Unfortunately, most athletes must experience the heartache of committing crucial mental and physical errors causing defeat and underachievement, first-hand, before prioritizing these multiple variables that are prerequisites for superior conditioning in training as well as peak performance in competition.

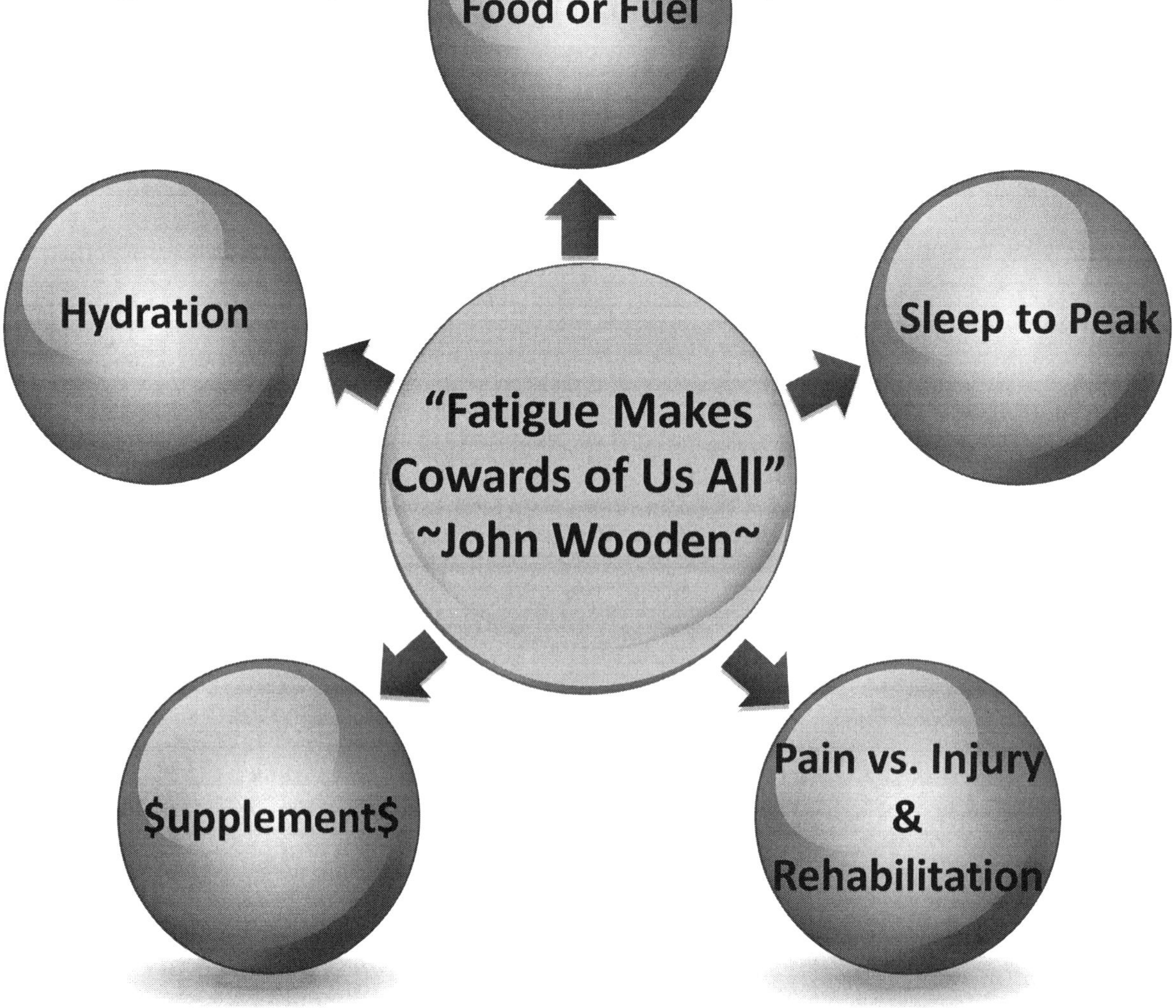

Food or Fuel

Hydration

Sleep to Peak

"Fatigue Makes Cowards of Us All" ~John Wooden~

$upplement$

Pain vs. Injury & Rehabilitation

Diet:
Food ~ Intake
~ Nourishment ~
~ Regimen ~

Diet & Nutrition

The Thrill of Victory or the Agony of Defeat just may depend on what, when or how much you eat.

Nutrition:
~ Nourishment ~
Diet ~ Food
~ Sustenance ~

Interpretations and mindsets rule here. DON'T get overly fixated on the initial word: **Diet**. It invokes thoughts of restriction, limitation, sacrifice and hunger pangs. Too often our interpretation of the word hinders our focus of the true meaning and impact of the entire term: **Diet & Nutrition**. In fact, and by definition, this two-word phrase is synonmous. We are on a diet at all times. **A diet is simply what we consume through our mouths. Nutrition is the most critical component of the phrase; the sustenance to sustain!**

The Mental Athlete Term: FUEL! Only top quality high-octane fuel for a Porsche!!

Peak Performance Athletes require proper fuel to sustain them before during and after training and competition. G'$ Quip: My Body is My Paycheck! Perpetual choices that can catapult or cripple us.

Fact: You Can't Out-train a Bad Diet

Three reasons I can not tell anyone what to eat!!!

1. While I'm not a doctor, as a Health & Fitness pro I follow the credo: **First, do no harm!**
2. My metabolic testing results directed I **limit** many foods that G'$ **constantly** consumed!
3. If Michael Jordan ate steak before every game, who am I to say anything to the contrary!
Simply put, it is not the food source, but how each body REACTS to the fuel source!

Metabolic Dominance: Oxidative System or Autonomic Nervous System

How the body digests and converts Protein, Fats & Carbohydrates to energy.

- **Protein, Fats & Carbs Mix? FUEL: Seek to get in tune with your own body.**
- **Organic Foods**
- **Whole Foods**
- **Processed Foods ~ Fast Foods ~Nutrient Values ~ Preservatives ~ Calories**
- **Preparation: Grilling, Baking & Broiling vs. Frying ~ Saturated/Non Fats**

Produce is a vehicle for our souls

OVERDOSE ON FRUCTOSE ~ I GET NAKED: NAKED JUICE ~ LOVE THY SMOOTHIE

Produce Soothes the Soul & Fuels the Body: 5+ servings of fruit or veggies per day!

Game Day of young G'13 ~ Oatmeal Fuel
G'13 "It just doesn't taste good Daddy."
G' 'Do you know what tastes best, G'13? The Sweet Taste of Victory. So eat it.' 'Or, you may face the agony of defeat!'

Americans choose what they eat based on:
1. *Taste*
2. *Price*
3. *Health*

CNN~May 6, 2011

2015 Mental Athlete Addendum: Convenience!

First Things First

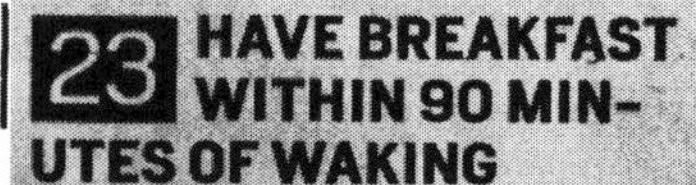

BREAK (THE) FAST: BY DEFINITION

Baseline Premise: 2013 TV commercial

A young girl, around 10 years old, speaks with volumes of knowledge.

"Malcolm, have you eaten yet today? You seem to be acting a little grumpy."

- **What we eat; When we eat; (and, if we DON'T eat), dictates our mood, energy, focus, temperament, patience and personality.**
- Another commercial chants: **"You're not who you are when you're hungry!"**
- **We are not automobiles**! Our fuel level when we park is not equal to our fuel level (minus evaporation) when it's time to drive again. At rest, our motor runs.
- Breakfast is the most important meal of the day, hence, 'Breakfast of Champions'.

Break 'the' Fast: Defined Beyond Cultural & Social Conditioning

Fast basically means to go without food and water, voluntarily, or in this case, during our sleep. So, **'breakfast'** is an 'action of consumption' more than a specific 'menu type' meal.

- **It's not necessarily 'a morning meal'**. Simply, the first meal after extended sleep.
- 'Breaking the Fast' isn't limited to eating. **Yet, caffeine jolts do not break a fast!**

"I remember the first time I saw G' actually drink his breakfast.
It was 'Championship Sunday' of the '94 'Gus Macker' 3-on-3 tourney.
We'd had a long night out, despite having an early morning game looming.
So, while I'm in the kitchen making a typical breakfast, G' only used a blender."
Michael Coleman ~ 'Still Got It' ~ 1994 Gus Macker Champions

You can't display superior skill, dominant will, or mental toughness without the proper fuel; which begins with 'breakfast'. Failing to Prepare is Preparing to Fail.

Food or Fuel??

All Around the World Same Song! *<u>POST GAME</u>
"Two all-beef patties, special sauce, lettuce, cheese, pickles, onions, on a sesame seed bun."

You can't tell me you want that, if you're not willing to do this!

Planning your Meals, Snacks <u>and</u> Workout Fuel with VISION!

Training & Competion Fuel & Nutrition: Pre ~ During ~ Post

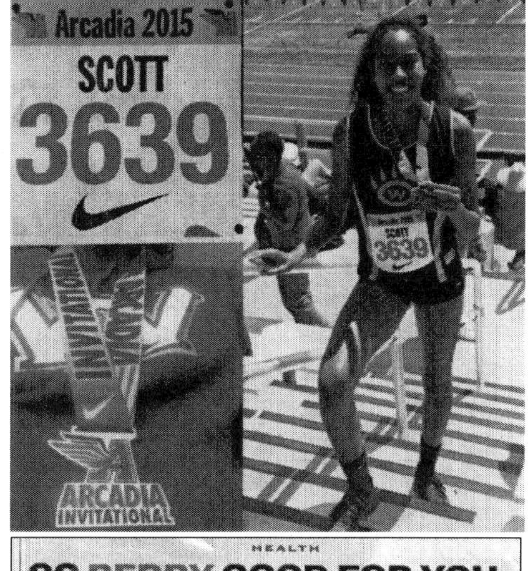

Body Type & Sport Specific Fuel

- Nature & Nurture
- Genetic Potential
- The Skewed Lens of Our Self-Image

Gaby Scott inherited my lean G'$ Body-Type; and my clean G'hoops 'Diet'!

Cultural Challenges

- Cushioning Family Customs & Traditions
- Adapting Peak Performance Requirements

Geographical Challenges

Road Trips & Travel Challenges ~ Multiple Events; Same Day

Beware of: Condiments, Sauces, Dips, Creams, Toppings, etc.

Curb your sweet tooth! "How many licks does it take to get to the center of a Tootsie Roll Pop? The world may never know."

<u>Plan Your Fuel</u> via training and competition calendars. Covet your 'vacation' time! I love pizza! L.A.'s Shakey's, UA Dominoes & UHH Pizza Hut! Canals of Venice, Italy: No presentation! Best ever!

Preparing a hearty homemade multi-course meal so that all components are completed at 'meal time' is all about timing. Parents and caregivers get tremendous **intrinsic value** watching their loved ones enjoying the <u>warm</u> meal they dutifully took the time to cook. **Now, as a parent, I understand the angst my mom felt when we were late to the table.**

Hydration

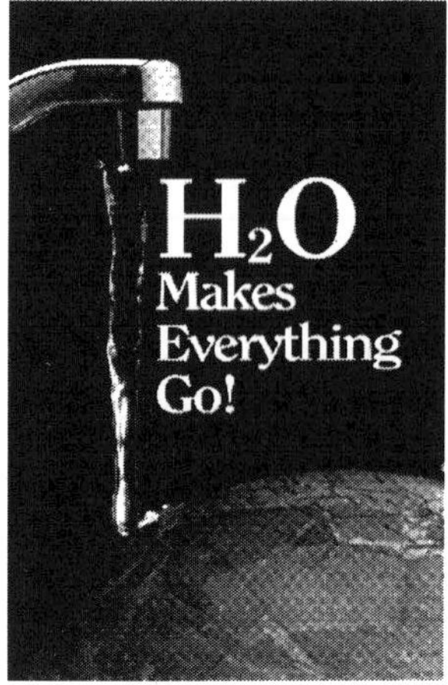

1. What percentage of the world is covered by water?________________

2. What percentage of the world's water is readily available for humans to use? _____

3. How much water is contained in the human body? ________________

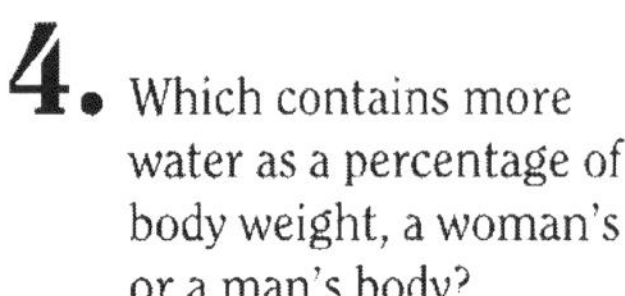

4. Which contains more water as a percentage of body weight, a woman's or a man's body?____________

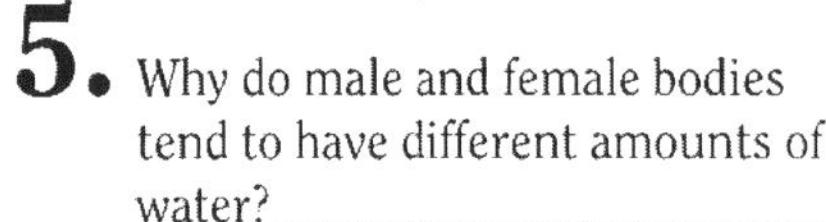

5. Why do male and female bodies tend to have different amounts of water? ________________

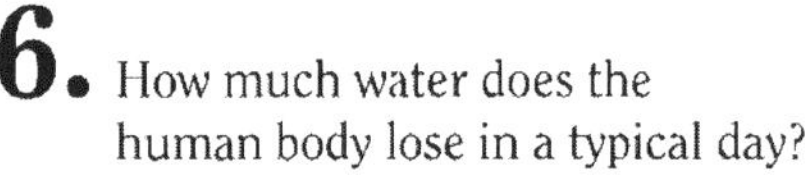

6. How much water does the human body lose in a typical day? ________________

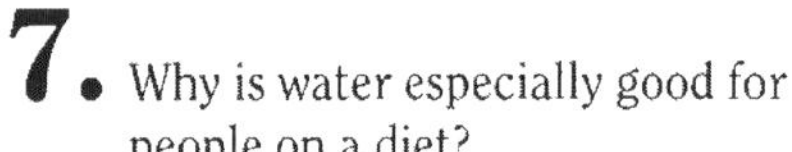

7. Why is water especially good for people on a diet?____________

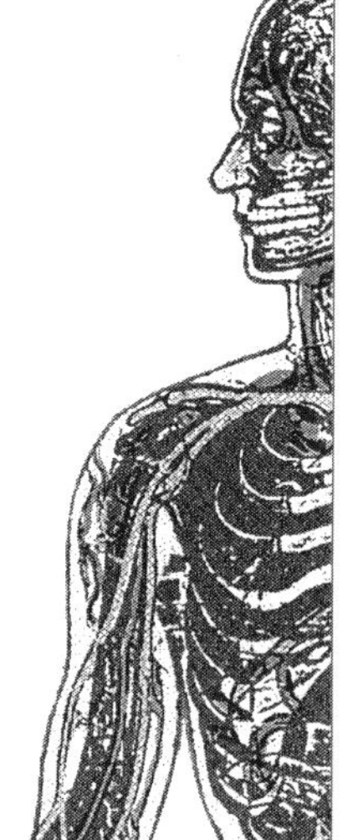

For Optimum Health, Fitness, Well-Being and Peak Performance:

- **CONSUME HALF OF YOUR BODY WEIGHT IN OUNCES DAILY; PLUS, 8 ounces DURING EVERY 20 mins. of EXERCISE/TRAINING/COMPETITION!**
- **SIMPLE MATH ~ 'Jusr Do It'!**
- **NO EXCUSES: ½ wt. =___ozs.**
- **Muscles are over 70% WATER**
- **The BRAIN is a MUSCLE!**
- **"MAXIMIZE YOUR ROI"**
- **REHYDRATE Post Training**
  - **Monitor Body Weight!**
- **Clear Urine = A Clear System!**
- **Take pride in your water bottle!**
- **How many sips does it take…?**
- **Don't be the one to cramp up!**
- **'Inherent Porsche Performance'**
- **You can't tell me you want that if you're not willing to do this!!**

Answers

1. Some 80% of the world is covered by water or ice. Only about 20% is dry land.
2. 97% of the water on earth is salty ocean and 2% is frozen. The remaining 1% is available to meet human needs.
3. If you're an adult, your body contains about 40 quarts or 10 gallons of water.
4. A man's body is 60–65% water. A woman's is 50–60% water. The human brain is about 75% water.
5. Muscle tissue contains a large amount of water. Fat tissues contain virtually no water. Men tend to have more muscle as a percentage of body weight while women have more fat.
6. You lose 2½ to 3 quarts of water per day through normal elimination, sweating and breathing. If you exercise or live in a humid climate, you may lose another quart.
7. It has zero calories and zero sugar, but a good drink of water can reduce hunger. Water also helps your body metabolize stored fats, helps maintain proper muscle tone, and helps rid the body of wastes.

Hydration vs. Thirst

Control your Carbonation Cravings: Bennie Davenport: Clear Sodas Only!

THIRST IS NOT AN ACCURATE INDICATOR OF OUR BODY'S NEED FOR PROPER HYDRATION.

We've all been guilty of turning down water while uttering or thinking, "I'm not thirsty". Well, know this: Your thirst mechanism can and will deceive you. So I repeat, thirst is not an accurate indicator of your body's need for proper hydration! Got it?! Just because you're consuming liquids does not necessarily mean that you're hydrating your body. On the contrary, 'liquids' such as soda, coffee, tea and energy drinks which contain caffeine, are all diuretics which are counterproductive to proper hydration and peak performance. This science-based fact dictates that you constantly monitor what, when, and how much you drink; beyond media hype, social conditioning, and especially beyond your sense of thirst!

Further compensation is required based on the amount of sodium/salt we may consume. Note: Since childhood I've had an obsession to sunflower seeds; 'Polly seeds' per Sparks.

Alcohol: Know Thy Self! Consequences & Ramifications Loom!

Be it peer pressure, genetic dispositions, media advertising onslaughts or social infulence we must be wary of the choices we make regarding alcohol libations. But, I had my noble elder role models (Mark, Dave Lewis & Marvin Mensies) to emulate. So, I easily abstained from drinking alcohol until I went off to college. Bless all my three 'bros'!

Then, by His grace, my first week at U of A, a man approached me during *'Rush Week'* by the name of, Donald Sage Sparks. He taught me his 'Prudent Partying 101':

Tolerance Levels ~ Public Behavior
Self Awareness ~ Exit Strategies
*Truth Syrum! ~ *Idiocy Enticment!
*Head Acher! ~ *Reaper of Regrets!

2014 & 2015

You can't run with the Big Dogs . . .
if you pee like a Puppy

Supplements

By definition, supplement means 'in addition to'. It does not mean 'in place of'!

Because we all have a unique metabolic makeup, unique dietary needs, alergic reactions, medical conditions and medications, all in flux within us, supplements are a mainstay for our well-being and our quest for a competitive edge. This multi-billion dollar industry is driven by marketing hype, profit margins, and the placebo effect. It prays on internal and external pressures to lose or gain weight, increase strength and stamina, train smarter and harder, and compete at increasingly higher levels; with delusions of grandeur. Advertising psycho-babble can warp our thinking and negatively impact our choices. Buyer Beware!

Lets start by piggy-backing off of the Hydration section. There, I insist upon water, H_2O, for proper hydration as a part of your lifestyle; plain and simple. However, endurance athletes reach a point that requires additional or supplemental means to combat fatigue. During prolonged high-intensity exercise our bodies lose vital electrolites which must be replaced for sustained performance. That's where supplements such as Gatorade come into play; pun intended. Conversely, **caffeine is both a diretic** that dehydrates the body, **and a stimulant** that induces blood-sugar spikes; **both of which impair performance.**

*Two Commercials: Science vs. Hyperbole (*with fine print)*

GATORADE "TO AID THE GATORS": TRUISMS VS. 'ADVERTISING'

By the historical account in their enlightening commercial, **Gatorade** was originally created based on science in a quest for sustained peak performance. As an electrolite replacement to 'aid' the Florida Gators Football teams in combating the debilitating chronic dehydration they suffered from due to the humid 'swamp-like' climate of their home field, this Sports Drink was a GAME CHANGER. **Aided the Gators & Aided Global Hoops!**

"5-HOUR ENERGY IS FOCUS": BALDERDASH & PSYCHOBABBLE

By inspirational merit, verbiage and images of excellence, the 5-hour energy commercials are on point. What is focus? Focus is this… Focus is that… Focus is blah blah blah. But, **"5-hour energy is focus!" Whatda....? Simply freeze-frame and read the fine print! "These statements have not been evaluated by the Food & Drug Administration" "Provides a feeling of alertness and energy." "Does not provide caloric energy." *** "Not proven to improve athletic performance, dexterity or endurance." *** "Contains caffeine comparable to a cup of the leading premium coffee." "Limit caffeine....to avoid nervousness, sleeplessness and occasional rapid heartbeat." Facts: 5-HOUR energy fine print. Mom Quote: "The Eyes are there but See, Not."**

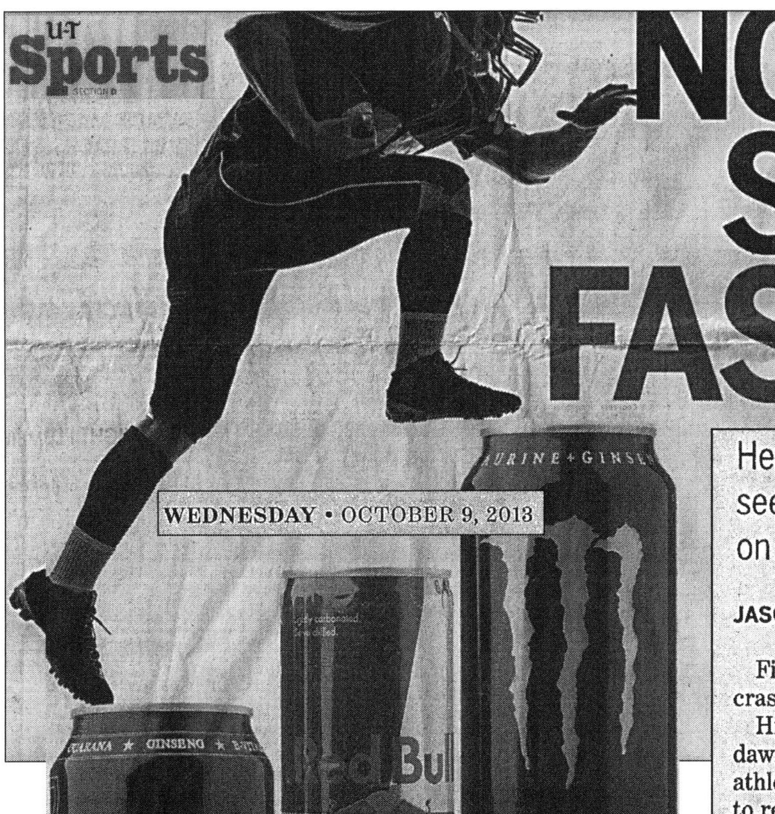

G' Propaganda

This keen article speaks volumes about the true perils, deceptive media hype and psycho-babble regarding today's 'energy' drinks.

Protect Our Kids!

Health experts cite risks, seek ban of energy drinks on high school campuses

JASON COWAN • U-T

First comes the rush. Then comes the crash.

High school students waking before dawn to a day of classes, homework and athletic competition might be tempted to reach for a boost in the form of energy drinks.

Health experts say it's not a good idea, and some high school administrators say the drinks should be banned from campuses.

Bill Beacham, executive director of the Center for Drug-Free Communities, said energy-drink consumption among adolescent athletes can be more dangerous than a simple crash — possibly causing arrhythmia, tachycardia or a stroke.

"You really don't know what you're getting," he said. "The energy drinks that are on the market today are not regulated by the Food and Drug Administration."

Representatives from Rockstar Energy Drink, Monster Energy Drink and Red Bull did not return phone calls or emails seeking comment.

Beacham, who spoke over the summer to a gathering of San Diego Unified School District athletic directors and coaches, said athletes who consume energy drinks before a game or workout receive an immediate boost followed by a very quick drop-off.

SEE **DRINKS** • D4

What is an energy drink?

Marketed as a quick and easy means of relieving fatigue and improving performance. Often contains higher concentrate of carbohydrates, adding calories. Also contains high amounts of caffeine and in some cases other nutritional supplements.

Not Regulated by the Food and Drug Administration.

What is a sports drink?

Designed to provide rehydration during athletic activity. Most contain a mix of carbohydrates and electrolytes, formulated to allow maximal absorption of the fluid by the gastrointestinal tract.

Regulated by the Food and Drug Administration.

Source:
National Federation of State High School Associations

Teenagers often make their choices based on misguided media hyperbole spewed via **unregulated** sources; disregarding asterisks, 'fine print', and science. **Counterproductive** to athletic performance!

Focus ~ Calm Under Fire ~ Poise

Caffine is a Drug

We all are guilty, me too!

"Mom Quote:

"The Eyes Are There; But See Not."

Kicking the Caffeine Habit

Caffeine is a drug that acts as a central nervous system stimulant and a diuretic. Caffeine is present in coffee, tea, soft drinks, cocoa, chocolate and kola nuts. There is no human requirement for caffeine in the diet. Although caffeine is safe to consume in moderation, it may negatively affect one's health and nutritional status. As an appetite suppressant, caffeinated beverages may be replacing nutrient-dense foods such as fruit juices and milk.

Excessive caffeine intake can lead to an increased heart rate, diuresis (excessive excretion of fluids), nausea and vomiting, restlessness, anxiety, depression, tremors, and difficulty sleeping. It is beneficial to cut back on your caffeine intake gradually to prevent any symptoms of withdrawal. Sudden cessation of caffeine intake may cause headaches, drowsiness, irritability, nausea and vomiting, and other symptoms.

Cut back caffeine intake if consuming caffeinated beverages in place of juice or milk or intake is more than 200 to 300 milligrams a day (about two cups of coffee). Start slowly by mixing half a cup decaffeinated and half a cup regular coffee. Or, replace your afternoon soda with a glass of juice – you'll get more nutrients without the caffeine. Other alternatives include:

* Fruit juice with seltzer water, or drop a slice of lime in your glass for flavor; mix fruit and ice in the blender for a cool slush.
* Freeze fruit juice into cubes and add to your glass of water.
* Fruit juice popsicles also provide a flavorful twist.
* Another thirst-quencher is flavored decaffeinated iced tea or green tea.
* Water, of course, is always the best way to cut out caffeine as well as stay hydrated. The best part about water is, it's always available and it's FREE.

There are many varieties of tea available from fruit to herb – just be sure to check labels for added sugars, which can increase calories. When you look at the options, choose fruit juice, decaffeinated teas and coffees, and water. When using a little imagination, quenching your thirst caffeine-free is easy. **OQ**

OFFICIALS' QUARTERLY | SPRING 2009 17

Sleep To Peak

Michael Coleman: "G' was not at all a morning person."
G' Truism: 'My mom woke me with a warm washcloth!!'

Baseline Premise: Quote from the film 'Ms. Congeniality'

"Excuse me. I am in the middle of a REM cycle over here."

As she is awoken, pleading with her noisy and oblivious co-contestants, she speaks with the knowledge of REM sleep providing a critical and tangible competitive edge in her personal quest for victory. Maximum ROI: Rest does not equal REM.

- When we sleep, how long we sleep, and how deeply we sleep, dictates our mood, energy, focus, temperament and personality. As well as IQ abilities.
- Our bodies rejuvenate and our muscles grow during the REM sleep period.
- Sleep Deprivation: A precursor to accidents, injuries & underachievement!
- Cat-naps can do wonders: 20 to 60 minutes recharges without any malaise.

We are not automobiles! As with our bodies, our minds don't 'park' either. While REM is a close ally to 'park', as it is the deepest level of sleep, simultaneously, the body renews.

Maximizing your ROI: Mainatain a consistent sleeping pattern!

We train, lift, grind and sweat. REM dictates the return on all investments!

- Yes, Tomorrow Starts Today. Yet, REM capitalizes on the labor of today.
- To bear the fruit of our labor today, we must rest and renew for tomorrow.
- The best sleeping pill: Peace of Mind. Today is past~tomorrow is planned.
- Create a 'throttle-down' period before bedtime. Minimize light and stimuli.
- Don't fight an active mind at sleep time. Assign the tasks, and let them go!

Full Disclosure Confessions of a Nite-owl & Nite-life Connoisseur

- The recommended eight hours was often unrealistic: G'$ & Sporty G'!
- In college and as a paid global pro, enduring late nights was a given!

Relaxation & Proper Breathing

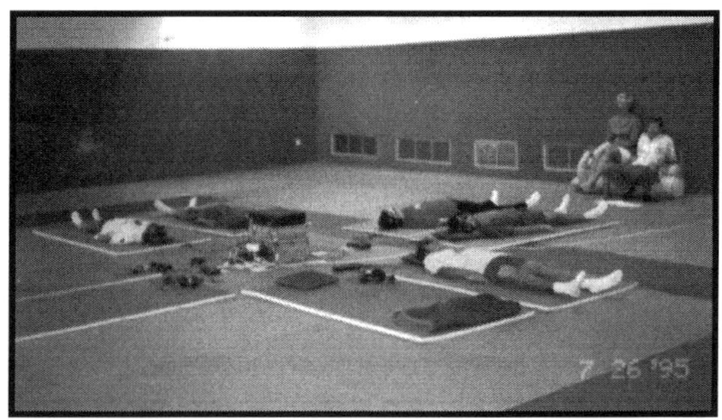

SportShule, Munchen, Germany: 'We all must commit time to decompress.' I enter mid-afternoon during Detlef's adidas camp feeling alert and energized. The lady has me lay down and put on the cool sunglasses and headphones. As the weird cosmic sounds mix with the cosmic IMAX space visuals, I am skeptical to say the least. The next thing I recall, the lady is gently awakening me from my neuro-based, REM induced (surgery-like) state. It was 30 minutes later! They told me that I was softly snoring. An amazing session!

Mindfulness ~ Relaxation ~ Meditation ~ 'Chillax' ~ Verbal Judo

Positive Intent Creates Miracles. Alas, nobleness has its limitations and challenges.

- It falters for me at the DMV. Geico Commercial: Atleast I know I'm not alone!
- I get irked stuck behind a 55 mph Prius smart-(ass)-car driver in the FAST lane.

Know Thy Self: Stress and Angst Hinder Health, Well-Being, Performance and Longevity!

LIFE CHANGING BREATHING ELIXIR: 'BLAB' & 'BOSS'

BLAB: 'BREATHE LIKE A BABY'
BOSS: 'BELLY OUT' ~ 'SHOULDERS STILL'

2003: After othroscopic shoulder surgery, typical deep breathing with my 'shoulders rising' caused spasms when I exhaled. Counter Productive. Trust Mother Nature: BLAB & BOSS!

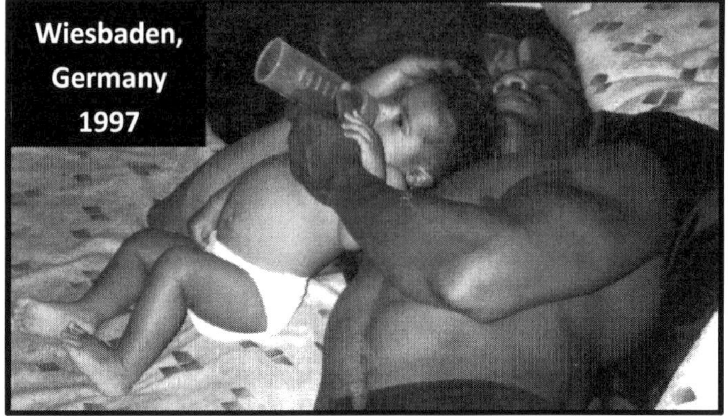

BREATHE

INHALE
3-COUNT
EXHALE
3-COUNT

G'enius Rx!
VOILA!!!

Pain vs. Injury

Mental Athlete: If you can't embrace those first few agonizing minutes of 'icing' until the area gets numb, Then Don't Play Sports!

Oust the naieve notion of 'No Pain, No Gain'!!

Embrace the G'$ truism of 'Know the difference between Pain & Injury'!

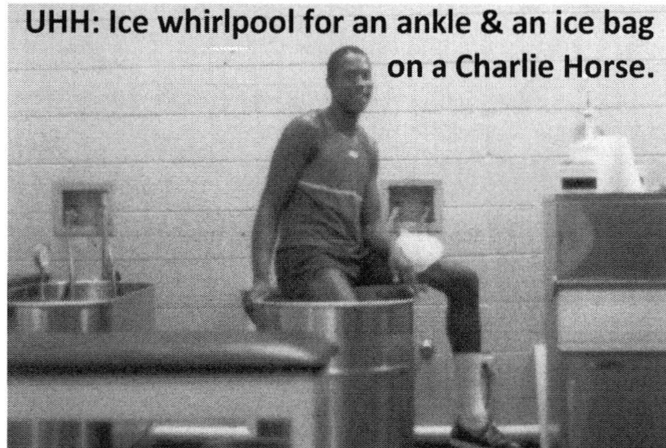
UHH: Ice whirlpool for an ankle & an ice bag on a Charlie Horse.

Pain, injuries and rehab are a part of sports! Ultimate tests of courage, commitment and coping skills. In fact, it is the cultivated ability to manage our pain and overcome the adversity of injuries, both mentally and physically, that breeds the champions mettle. The Mental Athlete faces each test with mental toughness, physical preparation, proper fuel and apt rehab. It is a perpetual cycle. No matter how well we train and protect our bodies, sooner or later we experience injuries that inhibit our ability to perform. A reality of sports.

The Current Era of Sports Concussion Awareness & Protocols

- First, differentiate between pain and injury. We all experience the bumps, bruises, strains and sprains that come with intense training and competition. It is important that we communicate lingering or significant ailments to coaches or trainers so that THEY may determine the severity of the situation. **Still, exhibit guts to play hurt.**
- Different athletes have different levels of pain tolerence. 'Soft' teammates irk me!!

Playing doctor on ourselves and deciding that we "can handle it" has dire consequences. G' Trainer: Altering your gait, stride, form or technique to compensate for an injury can absolutely cause an injury to another part of your body. Limping on a sore lower left leg, foot, heel or toe can cause an (unrelated?) injury to your right knee, hip or lower back. The net result often becomes a more serious injury and a longer healing process; in addition to the original root ailment. So, don't guess! Get qualified input from team trainers and doctors. Humbly, heed to their diagnosis.

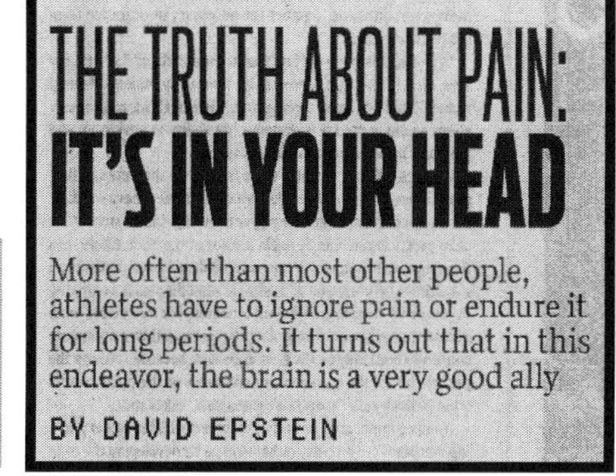
THE TRUTH ABOUT PAIN: IT'S IN YOUR HEAD

More often than most other people, athletes have to ignore pain or endure it for long periods. It turns out that in this endeavor, the brain is a very good ally

BY DAVID EPSTEIN

English as a Strange Language:

The icepack stings deeply as the compress is *wound* around the *wound*.

Rehabilitaion

"Skipping Rehab is like Skipping Training! 'You're only cheating yourself!' G' Hoops!

We must decompress. There is nothing more frustrating and challenging than injuries and illnesses that take us away from our sport. The ultimate test of our commitment and will as an athlete. Rehab and 'Treatment' are most often painful, grueling workouts or therapy sessions that every athlete must persevere through to some degree. It's Inherent! GRIND!

Sports Medicine ~ My Fav: Electro Stimulation Acupuncture!

If possible utilize a sports medicine doctor! YOUR FUTURE DEPENDS ON IT!

- **Kinesiology ~ Chiropractic ~ Muscle Stimulation ~ Ultrasound ~ Acupuncture Massage Therapy ~ Hydro-Therapy ~ Flexibility Therapy ~ Feet Reflexology**
- **Doctors ~ Surgeons ~ Therapists ~ Physios ~ Trainers ~ Gurus ~ Healers Strength Coaches ~ Nutritionists ~ Sports Psychologists ~ Rehab Specialists**

Heed to Prudent Timetables for Comebacks! Re-Injuries Loom!

Fool's Gold: Don't risk re-injury or compensatory injuries trying to come back too soon.

AFFRIMATIONS FOR HEALTH AND HEALING

- **I am caring for my body and my health.**
- **I am free of illness.**
- **I remain fit and strong while healing.**
- **I rehab with focus and intensity.**
- **I am healing well and quickly.**
- **I appreciate my body and my health.**
- **I am healthy in mind and body.**
- **My fitness level remains high even while I'm injured and healing.**
- **I will be a supportive and sincere teammate while I rehabilitate. 'WE before Me'**
- **My (injured part) heals quickly and well through my committed rehabilitation.**
- **I am getting well and remaining healthy in other areas of my body.**
- **I keep my mind focused on my goals as my body heals.**
- **My body is rested and rejuvenated.**
- **I can comeback…better than ever!**
- **I am what I think!**
- **I am paying my dues.**

Returning from an Injury or Illness is a Mental Game of Trusting Your Rehab!

YOUR BEST ABILITY IS AVAILABILITY

Cultivating Tangible Intangibles

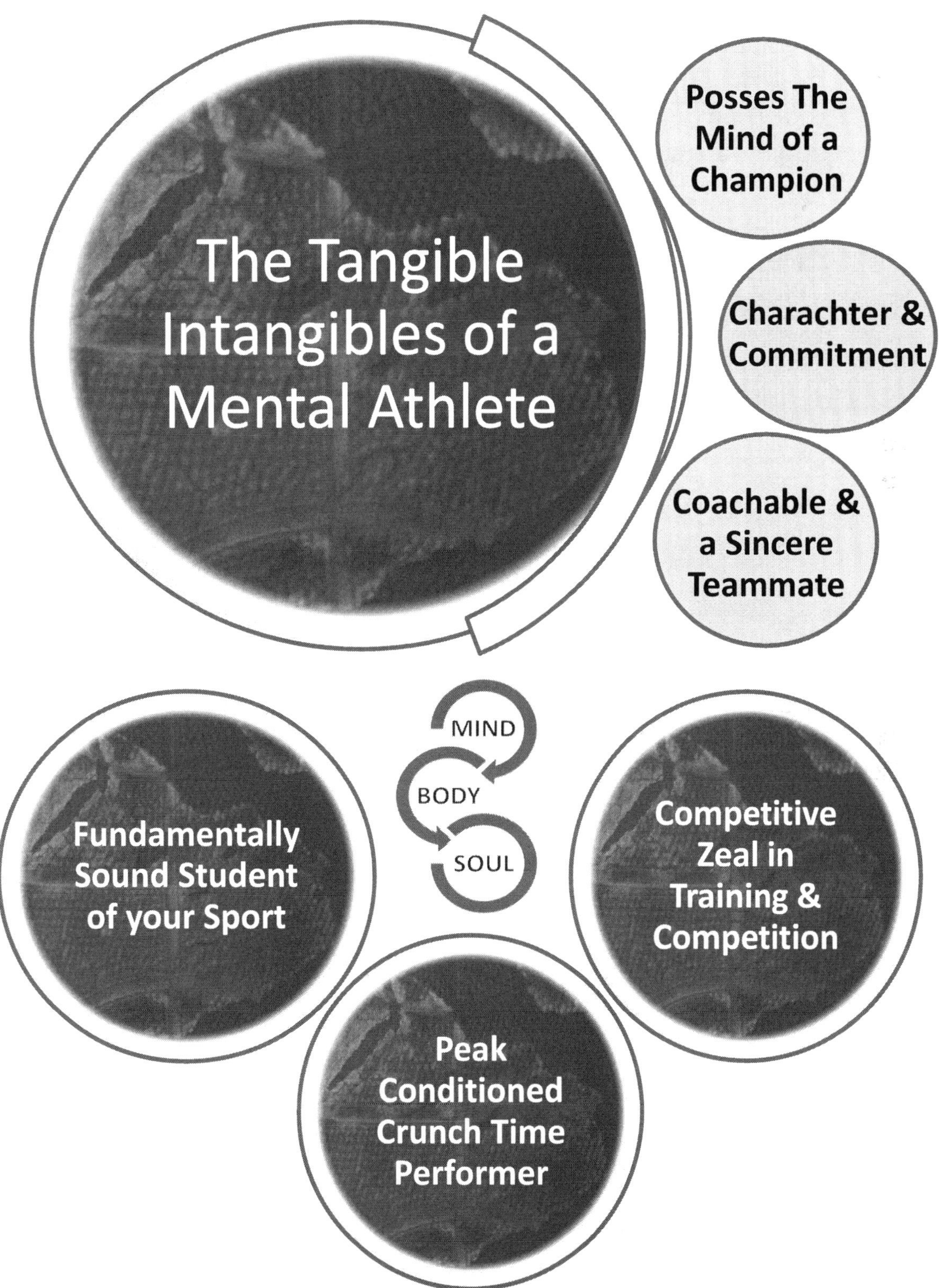
The Tangible Intangibles of a Mental Athlete
Posses The Mind of a Champion
Charachter & Commitment
Coachable & a Sincere Teammate
MIND
BODY
SOUL
Fundamentally Sound Student of your Sport
Competitive Zeal in Training & Competition
Peak Conditioned Crunch Time Performer

Rankings, Resumes & Reputations Don't Suit Up!

AFTERWORD ~ ABOUT THE AUTHOR

October 3, 2015: Clemson upset Irish! Dabo Swinney "B.Y.O.G."

"What I told them tonight was: We give you scholarships. We give you stipends and meals and a place to live. We give you nice uniforms. I can't give you guts! And, I can't give you heart. And, tonight it was B.Y.O.G.! Bring Your Own Guts! And, THEY BROUGHT SOME GUTS AND SOME HEART! And, they never quit until the last play!" ~ "I'm just so proud of my team!"

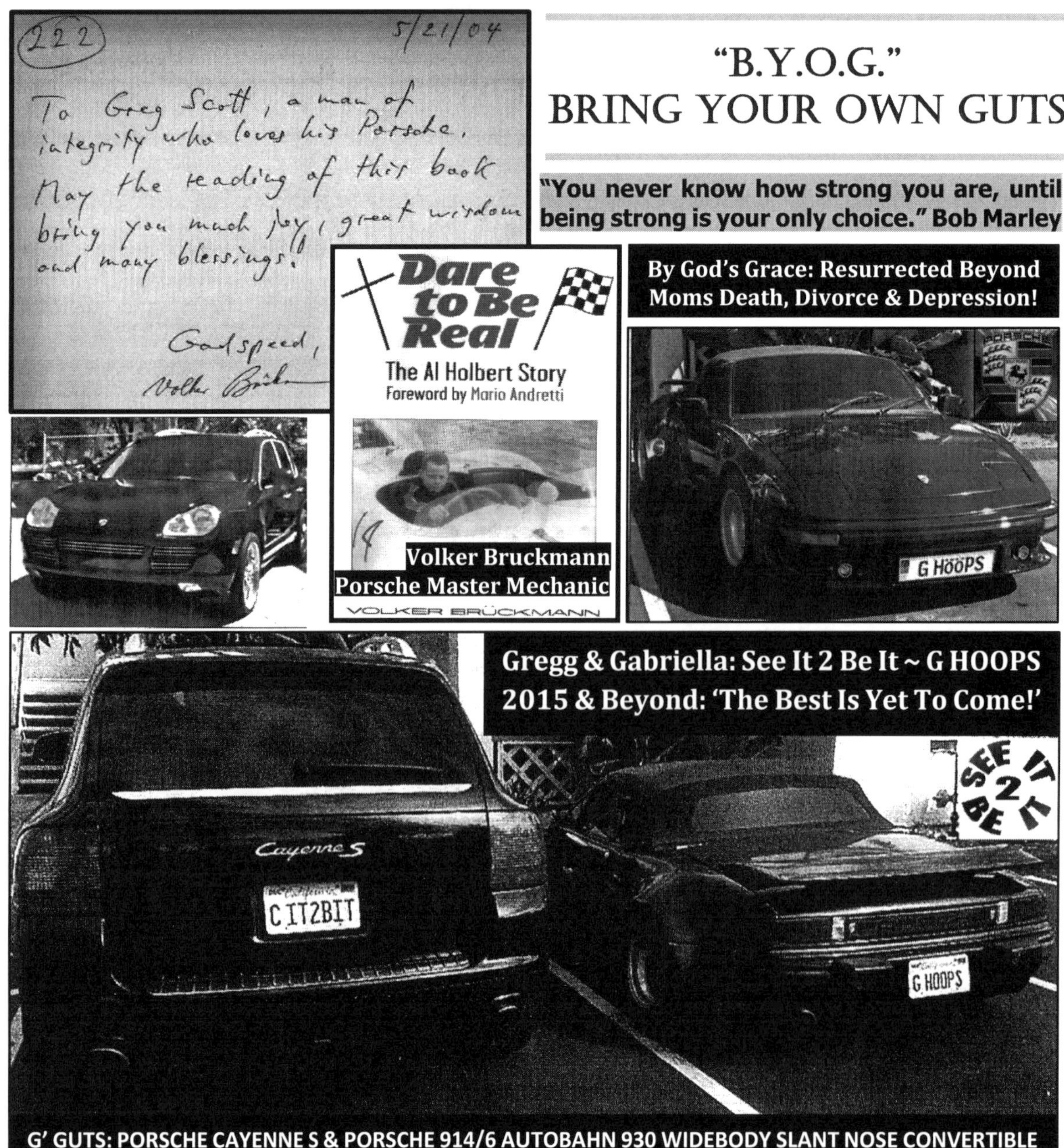

G' GUTS: PORSCHE CAYENNE S & PORSCHE 914/6 AUTOBAHN 930 WIDEBODY SLANT NOSE CONVERTIBLE